Who Decides What: The Citizen's Handbook

Who Decides What: The Citizen's Handbook

Klaus Boehm and Brian Morris

© Klaus Boehm and Brian Morris 1979

Softcover reprint of the hardcover 1st edition 1979

All rights reserved. No part of this publication may be reproduced or transmitted, in any form or by any means, without permission.

First published 1979 by
THE MACMILLAN PRESS LTD
London and Basingstoke
Associated companies in Delhi Dublin
Hong Kong Johannesburg Lagos Melbourne
New York Singapore and Tokyo

British Library Cataloguing in Publication Data
Boehm, Klaus
  Who decides what.
  1. Associations, institutions, etc. – Great Britain –
Directories
  I. Title   II. Morris, Brian
  068'.41   AS 118

ISBN 978-1-349-03009-5   ISBN 978-1-349-03007-1 (eBook)
DOI 10.1007/978-1-349-03007-1

This book is sold subject to the standard conditions of the Net Book Agreement.

Contents

	page
How to use the book	vi
Preface	vii
Acknowledgements	viii
Entries A–Z	1
Address List	365
Index	443

How To Use the Book

Who Decides What is in three sections – subject entries arranged alphabetically, an Address Section and a comprehensive index.

To use *Who Decides What*, first look up the most obvious entry heading (to repeat, they are arranged alphabetically). If this fails to identify the relevant subject (either directly or by using the cross-reference shown in bold type, e.g. **Social security benefits**), turn to the index, which covers the scope of the book in much more detail. For further information, consult the italicised enquiry point (or points) in each entry, e.g. *Department of Health and Social Security* – they will be found in the address section. Also check whether the facts have changed since the entry was approved for publication; in very many cases the relevant authority will be able to provide (usually free) leaflets or advice.

Preface

We all need, throughout our lives, to make contact with the numerous regulatory authorities which provide grants and services, issue licences and certificates, and otherwise help or hinder us – often in ways that baffle or annoy. *Who Decides What* charts this network of authorities – usually by starting from human activities and relating to them the authorities which impinge upon our lives.

Who Decides What is not a neat academic study of the way policy is formulated; its untidiness reflects contemporary British society, which has grown for the most part piecemeal and without elegant structure. Thus *Who Decides What* can be seen as a map, or gazetteer, rather than as an encyclopaedia or law book. Certainly the entries are intended to include only sufficient information to assign the right activities to the right authorities; they do not purport to be a full account of the relevant rules, regulations and laws. Almost all the entries have been verified by the appropriate authority – often the government department most directly concerned, or otherwise by the relevant professional, sporting or other public body. All these organisations helped us enormously, but the errors and omissions which are inevitable in a first edition of this kind are of course entirely the responsibility of the editors. Suggestions for subsequent editions are most welcome.

Klaus Boehm
Brian Morris

Acknowledgements

We would like to express our appreciation of the kindness and encouragement we have widely received in the preparation of *Who Decides What*, and convey our thanks to those in the many organisations we approached who helped us in its completion as far as their official duties permitted. We are indebted to the institutions, including those listed below this acknowledgement, which agreed to provide us with information and checked the content of the entries.
It is also a pleasure to acknowledge the help we have received editorially. Andrew Pates and Fay Sharman played a critical part in planning the book. Sarina Turner, Helen Watkins and Jennifer Lees-Spalding made a major contribution in organising much of the material and preparing many of the entries. Valuable criticism, information and support were provided by Rohan Bolton, Gillian Drake, and Peter Walsh. Jessica Orebi Gann of the Macmillan Press was a constant support throughout the preparation of this book. We are very grateful to them.
Organisations which helped in a variety of ways with *Who Decides What*, and to which we are greatly indebted, include:

>Acupuncture Association and Register Ltd
>Advertising Standards Authority Ltd
>Advisory Conciliation and Arbitration Service
>Agricultural Research Council
>Agriculture, Fisheries and Food, Ministry of
>Aircraft Owners and Pilots Association
>All England Lawn Tennis and Croquet Club
>All England Netball Association
>All England Women's Hockey Association
>All England Women's Lacrosse Association
>Alliance Party of Northern Ireland
>Amateur Boxing Association
>Amateur Fencing Association
>Amateur Rowing Association
>Amateur Swimming Association
>Amnesty International
>Architects Registration Council of the UK
>Arts Council of Great Britain
>Association of Certified Accountants
>Australian High Commission
>Auto-Cycle Union
>Automobile Association
>Badminton Association of England
>Baltic Exchange
>Bank of England
>Banking Information Service
>Billiards and Snooker Control Council
>Adam and Charles Black Ltd
>Boundary Commission for England
>Boundary Commission for Wales
>British Academy
>British Airways
>British Amateur Baseball Federation
>British Amateur Gymnastics Association
>British Amateur Weight Lifters' Association

Acknowledgements

British Association of Concert Agents
British Association of Occupational Therapists
British Aviation Authority
British Balloon and Airship Club
British Board of Film Censors
British Bobsleigh Association
British Boxing Board of Control
British Broadcasting Corporation
British Canoe Union
British Commonwealth Games Federation
British Council
British Cycling Federation
British Equestrian Promotions Ltd
British Federation of Sand and Land Yacht Clubs
British Field Sports Society
British Film Institute
British Gas Corporation
British Gliding Association
British Handball Association
British Hang Gliding Association
British Horse Society
British Hypnotherapy Association
British Ice Hockey Association
British Institute of Embalmers
British Insurance Brokers' Association
British Judo Association
British Library
British Market Research Bureau Ltd
British Mountaineering Council
British Museum
British Music Information Centre
British Olympic Association
British Orienteering Federation
British Orthoptic Society
British Overseas Trade Board
British Parachute Association Ltd
British Sports Association for the Disabled
British Standards Institution
British Sub-Aqua Club
British Surfing Association
British Tenpin Bowling Association Ltd
British Tourist Board
British Trampoline Federation Ltd
British Water Ski Federation
British Waterways Board
Buckingham Palace Press Office
Building Societies Association
Camping Club of Great Britain and Ireland Ltd
Canadian High Commission
Central Council for Physical Recreation
Central Midwives Board
Central Office of Industrial Tribunals
Central Statistical Office
Charities Aid Foundation
Charity Commission
Chartered Institute of Physiotherapy
City Communications Centre
Civil Aviation Authority

Civil Service Department
Clay Pigeon Shooting Association
College of Arms
Commission for Local Administration in England
Commission for Racial Equality
Commonwealth Development Corporation
Commonwealth Foundation
Commonwealth Secretariat
Commonwealth War Graves Commission
Communist Party of Great Britain
Confederation of British Industries
Conservative and Unionist Central Office
Co-operative Party
Corporation of Insurance Brokers
Council for Small Industries in Rural Areas
Council of Engineering Institutions
Council of Legal Education
Council on Tribunals
Countryside Commission
Crafts Advisory Committee
Criminal Injuries Compensation Board
Croquet Association
Crown Agents for Overseas Governments and Administrations
Crown Estate Commissioners
(HM) Customs and Excise
Defence, Ministry of
Design Council
Director of Public Prosecutions, Department of
Douglas Ltd, Basil
Duke of Edinburgh's Award
Education and Science, Department of
Electricity Council
Employment, Department of
Energy, Department of
English Basket Ball Association
English Bowling Association
English Curling Association
English Olympic Wrestling Association
English Table Tennis Association
English Volleyball Association
Entertainment Agents Association
Equal Opportunities Commission
European Communities Commission
Export Credits Guarantee Department
Faculty of Advocates
Fair Trading, Office of
Fellowship Party
Finland, Embassy of
Football Association
Football League Ltd
Foreign and Commonwealth Office
Foreign Compensation Commission
Forestry Commission
Gabitas Thring Educational Trust
Gaming Board for Great Britain
General Council and Register of Osteopaths Ltd
General Dental Council
General Medical Council

Acknowledgements

General Nursing Council for England and Wales
General Optical Council
Grand National Archery Society
Guild of Air Pilots and Air Navigators
Headmasters' Conference
Health and Safety Executive
Health and Social Security, Department of
Hockey Association
Home Office
Honourable Society of the Inns of Court of Northern Ireland
House of Commons
House of Lords
Immigration Appeals: the Appellate Authorities
Incorporated Association of Preparatory Schools
Incorporated Law Society of Northern Ireland
Incorporated Society of Valuers and Auctioneers
Independent Broadcasting Authority
Independent Schools Information Service
Industry, Department of
Inland Revenue
Institute of Actuaries
Institute of Chartered Accountants
Institute of Chartered Accountants in Ireland
Institute of Chartered Shipbrokers
Institute of Medical Laboratory Sciences
Institute of Practitioners in Advertising
Institute of Preventive Medicine
Institute of Psycho-analysis
Institute of Trichologists
International Defence and Aid
Intervention Board for Agricultural Produce
Irish Embassy
Israel Information
Jamaican High Commission
Keep Fit Association
Kennel Club
Labour Party
(HM) Land Registry
Landscape Institute, incorporating Institute of Landscape Architects
Lands Tribunal
Law Officers' Department
Law Society
Law Society of Scotland
Lawn Tennis Association
Liberal Party Organisation
Liberal Party of Wales
Library Association
Lloyd's of London
Lloyd's Register of Shipping
Local Government Boundary Commission for England
Location of Offices Bureau
London Tourist Board
London Transport Executive
Lord Chancellor's Office
Malta Government Tourist Office
Manpower Economics, Office of
Manpower Services Commission
Martial Arts Commission

Medical Research Council
Metrication Board
Modern Pentathlon Association
Monaco Information Centre
Muzzle Loaders' Association of Great Britain
National Air Rifle and Pistol Association
National Anglers' Council
National Caving Association
National Council for Civil Liberties
National Enterprise Board
National Front
National Greyhound Racing Club Ltd
National Research Development Corporation
National Rifle Association
National Savings, Department for
National Skating Association of Great Britain
National Ski Federation of Great Britain
National Smallbore Rifle Association
National Trust
National Trust for Scotland
National Water Council
Natural Environment Research Council
Nature Conservancy Council
Northern Ireland Commissioner for Complaints, Office of
Northern Ireland Labour Party
Northern Ireland Office
Occupational Pensions Board
Official Board of Ballroom Dancing
Offshore Supplies Office
Ordnance Survey
Overseas Development, Ministry of
Parliamentary Commissioner for Administration, Office of
Parole Board for England and Wales
Performing Rights Tribunal
Pharmaceutical Society of Great Britain
Plaid Cymru
Population Censuses and Surveys, Office of
Post Office
Press Council
Price Commission
Prices and Consumer Protection, Department of
Prime Minister's Office
Principal Registry of the Family Division
Privy Council Office
Public Record Office
Public Trustee Office
Race Relations Board
Racing Information Bureau
Ramblers' Association
Regatta Headquarters
Royal Academy of Arts
Royal Aero Club
Royal and Ancient Golf Club of St Andrews
Royal Automobile Club
Royal College of Veterinary Surgeons
Royal Commonwealth Society
Royal Fine Art Commission
Royal Greenwich Observatory

Acknowledgements

Royal Horticultural Society
Royal Hospital Chelsea
Royal Institution of Chartered Surveyors
Royal Institution of Naval Architects
Royal Mint
Royal Ocean Racing Club
Royal Society of London
Royal Yachting Association
Rugby Football League
Rugby Football Union
Samaritans
Schools Council
Science Research Council
Scottish Conservative Party
Scottish Football Association
Scottish Information Office
Scottish Liberal Party
Scottish National Party
Scottish Office
Scottish Record Office
Secretary of the Senate
Sinn Fein
Ski Club of Great Britain
Social Democratic and Labour Party
Social Science Research Council
Society of Chiropodists
Society of Industrial Artists and Designers
Society of Radiographers
Society of Remedial Gymnasts
South African Embassy
Speedway Control Board Ltd
Sports Council
Squash Rackets Association
Sri Lanka, High Commission for the Republic of
(HM) Stationery Office
Stock Exchange
Sunday Times
Television Licensing Organisation
Test and County Cricket Board
Trade, Department of
Trades Union Council
(HM) Treasury
Trinity House Lighthouse Service
Tug-of-War Association
UK Atomic Energy Authority
Ulster Liberal Party
Ulster Unionist Party
Union Movement
United States of America Embassy
Welsh Office
Wildfowlers' Association of Great Britain
Women's Cricket Association
Women's National Commission
Zoological Society of London

A

Abandoned Vehicles should be reported to the police; for removal apply to the relevant **local authority**.

Abattoirs The licensing of knacker's yards, slaughterhouses and slaughterers (who must not be under 18 years of age) is the responsibility of **local authorities** as is the implementation of much of the legislation dealing with the slaughter of animals.

Abortion Except in the case of an emergency operation, an abortion may be performed only if, before it takes place, two **doctors** (registered medical practitioners) certify their opinion that it comes within the provisions of the Abortion Act 1967. The consent of the woman, or of the parents or guardians of a minor under 16 years of age, is required to the legal performance of the operation and the administration of a general anaesthetic. For an abortion to be legal the continuance of the **pregnancy** must involve risk to the life of the pregnant woman or injury to her physical or mental health or that of any existing children of her family, greater than if the pregnancy were terminated; or a substantial risk that if the child were born it would suffer from such physical or mental abnormalities as to be seriously handicapped (Abortion Act 1967, Section 1 (1)(a) and (b)). In determining whether the continuance of pregnancy would involve such risk of injury to health, account may be taken of the pregnant woman's actual or reasonably foreseeable environment. The safest time for termination of pregnancy is (statistically) before the 12th week of pregnancy. Apply in first instance to your **doctor**. Private facilities for the termination of pregnancy must be approved by the Secretary of State for Social Services. Advice on private medical facilities from *British Pregnancy Advisory Service* or the *Pregnancy Advisory Service*.

Accommodation Addresses People proposing to carry on a business of receiving for reward letters, telegrams or other postal packets for delivery or forwarding to other addresses must be registered under the Official Secrets Act 1920. Apply to police.

Accommodation Vessels Those used in relation to offshore oil and gas exploration and exploitation, and moored within certain designated sea areas off the coast of Scotland, must be licensed by the *Scottish Development Department, Marine Advisers Unit*.

Accountants Accountants may practise in the UK without qualifications. Some statutory accounting activities, however, including auditing company accounts can be undertaken only by a member of one of the four major accountancy bodies recognised under the Companies Acts 1948–76. All four professional bodies have their own qualifications as follows: the *Association of Certified Accountants, Incorporated by Royal Charter* (ACCA and FCCA), the *Institute of Chartered*

Accountants in England and Wales and the *Institute of Chartered Accountants in Ireland* (ACA and FCA) and the *Institute of Chartered Accountants of Scotland* (CA). All these qualifications are awarded on the basis of a written examination and on completion of a required period of practical training (minimum three years). For the Association, training can be either with a firm of practising accountants (with or without articles) or in commerce, industry or the public service. For the three Institutes training has to be with a practising member of the professional body concerned.

There are two specialist professional bodies whose members are normally employees rather than in private practice; they are the *Institute of Cost and Management Accountants* and the *Chartered Institute of Public Finance and Accountancy*. They award their own qualifications (ACMA and FCMA and IPFA respectively) requiring a combination of examination passes, practical experience, and full-time education.

Lists of members are published annually by all six bodies and are available in public libraries. There is no central list.

Complaints about professional misconduct of members are investigated by each professional body.

Actuaries Actuaries give advice on life and non-life assurance, pension funds, friendly societies, social insurance, investments and statistical matters; certain statutory duties in these fields can be undertaken only by qualified actuaries.

Basic professional qualification is fellowship of the *Institute of Actuaries* or the *Faculty of Actuaries* (Scotland) whose yearbooks include lists of their members. Names of consulting actuaries can be obtained from the Institute and the Faculty.

Complaints regarding professional misconduct are investigated by the Institute and the Faculty.

Acupuncture may legally be practised by anyone in the UK without qualification, but the recognised basic qualification is the Licenciate Diploma in Acupuncture (LIcAc) obtained after two years' study at the *College of Acupuncture*. Before acceptance for the course, one must be a registered chiropractor, naturopath, osteopath, physiotherapist, doctor (i.e. medical practitioner) or state registered nurse.

The *Acupuncture Association and Register Ltd* publishes a yearbook and directory which the public can consult to find information about acupuncture and a practitioner.

Complaints about professional conduct are investigated by the Ethical Committee of the AAR Ltd.

Administrative Tribunals: Appeals and Complaints Administrative tribunals consist of people or bodies exercising judicial or quasi-judicial functions outside the ordinary hierarchy of the courts. As a rule, they are set up by Act of Parliament or under powers conferred by statute or statutory instrument, which also govern their constitution, function and procedure. There are now over 2000 such tribunals, hearing over 200,000 cases a year. They include tribunals concerned with land and property; with **national insurance** and **supplementary benefits**; with the **National Health Service**; with industry and employment; with transport; with taxation; and many which do not fall into any specified group. (There are also tribunals which enforce professional discipline, such as the General Medical Council and the Disciplinary Committee of the Law Society, but these are entirely different in constitution from the statutory tribunals and have no jurisdiction over the general public).

Although there is no general provision respecting appeals from statutory tribunals, the Tribunals and Inquiries Act 1971 (which requires tribunals covered by its provisions to give the reasons for their decisions) and other Acts provide for an appeal, at least on a point of law, from all the more important tribunals to the High Court. An appeal may also lie to a specially constituted appeal tribunal, to a Government minister, or to an independent referee. In addition, even where there is no right of appeal to a court of law, an aggrieved person may challenge the decision by pro-

ceedings for a declaration or a prerogative order (see **Disputes with public authorities**).
In Scotland appeals on points of law may be taken to the Court of Session from most tribunals. Where there is no specific right of appeal, a challenge may still be possible on a number of grounds.
See also **Civil law disputes**.

Admiralty Charts These are navigational charts covering the world, suitable for all ocean-going shipping. Royal Navy survey ships are the principal sources of information for them and for other publications, such as sailing directions, tide-tables, light and radio signal lists, etc., which are produced by the *Ministry of Defence Hydrographic Department*. The charts are sold in the UK and in most other countries of the world by officially appointed admiralty chart agents. Port and harbour authorities and customs officers will give the names of local agents. Lists of agents and catalogues of charts (specify whether world or home waters) are available from the MoD Hydrographic Department.

Adoption In England and Wales an adoption order comes from magistrates', county or high courts, with directions to the *Registrar General of England and Wales* to make an entry in the *General Register Office's Adopted Children Register* kept in Hampshire. Adoptions of English- and Welsh-born children in certain foreign countries can also be registered there. People wishing legally to adopt a child should approach their local court for advice. Briefly, when natural parents have consented to free a child for adoption, legal adoption transfers to the adopters all the rights, responsibilities, jurisdiction, etc., of the parents.
In Scotland a certified copy of the adoption order is sent from the sheriff court or the Court of Session with a direction to the *Registrar General for Scotland* to make an entry in the Scottish Adopted Children Register kept in the *General Register Office (Scotland)*. Adoptions of Scottish-born children in certain foreign countries can also be recorded there.
Adoptions authorised by the courts in Northern Ireland and of children born in Northern Ireland but adopted in certain foreign countries are registered in the Adopted Children Register maintained at the *General Register Office (Belfast)*.
Entries in all the Adopted Children Registers contain the child's adopted name(s); date and country of birth; name(s) and surname(s) and address of the adopters; male adopter's occupation; date when and court where the adoption order was made (or place where adopted); registration district (never given in Scotland) or country of birth. A full copy of the entry shows all these particulars; a short certificate shows only the child's adoptive name(s), surname and date and place of birth, and contains no evidence of adoption. Anyone who can give sufficient information to identify an entry in an Adopted Children Register can obtain a full or short certificate from the relevant General Register Office on payment of the statutory fee.
In England, Wales and Scotland the Adopted Children Registers are not open to public inspection, although anyone can inspect the indexes to the General Register at the General Register Offices, while in Northern Ireland searches may also be made in the indexes to the Adopted Children Register.
Normally no information is made available which would enable a link to be made between an entry in the Adopted Children Register and the corresponding original entry in the general register of births, but in England and Wales adopted people over the age of 18 can apply to the Registrar General at the General Register Office in Hampshire to find out about their original **birth certificate**.
People adopted before 12 November 1975 must have an interview with a counsellor (interviews held locally or in London) who will help with enquiries about origins and discuss the implications. This is to protect natural parents who believed that their children would never be able to trace them.
In Scotland, an adopted person aged 17

or over may be given information about his original birth entry, on application in person or in writing to the General Register Office (Scotland). In Northern Ireland no facilities are given in the General Register Office to enable the original birth entries of adopted children to be traced.
Prospective adoptive parents should apply to *local authority* (Director of Social Services) or to a registered adoption society. Useful booklet 'Adopting a Child' including a list of adoption agencies available from *Association of British Adoption and Fostering Agencies*.
See also **Birth registration; Illegitimate children.**

Adult Education Generally taken to mean post-school education outside the main areas of higher, professional and technical education. Most of the courses are introductory and part-time and do not lead to any recognised educational or vocational qualification, but the term is also extended to cover certain full-time and residential courses offering special opportunities to persons without formal educational qualifications.
Adult education courses are provided by *local education authorities*; various voluntary and statutory bodies, including the *Workers' Educational Association*; certain residential colleges; and the adult education (extra-mural) departments of universities. Many of the voluntary bodies are grant-aided.
Enquiries to local education authority, university extramural departments or the *National Institute of Adult Education*, which provides a national centre for information, research and publication on adult education.
State bursaries (i.e. scholarships) for full-time one- or two-year liberal adult courses at adult colleges are available on application to Awards Division 11 at the *Department of Education and Science, Higher and Further Education IV*, the *Scottish Education Department* and Scholarships and Students Awards Branch at the *Department of Education, Northern Ireland*. Applicants must be over 20, have been offered a place at one of the colleges, and have been resident in the UK at least three years previously. Grants are at the same rate as **student grants**: first degree.
See also **Education: Scotland; Education: Northern Ireland; Further Education; Universities.**

Adult Publications The *British Adult Publications Association Ltd*, a trade association representing publishers and distributors of magazines for sale to adults only, has established and financed the independent *British Adult Publications Control Board*. It operates on the basis of accepted guidelines. If a complaint is received about a publication it is considered by the Board's examiners who will make an adjudication. If a complaint is upheld the publisher is required to submit the next three issues of the publication for examination before publication. If there is continuing contravention of the guidelines the publication will not be handled by the distributors.
See also **Film censorship; Obscene publications.**

Advertising Controls There are more than 60 separate UK legislative controls, from general prohibitions of misleading claims to specific requirements for labelling products. *Local authorities* enforce much of this. Their trading standards or consumer protection departments advise both advertisers and consumers.
The advertising industry and the media have devised the British Code of Advertising Practice, which is implemented by the *Advertising Standards Authority*. The *Independent Broadcasting Authority* operates its own statutory Code of Advertising Standards and Practice under the Independent Broadcasting Authority Act. The codes lay down general rules (e.g. decency, honesty, freedom from violence) and specific requirements (e.g. for **alcohol** and **medicines**). They also outlaw certain practices (e.g. switch selling). All scripts for television and radio advertising have to be cleared by the IBA. In practice all cinema advertisements have to be approved by the *British Board of Film Censors* (see **Film censorship**).
Complaints against specific radio and

television advertisements are investigated by the IBA. Complaints against specific press, poster or other advertisements are investigated by the *Advertising Standards Authority*. If the complaint is upheld the advertisement is withdrawn or amended. The ASA and the Code secretariat also monitor a wide variety of advertisements, give prepublication advice to advertisers, and provide a forum for advertisers to criticise rival advertising.

Advertising Practitioners It is possible to work in advertising without formal professional qualification, but the diploma of the *CAM Education Foundation* (DipCAM) is the basic UK professional qualification for those concerned with the creation, production and placing of advertisements. The *Institute of Practitioners in Advertising* is the trade association of the advertising agencies, guaranteeing certain minimum standards of service, and the professional body representing people working in them. It advises manufacturers on the selection of advertising agencies and publishes a list of member agencies. The IPA investigates breaches of its byelaws (available on request) which are concerned with the business practices of members.

Advertising: Sandwich Boards Boards require a licence from the police in London thoroughfares within the Metropolitan Police District. Applications to the Commissioner of Police at the *Metropolitan Police Force Headquarters*.

Advice Impartial confidential advice on any subject is available free to all individuals at any of the 700 UK *Citizens' Advice Bureaux*. The CAB service aims to provide a source of guidance, support and representation to help solve peoples' problems, referring them on to other sources of help where necessary. Many CABs hold specialist sessions dealing with legal, financial or consumer problems. Each CAB is autonomous but the *National Association of Citizens' Advice Bureaux* controls work standards through a registration scheme (registering bureaux) and a training programme.

CABs are 90% volunteer staffed. Contact your local bureau or NACAB Area Office to enquire about joining the service.

Afghanistan For **exchange control** is a non-scheduled territory outside the **overseas sterling area** and the **EEC**. UK nationals travelling direct from the UK normally need only the following (but check): **passports**; **visas**; international certificates of **vaccination** against smallpox; **work permits** (if taking a job); green cards for motor insurance (if bringing a car); international driving permits (if intending to drive: see **Motoring abroad**).
The UK has no reciprocal health or social security arrangements.
Enquiries to *Afghanistan Embassy* in London.
British diplomatic mission to Afghanistan is *British Embassy* in Kabul.

Agricultural Finance Grants are available under various schemes in the UK on application to the nearest *Ministry of Agriculture, Fisheries and Food Divisional Office* in England and Wales; the *Department of Agriculture and Fisheries for Scotland*; or to the *Department of Agriculture for Northern Ireland*. The farm and horticulture development scheme − designed to modernise agricultural and horticultural businesses whose incomes per labour unit are below UK average for non-agricultural industry − makes grants available for a wide range of investments (e.g. equipment, farm buildings, machinery, drainage works, reclamation, roads, water supply, purchase of livestock and the keeping of farm accounts) and for the breeding or keeping of cattle and sheep for meat production.
The payments to outgoers scheme provides grants for occupiers who relinquish 'uncommercial' holdings (roughly, a one-man farm), either for approved amalgamations in cases where development plans have been approved under the farm and horticulture development regulations or, in certain circumstances, for afforestation or public use.
The farm capital grant scheme covers capital expenditure on farm buildings,

silos, yards, farm waste disposal, gas and electricity supply, field drainage, water supply, roads, bridges, pens, orchard grubbing, etc. Preferential rates of grant are available to applicants in less-favoured areas (hill land areas) for certain works. See **Hill livestock allowances**.

The horticultural capital grant scheme covers improvements to land and buildings and for plant and equipment. See **Horticultural crops**.

Development loans for purchase or improvement of farms are available from the *Agricultural Mortgage Corporation*, either long-term for up to two-thirds valuation or short-term for up to half valuation. Loan guarantees for agricultural development are available from the *Agricultural Credit Corporation*.

Information about production and marketing grants, including those under EEC regulations, available to co-operatives can be obtained from the *Central Council for Agricultural and Horticultural Co-operation*.

Appeals against official decisions on grants and subsidies by MAFF are judged by a regional panel. Write giving notice of appeal to *MAFF Divisional Office*.

See also **Agriculture: Northern Ireland**; **Agriculture: Scotland**.

Agricultural Land Tenure Disputes between landlords and tenants about statutory regulated matters (e.g. variation of rent, claims on termination of tenancy, liability for maintenance, repairs and insurance, security of tenure) may be referred to abitration. Parties who fail to agree on the appointment of an arbitrator may apply to the *Ministry of Agriculture, Fisheries and Food* to appoint one (for holdings in England to *MAFF Headquarters*, for holdings in Wales to *MAFF Welsh Department*). Other matters (e.g. family succession to agricultural tenancies and certain notices to quit) are referrable to the area *Agricultural Land Tribunal*. Application may be made to the *MAFF Divisional Offices* for consent to a letting for less than from year to year or to a licence to occupy land.

See also **Agriculture: Scotland**; **Agriculture: Northern Ireland**.

Agricultural Loans Loans secured on agricultural assets (e.g. farm machinery and livestock) are registerable against the name of the debtor farmer in cases where the farm is situated in England or Wales. Registration must be made with the Agricultural Credits Superintendent at *Her Majesty's Land Registry, Land Charges Department* within seven days of the date of the deed or it will be void against any person other than the borrower. Loans for farm improvements are made mainly by banks. The agricultural loans register is comparable to the register of land charges, with similar registration and search procedures.

See also **Land charges on unregistered land**.

Agricultural Prices Information for a wide range of agricultural and horticultural commodities is published weekly in the Agricultural Market Report, available from Statistics Division IIA at the *Ministry of Agriculture, Fisheries and Food, Main Headquarters*. Prices are also published in the national farming press.

Agricultural Produce: EEC Subsidies Market support subsidies are paid for the storage, stockholding, sale or withdrawal from sale within the EEC of milk and milk products, sugar, fruit, vegetables, beef, pig meat, fish and oilseeds. Subsidies include stockholding allowances; sugar levies on manufacturers to support storage; and beef premium schemes. Claims to *Intervention Board for Agricultural Produce*. Registration with IBAP is necessary to claim subsidies for fruit, vegetables and fish; and use of **abattoirs** and storage approved to EEC standards to claim subsidies for meat. Advice from *Central Council for Agricultural and Horticultural Co-operation*.

EEC production subsidies are payable on the production of starch from cereals; sugar for chemical products; herbage seeds; field bean seeds; casein and caseinates; dehydrated fodder and potatoes; flax and oilseeds for crushing. The subsidies include a levy on production of maize for seed. Claims to IBAP.

See also **Cattle and beef: support; Food: EEC intervention.**

Agricultural Produce: Exports Export produce to non-EEC countries which is subject to EEC grading rules must be at least Class II quality and be certificated accordingly. Apply in England and Wales to Horticultural Marketing Inspectorate at *Ministry of Agriculture, Fisheries and Food Regional Offices*, at least three days before export. Most consignments to other areas of the EEC must also be notified. Plants and plant produce may also require a certificate of health (phytosanitary certificate) under regulations of the importing overseas country; apply to Plant Health and Seeds Inspectorate at most MAFF Regional Offices at least five working days before export.
See also **Agriculture: Scotland; Agriculture: Northern Ireland; Exporting.**

Agricultural Produce: Grading Under EEC regulations a wide range of fresh fruit, vegetables, live plants, flowers and bulbs, tubers, corms and rhizomes are graded by quality into one of up to four classes depending on the product. All such produce, whether imported or home-grown, is liable to inspection by Horticultural Marketing Inspectors at the *Ministry of Agriculture, Fisheries and Food Regional Offices* in England and Wales. Leaflets on grading requirements from *MAFF Publications* and from *MAFF Regional and Divisional Offices*.
See also **Agriculture: Scotland; Agriculture: Northern Ireland.**

Agricultural Produce: Support Production price support is available in the UK for fat sheep (through the Sheep Guarantee Scheme administered by the *Ministry of Agriculture, Fisheries and Food, Headquarters*, the *Department of Agriculture for Northern Ireland*, and the *Meat and Livestock Commission*); for milk (through the *Milk Marketing Board*); and for wool (through the *British Wool Marketing Board*). Support for beef, milk products, pigmeat, cereals, oilseed rape, fodder, hops, herbage seed, field beans and peas, linseed, fresh fruit and vegetables is available under the EEC common agricultural policy and is administered by the *Intervention Board for Agricultural Produce* (see **Agricultural Produce: EEC Subsidies**). The *Home-grown Cereals Authority* undertakes agency work for the IBAP for cereals and oilseed rape.
See also **Agriculture: Scotland; Agriculture: Northern Ireland.**

Agricultural Safety Health and safety in agriculture, including horticulture and forestry, is dealt with by the *Health and Safety Executive Agricultural Inspectorate*. Inspectors give advice on the safe design, construction and operation of agricultural tractors and machinery; on the safe design and construction of agricultural buildings; on the safe packaging, use, handling, transport, and storage of agricultural chemicals; and on the safe housing, handling and control of farm animals. They also deal with EEC and UK tractor and safety cab approval certificates, and prepare new legislation and codes of practice. Advice at a local level is available from the Health and Safety Executive Agricultural Inspectorate regional office.

Agricultural Services The *Ministry of Agriculture, Fisheries and Food Agricultural Development and Advisory Service Centres* in England and Wales provide agricultural services (agronomy, farm mechanisation, beekeeping, farm management, dairy husbandry (including milk hygiene), livestock husbandry, horticulture, socio-economics, experimental husbandry farms and experimental horticulture stations); a horticultural marketing inspectorate; a land drainage service (field drainage, farm water supply and arterial drainage, including flood protection and sea defence); a land service (estate management, design and layout of farm buildings, land use, land classification and land economics); a veterinary service (control of notifiable diseases, disease investigations, licensing of medicines, meat hygiene, animal productivity and welfare of animals); and an agricultural science service (analytical services, entomology, micro-biology, nutrition

Agricultural chemistry, plant pathology, soil science, pest infestation control laboratory, plant pathology laboratory, plant health and seeds inspectorate, pollution science, and farm waste). See also **Agriculture: Scotland; Agriculture: Northern Ireland.**

Agricultural Wages Minimum wages and conditions of service in England and Wales are prescribed by the *Agricultural Wages Board*. In addition, local Agricultural Wages Committees at the *Ministry of Agriculture, Fisheries and Food Divisional Offices* issue permits of exemption authorising payment of specific lower minimum wages to workers who are physically or mentally handicapped; approve agreements for payment of premiums to employers for teaching learners; revalue the amount that may be reckoned as part payment of minimum wages for employers' houses occupied by agricultural workers under the terms of their employment; and issue craft certificates under the Statutory Wages Structure Scheme which can entitle workers to higher minimum rates of pay. There is also a *Scottish Agricultural Wages Board* and a *Northern Ireland Agricultural Wages Board*.

Agriculture: Northern Ireland The *Department of Agriculture for Northern Ireland* operates partly as an agent for the Ministry of Agriculture, Fisheries and Food, as regards economic support for agriculture and the implementation of EEC agricultural policies; and partly as a Northern Ireland Department in its own right, in respect of all other aspects of work involved in the development of agriculture, forestry and fisheries. All queries about how specific schemes affect Northern Ireland and about Northern Ireland agriculture in general to DANI. A free booklet outlining services, grants and subsidies is available on application to the Information Division at DANI.

Agriculture: Scotland The administration of agriculture and fisheries in Scotland is the responsibility of the *Department of Agriculture and Fisheries for Scotland*, with the exception of the operational control of outbreaks of certain animal diseases (e.g. foot and mouth disease) and of certain food functions, for both of which the *Ministry of Agriculture, Fisheries and Food* is responsible throughout the UK. Advisory and development services (in England and Wales an integral part of MAFF) are provided by the *East of Scotland College of Agriculture*, the *West of Scotland Agricultural College* and the *North of Scotland College of Agriculture*. They are grant-aided by DAFS.
In general the same or equivalent grants, schemes, services, regulations, etc. as from MAFF are available or applicable to the agriculture, horticulture and fishing industries in Scotland; variations in appropriate cases suit particularly Scottish conditions, and special provisions exist for uniquely Scottish occupations (e.g. crofting). Applications or enquiries to *DAFS Head Office* or to the nearest *DAFS Area Office*. A ready reference to the grants, schemes and services available to farmers in Scotland and a booklet containing a description of Scottish farming, details of the nature and volume of production, and sections on the roles of government and DAFS, are available from DAFS free of charge.

Air Fares International scheduled air fares are agreed by the airlines, in accordance with bilateral agreements between the UK (represented by the *Civil Aviation Authority*) and foreign governments; the airlines work where possible through the *International Air Transport Association*, and submit their final fare agreements to each government. Agreed international fares to and from the UK, UK cabotage and UK domestic air fares need to be approved by the CAA before they can come into effect. Charter air fares are now only subject to market forces; charters (normally tour operators) negotiate a price for the flight with the airline.

Air Pilots and Air Navigators (Civil) Pilots and navigators flying British-registered aircraft engaged in commercial operations must be registered with the *Civil Aviation Authority* as holding a valid commercial pilot's licence, a senior commercial pilot's licence, an airline transport pilot's licence or a flight navigator's licence. These are awarded by the CAA (see **Aircraft registration**).

The *Guild of Air Pilots and Air Navigators* awards master air pilots and air navigator certificates for exceptional skill, experience and service. Complaints about professional misconduct are investigated by the CAA.

Air Pollution To control air pollution, certain industrial processes are scheduled under the Alkali and Works Regulation Act 1906. Industry can only operate these processes when registered with and granted a certificate (renewable annually) by the *Health and Safety Executive, HM Alkali and Clean Air Inspectorate*. The Inspectorate is ultimately responsible to the Secretary of State for the Environment. Scheduled works must use the best practicable means to prevent the emission of noxious or offensive substances and to render harmless and inoffensive any substances that are discharged. Reports of pollution should be made to the Inspectorate's district offices which will provide advice and publications. See also **Smoke control; Work: health and safety**.

Air Traffic Control The responsibility of a joint civil/military authority, the *National Air Traffic Services*. It provides en route services, to ensure safe separation for all aircraft within defined geographical limits, and the necessary air navigation services for approach and landing at the main UK airports.

Air Travel British airlines require an air transport licence from the *Civil Aviation Authority* before providing scheduled or charter services, as does any flight for the carriage for reward of passengers or cargo by a UK-registered aircraft, and any flight beginning or ending in the UK by an aircraft registered in a relevant overseas territory. The CAA may refuse, revoke or suspend a licence if not satisfied that an applicant is fit (this includes financial and general competence) to hold such a licence or if it considers that the service to be provided is not appropriate. Other airlines can lodge objections to the grant of a licence and a public hearing is then held by the CAA.

Airline users' complaints should be made in the first instance to the Customer Relations Manager of the airline involved. If dissatisfied, write to the *Airline Users Committee*. The AUC cannot become involved in claims for refunds or compensation; these are matters for direct negotiation between the parties involved or, failing that, for legal action (see **Civil law disputes**).

Air travel organisers' licences, issued by the CAA, which first vets organisers for financial adequacy and fitness, must be held by those (e.g. charterers of aircraft) who buy seats from airlines and resell them to the public. Licence holders, other than those who are merely brokers on behalf of airlines, must enter into a bond which makes money available to trustees (e.g. the *Tour Operators Study Group Trust Fund Ltd*, the *Association of British Travel Agents* or the CAA's own trustee) to repatriate passengers stranded abroad or who had paid money in advance, in the event of a licence holder going out of business. If this bond is not enough, further funds may be made available by the *Air Travel Reserve Fund Agency*.

Airlines and commercial operations lease their land and facilities from the airport owner. An airline either has staff based at the airport or commissions a handling agent to look after its passengers on the ground (e.g. dealing with baggage, boarding passes, etc.). Handling agents normally operate at the smaller airports. One agent may act for a number of airlines, or one airline act for another. Complain about loss or damage to baggage to whichever firm was handling it; they are responsible.

Aircraft Accidents Civil aircraft accidents involving British-registered or British-manufactured aircraft abroad, and all civil aircraft accidents in the UK, are investigated by the *Department of Trade Accidents Investigation Branch*.

To report an accident in the UK, telephone 999 and ask for 'police'. To enquire about missing persons who might be concerned in a UK accident, telephone the airline offices; for an accident abroad, telephone the *Consular Department, Foreign and Commonwealth Office*. A register of births, deaths and persons missing in UK-registered aircraft is maintained by *Civil Aviation Authority UK Register of Civil Aircraft and of Aircraft Mortgages*.

Aircraft: Charter, Sale and Purchase Aircraft can be chartered for freight and passenger flights throughout the world, and can be bought and sold, through airbrokers, many of whom can be contacted through the *Baltic Air Charter Association* or the secretary of the *Baltic Exchange*.
Most major airlines have their own Charter Department, which can be found in the telephone book or by telephoning Directory Enquiries (most airlines have a London office). For air taxis or executive jets look up Air Charter and Rental in the telephone directory Yellow Pages, or contact the *Air Taxi Operators' Association*.

Aircraft Registration The *Civil Aviation Authority* maintains the UK Register of Civil Aircraft and the Register of Aircraft Mortgages. Any aircraft which is to be flown over the UK must be registered either in the UK or in its country of origin. It is also compulsory to inform the CAA of any change of particulars (i.e. change of ownership). The registration certificate is not proof of legal title but of nationality. No aircraft registered in the UK Register of Civil Aircraft operating for public transport may fly unless holding a current certificate of airworthiness from the *Civil Aviation Authority, Airworthiness Division*. This includes air taxis, agricultural aviation, flying clubs, flying schools, sporting and recreational flying. Registration of mortgages is not compulsory. The initiative rests with the mortgagees and the register was set up to protect their interests in case of dispute. The register works on a 'first come, first serve' philosophy. Air operational safety is the responsibility of the Directorate-General of Safety of the CAA, which issues air operators' certificates signifying competence for public transport operators (aircraft over 2,300 kg).

Airfreight Containers Those of minimum internal capacity of 35 cubic feet or over are approved by and registered with International Air Transport Association and marked accordingly. Apply: *International Air Transport Association* (Geneva).

Airports and Aerodromes In the UK these are owned and operated either by (military) the *Ministry of Defence* or (civil) the *British Airports Authority*, the *Civil Aviation Authority*, local authorities or private companies. All aerodromes (including airports, which are large, well-equipped aerodromes usually with customs facilities) in the UK used for public transport, joy riding or flying instruction must be licensed annually by the CAA; only exceptions are MOD and CAA aerodromes. International airports are designated by Her Majesty's *Customs and Excise*, and are bound by customs and immigration regulations; duty free shops operate in airports normally handling more than 20,000 alien departures a year. For major UK airports see *airports* in address section. A list of private airports is available from *Air Touring International*.
Landing fees must be paid by pilots or airlines every time their aircraft lands at an aerodrome, whether the flight is scheduled, charter or private. Charges vary and are decided by the airport owner or operator. Airlines and commercial operations lease their land and facilities from the airport owner.

Airports: VIP Lounges There are two different types. Airport VIP lounges are used by the airport owners to entertain guests of the airport; to check whether you are eligible enquire at the airport's Public Relations Department. Airline VIP lounges are sometimes established by airlines at airports where they have large-scale operations. Qualifications for eligibility vary from airline to airline. People flying frequently may be invited to join a club entitling them to use the lounge. Ask the Customer Relations Department of the airline for further information.

Albania Albania has no diplomatic relations with the UK. Contact through the *Albanian diplomatic mission* in Paris, France. **Visas** always necessary. Tourist matters handled by *Albtourist*, Albania.

Alcohol Wholesale sale of intoxicating liquor (see **Spirits**) except a for which a dealer's excise licence is held. A licence to manufacture intoxicating liquor (see **Spirits**) except a limited licence to brew (see **Brewers**), also authorises wholesale dealing in the liquor manufactured. Apply to *Her Majesty's Customs and Excise*. A licence is not required for bulk sale of imported **wines** and **spirits** in a **bonded warehouse**; details in HMCE Notice 26.
Retail sale of intoxicating liquors does not require an excise licence but, with a few minor exceptions, such sales may take place only under the authority of a justices' licence in England, Wales and Northern Ireland, or a licence granted by a licensing board in Scotland; apply to the local authority. The sale of **spirits** by retail to a rectifier, dealer or another retailer, however, requires a separate spirits dealer's licence; apply to HMCE, details in Notice 87.
See also **Liquor licences**.

Alcoholism Treatment is provided for alcoholics as part of the general psychiatric service within the **National Health Service**. There are also in the NHS some 24 specialised treatment units and a day hospital for the treatment of alcoholism. The Department of Health and Social Security is sponsoring three experimental detoxification centres (in Leeds, Manchester and London) to assess whether habitual drunken offenders could be detoxified as part of treatment and rehabilitation services rather than imprisoned.
Closely linked with treatment are community services covering prevention, advice to alcoholics and their families and rehabilitation, including residential care where necessary. Provision of these facilities involves co-operation between health and local authorities and voluntary organisations.
Enquiries to NHS family **doctor**, *Regional Health Authority, Alcoholism Treatment Units* or various voluntary organisations including *Alcohol Education Centre, Alcoholics Anonymous, Al-anon, Federation of Alcoholics Residential Establishments* (FARE), *Medical Council on Alcoholism, National Council on Alcoholism*.

Algeria For **exchange control** is a non-scheduled territory outside the **overseas sterling area** and the EEC. UK nationals travelling direct from the UK normally need only the following (but check): **passports** without Israeli stamp; international certificates of **vaccination** against smallpox or yellow fever; **work permits** (if taking a job); green cards for motor insurance (if bringing a car); international driving permits (if intending to drive: see **Motoring abroad**).
The UK has no reciprocal health or social security arrangements.
Enquiries to *Algerian Embassy* in London and *Algerian National Tourist Office* in London.
British diplomatic mission to Algeria is *British Embassy* in Algiers.

Alliance Party of Northern Ireland Membership is open to anyone who supports its principles. The party was formed in 1970 to establish a non-sectarian centre in Northern Ireland politics. Its official aims are to be a pragmatic, non-doctrinaire party but to have social and economic policies which are broadly social democratic. The party fought its first elections in 1973 when it won 65 out of 500 local government seats and eight of 78 Regional Assembly seats. It is the third largest political grouping in Ulster.
The party has a youth wing, Young Alliance. To join this or the main party contact *Alliance Party of Northern Ireland Headquarters*.

Allotments Applications by private individuals for allotments should be made to local allotment authorities, i.e. in England parish councils (or parish meetings) where they exist, otherwise district councils (or in Greater London, the London borough councils). In Wales the district and county council have concurrent powers. Outside Inner London, allotment authorities have a duty to provide land for this purpose and land allocated for allotments (statutory allotments) may not be withdrawn for use for other purposes without the consent of the appropriate Secretary of State (Environment, Scotland or Wales).

Ancient Monuments and Historic Buildings Those in England in government ownership and open to the public are in the charge of *Department of the Environment*. In Scotland and Wales they are in the charge of the *Secretary of State for Scotland* and the *Secretary of State for Wales*. Season tickets, valid for a year from the date of issue, admit their holders to all ancient monuments and historic buildings in the care of the State. Tickets and a 'List and Map of Historic Monuments open to the Public' (free to purchasers of season tickets) containing locations, hours of visiting are obtainable from *HMSO bookshops*, from the *Historic Monuments Centre*, at most monuments, or apply to *Department of the Environment (Saville Row)*.

Andorra For **exchange control** is a non-scheduled territory outside the **overseas sterling area** and the **EEC**. UK nationals travelling direct from the UK normally need only the following (but check): **passports; work permits** (if taking a job); green cards for motor insurance (if bringing a car: see **Motoring abroad**).
The UK has no reciprocal health or social security arrangements.
Enquiries to *Andorran Delegation* in London.
British diplomatic mission to Andorra is *British Consulate-General* in Barcelona, Spain.

Angling The *National Anglers' Council* represents the sport as a whole in England and Wales. Coarse fishing is controlled by the *National Federation of Anglers*, sea fishing by the *National Federation of Sea Anglers* and game fishing by the *Salmon and Trout Association*. Records are decided by the British Record (rod-caught) Fish Committee of the NAC.
Within this structure, specific bodies for Wales are the *Welsh Angler's Council*, the *Welsh Federation of Coarse Anglers*, the *Welsh Federation of Sea Anglers* and the *Welsh Fly Fishing Association*.
In Scotland the *Scottish Joint Committee for Anglers* is a forum for the representation of all freshwater anglers.
Sea fishing is represented by the *Scottish Federation of Sea Anglers*; coarse fishing by the *Scottish Federation of Coarse Angling*.
In Northern Ireland governing bodies are the *Ulster Angling Federation Ltd* and the *Ulster Province Irish Federation of Sea Anglers*.

Angling Licences These are always required in England and Wales for the use of rod and line, nets and other instruments to catch salmon, trout, eels and other freshwater fish. They are issued by the 10 regional *Water Authorities* in England and Wales. In addition a permit to fish is usually required from the riparian owner.
A person wanting a day's fishing on canals and rivers should obtain a licence from the relevant *Water Authority* (see also **Canals and rivers**) and a day ticket from the owner or manager of the fishery (e.g. a fishing club). Angling clubs which wish to lease sections of a British Waterways Board canal towpath for fishing should apply to the *British Waterways Board Fisheries Officer*. In Scotland permission is required only from the riparian owner. Salmon fishing rights may be held separately from other fishing rights.
See also **Angling**.

Angola For **exchange control** is a non-scheduled territory outside the **overseas sterling area** and the **EEC**. UK nationals travelling direct from the UK normally need only the following (but check): **passports; visas;** international certificates of **vaccination** against smallpox; **work permits** (if taking a job); green cards for motor insurance (if bringing a car); inter-

national driving permits (if intending to drive: see **Motoring abroad.**)
The UK has no reciprocal health or social security arrangements.
Diplomatic relations with the UK have not yet been established.

Animal Diseases: Notification Livestock diseases notifiable to the police as soon as they are suspected are: African horse sickness; anthrax; cattle plague in ruminating animals and swine; dourine; epizootic lymphangitis in horses, asses and mules; equine encephalomyelitis; equine infectious anaemia; foot-and-mouth disease in ruminating animals and swine; fowl pest (fowl plague and Newcastle disease) in all kinds of poultry; glanders and farcy in horses, asses and mules; parasitic mange in horses, asses and mules; pleuro-pneumonia in cattle; rabies; sheep pox; sheep scab; swine fever; swine vesicular disease; Teschen disease of pigs; tuberculosis (certain forms only) in cattle. In England and Wales after receiving a report that one of these diseases is suspected the police ask Divisional Veterinary Officer at the *Ministry of Agriculture Fisheries and Food Divisional Office* to arrange for the animals to be examined without charge to the owner.
Restrictions on movement of livestock may be imposed by either MAFF, the local authority or the police from or to an area or premises where there is disease or where disease is suspected.
For certain diseases the slaughter of all infected and contact animals is compulsory and compensation is paid to the owner via MAFF. For sheep scab disease compulsory dipping and marketing controls may also be imposed nationally, or within the infected area.
See also **Agriculture: Scotland; Agriculture: Northern Ireland.**

Animal Experiments Those which may cause pain can be conducted on living animals only if a licence to do so has been obtained from the *Home Secretary* under the Cruelty to Animals Act 1876. The experiment must be conducted in a place registered for such a purpose by the Home Secretary. For a licence or registration of premises apply to H3 Division of the *Home Office*.

Animal Welfare Domestic and captive animals are protected from ill treatment under the Protection of Animals Act 1911–1964. Complaints or reports of suspected ill treatment should be made to the *police* or *Royal Society for the Prevention of Cruelty to Animals*. In Northern Ireland, domestic animals are protected from unnecessary suffering under the Welfare of Animals Act 1972. Complaints or reports of suspected ill-treatment to the *police* (Royal Ulster Constabulary) or the *Ulster Society for the Prevention of Cruelty to Animals*.

Animals Abroad The *Ministry of Agriculture Fisheries and Food Animal Health Division II* issues certificates of health for animals going abroad. They must be submitted to the diplomatic mission in the UK of the country to be visited, which is responsible for the issue of the necessary permit (see entries for each country). MAFF also provides information about importation of animals into the UK (see **Animals, birds and pets: importation**).

Animals, Birds and Pets: Importation To prevent the spread of rabies, animals and pets imported into the UK must have a licence prior to importation and must then be quarantined in the UK for six months, except in the case of vampire bats which are subject to quarantine for life. Penalties for evasion and animal smuggling are an unlimited fine; up to a year's imprisonment; and the destruction of the animal concerned.
For importation of farm ruminating animals and swine, special veterinary conditions, usually incorporating up to 28 days post-import quarantine (or up to 12 months in the case of zoo ruminating animals and swine) in previously approved premises, is necessary.
Imports of exotic poultry and captive birds are also subject to conditional licence, including being isolated or quarantined on previously approved premises for at least 35 days.
Apply to import such animals and birds to the *Ministry of Agriculture*

Fisheries and Food, Animal Health Division I.
See also **Agriculture: Scotland**; **Agriculture: Northern Ireland**.

Animals, Dangerous Animals designated under the Dangerous Wild Animals Act 1976 (i.e. lions, tigers, crocodiles, bears and poisonous snakes) should be kept only with a licence from the local authority, to whom objections (e.g. by a neighbour on the grounds of danger or nuisance) against the issue of the licence may be made. Circuses, zoos, pet shops and laboratories are exempt.

Antiques: Imports   Customs duty and **value-added tax** are not charged on goods which are proved to have been manufactured or produced more than 100 years before the date when they are brought into the UK (with the exception of pearls and loose gemstones, which are liable to VAT, and **spirits** and **wine**, which are liable to duty). Documentary evidence of age must be produced and you will be required to make a written declaration on a form which will be provided by the customs officer; details from *Her Majesty's Customs and Excise*.

Apple and Pear Production Growers in England and Wales with two hectares or more of land planted with 50 or more apple and pear trees (other than cider apples and perry pears) must register with the *Apple and Pear Development Council*, which promotes consumption of home-grown produce and researches marketing and distribution. Its expenses are covered by growers.
See also **Agriculture: Scotland**; **Agriculture: Northern Ireland**.

Archaeological Finds In Great Britain these should be registered with the national archaeological records held by the *Ordnance Survey* at Southampton. The records, by prior arrangement, are open to inspection by bona fide students of archaeology.

Archery Controlled internationally by the International Archery Federation (FITA). The UK governing body is the *Grand National Archery Society*. It interprets rules, selects British teams, organises championships and open tournaments, administers handicap schemes, appoints judges and organises coaching. Membership is open to local UK clubs, via county associations, six regional societies in England and the *Welsh Archery Federation*, the *Scottish Archery Association* and the *Ulster Archery Association* in Wales, Scotland and Northern Ireland and to clubs of British nationals abroad. It welcomes the disabled. In Scotland field archery is separately governed by the *Scottish Field Archery Association*.

Architects Before a person may practise under a style containing the word 'architect', either on his own account or in salaried employment, he must be listed on the register of architects maintained by the *Architects Registration Council of the UK* under the Architects (Registration) Acts 1931 to 1969. For this, he must either pass one of the examinations recognised by ARCUK; or be the holder of a certificate from the National Council of the Architects Registration Board; or have passed examinations in architecture in a country outside the UK that, in the opinion of ARCUK, are equivalent in standard and scope to the examinations recognised by ARCUK. The British examinations recognised by ARCUK include the qualifying examination of the *Royal Institute of British Architects* and of other professional architectural institutions, including the *Royal Incorporation of Architects in Scotland*, the *Incorporated Association of Architects and Surveyors*, the *Faculty of Architects and Surveyors* and the *Institute of Registered Architects*. Every applicant for registration must also have passed in the UK a recognised examination in professional practice and practical experience.
The register of architects is published annually by ARCUK.
Complaints against an architect should be addressed in the first instance to the registrar, ARCUK.

Architectural Aesthetics In England, Wales and Northern Ireland, the official final arbiter in matters of taste is the *Royal Fine Art Commission*. It advises government, planning officials, architects, civic societies, conservationists and property developers on the quality of developments affecting national and public buildings or amenities, but has no official powers to implement its judgments. It gives its expert opinion free. Enquiries to the secretary.

The official arbiter in matters of taste in Scotland is the *Royal Fine Art Commission for Scotland*. It advises government on the quality of the built environment and on works of art in relation to the exteriors and interiors of buildings where these matters affect the public interest. Though not officially empowered to implement its judgments, it may call witnesses and invite planning officials, architects, civic societies and property developers to discuss matters with it. It gives its expert opinion free. Enquiries to the secretary.

Argentine Republic For **exchange control** is a non-scheduled territory outside the **overseas sterling area** and the **EEC**. UK nationals travelling direct from the UK normally need only the following (but check): **passports; work permits** (if taking a job); green cards for motor insurance (if bringing a car); international driving permit (if intending to drive: see **Motoring abroad**).

The UK has no reciprocal health or social security arrangements.

Enquiries to *Argentine Embassy* in London and *Argentine Consulate* in Liverpool.

British diplomatic missions to Argentine Republic are *British Embassy* in Buenos Aires, *British Consulate* in Rosario and *British Vice-Consulates* in Cipolletti, Comodoro Rivadavia, Rio Gallegos, Rio Grand (Tierra Del Fuego).

Armed Forces: Display Teams Application for a military display team to perform at a public event must be made in advance, preferably before September of the year preceding the event. For Royal Navy or Royal Marines vehicles or teams, apply to local Navy Careers Information Office (see telephone directory) or to the *Royal Navy Director of Recruiting*; for RAF, to the *RAF Participation Committee*; for Army display teams apply, if possible, direct to the team if address is known or to *Army Careers*.

Armed Forces: Pay and Allowances In all services and up to the rank of brigadier or equivalent, these are reviewed by the Review Body on Armed Forces' Pay at the *Office of Manpower Economics*. It makes its recommendations to the Prime Minister. If accepted, they are implemented by the *Ministry of Defence*. Senior officers are included in the arrangements for **public servants' top salaries**.

The government has undertaken to accept the recommendations of the review body unless there are clear and compelling reasons for not doing so.

Armed Forces: Recruitment Any British subject over 16 – male or female – may be able to join any of the armed forces. To find out more either write to the *Royal Navy, Director of Recruiting* for both the Navy and Royal Marines; the *Royal Air Force, Inspectorate of Recruiting*; or *Army Careers*; or, preferably, go to the nearest Careers Information Office (under Army, Navy or RAF in telephone directory). For both commissioned and non-commissioned recruits, entry into a particular service, regiment or trade depends on vacancies and ability. Without committing yourself you can take short tests which establish your suitability for training.

Armorial Bearings Arms for citizens of England, Wales, Northern Ireland and the Commonwealth are granted by the three senior heralds of the *College of Arms*, the Kings of Arms. They are individually authorised by the Queen to grant arms to 'eminent men' (includes women and corporate bodies). Some people automatically qualify for arms, e.g. peers, knights and members of orders of chivalry, and holders of eminent office under the Crown; others gain them through attaining eminence in their own fields, e.g. commissioned officers in the armed services, high ranking civil servants, eminent people in scientific, academic, legal, professional, artistic or local government work. Humble origins do not matter.

In Scotland, the Lord Lyon King of Arms at the *Court of Lord Lyon* is responsible for armorial matters, and it is a punishable offence to use or display bearings which are not in the 'Public Register of All Arms and Bearings in Scotland'. In Eire the *Chief Herald of Ireland* in Dublin is responsible for arms.

The right to arms by inheritance depends on proving a direct, legitimate, male-line descent from an ancestor who was entitled to arms. This is established by the College of Arms for English, Welsh, Irish and Commonwealth ancestors from its registers of arms and **pedigrees** to which only the College officers and their assistants have access. They will make a search for a (variable) fee.

Commonwealth citizens of Scots descent not resident in England, Wales or Northern Ireland, can apply to the Court of Lord Lyon to prove their right to arms in Scotland or for a grant of arms.

USA citizens who can prove direct male-line descent from a British subject can be granted honorary armorial bearings by the College of Arms (but not by the Court of Lord Lyon).
See also **Heralds**.

Arms: Sale and Purchase Before export sale, any UK equipment which could have a military application needs special permission from the *Ministry of Defence* and an export licence from the *Department of Trade*.

Advice to exporters and manufacturers about this and about potential purchasers is available from the *Ministry of Defence, Director of Marketing*.

To sell arms, equipment or services to the British armed forces, start with the *Ministry of Defence Procurement Executive, Director General of Defence Contracts*.
See also **Military surplus**.

Arrest and Questioning of Suspects
Warrants and orders are usually signed by a magistrate or a justice of the peace, directing police officers to arrest an offender (to be dealt with according to law) or to search premises. Warrants are issued on written information sworn by the informant.

A police officer may arrest without warrant anyone who is, or whom he suspects with reasonable cause to be, in the act of committing an arrestable offence (i.e. an offence which carries a penalty of at least five years' imprisonment on first conviction, e.g. arson, burglary, manslaughter, etc.).

The Judges' Rules are laid down by judges of the Queen's Bench Division as guidance for police in questioning persons suspected of an offence, or persons in custody.

Art Publishing: Arts Council Support
The *Arts Council of Great Britain* may provide subsidies for art magazines and art books, especially books about 20th century British artists or by living British artists. In England support includes direct grants to artists and authors to meet part of the pre-publication cost of books; grants to publishers in exchange for profits during the first three years after publication; and grants for a number of issues of an art magazine or the purchase of advertising space in magazines.

The *Scottish Arts Council*, the *Welsh Arts Council* and the *Arts Council of Northern Ireland* may assist publishers of books about artists from their areas or books written by resident art writers or art historians.

Artificial Insemination: Cattle and Pigs Available throughout England and Wales. Licences are required for the import, distribution or sale of cattle or pig semen. For address of nearest centre, and for licence, write to *Ministry of Agriculture, Fisheries and Food, Animal Health Division 111C*.
See also **Agriculture: Scotland; Agriculture: Northern Ireland**.

Artificial Insemination: Human
Available free to couples under the **National Health Service** (e.g. in some cases of male infertility or where there is a high risk of husband passing on serious genetic handicap). Apply in first instance to your **doctor**. Before

carrying out artificial insemination all doctors are likely to seek an indemnity and the husband's consent.

A man who wishes to offer himself as a donor should consult a doctor or family planning clinic.

Artists Abroad Variety, cabaret and other theatrical artists and musicians taking employment abroad should contact the *British Actors' Equity Association*, *Entertainment Agents' Association Ltd*, or the *Musicians' Union*, which have approved standard contracts for overseas engagements.

Arts Administration Training In Great Britain the *Arts Council of Great Britain* is associated with courses for professional arts administrators, and sometimes gives financial support to those being trained. Financial support is also available to Scottish and Welsh trainees through the *Scottish Arts Council* and the *Welsh Arts Council*.

Arts Centres The *Arts Council of Great Britain* subsidises a small number of professionally-run arts centres in England, and can help towards the capital cost of building or adapting and improving existing centres.

Regional Arts Associations can give grants to arts centres which engage professional performing arts companies.

In Scotland, the *Scottish Arts Council* annually allocates a substantial sum for offer to over 100 independent promoting organisations in Scotland (e.g. music clubs, arts guilds, local festivals).

In Wales, the *Welsh Arts Council* is responsible for 10 mixed programme theatres and arts centres. These are mainly theatre-orientated, with the emphasis on receiving rather than mounting productions, but all of them have the facilities to promote other art forms.

Arts, Royal Academy of The UK's oldest institution devoted to fine arts. It is a society of 75 practising artists, painters, engravers, sculptors and architects; members are elected by existing members. It holds many exhibitions, including the annual **Royal Academy summer exhibition**.

For a modest fee anyone can become a Friend of the Royal Academy and obtain free entry to all exhibitions: apply to the secretary, Friends of the Royal Academy, at the *Royal Academy of Arts*.

Arts Tours Overseas Overseas arts tours are organised by the *British Council*, which also assists financially a number of tours of drama, music, ballet and opera companies and groups to various parts of the world. The BC also sends exhibitions of painting and sculpture by British artists, photographic exhibitions and British films (documentary and feature) to international art festivals on extended tour. Much work is done through visiting individuals who produce plays, train musical groups, or give poetry readings or literary seminars. To promote the appreciation of literature the BC publishes booklets and provides teaching aids.

It also sponsors English literature and music recordings and sends copies of plays and musical scores to overseas posts. Enquiries to: Drama Department, Music Department, Fine Arts Department, Literature Department, as appropriate, at the *British Council, Headquarters* or the *British Council, Overseas Office*, in the country concerned.

Ascot, Royal For admission to the Royal Ascot Enclosure during the Royal Meeting obtain a voucher from Her Majesty's Representative, *Ascot Office*, and exchange it, on payment of a fee, for a badge of admission. There are special vouchers for young people (aged 17–25) at reduced rates (those under 17 are not admitted except on Fridays when children aged 10–16 may accompany a parent). Ladies must wear formal day dress with hats, gentlemen morning dress or service dress. Admission to other stands may be purchased without formality.

Assisted Areas These are designated in accordance with UK and EEC regional development policy (see also **Assisted areas: incentives**). There are

three categories of assisted area, offering different levels of incentive for the development of industry, including in some cases service industry; these are special development areas, development areas and intermediate areas. Assisted area benefits may also be available in **New Towns**.
Enquiries about the designation of assisted areas in the UK to *Department of Industry Headquarters* and *Department of Industry Regional Offices*.

Assisted Areas: Incentives Selective financial assistance can be made available to sound commercial and industrial projects which will improve the employment prospects in all types of **assisted area** in the UK. Normal forms of assistance cover employment-creating projects (loans at concessionary rates, interest relief grants, removal grants); employment-maintaining projects (loans at broadly commercial interest rates when these cannot be obtained from other sources) and limited assistance to service industries. Other incentives to industry and commerce in UK assisted areas include: expansion advice (see **Industry: expansion**); **regional development grants**; industrial mortgage and amortisation finance (see **Industry: mortgage and amortisation finance**); tourist industry finance (see **Tourist industry**); factory premises (see **Factories**); **public contracts preference**; finance from EEC funds (see **Industry: EEC finance**); key workers transfer grants (see below) and nucleus labour force grants (see below). Apply for all except the last two to *Department of Industry Regional Offices*, the *Scottish Economic Planning Department* or the *Welsh Office Industry Department*. Workers transferred to assisted areas may attract grants and allowances to assist their removal, with special additions in the case of key workers with dependants left behind with whom they would otherwise remain living. Nucleus labour force grants are available for employers establishing a new business in an assisted area, to help with the cost of temporarily transferring unemployed workers engaged at the new location to a parent factory for retraining. Apply to local *Department of Employment Office* or *Employment Service Agency*.

For assistance and incentives in Northern Ireland, see **Industry: Northern Ireland**.

Astronauts Selected in the UK by the *Department of Industry* for participation in the European Space Programme.

Astronomy The major UK astronomical societies are the *Royal Astronomical Society* (mainly professional) and the *British Astronomical Association* (mainly amateur); the *International Astronomical Union* is the international co-ordinating body. The *Royal Greenwich Observatory* at Herstmonceux Castle, East Sussex, manages telescopes and certain other equipment as 'national facilities' on behalf of the *Science Research Council*.
Use of the Isaac Newton telescope is allocated by the Panel for the Allocation of Telescope Time of the SRC. Use of other telescopes, etc., is available only for qualified people; apply to the telescopes manager or the director at the RGO. Other services available on application to the RGO are vacation courses for undergraduates; industrial training for sandwich students; graduate study in association with the University of Sussex; talks and lectures about the RGO; visits to the grounds of Hertsmonceux Castle and to the Isaac Newton telescope.
Central co-ordination of UK astronomical activities is carried out by the Astronomy Space and Radio Division at the SRC.

Athletics The world governing body for amateur athletics is the *International Amateur Athletic Federation* and the UK body is the *British Amateur Athletic Board*. The BAAB sets a uniform policy for all its member associations and is also responsible for international matches and competitions, selecting UK teams, dealing with infringements of the international rules, deciding UK records and submitting applications for world and European records to the IAAF and European Athletic Association respectively.
BAAB member associations are the *Amateur Athletic Association*, the *Northern Ireland Amateur Athletic*

Association, the *Scottish Amateur Athletic Association*, the *Welsh Amateur Athletic Association*, the *Women's Amateur Athletic Association*, the *Northern Ireland Women's Amateur Athletic Association*, the *Scottish Women's Amateur Athletic Association* and the *Welsh Women's Amateur Athletic Association*.

Attack on the UK Advance warning of an attack on the UK by air or nuclear submarine, or of the approach of nuclear fall-out, would be given by the UK Warning and Monitoring Organisation. Warnings would be based on information from the Ballistic Missile Early Warning System and other UK, NATO and North American sources. The UK warning and monitoring organisation comes under the direct control of the *Home Office*. Its three main functions are to warn the public of any air attack or of the approach of nuclear fall-out, and to supply the UK and neighbouring NATO countries with details of nuclear bursts and scientific assessment of the path and intensity of fall-out.

Attendance Centres When an offence has been committed, the courts can issue an attendance centre order, if the offender is a boy and a centre is available to the court. There are 60 centres in England and Wales for boys between the ages of 10 and 17 found guilty of offences for which older people could be sentenced to imprisonment. Boys ordered to attend must do so during their spare time on Saturdays; they may be required to attend for up to three hours on any one occasion and for a total of not less than 12 hours (with certain exceptions) and not more than 24. The activities include physical training and instruction in handicrafts or some other practical subject. Efforts are made at the centres to induce the boys to join a youth club or other suitable organisation. There are two attendance centres in England and Wales for young men aged 17 and under 21. The one attendance centre in Northern Ireland operates on similar lines, but caters for boys between the ages of 12 and 17.
See also **Young adult offenders**.

Au Pair Arrangements These are not subject to official control, nor is a work permit necessary for a maximum period of two years, but a code of practice is available from the *Home Office*. Au pairs are not required to pay social security contributions although it may be advantageous to do so if their home country has a reciprocal social security agreement with UK. Advice from *Department of Health and Social Security local office*. General information from *International Catholic Girls Society* or *Young Women's Christian Association of Great Britain*.

Auditors Auditors of companies in Great Britain must normally be members of an accountancy body (see **Accountants**) recognised by the Companies Administration Division at the *Department of Trade Headquarters* (2) or must be individuals authorised by the same division. Every company must appoint auditors at each general meeting at which accounts are laid. They hold office until the end of the next such meeting; automatic reappointment of auditors is not permitted. A company has the right to remove an auditor before the expiration of term of office by ordinary resolution requiring special notice, subject to certain safeguards.
An auditor who resigns must state in writing whether circumstances connected with his resignation should be brought to the attention of shareholders or creditors. If so the auditor must say what they are, and a copy of his statement must be sent to the shareholders and filed with the *Registrar of Companies*. A 'nil' return must also be filed. A resigning auditor has the right to requisition a meeting of the company to consider the circumstances which caused him to resign. Where a holding company has a subsidiary which is a body corporate incorporated in GB, the subsidiary and its auditors must give the auditors of the holding company such information as those auditors may reasonably require. In any other case, the holding company must, if required by its auditors, take all such steps as are reasonably open to it to obtain such information from the subsidiary. It is a criminal offence for an officer of a company knowingly or

recklessly to make false or misleading statements to an auditor.

Australia   Commonwealth member. For **exchange control** is a non-scheduled territory in the **overseas sterling area** but outside the EEC. UK nationals travelling direct from the UK normally need only the following (but check): **passports; visas; work permits** (if taking a job); green cards for motor insurance (if bringing a car); international driving permits are recommended (if intending to drive: see **Motoring abroad**).
UK reciprocal arrangements cover social security (see leaflet SA5 obtainable from *Department of Health and Social Security, Overseas Group*) but not health.
Enquiries to *Australian High Commission* in London.
British diplomatic missions to Australia are *British High Commission* in Canberra and *British Consulates* in Adelaide, Brisbane, Melbourne, Perth and Sydney.

Austria   For **exchange control** is a non-scheduled territory outside the **overseas sterling area** and the EEC. UK nationals travelling direct from the UK normally need only the following (but check): **passports; work permits** (if taking a job).
UK reciprocal arrangements cover social security (see leaflet SA25 obtainable from *Department of Health and Social Security, Overseas Group*) and health. In-patient hospital treatment free on production of UK passport; small charge for dependants. (Charges for all other services.)
Enquiries to *Austrian Embassy* in London or *Austrian National Tourist Department* in London.
British diplomatic missions in Austria are *British Embassy* in Vienna and *British Consulate* in Innsbruck.

Authorised Banks   These are the offices and branches in the UK (including the Channel Islands and the Isle of Man) of **banks** which have been authorised by an Order of *HM Treasury* to act for all purposes of the Exchange Control Act 1947 as authorised dealers in **gold** and **foreign currencies** and to which various general permissions have been given to implement certain **exchange control** transactions. Authorised banks include many of the commercial banks in the UK (both British and foreign) but not their offices abroad.

Authorised Depositaries   These are persons authorised by an Order of *HM Treasury* to receive securities into deposit in accordance with the Exchange Control Act 1947, and to whom various general permissions have been given covering transactions in securities. These persons include **authorised banks,** UK resident members of the **Stock Exchange,** and **solicitors** practising in the UK. Full list available from *Her Majesty's Stationery Office*; guidance in Notice EC1 from the *Bank of England*.

B

Badger Carcasses Badgers can spread bovine tuberculosis in cattle. In England and Wales carcases should be reported to the local Animal Health Office through the *Ministry of Agriculture, Fisheries and Food Divisional Office*, which will arrange for their collection and post-mortem examination, to establish whether or not bovine tuberculosis was present at the time of death and whether control measures should be put into effect.
See also **Agriculture: Scotland; Agriculture: Northern Ireland**.

Badgers The catching, marking, or killing of badgers requires a licence from the *Nature Conservancy Council* or in some cases from the *Ministry of Agriculture, Fisheries and Food*, or in Scotland from the *Scottish Department of Agriculture*.

Badminton Controlled internationally by the International Badminton Federation, and in England by the *Badminton Association of England*, an amateur association which administers rules and amateur status regulations, and organises the inter-county championship, international fixtures, television events, sponsorship and coaching. It selects English teams, sanctions all county open tournaments, approves equipment and arranges national and international tournaments. Scotland, Wales and Ireland have separate associations, the *Scottish Badminton Union*, the *Welsh Badminton Union* and the *Badminton Union of Ireland* (Ulster and Eire). There is no UK team.

Bahamas Commonwealth member. For **exchange control** is a non-scheduled territory in the **overseas sterling area** but outside the **EEC**. UK nationals travelling direct from the UK normally need only the following (but check): **passports; work permits** (if taking a job).
The UK has no reciprocal health or social security arrangements.
Enquiries to *Bahamas High Commission* in London.
British diplomatic mission to the Bahamas is *British High Commission* in Nassau.

Bahrain For **exchange control** is a non-scheduled territory in the **overseas sterling area** but outside the **EEC**. UK nationals travelling direct from the UK normally need only the following (but check): **passports** without Israeli stamp; **work permits** (if taking a job); green cards for motor insurance (if bringing a car); international driving permits (if intending to drive: see also **Motoring abroad**).
The UK has no reciprocal health or social security arrangements.
Enquiries to *Bahrain Embassy* in London.
British diplomatic mission in Bahrain is *British Embassy* in Bahrain.

Ballooning In line with other forms of aviation, ballooning comes under the international jurisdiction of the Fédération Aeronautique Internationale and in the UK is mostly under the jurisdiction of the *British Balloon and Airship Club*. The BBAC liaises with the *Civil Aviation Authority* on technical matters (e.g. airworthiness), flying (e.g. licensing pilots) and safety (e.g. incident reports), publishes a bi-monthly magazine, organises balloon meets and publishes a list of owners whose balloons are available for hire.

Baltic Exchange An international mercantile and shipping exchange with a membership of 700 British and foreign companies whose main business activities are chartering of ships; sale and purchase of ships; finance for shipping; towage and salvage; port services and information; shipping statistics; general shipping services; commodity trading, particularly in grain, oils, oilseeds and tallow; chartering of aircraft; sale and purchase of aircraft; futures trading in wheat and barley; maritime arbitration.

The Exchange's proper name is the Baltic Mercantile and Shipping Exchange. Membership (by proposal, seconding, and election by the directors) is open to companies and individuals; conditions of membership from the secretary at the *Baltic Exchange*. Organised groups (but not individuals) can visit the Exchange; apply to the secretary.

Bangladesh **Commonwealth** member. For **exchange control** is a non-scheduled territory in the **overseas sterling area** but outside the EEC. UK nationals travelling direct from the UK normally need only the following (but check): **passports**; **visas**; international certificates of **vaccination** against smallpox; **work permits** (if taking a job); green cards for motor insurance (if bringing a car); international driving permits (if intending to drive: see **Motoring abroad**).
The UK has no reciprocal health or social security arrangements.
Enquiries to *Bangladesh High Commission* in London and *Bangladesh Assistant Commissioners* in Birmingham and Manchester.
British diplomatic mission to Bangladesh is *British High Commission* in Dacca.

Bank Accounts To open a bank account, go to the bank where you wish your account to be; be prepared to prove your identity, your responsibility and honesty, and to supply the name and address of your employer and a referee. The bank will also want a specimen of your signature, your address and details of your requirements (e.g. how often you need a statement, the type of cheque book, transfer of money for savings, etc.).
If you open a current account you will be given a cheque book (see **Cheques**); for a deposit or savings account no cheque book is issued and you may have to deposit an initial balance (possibly only a pound). You can open any number of bank accounts in any number of banks, provided that the bank manager accepts the accounts. A court order needs to be produced before the manager is relieved of his responsibility to keep your affairs secret.

See also **National savings bank accounts**.

Bank Accounts Overseas Under **exchange control** regulations, UK residents cannot normally open foreign currency accounts with banks or other organisations outside the scheduled territories. But accounts for the receipt of travel funds may be permitted on application to an authorised bank. Balances on these accounts must be surrendered when the resident returns home and the account closed, unless specific permission has been given by the *Bank of England*.
The BE normally gives permission to operate retained foreign currency accounts, subject to supervision, to firms with trading interests abroad and to persons who have a source of income abroad with regular commitments to meet of a type for which permission for a remittance from the UK would be granted; any balances surplus to normal requirements must be offered for sale to an authorised bank at the current market rate in the official foreign exchange market.

See also **Direct investment overseas**; **Foreign currency and credit**; **Swiss bank accounts**.

Bank Holidays Apart from the common law holidays (i.e. Christmas and Good Friday), bank holidays in the UK are fixed by the *Department of Employment*. Under the Banking and Financial Dealings Act 1971, only banks and financial institutions must by law close on bank holidays; in other sectors the holidays can be taken (or varied) by voluntary agreement between employers and employees. Wages Council orders, however, as well as national collective agreements (see **Wages**) often specify that the official bank holidays must be taken. Bank holidays and common law holidays make up the normal annual public holidays shown below; extra bank holidays may be declared by the DEm.

by the BE for its loans to the banking system. The rate is calculated from an actual market rate by taking the average rate of discount at the Friday Treasury Bill tender, adding one-half per cent and rounding up to the nearest quarter per cent. Banks individually determine their own base rates and tie their lending rates to this, which may or may not move as MLR changes according to the flow of funds in the market generally.

Banknotes: Mutilated Slightly mutilated notes may be exchanged at **banks** and **post offices**; to qualify for payment in this way a note must be in not more than four pieces, must consist of more than half the original area and

Bank Holidays	England	N. Ireland	Scotland	Wales
New Year	1	1	2	1
St Patrick's Day	–	1	–	–
Good Friday	1	1	1	1
Easter Monday	1	1	–	1
May Day	1 (1 May)	1 (1 May)	1 (end May)	1 (1 May)
Spring Bank	1 (end May)	1 (end May)	1 (beginning May)	1 (end May)
12 July (Battle of Boyne)	–	1	–	–
Summer	1 (end August)	1 (end August)	1 (beginning August)	1 (end August)
Christmas Day	1	1	1	1
Boxing Day	1	1	1	1

Bank Loans For a bank loan from a place where you have a **bank account** your bank manager will require to know how much money you want; what you need the money for; when you will repay; where the money for repayment will come from; and what your commitments are. This information must be based on current, not anticipated, income and assets. The bank manager will be concerned with your character, capability and capital when discussing the loan proposition.

Bank Rate The original name for the *Bank of England*'s discount rate. It is now called Minimum Lending Rate and is the minimum rate charged

contain the 'promise to pay' with at least one-third of the signature and, where applicable, rather more than one complete number (which appears in two places on each note). Mutilated notes which do not satisfy these requirements (and all mutilated notes of the old black-and-white type) must be submitted to the *Bank of England* accompanied by a form obtainable from any bank or post office. Successful claims are paid either by credit to the applicant's bank or **National Giro** account, or through a post office.

Bankruptcy and Liquidation Bankruptcy is a declaration by a court of law that an individual or company is insolvent. A bankruptcy petition may be filed either by the debtor or by his creditors requesting a receiving order.

An enquiry into the debtor's affairs is then conducted by the nearest *Department of Trade Official Receiver's Office*, which retains temporary control of the debtor's affairs. Enquiries to nearest DoT Official Receiver's Office.

Banks   Clearing banks are the 'high-street' banks with branches in nearly every town. The London clearing banks are *Barclays Bank, Lloyds Bank, National Westminster Bank, Midland Bank* and *Williams and Glyn's Bank*. The Scottish clearing banks are *Bank of Scotland, Clydesdale Bank* and the *Royal Bank of Scotland*. In Northern Ireland the clearing banks are *Allied Irish Banks, Bank of Ireland, Northern Bank* and the *Ulster Bank*. These banks comprise the largest section of the primary banking sector, but some other banks offer similar services, e.g. the *Yorkshire Bank* and the *Co-op Bank*.

Basic 'high-street' banking services include taking deposits on current and deposit accounts; lending on loan or overdraft; transmission of money (**cheques**, credit transfers, standing orders and providing cash for personal and business purposes); foreign exchange services (travellers' cheques, **foreign currency**, remissions of money abroad); finance for foreign trade (documentary credits, bills of exchange, reports on overseas buyers and **exchange control** services); personal and business financial references; safe custody of documents and valuables; acting as executor or trustee; advice on taxation; purchase and sale of **stock exchange** investments; registrar work; night safes; leasing; factoring; payroll; external computer services; and managerial advice.

The branch manager is the first point of contact for all these services. Managers will also introduce their customers to merchant banks and other specialist financial institutions.

Merchant banks do not provide retail banking services for private individuals. Traditionally, as their name implies, they accept credit for the financing of international trade, but they have diversified in the field of domestic and international company finance, e.g. amalgamations, takeovers, investment management, flotations, stock management and eurocurrency markets and parallel sterling money markets. The 17 principal merchant banks are members of the *Accepting Houses Committee* and include names such as *Baring Bros & Co., Hambros* and *Rothschilds & Sons*.

British overseas banks have head offices in Britain, but their activities and branches are mostly located overseas. Most deal extensively in the wholesale money markets and the foreign exchange markets. Some are part or wholly-owned subsidiaries of the clearing banks (see **Bank accounts overseas**).

Foreign banks (nearly 300 registered banks from some 60 countries) serve the needs in the UK of their domestic customers, participate in the eurocurrency markets, and undertake banking business for company customers.

Trustee Savings Bank Association has branches in most cities and large towns in the UK. They are predominantly for savings, transmission and private borrowing requirements.

Secondary banks specialise in loans to house owners. Their services are similar to finance houses and they are only termed banks because they accept deposits from the public.

See also **Exchange control**.

Barbados   **Commonwealth** member. For **exchange control** is a non-scheduled territory in the **overseas sterling area** but outside the **EEC**. UK nationals travelling direct from the UK normally need only the following (but check): **passports**; **work permits** (if taking a job).

The UK has no reciprocal health or social security arrangements.

Enquiries to *Barbados High Commission* in London.

British diplomatic mission to Barbados is *British High Commission* in Bridgetown.

Barristers   The specialist branch of the legal profession in England and Wales, barristers, or members of the Bar, provide advocacy services when instructed by solicitors on behalf of clients. The public should only contact a barrister through a solicitor. In the superior courts only barristers have the right of audience. Every barrister is a member of one or other of the ancient voluntary societies known as the Inns of Court: Lincoln's Inn, Inner Temple, Middle Temple and Gray's Inn. The Inns have always been responsible for educating Bar students and calling them to the Bar, and exercising discipline over their members.

The central governing body of the profession is the *Senate of the Inns of Court and the Bar*, consisting of representatives nominated by the Inns and of representatives elected by the Bar; the latter also constitute an autonomous Bar Council. The Senate controls the *Council of Legal Education*, which conducts the Bar examinations and runs the Inns of Court School of Law. A charge of professional misconduct against a barrister is tried by a disciplinary tribunal appointed by the Senate.

Entry into the profession is confined to graduates, except for certain 'mature students'. Those with law degrees may proceed at once to the vocational stage of training. Those with degrees in other subjects, and mature students, must first obtain the Diploma in Law from the *City University* or the *Polytechnic of Central London*. The vocational stage of training, which lasts one year, is conducted by the *Council of Legal Education*. On completion of that stage the student may be called to the Bar by his Inn but, before undertaking independent practice, he must spend a year as the pupil of an established barrister.

In Northern Ireland barristers belong to the *Inn of Court of Northern Ireland* which is responsible for admitting students and calling them to the Bar in Northern Ireland. All barristers must hold a degree, and the vocational training of Bar students is prescribed by the *Institute of Professional Legal Studies* which is governed by the *Council of Legal Education (Northern Ireland)*.

The equivalent to a barrister in Scotland is an advocate. Advocates are all members of the *Faculty of Advocates* which deals with complaints about professional conduct. All advocates must pass examinations equivalent to a law degree from a Scottish university, followed by a period of up to 21 months in a solicitor's office and a further nine months devilling or in pupillage.
See also **Solicitors**.

Baseball British baseball follows American professional rules, which are determined by the USA Baseball Commissioners Office. The governing body in the UK is the *British Amateur Baseball Federation*, which is affiliated to the International Association of Amateur Baseball and the European Baseball Federation. BABF selects British teams and organises the British championship. Baseball in England is organised in four self-governing areas – the Southern Baseball League, the Humberside Baseball League, the Merseyside Baseball League and the Midlands Baseball League. Each runs a league and trains its own umpires and coaches. There is also a *Welsh Baseball Union*.

Basketball Amateur basketball is governed worldwide by the Fédération Internationale de Basketball Amateur, and in the UK by the *English Basketball Association*, the *Welsh Amateur Basketball Association*, the *Amateur Basketball Association of Scotland* and the *Amateur Basketball Association of Ireland* (N. Ireland and Eire). These four national associations are autonomous, but together form the *British and Irish Basketball Federation* which is responsible for joint matters, e.g. British teams, British International Championships, etc.

Beekeeping Inspection facilities in England and Wales from *Ministry of Agriculture, Fisheries and Food Divisional Offices* help control disease. Imported bees have to be certified free of disease by the authorities in the country of origin. Health certificates for the export of bees are issued by MAFF.
See also **Agriculture: Scotland; Agriculture: Northern Ireland**.

Belgium EEC member. For **exchange control** is a non-scheduled territory in the EEC but outside the **overseas sterling area**. UK nationals travelling direct from the UK normally need only the following (but check): **passports** (British visitors' passports acceptable).
EEC or bilateral social security arrangements are applicable; leaflets and EEC Guides obtainable from *Department of Health and Social Security Overseas Branch*. Apply to local social security office for a leaflet SA28 E111 which will explain who is entitled to reduced-cost medical treatment under EEC health arrangements, and how to get a certificate of entitlement (form E111).
Enquiries to *Belgian Embassy* in London, *Belgian Consulate-General* in Manchester, *Belgian Trade Office* in Birmingham or *Belgian National Tourist Department* in London.
British diplomatic missions in Belgium are *British Embassy* in Brussels and *British Consulates* in Antwerp, Ghent, Liège and Ostend.

Benin For **exchange control** is a non-scheduled territory outside the **overseas sterling area** and the **EEC**. UK nationals travelling direct from the UK normally need only the following (but check): **passports**; **visas**; international certificates of **vaccination** against smallpox and yellow fever; **work permits** (if taking a job).
The UK has no reciprocal health or social security arrangements.
Enquiries to *Benin Diplomatic Mission for UK, Benin Embassy* in Paris, France. Visas can be dealt with by the *Benin Honorary Consulate* in London.
British diplomatic mission for Benin is at the *British High Commission* in Lagos, Nigeria.

Bermuda UK dependency. For **exchange control** is a non-scheduled territory in the **overseas sterling area** but outside the EEC. UK nationals travelling direct from the UK normally need only the following (but check): **passports**; **work permits** (if taking a job).
UK reciprocal arrangements cover social security (see leaflet SA23 obtainable from *Department of Health and Social Security, Overseas Branch*), but not health.
Enquiries to *Bermuda Department of Tourism* in London.
The Queen's representative in Bermuda is the *Governor and Commander in Chief* in Hamilton.

Betting Businesses These must notify *Her Majesty's Customs and Excise* local offices not less than one week before commencing business; form BD75 available from HMCE local offices. An official betting duty reference number is issued for the business premises, and use of new premises must be similarly notified. Track occupiers may not permit any person to carry on bookmaking at the track unless in possession of a valid certificate of approval or a betting duty card and sheet; details in HMCE notices 451 and 455.
See also **Betting duty; Bookmaking licences; Gaming licences; Gaming premises.**

Betting Duty Payable on the stake money on bets with a bookmaker or by means of a totalisator, excluding bets liable to **pool betting duty**. The rate of general betting duty is 5 or 6% (on course) and 7½% (off course). Laid-off bets are chargeable. Duty is payable by bookmakers, either by purchase of betting duty sheets from *HM Customs and Excise, Collections*, or by submission of monthly returns (for which a certificate of approval is issued). Failure to pay may lead to recovery of the duty either from others concerned in the management of the bookmaking business or from the premises where the bet was made. Duty is due when the bet is made. General enquiries to *HM Customs and Excise, Collections*. See C & E notices 451, 455.
See also **Football pools: charity; Lotteries.**

Billiard Tables and Bagatelle Boards For public use these require a billiard licence, or a publican's licence in respect of the premises on which public billiards is played. Apply to the clerk

to the licensing justices at the local magistrates' court.
See also **Gaming licences**.

Billiards The UK and worldwide governing authority for English Billiards and any other game – professional or amateur – played on an English Billiard table is the *Billiards and Snooker Control Council*. Its responsibilities include representation, regulating rules and implements, controlling referees, players' status, etc. The UK associations referee their own tournaments. They are the BSCC, the *Scottish Billiards Association and Control Council*, the *Welsh Billiards and Snooker Association and Control Council* and the *Northern Ireland Billiards and Snooker Control Council*.

Bingo Any person who intends to promote dutiable bingo in the UK must apply to *Her Majesty's Customs and Excise, Collectors*, for registration as a bingo promoter; details in Notice 457 from HMCE. Bingo duty is payable upon the total of the money taken by or on behalf of the promoter, plus the amount by which the value of prizes won exceeds the money taken after deduction of duty. The duty applies to all bingo played in the UK, with specified exceptions. Enquiries to *Her Majesty's Customs and Excise* local offices.
See also **Gambling clubs; Gaming licences; Gaming premises; Lotteries; Pool betting permits**.

Birth Under **National Health Service** medical care, birth may take place at home or in hospital, the decision usually being made by the expectant mother's doctor. Different NHS hospitals provide different kinds of treatment and service. Fathers are allowed to be present at the birth in most NHS hospitals. All hospitals with maternity units provide ante-natal and post-natal services. Enquiries to NHS family doctor.
See also **Birth certificates; Birth registration**.

Birth Certificates: England and Wales After the birth (see **Birth registration**), a short certificate is issued free by the *Registrar of Births, Deaths and Marriages* to the informant. This shows only the child's names, surname, sex and date and place of birth. Full certificates costing £1.25 may also be obtained after registration, as may additional short certificates also at £1.25. Certificates obtained after the register has been passed to the *Superintendent Registrar of Births, Deaths and Marriages* (usually after two or three months) cost £2.50 (full) and £1.25 (short).

Birth Certificates: Northern Ireland After the birth has been registered (see **Birth registration: Northern Ireland**), a short birth certificate is issued free by the *Registrar of Births, Deaths and Marriages* to the informant. It shows only the child's names, surname, sex and date and district of birth. Further short certificates at 50p each and full certificates at £1, or reduced-fee certificates (30p and 50p) for certain statutory purposes, may also be obtained on registration, or from the *General Register Office (Belfast)* in the week following. A fee of 50p is payable for full certificates if a search has to be made. Registrars retain duplicate records for one year and can issue certificates during that period.

Birth Certificates: Scotland When the birth is registered (see **Birth registration: Scotland**) a short birth certificate, showing child's names, surname, sex, and date and place of birth, is issued by the *Registrar of Births, Deaths and Marriages* free of charge to the informant. A full certificate issued at the time of registration costs £1.25. A certificate obtained from the Registrar or the *General Register Office (Scotland)* subsequent to the time of registration costs £2.50 (full) and £1.25 (short). If more than one full certificate is purchased, either at the time of registration or thereafter, the cost of the second and each subsequent certificate is £1.50.

Birth Registration: England and Wales Births must be registered within 42 days. Persons qualified to give information for the registration of a birth, in order of preference, are the mother; the father of a legitimate child; the occupier of the house or institution in which the birth occurred; a person present at the birth; the person in charge of the child.

A birth must be registered at the office of the *Registrar of Births, Deaths and Marriages* for the sub-district in which the birth occurred, but the informant may make a declaration of the particulars before any Registrar in England and Wales. If a birth is registered after three months the *Superintendent Registrar of Births, Deaths and Marriages* of the district should be in attendance at the registration.

The informant is responsible for all information included in the entry and signs the register when the entry is completed. Information required is the date and place of birth, names, surname and sex of the child; names, surname and place of birth of both parents; the father's occupation; the mother's usual address.

See also **Adoption; Illegitimate children; Foundlings; Still births.**

Birth Registration: Northern Ireland Births should be registered within 42 days. Persons qualified to give information for the registration of a birth, in order of preference, are the mother; the father of a legitimate child; any aunt, uncle or grandparent of the child who has knowledge of the birth; the occupier of the premises in which the birth occurred; a person present at the birth; the person in charge of the child. A birth may be registered with the *Registrar of Births, Deaths and Marriages* in the district in which the child was born or, if different, in the district in which the mother of the child was ordinarily resident at the time of the birth, if that is in Northern Ireland. Registrars attend at hospitals to register births occurring there.

The informant is responsible for all information included in the entry and signs the entry when it is completed. Information required for registration is names, surname, sex and date and place of birth of child; names, surname and occupation of father; names, surname, usual address, maiden surname and surname at marriage of mother.

The authority of the *Registrar General for Northern Ireland* is required for the registration of any birth after the expiration of one year from the date of birth.

See also **Adoption; Illegitimate children; Still births.**

Birth Registration: Scotland Births must be registered within 21 days, preferably by the father or mother of a legitimate child or the mother of an illegitimate child; or otherwise by any relative of either parent of the child who has knowledge of the birth; the occupier of the premises in which the child was, to the knowledge of the occupier, born; any person present at the birth; any person having charge of the child.

A birth must be registered at the office of a *Registrar of Births, Deaths and Marriages* – either the one for the district in which the birth took place or the one for the district in which the mother's usual residence is situated, if that residence is in Scotland.

The Registrar for the district in which the birth occurs has a duty to ensure that it is registered in due time and otherwise can require an informant to attend at his office. A birth may not be registered beyond three months without the authority of the *Registrar General for Scotland*.

The informant is responsible for the accuracy of all the information included in the entry and signs the register when the entry has been completed. Information required is date and place of birth; names, surname and sex of the child; names, surname and occupation of the father; names, surname, maiden surname and usual residence of the mother; and date and place of parents' marriage.

See also **Adoption; Illegitimate children; Still births.**

Blindness Blind people can register with the local authority (Social Services Department) when certified blind or partially sighted by a hospital consultant. Special services for blind people (e.g. special training, accommodation, holidays and special homes for the deaf-blind) are provided by local authorities (Social Services

Departments and Education Departments), the *National Health Service* and the *Royal National Institute for the Blind*. Advice from RNIB, local authorities (Social Services Departments) and Blind Persons Resettlement Officers of the *Employment Services Agency*.
There are many special financial concessions for blind people. Apply to *Inspector of Taxes* for special income tax allowance; to *Department of Health and Social Security* local offices for special rates of supplementary benefit; to *post offices* for free postage on items sent as 'articles for the blind' and for a reduced television licence fee; to local authorities (Social Services Department) for travel concessions, parking concessions under the car badge scheme (see **Disablement**) and certificates for presentation to travel operators (e.g. for British Airways internal flights). Some travel concessions are for specified purposes only and may relate only to a blind person's guide and not to a blind person. No **dog licence** is required for a guide dog kept by a blind person. See also **Disablement**.

Blindness: Aids   Low vision aids can be issued on free loan under the National Health Service Hospital Eye Service; apply NHS family **doctor**. Radios are provided on permanent free loan to registered blind people by the British Wireless for the Blind Fund; apply local authority (Social Services Department). Special aids and appliances at reduced prices are available from the *Royal National Institute for the Blind*. The *Telephone for the Blind Fund* may help pay for installation or rental of a telephone.
See also **Disablement**; **Eyes**; **Eye treatment**; **Spectacles**.

Blindness: Books   Books in Braille or Moon may be obtained on free loan from the *National Library for the Blind*, and for students from the Students' Braille and Tape Libraries of the *Royal National Institute for the Blind*; books and periodicals in Braille and Moon type are published by RNIB and in Braille by *Scottish Braille Press*; large print books are stocked by public libraries and NLB. 'Talking books for the blind' services are operated by certain voluntary societies.
See also **Disablement**.

Blindness: Postal Services   Certain items for use by the blind can be sent free by first-class letter post: impressed (e.g. Braille) books, papers and letters; machines for making impressions; Braille instructional devices; writing frames; relief maps. Other articles, e.g. talking books and guide-dog harnesses, can be sent free to and from institutions which have agreed this with the *Post Office, Central Headquarters*. Packets must be marked 'articles for the blind' and carry the name and address of the sender. Their contents must be visible or in an easily removable cover. Full details in the '*Post Office Guide*'.

Blood Donors   Blood transfusion gives life to injured people, permits life-saving hospital treatment, counteracts disorders like blood-clotting failure, and enables 'Rhesus' babies to survive and lead normal lives. Donors are always needed. They should be between 18 and 65, in normal health, and should not have suffered from jaundice or undulant fever. Contact: *National Blood Transfusion Service*.
See also **Eye donations**; **Kidney donations**.

Boating and Cruising   The UK representative body for all pleasure boating (including sailing and motor cruising) is the *Royal Yachting Association*. It initiates training programmes; recognises teaching establishments; regulates UK yacht racing (see **Yachting**); issues booklets (e.g. on international flag etiquette and collision regulations); controls UK power boat racing (see **Power boat racing**).
See also **Canals and rivers**.

Bobsleigh   The world governing body is the Fédération Internationale de Bobsleigh et de Tobogganing; the British body is the *British Bobsleigh Association*. There are no tracks and so no races in Britain, but the BBA runs British training, selects British teams for international and Olympic events and holds a championship each year on a European track. All races are under FIBT rules. The armed forces run inter-service tournaments within the British Championships.

Bolivia For **exchange control** is a non-scheduled territory outside the **overseas sterling area** and the **EEC** UK nationals travelling direct from the UK normally need only the following (but check): **passports**; **work permits** (if taking a job); green cards for motor insurance (if bringing a car); international driving permits (if intending to drive: see **Motoring abroad**). The UK has no reciprocal health or social security arrangements.
Enquiries to *Bolivian Embassy* in London.
British diplomatic mission to Bolivia is *British Embassy* in La Paz.

Bombs The Police Bomb Squad disposes of bombs. If necessary, it summons help from the Ordnance Explosive Disposal experts of the armed forces. If you find a bomb, a shell or a bullet leave it alone, keep people away from it and dial 999 for the *police*.

Bonded Warehouses Normally provided by commercial enterprises or public authorities for the general use of anyone wishing to store goods which are liable to **customs duty** (including charges having equivalent effect and the agricultural levy) and **excise duty**. A few warehouses are approved in special circumstances for their owners' sole use. Control of bonded warehouses is regulated by law and an applicant for a warehouse is required to enter into a bond sufficient to cover any duty liability.
For purposes of revenue control, warehouses may be 'crown-locked' (secured by both Crown and warehousekeeper's locks with access obtainable only in the presence of a customs official) or 'open' (control more relaxed). Certain duties may be paid or accounted for before or during deposit at the warehouse; all duties must be cleared at the time of removal from it. Approval of any premises is at the discretion of the Commissioners of *Her Majesty's Customs and Excise*; apply to HMCE local office which will provide copies of appropriate customs notices. Approval is for a specified period and requires renewal.

Bookmakers' Levy All bookmakers whose business includes betting transactions on horseraces are liable for payment of a levy. Under the Betting, Gaming and Lotteries Act 1963 (as amended by the Horserace Betting Levy Act 1969), the *Horserace Betting Levy Board* assesses and collects each year a levy on bookmakers' horserace betting turnover in accordance with a scheme drawn up annually in agreement with the *Bookmakers' Committee* or, in the event of disagreement, in accordance with a scheme determined by the *Home Secretary*.
Bookmakers in disagreement with assessments to liability of levy have the right of appeal either to the Appeal Tribunal for England and Wales or to the Appeal Tribunal for Scotland. The contribution payable by the Tote Board is determined following consultation between that Board and the Levy Board or in the event of disagreement between the two Boards by the Home Secretary.
See also **Horseracing**.

Bookmaking Licences Bookmakers and betting agencies require licences which are granted by magistrates' courts in England and Wales. Licences run from 1 June to 31 May. A bookmaker's permit authorises a person to act as a bookmaker on his own account, but a person who receives a bet as the agent of another bookmaker, or of the Totalisator Board, and who wishes to obtain a betting office licence requires a betting agency permit. A separate betting office licence is needed for each shop.
See also **Betting businesses; Bingo; Horseracing; Pool betting permits**.

Books: Bestsellers The 'Sunday Times' list of bestselling books in Britain is compiled from sales figures supplied by a nationwide panel of 130 bookshops. The list is presented in three groups (non-fiction, fiction and paperbacks) and appears weekly in the

ST and on posters in selected bookshops. Enquiries: 'Sunday Times' (Bestsellers). A list of Scotland's best-selling books is compiled on behalf of the 'Scotsman' by the ST and appears in the 'Scotsman' every Monday. Lists are also compiled for the 'Evening Standard' (London) and the 'Manchester Evening News'.

Boroughs District councils (see **Local authorities**) which have received a royal charter granting borough status; the chairman of the council is known as the mayor. About 190 districts in England and Wales have borough status. Petitions for the royal charter must be prepared in consultation with the *Privy Council Office*. Former boroughs in England which are too large to have parish councils and yet are in districts without city or borough status have charter trustees, district councillors representing the former borough area, who may elect a town or city mayor and who are responsible for the charters, insignia and civic plate of the former borough.

Borstal Training The crown court can place an offender in borstal training, which is available for offenders aged 15–20 years (16–20 in Scotland and 16–21 in Northern Ireland). Offenders are placed as near their home area as possible so as to maintain and foster ties with the local community. Courts rarely order borstal training unless they have tried fines, probation or detention centre training, perhaps all three, and it is primarily intended for offenders of at least 17 years of age. In England, Wales and Northern Ireland the period of training ranges from six months to two years, and is followed by supervision for two years (to be reduced to one year by the Criminal Law Act 1977; it is already one year in Northern Ireland). The actual term of a boy's custodial care depends on his response to training; on average it is less than a year. In Scotland, where there is no minimum period of training, the maximum is two years, and the supervision order lasts for one year.
Borstal training aims to develop the trainee's character and capacities, progressively providing increasing scope for personal decision, responsibility and self-control, and enabling the trainee to develop as an individual. The daily routine generally includes a 40-hour working week with opportunities for suitable trainees to undertake vocational training, e.g. construction industry training courses, physical education, general education at evening classes, and recreation. Outside activities are encouraged and services provided to the community are increasing. There is considerable freedom of movement, and many borstals are open establishments.

Botswana **Commonwealth** member. For **exchange control** is a non-scheduled territory in the **overseas sterling area** but outside the **EEC**. UK nationals travelling direct from the UK normally need only the following (but check): **passports**; international certificates of **vaccination** against yellow fever; **work permits** (if taking a job); green cards for motor insurance (if bringing a car); international driving permits (if intending to drive: see **Motoring abroad**).
The UK has no reciprocal health or social security arrangements.
Enquiries to *Botswana High Commission* in London.
British Diplomatic mission to Botswana is *High Commission* in Saborone.

Boundaries There is a statutory requirement for the *Ordnance Survey* to show certain specified boundaries on maps including national, county, district, borough, parish, electoral division, ward and constituency boundaries. Foreshore boundaries are also shown on OS maps; in England and Wales the boundaries are legally defined as following the high and low water marks of a medium or average tide and in Scotland, by custom, the boundaries are the high and low water marks of mean spring tides.
See also **Foreshore and seabed: ownership**; **Local government: boundaries and electoral arrangements**.

Bowls The internationally recognised game is level-green amateur bowls which is played in 22 countries. It is controlled internationally by the International Bowling Board and within Great Britain by the British Isles Bowling Council. The BIBC is composed of the *English Bowling Association*, *Irish Bowling Association*, *Scottish Bowling Association* and *Welsh Bowling Association*. Each association arranges national championships, coaching and training schemes and national umpires, and the national teams play each other annually in an international series. Women's bowls is based on a similar patern: in England it is governed by the *English Women's Bowling Association*; in Scotland by the *Scottish Women's Bowling Association*; in Wales by the *Welsh Women's Bowling Association*; and in Ulster by the *Irish Women's Bowling Association*.

For men's level-green indoor bowls, the *National Indoor Bowls Council* co-ordinates the *English Indoor Bowling Association*, the *Welsh Indoor Bowling Association*, the *Scottish Indoor Bowling Association* and the Indoor Section of the IBA. The women's indoor bowling associations (the *English Women's Indoor Bowling Association*, the *Welsh Ladies Indoor Bowling Association*, the *Scottish Women's Indoor Bowling Association*, and the *Irish Women's Indoor Bowling Association*) have no UK co-ordinating body.

Crown bowls – a regional game, mainly in the north-west of England – is controlled by the *British Crown Green Bowling Association*. Federation bowls – played in the Midlands and eastern counties – is controlled by the *English Bowling Federation* and the women's game is controlled by the *English Women's Bowling Federation*.

Boxing Professional boxing is controlled internationally by the World Boxing Council (which controls world championships) and the European Boxing Union (European championships). In the UK the governing body is the *British Boxing Board of Control*. All professional boxers, promoters, referees, managers, trainers, seconds, etc., have to hold BBB of C licences, and all tournaments have to be sanctioned by the BBB of C, which is responsible for the complete control and regulation of British boxing including rules, discipline, selection of boxers for British championships, and for putting forward challengers for European and world championships. Amateur boxing is controlled internationally by the Association International de Box Amateur and in England by the *Amateur Boxing Association*. The ABA governs rules and regulations, holds tournaments, championships, etc., fosters youth boxing, administers an obligatory medical scheme for examination and registration of boxers, determines amateur status, selects English teams. In Scotland and Wales the *Scottish Amateur Boxing Association* and the *Welsh Amateur Boxing Association* have similar powers. The co-ordinating body for Great Britain is the *British Amateur Boxing Association* which selects British teams. The *Irish Boxing Association* (Ulster and Eire) is autonomous.

Boxing and Wrestling Premises Premises to be used for public boxing or wrestling entertainments may need a licence. Apply to local authority. Classes which are not public do not require a licence.

Brazil For **exchange control** is a non-scheduled territory outside the **overseas sterling area** and the **EEC**. UK nationals travelling direct from the UK normally need only the following (but check): **passports**; international certificates of **vaccination** against smallpox; **work permits** (if taking a job); green cards for motor insurance (if bringing a car); international driving permits (if intending to drive: see **Motoring abroad**). For stays of longer than three months they may also need **visas**.

The UK has no reciprocal health or social security arrangements.

Enquiries to *Brazilian Embassy* in London and *Brazilian Consulate-General* in Liverpool.

British diplomatic missions to Brazil are *British Embassy* in Brasilia and *British Consulates-General*, *British*

Consulates or *British Vice-Consulates* in 12 provincial centres in Brazil.

Breath Tests may be administered by the *police* when they have reasonable cause to suspect drivers of having excess alcohol in their body, or of having committed a moving traffic offence, or of having been involved in a motor accident. What the police do within the law is an operational matter and entirely for each individual chief officer of **police** of each police force in the UK.
Anyone driving or attempting to drive or in charge of a motor vehicle while unfit through drink or drugs, or who has provided a positive breath test or has refused a breath test, may be arrested without warrant (except while a patient in hospital). Once arrested a person is taken to a police station where the drinking and driving procedure is continued.
See also **Arrest and questioning of suspects**.

Brewers A person who brews beer for sale must be licensed under arrangements for payments of **excise duty**. The licence is granted for one set of premises only but a person may hold more than one brewer's for-sale licence. Before brewing can begin, all premises, rooms, places and vessels intended for brewing purposes must be entered and marked in a manner directed by the Commissioners of *Her Majesty's Customs and Excise*. A 'limited' licence to brew is issued to people who brew beer not for sale but for supply free of charge (e.g. to their employees in factories and work canteens); licence duty and beer duty are payable.
A person who brews beer only for his own domestic use or for consumption by farm labourers employed by him in the course of their employment only has to take out a licence or to pay beer duty when he also deals in or retails beer.
There is relief of excise duty, in the form of 'drawback', on beer removed to a warehouse on the premises of a licensed producer of made-wine or on beer exported, removed to the Isle of Man or shipped as stores. Enquiries: HMCE.
See also **Alcohol**.

British Library Reading Room Passes are available to those engaged in reference work and research beyond first degree level who cannot readily obtain the facilities they need in other libraries. The BL is one of the world's largest collections. Passes give access for reference (not for loan) to, among other items, all UK copyright material, including maps, music, newspapers and scientific publications. Applications in person, with proof of identity (e.g. passport, banker's card or letter of recommendation from person of standing), to the *British Library, Readers Admissions Office*. Newspapers are held at the *British Library, Newspaper Library* and scientific material of the last 50 years in the *British Library, Science Reference Library*.

British Protected Person is a person born, or whose father was born, in a protectorate, or who is the subject of a protected state. British protected persons receive the protection of the UK government and are not subject to the restrictions imposed on foreigners by the Aliens Restriction Acts and the Aliens Order; they do not, however, outside their own country ordinarily possess the other privileges of a British subject. In order to become a citizen of the UK and colonies, they have to apply for **naturalisation**.
Enquiries to *Home Office Immigration and Nationality Department*.
See also **British subjects; Citizenship of the UK and colonies; Passports**.

British Savings Bonds These are issued by *Her Majesty's Treasury* and administered by the *Department for National Savings*. The Jubilee Issue ($8\frac{1}{4}$%) is available from *post offices* and banks. Anyone can purchase savings bonds up to a maximum holding of £10,000. The interest is taxable. Bonds mature after five years, when there is a 4% bonus.

British Standards Certified standards for the construction and performance of a wide range of products, and codes of practice for many technical processes (e.g. tunnelling), are compiled in the UK by committees of the *British Standards Institution*. BSI incorporates international and European standards into British Standards, which are becoming increasingly international in origin. BSI operates testing and inspection services, and provides assurance of compliance with British Standards through certification schemes which provide for the marking of complying products (e.g. Kitemark, Safety Mark). A buyer's guide, listing manufacturers and products covered by certification schemes, is available from BSI offices.

British Subjects Each **Commonwealth** country defines its own citizenship but recognises citizens of every Commonwealth country as possessing the common status of British subject or 'Commonwealth citizen' (which in the UK has the same meaning as British subject). All British subjects have British nationality, but not necessarily citizenship of the UK and colonies. When a colonial territory achieves independence within the Commonwealth it is usual for a separate citizenship to be embodied in its constitution and for its citizens to become British subjects in UK law. At the same time citizenship of the UK and colonies is withdrawn; a person only retains citizenship of the UK and colonies if he possesses a specified connection with the UK or a remaining colonial territory.

There are in addition two classes of British subjects who do not possess citizenship of any Commonwealth country. They are 'British subjects without citizenship' (people connected with former British India by birth, naturalisation or ancestry in the male line, who have not become citizens of any Commonwealth country or the Irish Republic) and British subjects of Southern Irish origin (certain citizens of Eire who have formally made a claim to remain a British subject). Alien women who have been married to people in these two classes are entitled on application to be registered as British subjects.

In general, all British subjects are treated alike in UK law except for purposes of **immigration** and issue of **passports**. All British subjects may vote at Parliamentary and local government elections if they have the necessary residence qualifications. Citizens of the Irish Republic have all the rights of British subjects in the UK and may obtain citizenship of the UK and colonies on the same terms as citizens of Commonwealth countries. Enquiries to *Home Office Immigration and Nationality Department*.

See also **Citizenship of the UK and colonies**; **Commonwealth**; **Immigration into the UK**.

British Summer Time begins at 02.00 hrs Greenwich Mean Time on the day following the third Saturday in March when all clocks are put forward one hour. They go back one hour at 03.00 hrs GMT on the day following the fourth Saturday in October. Enquiries to the *Home Office*.

Broadcast Charity Appeals are made nationally on BBC 1 and BBC Radio 4, and by local radio stations. Separate appeals may be broadcast in Scotland, Wales and Northern Ireland. First preference is given to causes concerned directly with the relief of human distress and with the preservation of life and health. Second come those causes which aim to promote social, physical, cultural, mental or moral well-being but which do not necessarily deal with individual cases of distress (e.g. organisations promoting research into the causes and treatment of disease and of mental or physical handicap). Further information from Appeals Secretary, *BBC Headquarters*, or Manager, *BBC local radio station*.

Broadcast Relay Systems Licences Licences for running any broadcast relay system (including communal aerials), such as a radio taxi network, are required separately from the *Post Office* and from the *Home Office Broadcasting Department*.
See also **Radio apparatus**.

Brunei Commonwealth member. For **exchange control** is a non-scheduled territory in the **overseas sterling area** but outside the **EEC**.

UK nationals travelling direct from the UK normally need only the following (but check): **passports**; international certificates of **vaccination** against smallpox; **work permits** (if taking a job).
The UK has no reciprocal health or social security arrangements.
Enquiries to *Brunei High Commission* in London.
British diplomatic mission to Brunei is the *British High Commission* in Bandar Seri Begawan.

Buckingham Palace The public is admitted to the Queen's Gallery (art) and to the Royal Mews (horses and carriages on view) for an admission charge. Times of admission are: the Queen's Gallery, Tuesday to Saturday 11.00–17.00 hours, Sunday 14.00–17.00 hours; the Royal Mews, Wednesdays and Thursdays only 14.00–16.00 hours. The changing of the guard takes place daily at 11.30 hours (no charge).
See also **Royal garden parties**.

Building In England (except Inner London) and Wales, most building work, apart from straightforward maintenance and repairs, requires approval under building regulations, irrespective of whether **planning permission** is also required. Plans must be deposited with the relevant district council before work begins. Building regulations aim to ensure that the erection of new buildings and the structural alteration and extension of existing ones are carried out in such a way that the buildings are safe and not a danger to the health of those who occupy them; the regulations also apply to certain changes of use.
Enquiries to the building control section of local authorities (district councils). Appeals against rejection of building plans can be made to magistrates' courts, or in Scotland to sheriffs' courts. Applications for discretionary relaxation of the regulations in particular cases are decided by the local authority, except those relating to structural stability and to structural fire precautions in large buildings, which are dealt with in England by the *Department of the Environment* and in Wales by the *Welsh Office*; all such applications must be made in the first instance to the district council. There is also a right of appeal to these departments where the council refuses an application for relaxation which it is empowered to decide, or if it has not made a decision on the application after two months. In addition the person proposing to carry out the work and the council may join in an application to the department for a determination on whether or how the regulations apply in a particular case, and the department's decision is binding.
In Scotland, responsibility for granting relaxations is shared between the local authority (usually the district council) and the *Scottish Development Department*, with the latter being responsible generally for all new buildings and major extensions. SDD also deals with appeals against refusal by local authorities of relaxation applications within their powers. There is no provision for determination as in England and Wales.
Inner London has its own building byelaws; enquiries to the *Greater London Council District Surveyor*.
See also **Local authorities**.

Buildings and Fixtures: Dangerous Buildings or fixtures suspected of being in a dangerous condition should be reported to *police* or local authorities. Local authorities have power to deal with dangerous buildings and structures.
See also **Local authorities**.

Buildings of Special Architectural or Historic Interest These are listed by the *Department of the Environment*, the *Welsh Office* and the *Scottish Office* as a guide for local planning authorities. 'Listed buildings' are classified into Grades I, II* and II to indicate their relative importance. A listed building cannot legally be demolished or altered in any way which might affect its character without the consent of the local planning authority or the appropriate Secretary of State. (In Scotland see booklet 'Scotland's listed buildings: A guide to their protection'.) The *Historic Buildings*

Councils for England, Wales and Scotland advise their respective Secretaries of State on giving discretionary grants or loans towards the cost of repairing buildings of outstanding architectural or historic interest. Any owner of an historic building may apply for a grant by writing to the appropriate HBC. Since 1953 about 1,800 buildings in England have received grants on condition that the public should have reasonable access to view the building. A town scheme is an arrangement whereby the appropriate Secretary of State and local authorities make joint grants to owners for repairing selected buildings in historic towns. The joint grants normally meet half the cost of structural repairs. Apply to: local authority. (See also **Ancient monuments and historic buildings**.)

Whole districts can be designated as legally protected conservation areas. Planning and other authorities concerned have a duty to safeguard the character and appearance of conservation areas.

Under the Field Monuments Act 1972 the DoE can make annual tax-free payments to arable farmers and timber growers who agree not to disturb earthworks and similar monuments on their land. There is similar provision in Scotland.

In Northern Ireland the *Department of the Environment (NI)* is responsible for the listing of historic buildings and for the designation as conservation areas of areas of special architectural or historic interest.

Bulgaria   For **exchange control** is a non-scheduled territory outside the **overseas sterling area** and the **EEC**. UK nationals travelling direct from the UK normally need only the following (but check): **passports; visas; work permits** (if taking a job); green cards for motor insurance (if bringing a car: see **Motoring abroad**). Petrol and diesel coupons for private cars are obtainable at frontier posts in unlimited quantities at a reduction of about 8%.

UK reciprocal arrangements cover health but not social security. Hospital and general medical treatment are free for those normally living in the UK, on production of UK passport and National Health Service Medical card. (Charges for medicines.)

Enquiries to *Bulgarian Embassy* in London or *Bulgarian National Tourist Office* in London.

British diplomatic mission to Bulgaria is *British Embassy* in Sofia.

Burial and Cremation: England and Wales   The authority for the burial of a body can be issued by the *Registrar of Births, Deaths and Marriages* (either certificate for disposal before registration, certificate for disposal after registration or certificate of no liability to register) or issued by the coroner (coroner's order for burial). The coroner may issue his order for burial only where he holds, or intends to hold, an inquest. See also **Death registration; Death registration: coroners**.

For cremation neither the registrar nor the coroner can issue a document which, by itself, is sufficient authority. A registrar's certificate for disposal after registration or a coroner's certificate for cremation is required but a medical referee at the crematorium must give final authority for cremation. The coroner's certificate for cremation is issued after he has held a postmortem or after he has opened an inquest.

Burial and Cremation: Northern Ireland   The authority for burial of a body may be issued by the *Registrar of Births, Deaths and Marriages* (a certificate that he has registered or received written notice of the death together with a medical certificate of the cause of death) or by the coroner, where he considers an inquest unnecessary.

See also **Death registration; Death registration: coroners**.

Burial and Cremation: Scotland   If a body is to be disposed of by burial, the burial can take place either before or after the death is registered. See also **Death registration** and **Death registration: coroners**. If, as is usual, the death is registered before burial, the *Registrar of Births, Deaths and Mar-*

riages issues a certificate of registration of death for production to the burial ground keeper. If the burial takes place before the death is registered, the burial ground keeper notifies the Registrar for the district in which the death occurred so that he can arrange for the death to be registered.
The certificate of registration of death is not sufficient authority on its own to allow cremation to take place.
Cremation may take place if an application is made to the cremation authorities and there is produced to them a medical certificate given by a medical practitioner who attended the deceased during his last illness, a confirmatory medical certificate from an independent medical practitioner and a certificate that the death has been registered.

Burials at Sea Authorisation and advice on suitable areas from Fisheries Division IC at the *Ministry of Agriculture, Fisheries and Food, Headquarters (2)*.

Burma For **exchange control** is a non-scheduled territory outside the **overseas sterling area** and the **EEC**. UK nationals travelling direct from the UK normally need only the following (but check): **passports**; **visas**; international certificates of **vaccination** against smallpox; **work permits** (if taking a job); green cards for motor insurance (if bringing a car); international driving permits (if intending to drive: see **Motoring abroad**).
The UK has no reciprocal health or social security arrangements.
Enquiries to *Burmese Embassy* in London.
British diplomatic mission to Burma is *British Embassy* in Rangoon.

Burundi For **exchange control** is a non-scheduled territory outside the **overseas sterling area** and the **EEC**. UK nationals travelling direct from the UK normally need only the following (but check): **passports**; **visas**; international certificates of **vaccination** against smallpox; **work permits** (if taking a job); green cards for motor insurance (if bringing a car); international driving permits (if intending to drive: see **Motoring abroad**).
The UK has no reciprocal health or social security arrangements.
Enquiries to *Burundi Diplomatic Mission to UK*, *Burundi Embassy*, Brussels, Belgium.
British diplomatic mission to Burundi is *British Consulate* in Bujumbura. The responsible British main mission is *British Embassy* in Zaire.

Bus Conductors On public service vehicles conductors who are not also drivers must hold a conductor's licence from the *Traffic Commissioners*; or, in London, from the Commissioner of Police at the *Public Carriage Office*. Appeal against refusal of licence to a magistrates' court (sheriff's court in Scotland).
See also **Public service vehicle operators**; **Public service vehicles**.

Bus Services and Subsidies The operators of bus and coach services in Great Britain are the *London Transport Executive* in London; the *Passenger Transport Executive* in the other six major conurbations; district councils (regional councils in Scotland) in many of the other major cities; the *National Bus Company* (*Scottish Bus Group* in Scotland) for the vast majority of rural services; and private companies. The *Traffic Commissioners*, who are statutorily independent, have to approve routes, stopping places and (with the exception of the LTE to which special arrangements apply) fare levels in order to exercise control in the interests of safety and prevent any unreasonable competition which may also not be in the public interest (see also **Public service vehicle operators**).
Central government sets the broad policy and financial framework for the nation's bus operations, but determination of bus networks to meet local needs is the responsibility of the metropolitan and shire counties (regional/island councils in Scotland) which can subsidise bus services within the overall resources available for this purpose. Local authorities' financial support for loss-making services is eligible for central government grant.

There is additional government financial assistance in the form of a fuel duty rebate to operators on all stage carriage services and, until 1985, a bus grant which is payable to operators at the rate of 50% to help them buy new vehicles for stage carriage work.
See also **Local authorities; Public serice vehicle operation: complaints; Public service vehicles.**

Business Names   Any business which is not conducted under the proprietor's own name must be registered under the Registration of Business Names Act 1916 with the *Registrar of Business Names*. He has the power to refuse the registration of any business name which in his opinion is undesirable, a power which is co-extensive with that of the *Department of Trade* to refuse the registration of undesirable names of companies.
See also **Companies: formation and registration.**

Business Registration: VAT   Anyone carrying on a business which has a taxable turnover at or above specified limits (broadly £7,500 per annum), must notify *Her Majesty's Customs and Excise* on form VAT 1.
See also **Value-added tax.**

Business Security: Keys   In the interest of crime prevention, keyholders of business premises are advised to register with the local *police*. Changes should be notified to police immediately.

Businesses, Small   Throughout Great Britain, the *Department of Industry Small Firms Information Centres* (run by the DT in association with the *Scottish Office* and *Welsh Office*) offers a free advice service to small firms and people wishing to establish a business, and assists small firms in finding the right sources of help for their problems.

Byelaws   Under the Local Government Act 1972 the *Home Secretary* has power either to confirm or to refuse byelaws, and also to cause a public local enquiry to be held, before he reaches his decision. Representations about the byelaw are taken into full account and, at least one month before the application for confirmation of the byelaw is made, notice must be given in one or more local newspapers. Enquiries to the relevant local authority in the first instance, and then to the *Home Office*; in Northern Ireland to relevant district council, then to the *Department of the Environment for Northern Ireland.*
See also **Local authorities.**

C

Calibration Official calibration certificates are provided by laboratories approved by the *British Calibration Service*. BCS provides authenticated calibration of scientific instruments and other measuring devices and certification of measurements of all kinds. Laboratories are specially approved for particular measurements, for which they are authorised to issue BCS certificates. These provide a very high degree of assurance of the correctness of the calibration and guarantee traceability to national standards of measurement. Copies of the 'Directory of Approved Laboratories' and details of other BCS facilities available on request to BCS.

Cameroon For **exchange control** is a non-scheduled territory outside the **overseas sterling area** and the **EEC**. UK nationals travelling direct from the UK normally need only the following (but check): **passports; visas;** international certificates of **vaccination** against smallpox and yellow fever; **work permits** (if taking a job); green cards for motor insurance (if bringing a car); international driving permits (if intending to drive: see **Motoring abroad**).
The UK has no reciprocal health or social security arrangements.
Enquiries to *Cameroon Embassy* in London.
British diplomatic missions to Cameroon are *British Embassy* in Yaoundé and *British Consulate* in Douala.

Camping The Fédération Internationale de Camping et Caravanning represents camping internationally. In the UK there is no official representative body, but among the many clubs for different aspects of camping, the *Camping Club of Great Britain and Ireland* is the most all-inclusive. It is open to users of tents, trailers, trailer caravans and motor caravans and is represented on most UK amenity bodies. It operates many camp sites; some are open to non-members. The *Forestry Commission, National Trust* and regional tourist offices (see **Tourism**) provide details of camp sites in national parks. Apart from organised sites the position is complicated (local byelaws differ) but the general rule is that permission to camp should be obtained in advance from the landowner and one cannot camp on roads or car parks.
International Camping Carnets are issued to members of clubs which are affiliated to either the Alliance Internationale de Tourisme, the Fédération Internationale d'Automobile or the FICC. The carnet is required for camping in Denmark, Holland, certain areas of Belgium, and in the state forests of France. It entitles holders to reductions in site fees at many sites, and to the privileges of local club members; is proof of membership of a recognised club; is a guarantee to the site management that the holder is covered for third-party risks up to a total of £100,000; and may usually be left at site reception offices instead of a pass-

port for police registration purposes. In the UK, issuing clubs are the *Automobile Association*, the *Royal Automobile Club*, the *Camping Club of Great Britain and Ireland*, the *Caravan Club*, the *Motor Caravanner's Club*, the *Civil Service Motoring Association* and the *Cyclists' Touring Club*.

Camping and Caravanning Sites Campers and caravanners should seek permission from landowners before camping in any location. Landowners must obtain **planning permission** and a site licence for use of land as a camping or caravan site from **local authorities**. Appeal against conditions attached to, or a refusal of, planning permission may be made to the appropriate *Secretary of State* (Environment, Scotland or Wales). Appeal against conditions attached to a site licence to magistrates' courts (or in Scotland sheriff courts). Certain recreational organisations are exempt from the normal requirements to obtain planning permission and a licence. The issue of exemption certificates and their control is a matter for the appropriate Secretary of State. Model standards for static holiday caravan sites are specified by the appropriate Secretary of State. Complaints concerning site conditions to local authorities.

Canada **Commonwealth** member. For **exchange control** is a non-scheduled territory outside the **overseas sterling area** and the **EEC**. UK nationals travelling direct from the UK normally need only the following (but check): **passports; work permits** (if taking a job); green cards for motor insurance (if bringing a car); international driving permits (if intending to drive: see **Motoring abroad**).
UK reciprocal arrangements cover social security (see leaflet SA20 obtainable from *Department of Health and Social Security, Overseas Branch*), but not health.
Enquiries to *Canadian High Commission* in London and *Canadian Consulates* in Belfast, Birmingham, Glasgow and Manchester.
British diplomatic missions to Canada are *British High Commission* in Ottawa and *British Consulates* in Edmonton, Halifax, Montreal, Quebec, Toronto, Vancouver and Winnipeg.

Canals and Rivers Canals and rivers in the UK have some commercial use and are extensively used for recreation. They are controlled by a variety of bodies, but most canals and some rivers are controlled by the *British Waterways Board*. The BWB maintains its canals, produces maps and guides to waterways and other publications, arranges canal holidays and can provide a list of hire cruiser operators.
All boats on BWB waterways, from canoes and inflatable dinghies to houseboats and passenger boats, require a licence or registration certificate (where appropriate) from the *BWB Craft Licensing Office*. Houseboat certificates are rigidly restricted. Hire cruiser operators on BWB waterways also require BWB approval for their sites (which should be off the main line of the canal) and for certain other facilities.
On most rivers the BWB is a navigation authority only, and has limited control over mooring. On BWB canals mooring on the towpath side is allowed for 14 nights without a permit. On the offside mooring is permitted provided the landowner has a permit and his permission is obtained. The site must meet navigational and other criteria. All permits are obtained through the local *British Waterways Board, Area Amenity Assistant*.
See also **Angling licences; Canal towpaths**.

Canal Towpaths Towpaths alongside *British Waterways Board* canals are normally private (BWB) property. Some carry scheduled public **footpaths** or are walkways by agreement with local authorities. Licences for access for nature walks, etc., (but not for boating and fishing) are issued by the local *British Waterways Board, Area Amenity Assistant* and other offices of the Board.
See also **Canals and rivers**.

Canoeing is governed internationally by the International Canoe Federation which sets rules for competitive canoeing and the conduct of world championship events. In Britain the *British Canoe Union* trains and selects UK teams, organises international events, supervises domestic competitions, trains and examines instructors and coaches, operates a system of personal performance tests, and represents canoeing interests. National divisions of the BCU are the *Welsh Canoeing Association*, the *Scottish Canoe Association* and the *Canoe Association of Northern Ireland*.

Capital Gains Tax is a UK tax on the gains of individuals which are not chargeable to **income tax**. There are various exemptions (including the individual's residence and car) and thresholds before liability arises. Liability may arise on a disposal when any chargeable gain (or allowable loss, as losses can in some circumstances be set against gains) has to be determined. The gain or loss is, broadly, the rise or fall in value between the date of acquisition of the asset (or 6 April 1965, when CGT came into effect, whichever is the later) and the date of disposal. The disposal can be by way of gift, so a chargeable gain is not necessarily one evidenced by hard cash following a sale. A gift can give rise both to CGT and to **capital transfer tax**.
The *Inland Revenue Inspector of Taxes* assesses CGT, which is payable to the *Inland Revenue Collector of Taxes*. There is a right of appeal to the Appeal Commissioners; tell your Inspector if you wish to appeal.

Capital Transfer Tax was introduced in the UK by the Finance Act 1975, it embodies features of both a gifts tax (payable on gratuitous dispositions between living people) and a death duty (chargeable on assets passing on the death of a person). The principle is that the value of chargeable transfers made by a person is logged up during his life with a final cumulation of the value of his estate at death. The tax is payable on a rising scale, according to the level of the cumulation immediately following a chargeable transfer. The tax is payable by either the tranferor or the recipient. In the former case the value of the gift has to be 'grossed up' to include the amount of the tax, for that represents part of the loss to the transferor. There are many exemptions, the principal one relating to transfer in life or on death between spouses. Small gifts, habitual gifts and wedding gifts can also be exempt, depending upon value, and there is an annual exemption for other gifts which means that up to a certain amount gifts are not chargeable and do not count in the cumulation of chargeable transfers. There is also a threshold, (currently £15,000), i.e. no CTT can become payable until the cumulation of chargeable transfers exceeds it.
CTT is administered by *Inland Revenue Capital Taxes Offices*. Appeals can be made to the Appeal Commissioners and/or the High Court, depending upon the nature and topic of the matter in dispute. Notice of appeal should be given to the Capital Taxes Office.

Car Sales: Tax Free Cars may be sold free of both **value-added tax** and **car tax** to anyone who intends to live outside the UK for at least 12 consecutive months. Such vehicles may be used for six months (overseas visitors to UK for 12 months) in the UK before the owner takes up residence abroad. Vehicles must be supplied by approved UK manufacturers or sole selling agents of manufacturers overseas (approval from *Her Majesty's Customs and Excise*). Apply for permission to acquire tax free vehicle via the supplier (form VAT 410 or 411). Details in HMCE notice 705.

Car Tax Payable once only on all new and imported cars and motorised caravans, including three-wheeled and privately assembled vehicles, which are made or registered for road use in the UK. Any person who in any calendar year makes or imports 10 or more chargeable vehicles must notify *Her Majesty's Customs and Excise* for possible registration, but tax is also due on cars made or imported by non-registered persons. Car tax, which is separate from and additional to **value-added tax**, is charged on the assessed wholesale value, including accessories and optional extras fitted to the car when supplied; disputes about value may be taken to arbitration before an independent referee. The tax does not apply to motor cycles (even those with side-cars), taxi-cabs, ambulances, certain special purpose vehicles and in general to commercial vehicles, nor to vehicles over 20 years old, but tax is payable upon conversion of a non-chargeable vehicle into a chargeable one. Special provisions exist for direct and personal car exports, and for temporary importation of private and commercial motor vehicles. Details in HMCE notice 670 (Car tax general guide); 671 (Cars made or imported by non-registered persons); 672 (Car tax on conversion of vehicles); 705 (Tax free sales of motor vehicles for use before export). Registration for road use of chargeable vehicles may be refused without proof of car tax payment.

Car Wash Plant   Water supplied to a car wash plant is metered and charged for by volume by the local *water authority* or *water company*.
See also **Water services**.

Cargo at Sea   Carriage of certain types of cargo is controlled by the *Department of Trade* (Marine Division); see 'Carriage of Dangerous Goods in Ships' from DoT. Guidance on storage is issued by Merchant Shipping Notices (see **Shipping notices**).

Cattle and Beef: Support   Under EEC rules for cattle and beef, UK producers are supported by the payment of variable premiums, calculated to maintain average returns at the level of seasonally adjusted target prices. In the EEC the market is underpinned by intervention-support buying of specified qualities of beef and, when necessary, by assistance towards the private storage of beef. The prices of imports for non-EEC countries are regulated by a system of tariffs and variable levies. Information on all forms of support from the *Intervention Board for Agricultural Produce*.
See also **Agricultural produce: EEC subsidies**.

Cattle: Bovine Tuberculosis   All cattle in Great Britain are subjected to a tuberculin test at regular intervals. In England and Wales the Divisional Veterinary Officer at the *Ministry of Agriculture, Fisheries and Food, Divisional Office* decides, on the basis of the herd test, whether to put in action the Minister's power of compulsory slaughter of any animal which is infected, has reacted to the tuberculin test or has been exposed to infection by contact.
See also **Agriculture: Scotland; Agriculture: Northern Ireland**.

Cattle: Brucellosis   An official register, the British Register of Brucellosis Accredited Herds, is maintained by the *Ministry of Agriculture, Fisheries and Food*. County sections of the Register are kept at the *Ministry of Agriculture, Fisheries and Food, Divisional Offices* in England and Wales. For an entry an owner must submit his herd to a series of qualifying blood tests. Under the voluntary Brucellosis Incentives Scheme *MAFF* pays incentives to owners of herds who achieve accredited status, in the form of premiums on milk sales or a headage payment on breeding animals in beef breeding herds. Owners of herds dealt with under the compulsory eradication measures are not eligible for incentives but receive compensation for reactors and dangerous contacts which have to be slaughtered.
Under the conditions of an EEC directive, exports of cattle to the EEC must be from herds declared 'officially brucellosis-free'. To obtain entry on the British Officially Brucellosis-Free Register herds must meet other requirements (e.g. must not contain any animals which have been vaccinated during the previous three years).
See also **Agriculture: Scotland; Agriculture: Northern Ireland**.

Cattle: Calf Subsidies   Stage A subsidy is payable on live calves of beef type born in the UK. They must be at least eight months old (six months for spring-born calves in approved hill areas) but not have cut an incisor tooth. Stage A subsidy calves are marked in the right ear and any other mark likely

to be confused with the subsidy marking forfeits the subsidy unless registered as a confusion mark. Stage B subsidy is payable on carcases of clean, home-bred cattle slaughtered for beef. Animals must be presented for certification at approved deadweight centres. Enquiries to *Ministry of Agriculture, Fisheries and Food, Divisional Offices* in England and Wales; the *Department of Agriculture and Fisheries* for Scotland; or the *Department of Agriculture for Northern Ireland*.
See also **Agricultural produce: support; Cattle and beef: support.**

Caving Caving is an individualistic sport and has no international government. In the UK it is represented by the *National Caving Association*. This is a federation of regional Caving Councils, the British Cave Research Association, the British Association of Caving Instructors, the Cave Diving Group, the Cave Rescue Council, and the William Pengelly Cave Studies Trust. Apply to the NCA for their addresses.

Cellar Flaps must be properly guarded when open. When shut they must conform to specified regulations. Report suspected dangers or hazards to the relevant local authority. In London, it is an offence under the Metropolitan Police Act of 1839 to have an open cellar or vault without an adequate fence or handrail.

Censuses The *Registrar General of England and Wales* and the *Registrar General for Scotland* are responsible for taking the national censuses of the population of Great Britain. Censuses have been taken every 10 years since 1801 (bar 1941) and include every man, woman and child (British and foreign) in Great Britain on a set night. There was also a census of 10% of the population in 1966. In Northern Ireland, the *Registrar General for Northern Ireland* is responsible for censuses of population. Censuses were taken in Ireland every 10 years from 1841 to 1911 and in Northern Ireland in 1926, 1937, 1951, 1961, 1966 and 1971.
Filling up the census form is compulsory but information given about named people is not divulged to anyone outside the census organisation. Information generally includes name; date of birth; sex; marital status; usual address and addresses at previous dates; country of birth; economic activity; education; housing; transport. Census results are available in formal reports published by *Her Majesty's Stationery Office* and in other tables obtainable from the *Office of Population Censuses and Surveys*, the *General Register Office* (Scotland) and the *General Register Office* (Belfast).

Central African Empire For exchange control is a non-scheduled territory outside the **overseas sterling area** and the **EEC**. UK nationals travelling direct from the UK normally need only the following (but check): **passports**; **visas**; international certificates of **vaccination** against smallpox and yellow fever; **work permits** (if taking a job); green cards for motor insurance (if bringing a car); international driving permits (if intending to drive: see **Motoring abroad**).
The UK has no reciprocal health or social security arrangements.
Enquiries to *Central African Empire Diplomatic Mission to UK*, at *French Consulate-General* in London.
British diplomatic mission to Central African Empire is *British Consulate* in Bangui. The main mission with overall responsibility is *British Embassy* in Yaoundé, Cameroon.

Cereals The *Home-Grown Cereals Authority* raises a levy on all first-hand purchases by dealers and processors of home grown wheat, barley and oats. The dealers and processors may recover 50% of the levy from the grower concerned and a further 25% from the dealer or processor to whom the cereals are sold. The current rate of levy is 2p per tonne. The HGCA provides a market intelligence service, sponsors research and operates a wheat classification scheme.
The *Intervention Board for Agricultural Produce* is responsible for the administration of EEC cereal support buying arrangements. Under these arrangements IBAP is obliged to purchase wheat or barley of EEC origin,

which meets certain quantity and quality requirements, and is offered to them for delivery to a designated intervention centre. Enquiries to IBAP or the HGCA.

Certificates of Origin These may be required of UK exporters by certain overseas countries for particular products. They are available from chambers of commerce authorised by the *Department of Trade*; apply to *Department of Trade Headquarters 3*, for list.

Certificate of Secondary Education Examinations are set by the *South-Western Examinations Board*; *Southern Regional Examinations Board*; *South-East Regional Examinations Board*; *Metropolitan Regional Examinations Board*; *Middlesex Regional Examining Board*; *East Anglian Examinations Board*; *West Midlands Examinations Board*; *East Midland Regional Examinations Board*; *North West Regional Examinations Board*; *Associated Lancashire Schools Examining Board*; *West Yorkshire and Lindsey Regional Examining Board*; *Yorkshire Regional Examinations Board*; *North Regional Examinations Board*; *Welsh Joint Education Committee*; and *Northern Ireland Schools Examinations Council*. CSE examinations are normally taken in any number of subjects after completion of five years of secondary education. Control of the examination is under the examining bodies above. A grade one result in CSE is regarded as equivalent to at least grade C at 'O' level in the General Certificate of Education.
See also **Education: Scotland**; **Education: Northern Ireland**.

Chad For **exchange control** is a non-scheduled territory outside the **overseas sterling area** and the **EEC**. UK nationals travelling direct from the UK normally need only the following (but check): **passports**; **visas**; international certificates of **vaccination** against smallpox; **work permits** (if taking a job); green cards for motor insurance (if bringing a car); international driving permits (if intending to drive: see **Motoring abroad**).
The UK has no reciprocal health or social security arrangements.
Enquiries to *Chad Diplomatic Mission to UK* at *French Consulate-General* in London.
British diplomatic mission to Chad is *British Consulate* in Ndgamena.

Channel Islands The Islands comprise two main administrative units, the Bailiwick of Jersey and the Bailiwick of Guernsey (including respectively the islets of Herm and Jethou, and Alderney and Sark). In each of the Bailiwicks the Queen's personal representative is the Lieutenant Governor, who is responsible for issuing **passports**. Other Crown officers in each Bailiwick are the Bailiff and Deputy Bailiff, who head the Islands' administrations and share the duties of presiding over the legislatures and the Royal Courts of Jersey and Guernsey; and the Attorney General and Solicitor General, legal advisers to both the Crown and Islands' authorities.
The Islands have their own legislative assemblies and their own fiscal, administrative and legal systems; they have no representatives in the UK Parliament. In the UK the Privy Council is responsible for decisions on Channel Island affairs and deals with legislation submitted to it for royal approval. Primary legislation passed by the Islands' assemblies requires this assent. Enquiries to the *Home Office*.
The Channel Islands, together with the UK and Eire, form a common travel area; there is no immigration control between the UK and the Islands. For **exchange control**, the Islands are part of the scheduled territories.

Charitable Funds These may be entrusted for safe custody to the *Official Custodian for Charities*, who accepts the transfer of investments into his corporate name to ensure continuity of title, and collects on behalf of charity trustees the income (from which UK **income tax** is deducted at source) and any other benefits accruing on their holdings. Charity trustees retain control and responsibility as if the investments were held in their own names, and the OCC is statutorily prohibited from exercising powers of investment management. Enquiries to: OCC.

Charities and Voluntary Organisations Local authorities (except in Scotland) register charities whose main aims include the promotion of the welfare of disabled people. Local authorities can only use and contribute to registered voluntary organisations.
Enquiries to local authority Social Services Department or to *National Council of Social Service*. Informative publications include 'Voluntary Social Services' published annually by NCSS, and 'Guide to the Social Services' and the comprehensive 'Charities Digest', both obtainable from *Family Welfare Association*.
See also **Local authorities**.

Charities: Complaints Complaints about breaches of trust, unsatisfactory presentation of accounts, excessive expenditure on fund-raising or administration, or maladministration may be made to the *Charity Commission*. The Commission normally investigates complaints informally but has powers to institute an inquiry where considered necessary.

Charities Overseas British consular officers are not directly responsible for the administration of local British charities but they frequently serve as ex-officio members of the bodies administering such charities and other community organisations. Addresses of British consulates are listed under *British diplomatic missions*.

Charities: Registration Institutions for the relief of poverty, for the advancement of education or religion, or for other purposes beneficial to the community may be registered as charitable trusts. Non-exempt charities in England and Wales must be registered with the *Charity Commission* if they have any permanent endowment, or income from property of more than £15 p.a. or the use and occupation of land. The Commission may institute inquiries (see **Charities: complaints**) and call for annual accounts and documents. Advice from the Charity Commision or a **solicitor**.

Chelsea Flower Show Held by the *Royal Horticultural Society* in May each year for four days. Exhibits include complete gardens, trees, shrubs, flowers, vegetables, fruit, garden machinery and equipment, glasshouses, sheds and horticultural sundries. Exhibitors should apply for space to the secretary of the RHS. First day viewing is reserved for holders of tickets issued free to fellows of the RHS. The public may attend on payment for the last three days.
See also **Horticulture; Royal Horticultural Society**.

Chelsea Pensioners live at the *Royal Hospital*, Chelsea, which is not a hospital, but a home for old soldiers (built by Sir Christopher Wren and opened in 1692). To qualify for admission a man has to be in receipt of a British Army pension (either long service or disability) and be over 65 (55 in case of disability). There is no accommodation for wives. On entry you surrender your Army Pension in return for free board, lodging, clothes and medical attention, but retain your contributory state **retirement pension**.

Chemical Analysis Services are provided to government departments and other public bodies by the *Laboratory of the Government Chemist*; enquiries to the Laboratory.

Cheques are bills of exchange payable on demand and drawn on a banker; they are valid throughout the world. Cheque cards, used by customers of the 20 UK banks in the cheque card consortium, guarantee cheques up to a limit of £50.
See also **Banks; Credit cards**.

Child Care and Welfare The responsibility of local authority (Social Services Departments), which must receive into their care any child under 17 who has no parents or has been abandoned, or whose parents are unable for any reason to provide for his proper accommodation, maintenance, and upbringing; always provided that intervention is necessary in the interest of the child's welfare. Although no court order is involved in such reception into care, it is normally done with the consent of any parent whose whereabouts is known or can be traced. Local authorities can give advice, guidance and assistance to families to prevent children from coming into or remaining in care, or being brought before the courts, whether as offenders or as being in need of care or protection. Anyone (e.g. neighbours) who believes a child to be at risk of improper care should report it to the local authority (Social Services Department), which has a duty to investigate any report suggesting that there are grounds for bringing care proceedings in respect of a child in their area, unless they are satisfied that enquiries are unnecessary. They would then decide whether care proceedings were appropriate in that case. Reports of ill-treatment or neglect are also received by the *National Society for the Prevention of Cruelty to Children* and the *police.*

Having received a child into care on the basis indicated above (i.e. without a court order), the local authority may assume full parental rights if either or both parents of a child in its care are dead, or have abandoned the child, or when a parent suffers from a disability which renders him or her incapable of caring for the child properly, or is otherwise unfit to have its care, or, finally, if the child has remained in local authority care (including any intervening period spent in the care of a voluntary organisation) throughout the preceding three years. The authority may also assume the rights of a second parent in order to prevent a child living in a household comprising that parent and a parent whose rights they have already assumed.

Where the child is in voluntary care, and the local authority has not assumed parental rights, the parent may remove the child from care at any time, unless the child has been continuously in care throughout the preceding six months, in which case the parent must give the authority 28 days' notice of his intention to remove the child from care. This requirement may be waived or the period reduced by the local authority if it thinks fit.

If challenged by a parent, whom the local authority must notify immediately of its assumption of parental rights, the parent may serve on the authority counter notice of objection whereon the authority's rights must be confirmed by the juvenile court. An application for a care order is made by the authority, the police, or the NSPCC. (This is the only statutory function of the NSPCC, which is a voluntary children's organisation working in the field of child protection and co-operating closely with local authorities to this end.)

The child (or, if the child is not legally represented, the parent acting on the child's behalf) may contest the care proceedings before the court; or may appeal to the crown court from the decision of the juvenile court; or may subsequently apply to the juvenile court for the variation of discharge of the care order. A parent is not in his or her own right a party to the proceedings. Under new powers (at present in limited operation) designed to protect children in cases where there appears to be a conflict of interests between the child and the parent, a court may order that the child shall not be represented by the parent and may appoint a guardian *ad litem* to look after the child's interests before the court. Where the court makes such an order, it may also order that the parent shall be given **legal aid** for the purpose of taking such part in the proceedings as may be allowed by rules of court.

The local authority may obtain a care order from a juvenile court when a child under the age of 17 is being neglected or ill-treated, is exposed to moral danger, is beyond parental control or fails to attend school. A juvenile court may commit a child aged 10 and under 17 who has committed an offence other than homicide to the care of the authority. The court must be satisfied not only that one of these grounds is proved but also that the child is in need of care or control which will not be received unless such an order is made. On the care order the local authority Social Services Department is fully responsible for the child's care and welfare and makes decisions normally the prerogative of the parent. In making any decision in relation to a child in their care (whether subject to a care order or in voluntary care, and in the latter case whether or not the authority has assumed parental rights), the authority is required by law to give first consideration to the need to safeguard and promote the child's welfare throughout childhood; also to ascertain the child's wishes and feelings regarding the decision as far as is practicable and to give due consideration to them having regard to the child's age and understanding. A local authority will normally try to the fullest extent practicable and consistent with the child's welfare to involve the parent in any plans and decisions affecting the child and to keep the parent in close touch with the child. The parent has a duty to keep the authority aware of his or her whereabouts.

Children in trouble, whom a juvenile court has placed under the supervision of the local authority or a probation officer, usually remain at home. The court making the supervision order may also specify that the child participates in 'intermediate treatment'. In intermediate treatment the child attends activities of a recreational, educational, cultural or social nature in charge of a responsible person and may have to attend a residential establishment for up to 90 days. Intermediate treatment facilities can also be used on a voluntary basis for children in trouble or at risk but not in care or under a supervision order.

A child remains in local authority care for as long as his welfare requires it, or up to the age of 18 (or in certain circumstances 19). The authority has a duty to provide for accommodation and maintenance of a child in its care (e.g. through foster parents or a community or voluntary home), and to appoint an independent visitor to any child in a residential home who does not go out to school or work and who has little or no contact with the parents. A child may, at the discretion of the authority, be allowed, either for a fixed or an indefinite period, to be under the charge and control of a parent, guardian, relative or friend while residing in the authority's care. Every six months the authority reviews the child's need to remain in care.

The parents of a child in local authority care are legally liable to make a parental contribution to the authority towards the cost of the child's maintenance so long as he or she is under the age of 16. This liability is suspended for any period during which the child is allowed to be under the charge and control of a parent, guardian, relative or friend.

A parent may at any time ask the authority to rescind a resolution under which it has assumed that parent's rights, and if the authority is unwilling to do so, the parent may complain to the local juvenile court which will determine whether or not the resolution should remain in force.

Voluntary and compulsory child care operates in Scotland under the Social Work (Scotland) Act. There are no juvenile courts. A system of childrens' hearings operates, though some children do go before the courts – mainly the sheriff court. Children in need of compulsory measures of care go to D schools. Information from: *Scottish Information Office.*

See also **Adoption; Child health services; Fostering; Local authorities.**

Child Community Homes These homes constitute a comprehensive system of residential establishments organised by **local authorities** on a regional basis. They provide residential accommodation for children in the care of local authorities and voluntary organisations who, for a variety of reasons, cannot live at home or be boarded out with foster parents. The placing of a child in the care of a local authority or voluntary organisation in a community home is at the discretion of the authority or organisation concerned. A substantial proportion of community homes provide long-term residential accommodation for children with no special difficulties who attend local schools or go out to work or to further education. For children with special needs or difficulties, certain community homes provide between them a wide range of residential facilities, often shared by several local authorities on a regional basis. They include observation and assessment centres, community homes with education on the premises, secure accommodation, hostels for children of working age and residential nurseries. Community homes may be provided either by a local authority or by a voluntary organisation. The latter may also provide residential accommodation for children outside the community home system. Where this is so, the homes are registered with the *Department of Health and Social Security*, which also inspects them. For a very small minority of children in the care of local authorities who are too disturbed to be accommodated even in the more specialised community homes, the Department of Health and Social Security is providing three youth treatment centres.

See also **Adoption; Child care and welfare; Child health services; Disablement: handicapped children's education; Fostering; Local authorities.**

Child Day Care Responsibility for the provision and regulation of day care services rests with the **local authorities**, who provide day care facilities, including **day nurseries**, as part of the arrangements they make for the care of children under 5 years of age, under section 22 of the National Health Service Act 1946 (as amended). Priority for places in local authority day nurseries is given to children who have a special social or health reason for day care (e.g. children whose mothers have no option but to go to work; whose mothers are unable to look after them adequately; whose home conditions are unsatisfactory; or who have a mental or physical handicap). For handicapped children, such care may help develop potential ability. Day nurseries are increasingly being used as day care centres and as such provide a focus for all day care services in their area and a meeting place for local groups of parents and **childminders** as well as for parent/toddler groups and **playgroups**.

In addition to local authority day care facilities, there are private day nurseries, child minders and playgroups. All private day care provision is required to be registered with local authorities (Social Services Department) under the Nurseries and Childminders Regulation Act 1948 (as amended). Local authorities keep lists of all private facilities in their area. Day care may be available for older children during out-of-school hours and school holidays. Apply to local authority (Social Services Department) for details. Day care provision, including childminding and playgroups, is broadly similar in Scotland.

Child Dental Services The School Dental Service is provided under the **National Health Service** as part of the School Health Service. Its aim is to ensure that, as far as possible, children attending *local education authority* schools obtain the care and treatment necessary to help them maintain a high standard of dental health during and after school life.

The service has three main functions. First, dental inspection: arrangements are made for Dental Officers of the *area health authority* to visit schools to carry out inspections of each child's gums and teeth. Such inspections enable the Dental Officer to decide whether the child should attend a detailed examination in a dental surgery, with a view to further treatment. Secondly, dental treatment: after the inspection parents are normally notified in cases where the Dental Officer considers that there is a need for treatment or for a fuller examination, and are asked to indicate whether they intend to make arrangements for the child's treatment by a general dental practitioner under the NHS or privately, or whether they wish the necessary treatment to be carried out by the school. Thirdly, dental health education: in addition to inspection and treatment, it is the job of the School Dental Service, with the help of school teachers and parents, to show children how dental disease can be reduced by observing simple rules of dental care. Parents who are dissatisfied with the treatment provided under the School Dental Service may complain to the *area health authority*.

See also **Dental treatment.**

Child Health Services Children may be registered at birth with a National Health Service family **doctor**. He should be contacted if the child becomes ill.

Child health clinics, provided by all health authorities and staffed by doctors and health visitors, give advice on the health and development of babies and young children up to school entry, and perform screening tests and examinations to detect anything unusual. A list of child health clinics can be obtained from the *area health authority*. All new babies are visited at home by a **health visitor** who advises mothers about the nearest clinic and other facilities. Some doctors and health visitors run the clinics at health centres or surgeries.

Vaccinations and immunisations can be obtained at a child health clinic or from your NHS family doctor. In addition, handicapped children receive help from district nurses and social workers (see **Disablement**).

The School Health Service is responsible for the provision of medical and dental inspections, and for treatment, of pupils attending schools maintained by *local education authorities*. The SHS developed independently from its inception in 1907 until the NHS Reorganisation Act 1973. It continues the process of health surveillance provided in pre-school years by child health centres and in the home by health visitors. The SHS's aim is to identify as early as possible health problems likely to interfere with normal learning (e.g. need for glasses to see the blackboard, hearing impairment). Any deviation noted by a school nurse during her assessment would be referred to the SHS doctor, who would ensure that appropriate advice and treatment is obtained; the local education authority, the school, parents and pupils would also be advised.

Parents are asked to sign a form giving their consent to medical and dental inspections and treatment and they can refuse to do so. They are invited to attend the medical examination. Records of medical and dental inspections are kept.

Complaints about the SHS should be addressed to the head teacher of the child's school who pursues the matter with the doctor or nurse concerned. It is also open to the parent of any child to seek advice from NHS family doctor or from the other services provided by the NHS.

See also **Child care and welfare**; **Doctors**; **Health authorities**; **National Health Service**.

Child Minders People who look after children under the age of 5 for two hours or more a day in their own (i.e. the child minder's) home for reward must be registered with the local authority (Social Services Department) unless the children are relations. Local authorities inspect and supervise minders and are empowered to lay down various requirements (e.g. as to the number of children who can be looked after) with the object of protecting the children from conditions which could endanger their health and welfare. Many local authorities provide support and advisory services for minders, including in-service training, and material assistance such as basic equipment and toy kits. Day fostering/sponsored childminding schemes have been set up by a number of local authorities. Under these, local authorities recruit and pay allowances to selected people to look after children under 5, most of whom are within prescribed authority day care groups, for the day or part of the day.

See also **Playgroups**.

Child Social Security Benefits Child benefit is a tax-free weekly cash payment for all children, at the rate of £2.30 for each child (£3 from November 1978; £4 from April 1979). It is normally paid to the mother. An additional £1 (£2 from November 1978) is payable for the first child in certain one-parent families. A child, for child benefit purposes, is someone under the age of 16 (or 19 if undergoing full-time secondary education at a recognised educational establishment). Since 30 October 1977 child benefit is not payable for children under 19 in advanced education; such students are usually entitled to **student grants**. Claim for benefit from *Department of Health and Social Security local offices*; once approved, benefit is usually payable through **post offices**. See leaflet CH1B from DHSS. Divorced women can receive a Child's Special Allowance after the death of a

former husband who was contributing or was liable to contribute to the support of her child or children. Low income families are entitled to Educational Maintenance Allowances to help keep a child at school beyond the age of 16. There may be supplements if the child is handicapped. Apply to local authority Education Welfare Officer, details in DHSS leaflet M2.
See also **Disablement; Family income supplement; Families on low incomes; Orphans; Social security benefits.**

Children and Young People's Orders
The following orders are available to the juvenile courts in England and Wales in both care proceedings (see **Child care and welfare**), and criminal proceedings:
(a) A care order commiting the child to the care of a local authority. The effect of this type of order is that the local authority has legal custody of the child, and has power to restrict his liberty where necessary. The authority is responsible for deciding where the child should be accommodated – for example, with foster parents or a community home (see **Child community homes**).
(b) A supervision order for a specified period of up to three years. Supervision of a child under 13 years is carried out by a local authority social worker (a probation officer may be appointed if he or she is already working with the child's family). For children aged 13–16 supervision is (at the discretion of the court) by either a social worker or a probation officer. Any one of the following conditions may be attached to a supervision order: (i) a requirement to submit to treatment for a mental condition; (ii) a requirement to reside with a named individual – for example, a relative; or (iii) an 'intermediate treatment' requirement. Intermediate treatment – which is in between those measures which involve complete removal from home and those which do not – consists of participation, under a supervisor in a variety of constructive and remedial activities either through a short residential course or through attendance at a day or evening **attendance centre**. The object is to bring the child into contact with a new environment giving an opportunity to develop new interests. Often treatment involves the child with other children who have not been before the courts.
(c) An order requiring the child's parents or guardian to take proper care of him and to exercise proper control over him.
(d) A hospital or guardianship order in accordance with the mental health legislation.
(e) Payment of compensation (an offence must be proved and the maximum amount which can be ordered is £400 in criminal proceedings and £100 in care proceedings).
The following additional orders are available to the courts in criminal proceedings:
(a) Binding over.
(b) Absolute or conditional discharge.
(c) Fines.
See also **Young adult offenders.**

Chile For **exchange control** is a non-scheduled territory outside the **overseas sterling area** and the **EEC**. UK nationals travelling direct from the UK normally need only the following (but check): **passports; visas; work permits** (if taking a job); green cards for motor insurance (if bringing a car); international driving permits (if intending to drive: see **Motoring abroad**). The UK has no reciprocal health or social security arrangements.
Enquiries to *Chilean Embassy* in London.
British diplomatic missions to Chile are *British Embassy* in Santiago and *British Consulates* in Antofagasta, Arica, Concepcion, Coquimbo, Punta Arenas (Magallanes) and Valparaiso.

Chiltern Hundreds A member of the House of Commons cannot officially resign but acceptance of the office of steward or bailiff of Her Majesty's three Chiltern Hundreds of Stoke, Desborough and Burnham, or of the Manor of Northstead, involves dis-

China For **exchange control** is a non-scheduled territory outside the **overseas sterling area** and the EEC. UK nationals travelling direct from the UK normally need only the following (but check): **passports**; **visas**; international certificates of **vaccination** against smallpox; **work permits** (if taking a job).
The UK has no reciprocal health or social security arrangements.
Enquiries to *Chinese Embassy* in London.
British diplomatic mission to China is *British Embassy* in Peking.

Chiropodists Chiropodists employed by the **National Health Service** must be state registered by the Chiropodists' Board of the *Council for Professions Supplementary to Medicine*; the basic qualification for registration is the three-year course of the *Society of Chiropodists*. Chiropodists in private practice need not be registered. The Chiropodists' Board publishes an annual register which is available at public libraries, while some private practitioners are listed in the telephone directory. Patients do not need a doctor's reference to consult a chiropodist.
Complaints about professional misconduct of state registered chiropodists should be made to, and are investigated by, the Chiropodists' Board of the CPSM. The Society investigates complaints about its members and fellows. Complaints about disciplinary matters relating to NHS employees should be made to, and are investigated by, the employing authority (the *Area Health Authority* or Board of Governors in England and Wales, the *Health Board* in Scotland).
See also **Disputes with public authorities**.

Christmas Mail The **Post Office** recruits temporary postmen/postwomen to help out before Christmas and gives preference to people registered as unemployed (see **Unemployment**). Application forms from: *Post Office, Head/District Postmaster*.

Church of England: Crown Appointments Archbishops and diocesan bishops are chosen by the Crown acting on the advice of the *Prime Minister*. The Crown issues a licence to the appropriate dean and chapter to elect the Crown's nominee and the election is certified for confirmation and consecration by the appropriate archbishop. Suffragan bishops are appointed by the Crown following the submission of two names (the first is customarily chosen) by the diocesan bishop. Deans of cathedrals are appointed by the Crown under letters patent. Some canonries and a considerable number of livings are in the patronage of the Crown, which is exercised broadly in the same way as private patronage. Appointment of Crown nominees involves the continuous consultation of a range of people and organisations by the Secretary for Appointments at the *Prime Minister's Office*. A *Crown Appointments Commission* is responsible for submitting names to the PM for vacant diocesan bishoprics. Each diocese now has a Vacancy-in-See Committee, which can be contacted through the Registrar of a diocese, and the Archbishops of Canterbury and York can be approached through the *Archbishops Appointments Secretary*.

Cider and Perry Makers of cider or perry for sale must register with *Her Majesty's Customs and Excise, Collectors*; however, if they make less than 1,500 gallons a year they may claim exemption. Cider and perry are subject to revenue controls similar to those on **wine** and made-wine, but the entry book for makers of less than 20,000 gallons a year is designed to reduce documentation to a minimum; all details in notice 163 from HMCE.

Cinemas Premises used for the public, commercial exhibition of films are required under the Cinematograph Act 1909 to be licensed by the local authority (in London the *Greater London Council* and elsewhere usually the district council).
See also **Film: censorship**.

Cities District or parish councils (see **Local authorities**) which have been granted city status by letters patent, which also specify whether there is the right to call the mayor 'lord mayor'. There are 47 cities in England and Wales, 19 of which have lord mayors. Petitions should be prepared in consultation with the *Home Office*.

Citizenship of the UK and Colonies Governed by the British Nationality Acts 1948–65. The UK and colonies form a distinct single unit for citizenship purposes. Like citizens of most **Commonwealth** countries, citizens of the UK and colonies are **British subjects** and have British nationality; they are treated in the same way as all British subjects in UK law except for purposes of immigration and issue of passports (see **Immigration into the UK** and **Passports**).

Citizenship was conferred on certain people who were British subjects when the British Nationality Act 1948 came into force on 1 January 1949. They were persons born or naturalised in the UK and colonies: people born elsewhere whose fathers were so born or naturalised; British subjects born in a protectorate, protected state, or UK trust territory; other British subjects (bar those without citizenship or of Southern Irish origin) who were not at that date citizens of a self-governing Commonwealth country and did not subsequently become such citizens when the citizenship law of another Commonwealth country took effect; and women married to people who acquired UK citizenship or would have acquired it if alive at that date.

Citizenship is now acquired by birth by all people born in the UK and colonies (bar children of parents with certain degrees of diplomatic immunity and those born in places under enemy occupation to alien enemy fathers); and by descent, if at the child's birth his father is a UK citizen other than by descent. Where the father is a UK citizen by descent, citizenship is acquired by descent if the child or his father was born in a place then under UK protection or where the Sovereign then exercised jurisdiction over British subjects, or if the birth is registered at a British Consulate (normally within one year), or if the father is in Crown service. It is also automatically acquired by adoption for someone adopted in the UK, Channel Islands or Isle of Man by a citizen of the UK and colonies, or jointly by a husband and wife, the husband being such a citizen. Citizenship can also be acquired by **naturalisation** or registration.

Citizenship may be lost by legislation passed by the UK Parliament (e.g. when a colonial territory attains independence); by a voluntary act of renunciation formally made by a person who possesses or is about to acquire another citizenship; or by an order of deprivation which may be made in special circumstances by the *Home Secretary* or a Colonial Governor taking away the citizenship of a person who had been naturalised or registered as a citizen. Otherwise citizenship of the UK and colonies cannot be lost. Such citizenship is not forfeited (as was British nationality in most cases before 1949) as a result of marriage to an alien or naturalisation in a foreign country.

Individuals who want information about their own position in UK law should consult the *Home Office Immigration and Nationality Department*. Enquiries about the law of other Commonwealth countries to the authorities of those countries in the UK, i.e. the appropriate High Commissioner (for address see under country name in the address section).

The British Nationality Acts are currently under review with a view to replacing citizenship of the UK and colonies with 'British citizenship' for those who have close ties with the UK and 'British overseas citizenship' for the remainder of those who are now citizens of the UK and colonies. Information from Nationality Division at the HOIND.

Citizenship of the UK and Colonies: Registration Certain people who do not otherwise possess **citizenship of the UK and colonies** may be registered as a citizen. A **British subject** or citizen of the Irish Republic is entitled to registration on completion of five years' ordinary residence in the UK (or appropriate colonial territory) or five years' Crown service, or partly the one and partly the other (in special circumstances a shorter period may be accepted).

A British subject or citizen of the Irish Republic may be registered at discretion on the grounds of service (usually for five years) under various international organisations or in the employment of a company, etc., established in the UK or in a colony or protectorate, if he also possesses a close connection with the UK and colonies.

A woman, whatever her nationality or citizenship, who has been married to a citizen of the UK and colonies is in general entitled to registration as such a citizen.

Minor children may be registered as citizens of the UK and colonies at the discretion of the Home Secretary, Colonial Governors, or British High Commissioners.

A person who has renounced citizenship of the UK and colonies as a condition of acquiring or retaining citizenship of another Commonwealth country may be registered as a citizen of the UK and colonies without fulfilling the residence or service requirements above.

Certain persons possessing defined connections with the UK and colonies are entitled to be registered as citizens if they are and have always been stateless.

Detailed information about qualifications and procedure for registration in *Home Office* leaflets N356 (Commonwealth citizens); N376 (Married women); N332 (Minors).

See also **Naturalisation**.

City and Guilds Certificates Awarded by the *City and Guilds of London Institute* for success in examinations at operative, craft and technician level. City and Guilds courses are available in over 200 subjects; most are part-time (one to five years depending on the subject) and many have no entry requirements. Technician Full Technological Certificates are accepted for entry to degree and other higher level courses at some universities and polytechnics. Entry to examinations is controlled by colleges.

See also **Adult education**; **Further education**.

City of London The 'Mayor and Commonalty and Citizens of the City of London', the City Corporation, is a specially constituted form of **local authority**. The Corporation acts through three courts – the Court of Common Council, the Court of Aldermen and the Court of Common Hall – over each of which the Lord Mayor presides. The Court of Common Council is the main administrative and executive body with functions similar to those of the London borough councils. The court comprises the Lord Mayor (who is an alderman), 25 other aldermen and 155 common councilmen. Both aldermen and councilmen are elected by the some 12,500 voters of the City whose right to vote is based on residential qualifications or occupation of business premises. The Court of Aldermen – comprising the 26 elected aldermen – elects the Lord Mayor from the two candidates nominated by the third court, the Court of Common Hall. The latter court comprises the Lord Mayor, aldermen and sheriffs of the City and the freemen and liverymen of the ancient City companies (survivors of the medieval merchant guilds or associations of craftsmen).

The Lord Mayor of London must be a freeman of the City, a liveryman and an alderman at the time of his election; he holds office for one year. During his term of office he is, ex officio, a member of the Privy Council; he summons and presides over the several courts and meetings of the corporation; he is the chief magistrate of the City, one of the custodians of the City seal, and, by tradition, holds several ancient offices; for instance, he is the head of the City lieutenancy, Admiral of the Port of London and a trustee of the fabric of St Paul's Cathedral. He also attends every civic and ceremonial function in the City and is regarded as the dispenser of the hospitality which frequently devolves upon the corporation.

Enquiries to *Corporation of London*.

Civil Defence Statutory responsibility for civil defence rests with local authorities.

Civil Law Disputes: England and Wales Civil law relates to the rights, duties and obligations of individuals between themselves. Its main sub-divisions are: family law, which includes the laws governing **marriage**, **divorce**, and the custody of children; the law of property (including intangibles), which governs ownership and rights of enjoyment, the creation and administration of trusts, and the devolution of property on death; the law of contract, which regulates, for instance, the **sale of goods**, loans, partnerships, insurance and guarantees; and the law of torts, which governs such actionable wrongs as negligence, defamation, malicious prosecution, nuisance and trespass – injuries suffered by one person at the hands of another, irrespective of any contract between them.

Admiralty law was originally concerned with crime, as well as with tort and contract upon the high seas. It is now limited to civil matters but, because it deals with cases involving foreign as well as British vessels, its rules differ from those which would apply in the same matter occurring on land:

Magistrates' courts have certain powers in civil law in matrimonial proceedings to make separation, maintenance and affiliation orders and to deal with the custody of children. Appeals on points of law are made to the Family Division of the High Court. Committees of magistrates exercise semi-administrative functions in relation to the licensing of public houses and betting shops and clubs. Appeals usually lie to the crown court with a further (or alternative) appeal on legal points to the High Court.

County courts' civil jurisdiction includes actions founded on contract and tort (with some exceptions such as defamation cases), where the amount claimed is not more than £1,000; equity matters such as trusts, mortgages and dissolution of partnerships, where the amount does not exceed £5,000; and actions for the recovery of land where the net annual value for rating purposes does not exceed £1,000. Cases outside these limits are usually heard in the High Court, but may be tried in the county court by consent of the parties, or they may be transferred from the High Court in certain circumstances. Other matters dealt with by county courts include hire purchase, the Rent Act legislation, landlord and tenant questions and **adoption** cases. In addition, undefended divorce cases are heard and determined in county courts designated as divorce county courts (defended cases are heard by the High Court); outside London bankruptcies are dealt with in certain county courts; and complaints of **racial discrimination** brought by the Race Relations Board and complaints alleging some forms of **sex discrimination** are heard in selected county courts.

Every county court has a registrar who deals with procedural matters and the various steps that have to be taken before an action is tried. The registrar also acts as an assistant judge, and tries most small actions. A circuit judge tries the larger actions, and hears appeals from decisions by the registrar.

The High Court – has three divisions – the Queen's Bench Division, the Chancery Division and the Family Division. Although exclusive jurisdiction in a particular matter is not normally given to any one division, in practice each division has a separate jurisdiction. Matters that must go to the Chancery Division include: the administration of estates, including those of deceased persons; partnerships and mortgages; contractual rights; and the execution of trusts and settlements. The division also deals with the 'revenue list' which consists mainly of **income tax** cases, with the special law affecting **companies** (including winding-up) and with some **bankruptcy** matters when they have been dealt with in the county courts. The Family Division deals with all jurisdiction of a family kind, including matrimonial cases and cases related to wardship, adoption, and guardianship. Most other civil litigation comes before the Queen's Bench Division. Specialisation within this division is recognised to some extent by the assignment of particular cases to different lists. Thus, commercial cases are placed on the 'commercial list' and are heard by one of two or three judges of the division with special experience of this type of litigation. Admiralty and prize jurisdiction (dealing with naval matters and claims over captured ships or aircraft) rests with a specially constituted Admiralty Court within the Queen's Bench Division.

The High Court sits in London at the Royal Courts of Justice and is juxtaposed with the crown court at certain provincial centres, where, besides hearing civil cases, High Court judges deal with serious criminal proceedings. In London the High Court has four sittings: *Michaelmas*, which normally begins on 1 October and ends on 21 December; *Hilary*, which begins on 11 January and ends on the Wednesday before Easter; *Easter*, which begins on the second Tuesday after Easter and ends on the Friday before the Spring Bank Holiday; and *Trinity*, which begins on the second Tuesday after the spring holiday and ends on 31 July. Two judges are selected at the beginning of each Long Vacation (during the summer) for the hearing of all cases needing prompt attention.

Apellate Courts – appeals in matrimonial proceedings heard by magistrates' courts go to a Divisional Court of the Family Division of the High Court. Affiliation appeals are heard by the crown court, as are appeals from decisions of the licensing and betting committees of magistrates.

Appeals from the county courts and the High Court are heard in the Court of Appeal Civil Division, and may go on to the House of Lords (with the leave of the court or of the House). On a point of law of exceptional difficulty calling for a reconsideration of a binding precedent, an appeal may in some cases and with the leave of the House lie directly from the High Court to the House of Lords.

Civil Law Disputes: Judicial Procedure
Civil proceedings are instituted by the aggrieved person (the 'plaintiff'); no preliminary inquiry into the authenticity of the grievance is required. The most common form of proceedings is an action commenced in the High Court by a writ served on the defendant by the plaintiff or his representative, or in the county court by a summons served on the defendant through the court. The writ or summons states the nature of the plaintiff's claim against the defendant and the remedy he seeks to obtain. This may be damages, or the recovery of a debt, or an injunction restraining the defendant from carrying out a course of conduct. If the defendant intends to contest the claim, he 'enters an appearance' by informing the court to this effect on the appropriate form. The next step is the delivery to the court of the 'pleadings' – documents setting out the precise question in dispute, which may be (and in the High Court normally are) drafted by counsel. Prior to the trial, either party may apply for an order that the other should clarify his pleadings or disclose additional documents relevant to the dispute.

Because civil proceedings are a private matter, they can usually be abandoned or compromised without the court's leave, and in the great majority of cases, the parties to a dispute settle their differences through solicitors before actual trial is reached. Divorce proceedings are exceptional in that a decree of divorce (even if the case is undefended) can only be granted in court, either after a hearing or (in certain limited classes of case) on a certificate by the registrar that the grounds for divorce have been established. Actions that are brought to court are usually tried by a judge without a jury, except in cases involving claims for defamation, false imprisonment, or unlawful arrest, when either party may insist on trial by jury, or in cases of fraud, when the person charged may also claim this right.

Judgments in civil cases are enforceable through the authority of the court. Most of them are for payment of sums of money, and these may be enforced in cases of default by seizure of the debtor's goods. Under the Administration of Justice Act 1970 a judgment may also be enforced by attachment of earnings – that is to say, by an order of a court (usually the county court) addressed to an employer to require him to make periodic payments to the court by deduction from the debtor's wages. A judgment for the possession of land is enforced by an officer of the court entering upon the land and putting the plaintiff in possession. Refusal to obey a judgment directing the defendant to do something or to abstain from doing something may result in imprisonment for contempt of court. Arrest under an order of committal may be effected only on warrant of the court.

Costs: the general rule is that the costs of an action (the barrister's fees, the solicitor's charges, court fees and other disbursements) are in the discretion of the court, but normally the court orders costs to be paid by the party losing the action.

General advice from **solicitors**. See also **Legal aid**.

Civil Law Disputes: Northern Ireland Inferior courts in Northern Ireland are the county courts and the magistrates' courts, both of which differ in a number of ways from their counterparts in England and Wales. The general civil jurisdiction of the courts includes the determination of most actions (not divorce cases) in which the amount or the value of specific articles claimed is not very large. The courts also deal with minor actions involving title to or the recovery of land, equity matters such as trusts and estates, mortgages, the sale of land and partnerships; contentious probate matters; criminal injury cases embracing both personal injuries (which in England, Wales and Scotland are dealt with by the Criminal Injuries Compensation Board) and damage to property; certain rent matters; and adoption orders. Appeals lie from county courts to the assize judge or High Court.

Superior courts in Northern Ireland comprise the Supreme Court of Judicature and the Court of Criminal Appeal. The Supreme Court of Judicature in turn consists of the Court of Appeal and the High Court of Justice (the superior court of first instance). The practice and procedure of the Court of Appeal and the High Court are virtually the same as in the corresponding courts in England and Wales. Both courts sit in the Royal Courts of Justice in Belfast. The Court of Appeal has power to review the civil law decisions of the High Court, and may in certain cases review the decisions of county courts and magistrates' courts. Subject to certain restrictions, appeal from a judgment of the Court of Appeal lies to the House of Lords.

The High Court is divided into a Queen's Bench Division, dealing with all criminal and many civil law matters, and a Chancery Division, dealing, for instance, with trusts and estates, title to land, mortgages and charges, wills and company matters.

Civil Law Disputes: Scotland The two main civil courts in Scotland are the sheriff court, the principal local court; and the Court of Session, the supreme central court (subject only to the House of Lords in London).

The sheriff court's jurisdiction is very wide. The value of the subject matter with which the court can deal has, with very few exceptions, no upper limit, and a wide range of remedies may be granted concerning, among other things, debt, contract, reparation (damages), rent restriction, possession and the use of property, leases and tenancies, and the custody of children. The court deals with most actions for alimentary debt and for separation. It also has jurisdiction, to the exclusion of the Court of Session, in cases below a value of £50. These, and actions of a value between £50 and £500, are 'summary causes' and involve an abbreviated procedure. The sheriff hears cases in the first instance in the sheriff court of a district and an appeal may be taken from his decision to the sheriff principal, and thereafter to the Inner House of the Court of Session. Alternatively a litigant may appeal direct from the sheriff to the Inner House, although he must in certain cases obtain leave to make the appeal.

The Court of Session sits in Edinburgh and is divided into an Inner House and an Outer House. The Inner House is sub-divided into two divisions, the First Division presided over by the Lord President of the Court of Session and the Second Division by the Lord Justice-Clerk. The main business of the Inner House is to hear appeals from the judges of the Outer House (who are called Lords Ordinary) and from the sheriff courts and other inferior courts and tribunals. The Lords Ordinary, who sit as single judges, hear cases when they are first brought into the court. The Inner House Divisions and Lords Ordinary do not specialise in specific categories of business. Officials of the General and Petition Departments of the Court of Session allocate cases to particular Lords Ordinary and the Divisions of the Inner House. It is, however, possible for parties, by agreement, to refer for summary trial a dispute not affecting status to a judge chosen by them.

There are certain matters with which the Court of Session alone can deal – for example, actions to alter or determine personal status, such as actions for divorce and actions for declarator of marriage, of nullity of marriage, and of legitimacy. The court has also exclusive jurisdiction in actions to 'reduce' (to set aside or annul) judicial decrees, and in petitions to vary private or public trusts or to wind up companies having at least £10,000 paid-up capital. A wider range of actions may be brought either in the Court of Session or sheriff court: examples include actions of damages and actions for recovery of debt (exceeding £50 in value), actions relating to the interpretation and implementation of contracts and other writings, certain actions concerning family matters (for instance, aliment of wives or children, or custody of children), and possessory actions (to attain, retain or recover possession of land or moveable property).

Appeals on questions of law or fact may be taken from the Inner House of the Court of Session to the House of Lords sitting in the Palace of Westminster in London. The House includes Lords of Appeal in Ordinary who are Scots lawyers.

Court of Session proceedings are nearly all either 'actions' or 'petitions'. The object of an action is to enforce a legal right against a defender who resists it, or to protect a legal right which the defender is infringing. The object of a petition is generally to obtain from the court power to do something or to require something to be done, which it is just and proper should be done, but which the petitioner has no legal right to do, or to require, in the absence of judicial authority. Actions in the Court of Session are begun when one litigant, the 'pursuer', serves (usually by post) a signeted summons on the other litigant, the defender, and lodges a copy, together with other papers for the court's use, in the offices of court. The signet is a seal by which certain writs in the name of the Sovereign, including a Court of Session summons, are authenticated. The summons warns the defender that, if he does not appear before the court and defend the action, the court will grant a decree in his absence in favour of the pursuer. To the summons is attached a request to the court to grant the remedy sought by the pursuer, called the conclusion of the summons; a detailed statement of the facts upon which the pursuer relies, called the condescendence; and finally a brief statement of the legal grounds, called the pleas-in-law, which, if the facts are proved, would entitle the pursuer to the remedy he seeks. The defender has a chance to put forward his statement of the facts, either accepting or rejecting the pursuer's statement, together with the pleas-in-law in support of his argument. Thereafter both pursuer and defender adjust their own cases in the light of the statement and allegations put forward by the other side. These written pleadings clarify the area of disagreement between the litigants and give each party fair notice of the case to be answered. The pleadings are then made into a 'closed record' which sets out one against the other the numbered allegations, admissions and denials of each party, and the matter goes forward for determination by the Court. If the dispute concerns questions of law, the court hears a debate between counsel on those legal questions and, if the parties agree about the facts, thereafter issues its decision granting or refusing the remedy sought by the pursuer. Where there is a dispute over the facts, evidence is led before the judge sitting without a jury or in certain cases, usually damages actions, before the judge sitting with a jury.

A petition in the Court of Session is strictly an *ex parte* application to the court. Examples include petitions for the sequestration of an insolvent person, for the liquidation of a company, for an order enabling a person to adopt a child, for the appointment of a judicial factor to administer property, or for the variation of trust purposes. The petitioner and the respondents to the petition may not be in dispute, the court's approval to some matter nevertheless being required by law. Petitions can be contentious, such as those concerning custody of children. A petition is presented to the court, and the court decides which people should receive service or intimation of the petition. Any respondent to the petition may lodge answers in much the same way as any defender to a summons can lodge defences.

Ordinary procedure in the sheriff court is modelled on Court of Session procedure. For small debt cases, a simplified form of procedure (available in the sheriff's small debt court) is used, of which the aims are speed, cheapness and finality of judgment. Under the Sheriff Courts (Scotland) Act 1971, the small debt court will in due course be replaced by a new summary procedure. General advice from a **solicitor**.

Civil Servants Recruitment to all permanent appointments in UK Government departments, including period appointments for more than five years, is the responsibility of the *Civil Service Commission*. The CSC acts independently of other departments in recruitment matters to ensure that appointments are made purely on merit and are free from patronage. Vacancies are publicly advertised and filled by fair and open competition.

For junior appointments in specific locations (e.g. clerical, typing and industrial grades) the employing departments are empowered to recruit direct in accordance with detailed instructions issued by the CSC; even where this is done, the CSC issues a Certificate of Qualification as formal approval of an appointment.

All permanent civil servants must satisfy the Civil Service nationality rules; aliens cannot be appointed, other than in exceptional circumstances and short-term in accordance with the Aliens Employment Act 1955. They must obtain a certificate from the *Civil Service Department*, which consults the Department of Employment and the Home Office. Advice, etc., from the CSC.

The CSC's requirements on nationality, age, health, character and knowledge and ability are set out in their general regulations which are made with the approval of the Minister for the Civil Service under the authority of the Order in Council. Copies of these are available from the CSC; detailed requirements for each post are sent when enquirers respond to advertisements. Advice about vacancies from: *Civil Service Commission*.

Claims against Foreign Governments If a UK national suffers loss, injury or damage as a result of an act or omission by a foreign government or its servants which constitutes a breach of international law, the UK government may at its discretion assist with or take up the claim against the other government if all the legal remedies in the state concerned have been shown to be exhausted or ineffective. Seek the advice of lawyers versed in the foreign country's law before contacting the *Foreign and Commonwealth Office, Claims Department*, or, if overseas, the nearest *British diplomatic mission*; provide the fullest details regarding the loss, injury or damage and include any documents in support of the claim.

Claims by Foreigners against the UK Government These should be directed to the appropriate central government department, local authority or the courts.
See **Civil law disputes**.

Closed Shop The term means that workers in a specific workplace have decided that no one may work there other than members of a specified trade union. Enquiries in workplace.
A pre-entry closed shop is one in which only existing members of the specified union may be recruited. A post-entry closed shop is one in which all recruits will be expected to join the union. Recent legislation affecting the status of the closed shop includes the 1974 Trade Union and Labour Relations

Clothing at Work General UK policy on protective clothing for work purposes (including eye protection), consideration of changes to legislation and new codes of practice is the responsibility of the Safety and General Branch A at the *Health and Safety Executive Head Office*. Advice at a local level on suitable and recommended protective clothing and eye protection from *Health and Safety Executive, HM Factory Inspectorate, Area Offices*.
See also **Work: health and safety**.

Clubs: Liquor Licensing Clubs supplying intoxicating liquor must either hold a justices 'on licence' for the premises or a registration certificate issued by the magistrates court. Apply to clerk to the magistrates court. Certain specified persons (e.g. the police and local authority) can object to award of a certificate. Appeal against refusal to issue or renew a registration certificate, or against the conditions attaching to its issue, is to the crown court.
See also **Alcohol; Liquor Licences**.

Coal Mining To mine coal, either by underground or opencast methods, you must obtain: a licence from the *National Coal Board*; **planning permission** under the Town and Country Planning Acts; and permission of the coal owners and occupiers concerned. The NCB may attach whatever conditions it chooses to a licence. There is no right of appeal against the NCB's decisions. Objections to proposals by private firms to work opencast sites under licence should be made to the planning department of the local authority (normally the county council). To object to a proposal by the NCB for an opencast coal site, write to the *Department of Energy*, or to the *Welsh Office* if the site is in Wales. The NCB must publish a notice of the proposal in local newspapers, and in the 'London Gazette' (for sites in England and Wales) and in the 'Edinburgh Gazette' (for Scotland).

Coins UK coins are minted by the *Royal Mint* which also strikes coins for many foreign governments. Enquiries to the Marketing Manager at the RM in London. Coins especially struck by the RM for collectors, including proof sets, can be purchased from the *Royal Mint Numismatic Bureau*. The Royal Mint Advisory Committee is consulted on the designs for UK coinage. Foreign gold coins (see **Gold**) struck after 1937 are subject to **exchange control**.

Cold Stores Certification is undertaken by *Lloyd's Register of Shipping*, which inspects and classes refrigerated plant in many countries and re-inspects periodically.
See also **Shipping registration**.

Colombia For **exchange control** is a non-scheduled territory outside the **overseas sterling area** and the **EEC**. UK nationals travelling direct from the UK normally need only the following (but check): **passports; work permits** (if taking a job).
The UK has no reciprocal health or social security arrangements.
Enquiries to *Colombian Embassy* in London.
British diplomatic missions to Colombia are *British Embassy* in Bogota and *British Consulates* in Barranquilla and Cali.

Commodity Markets London's commodity markets facilitate international dealing in many foodstuffs and raw materials and act as centres of information on production, supplies, trade and prices. Most of the London commodity markets operate at the *London Commodity Exchange*. In some markets or 'exchanges' (e.g. sugar, cocoa, coffee, non-ferrous metals and vegetable oils) the commodity itself is not seen by the dealers, but is sold on description as to quality, weight and international standard. Some such transactions are for delivery at a future date and in some commodities there is a lively 'futures' market in which contracts for future delivery or receipt are bought and sold.
Commodities in which the size of consignments is relatively small, or where the quality is most important or not

Commodity Market Associations

	Trade Associations	Future/Terminal Market Associations or Exchanges
Cocoa	Cocoa Association of London	London Cocoa Terminal Market Association
Coffee	Coffee Trade Federation	Coffee Terminal Market Association of London
Cotton	Liverpool Cotton Association	—
Grains, Feeding Stuffs and Soya Bean Meal	Grain and Feed Trade Association	London Grain Futures Market and Clearing House GAFTA Soya Bean Meal Futures Association
Jute	London Jute Association	—
Non-ferrous Metals	London Metal Exchange	London Metal Exchange
Rubber	Rubber Trade Association of London	London Rubber Terminal Market Association
Sugar	Sugar Association of London	United Terminal Sugar Market Association
Tea	Tea Trade Committee	Tea Centre (auctions)
Timber	Timber Trade Federation	—
Vegetable oils, Oilseeds, Animal Fats and Marine Oils	Federation of Oils, Seeds and Fats Associations	London Vegetable Oil Terminal Market Association
Wool	British Wool Confederation	London Wool Terminal Market Association

assessable except by inspection (e.g. tea, furs) are handled in auction rooms, where the value of the goods is established by competitive bidding.

Sale rooms cover commodities which are usually not sufficiently uniform in quality to permit trading on description only (e.g. fibres, spices, herbs, gums, nuts, citrus juices); transactions are primarily a series of bilateral deals, with the producer's agent and the consumer's agent meeting each other to establish a bargain.

The conduct of trade is governed by the rules, regulations and contract of the appropriate trade associations. The *International Commodities Clearing House* is an independent service which provides clearing and guarantee arrangements for 'future' contracts in sugar, cocoa, rubber, coffee, vegetable oils, soya bean meal and wool; the *London Metal Exchange* and the *Grain and Feed Trade Association* fulfil a similar function for their commodities. London is a world centre for arbitrations in the case of disputes according to the rules and regulations of the appropriate markets. Enquiries to *Federation of Commodity Associations*.

Common Entrance Examination The entrance examination to boys' public schools is administered by the subcommittee of the Joint Standing Committee of the *Headmasters' Conference* and the *Incorporated Association of Preparatory Schools*. It is not a public examination such as the General Certificate of Education and candidates may normally only be entered for it if they have been offered a place at a public school, subject to their passing the examination; if they have been required to take it as a preliminary to sitting a scholarship examination; or if they have been entered for a trial run, in which case their preparatory school corrects the papers. The papers are set by examiners appointed by the subcommittee but the answers are marked at the public school to which the candidate is seeking admittance. The examination is normally taken in the

term immediately preceding the one for which candidates are registered to enter public school. Enquiries: Administrative Secretary, *Common Entrance Office*; *Independent Schools Information Service*.
There are parallel arrangements for girls' public schools. Enquiries to *Common Entrance Examination for Girls' Schools*; *Association of Head Mistresses of Preparatory Schools*; or the *Independent Schools Information Service*.
See also **Education: Scotland; Education: Northern Ireland; Independent schools.**

Common and Open Spaces Common land is often privately owned but local people have certain rights on or over it and the public has access to most of it. Under the Countryside Act 1968 **local authorities** can provide facilities for enjoyment on any common land to which the public has access. The Commons Registration Act 1965 provided for the registration of all common land and common rights and of town and village greens. Registers are kept open for public inspection by local authorities, which refer provisional registration disputes to a Commons Commissioner for settlement. It is not lawful to enclose or erect buildings on common land without the consent of the *Secretary of State for the Environment*. Application forms and details of procedure from *Department of the Environment*. In Wales, the responsible Minister is the *Secretary of State for Wales* and application forms are available from the *Welsh Office*.
Advice can also be sought from the *Commons, Open Spaces and Footpaths Preservation Society*.
See also **Footpaths, bridleways and rights of way**.

Commonwealth Members of the Commonwealth are Australia, the Bahamas, Bangladesh, Barbados, Botswana, Canada, Cyprus, Fiji, the Gambia, Ghana, Grenada, Guyana, India, Jamaica, Kenya, Lesotho, Malawi, Malaysia, Malta, Mauritius, Nauru, New Zealand, Nigeria, Papua/New Guinea, Seychelles, Sierra Leone, Singapore, Sri Lanka, Swaziland, Tanzania, Tonga, Trinidad and Tobago, Uganda, UK, Western Samoa and Zambia.
There are a number of dependencies of, or states associated with, Commonwealth countries, mostly small islands or sparsely populated territories. Most are dependencies of Britain although Australia and New Zealand are each responsible for a few overseas territories. The Queen is acknowledged as head of the Commonwealth by all member countries. In 11 she is head of State; 21 are republics within the Commonwealth; and Malaysia, Lesotho, Swaziland and Tonga have their own monarchs.
Outline guides on most Commonwealth countries are published by the *Royal Commonwealth Society* and the *Commonwealth Institute*; otherwise make enquiries at the country's diplomatic mission in the UK (see entry for each country).
The *Commonwealth Secretariat* is the central organisation for joint consultation and co-operation between Commonwealth governments. Its main areas of operation are international and economic affairs, development co-operation (through the Commonwealth Fund for Technical Co-operation), food production and rural development, youth education, information, applied studies in government, science and technology, law and health.
The *Commonwealth Foundation*, an autonomous international organisation registered as a charity under English law, supports pan-Commonwealth professional activity and associations. It currently backs the *Commonwealth Association of Architects*, the *Commonwealth Association of Planners*, the *Commonwealth Association of Surveying and Land Economy*, the *Commonwealth Magistrates' Association*, the *Commonwealth Legal Education Association*, the *Commonwealth Legal Bureau*, the *Commonwealth Medical Association*, the *Commonwealth Nurses Federation*, the *Commonwealth Pharmaceutical Association*, the *Commonwealth Society for the Deaf*, the *Commonwealth Veterinary Association*, the *Commonwealth Council of Educational Administration*, the *Commonwealth Library Association*,

the *Association for Commonwealth Literature and Language Studies*, the *Commonwealth Association of Museums*, the *Commonwealth Geographical Bureau*, the *Commonwealth Engineers' Council*, the *Commonwealth Human Ecology Council*. The CF also finances individuals attending professional conferences and exchange visits; applications to the director.
The Commonwealth Scholarship and Fellowship Plan has 1,500 places available each year. It works through bilateral arrangements under which governments provide scholarships to men and women from other Commonwealth countries. Most awards are for postgraduate study. Each country has an administering body: in Britain apply to the Commonwealth Scholarship Commission at the *Association of Commonwealth Universities*.

Commonwealth Games The Games, held every four years, are under the overall control of the *British Commonwealth Games Federation*. In the UK there are separate *Commonwealth Games Councils* in England, Scotland, Wales, Northern Ireland, the Isle of Man, Jersey and Guernsey. Membership of these Councils is drawn mainly from the national governing bodies of the sports included in the Games. Each Council is responsible for organising and selecting teams and raising funds.

Communist Party Membership is open to British citizens and permanent residents of Britain aged 18 and over who accept the aims, constitution and policy of the *Communist Party of Great Britain*. There is also a Communist Party of Ireland covering both Eire and Northern Ireland.
There are about 28,000 members in England, Scotland and Wales, organised into branches in places or work, in local areas, colleges and universities. To join, contact either the district offices (see Communist Party in telephone directory in most cities) or the *Communist Party of Great Britain Headquarters* and *Communist Party of Ireland Headquarters*.
The party's official aims are: to achieve a socialist Britain in which the means of production, distribution and exchange will be socially owned and utilised in a planned way for the benefit of all. They consider that in the conditions of Britain socialism can be achieved without civil war and by democratic means, including the election of a parliamentary democracy pledged to socialism and reflecting the extra-parliamentary struggles of the people.
The party's youth organisation is the Young Communist League.

Community Arts In 1975, for an experimental period, the *Arts Council of Great Britain* introduced subsidies to professional artists working with communities in England. The aim was to encourage local people to create their own artistic and cultural expression. Assistance has been provided for touring community arts groups working in a variety of media, and also for individuals on long-term projects, e.g. setting up community workshops and festivals. Regional Arts Associations assist community artists in England with specific projects in certain cases.
In Scotland, the *Scottish Arts Council* supports several community arts organisations and events, preferably those which are professionally run and attract local support.
In Wales, the *Welsh Arts Council* primarily assists community theatre groups.
See also **Arts: support.**

Community Centres and Village Halls These may receive grants towards capital expenditure from the *Department of Education and Science* or the *Department of Education, Northern Ireland*. Apply in first instance to the *local education authority* in England and Wales; to the area's *education and library board* in Northern Ireland.
See also **Education: Scotland; Education: Northern Ireland.**

Community Land Scheme The scheme enables certain authorities to acquire land needed for development and then to dispose of it, whether leasehold or freehold, on the private market. As no **development land tax** is payable by the seller on any land acquired by these authorities, the price ultimately paid by them for land for development tends to be equivalent to what the seller would have been left with had he sold the land privately and paid the development land tax due. The scheme does not affect land transactions which do not involve development.

For land scheme purposes the authorities in England are all local authorities, the *New Town Development Corporations*, the *Peak Park Joint Planning Board* and the *Lake District Special Planning Board*; in Scotland the regional, general and district planning authorities and *New Town Development Corporations*; and in Wales *Land Authority for Wales* and *New Town Development Corporations*.

Land acquired by authorities for disposal for private development must be firmly based on their planning policies. Authorities other than new town development corporations have prepared land policy statements including the estimated land development needs in their area; the quantity of land available to meet those needs; and the extent to which the authority intends to intervene through the land scheme to make land available for private development. For current land policy statements, apply to the relevant authority.

Authorities acquire development land either as a part of their normal activities, or as a result of planning applications to carry out development: authorities are generally concerned only with land for major development. If a proposed acquisition results from a planning application and the authority decides to grant **planning permission**, that permission will be 'suspended' (i.e. it cannot be acted on) to enable acquisition procedures to begin. Authorities acquiring land under the land scheme do so in the normal way – either by agreement or, if necessary, by means of **compulsory purchase**. The landowner may object to a compulsory purchase order, although in certain specified circumstances the relevant *Secretary of State* may disregard an objection or dispense with holding a public inquiry.

Authorities proposing to develop or re-develop an area may declare it a 'disposal notification area'. Intended sales of land, other than by owner-occupiers of up to one acre, must then be notified to the authority, which may seek to acquire it. The declaration of a disposal notification area must be advertised in local newspapers.

Booklets on the community land scheme are available free of charge from authorities, or, in England, from the *Department of the Environment*; in Scotland from the *Scottish Information Office*; and in Wales from the *Welsh Office Conservation and Land Division*.

See also **Compulsory purchase: compensation**.

Community Service Orders These give the courts an alternative to shorter custodial sentences in cases where the need to safeguard the public interest is not an overriding consideration and enable offenders to repay their debt to society in a positive manner. Offenders aged 17 or over who are convicted of an offence punishable with imprisonment may be ordered, subject to their consent, to carry out in their spare time unpaid work of benefit to the community. Between 40 and 240 hours of work may be ordered. Sanctions exist for breach of a Community Service Order: the offender can be fined up to £50 or resentenced for the original offence.

See also **Criminal courts; Criminal justice**.

Companies: Annual Accounts and Return In each calendar year every company must send to the *Registrar of Companies* an annual return made up to the 14th day after the annual general meeting. The return must be filed within 42 days of the meeting.

Every company may if it wishes notify the RoC of the date on which its accounting reference period will end in each year, and this will be the company's accounting reference date. Without this notification, the RoC regards the company's accounting reference date as being 31 March. Each year the company must produce its accounts made up to the accounting reference date or to a date within seven days of the accounting reference date. The financial year is the twelve-month period covered by the accounts, and may end up to seven days before or after the accounting reference date.

A new company's first accounting reference period begins on its incorporation and runs until the accounting reference date as notified to (or imposed by) the RoC is first reached. If this would result in the period being less than six months in duration, it will run to the second occasion on which the accounting reference date is reached. The first accounting reference period should not exceed 18 months.

Companies are also required to lay before the company's members in general meeting the accounts prepared for each accounting reference period and deliver a copy of the accounts to the RoC (unless throughout the accounting reference period the company was unlimited, not a subsidiary of, or the holding company of, a limited company, and had not carried out business as a trading stamp scheme promoter). The accounts must be laid before the company and delivered to the RoC within 10 months of the end of the accounting reference period in the case of private companies, and seven months in the case of public companies; but companies (private and public) with overseas interests may claim a three month extension from the RoC. Where a newly incorporated company has as its first accounting reference period a period in excess of 12 months, the period allowed for laying and delivering of accounts will be reduced by the amount of time by which the accounting reference period exceeded 12 months; in no case, however, will less than three months be allowed. Accounts must also be audited (see **Auditors**).

Companies: Articles of Association
The articles of association of a private company adopting certain restrictions must be registered with the *Registrar of Companies*, together with the **memorandum of association**. The restrictions cover the right to transfer its shares; to limit the number of its members to 50 (not including members who are employees of the company); and to prohibit any invitation to the public to subscribe for its shares and debentures. In addition all or any of the regulations contained in Table A in the First Schedule to the Companies Act 1948 may be adopted. Any of these regulations not specifically excluded or modified by the articles registered will be taken as applying to the company. The articles must be printed, divided into paragraphs numbered consecutively and must also be executed and dated like the memorandum. Articles of association are intended to show the regulations for the internal arrangements and management of the company; they should not contain anything beyond the powers or rights possessed by the company as stated in the memorandum.

For public companies the requirements as to articles are similar to those for private companies, but Part 2 of Table A in the First Schedule to the Companies Act 1948 is not applicable.
See also **Companies: formation and registration**.

Companies: Directors and Secretaries
Under the Companies Acts details of any changes in directors or secretaries of registered companies must be sent to the *Registrar of Companies* (on form 9B) within 14 days of the changes occurring. In their annual report, the directors should deal with the state of the company's affairs and indicate the dividend they recommend and the amount they propose to carry to reserves. Matters of a general nature to be dealt with in the directors' report are set out in Section 16 of the Companies Act 1967 and other matters are prescribed in Sections 17 to 20. Circumstances in which the information has to be given vary and, for details, reference should be made to the Sections of the 1967 Act mentioned against each item. Broadly information required is as follows: names of persons who have been directors during the financial year (16(1)); principal activities of the company and its subsidiaries during the year and any significant changes therein (16(1)); particulars of any significant changes in the fixed assets of the company or any of its subsidiaries (16(1)(a)); details of shares and debentures issued during the year and the reasons for the issues (16(1)(b)); particulars of significant contracts with the company

in which a director thereof has a direct or indirect interest (16(1)(c)); statement of the arrangements to which the company is a party under which directors of the company are or were during the year enabled to acquire shares or debentures in the company or any other body corporate (16(1)(d)); information regarding directors' interests if existing at the end of the year, in shares or debentures of the company or its holding company's subsidiaries, etc. (16(1)(e)); particulars of any other matters material for the appreciation of the state of the company's affairs (16(1)(f)); if the company has carried on business of two or more classes that differ substantially from each other, the turnover and the profit (or loss) attributable to each of those classes, unless the company is neither a holding company nor a subsidiary company and its turnover does not exceed £250,000 (section 17 and para 13A of the Schedule as amended by the Companies (Accounts) Regulations 1971); if the number of employees of the company exceeds 100, a statement of the average number employed during the year together with their aggregate remuneration (18); particulars of contributions made by the company for political or charitable purposes (or both) if the total exceeds £50 in the year (19); if the company supplies goods, the value of goods exported by the company during the year or a statement that no goods were exported (unless it is neither a holding company nor a subsidiary company and its turnover does not exceed £250,000, or it is a subsidiary company but not a holding company and its turnover as shown in the accounts does not exceed £50,000; or it is a holding company (whether or not it is also a subsidiary company) which presents consolidated accounts, and its consolidated turnover as shown in the accounts does not exceed £50,000).

Every member of a company and any other person entitled to receive notice of a general meeting is entitled to receive a copy of the directors' report. Every company must keep a register of directors' interests: directors must notify the company within five days of any interests they have in shares or debentures of the company, its holding company or any subsidiary; interests of directors' spouses and infant children must also be stated. If this register is not kept at the registered office of the company, then notification of the address at which it is kept, and any changes in that address, must be sent to the *Registrar of Companies*.

A company listed on a recognised stock exchange must notify that stock exchange of any acquisition, etc., by a director of such of its shares or debentures as are listed on that stock exchange. Notification must be made by the following day, excluding a Saturday, Sunday or bank holiday.

The *Secretary of State for Trade* has the power to apply to the court for an order disqualifying a person from acting as a director of a company for up to five years if he has been in default in filing returns on at least three occasions in five years. A public register of disqualified persons is open to inspection (fee payable) at the *Companies Registration Office* (Cardiff), the *Companies Registration Office, London Search Room*, the *Insolvency Service* (for England and Wales) or at the *Companies Registration Office* (Edinburgh) for Scotland.

Companies: Enquiries Enquiries relating to the registration of companies having their registered offices in England and Wales should be addressed to the *Registrar of Companies (London)* and for those in Scotland to the *Registrar of Companies (Edinburgh)*. Northern Ireland operates its own entirely independent Companies Acts and all enquiries about companies registered there should be addressed to the *Registrar of Companies (Belfast)*.

All documents kept by the RoC relative to individual companies may be inspected at a cost of 5p for each company file searched, including documents submitted in connection with the incorporation of a company which can be inspected at the *Companies Registration Office (Cardiff)*, the *Companies Registration Office, London Search Rooms* (for companies registered in England and Wales) or the *Companies Registration Office (Edinburgh)* (for companies registered in Scotland).

See also **Companies: formation and registration**.

Companies: Formation and Registration Every company registered on or after 1 November 1929 (other than a private company) must have at least two directors, while every company registered before that date and every private company must have one director (see **Companies: directors and secretaries**). Any two or more persons may form and carry on a private company, which must by its articles restrict the right to transfer its shares; limit the number of its members to 50 (this does not include members who are employees of the company); and prohibit any invitation to the public to subscribe for any shares or debentures of the company. Documents which must be delivered to the *Registrar of Companies* for the registration of a private company are the memorandum of association (with at least two signatories); the articles of association; a statement of capital; a statement of first directors and secretary and intended situation of registered office; and a declaration of compliance (a statutory declaration by a solicitor engaged in the formation of the company, or by a person named as director or secretary of the company that all the requirements of the Companies Acts in respect of registration have been complied with).

The documents to be delivered to the RoC for the registration of a public company are similar, except that the memorandum of association must have at least seven signatures. A public company having a share capital must, before it commences business or exercises any borrowing powers, obtain the RoC's certificate that it is entitled to commence business.

See also **Business names; Companies: articles of association; Companies: memorandum of association; Stock Exchange listing**.

Companies: Investigation Investigation of companies is provided for in certain circumstances under the Companies Acts. Enquiries and applications to the *Department of Trade Headquarters*. The DoT's powers are aimed principally at fraud, misfeasance and misconduct; they are not used solely to investigate insolvency, or as a substitute for civil remedies through the courts.

Companies: Memorandum of Association The memorandum of association of a private company, in addition to containing the particulars required by section 2 of the Companies Act 1948, must be signed by at least two persons whose addresses and description must be stated. Each of them must write opposite to his name in his own handwriting the number and class of shares taken. The signatures must be witnessed and the date of execution given. This memorandum forms the company's charter, and indicates the nature of the company's business, its capital and its nationality. For a public company, the requirements are similar but the memorandum must be signed by at least seven persons. The memorandum must be delivered to the *Registrar of Companies* for registration of the company.

See also **Companies: formation and registration**.

Companies Registered in Wales Companies with registered offices in Wales may, under Section 30 of the Companies Act 1976, state in their **memorandum of association** that their registered office is to be situated in Wales rather than England. A company that makes this statement in the memorandum of association may use the word 'Cyfyngedig' instead of 'Limited' as the last word of its name and deliver documents to the *Registrar of Companies* in Welsh. These should be accompanied by an English translation certified by a notary public in England or Wales, or a solicitor of the Supreme Court.

See also **Companies: formation and registration**.

Companies: Registration Changes In Great Britain every registered company must submit certain particulars to the *Registrar of Companies*. Changes to these particulars must also be submitted to the RoC, within certain specified time limits, as follows:

Change	Notification to RoC
Acquisition of most mortgages or charges on properties	Within 21 days of acquisition (with certified copy of relevant instrument, if any) (form 47B)
Address of registered offices	Within 14 days of change (form 4A)
Address where register of debenture holders is kept	Within 21 days (form 102)
Address where register of directors' interests is kept	Within 14 days (form R5)
Address where register of members is kept	Within 14 days (form 103)
Allotment of shares	Within one month (form PUC 2, 3 or 7)
Alteration of company's objects in memorandum or articles of association	Within 15 days of special resolution
Becoming public	Within 14 days (form 55A)
Company's secretary or directors	Within 14 days of appointment (form 9P)
Consolidation of shares into stock	Within one month (form 28)
Creation of certain mortgages and charges	Within 21 days (with relevant instrument, if any) (form 47)
Increase in capital	Within 15 days of resolution (copy of resolution and details of increase) (form 10)
Increase in members (by unlimited or limited guarantee company)	Within 15 days of resolution (form 11)
Name	Within 14 days of special resolution (approval needed by *Secretary of State for Trade* and fee payable)

Unlimited companies can re-register with the RoC as limited companies (provided they were not converted from limited to unlimited in the first place) after the directors have passed a special resolution. Limited companies can re-register as unlimited (provided they were not previously converted from unlimited to limited) with the signed assents of all members of the company. Copies of the revised memorandum and articles of association must be forwarded to the RoC with the application.

See also **Companies: articles of association; Companies: formation and registration; Companies: memorandum of association.**

Companies: Stationery Every company registered on or after 23 November 1916, and overseas companies establishing a place of business in Great Britain on or after that date, must show on all trade catalogues, trade circulars, showcards and business letters the names of all directors (including any corporate directors) and their nationality if not British. The nationality of a director who is a citizen of an EEC member state need not be stated.

Companies must also show, under the European Communities Act 1972, on business letters and order forms the place of registration of the company, the number with which it is registered and the address of its registered office. Place of registration should be indicated by printing on stationery either 'registered in England and Wales', 'registered in Cardiff' or 'registered in Wales'. Companies using 'England' or 'London' for these purposes need not change their letter paper as a result of the move of the *Companies Registration Office* to Cardiff. For companies registered in Scotland, 'registered in Scotland' or 'registered in Edinburgh' is acceptable. The registered number of a company is shown on its certificate of incorporation. If a business letter or order form shows more than one address, it is advisable, to avoid con-

fusion, to indicate which is the registered office.
A limited company which is exempt under Section 19 of the Companies Act 1948 from the obligation to use the word 'limited' as part of its name must show that it is a limited company. This does not alter the company's right to omit the word 'limited' from its name. If there is any reference to the amount of share capital on a business letter or order form, the reference must be to paid-up share capital.

Companies: Trading and Non-trading
Once a company has incorporated in Great Britain (see **Companies: formation and registration**) and before it begins trading, or borrowing or raising capital, it must obtain a certificate of trading from the *Registrar of Companies*. It must first furnish the RoC with a document stating that the minimum capital has been subscribed, that directors have paid for their shares and that the requirements of the Companies Acts have been met. With a private company, minimum capital comes mainly from the directors; with a public company the capital must be obtained by inviting members of the public and institutions to buy shares.
The invitation and relevant details of the company are given in a 'prospectus' which must be lodged with the RoC on or before its publication. If minimum capital is not subscribed and the issue of shares has not been underwritten against this risk, the company cannot commence trading and has to return any subscriptions received; advice from RoC.
The RoC has power to strike companies off the register when he has reason to believe they are not carrying on business or in operation.

Companies: Winding up The winding up of a company may be carried out either by the court, by members voluntarily, by creditors voluntarily, or subject to the supervision of the court. Notice of a meeting of creditors called for voluntary liquidation by creditors must be advertised once in the 'London Gazette' (in the case of companies registered in England and Wales) and once at least in two local newspapers circulating in the district of the registered office or principal place of business of the company. Notice of all resolutions to wind up voluntarily must be similarly given within 14 days of their passing, by advertisement. A copy of the resolution to wind up voluntarily must be filed with the *Registrar of Companies* within 15 days of the passing of the resolution.
In the case of a proposal to wind up a company as a members' voluntary winding up, a meeting of the directors should first be called at which a 'declaration of solvency' must be made. This declaration should include a statement of the company's assets and liabilities at the latest practicable date before the declaration is made. The declaration of solvency must be made within five weeks before the date of passing the resolution to wind up, and be filed with the RoC before the resolution is passed.
Notes for guidance on voluntary liquidation from the RoC.

Company Law and EEC Harmonisation of company law in the EEC is progressing slowly. A directive on disclosure, nullity and powers of companies was adopted by the EEC in 1968 and incorporated in UK law through Section 9 of the European Communities Act 1976. A directive on company capital was adopted in December 1976, to be incorporated into UK law within two years. Other draft directives (e.g. on mergers and on company accounts) are being developed. Enquiries to the Market Information Country Section of the Export Services Promotion Division at the *Department of Trade headquarters*.

Compensation from Criminals In England and Wales the courts may order an offender to pay compensation for any personal injury, loss or damage resulting from his offence and, in certain circumstances, may order the forfeiture of property used, or intended for use, in the commission of a crime. In the case of major crimes against property a criminal bankruptcy order against the offender can form the basis of bankruptcy proceedings against him. A committee has recommended that a

compensation scheme similar to that in England and Wales should be started in Scotland.
See also **Criminal injuries: compensation.**

Compulsory Purchase: Compensation
Compensation is payable for land and property wanted for public development and acquired under a compulsory purchase order.
If the whole of a property is needed, compensation may include the market value of the owner's interest in the property. No reduction is made in compensation on account of any decrease in value caused by the scheme for which the authority wants the land. Similarly any increase in value caused by the scheme is disregarded. Displaced persons may also be entitled to some compensation for disturbance; reasonable removal and other expenses; 'home-loss' payments for those who have lived in their present home for at least five years, and if certain other conditions are satisfied; rehousing or a local authority mortgage if suitable alternative accommodation is not otherwise available; an advance payment, within three months of asking for it, of 90% of the compensation – less any outstanding mortgage (see 'Your home and compulsory purchase', Booklet 1 from *Department of the Environment*).
If only part of the property is needed compensation may include: the market value for the owner's interest in the property taken and compensation for depreciation in the value of the interest in the remainder; an advance payment, within three months of asking for it, of 90% of the compensation – less any outstanding mortgage; in most cases replacement of hedges, fencing and gates, subject to any benefit arising being taken into account in assessing compensation; liability by the authority to buy the whole of the property.
If none of the property is needed, the authority may still be prepared to buy it if the enjoyment of the property is seriously affected by nuisance from construction on nearby land or new operations on recently developed land (if reported within one year of their start). Compensation may also be payable if, one year after start of use, e.g. one year after a new or altered road is open to public traffic, the value of the claimant's interest in the property for its present use is depreciated by more than £50 by physical factors such as noise, dust or fumes arising from the use of the new works. Those selling privately during this first year, and who wish to claim, must lodge the claim with the appropriate authority after exchanging a contract to sell but before completion of the sale.

Owners and occupiers of property which a local authority has indicated it may need to acquire may be able to serve a 'blight notice' to force the local authority to purchase the property in advance of its requirements. They must be able to show that they cannot sell the property except at a depreciated price because of the authority's proposals. Blight notices may also be served if the authority only wants part of the land. Compensation for acquisition resulting from a blight notice is at market value.

Noise insulation: if the traffic using a new road or a road to which a carriageway has been added is calculated to produce noise at or above a specified level after the erection of any noise mounds or barriers, insulation may be provided for affected dwellings in living rooms and bedrooms. This comprises double glazing, ventilation and, if necessary, venetian blinds. Insulation may also be provided against construction noise or noise from the use of altered roads.

Temporary accommodation: persons disturbed by construction works to the extent that continued occupation of the dwelling is not reasonably practical may be able to get repayment of expenses incurred by living elsewhere temporarily, but only if this is agreed in advance with the appropriate authority.

Tenants of residential accommodation: if required to leave home, tenants may be entitled to a home loss payment, to receive reasonable removal expenses, to be rehoused or, if they decide to buy their own house, to receive assistance with costs such as legal expenses incurred in connection with its purchase (see Booklet 1 as above). Tenants who do

not have to move but whose home is badly affected by traffic noise from a new or altered road may be entitled to noise insulation (see Booklet 5 – 'Insulation against traffic noise'). Tenants very seriously disturbed by construction works (see above) may be able to get repayment of the expenses incurred by living elsewhere temporarily (see Booklet 2 – 'Your home and nuisance from public development').
There are special provisions for businessmen and farmers (see Booklet 3 – 'Your business and public development' and Booklet 4 – 'The farmer and public development'). General information is available from **local authorities** or DoE. The position in Scotland is explained in 'Compensation, a guide for house-owners and tenants' from the Scottish Development Department, Professional advice may be needed, from a **solicitor** or **surveyor**.
See also **Community land scheme**; **Mortgages: local authority**.

Computers and Privacy A Data Protection Committee has been established through the *Home Office* to prepare the way for legislation to secure that all existing and future computer systems in which personal information is held, in both the private and public sectors, are operated with appropriate safeguards for the privacy of the subject of that information. The DPC's functions are to advise the government on the form of the permanent control machinery, and to consider and refine the objectives to be incorporated in legislation establishing permanent safeguards.
This follows the government white paper 'Computers and Privacy' (1975) which identified a need for legislation involving two elements: the establishment of a set of objectives, to set standards governing the use of computers that handle personal information; and the establishment of a permanent statutory agency (provisionally called the Data Protection Authority) to oversee the use and operation of computers.

Concert Agencies Anyone may start a concert staff employment agency, but under the Employment Agencies Act 1973 a licence is required from the *Department of Employment, Regional Offices*. After six consecutive months of practice, agents are eligible for provisional membership, and after three years for full membership, of the *British Association of Concert Agents*. It publishes a list of the artists exclusively managed by its members, administers a code of professional conduct, and holds regular meetings for the discussion of matters of mutual interest.

Congo For **exchange control** is a non-scheduled territory outside the **overseas sterling area** and the **EEC**. UK nationals travelling direct from the UK normally need only the following (but check): **passports**; **visas**; international certificates of **vaccination** against smallpox; **work permits** (if taking a job); green cards for motor insurance (if bringing a car); international driving permits (if intending to drive: see **Motoring abroad**).
The UK has no reciprocal health or social security arrangements.
Enquiries to *Congolese Embassy* in Paris, France.
British diplomatic mission to Congo is *British Consulate* in Brazzaville. The main British mission responsible is *British Embassy* in Kinshasa, Zaire.

Conservation: Beauty Spots The *Countryside Commission* helps to safeguard the most attractive country in England and Wales by designating areas of outstanding natural beauty. There are currently 33 such areas. They tend to be smaller and less spectacular than **national parks** and have no special administrative arrangements.

Conservation: Coasts Under the Heritage Coasts Scheme, the *Countryside Commission* is currently trying to identify the finest lengths of unspoilt coastline in England and Wales so that they may be effectively preserved.

Conservative Party Membership is open to all who believe in Conservative principles. Members subscribe directly to the Conservative Association of the constituency in which they reside or have a special interest (address in local telephone directory). Age limits for Young Conservative branches extend from 15 to 30 years.

The party organisation is based on constituency associations in the 552 parliamentary constituencies in England and Wales. Scotland with 71 constituencies is separately organised (see **Scottish Conservative Party**), as is Northern Ireland with 12 constituencies. Each association is autonomous and is responsible for selecting its own parliamentary and local government candidates, for raising money to run local party headquarters and campaigns and for employing staff, which often includes a full-time constituency agent.

Conservative and Unionist Central Office provides specialist services (organisation, community affairs, publicity, research, local government and political education) for the constituencies and the parliamentary party.

Conservative policy has been defined as 'a regard for the lessons of experience, a respect for tradition, a reluctance to destroy established beliefs and institutions and a belief in freedom of the individual'. Further information from the Central Office.

Constituency Boundaries: European Assembly The *Boundary Commissions* for England, Scotland and Wales recommend the boundaries of the directly elected European Assembly constituencies in Great Britain. There are 78 single-member 'Euro-constituencies' in Great Britain (England 66, Scotland 8, Wales 4) for the simple majority system of elections. These are formed by grouping parliamentary constituencies so that the number of electors in the Euro-constituency is as close to the electoral quota (average) as possible, taking account of any special geographical considerations. The electoral quota is calculated separately for each country. The procedure is similar to that for parliamentary constituencies (see **Constituency boundaries: UK Parliament**) with some exceptions relating only to the first direct elections to the European Assembly, in June 1979. In Northern Ireland three representatives are elected by the single transferable vote system, which does not entail the division of the province into Euro-constituencies.

Constituency Boundaries: Scottish and Welsh Assemblies If responsibilities are devolved upon Scottish and Welsh Assemblies, it seems likely (at the time of going to press) that the *Boundary Commission for Scotland* and the *Boundary Commission for Wales* will have to recommend constituencies for the election of members for the Assemblies; constituencies will probably be based on Westminster parliamentary constituencies, which will be divided to form Assembly constituencies.

Constituency Boundaries: UK Parliament Parliamentary constituency boundaries are reviewed by each of the four *Boundary Commissions* (for England, Scotland, Wales and Northern Ireland). They submit recommendations to the relevant Secretary of State (e.g. *Home Secretary, Secretary of State for Scotland*) between 10 and 15 years after the completion of their last general review. The rules for redistribution of seats limit the total number of parliamentary constituencies (currently – England 516, Scotland 71, Wales 36 and Northern Ireland 12). County and London borough boundaries and the major local government boundaries in Scotland must be followed as far as is practicable without causing an excessive disparity between the electorates of constituencies; the electorates must be as near the electoral quota as possible (i.e. the total electorate of that part of the UK, divided by the existing number of constituencies). The BCs may depart from these basic rules for special geographical reasons (e.g. in particular the size, shape and accessibility of a constituency) and have to take account of inconveniences likely to be caused by alterations and of any local ties which would be broken.

A BC's provisional recommendations must be published, giving opportunity for representations against them. If a local authority within an affected con-

stituency or a body of 100 or more electors object to the proposals, a local inquiry must be held. Any subsequent revised proposals by the BC are also published and representations invited upon them. The Home Secretary (or the Secretary of State for Scotland as appropriate) has to lay a BC's report of its review before Parliament. To modify the recommendations, he must lay a statement of the reasons for the modification with the accompanying draft Order in Council for consideration with the report. The draft Orders are subject to the approval of both Houses of Parliament and the new constituencies come into operation at the next general election.
See also **Local government: boundaries and electoral arrangements**.

Construction Safety General UK policy on safety in construction work, including the preparation of new legislation, codes of practice and EEC directives on construction work, is the responsibility of Safety and General Branch B at the *Health and Safety Executive Head Office*. The *Health and Safety Executive HM Factory Inspectorate Consultant Section 6* is responsible for giving technical advice on safety in construction work, including the construction and demolition of all types of buildings, bridges, chimneys, tanks, etc., and allied aspects of construction such as scaffolding, excavation, etc. General advice on safety in construction work, including compliance with legal requirements, is available from the *Health and Safety Executive HM Factory Inspectorate Area Offices*.
See also **Work: health and safety**.

Construction Works in Tidal Waters The issue of licences under the Dumping at Sea Act 1974 is by Fisheries Division 1C at the *Ministry of Agriculture, Fisheries and Food Headquarters (2)*.
See also **Foreshore and seabed: ownership**.

Consuls Services available to UK citizens abroad from British consulates include statutory duties (e.g. registration of births and deaths and the performance of notarial acts) and non-statutory work which has evolved over the years (e.g. issuing **passports, visas** and entry certificates); the occasional administration of estates of deceased persons (see **Overseas estate administration**); and the protection of UK citizens (see **Imprisonment and detention abroad**). Consuls should not be asked to do the work of travel agents, lawyers, banks, telegraph offices, information bureaux or hotels. There are consular officers at nearly all British embassies in foreign capitals and at consulates in some provincial centres (addresses under *British diplomatic missions*). Consular officials in **Commonwealth** countries do not perform the full range of services carried out by their counterparts in non-Commonwealth countries. In countries with which the UK has no diplomatic relations, consular services are ordinarily provided, but on a restricted scale, by the diplomatic mission of another country. The *Foreign and Commonwealth Office, Consular Department* should be consulted before departure for such countries.
See also entry for each country.

Consumer Credit Licences are required by anyone in the UK conducting a consumer credit business; consumer hire business; credit brokerage; debt adjusting or debt counselling; debt collection; or a **credit reference agency**. A consumer credit business is any business so far as it comprises or relates to the provision of credit under regulated consumer credit agreements, i.e. a business involved in providing individuals with a cash loan or other form of credit or not more than £5,000 (e.g. retailers, trade suppliers, banks, finance houses, mutual loan clubs, employers offering loans to employees, moneylenders and pawnbrokers). But normal trade credit, low cost credit, finance of foreign trade, certain mortgage lending and land transactions (as defined in the Consumer Credit (Exempt Agreements) Order 1977) and, at present, small traders whose credit transactions involve advances of £30 or less are excepted.
A consumer hire business is any business so far as it comprises or relates to

the bailment, leasing, hiring or renting of goods under regulated consumer hire agreements, i.e. a business which hires out, leases or rents goods to individuals under transactions which may last for more than three months and where the total amount of the payments come to no more than £5,000. 'Individual' includes a partnership or other unincorporated body of persons. Applications for a licence should be made to the Licensing Branch of the *Office of Fair Trading*. Application forms and a booklet giving further information are obtainable from the *OFT* or from local authority trading standards, consumer protection or weights and measures departments. In Northern Ireland application forms may be obtained from the Trading Standards Branch of the *Northern Ireland Department of Commerce*.

The Consumer Credit Act gives the courts power to grant relief to people who have entered into extortionate credit transactions. Consult a **solicitor**. The Act also provides for the disclosure of the annual percentage rate of the total charge for credit in regulated consumer credit agrements. The items which constitute the total charge for credit and the formula for calculating the annual percentage rate are laid down in the Consumer Credit (Total Charge for Credit) Regulations 1977. Further regulations are in preparation by which the annual percentage rate and the total charge for credit will have to be disclosed in advertisements, quotations and credit and hire agreements. Enquiries to the *Office of Fair Trading*.

See also **Consumer protection**.

Consumer Products Well-designed modern British consumer products are exhibited at the Design Council's *Design Centres* in Glasgow and London. The Centres occasionally stage thematic exhibitions to illustrate new design developments (details of display charges from the manager) but otherwise all products on display have been included in the Council's 'Design Index.' To be included, products are initially submitted by manufacturers through the Council's industrial officers and then selected as well designed by the Council's independent committees of outside experts on design and engineering. The Index records some 9,000 products and is available at the Centres and at the *Building and Design Centre* in Liverpool. Only products listed in the Index can use or advertise the black and white triangular Design Centre label (adhesive or tie on – details from *DC* managers).

Consumer Protection Local authorities in Great Britain are generally responsible for enforcing the laws protecting shoppers. Their Trading Standards Officers police the laws concerning fair trading and investigate complaints from buyers or other traders. In Northern Ireland these laws are enforced by central government operating through area offices. Any complaints concerning the specific obligations of sellers in Great Britain should be made to the local authority. The *Office of Fair Trading* collects information about methods of trading and investigates traders who persistently commit offences or breach obligations to customers; if necessary it takes legal action or withholds consumer credit licences. The *Price Commission* monitors prices (**see Price control**) and is responsible for ensuring that prices do not rise beyond any statutory limits. The *Metrication Board* gives advice to traders and shoppers concerning **metrication**. The *National Consumer Council*, the *Welsh Consumer Council* and the *Scottish Consumer Council* represent the views and concerns of consumers in England, Wales and Scotland respectively. The *Department of Prices and Consumer Protection* is the responsible central government department. The *Consumers Association* offers detailed help and advice to its members; its independent magazine 'Which?', published monthly, tests and compares many different goods and services. *Citizens Advice Bureaux* will act as referees between a buyer and a trader to settle differences over specific purchases.

Specific complaints may also be taken up with various trade or professional associations (see details below). The trade associations of certain industries have voluntary codes of practice for

member firms to ensure a standard of service to customers; these are indicated with an asterisk (*).
Advertising: *Advertising Standards Authority*; *Independent Broadcasting Authority*; *Independent Television Companies Association*.
Agriculture: *Consumers Committees for Great Britain, England and Wales, and Scotland*.
Building and decorating: *National House Building Council*; *British Decorators Association*.
Caravans and sites: *National Caravan Council*.
Carpets: *Federation of British Carpet Manufacturers*.
Cars and drivers: *Motor Agents Association**; *Scottish Motor Trade Association**; *Council for Vehicle Servicing and Repair*; *Society of Motor Manufacturers and Traders**; *Vehicle Builders and Repairers Association**.
Electrical goods: *Association of Manufacturers of Domestic Electrical Appliances**.
Furniture: *National Association of Retail Furnishers*.
Hearing aids: *Hearing Aids Council*.
Insurance: *British Insurance Association*.
Laundry and cleaning: *Association of British Launderers and Cleaners**; *National Association of Laundrette Industry*.
Mail order: *Newspaper Publishers Association*; *Newspaper Society*; *Periodical Publishers Association*; *Scottish Newspaper Proprietors Association*; *Scottish Daily Newspaper Society* (jointly operate a mail order protection scheme to reimburse readers losing money sent to advertisers who go bankrupt before the goods are received).
Nationalised industries: Gas, *Regional Gas Consumers Council*; Electricity, *Electricity Consultative Council*; Post Office, *Post Office Advisory Committee*; British Rail, *Transport Users Consultative Committee*; Coal and solid fuels, *Approved Coal Merchants Scheme*; Airlines, *Airline Users Committee*; Airports, Heathrow/Gatwick/Stansted/Prestwick/Aberdeen/Edinburgh/Glasgow Consultative Committee; otherwise airport manager.
Radio and television: *Radio and Television Retailers Association**.
Shoes and shoe repairs: *Footwear Distributors Federation*; *National Association of Shoe Repair Factories*; *St Crispin's Boot Trades Association*.
Solicitors: *Law Society*; *Law Society of Scotland*; *Incorporated Law Society of Northern Ireland*.
Toys: *British Toy Manufacturers Association*.
Travel: *Association of British Travel Agents**.

Most other trade and professional organisations will provide advice and consider complaints about their members, although such associations cannot be expected to represent the consumer's interest against their own members. Consumer organisations with the buyer's interest as their prime concern are: *Good Housekeeping Institute*; the *Housewife's Trust*; the *National Consumer Council*; the *National Federation of Consumer Groups*; and the consumer standard advisory committee of the *British Standards Institution*. See also **Sales of goods**; **Goods: unsolicited**.

Contraception   Advice and contraceptive appliances (including contraceptive pills) are free to both men and women under the **National Health Service**. Most doctors in general practice provide family planning services for women; see list of doctors published by each *Family Practitioner Committee*. NHS Family Planning Clinics provide a free service for both men and women. A list of these clinics is kept by the *area health authority* (or look in the telephone directory under Family Planning Service).

Co-operative Party   Membership is open to British citizens over the age of 16 who accept the party's declaration of loyalty, which includes abstention from membership of opposing parties. The party is a department of the Co-operative Union (the national advisory organisation for the British Co-operative Movement to which nearly all retail co-operative societies are affiliated). It works in close liaison with the Labour Party and has agreed with it that the Co-operative party should not sponsor more than 30 parliamentary candidates. Membership is handled centrally by the *Co-operative Party* in London.

Copyright The Copyright Act 1956 gives protection to every literary, dramatic, musical or artistic work before and after publication. Generally the author of the work is the first owner of the copyright and it lasts for his lifetime and 50 years thereafter. The Act applies automatically (no registration or fee is needed) and protects the copyright holder against reproduction of his work and its public performance without permission. The government department responsible for copyright matters is the *Department of Trade, Industrial Property and Copyright Department.* Cases of alleged infringement of copyright which cannot be settled privately can only be dealt with in the courts, since there is no provision in the Act for government intervention. Sound recordings, cinema films and TV and radio broadcasts can also have copyright.
See also **Crown copyright; Libraries.**

Corporation Tax In much the same way as **income tax** is charged on an individual's net taxable income, corporation tax is charged in the UK on a company's profits (both income and capital gains, although effectively gains are charged at a lower rate) after allowable deductions. Deductions are allowed in respect of the normal operating costs of a business (rent, wages, cost of materials, etc.) and there are also 'capital allowances' where plant and machinery have been purchased. For tax a company means any body corporate or unincorporated association. 'Small companies' (the definition, relating to size of profits, has varied from time to time) are charged at a reduced rate compared with the normal as regards income only.
Corporation tax is also payable (though at a special rate) by industrial and provident societies, **housing associations** and building societies.
Assessment, collection and appeals are much the same as for income tax.
See also **Businesses, small.**

Correspondence Colleges Anyone may start, run and teach at a correspondence college in England and Wales without qualification, but the *Council for the Accreditation of Correspondence Colleges,* an independent body set up by the colleges, accredits colleges reaching CACC standards for postal tuition. Complaints against accredited corespondence colleges can be investigated by the CACC.
See also **Education: Scotland; Education: Northern Ireland.**

Costa Rica For **exchange control** is a non-scheduled territory outside the **overseas sterling area** and the **EEC.** UK nationals travelling direct from the UK normally need only the following (but check): **passports; work permits** (if taking a job); green cards for motor insurance (if bringing a car); international driving permits (if intending to drive: see **Motoring abroad).**
The UK has no reciprocal health or social security arrangements.
Enquiries to *Costa Rican Embassy* in London.
British diplomatic mission to Costa Rica is *British Embassy* in San Jose.

Country Code A guide to the behaviour of visitors to the countryside is prepared and distributed by the *Countryside Commission.* Copies can be obtained post-free from the CC or from the *Countryside Commission for Scotland.*

Country Parks These are created in Scotland by the *Countryside Commission for Scotland* in order to give priority in the areas so designated to recreational needs. Enquiries to CCS.
See also **Conservation: beauty spots.**

Countryside Conservation: Recreation Grants These can be provided in certain circumstances by the *Countryside Commission* to private landowners or **local authorities** in England and Wales. Grants are payable towards the capital costs incurred in establishing country parks and picnic sites; providing public access to open country; clearing eyesores; providing transit caravan and camping sites, hostels, visitor information centres; and providing wardening services. Grants for specific objectives are also available to voluntary organisations which promote conservation and recreation. Similar grants are available to private landowners in Scotland either directly from the *Countryside Commission for Scotland,* or from the *Scottish Develop-*

ment Department on the recommendation of the CCS.

Coursing Represented by the *National Coursing Club*, which governs and controls all competitive coursing, and is affiliated to the *British Field Sports Society* (see **Field sports**).

Covenants Any company or individual paying tax on income earned in the UK and making a gift to charity can give extra money to the charity at no extra cost to themselves by making their gift in a deed of covenant. For every £100 net which the charity receives as a covenanted gift, £51.52 can be recovered from the Inland Revenue. The requirement is that the donor should make a commitment to pay a fixed sum (e.g. £100) or a fixed computation (e.g. 5% of royalties, fees or profits) to a body recognised as charitable for tax purposes. The period of commitment should be capable of exceeding six years (i.e. in some circumstances the covenant's duration may be less if this condition is written into the deed). By covenanting to the *Charities Aid Foundation*, which is not an end-user of covenanted funds, donors can have an account gross of tax from which they can make payments to any UK charity or **charities** and vary the amounts from year to year. Advice from CAF.

Crafts Pottery, weaving, bookbinding, handmade paper, private presses, embroidery, knitting, fabric printing, wood turning and carving, furniture making, glass – painted, engraved or blown, metalwork, jewellery, calligraphy, lettering are supported financially in England and Wales by the *Crafts Advisory Committee*, in Scotland by the *Scottish Development Agency* and in Northern Ireland by the *Local Enterprise Development Unit*.
The aim of the CAC is to publicise Britain's professional artist craftsmen; to help them improve their standards; to sell their work; and to make them better known to the public, in Britain and overseas. Grants are given to individual craftsmen to take on trainees; to craftsmen just setting up; for exhibitions or publications by craft societies and regional arts associations; for study and experiment by established craftsmen; and for conservation of craftwork of the past (e.g. hangings, stained glass or stonework). Loans to established craftsmen for workshop expansion are available at favourable interest rates.
Similarly in Northern Ireland the LEDU, sponsored by the Northern Ireland Department of Commerce, gives grants and loans; makes available government factories and sites; and gives business advice on marketing, technology, accountancy and design.
The CAC gives a grant to the *British Crafts Centre* which displays work for sale at its retail shop in London; and to the *Federation of British Craft Societies*, a voluntary organisation open to all British craft societies and guilds, which represents their interests and sends out information and a newsletter.

Credit Cards It is not necessary to have a **bank account** to have a credit card. Most of the big banks are involved with the ownership or part ownership of credit card companies. Application forms for a credit card from a credit card company can be obtained from most banks or by writing direct to the credit card company, e.g. *Barclaycard* and *Access*.

Credit Reference Agencies Any UK business which supplies information about the financial standing of individuals and which has collected the information for that purpose is, statutorily, a credit reference agency and must have a licence (see **Consumer credit**). Names of licensed agencies are included in the Consumer Credit Public Register which can be inspected at *Office of Fair Trading*. An individual who applies to a trader for credit or hire under a prospective regulated consumer credit or consumer hire agreement can, within 28 days, ask for the name and address of any credit reference agency consulted about him. The trader must provide this information within seven working days whether the credit or hire was granted or not. Credit includes cash loans, hire purchase agreements, subscription accounts, **mortgages, credit cards,** trading checks, etc. Anyone can write to a credit reference agency, at any time, enclosing 25p, and receive a copy of all the information the agency holds about him; if he considers the information is wrong and likely to cause him harm, he can ask the agency to correct it. If the agency say they will not alter the file, or the alteration is unsatisfactory, the individual can write a note of correction of up to 200 words and ask the agency to add the note to the file and include a copy with any information supplied to inquirers. If the agency does not accept the correction the individual can ask the *Director General of Fair Trading* to intervene in the dispute.

Advice from local authority trading standards departments (or consumer protection or weights and measures departments) in Great Britain or from the *Northern Ireland Department of Commerce.*

Cricket Administered worldwide by the International Cricket Conference which approves the official programme of international Test Matches; countries have to be full ICC members to participate. World custodian of the laws of cricket is a private club, the *Marylebone Cricket Club.* There is no distinction between amateur and professional.

In the UK the men's game is administered by the *Cricket Council* which consists of representatives of the Marylebone Cricket Club, the *Test and County Cricket Board,* the *National Cricket Association* and the *Minor Counties Cricket Association.*

The MCC guards the rules, owns Lord's Cricket Ground and provides the headquarters for UK cricket administration.

The TCCB is responsible for the professional game which includes selecting England teams (known as MCC teams when abroad), appointing umpires, and staging Test Matches, the County Championships and all sponsored competitions played by the 17 first-class clubs. It also negotiates all sponsorships, television and radio contracts, and raises money for distribution to its constituent members, which are the 17 first-class clubs, the MCC and the MCCA.

The MCCA represents the 19 minor counties and controls the Minor Counties Competition.

The NCA administers and develops amateur cricket at all levels below first-class and minor county. It is responsible for a national coaching scheme, junior and club competitions, and tours and matches for UK teams under 19. It is organised through county associations, the *Welsh Cricket Association,* the *Scottish Cricket Union* and the *Irish Cricket Union* (all Ireland).

Women's cricket follows the same rules as men's except that a five-ounce ball is used. The *International Women's Council* is the world body which co-ordinates international tours, etc. Its founder member, the *Women's Cricket Association,* administers and governs the game as played by women in England, Wales, Scotland and Northern Ireland. Coaches qualify by taking the NCA awards.

Umpires (men and women) qualify through the *Association of Cricket Umpires* examination.

Crime Prevention Each police force has Crime Prevention Officers who give free advice to the public on all aspects of security (e.g. the installation of security devices in domestic and business premises). The CPO organises campaigns on problems such as how to curb vandalism, car thefts and house burglaries. Enquiries to local police station. To help the police in the prevention of crime most police forces have a Crime Convention Panel, made up of members of the public; contact the Panel through the CPO.
See also **Police.**

Criminal Court Proceedings In the UK an accused person is presumed innocent until proved guilty beyond reasonable doubt in a criminal court. Criminal trials take the form of 'adversary procedure' under which the court reaches a decision on the basis of legal arguments and the facts alleged and proved by the prosecution and the defence, who are responsible for the presentation of their respective cases, including calling and examining witnesses. In criminal trials by jury the judge determines questions of law but the jury alone decides the issue of guilt. The judges passes sentence. The prosecution cannot appeal against a verdict of not guilty; the defendant cannot be tried again for the same offence.

There is normally public right of access to every criminal court, except in special circumstances, e.g. cases involving children (where the child's right of privacy is considered paramount) or state security. Court proceedings are reported in the press, and, when a trial has finished (but not before), comments may also be published, provided that they are not calculated to bring a court or a judge into contempt, or to interefere with the course of justice. In any matter of criminal court proceedings consult a **solicitor**.

Criminal Courts: England and Wales
Magistrates' courts deal with 97% of all people charged with criminal offences and conduct preliminary investigations into the more serious offences. The crown court takes all criminal work above the level of magistrates' courts; hears appeals against conviction and sentence by magistrates' courts and sentences those committed for sentencing by magistrates' courts. The Court of Appeal (Criminal Division) normally takes appeals against conviction and sentence by the crown court. The House of Lords takes appeals from the Court of Appeal (Criminal Division) on points of law of general public importance. This summarises the general position but there are many complications: consult a **solicitor**.

Criminal Courts: Northern Ireland
The superior courts in Northern Ireland are the Supreme Court of Justice and the Court of Criminal Appeal. Both sit in Belfast. The High Court is the superior court of first instance, and comprises the Lord Chief Justice and five judges. The Court of Criminal Appeal, which is the appellate tribunal in criminal cases tried on indictment, consists of the Lord Chief Justice and all the judges of the Supreme Court, but sittings normally comprise two or three judges. Appeals to the House of Lords from the Court of Criminal Appeal lie under similar conditions as from the English Court of Appeal (Criminal Division). See **Criminal courts: England and Wales**.

The inferior criminal courts are the county courts and courts of summary jurisdiction, 'petty sessions'. The county courts are presided over by judges, of whom there are ten, who sit with a jury to try cases of the more serious sort on indictment. The county court judge sits alone to hear appeals from the magistrates' courts. Magistrates' courts are presided over by a resident magistrate who sits alone, and corresponds to a stipendiary magistrate in England and Wales. As a temporary arrangement in Northern Ireland certain offences involving violence or explosives may be tried by a High Court or county court judge sitting without a jury. Consult a **solicitor**.

Criminal Courts: Scotland Scotland has three levels of court – summary courts, sheriff courts, and the High Court of Justiciary. Criminal cases in Scotland are heard either under solemn procedure, when proceedings are taken on indictment and the judge sits with a jury, or under summary procedure, when the judge sits without a jury. All cases in the High Court of Justiciary and the more serious ones in the sheriff court are tried under solemn procedure. Proceedings are taken under summary procedure in the less serious cases in the sheriff court, and in the lay summary courts.

A person convicted in the High Court or in a sheriff court on indictment may appeal to the High Court of Justiciary (a) against his conviction on any ground which involves a question of law alone, or, with leave of the High Court or upon the certificate of the judge who presided at the trial that it is a fit case for appeal, on any ground, and (b) against his sentence, with the leave of the High Court, unless the sentence is one fixed by law. Appeals are heard by three or more judges, and there is no further appeal to the House of Lords.

A person convicted summarily may

appeal to the High Court, but only on questions of law and procedure, and not on issues of fact.

In Scottish trials on indictment, the first 'pleading' proceedings take place in the sheriff court, when the accused person is called upon to plead guilty or not guilty. If he pleads not guilty, the case is continued to the second 'trial' proceedings in the appropriate court. If he pleads guilty, and it is a case which is to be dealt with in the sheriff court, the sheriff may dispose of it at once. If it is a High Court case it is continued to the second proceedings in the High Court for disposal.

The second proceedings are held at least nine days after the pleading proceedings, either before the sheriff or the High Court, with a jury of 15 members. Evidence is led (without opening speeches) and there are closing speeches for the prosecution and the defence, followed by the judge's charge to the jury. The jury may return a verdict of 'not guilty' or 'not proven', both of which result in acquittal, or they may find the accused 'guilty', in which case the court proceeds to deliver sentence. The verdict may be by a simple majority. Fairness to the accused is ensured by the fact that, with a few minor exceptions, no person may be convicted without the evidence of at least two witnesses, or corroboration of one witness by facts and circumstances which clearly implicate the accused in the crime.

At summary trials in Scotland the accused is asked to plead to the charge at the first calling of the case, and, if he pleads guilty, the court may dispose of the case. Where the plea is 'not guilty', the court may proceed to trial at once or it may appoint a later date. Consult a **solicitor**.

Criminal Injuries Compensation

Compensation may be claimed in Great Britain for personal injuries (including loss of earnings) resulting from being the victim of a crime of violence; from trying to prevent a crime; or from attempting, or helping the police, to arrest a suspected offender. Dependants may apply if the victim's injuries were fatal. Apply to *Criminal Injuries Compensation Board* whether or not the assailant is known.

Incidents involving criminal injuries must be reported to the police without delay. In Northern Ireland the *Secretary of State for Northern Ireland* is responsible for the payment of compensation; apply *Northern Ireland Office* (Personal Injuries Board). Dissatisfied claimants may appeal to the courts.

See also **Compensation from criminals**.

Criminal Justice Criminal law deals with acts punishable by the state. England and Wales have their own distinctive system of criminal law, law courts and penal procedures; Scotland has another; Northern Ireland criminal justice resembles that in England and Wales with the exception of special measures introduced to cope with the present situation.

Criminal guilt or innocence is decided in the criminal courts; so are criminal sentences. Sentences are increasingly based on the idea that custodial sentences should only be imposed when necessary for the protection of society or the punishment of a serious offence. Growing emphasis in the attempt to reduce crime is placed on treatment within the community rather than within a custodial establishment.

Government departments concerned with criminal justice include the *Home Office*, the *Lord Chancellor's Office*, the *Law Officers Department*, the *Scottish Home and Health Department*, the *Lord Advocate's Department* and the *Northern Ireland Office*.

See also **Criminal courts; Pardons**.

Criminal Justice and Discipline: Armed Forces Service law is codified in Acts of Parliament for the Royal Navy, the Army and the Royal Air Force (and in the delegated legislation under them). It is administered by courts-martial and applies to all serving members of the armed forces of the Crown throughout the world. Its purpose is the preservation of essential discipline, and no change of substantive law can be made except by Parliament. A person subject to military law does not cease to be subject to the ordinary law, his obligations as a member of the armed forces being in addition to, and not in lieu of, his duties as a citizen.

Courts-Martial have jurisdiction over

members of the armed forces and, in certain circumstances, their dependants and civilians employed by the armed forces who accompany them outside the UK. The courts do not have power to deal with offences of treason, murder, manslaughter; treason, felony or rape and other non-military criminal offences committed by servicemen in the UK are in practice normally dealt with in the ordinary courts.

A court-martial (which consists of a president and a number of serving officers although a court trying a civilian may have a proportion of civilian members) may be convened by an authorised officer. A judge advocate is appointed to sit with the court in more serious Army and Air Force cases (and at every Navy trial) to advise on law and procedure and, in the former case, to sum up the evidence. The judge advocate in the case of the Army and the Air Force is normally a member of the judicial staff of the *Judge Advocate General of the Forces*, a civilian department responsible to the Lord Chancellor. Members of the staff must be barristers of at least five years' standing. In the case of the Navy, the judge advocate is a legally qualified serving officer.

A person convicted by court-martial may petition the military authorities responsible for confirming or reviewing the finding and sentence of the court-martial against the finding or sentence. Appeal also lies to the *Courts-Martial Appeal Court* (and from there to the House of Lords if the court certifies that a point of general public importance is involved and it appears to the court or to the House that the point is one that ought to be considered by the House). Servicemen can appeal to the Courts-Martial Appeal Court only against finding. Civilians, however, in addition to their general right to petition a confirming or reviewing authority, can also appeal to the Courts-Martial Appeal Court against sentence. Certain specified minor charges may be dealt with summarily by commanding officers (in the case of offenders who are soldiers or non-commissioned officers) or by a senior officer known as an Appropriate Superior Authority (in the case of offenders who are either officers below the rank of Lieutenant Colonel, Warrant Officers or civilians). If the officer dealing with the case decides to impose a punishment which involves a financial penalty then the offender has the right to elect to be tried by court-martial.

Standing Civilian Courts are new courts, operating at present only in Germany, Belgium and Holland, which may deal with civilian offenders who would be amenable to trial by court-martial. They deal with offences which, generally speaking, are less serious than those normally dealt with by court-martial but more serious than those dealt with by an Appropriate Superior Authority. The court consists of one magistrate who is a member of the judicial staff of the Judge Advocate General of the Forces who sits either alone or, in juvenile cases, may sit with lay assessors. There is a right of appeal from this court to a court-martial.

Criminal Justice: Children and Young People   In England, Wales and Northern Ireland criminal proceedings involving children and young people under 17 years of age are held before special types of magistrates' courts known as 'juvenile courts'. The case of a young person charged jointly with someone over 17 is heard in a normal magistrates' court or higher court; if the young person is found guilty and not discharged or fined, the court remits the case to a juvenile court. If a child or young person is charged with an offence which, in the case of an adult, is punishable on indictment with 14 years' imprisonment or more, a juvenile court may commit him for trial in the crown court. In the very rare event of a child being charged with homicide, the case is only triable on indictment at the crown court, but committal takes place in a juvenile court unless there is a joint charge against a person over 17 years of age. Juvenile courts exercise their powers subject to the overriding principle of the welfare of the child. They comprise not more than three magistrates – nearly always including at least one man and one woman drawn from a panel of those most suited to dealing with children – and must sit in a different place from other courts or at a different time. Proceedings are less formal than in an adult court, and the public is excluded. Accredited press representatives may be present, but they are not allowed to publish any details that might lead to the identification of the child unless the court or the Home Secretary expressly dispenses with this requirement in the interests of justice. The courts must explain the substance of the charge or application in language which the child can understand, and parents or guardians may be required to attend during all stages of the proceedings. Having determined the guilt of a young offender on the evidence, the court must, before deciding on a method of treatment, consider any information concerning school record, health, character and home conditions that may be provided by a probation officer or the local authority. Consult a **solicitor**.

In Scotland the age of criminal responsibility is eight years, but prosecution is the exception, and no child can be prosecuted for an offence other than at the instance of the Lord Advocate. Children who have committed an offence or need care and protection are generally brought before an informal children's hearing; social workers, doctors, friends or neighbours, the child's parents, the police or the local authority may all refer a case to a local authority employee known as the 'reporter', who administers hearings and decides whether cases should be brought before a hearing or not. Investigations can be helped by the police or the local authority social work department.

Each hearing comprises three members of the local community (one of whom must be a woman) from a local panel. The child, his (or her) parent and a representative from the local social work department normally attend, and proceedings are kept as informal as possible.

The hearing may decide that the child needs compulsory measures of care, and commit him to supervision by the local authority, a voluntary organisation or an individual. All aspects of the supervision requirement are discussed with the parents and the child. Conditions appropriate to the child's needs may be attached to the requirement – these may include, for example, residence away from home, participation in recreational activities or evening classes, or help for the aged or handicapped.

Other powers of children's hearings include reporting to the local education authority that a child may have special educational needs, and reporting to the local mental health officer that a child may need hospital treatment.

See also **Child care and welfare; Young adult offenders.**

Criminal Sentences: Non-custodial Except in cases of murder (and of one or two rarely prosecuted offences), for which the penalty is prescribed by law, the judges who preside at the offender's trial have discretion to select the most suitable penalty in the light of the nature and gravity of the offence and the information available about the character and needs of the offender, within the limits laid down by Parliament. To help courts to decide the best possible way of dealing with cases in the interests of both offenders and the community, probation officers at the request of the courts prepare social inquiry reports on the social and domestic background of many accused people, their character, personality, education and employment. There is a variety of different sentences: traditional non-custodial penalties include fines; probation; absolute or (in England, Wales and Northern Ireland) conditional discharge for up to three years (one year in Northern Ireland in circumstances in which there is properly a conviction but the court feels that there is no need to impose punishment) and 'binding over', under which an offender is required to pledge money, with or without sureties, 'to keep the peace and be of good behaviour'.

The main non-custodial measures used in dealing with young adults are generally the same as those used in dealing with adults – that is to say, absolute and conditional discharge, binding over, fines, **probation** and, in some areas, **community service**. An additional measure, available only to courts in the Greater London and Manchester areas, is the **attendance centre** order, which is more commonly used for younger boys.

Croquet Association croquet is played in the British Isles, New Zealand, South Africa and a few clubs in North America. The laws are the responsibility of the English *Croquet Association*. In the UK the CA (individuals are members) co-ordinates a calendar of club tournaments; provides referees, whom it qualifies; selects teams for the international competition held every few years; and organises tournaments including Open Championships, the President's Cup and one tournament for golf croquet (a faster, less serious game). The *Scottish Croquet Association* is affiliated to the CA. The game is developing in Northern Ireland; apply to the *Sports Council for Northern Ireland*.

Crown Copyright is vested in the Controller, *Her Majesty's Stationery Office* to whom application should be made for permission to use material. Crown copyright subsists, under the Copyright Act 1956, in all material produced by or under the control or direction of a UK government department or first published by a UK government department. Day-to-day administration of Ordnance Survey copyright has been delegated to the *Ordnance Survey* (Copyright Branch).

Crown Estates are managed by the *Crown Estate Office*; it deals with all enquiries about leases and recreational use.

Cruelty to Animals Police may arrest without warrant anyone believed guilty of an offence under the Protection of Animals Act, 1911. Offences may also be reported to the *Royal Society for the Prevention of Cruelty to Animals*.

Cruelty to Children Cases should be reported to the police, the Children's Officer at the Social Services Department of the local authority, and the nearest local group or advisory centre of the *National Society for the Prevention of Cruelty to Children*.

Cuba For **exchange control** is a non-scheduled territory outside the **overseas sterling area** and the EEC. UK nationals travelling direct from the UK normally need only the following (but check): **passports; visas; work permits** (if taking a job).
The UK has no reciprocal health or social security arrangements.
Enquiries to *Cuban Embassy* in London.
British diplomatic mission to Cuba is *British Embassy* in Havana.

Cup Final The *Football Association* organises the FA Cup Competition, for which about 450 clubs enter, and allocates tickets for the match between the two finalists. Tickets go only to the two competing clubs, full-member clubs of the FA and county FAs and are not available to members of the public. They are usually allocated to season-ticket holders and administrators. Unless you are a supporter of one of the competing teams, you are unlikely to obtain a ticket. The ground is hired for the day from Wembley Stadium Limited, which is responsible for printing and distributing tickets; and for ground security in conjunction with the police.
See also **Football; Scottish Cup Final**.

Curling International competition is controlled by the International Curling Federation. The *Royal Caledonian Curling Club* controls the rules and governs the sport in Scotland. It is recognised as the mother club of curling and all national associations affiliate to it, including the *English Curling Association* and the *Welsh Curling Association*.

Customs: Airmail Parcels Traders who regularly import goods liable to **customs duty** by air parcel post may participate in the Advance Documentation Scheme for customs clearance. Apply for registration to *Her Majesty's Customs and Excise*.
See also **Postal imports: customs clearance**.

Customs: Containers Containers, pallets and packings otherwise liable to **customs duty** and **value-added tax** may be entitled to temporary admission to the UK without payment of duty, etc. Apply to *Her Majesty's Customs and Excise*; details in HMCE notice 309.
See also **Customs: TIR carnets**

Customs Co-operation Council Nomenclature Formerly the Brussels Tariff Nomenclature. This is an internationally agreed system of classification for all goods in international commerce. More than 130 countries (including all EEC countries) use it as the basis for their national tariff structures. The system is supervised by the Nomenclature Committee of the Customs Co-operation Council in Brussels. The UK is represented by *Her Majesty's Customs and Excise*.

Customs: Continental Shelf Operations Companies licensed by the *Department of Energy* to explore and exploit UK designated areas of the continental shelf and other traders who have, or expect to have, a continuing trade in continental shelf goods, may apply at the office of *Her Majesty's Customs and Excise* nearest to their main base for authority to import, process and subsequently export to the designated areas without payment of **customs duties** any goods necessary for exploring and exploiting natural resources. Details in HMCE notice 156. Products won from UK designated areas, when brought into the UK and properly entered for customs purposes, are treated, for any charge to import duty under the Import Duties Act 1958, as if the goods had not been imported.
See also **Customs controls; Imports**

Customs Controls Customs clearance is required before entry into the UK for all ships, aircraft, road vehicles, goods, travellers' personal baggage and postal packages arriving from overseas or across the Irish Land Boundary into Northern Ireland. Import of certain goods is prohibited or restricted, e.g. controlled drugs; counterfeit coins; gold coins, medals, medallions and similar gold pieces; firearms (including gas pistols); ammunition and explosives; flick knives; horror comics; indecent and obscene books, magazines, films and other articles; meat and poultry (not fully cooked); walkie-talkies, microbugs and radio microphones; plants, bulbs, trees and certain fruit and vegetables; live animals and birds and certain derivatives of rare species including certain furskins (and garments thereof) and plumage.

Customs Controls: ATA Carnets ATA carnets facilitate customs clearance of certain classes of temporary imports and exports by replacing normal customs documentation. The initials stand for 'Admission Temporaire – Temporary Admission'. They may not be used for goods sent to or from the UK by post. Carnets are issued by chambers of commerce or similar organisations approved by *Her Majesty's Customs and Excise*. Apply for issue of carnet to cover goods to be sent overseas to the Exports Documents Service Department (Carnets) at the *London Chamber of Commerce and Industry*, which also supplies details of local chambers of commerce issuing carnets either in the UK or abroad to cover temporary importation of goods into UK. Details in HMCE notice 104.

Customs Controls: Cargo Cargo landed in the UK from a ship or aircraft must be the subject of a written customs declaration (an 'entry') by the importer, on specified entry documents. Various entry procedures provide for the special needs of different kinds of traffic. Enquiries to *Her Majesty's Customs and Excise*; details in HMCE notice 461 (General information for importers). Further information and rates of duty in 'HM Customs and Excise Tariff and Overseas Trade Clarification' from *Her Majesty's Stationery Office*; more detailed information on entry procedure in HMCE notice 465. Special provisions include duty deferment (101), reimported goods (207), export reliefs (221, 223), valuation (252), transhipment (198), EEC community transit (750, 750A, 750B, 752, 753, 755), EEC end use control (770), tariff quotas (771), and EEC Common Agricultural Policy (780, 780A, 800). See also **Customs controls.**

Customs Controls: Shipping and Aircraft For clearance inwards shipping and aircraft are required to arrive in the UK first at a customs-entry port or aerodrome, and to report to customs immediately on arrival with the necessary documents (customs clearance outwards from the country last left; a general declaration; a cargo manifest; and a list of stores on board). Clearance outwards upon departure from the UK requires submission of similar documentation and once clearance has been obtained, further calls may not be made within the UK unless provision for such was made at the time of clearance. Clearance is given by *Her Majesty's Customs and Excise.* Details in HMCE notices 29, 68.
See also **Customs controls.**

Customs Controls: TIR Carnets These enable goods in customs-sealed road vehices or in customs-sealed containers carried on road vehicles to travel across one or more national frontier with the minimum of customs interference. Goods covered by a Transport International Routier carnet from countries which are parties to the international TIR Convention may normally pass through the territory of other contracting parties without payment of, or security for, **customs duties** and other taxes and without customs examination.
Countries in which the Convention operates are the UK, Afghanistan, Albania, Austria, Belgium, Bulgaria, Canada, Czechoslovakia, Denmark, Federal Republic of Germany, German Democratic Republic, Finland, France, Greece, Hungary, Iran, Israel, Italy, Japan, Jordan, Liechtenstein, Luxembourg, Morocco, Netherlands, Norway, Poland, Portugal, Republic of Ireland, Roumania, Spain, Sweden, Switzerland, Turkey, the USA, USSR and Yugoslavia.

Goods must be transported in approved road vehicles or containers constructed to specified standards and be documented on a TIR carnet issued by an approved guaranteeing association. Guaranteeing associations issuing TIR carnets in the UK are the *Road Haulage Association* and the *Freight Transport Association.* Vehicles are approved by the *Department of Transport*; containers by approved certifying organisations. Apply for approval as a container certifying organisation to *Her Majesty's Customs and Excise.*

Customs Controls: Travellers Travellers must make a declaration orally to customs on arrival if necessary in respect of accompanied baggage; articles to be declared should be packed so that they can be produced quickly for examination (written lists of items may be helpful but do not exempt the traveller from examination). A written customs declaration (form C3) is required in respect of any unaccompanied baggage and household effects. Well-used effects for personal or household use, brought into the UK solely for the use of the traveller, are not liable to **customs duty** or **value-added tax** if they are properly declared. Recently acquired articles to be retained in the UK, and consumable items in excess of the **duty-free allowances** are liable to customs charge. Customs charges are levied in respect of accompanied baggage only on the amount carried in excess of the duty-free allowances. (Customs charges for alcoholic drinks, tobacco products, lighters, perfume and toilet waters, may be substantially more than the price originally paid). Articles are not released from customs control until any duty and/or tax due has been paid; if payment cannot be made immediately, the articles are detained and a receipt given pending subsequent payment within a specified time. Enquiries to *Her Majesty's Customs and Excise*; details in HMCE notice 12 (Passengers' baggage; personal and household effects).

Customs Duty Duty is chargeable on UK imports in order to protect home suppliers and to raise revenue.

Rates of duty and general information are contained in 'Customs and Excise Tariff' available from *Her Majesty's Stationery Office*, and in Customs and Excise notices obtainable free from *Her Majesty's Customs and Excise*. The reference number of each of these notes is included in brackets after the relevant items.

Imports from specified countries are relieved from duty under the EEC generalised system of preferences (HMCE notice 343), Commonwealth preference (27A, 27B), EEC preferences (810), African, Caribbean and Pacific states (ACP)/EEC Convention of Lomé tariff preferences (825) or by tariff quota relief (771). Other general reliefs from duty cover personal luggage; containers; registered shipbuilding yards; continental shelf operations; yachts' stores; exhibits for museums and galleries; antiques (362); awards for distinction (364); blind welfare goods (372); educational and UN films (59, 370); organic intermediate projects (341); imports for non-commercial use in scientific research, learning, art or sport (342); industrial research (425); legacies (368); re-imports (207); cotton and silk handloom goods (65); goods imported for exhibitions and meetings (212); samples (105, 118); goods for testing (374, 214, 332); USA government expenditure in the UK (431); temporary imports of professional effects (48); private and commercial motor vehicles (115A, 115C); yachts (8A); aircraft (115B); tourist publicity materials (208); equipment on hire or loan (209); films and tapes (210, 211); promotion of export trade (221, 221A, 223, 234); and when use is for particular purposes ('end-use reliefs' 770). Imports may be liable to **excise duty** and **value-added tax** in addition to customs duty. General enquiries: *Her Majesty's Customs and Excise*.

See also **Customs controls; Customs: containers; Customs: continental shelf operations; Customs: travellers; Yachts' duty-free stores.**

Customs Entry Points Ports, airports and road routes (across the Irish Land Boundary) are approved by *Her Majesty's Customs and Excise*.

Customs: Goods in Vehicle or Container Customs clearance inwards and outwards of goods transported in secure vehicles or containers may take place at any approved inland clearance depot. For approval of depot, or for extension of approval for the purpose of any existing customs wharf or airport, apply to *Her Majesty's Customs and Excise* and local planning authority (before committing any investment). Apply for removal of vehicle or container from place of importation to inland clearance depot at port of importation; details in HMCE notice 464.

See also **Customs controls; Customs controls: TIR carnets.**

Cycle Races and Time Trials These require either prior authorisation or 28 days' notice in advance. Apply to police.

Cycling is controlled internationally by the Union Cycliste Internationale. In Britain the *British Cycling Federation* is responsible for the control of road racing and track racing. The *Road Time Trials Council* controls time trialling. The *Scottish Cyclists' Union*, the *Welsh Cycling Union* and the *Northern Ireland Cycling Federation* are responsible for the control and administration of cycling in their own countries. The *British Cyclo-Cross Association*, *British Professional Cycle Racing Association* and *Cycle Speedway Council* control their own branches of the sport but are affiliated to the BCF.

The *Cyclists' Touring Club* is the national association for recreational cycling in the UK.

Cyprus **Commonwealth** member. For **exchange control** is a non-scheduled territory in the **overseas sterling area** but outside the **EEC**. UK nationals travelling direct from the UK normally need only the following (but check): **passports; work permits** (if taking a job); green cards for motor insurance (if bringing a car: see **Motoring abroad**).

UK reciprocal arrangements cover social security (see leaflet SA12 obtainable from *Department of Health*

and Social Security, Overseas Group), but not health.
Enquiries to *Cyprus High Commission* in London and *Cyprus Tourism Public Relations Office* in London.
British diplomatic mission to Cyprus is *British High Commission* in Nicosia.

Czechoslovakia For **exchange control** is a non-scheduled territory outside the **overseas sterling area** and the **EEC**. Uk nationals travelling direct from the UK normally need only the following (but check): **passports; visas; work permits** (if taking a job); green cards for motor insurance (if bringing a car).

Tuzex petrol coupons for private cars may be purchased for sterling or other non-Czechoslovak currency, in London from the *Czechoslovak Tourist Bureau, Cedok (London) Ltd*, the *Zunostenska Bank* and the *Royal Automobile Club* and in Czechoslovakia from frontier posts and Tuzex shops and banks (see **Motoring abroad**).
There are reciprocal arrangements for health but not for social security.
Enquiries to *Czechoslovak Embassy* in London or *Czechoslovak Travel Bureau* in London.
British diplomatic mission to Czechoslovakia is *British Embassy* in Prague.

D

Dancing Ballroom dancing is controlled internationally by the International Council of Ballroom Dancing and the International Council of Amateur Dancers. In the UK the governing body is the Council of the *Official Board of Ballroom Dancing*, which represents 16 amateur, professional and entertainment organisations, including the *British Amateur Dancers' Association* and the *Scottish Amateur Ballroom Dancers' Association*. In Northern Ireland the amateur body is the *Ulster Society of Amateur Dancers*.

Folk dancing is largely social and non-competitive in the UK. It is represented and controlled by the *English Folk Dance and Song Society*, the *Royal Scottish Country Dance Society*, the *Scottish Official Board of Highland Dancing* and the *Welsh Folk Dance Society*.

Day Centres Centres for elderly and handicapped people are run by many local authorities (Social Services Department) and voluntary bodies. They offer opportunities for social and recreational activities and the larger centres may also provide meals and facilities for handicrafts and light work. Some centres are open throughout the week including weekends and evenings; in some areas special transport to and from the centre is provided.

Day Nurseries Day nurseries are administered by, or if independent must be registered with, the local authority (Social Services Department). Lists of nurseries are available from local authorities.
See also **Child day care; Child minders.**

Deafness Deafness arising from noise at work may qualify the deaf person for Disablement Benefit. Deaf people may obtain help from local authorities (Social Services Departments) and from voluntary organisations. Local authorities will also provide the names and addresses of local branches of voluntary societies which run social and cultural clubs, recreational facilities and special religious services for deaf people. Additional information is given in leaflet HB1 from the *Department of Health and Social Security* local office or from the local authority.
See also **Disablement; Hearing aids.**

Deafness: Children Teachers of the deaf are often closely involved with the clinical as well as the educational assessment of deaf and partially hearing children. They can offer expert help and reassurance to the deaf child and his parents. Further information about the services of teachers of the deaf can be obtained from the *local education authority*.
See also **Disablement; Disablement: handicapped children.**

Death Abroad When a UK national dies abroad and if no relative, friend, tour operator's representative or other responsible person is available, consular officers (addresses given under *British diplomatic missions*) will notify the next of kin and provide details of local facilities and charges for burial and cremation, and estimate the cost of repatriation of the remains. Normally the next of kin then make arrangements on the basis of this information.

Under EEC regulations on social security, if a UK national dies in another EEC country the death may be treated as if it had taken place in the UK. Any **death grant** is normally paid by the country in which the person on whose contributions the claim is based was last insured. If death occurs in Austria, Cyprus, Jamaica, Jersey or Guernsey, Norway, Spain, Turkey or Yugoslavia, it may also be treated as if it had taken place in the UK, and a death grant may be paid if all other conditions are satisfied.

A grant is also paid for deaths elsewhere abroad in certain circumstances (e.g. if the deceased was receiving a **national insurance** benefit at the time of his death or was ordinarily resident in the UK and died within 13 weeks of going abroad). Further information from *Department of Health and Social Security* local offices, or write to *DHSS Overseas Branch*.
See also **Registration of births and deaths overseas**.

Death at Sea A death on a UK registered ship or of a UK citizen on a ship calling at a UK port must be notified to the *Department of Trade local Mercantile Marine Office*, which informs the *Registrar General of Shipping and Seamen*, the police and, if the death occurred in territorial waters around Scotland, the procurator fiscal. In the event of a death occurring on an offshore installation, notification should be made to the *Department of Energy* instead of the Mercantile Marine Office.
See also **Burials at sea**.

Death Certificates: England and Wales After a death has been registered (see **Death registration**) certificates of the entry may be bought from the *Registrar of Births, Deaths and Marriages* at £1.25 each. Certificates obtained after the register has been passed to the *Superintendent Registrar of Births, Deaths and Marriages* cost £2.50. Cheap certificates are issued for certain statutory purposes.

Death Certificates: Northern Ireland After a death has been registered (see **Death registration**) full certificates may be obtained for £1 (or reduced-fee certificates for certain statutory purposes at 30p and 5p) from the *Registrar of Births, Deaths and Marriages* or from the *General Register Office (Belfast)* in the week following registration. A fee of 50p is payable for full certificates if a search is needed. Registrars retain duplicate records for one year and can issue certificates in that period.

Death Certificates: Scotland When a death is registered (see **Death registration**) a certificate of the entry may be purchased from the *Registrar of Births, Deaths and Marriages* for £1.25 and subsequently from the registrar or the *General Register Office (Scotland)* for £2.50. If more than one certificate is purchased, either at the time of registration or thereafter, the cost of the second and each subsequent certificate is £1.50. Cheap certificates may be obtained for certain statutory purposes.

Death Duties Since the Finance Act 1975, **capital transfer tax** is the only UK death duty; it is payable on a death but also provides for tax to be payable on certain transfers when the transferor is still living. Previous death duties (e.g. probate duty, legacy duty, succession duty and estate duty) are still payable on estates which have not yet been resolved and to which the duties were applicable.

Death Grant A death grant is a single lump sum benefit payable on the death of a **national insurance** contributor or certain of his dependants. For a handicapped person who has been unable to work, the grant may be paid on the contribution record of a

near relative. Apply to *Department of Health and Social Security* local office; details in DHSS leaflet N149.
See also **Social security benefits**.

Death in Hospital: Funerals In England and Wales, hospital authorities and **local authorities** can arrange for the burial or cremation of people who die in hospital within their area if no one else (e.g. a relative) will or can arrange the funeral. Any **death grant** which may be paid is then claimed by the authority making the arrangements, and the balance of the funeral costs can be claimed from the deceased's estate.

Death Registration: England and Wales A death should be registered within five days and must be registered with the *Registrar of Births, Deaths and Marriages* for the sub-district in which it occurred. People qualified to give information for the registration, where the death occurred in a house or public institution are, in order of preference, a relative of the deceased or other person present at the death; the occupier or any inmate of the house who knew of the death; the person causing the disposal of the body. For deaths elsewhere, or dead bodies found, qualified informants are any relative of the deceased; any person present at the death; any person who found the body; any person in charge of the body; the person causing the disposal of the body.
The informant supplies all the details for the register entry apart from cause of death which is copied verbatim by the registrar from the medical certificate.
If the deceased was attended by a **doctor** during his last illness that doctor must by law issue a medical certificate of cause of death to the registrar for the sub-district where the death occurred. This certificate is acceptable for registration unless the registrar decides to report the case to the coroner.
See also **Death registration (England and Wales): coroners.**

Death Registration (England and Wales): Coroners The *Registrar of Births, Deaths and Marriages* reports a death to the coroner if either the deceased was not attended during his last illness by a medical practitioner; the registrar has been unable to obtain a completed certificate of cause of death; it appears from the particulars contained in such a certificate or otherwise, that the deceased was not seen by the certifying doctor after death nor within 14 days before death; the cause of death appears unknown; the registrar has reason to believe the death was unnatural or caused by violence or neglect, or by abortion, or attended by suspicious circumstances; death appears to have occurred during an operation or before recovery from the effect of an anaesthetic; or death appears from the contents of any medical certificate to have been due to industrial disease or industrial poisoning.
The coroner decides whether to hold a **post-mortem**. If he does, he reports his findings to the registrar and the death is then registered in the usual way with the informant supplying details except that the cause of death is taken from a form completed by the coroner.
Sometimes a coroner holds an inquest. After it is completed, he issues a certificate to the registrar who registers the death by copying all the details from the certificate. No informant is needed for such registration.

Death Registration: Northern Ireland
Normally a death should be registered within five days with the *Registrar of Births, Deaths and Marriages* in the district of occurrence or, if different, in the district in which the deceased person was ordinarily resident, if that is in Northern Ireland. Qualified informants are, in order of preference, a relative of the deceased; a person present at the death; the executor or administrator of the deceased's estate; the occupier of the premises in which the death occurred; the person finding the body; the person taking charge of the body; the person procuring the disposal of the body. No informant is required where an inquest is held.
If the deceased died from natural illness for which he was treated by a **doctor** within 28 days prior to death, the

doctor is required to issue a medical certificate of cause of death to a qualified informant who delivers it to the registrar. In certain circumstances the death must be reported to the coroner. The informant supplies all the particulars for registration apart from the cause of death which is copied verbatim by the registrar from the medical certificate or coroner's statement or certificate (after post-mortem). Information required for registration is name and surname of deceased, sex, date of death, place of death, usual address, marital status, date and place of birth, occupation and maiden surname (of woman who had married).
See also **Death registration (Northern Ireland): coroners.**

Death Registration (Northern Ireland): Coroners A death must be reported by the *Registrar of Births, Deaths and Marriages* to the coroner if there is reason to believe that the death was directly or indirectly the result of violence or misadventure or unfair means; the result of negligence or misconduct or malpractice on the part of others; due to any cause other than natural illness or disease for which the deceased had been seen and treated by a NHS family **doctor** within 28 days prior to his death; or in circumstances requiring investigation, including death from administration of an anaesthetic.

The coroner either holds an inquest or decides that an inquest is unnecessary. In the latter case he issues either a statement or a certificate, following post-mortem examination, to the registrar and the death is then registered in the usual way (with the informant supplying details) except that the cause of death is taken from the coroner's statement or certificate.

If an inquest is held the coroner will issue a certificate to the registrar who will then register the death by copying all the details from the certificate. No informant is needed for such registration.

Death Registration: Scotland A death must be registered within eight days. It must be registered at the office of the *Registrar of Births, Deaths and Marriages* for the district in which the death occurred or at the office of the registrar for the district in which the deceased had his usual residence at the time of death, provided that residence was in Scotland.

Qualified informants are any relative of the deceased; any person present at the death; the deceased's executor or other legal representative; the occupier, at the time of death, of the premises where the death took place; or, failing any of these, any other person who has knowledge of the facts to be registered.

The informant supplies all the details for the entry in the register apart from the cause of death. This is copied verbatim by the registrar from the medical certificate of cause of death issued by the **doctor** for death registration purposes.

If the deceased was attended by a doctor during the last illness, that doctor must issue a medical certificate of cause of death to a qualified informant or to the registrar. Otherwise the certificate may be signed by any doctor who is able to do so.
See also **Death registration (Scotland): procurators fiscal.**

Death Registration (Scotland): Procurators Fiscal In Scotland the *Registrar of Births, Deaths and Marriages* reports a death to the procurator fiscal if a medical certificate of cause of death is not produced to him; or if it appears from the certificate that the death was sudden, violent or unexplained or was due to any of the causes set out in a list which includes certain types of accident and certain types of industrial diseases or industrial poisoning.

The procurator fiscal decides whether to hold an investigation and whether to call for a **post-mortem**. The results of the procurator fiscal's investigation are intimated to the *Registrar General for Scotland* and, where necessary, the entry in the register of deaths is then amended.

Defence, Ministry of: Claims Upon loss, injury or damage for which the armed forces or the Ministry of Defence are possibly to blame, write

immediately to the *Ministry of Defence, Claims Commission* giving the date, time, place and nature of the incident and its effects. Should animals be involved, veterinary and other evidence will be required, to accord with procedure agreed between the MOD and the National Farmers' Union. The Commission gives advice about evidence, etc.
The Commission has certain delegated powers, but high-value claims are passed to the Civil Service Department or the Treasury.

Defence Research Facilities Facilities at Ministry of Defence research and development establishments are sometimes opened to bona fide researchers on application to the establishment concerned or, failing that, to the *Ministry of Defence Procurement Executive, ER (Central) 1a*. Details of technical information and other services available from government departments and associated organisations are obtainable from the *Department of Industry*.

Degrees and Degree-Equivalents UK degrees are granted by royal prerogative. Only universities and a few other bodies (e.g. the *Council for National Academic Awards*) have been franchised by Royal Charter or Act of Parliament to award degrees.
There are now about 50 degree-giving bodies in the UK including universities, CNAA, the Royal College of Art, Cranfield Institute, the Open University. The *Department of Education and Science* has no statutory powers to accredit, recognise or approve qualifications for students above school-leaving age; it does, however, issue its own list of qualifications for mandatory **student grant** purposes. This covers England, Scotland, Wales and Northern Ireland. Bogus degrees are issued and sold in the UK (usually 'doctors' for overseas use). There is no central validation authority in the UK.
See also **Education: Scotland**; **Education: Northern Ireland**.

Demonstrations Public marches, lobbies, mass protests of any kind, pickets and meetings in a public place should be notified in advance to the police.

Denmark EEC member. For **exchange control** is a non-scheduled territory in the EEC but outside the **overseas sterling area**. UK nationals travelling direct from the UK normally need only the following (but check): **passports** (British Visitors' passports acceptable).
EEC or bilateral society security arrangements are applicable; leaflets and EEC Guides obtainable from *Department of Health and Social Security, Overseas Branch*. Apply to local social security office for a leaflet SA 28 which explains how to get reduced-cost medical treatment under EEC health arrangements, and how to get a certificate of entitlement (form E111).
Enquiries to *Royal Danish Embassy* in London and *National Travel Association of Denmark* in London.
British diplomatic missions to Denmark are *British Embassy* in Copenhagen and *British Consulates* in Aabenraa, Aalborg, Aarhus, Esbjerg, Klaksvik (Faroe Islands), Odense, and Thorshavn (Faroe Islands).

Dental Auxiliaries and Hygienists Those practising in the UK must be enrolled in the Rolls of Ancillary Dental Workers kept by the *General Dental Council*. The basic qualifications are a certificate of proficiency from the Committee of Management of the *School for Dental Auxiliaries*, or from the *Central Examining Board for Dental Hygienists*.

Dental Charges Under the **National Health Service** there is no charge for examination of teeth, arrest of bleeding, repairs to dentures or essential home visits. All treatment is free for: children under 16; people under 21 still attending a school full-time; people aged 16–21 who have left school (except dentures); expectant mothers; women who have had a child in the previous 12 months; people and their dependants receiving certain **social security benefits** because of low income; others with a low income (free or reduced charges). A special declaration has to be signed at the dentists by anyone entitled to free treatment. Others claiming help with charges must complete a form provided by the dentist and send it to the *Department of Health and Social Security* (local office). Details in leaflet M11 (M2 in Salop and Brighton only) from post offices and DHSS local offices.

All other patients must pay the dentist the full cost of each item of treatment or £5.00, whichever is less, excluding dentures and certain other items. For these the charges are:

1. for a denture or a bridge –

	Synthetic resin	Metal or porcelain
(a) 1, 2 or 3 teeth	£10	£15
(b) 4–8 teeth	£11	£16
(c) More than 8 teeth	£12	£17
Maximum for more than one denture (or bridge)	£20	£30

2. for crowns, inlays, pinlays and gold fillings –

(a) per tooth restored	£10 inclusive of any other restorations, in the same tooth, apart from root fillings
(b) maximum for more than 3 teeth restored	£30

3. all subject to a maximum charge for any combination of these.

Dental Treatment Any person normally resident in the UK is entitled to receive dental treatment under the **National Health Service**. A patient may seek NHS treatment from any dentist at any time (i.e. he does not have to register with a dentist as with a family doctor) but in general dental practitioners can accept or refuse anyone for treatment. Dentists may also take private patients; those wishing to be NHS patients should make this clear at the outset and sign a form at the start of each course of treatments. All treatment necessary for dental fitness is available under NHS arrangements, but the approval of the *Dental Estimates Board* has to be obtained by the dentist before he can proceed with some kinds of treatment. Any dentist or patient may appeal to the *Secretary of State for Health and Social Security* against a decision of the Board within one month of that decision being given. The majority of appeals are determined at hearings before two independent dentists, one of whom must be selected from a panel nominated by the *British Dental Association*. The form signed by a patient before NHS dental treatment commits the patient to examination by a Dental Officer of the Department of Health and Social Security if required.

See also **Child dental services; Dental charges; Dentists; Dentists: complaints**.

Dentists Dentists practising in the UK must be registered in the Dentists Register kept by the *General Dental Council*. Basic qualifications are a degree or licence in dental surgery from a UK or Irish university (Birmingham, Bristol, Leeds, Liverpool, London, Manchester, Newcastle-upon-Tyne, Sheffield, Cardiff, Dundee, Edinburgh, Glasgow, Belfast and Dublin), or a licence in dental surgery from the Royal Colleges of Surgeons of England and Edinburgh, the Royal College of Physicians and Surgeons of Glasgow and the Royal College of Surgeons in Ireland. **Doctors** registered as medical practitioners with the *General Medical Council* may legally practise dentistry but within the **National Health Service** they may not act as general dental practitioners.

Any registered dentist may enter into a contract with a *Family Practitioner Committee* (or, in Northern Ireland, the *Health and Social Services Board*) to provide National Health Service general dental services and have his name included on the FPC dental list.

To find a dentist, consult the register of the GDC. For NHS treatment, consult the local Family Practitioner Committee (or, in Northern Ireland, the *Dental Services Agency*) dental list at main post offices, public libraries and the FPC offices. A dentist on the FPC list can also provide private treatment.

See also **Dental charges; Dental treatment**.

Dentists: Complaints To complain about the service provided by a dentist under the **National Health Service**, the patient or his authorised representative should write to the local *Family Practitioner Committee*. Complaints are investigated by the FPC's dental service committee. There is a right of appeal to the *Secretary of State for Social Services* against an adverse decision. Complaints about professional misconduct are dealt with by the *General Dental Council*, and should be submitted within six months after completion of the treatment or eight weeks after the matter giving rise to the complaint was first noticed, whichever is the sooner. Late complaints may be investigated only if certain conditions are met.

Deportation from the UK Deportation may be ordered by the *Home Secretary* for a person who is not a patrial (see **Immigration: non-patrials**) if he has failed to comply with the conditions attached to his leave to enter the UK; stayed beyond the authorised time; or been recommended by a court for deportation after conviction; or if the Home Secretary deems his deportation to be conducive to the public good. A person may appeal to an adjudicator against a decision by the Home Secretary to make a deportation order on the first two grounds, or against a refusal by the Home Secretary to revoke a deportation order made under any of the above. The wife or child (under 18) of a person ordered to be deported may also be deported.
When a court has ordered deportation, the person concerned may appeal to a higher court. Appeal may be made to the *Appeal Tribunal* first if the appeal is against a decision to make a deportation order either on the grounds that deportation is conducive to the public good, or because the person belongs to the family of another person, or if appeal is against a refusal to revoke such a deportation order. An appeal against refusal cannot be exercised while the person concerned is in the UK.
See also **British subjects; Naturalisation**.

Design Awards Awards are made annually by the *Design Council* to British products of outstanding design. Winning consumer and contract goods are chosen from the DC's Design Index by a special committee. Award winners in the fields of engineering products and components, motor vehicle products and medical equipment are chosen, by panels of judges, from products submitted by manufacturers.
See also **Design: consumer products**.

Design: Consumer Products The Design Council publishes books and magazines on design for the general public, for professional designers and engineers and for schools and colleges. These and other publications on design are available from the bookshop at the *Design Centre* in London and Cardiff direct or by mail order. Well-designed modern British consumer products are exhibited at the Design Council's *Design Centres* in Cardiff, Glasgow and London. The Centres occasionally stage thematic exhibitions to illustrate new design developments (details of display charges from the manager) but otherwise all products on display have been included in the Council's Design Index.

Detention Centres The courts can issue detention centre orders for boys aged 14 or over. Detention centres provide a means of treating young male offenders for whom a long period of residential training away from home does not seem necessary or justified by the offence, but who cannot be taught respect for the law by such non-custodial measure as fines or probation. In England and Wales there are 11 senior detention centres providing accommodation for up to 1300 trainees (as well as six junior centres for boys aged 14–16 years providing 650 places). Detention may be for a period of three months (minimum) to six months; if consecutive sentences are passed, the total term must not exceed six months, or nine months in certain exceptional cases. A trainee is allowed remission of one-third of his sentence in senior and one-half in junior detention centres, which may be forfeited for misbehaviour. In Scotland, where there is only one senior centre, the fixed period for all detention centre sentences is three months and the age range is from 16 to 20 years. There are no detention centres in Northern Ireland. See also **Criminal justice: children and young people; Young adult offenders.**

Detention in an Approved Place The crown courts can sentence young offenders over 15 but under 18 to detention in a place approved by the Home Secretary. This power is only used in the case of very serious crimes. See also **Detention centres.**

Developing Countries: Overseas Agricultural Training Courses in agricultural business management for nationals of developing countries are provided at the *Commonwealth Development Corporation Mananga Agricultural Management Centre* in Swaziland. Apply to the Centre up to 18 months in advance. Grants for these courses are sometimes obtainable from the *Commonwealth Fund for Technical Cooperation, Commonwealth Secretariat*, and overseas agencies (e.g. United Nations agencies such as the *Food and Agriculture Organisation of the United Nations*).

Development Aid: Overseas The *Commonwealth Development Corporation* finances economic development in developing countries. It also holds financial interests in overseas companies involved in commerical and, in some cases, agricultural and property developments. A CDC associate company specialises in hotel development.

Development Aid: Procurement The *Crown Agents for Overseas Governments and Administrations* (sponsored by the Ministry of Overseas Development) purchase goods for countries and bodies receiving development aid. Services include dealing with tenders, from preparing specifications to evaluation, assisting in the award of contract and arranging inspection, shipping and insurance.

Development Land Tax A UK tax on the development value realised on land, operative from 1 August 1976. It is assessed centrally by the *Inland Revenue, Development Land Tax Office.*
Not all events relating to development give rise to liability to DLT and there are various exemptions and an annual threshold before any chargeable development value realised in the particular financial year becomes liable to payment of DLT. Appeals against assessments go to the Appeal Commissioners or the appropriate Lands Tribunal depending on the matter in dispute; notice of appeal should be sent to the Controller at the IR Development Land Tax Office.

Dietitians Dietitians practising in the **National Health Service** must be state registered with the Dietitians Board of the *Council for Professions Supplementary to Medicine.* Basic qualifications for registration are a dietitian's diploma or degree or a postgraduate diploma recognised by the CPSM. The Dietitians Board publishes an annual register which is available at public libraries. In the majority of cases NHS dietitians advise only those people who have been referred to them by a doctor.
Complaints about professional misconduct of state registered dietitians to the Dietitians Board of the CPSM, which will investigate. Complaints about disciplinary matters of NHS employees should be made to and are investigated by the employing authority (i.e. the *Area Health Authority* or Board of Governors in England and Wales, the *Health Board* in Scotland).
See also **Disputes with public authorities.**

Diplomatic Immunity The Diplomatic Privileges Act 1964 gives the force of law to the relevant provisions of the Vienna Convention on Diplomatic Relations and applies to every country's diplomatic mission in the UK. A diplomatic agent, as defined in the Act, enjoys immunity from UK criminal jurisdiction and, in defined respects, from civil and administrative jurisdiction. Seek legal advice in these matters from a **solicitor**.

Direct Investment: Exchange Control Permission is required for UK residents to make direct investments in countries outside the scheduled territories. Apply to the *Bank of England*. Such direct investments – where the investor participates in the management and operation of the overseas economic enterprise – are normally authorised provided the investor has expertise in the field involved, the investment will be financed in an appropriate manner, and it is likely to benefit the UK balance of payments. See also **Investment**.

Only investments which promote UK exports and promise exceptionally large and rapid benefits to the UK balance of payments may buy foreign currency at the official exchange rate. Other investments must be funded in other ways, e.g. by profits retained abroad by overseas subsidiaries, foreign currency borrowing, exports, or the purchase of investment currency (see **Foreign currency securities**). The complex criteria on which the availability of foreign currency at the official exchange rate depends are less demanding for investment in EEC member countries than for other non-scheduled territories. Consult an **authorised bank** (see **Exchange control**).

Direct investment in the UK by persons resident abroad and undertakings controlled by such persons is in general encouraged provided it is financed suitably, i.e. largely with foreign currency or with sterling from the account of the person resident abroad. Transfers resulting in the acquisition of less than 10% of the voting rights of a quoted UK company by non-residents are delegated to authorised depositaries, but transfers resulting in acquisitions of 10% or more of the voting rights of a quoted UK company must be referred to the Bank of England. Applications must also be made to the Bank to establish new concerns in the UK or to acquire any shares with a private UK company.

Foreign controlled companies in the UK which are involved in manufacturing or importing may, on application to the Bank of England, normally borrow sterling in the UK without restriction, but companies involved in other activities are normally limited in their access to sterling finance, depending on their function and the amount of foreign capital in the company. Foreign currency borrowing by non-resident controlled companies is normally allowed by the Bank, subject to the same conditions as for other UK borrowers.

Prospective investors should approach their bank or other professional advisers, through whom applications to the Bank of England for exchange control consent should be channelled, giving full details, including particulars of the capital structure and primary function of the UK undertaking and the extent and value of their proposed participation. If shares are being acquired in an existing unquoted company (see **Stock Exchange**) documentary evidence should be produced to show that a fair price has been paid.

Disablement People defined as disabled under the Chronically Sick and Disabled Persons Act 1970 are those who are blind, deaf or dumb, or who suffer from mental disorder of any description, and other persons who are substantially and permanently handicapped by reason of illness, injury, or congenital deformity. Chief causes of disablement are arthritis and rheumatism, organic nervous diseases, and injuries. A wide range of assistance is available to disabled people from local authorities, from the **National Health Service**, from various government departments, including the *Department of Health and Social Security*, the other Health Departments (see **Health authorities**), the *Manpower Services Commission*, education departments (see **Education authorities**), and from voluntary bodies.

Local authorities are required to inform themselves of the numbers of disabled people resident in their area and of their need for special services, and to publicise the services available. The latter generally include social work support and advice, **day centres** of various kinds, and occupational activities in centres or at home. Local authorities must also, if satisfied of need, make arrangements to assist disabled people with such matters as adaptations to their homes, additional facilities to secure greater safety, comfort or convenience, telephones and holidays. Enquiries to: local authority (Social Services Department).

Car badges showing the international symbol for the disabled allow certain parking concessions (e.g. free parking on meters with no time limits; no time limits in limited waiting areas; parking up to two hours on yellow lines). Badges are valid throughout the UK except for parts of central London; apply submitting a doctor's certificate to local authorities.

Exemption from tax on **motor vehicle excise licenses** may be given to seriously disabled people who are too disabled to drive but own a car driven on their behalf; enquiries to local *artificial limb and appliance centre*. They may also be exempted from rates on their garage; enquiries to local authority.

The National Health Service provides medical rehabilitation aimed at helping to restore normal living, as well as continuing treatment and care for the relief of pain and the cure of pathological conditions. Employment, industrial rehabilitation and vocational training of disabled people are the general responsibility of the Manpower Services Commission with some help in training from educational institutions. The public educational system provides special education for children who require it because of physical or mental disability. **Social security benefits** of various kinds are mainly the responsibility of the *Department of Health and Social Security*. A number of voluntary bodies provide specialised help in regard to particular aspects or problems of disablement or for people with particular disabilities. Enquiries to the co-ordinating body, the *Royal Association for Disability and Rehabilitation*.

See also subsequent entries on **Disablement** and separate entries on **Blindness, Deafness, Mental disablement, National Health Service**, and **Speech disability**.

Disablement: Aids and Equipment
Equipment is generally prescribed by hospital consultants (e.g. artificial limbs, crutches, walking sticks, walking frames, fabric supports). In addition items required at home in connection with medical and nursing care are supplied through the **National Health Service**; apply to NHS family **doctor**. Certain personal and domestic aids (including aids to toiletry, washing and dressing) are provided by local authority (Social Services Departments). *Local education authorities* and the *Employment Service Agency* supply aids for use in connection with education or employment respectively. Voluntary organisations also provide aids. People who have serious difficulty in walking may be provided with a wheelchair, non-powered tricycle or, in some cases, an electric indoor chair or invalid vehicle by the *Department of Health and Social Security* in England, by the *Welsh Office* in Wales, and by the *Scottish Home and Health Department* in Scotland: discuss needs in first instance with NHS family **doctor** who may make the necessary recommendation to the appropriate *artificial limb and appliance centre*. Electric indoor chairs are provided for people who cannot operate hand-propelled chairs, and electric outdoor chairs for users with attendants unable to push an ordinary wheelchair. Booklets are available from DHSS local offices, the *Department of Health and Social Security Physical Handicap Branch*. The *Oxford Regional Health Authority* publishes, on behalf of the DHSS, a series of illustrated booklets on aids and equipment under the title 'Equipment for the Disabled', and the *Disabled Living Foundation* publishes lists of aids and has an information service giving advice.

Very severely handicapped persons may be provided with devices which operate by minimal muscular action (e.g. light pressure or by sucking or blowing into a small tube) and enable patients to control electrical equipment

Who Decides What 97 Disablement

(e.g. alarm bells, lights, radio or television sets, telephones and typewriters). Apply: NHS family **doctor**.
See also **Disablement**.

Disablement: Children's Family Fund
The fund helps families with very severely handicapped children under 16. Help (i.e. goods, services or a grant of money for some definite purpose) is mainly for circumstances not covered by other benefits or services (e.g. assistance with transport, laundry, equipment, unusual adaptations and aids, help with holidays). Apply to the Family Fund at *Joseph Rowntree Memorial Trust*.
See also **Disablement: handicapped children**.

Disablement: Employment and Training Registration with the *Employment Service Agency* (not obligatory) may assist a disabled person to find employment. Rehabilitation courses are provided at 26 ESA centres and at others run by voluntary and local authority bodies. Vocational training is provided at Skill centres of the *Training Services Agency*, educational institutions and employers' establishments, and, for the seriously disabled, at residential colleges run by voluntary organisations with TSA help: grants are available and allowances are paid during courses. ESA industrial rehabilitation units provide employment rehabilitation and vocational guidance after illness. Advice on all the above from Disablement Resettlement Officers of the ESA.
These DROs try to place the disabled in suitable employment. They administer the quota scheme which requires employers to include a percentage of registered disabled people among their work force, and advise employers on grants for adaptation of equipment. DROs may also be able to arrange 'sheltered work' for those who are unlikely to obtain work except under special conditions. Disabled people are normally included in the employers' liability insurance on the same terms as other employees. Apply to the *National Association of Pension Funds* for advice about inclusion of the disabled in pension schemes. Registered severely disabled people whose disability involves high travel costs can receive help with fares to work.

Disablement: Further Education
Local education authorities usually provide special help, e.g. Braille writing machines, readers for blind students, interpreters for deaf students. Some special schools catering for particular handicaps have arrangements with nearby colleges to help handicapped students. Information from local education authorities.
See also **Disablement**.

Disablement: Handicapped Children
The family doctor, school doctor, and staff at child health clinics or hospitals advise on the health care and treatment of disabled children. The family doctor can refer the child for a comprehensive assessment by a team of doctors, nurses, therapists and educational and social work staff to work out a special programme for the child's health, educational and social needs as necessary.
Local authorities (Social Services Department) advise families on bringing up disabled children; work with health and education departments to give children and their families necessary support; and place parents in touch with voluntary bodies concerned with handicapped children (e.g. to discuss difficulties and exchange ideas with parents facing similar problems). When children are in hospital parents can receive help from the hospital social worker (e.g. over travelling or visiting problems when the hospital is at a distance). When children are home from hospital for a holiday, equipment (e.g. wheelchairs) or regular visits by the district nurse can be arranged by the family **doctor** or **health visitor**.
See also **Disablement; Disablement: handicapped children's education; Disablement: children's family fund**.

Disablement: Handicapped Children's Education Mentally or physically handicapped children, including maladjusted children, form one of the special categories of children for which *local education authorities* are bound to provide suitable special education, if it is needed (see **Schooling for children in special categories**). Advice on the need for special education for a handicapped child may be obtained from the *local education authority* (Special Education Department), from the child's NHS family **doctor** and from the school.

The decision as to whether a child needs such education rests with the authority, which may on request arrange a medical examination for any child over 2. Appeal against the authority's decision may be made to the appropriate *Secretary of State* (see **education authorities**). Special education at an independent school may also be arranged. Consult the *Independent Schools Information Service*.

There are 10 categories of handicapped pupils in England, Wales and Northern Ireland and nine in Scotland for whom local education authorities must provide special educational treatment: blind, partially sighted, deaf, partially hearing, delicate, educationally subnormal (mentally handicapped in Scotland), epileptic, maladjusted, physically handicapped and children suffering from speech defects. There is no separate category for the delicate in Scotland. As many children have multiple handicaps there is a growing tendency to relate educational needs to over-all medical condition and to use the system of categories for administrative purposes only.

Most severe handicaps should be detected by doctors at birth, or soon after. But a parent or guardian suspecting that a child has a handicap should consult a doctor. Help is available in overcoming educational disadvantages, e.g. hearing aids, pre-school teacher visits, special nursery education, and there should be continuous assessment of the child's educational strength and disabilities by the local education authority.

Handicapped children may attend ordinary classes or special classes in ordinary schools, or go to special schools suited to their disability, depending on the degree and type of handicap and the policy of the authority. Home tuition may sometimes be provided for children too handicapped to go to school. It has long been the policy of the education authorities not to send to special schools those handicapped children who can be educated satisfactorily at an ordinary school. However, there are still many special schools, including hospital schools and day and boarding schools. There are also boarding homes for handicapped children attending ordinary school.

Further education institutions and universities often provide special facilities for the handicapped; enquiries direct to the institution concerned.

For the financial and administrative arrangements for special education see **Schooling for children in special categories**. See also **Disablement: handicapped children** and **Mental disablement: children**.

Disablement: Housing Local authorities (Social Services Departments) may pay for or help disabled people to carry out adaptations to their homes, whether owner-occupied or rented, so as to make them easier to live in. They may, for example, move an electric switch, provide a bath handrail or install a downstairs toilet or a different heating system. Local authorities have specially designed council houses for the disabled (e.g. 'mobility housing' with normal space standards but including special features such as a ramped entrance and wider doors for people who do not need a wheelchair all the time; 'independent wheelchair housing' for people totally dependent on a wheelchair; and 'sheltered housing' for old people). Housing associations may also provide special types of accommodation. Apply to local authority housing advice centre. See also **Housing: local authority**.

Disablement: Laundry Some local authorities provide a laundry service, including supply of incontinence pads, to help households where there is a handicapped person. Further information from local authority (Social Services Department), National Health Service family **doctor**, district nurse or **health visitor**.

Disablement: Residential Accommodation Permanent places in homes managed by **local authorities,** or homes run by voluntary organisations and/or privately owned are arranged by local authorities (Social Services Department) for people who are too old, infirm or handicapped to be cared for at home even with help from relatives and the domiciliary health and social services. A charge is made for the accommodation according to residents' means. There are homes for the elderly, for certain classes of handicapped people with special needs and for the younger physically handicapped (i.e. aged 17–50). Most authorities have a waiting list for permanent admissions but will admit people for short-stay care to make a holiday for them and for those who normally care for them at home.

Anyone running a home for disabled or old people, including the mentally disordered, must register with the local authority in whose area the home is situated. The authority has power to refuse or to cancel registration in certain circumstances. Any person authorised by the Secretary of State for Social Services has power to enter and inspect registered homes, or any premises which it is believed are being used for the purposes of a home liable to registration.

Disablement: Social Security Benefits
Attendance allowance is a tax-free cash benefit for people who are severely disabled physically or mentally, and who need much looking after. For those who require attendance both by day and night there is a higher rate allowance. For those who require attendance either by day or night there is a lower rate allowance. Certain medical requirements have to be satisfied and claims are decided by the Attendance Allowance Board (or one of its delegates) which is an independent statutory authority. Apply to *Department of Health and Social Security local offices* (see leaflet NI 205).

Invalid Care Allowance is a non-means-tested benefit payable to men and single women unable to work because they are caring for a disabled relative receiving an attendance allowance. Married women are only eligible if they are not living with or being maintained by their husbands. Apply to **Department of Health and Social Security, Medical Care Allowance Unit.**

Mobility Allowance is a cash allowance replacing the Invalid Vehicle Scheme, which ended on 31 December 1975. Enquiries to DHSS local offices. See also **Disablement; Industrial injury and disease; Invalidity; War disablement.**

Disablement: Social Services Services may be provided by the local authority; they include home help, holidays for the severely handicapped and for convalescents, and aids and adaptations to help with mobility, dressing, eating and toilet. Services may be free or at reduced charges for those on low incomes. Apply to local authority (Social Services Department).
See also **Disablement; Families on low incomes.**

Disablement: Tourist Information
Accommodation and travel arrangements suitable for disabled people are provided by local authorities, by the *Royal Association for Disability and Rehabilitation* (RADAR), the *Welsh Council for the Disabled*, the *Scottish Council on Disability*, the *Tourist Boards* (regional), the *Automobile Association* and the *Royal Automobile Club*.
See also **Disablement.**

Disablement: Voting Disabled people are entitled to vote in local and general elections by post or proxy. See also **Disablement; Elections: returning officers.**

Disasters and Emergencies Overseas
Worldwide allocation and urgent dispatch of relief supplies is undertaken by the *Crown Agents for Overseas Governments and Administrations* (sponsored by the Ministry of Overseas Development). They have offices in the UK and overseas.

Disinfectants Manufacturers may apply for disinfectants to be govern-

ment approved for use against specific diseases and for general purposes. Suitability is determined by subjecting samples to various laboratory tests. Enquiries and applications in England and Wales to *Ministry of Agriculture, Fisheries and Food, Animal Health Division I.*
Lists of approved disinfectants are available from Animal Health Offices at *Ministry of Agriculture, Fisheries and Food Divisional Offices* and from *MAFF Animal Health Division I.*
See also **Agriculture: Scotland**; **Agriculture: Northern Ireland**.

Dismissal On request, employers must give to an employee, within 14 days, a written statement of the reasons for dismissal; this includes non-renewal of a fixed-term contract. If a complaint is made to an **industrial tribunal** (see below) and it agrees that a statement has not been provided or is inaccurate, it will award two weeks' pay as compensation.
An employee who feels he has been unfairly dismissed should complain to an industrial tribunal. The onus will be on the employer to show that the main reason for dismissal was fair according to the Trade Union and Labour Relations Act 1974 and that it was reasonable to dismiss the employee for that reason.
Fair reasons for dismissal are misconduct, lack of capability, redundancy, 'substantial reason of a kind which would justify dismissal', or if continuing employment would contravene the law. Dismissals shown to be on the grounds of racial, sex or marital discrimination, or of a past conviction that is spent (see **Rehabilitation of offenders**) are unfair. Dismissals arising from strikes and lockouts are generally fair if all employees concerned are treated alike. Employees complaining of constructive dismissal (i.e. that the employer's conduct forced resignation) must prove the dismissal was also unfair.
To complain to an industrial tribunal of unfair dismissal or of an employer failing to supply written reasons for dismissal, obtain form IT1 and leaflet ITL1 from *Employment Service Agency Employment Office* or *Employment Services Agency Jobcentre* or *Department of Employment Unemployment Benefit Office* and send the completed form to *Industrial Tribunals' Central Office* within three months of termination of employment. The ITCO sends copies to the former employer and to the *Advisory, Conciliation and Arbitration Service* which tries to arrange the settlement of the complaint by conciliation. Failing this, the complaint goes to a tribunal hearing which may, if it finds the dismissal unfair, order reinstatement, reengagement or compensation. If the employer does not comply with a tribunal order for reinstatement or reengagement, the tribunal can order additional compensation. Appeal against an industrial tribunal ruling, on a point of law only to *Employment Appeal Tribunal*; general advice from ACAS.
See also **Employment: terms and conditions**.

Disputes with Public Authorities (England and Wales) All agencies of the state – government departments, local authorities, statutory corporations, administrative tribunals and the like – exist to perform functions defined and limited in varying degrees of detail by legislation or rules of common law. The control exercised by the courts over these public authorities is primarily concerned to ensure that they keep within the limits of their powers; that is, that the authorities do not act ultra vires. If they act within those limits, then the courts will not intervene. A public authority acts ultra vires if it assumes a power which it does not by law possess, or if it uses its powers to defeat the objects for which the powers were conferred upon it or for purposes which differ from these prescribed by law; or if it fails to exercise its powers in accordance with the procedure laid down by law. Any person whose rights are injured, or threatened with injury, by an ultra vires or negligent act of a public authority, or by any failure of the authority to perform its statutory duties, may bring an action in the ordinary courts to obtain the appropriate remedy.

Liability: Public authorities, including central government departments (the Crown), are liable in ordinary civil action for torts (such as negligence or trespass), or breaches of contract, broadly as if they were private people (see **Civil Law disputes**). Actions for damages may be brought against public authorities or (in the case of the central government) the Attorney General if the complainant is in doubt which is the proper department. Sometimes criminal proceedings can be brought against public authorities (for instance, for breaches of the public health legislation). In addition implied requirements establish a number of principles applicable to all public authorities unless expressly excluded by relevant legislation; for example, 'rules of natural justice' as minimum fair standards of decision-making. The decision-maker must be free from bias – no one is to be a judge in his own cause – and all parties to a dispute are to be given a fair hearing.

Remedies: If an official body fails to carry out a duty, or exercises a power for an unauthorised purpose, or uses a power beyond the limits placed on it (although not for an illegal purpose), a wide range of remedies can be sought from the courts. These remedies comprise prerogative orders, injunctions, declarations, and those provided specifically by statute.

Prerogative Orders are: *certiorari* and *prohibition*, and *mandamus*. The decision whether or not to make such an order rests with the court on the basis of the facts put before it by the parties to the dispute.

Certiorari may be used to quash a decision (whether or not it affects the enforceable rights of an individual) that has already been made. It is available where an inferior court or administrative tribunal or authority has acted in excess or abuse of jurisdiction or contrary to the rules of natural justice, or where there is an error of law apparent on the face of the record of its proceedings. *Prohibition* may be used to prevent such bodies from acting or continuing to act in excess or abuse of jurisdiction or contrary to the rules of natural justice. Both *certiorari* and *prohibition* are limited to the enforcement of judicial functions and are not concerned with legislative functions. Neither may be used to control the jurisdiction of non-statutory private or domestic tribunals. A court may refuse leave to apply for an order of *certiorari* if the application has not been made within six months of the proceedings which it is sought to challenge, unless the delay can be satisfactorily explained to the court. It will also refuse to grant *certiorari* or *prohibition* if the matter in dispute is already the subject of appeal in an ordinary court of law. In addition, some administrative orders are statutorily excluded from judicial review and may be challenged only by means of the remedy expressly provided for in the Act concerned.

Mandamus may be granted to compel the performance of a public duty owed to an applicant with a sufficient legal interest in its performance; it may be used in respect of both legislative and judicial functions; and it is not subject to a time limit. As with the other prerogative orders, it lies only against public bodies, but it does not lie against the Crown nor against Crown servants, at least where they are acting as advisers to the Crown.

Injunctions are orders of the courts restraining a person from doing something injurious to another's interests or commanding something to be done for the protection of another's interests. They are available in disputes between private individuals as well as between the subject and public authority. They do not lie against the Crown, nor against Crown servants, but are the remedies most often used against local government authorities and chartered and statutory corporations. An injunction may be provisional, interlocutory, or perpetual.

Declarations may be issued to declare the invalidity of administrative orders and delegated legislation, or to declare the applicant's rights without necessarily referring to any decision of an administrative authority. Unlike a prerogative order it can be granted in respect of domestic tribunals. Its availability does not depend on whether the applicant has an independent cause of action, but he must assert a real interest recognised in law. A declaration may be refused by the court on the grounds that the right or privilege in respect of which it is sought has been conferred on the applicant by a statute which also provides a remedy for the protection of that right or privilege. A declaration is applied for in the same way and subject to the same procedure as an ordinary civil action. There is full interlocutory process, and there is no time-limit within which proceedings must be instituted.

Statutory remedies depend on each particular statute. In some cases a statute provides for an application to review and then annul an authority's action; in others it provides for an appeal to a court from an authority's decision, usually on a question of law. An important difference between review and appeal is that in the case of review the court simply annuls a decision and the authority is then free to reconsider the matter, whereas in the case of an appeal the court can usually substitute its own decision for that of the authority.

Advice from a **solicitor**.

See also **Civil law disputes**, entries on **Injustice**.

Disputes with Public Authorities (Scotland) The more important remedies are decrees of declarator, reduction, interdict, specific implement and damages, all of which are also available in actions between private persons.

Declarator protects some legally enforceable right of the pursuer. The decree may protect this right either directly by declaring that the pursuer has the right, or indirectly − for example, by declaring that the defender has no competing right. Unlike other remedies, a declarator does not order something to be done or prevent something from being done; it is merely declaratory of a particular state of affairs. It may, however, be obtained before some action is taken by a public authority, to ensure that some right of the pursuer is taken into account by that authority, but it may be refused if an alternative remedy exists or if there is no actual dispute between the parties.

Reduction is essentially a negative remedy by which the whole or any part of an act of a public authority may be reduced (that is, annulled or set aside) on the grounds that the authority has acted ultra vires. An action of reduction may only be brought in the Court of Session, and must be commenced within 20 years after the ultra vires act has been taken, although the court may refuse the remedy if there was delay in bringing the action, and its availability may be restricted by the statute under which the public authority is acting. The remedy may also be refused if lesser remedies would suffice.

Interdict is a preventive remedy by which a person may protect his rights when they are threatened by the proposed wrongful actions of a public authority. The decree prohibits the authority from infringing the rights in question. It may be refused where there is an alternative remedy, such as a statutory penalty. Interdict is not available against the Crown. Unlike reduction and declarator, however, the court may grant interim interdict to maintain the status quo pending the court's final decision. The court will grant or refuse interim interdict as the balance of fairness and convenience requires.

The Court of Session also has power to order a public authority, other than the Crown, to perform a statutory duty by making an order called an order for specific implement. The court may also prescribe such penalties (including fine and imprisonment) in the event of the order not being implemented as it considers to be appropriate. Generally a person may obtain a decree of specific implement only if the duty of the authority is judicially enforceable, and owed by the authority to that person. He cannot enforce the duty if it is owed to someone else or to the community as a whole.

A public authority is liable to make reparation (compensation) for any damage which it causes through the negligent exercise of its statutory powers and duties. A person injured in this way may bring an action of damages against the authority to determine the authority's liability and the amount of compensation due to him and to obtain an order for payment.

Statutory remedies arise from special legislative provision for an appeal against, or judicial review of, the decisions and other acts of a public authority. These specific statutory remedies sometimes exclude the ordinary remedies outlined above and may be accompanied by a statutory 'finality clause' excluding judicial challenge of the particular act of the public authority after a prescribed period.

See also **Civil law disputes: Scotland**, and entries on **Injustice**.

Dividend Control Generally a company incorporated in the UK may not declare dividends which amount to 10% more than the previous years' dividends. In exceptional circumstances higher dividends are permitted (e.g. a company defending a takeover bid); apply to *Her Majesty's Treasury, Dividends Section*. The Section will also on request help companies to calculate dividends within the legal limit. Enquiries about a company's dividends should first be addressed to the secretary of the company concerned.

See also **Companies: annual accounts and return**.

Diving All commercial divers working in UK waters must obtain a certificate of medical fitness after examination by a doctor approved by the Departments of Energy and Trade; lists of such doctors available from the *Health and Safety Executive, Employment Medical Advisory Service* or the *Department of Energy*. For training standards, certification of diving trainees, inspection and approval of courses, and payment of grants to employers sponsoring trainees to approved courses apply to *Training Services Agency*.

Divorce and Separation The sole ground for divorce or judicial separation is that the marriage has broken down irretrievably, on evidence that one spouse has committed adultery; one spouse has behaved in such a way that the other cannot reasonably be expected to live with him/her; one spouse has deserted the other for two years; the parties have lived apart for two years and consent to a decree being granted; or the parties have lived apart for five years. A registrar of a divorce county court or the *Principal Registry of the Family Division* in London will, when everything is in order and all the procedural steps have been complied with, recommend to the judge that a decree should be granted. Before a decree is made absolute, the judge must be satisfied about arrangements for any children of the family; he will also decide who is to have custody. The question of maintenance, lump sum and any transfer of property will probably be dealt with by a registrar. A leaflet giving details on how to obtain a divorce or separation may be obtained from any divorce county court, the *Principal Registry of the Family Division* or any *Citizens Advice Bureau*.

Docks and Cargo Gear: Survey Survey and classification of cranes, port handling equipment, dock gates, syncrolift and floating docks, etc., are undertaken by *Lloyd's Register of Shipping*.

Dock Work: Disputes Disputes in the UK under the Docks and Harbours Act 1966 (and about whether any place is in, or in the vicinity of, a port to which a labour scheme for the time being applies) may be referred for settlement to the *Industrial Tribunals' Central Office*.

Doctors Any fully-registered medical practitioner can practise as a **National Health Service** general practitioner and may in addition take private patients. To become an NHS patient, see **National Health Service**. To start in NHS practice, the doctor must submit an application to the local *Family Practitioner Committee*, which forwards it, after consulting the Local Medical Committee, to the Medical Practices Committee, which surveys the need for more doctors in each area. The doctor can appeal to the Secretary of State for Health and Social Security against the MPC's refusal to allow practice.

A doctor in single-handed practice can have up to 3,500 NHS patients; in partnerships he may have up to 4,500 patients, providing the average does not exceed 3,500 for each partner. With a full-time assistant he can, with the consent of the FPC, have a further 2,000 patients.

The *Department of Health and Social Security* gives general practitioners financial grants towards rent and rates of practice premises; employment of ancillary staff; and for group practices and health centres (i.e. with **nurses, midwives, health visitors**, etc., attached); and for setting up practices in areas where more doctors are needed.

See also **Doctors: complaints; Doctors: qualifications and registration**.

Doctors' and Dentists' Pay In the National Health Service pay is reviewed by the Review Body on Doctors' and Dentists' Remuneration at the *Office of Manpower Economics*. It makes its recommendations to the Prime Minister. If accepted, they are implemented by the *Department of Health and Social Security*, the *Scottish Home and Health Department*, the *Welsh Office Health and Social Work Department* and the *Northern Ireland Department of Health and Social Services*. The government has undertaken to accept the recommendations unless there are clear and compelling reasons for not doing so.

Doctors: Complaints Complaints about professional misconduct should be addressed to the *General Medical Council*. The GMC is empowered to investigate complaints about serious professional misconduct, and the Disciplinary Committee of the GMC may, if it thinks fit, remove a practitioner's name from the Register, or suspend his registration. To complain about a professional failing in a **National Health Service** family **doctor**, the patient or his authorised representative should write to the local *Family Practitioner Committee* within eight weeks of the event about which the complaint is being made. Late complaints may be investigated only under certain conditions. Complaints are investigated by the FPC's medical service committee. There is a right of appeal to the *Secretary of State for Social Services* against an adverse decision.

See also **Injustice: health services**.

Doctors: Qualifications Medical practitioners practising in the UK must be registered with the *General Medical Council*. The usual primary medical qualification is the degrees of both Bachelor of Medicine and Bachelor of Surgery (e.g. MB, ChB) from a UK university. With these two qualifications a doctor is entitled to provisional registration with the GMC. A newly-qualified doctor must then serve for one year as a resident house officer in approved hospital posts in medicine and surgery. On completion of this service he is eligible for full registration as a qualified practitioner. Registrable primary qualifications may also be obtained from certain non-university licensing bodies (e.g. the English Conjoint Board or the Society of Apothecaries of London).

Provision or full registration may also be granted to doctors holding overseas qualifications which the GMC recognises for this purpose (e.g. those obtained by EEC nationals in member states of the EEC). Temporary registration may be granted to doctors holding acceptable overseas qualifications; such doctors normally have first to pass a test of proficiency in the English language and in professional competence conducted by the GMC Temporary Registration Assessment Board.

Additional qualifications may be registered with the GMC, e.g. the postgraduate degrees of Doctor of Medicine and Master of Surgery. Memberships and fellowships of the Royal Colleges of Physicians, Surgeons, Obstetricians and Gynaecologists, Pathologists, Psychologists, Radiologists and General Practitioners, and of the Faculties of Anaesthetists and Community Medicine may also be registered. Higher qualifications and

appropriate training lead to accreditation with the Royal Colleges as specialists, and are necessary for career advancement.
The GMC register of all fully and provisionally registered doctors is published annually in the Medical Register.

Dog Breeding   Under the Breeding of Dogs Act 1973, breeders in Great Britain with more than two bitches for breeding commercially require registration with the local authority and must be licensed annually. Private dog breeders need not be licensed. Enquiries or complaints to local authority. In Northern Ireland there is no special legislation on dog breeding establishments.

Dog Licences   Licences may be obtained from many post offices in Great Britain. They are issued on behalf of the local authority; the *Ministry of Agriculture, Fisheries and Food* is responsible for legislation. In Northern Ireland they are obtainable from any Clerk of Petty Sessions.

Dog Shows and Registration   The *Kennel Club* is the controlling authority of dog shows, field trials, working trials and obedience classes in Great Britain. Some 3,500 dog shows are held in GB each year, licensed by the KC and organised by canine societies registered with the KC. Dog shows arrange their activities within KC rules and participating dogs must be individually registered with the KC. Details of the individual shows may be obtained from each society's show secretary; lists are published in the 'Kennel Gazette', available from the KC. Crufts is the KC's dog show; to qualify for entry a dog must have won one of a number of specified prizes at a championship show during the previous year. Tickets are available at the gate and from the KC.
For a dog to be registered with the KC, it must be pure-bred and both its parents must be registered. There is no KC pedigree as such, but the owner of a registered dog is provided with a KC registration certificate which sets out the dog's details: breed, registered name, sex, date of birth, colour, breeder and present owner. Dogs are first entered in the KC basic register and then transferred into the active register if they are to be shown, bred from, or exported with a view to registration with an overseas kennel club. Over 150 breeds of pure-bred dogs are recognised by the KC. Recognition is dependent on evidence of pure breeding over a long period.
See also **Dog breeding**.

Dominican Republic   For **exchange control** is a non-scheduled territory outside the **overseas sterling area** and the **EEC**. UK nationals travelling direct from the UK normally need only the following (but check): **passports**; international certificates of **vaccination** against smallpox; **work permits** (if taking a job); green cards for motor insurance (if bringing a car: see **Motoring abroad**).
The UK has no reciprocal health or social security arrangements.
Enquiries to *Dominican Republic Embassy* in London.
British diplomatic missions to Dominican Republic are *British Embassy* in Santo Domingo and *British Consulates* in Puerto Plata and San Pedro de Macoris.

Driving Instructors   Instructors who give professional tuition in driving motor cars must be registered with the *Department of Transport, Register of Approved Driving Instructors*, which is also responsible for issuing short-term trainee instructor's licenses. An applicant for a trainee licence must have held a substantive driving licence for at least four years out of the last six; not have been under a disqualification from driving at any time in the last four years; and be of good character. An applicant for registration must meet these conditions and pass the qualifying examination. Information about registration and licensing from the nearest *Department of Transport Traffic Area Office*; details of training as an instructor from *National Joint Council of Approved Driving Instructor Organisations*.

Driving Licences   Licences are required in Great Britain for all drivers

Driving

of mechanically operated vehicles on public roads. Applicants for full driving licences must have passed a driving test in GB and be aged at least 16 for invalid carriages and mopeds; 17 for motor cars, motor cycles, small passenger and goods vehicles up to 3.5 tonnes; 18 for goods vehicles up to 7.5 tonnes maximum weight; or 21 for large passenger vehicles and goods vehicles (special licences required for these). Mopeds include only motor cycles with an engine capacity of 500 c.c. or less, a maximum design speed of not more than 30 m.p.h. and a kerbside weight not over 250 kg; also certain older style mopeds with propelling pedals.

Until they have passed a test drivers must hold a provisional licence (fee £2, valid for one year) and drive only according to its conditions. Application form for driving licences from post offices; send completed form to *Department of Transport Driver and Vehicle Licensing Centre*. A single £5 fee covers all ordinary licenses (except provisional) for life.

Visitors from overseas may drive for up to one year from date of entry without holding a GB driving licence provided that they hold a valid driving licence in another country, or an International Driving Permit; those who take up residence in GB may only drive without a GB licence for three months from that date. During that time they may pass a GB driving test and obtain a full GB licence. If they do not, they must obtain a provisional licence. International Driving Permits for those travelling overseas may be obtained from the *Automobile Association*; the *Royal Automobile Club*; the *Royal Scottish Automobile Club*; or the *Department of the Environment for Northern Ireland*.

See also **Driving tests; Heavy goods vehicle driver's licence; Public service vehicle driver's licence; Vehicle licences.**

Driving Tests Tests may be taken at any driving test centre in Great Britain upon application to the nearest *Department of Transport Traffic Area Office*; the fee for each test is £6.75 (no fee for test on invalid carriage). For details of driving test requirements see leaflet DL68 available from the above office. The candidate must provide for the test a suitable vehicle of the kind for which he wants a full driving licence. Appeal about the conduct of a test (but not against failure to pass a test) may be made to a magistrates' court. Current copy of 'Highway Code' and manual 'Driving' available from *Her Majesty's Stationery Office*. There are special tests for **Public service vehicle driver's licences** and **Heavy goods vehicle driver's licences.**

Drought A drought order issued by the Secretary of State for the Environment (or Secretary of State for Scotland in Scotland) enables a *water authority* or *water company* to limit the supply of water to consumers, to prohibit or limit the use of water for specified purposes, and to reduce the flow in watercourses by varying the amount of compensation water supplied from reservoirs. In extreme cases of drought consumers' water may be cut off.

Drug Control Responsibility for the control of dangerous drugs rests with the *Home Office*. The Home Secretary is advised by the Advisory Council on the Misuse of Drugs which was set up in 1972 to advise on measures to prevent the misuse of drugs and to deal with the social problems connected with their misuse. Most controlled drugs (e.g. cocaine, morphine, opium (Class A) amphetamine, cannabis (Class B) and piprado (Class C) are listed in the schedules to the 1971 Misuse of Drugs Act, which provides a variety of controls, varying by class of drug, including controls on imports, exports, production, possession and cultivation. The *Home Secretary* can issue licences regarding these controls. Tribunals can be set up under the Act to deal with **doctors** who have allegedly contravened the regulations. Enquiries to the Secretary of the Advisory Council on the Misuse of Drugs at the *Home Office*.

See also **Drug dependence.**

Drug Dependence The hospital service plays an important role in the treatment of drug dependence. Treatment for narcotic addiction is provided mostly in out-patient treatment clinics under the **National Health Service**. Only doctors working in the drug addiction clinics are licensed by the *Home Secretary* (Secretary for Social Services in Northern Ireland) to prescribe heroin and cocaine to addicts for the purpose of treating their addiction. Most doctors, including general practitioners, are not licensed to prescribe these drugs; they can, however, send addicts to established drug treatment clinics. All medical practitioners are required to notify the *Home Office* of any patient they consider to be addicted to these and other narcotic drugs.

Hospital services similarly provide treatment services for multiple drug misusers including accident and emergency services for those who overdose. An experimental Short Stay Crisis Centre is being provided in London for this group.

Voluntary organisations provide many rehabilitation facilities, particularly residential accommodation, both for addicts receiving prescribed drugs and others withdrawing from drugs. These organisations also take the lead in providing day centres, advisory counselling centres and sheltered housing for married couples. The *Standing Conference on Drug Abuse* (SCODA) is the organisation which co-ordinates the activities of voluntary agencies concerned with drug misusers. It helps them when beginning new activities, encourages research into the problems of drug misuse and provides a forum for information on the changing pattern of drug misuse. Enquiries to: NHS family **doctor**, *SCODA* as above, or to *National Health Service Drug Dependence Centres*.
See also **Drug control**.

Dual Nationality and Citizenship
Nothing in UK law prevents a person from having another citizenship in addition to **citizenship of the UK and colonies** (e.g. resulting from birth in the UK to a foreign father or birth abroad to a British father). But under the generally accepted 'master nationality rule', when a dual citizen is in one of the countries whose citizenship he possesses, the authorities of the country have the right to treat him as if he possessed only the citizenship of that country, and the representative of the other country whose citizenship he possesses will be unable to afford him any assistance or protection against those authorities. It is advisable for people born or whose parents were born in the country they intend to visit and who have acquired UK citizenship by **naturalisation**, registration or descent to verify with the diplomatic mission of that country in the UK whether they, their wives or children possess as second nationality the citizenship of that country. Most foreign or Commonwealth countries are represented in London (addresses given under each country), but in the case of difficulty the *Nationality and Treaty Department of the Foreign and Commonwealth Office* may be consulted.

Although UK nationals who are also nationals of another country cannot be protected by HM Representatives while in the country of second nationality, this constraint does not normally affect the person's eligibility for UK passport services. It should be noted however, that the grant of a UK **passport** could prejudice the person's status as a citizen or national of the other country concerned or could affect the person's eligibility to be granted a passport of the other country. He should therefore check the position with the authorities of the country concerned before proceeding with his application for UK passport facilities.

Duke of Edinburgh's Award Scheme for Young People This provides UK and Commonwealth 14–25-year-olds with incentives to serve the community and develop their own leisure interests at their own pace. Success depends more on effort and persistence than on brains and brawn. Physical handicap or slow learning are not penalised.

Entry for the Bronze, Silver and Gold Awards is through schools, employers, and youth organisations or directly by applying to the nearest office of the *Duke of Edinburgh's Award*. Addresses of Commonwealth offices are available from the international head office. Organisations concerned with young people can be licensed by the international head office. This authorises them to grant Awards on behalf of HRH The Duke of Edinburgh.

Adults who are prepared to pass on their knowledge and interests to young people should apply to the nearest Duke of Edinburgh's Award office.

Dumping at Sea The permanent deposit of substances and articles below high water mark requires a licence under the Dumping at Sea Act 1974; this includes construction works. Apply to *Ministry of Agriculture, Fisheries and Food* in England and Wales; *Department of Agriculture and Fisheries for Scotland* in Scotland; and *Department of the Environment (Northern Ireland)*. Dumping of radioactive waste requires the additional consent, under the Radioactive Substances Act 1960, of the *Department of the Environment* (in England) or the *Scottish Development Department*.

Dust: Health Hazards General UK policy relating to health hazards from dusts (including asbestos, silica, cotton, man-made mineral fibres, vegetable and nuisance dusts) is the responsibility of the Hazardous Substances Division Branch at the *Health and Safety Executive Head Office*. Technical advice at a local level on safety in the handling of dust is available from the *Health and Safety Executive HM Factory Inspectorate Area Offices*. Advice on medical aspects of handling dust is available from the *Health and Safety Executive Employment Medical Advisory Service*. Advice on safe use of asbestos from *Asbestos Information Committee*. See also **Work: health and safety**.

Duty-free and Tax-free Allowances Certain goods carried in the baggage brought with them by persons arriving in the UK may be admitted free of duty and tax up to specified limits. Persons under 17 are not entitled to tobacco and drinks allowances. None of the allowances apply to goods brought in for sale or other commercial purposes. Reduced allowances apply to certain persons crossing the land boundary from Eire and to seamen and aircrew. Details from *Her Majesty's Customs and Excise*.

Articles which have previously been in the EEC and which have undergone no alteration, addition, non-essential repair or other process while outside the EEC are normally admitted free of duty if they were removed from the EEC by the traveller or on his behalf; are being returned within three years of their export; and were not exported free of duty. Articles which have previously been in the UK and which have undergone no alteration, addition, non-essential repair or other process while outside the UK are normally admitted free of **value-added tax** if they were removed from the UK by the traveller or on his behalf; and were not exported free of tax. When claiming relief, if possible, produce to the customs officer evidence of purchase (e.g. a bill from a shop), either in the EEC or in the UK as appropriate, or a duty receipt if duty and/or VAT has been previously paid. Otherwise you may be asked to make a written declaration. Details from *Her Majesty's Customs and Excise*.

See also **Customs duty**.

E

Earnings Related Supplement (And widow's earnings related benefit.) For **social security benefits** – sickness, unemployment, injury (where there is underlying right to sickness benefit), widow's allowance and maternity allowance – an extra payment may be made to a contributor (or the widow of a contributor) who has paid Class I **national insurance contributions** on annual earnings of more than 50 times the minimum weekly earnings on which contributions are payable in the current financial income tax year. The supplement is related to the contributor's former earnings on which Class I contributions have been paid, and may be payable after two weeks off work for up to six months. Apply to *Department of Health and Social Security* local offices; details in DHSS leaflet NI 155A.
See also entries on individual **social security benefits**.

Ecclesiastical Law Ecclesiastical law consists of such portions of the old canon law as continued in force after the Reformation in the 16th century, together with the post-Reformation statutes and canons of the English Church passed by Parliament, and the General Synod of the Church of England, which under its previous title of National Assembly was set up by Act of Parliament in 1919 and is the central legislative body of the Church, its measures being endorsed by Parliament. Ecclesiastical law formerly governed the clergy in all their affairs and the laity in matters of faith and morals and in those aspects of their lives in which the ministrations of the Church were required. Modern ecclesiastical law is concerned only with the regulation of church affairs, the discipline of the clergy in matters of doctrine and conduct, and control over the fabric of churches and over churchyards.
Since the constitution and law of the established Church of England are part of the public law of the country, the ecclesiastical courts are the Queen's courts and have the status of public courts of limited but, within their own sphere, exclusive jurisdiction. Their effective base is the court of the diocese, known as the consistory court, over which the Chancellor of the Diocese – who is a barrister appointed by the bishop, but possessing in his own right the authority of a judge of the Queen's court – usually presides. Above the consistory courts are the provincial courts of Canterbury and York, which are presided over by the same judge who is appointed jointly by the two archbishops. At the head of the whole system is the Judicial Committee of the Privy Council, which is assisted in ecclesiastical matters by a number of bishops summoned to attend as assessors.
See also **Civil law disputes; Injustice.**

Ecuador For **exchange control** is a non-scheduled territory outside the **overseas sterling area** and the **EEC**. UK nationals travelling direct from the

UK normally need only the following (but check): **passports; work permits** (if taking a job).
The UK has no reciprocal health or social security arrangements. Enquiries to *Ecuador Embassy* in London.
British diplomatic missions to Ecuador are *British Embassy* in Quito and *British Consulate* in Guayaquil.

Education Abroad Expenditure for this purpose is subject to **exchange control**. UK residents who undertake a course of education abroad should apply to an **authorised bank**. Remittances are normally allowed up to a total of £2,000 per person per academic year, to cover the cost of enrolment and tuition fees, boarding or accommodation and books. The amounts which may be remitted are reduced on a pro rata basis for courses of less than one academic year and by the value of any scholarships or fees or award monies from non-resident sources. Applications over these limits to the *Bank of England*. Incidental personal expenditure is expected to be met from the student's normal travel exchange allowance.
See also **Student grants; Travel: currency allowances.**

Education Authorities The *Secretary of State for Education and Science* is responsible for all aspects of education in England, for further education in Wales, and for universities, civil science and the arts throughout Great Britain. The *Secretary of State for Wales* is responsible for nursery, primary and secondary education in Wales; the *Secretaries of State for Scotland* and *Northern Ireland* have full educational responsibilities in their countries except that the Secretary of State for Scotland is consulted about Scottish universities but is not responsible for them.
Administration of publicly provided schools and further education is divided between the central government departments (the *Department of Education and Science*, the *Welsh Office*, the *Scottish Education Department*, and the *Northern Ireland Department of Education*), local education authorities (*education and library boards* in Northern Ireland), and various voluntary organisations.
The local education authorities are responsible for the provision of school education and most post-school education outside the universities, and provide grants to students proceeding to higher education (including the universities).
The universities are administratively independent and their governing bodies are appointed according to the terms of their individual charters or statutory provisions. The government exercises its financial responsibilities in relation to the universities through the University Grants Committee.
See also **Further education; Student grants.**

Education: Northern Ireland The *Department of Education, Northern Ireland*, is responsible for the development of primary, secondary, further and higher education, the library service and the youth service; oversight of the five *education and library boards* which are responsible to the Department for the local administration of the education, library and youth services; teacher training; examinations (including selection and review procedures); museums. The Department grant-aids the universities and the Ulster College. It is also responsible for formulating and sponsoring policies for the improvement of community relations and community services and grant-aids district councils and voluntary organisations in the provision of sporting, recreational and social facilities.

Education: Scotland Scottish educational arrangements are often different to those in the rest of the UK. The central institutions (colleges of higher education) and colleges of education (for teacher training), which are administered by independent governing bodies, are financed directly by the Scottish Education Department and grants to students are also paid by the department.
A description of the Scottish educational system is contained in: 'Scottish Education', and 'The Education

System of Scotland', both obtainable from the *Scottish Information Office*; also in 'Education in Scotland in 1976', published by *Her Majesty's Stationery Office*. Enquiries to *Scottish Education Department*.

Educational Technology Advice and training for overseas nationals is provided by the British Council both overseas and in Britain (where it runs practical four-month courses geared particularly to educational technology specialists from the developing countries). The BC also participates in educational broadcasting courses in many countries, and gives advice on media development.
Enquiries to: the *British Council, Media Department*, or the *British Council Overseas Office* in the country concerned.

EEC Legally, there are three European Communities which share the same institutions. The European Coal and Steel Community, set up by the Paris Treaty in 1951, established a common market for coal and steel. The European Atomic Energy Community (Euratom) was set up by the Rome Treaty in 1957 to promote the peaceful uses of nuclear energy. The European Economic Community (the Common Market) was set up by a second Rome Treaty in 1957. Founder-members of all three Communities are Belgium, France, West Germany, Italy, Luxembourg and the Netherlands. In January 1973 Denmark, Eire and the UK also became full members.
All of the Communities have complex ranges of grants, loans and subsidies; details in 'Grants and loans from the European Community' from the *Commission of the European Communities*. For businessmen, the *EEC Information Unit* answers all queries and publishes 'EEC: your questions answered'; its main concern is with aspects relevant to the Departments of Industry, Trade, and Prices and Consumer Protection, but it will refer the reader to relevant contacts in other government departments or outside bodies.

See also subsequent entries on the EEC, and **Company law and the EEC**.

EEC: Community Transit Full Community transit documents, T1 and T2, provide cover for movements of goods within a specified time limit to and across member states of the EEC and Austria and Switzerland. They also provide evidence of the Community status of goods and form T2 will support a claim to Community treatment in another member state. Where evidence of entitlement only is required, the system provides, with certain exclusions, for the issue of CT Movement Certificates – form T2L. Apply to *Her Majesty's Customs and Excise*.

EEC: Legislative Process The legislative process of the EEC differs from the pattern of UK legislation. The *Commission of the European Communities* makes proposals for EEC legislation and the *European Council of Ministers* takes the decisions, with the *European Parliament* and the Economic and Social Committee giving their formal opinions on the proposals.
In drawing up proposals, the Commission consults widely (through the European groupings of employers and trade unions, trade and industrial associations, etc.). Once it has determined the proposals, it sends them to the Council of Ministers, i.e. to the governments of all the member countries. At this stage the proposed legislation is published in the 'Official Journal of the European Communities' and interested parties wishing to influence the final decision should lobby the relevant UK government department.
The Council of Ministers does not take a decision until the European Parliament and the Economic and Social Committee have scrutinised the proposals and given their opinions, which often lead the Commission to modify its proposals, i.e. contacting and lobbying members of the European Parliament and of the Economic and

Social Committee is another way of effecting EEC legislation.
See also **Law: European Economic Community**.

EEC: Professional Qualifications Qualifications differ from country to country in the EEC. So far agreement has been reached by EEC national authorities to enable **doctors**, lawyers and **nurses** to work in other EEC countries. Discussions are under way to provide similar recognition for others, e.g. **architects, dentists, midwives, pharmacists** and chartered **accountants**.
At present professional people – apart from doctors and lawyers (from March 1979) and nurses (from July 1979) – need to check with their professional body (see entry for each profession) whether their diplomas are recognised in another country on a case-by-case basis.

EEC: Recruitment The *Commission of the European Communities* recruits by means of open competitions for all categories of staff. Advertisements are carried in the daily and weekly national press when these competitions are due to take place. Enquiries to the Recruitment, Appointments and Promotions Division at the *Commission of the European Communities* in Brussels.
The other Community institutions (i.e. the *European Council of Ministers*, the *European Parliament* and the *Court of Justice*) carry out their own recruitment in a similar way, but on a smaller scale.

EEC: Work and Residence Nationals of the member states of the EEC are free to work in any other EEC country. UK workers wishing to work and live in another member state do not (except for government service) need **work permits** but do need a valid **passport** endorsed 'holder has the right of abode in the United Kingdom'. Once they have a job, workers and their families automatically get residence permits, initially valid for five years and automatically renewable. Conditions of employment, social security, union rights and access to housing must all be on equal terms with nationals of the host country. Finding a job is up to the individual concerned, but *Department of Employment local offices* can find out about vacancies in EEC countries through the European Office for the Coordination of Vacancy Clearance.
A worker moving from one EEC country to another can transfer his **social security benefits** and has the right to live permanently in another EEC country if on retirement he is entitled by that country's law to an old age pension and has worked in the country for at least the last year, and has lived there more than three years; or if he has lived in the country for the past two years but can no longer work as a result of permanent incapacity. Further details in 'Working in Europe' free from *Job Centres* and all *Department of Employment local offices*, and in 'Working in other EEC countries' from the *Commission of the European Communities, UK office*.

Eggs Under EEC regulations concerning hen eggs, all persons engaged in egg packing and selling graded eggs to wholesalers and retail shops must register with the appropriate agricultural department; in England and Wales the Pigs and Poultry Division at the *Ministry of Agriculture, Fisheries and Food*, headquarters, in Scotland the *Department of Agriculture for Scotland*, in Northern Ireland the *Department of Agriculture for Northern Ireland*, and must comply with the marketing standards regulations for shell eggs. All breeding and hatchery establishments must also be registered with the appropriate agricultural department and comply with the regulations on the production and marketing of eggs for hatching. Hatchers and importers of chicks placed for egg production must pay a levy, calculated annually, to the *Eggs Authority*, which they can recover from the purchaser of the chicks. Enquiries in England and Wales to the regional Egg Marketing Inspectors at the *MAFF Regional Offices*, in Scotland to the DAS and in Northern Ireland to the DANI.

Egypt For **exchange control** is a non-scheduled territory outside the **overseas sterling area** and the **EEC**. UK nationals travelling direct from the UK normally need only the following (but check): **passports** without Israeli stamp; **visas**; international certificates of **vaccination** against smallpox; **work permits** (if taking a job); green cards for motor insurance (if bringing a car); international driving permits (if intending to drive: see **Motoring abroad**).
The UK has no reciprocal health or social security arrangements.
Enquiries to *Egyptian Embassy* in London.
British diplomatic missions to Egypt are *British Embassy* in Cairo and *British Consulate* in Alexandria.

Eire (Irish Republic) EEC member. For **exchange control** is a scheduled territory. UK nationals travelling direct from the UK do not need **passports**, nor any special permits or certificates; there are no restrictions on entry for people born in Britain. EEC or bilateral social security arrangements are applicable; leaflets and EEC Guides obtainable from *Department of Health and Social Security, Overseas Branch*. Apply to the local social security office for leaflet SA28 which explains who is entitled to free medical treatment. A certificate of entitlement (form E111) is not necessary.
Enquiries to *Irish Embassy* in London.
British diplomatic mission to Eire is *British Embassy* in Dublin.

El Salvador For **exchange control** is a non-scheduled territory outside the **overseas sterling area** and the **EEC**.
UK nationals travelling direct from the UK normally need only the following (but check): **passports**; international certificates of **vaccination** against smallpox; **work permits** (if taking a job); green cards for motor insurance (if bringing a car); international driving permits (if intending to drive: see **Motoring abroad**).
The UK has no reciprocal health or social security arrangements.
Enquiries to *El Salvador Embassy* in London.
British diplomatic missions to El Salvador are *British Embassy* in San Salvador and *British Consulate* in Acajutla.

Election Agents Candidates in Parliamentary or local government elections must nominate an election agent, even if only themselves, to the returning officer. In county Parliamentary constituencies, election agents may appoint one sub-agent. Election agents' statutory duties include responsibility for expenses and for submitting a true return of expenses to the returning officer not later than 35 days after the result has been declared.
See also **Election expenses; Elections: returning officers; Local government elections; Parliamentary elections**.

Election Expenses Expenses in Parliamentary and local government elections are strictly controlled by statute. **Parliamentary election candidates** may spend up to a maximum of £1,075 together with 6p per each six entries in the electoral register in county constituencies and 6p per eight entries in borough constituencies. Certain expenditures are illegal, including paying other candidates to withdraw. The total sum which a **local government election candidate** may incur by way of election expenses is also limited. At a Greater London Council election, the sum is £320 plus 2p for every entry in the register; at other elections the maximum is £72, plus an additional 1.5p for every entry.
Election agents are responsible for presenting the accounts, including the candidates' personal expenses.

Election Results Results are determined by a count conducted by the Returning Officer. In **Parliamentary elections** which are contested, the result is declared publicly; if uncontested the RO declares the result at the time of nomination.
Recounts in Parliamentary elections before the result has been declared can be undertaken by the RO when he thinks there has been an error in counting; candidates and election agents may require the RO to have a recount or a further recount but he may refuse if in his opinion the request is unreasonable. After the result has

been declared it can be challenged by an application to the court.
Tied votes in Parliamentary elections are settled by lot. The RO proceeds, after the lot has been cast, as if the candidate upon whom the lot has fallen had one extra vote. In **local government elections** procedure is the same. At local elections in Northern Ireland the procedures are very similar to Parliamentary elections but, as the single transferable vote system of proportional representation is used, the deputy returning officer notifies the candidates and election agents when each stage is completed of his intention to proceed to the next stage. If a candidate or agent so requests, the immediate preceding stage will be recounted. A deputy returning officer may also recount papers if he is not satisfied of the accuracy of a stage.
See also **Election agents; Elections: returning officers.**

Elections: Returning Officers In England and Wales returning officers for **Parliamentary elections** are normally county sheriffs, mayors of boroughs or the chairman of the district council, but in practice an acting returning officer normally discharges the returning officer's duties. Returning officers for **local government elections** must be appointed by the relevant local authority. In Scotland returning officers appointed for elections to regional and islands councils are also the returning officers for Parliamentary elections; they are appointed by the local authority concerned. In Northern Ireland the chief Electoral Officer is the registration officer and returning officer for Parliamentary, Northern Ireland Assembly and local government elections. At local government elections the clerk of a district council is the deputy returning officer for elections to that council.

Electoral Registration People who may vote in a **Parliamentary election** in a constituency are those resident in the constituency on the qualifying date who are on the electoral register and are **British subjects, Commonwealth** citizens or citizens of Eire (Irish Republic), and who are not otherwise disqualified (e.g. **peers,** prisoners or lunatics). Postal ballot papers or proxy votes may be available in certain circumstances to voters who will be absent from the constituency. All enquiries to the acting returning officer. Franchise at **local government elections** is similar, but includes peers. In local elections it is an offence to vote more than once in a county, district, London borough, parish or community; but it is possible to vote in more than one of these areas if one can claim residence. In Parliamentary elections it is an offence to vote twice even if the votes are cast in different constituencies. Every **local authority** appoints one of its officers as electoral registration officer.
The electoral register is prepared and published by the registration officer by 15 February each year and lists electors within the district for which the registration officer is responsible. For inclusion on the register you must be a British subject, a Commonwealth citizen or a citizen of the Republic of Ireland, over 18 years of age and resident at the address on the qualifying date of 18 October of the previous year. Peers are indicated by an 'L' against their name on the register. The registers are used for any poll after 16 February for a year, and are open for inspection at local authority offices, public libraries and main post offices.
Electoral lists or a draft register are published and open for inspection between 28 November and 16 December of the previous year to enable voters to check that they have been included. A copy of each register goes to the *British Museum.* A free copy is supplied on request to the Member of Parliament for the constituency, every councillor for the local government area and each candidate at a local government election. Two free copies go to Parliamentary election candidates and four free copies to any person who satisfies the registration officer that he requires them for use in connection with his own or some other person's prospective candidature at a Parliamentary election for that constituency. Copies can be bought for a small fee from the

registration officer at the local authority offices.

In Northern Ireland the qualifying date for registration is 15 September and electors must be resident in NI for the whole of the preceding three months. To qualify as an elector at NI Assembly or local elections a person must be a British subject aged 18 or over. Disqualifications are similar to those for Parliamentary elections, except that peers may vote. Persons qualified only at Parliamentary elections are indicated by an 'I' against their name in the register, while those qualified to vote only at NI elections are indicated by an 'N'. For NI elections an elector may have only one qualifying address; if he has more than one residence in NI he must choose the one for which he wishes to be registered.
See also **Constituency boundaries; Elections: returning officers.**

Electric Lines and Generating Stations
Before placing an overhead electricity line or constructing or extending a generating station, *Electricity Boards* in England and Wales must have the consent of the *Department of Energy*. In Scotland consent is given by the *Scottish Office* and in Northern Ireland by the *Northern Ireland Department of Commerce*.
Before consent is given the relevant district or borough council and the county council must be given the chance to object. If a local planning authority objects then the *Secretary of State for Energy* must hold a public inquiry. For other objections a public enquiry may be held at the discretion of the Secretary of State.
The *Department of Energy*, the *Scottish Office* or the *Northern Ireland Department of Commerce* may also grant compulsory easements to EBs to enable them to place electricity lines above or below ground, or to acquire land. Landowners and occupiers have the right to be heard before a decision is reached on an application for a compulsory easement.
See also **Electricity.**

Electrical Contractors The *National Inspection Council for Electrical Installation Contracting* publishes an annual roll of approved contractors in the UK which is available at all *Electricity Board Showrooms*. The NICEIC approval requires that the contractors work to standards set out in the 'Regulations for the electrical equipment of buildings' published by the *Institution of Electrical Engineers*.

Electrical Equipment: Approval Marks
Appliances often carry the approval mark of the *British Electrotechnical Approvals Board* which is an industry-backed body authorised by the Home Office. BEAB marks mean that appliances have been tested for safety and conform to British Standards 3456 (domestic equipment) or 415 (mains-operated household sound, vision and audio equipment). Although the Board cannot deal directly with consumers, it distributes lists of approved products.
Explosion safety certification of electrical equipment is undertaken by the *Department of Energy, British Approvals for Electrical Equipment in Flammable Atmospheres* to appropriate domestic and overseas standards. Apply to the Director.

Electrical Safety at Work General UK policy on all matters relating to electrical safety at work is the responsibility of Safety and General Branch A at *Health and Safety Executive Head Office*. The *Health and Safety Executive HM Factory Inspectorate Consultant Section 3* is responsible for determining practicable standards for electrical safety at work to meet policy objectives and for the preparation of technical codes of practice and other advisory literature with a technical content. Technical advice at a local level is available from the *Health and Safety Executive HM Factory Inspectorate Area Offices*.
See also **Work: health and safety.**

Electricity The *Central Electricity Generating Board* owns Great Britain's generating stations, high voltage transformer substations, overhead transmission lines supported on pylons, and underground cables. The generation, transmission and distribution of electricity in Northern Ireland is the responsibility of the *Northern Ireland Electricity Service*. These national generation and transmission systems supply power to the area *Electricity Boards*.

The EBs own the lower voltage overhead lines supported on small pylons or poles, the underground cables and transformer substations which form the local distribution network and supply lines to the consumer.

Deemed planning permission and ministerial consent are required for power stations, high voltage and most low voltage overhead transmission lines. Transformer substations require only **planning permission**. Underground cables require no statutory consent. Public enquiries about generating stations and overhead transmission lines can be called by Departments of Energy and Environment. Voluntary wayleaves (forms of consent, agreements, easements, etc.) are required for all overhead lines and underground cables where they cross privately-owned land. The annual rental and agricultural compensation rates payable to the owners or occupiers of agricultural land are agreed nationally by the CEGB with the *National Farmers Union* and *Country Landowners' Association*. Capital payments in return for permanent easements are negotiable.

The CEGB and the area EBs have statutory powers to purchase interest in land and carry out tree cutting, etc.

Electricity and Gas Bills Bills overdue for payment may result in disconnection (see **Electricity and gas disconnections**). But the *British Gas Corporation, Regions* and *Electricity Boards* offer a range of pay-as-you-go aids. They include regular budget payment schemes and purchase of gas or electricity savings stamps to enable consumers to budget in advance against their next bill. Information about these schemes is available at most *Gas showrooms* and *Electricity showrooms*. In cases of genuine hardship where other payment arrangements are not appropriate, the industries will provide to any consumer on request a prepayment meter provided it is safe and practical. Consumers are reminded, however, that they would be charged on the prepayment tariff.

Apply to local showroom, district office or accounts centre of relevant *EB* or *Gas region*.

Electricity Disconnections: see **Gas**.

Electricity: Enquiries and Complaints Enquiries and complaints about charges, accounts and appliances purchased (or serviced) through *Electricity Board Showrooms*, and *Electricity Board* contracting work, should be made first to the district manager at the EB showroom. He is in charge of all engineering and commercial activities in a district. If not satisfied, write to the secretary, the *Electricity Consultative Council*, or in Northern Ireland to the Secretary of the *Northern Ireland Electricity Consumers' Council*.

Electricity Meters Meters must be of a type approved by the *Secretary of State for Energy* and individually verified for accuracy by the electricity meter examiners of the *Department of Energy* before being used by an *Electricity Board* to register the value of the supply to an ordinary consumer. Meter accuracy is tested on request for any consumer who has reason to suspect that his meter is registering inaccurately; apply to the EB for your area. Where there is disagreement between a consumer and an EB regarding the accuracy of a meter, the disagreement can be referred to the DEn for determination by an area electricity meter examiner.

See also **Electricity; Electricity and gas bills**.

Electricity Supply The electricity supply for houses, factories and business premises in the UK is arranged through the Area *Electricity Boards* (in England and Wales), the *Electricity Boards* (in Scotland) and the *Northern Ireland Electricity Service* (in Northern Ireland). New circuits in houses and business premises must be checked – whoever did the wiring or rewiring – by the Installation Inspector at the area EB local office, who will make certain tests on the installation before it is connected to the mains. See also **Electricity**.

Embalmers Embalmers may practise in the UK without qualifications, but the recognised professional qualification is membership of the *British Institute of Embalmers* after successfully passing the examinations of the *National Examinations Board of Embalmers*. Embalmers are contracted through a funeral director. A list is maintained by the BEI by locations and names.
Complaints about professional misconduct should, in the first instance, be directed to the funeral director employing the embalmer but in the event of an unsatisfactory outcome then the National General Secretary of the BIE should be contacted.

Emigration For information on emigration to any country, write in the first instance to the appropriate diplomatic mission in the UK; see under relevant country entry.

Emigration: Exchange Control Emigrants, i.e. people leaving the United Kingdom to take up residence abroad for a period expected to be at least 3 years (see **Exchange control**), can take with them their household and personal effects, £1,100 per person for travelling expenses and any foreign securities, which they may hold. An emigrant family may also transfer to their new country of residence on departure up to £40,000 – or if it is a member country of the EEC £80,000 – of their sterling assets at the current official exchange rate; emigrants taking up employment in the EEC may be allowed additional funds if this is necessary to enable them to take up that employment.
Sterling assets in excess of the limits are subject to certain restrictions for four years from the date of redesignation, but may be made available by means of purchases of investment currency (see **Foreign currency securities**). In addition all emigrants, irrespective of age, may apply for releases from restricted funds if they face financial hardship caused by unforeseen difficulties after leaving the UK. Foreign nationals returning to their native country should apply for repatriation facilities which will, normally, enable them to transfer all their assets immediately at the current official exchange rates.
Consult an **authorised bank** (see **Exchange control**).

Employers' Grants Under the Youth Employment Subsidy employers receive a weekly subsidy of £10 for up to 26 weeks for each young person taken on who has been registered unemployed for six months or more; apply to the *Careers Office*, or *Employment Service Agency Employment Office* or *Employment Service Agency Job Centre*. Other grants are available for recruiting trainees and providing sandwich courses (see **Training: special grants**).
The Temporary Employment Subsidy provides employers in the private sector in Great Britain who defer impending redundancies affecting 10 or more full-time workers with a subsidy of £20 per week for 12 months for each job maintained. A subsidy supplement is sometimes available after 12 months. Details from *Department of Employment Regional Offices*, or *Department of Employment Unemployment Benefit Offices* or *Employment Service Agency Employment Offices* or *Employment Service Agency Job Centres*.

Employer's Insolvency Employees with certain debts owing to them (e.g. arrears of pay, holiday pay and payments in lieu of notice) can claim the amount due, within limits, from the Redundancy Fund (a central fund financed by employers' contributions). Apply to the insolvent employer's representative (e.g. the liquidator, trustee, receiver or official receiver). Complain to the *Industrial Tribunals Central Office*. Leaflet ITL1 and application form IT1 available from *Department of Employment Unemployment Benefit Offices* or *Employment Service Agency Job Centres* or *Employment Services Agency Employment Offices*.
See also **Bankruptcy**.

Employment Abroad Work permits are required in most countries, even for casual labour, and the *diplomatic missions* of the country in question should be consulted (see entry for each country). But in EEC member states, UK nationals resident in the UK are normally allowed to seek and take up employment without work permits; further information from *Department of Employment local offices*.

See also **EEC: work and residence; Employment abroad: developing countries; Employment abroad: international organisations; Employment abroad: voluntary service**.

Employment Abroad: Developing countries Two- or three-year-contracts for qualified professionals and experts are arranged at the request of overseas governments through the *Ministry of Overseas Development, Appointments Officer*. Almost half of the recruits work in education; the remainder in public works, communication, public administration, health, agriculture, industry and commerce, and social services.

See also **Employment abroad; Employment abroad: international organisations; Employment abroad: voluntary service**.

Employment Abroad: Exchange Control UK residents temporarily employed, i.e. for less than three years, anywhere outside the scheduled territories, i.e. the UK, including the Channel Islands, the Isle of Man, the Republic of Ireland and Gibraltar (see **Exchange control**), will continue to be treated as UK residents for the purposes of exchange control, but may normally have their salaries and allowances transferred abroad. People employed, or about to be employed, in the EEC may be allowed additional transfers (e.g. for accommodation) if they are necessary to enable them to take up or continue their employment. Special rules apply to civil servants and members of HM Forces working abroad for the UK Government and to staff of the United Nations and its agencies. See also **Emigration: exchange control**.

For further information, advice or help consult an **authorised bank** (see **Exchange control**).

Employment Abroad: Recruitment UK specialists employed abroad on work with official international organisations in developing countries are handled centrally in the UK by the *Ministry of Overseas Development, International Recruitment Unit*. Procedure can vary but generally the IRU circulates job specifications, and recommends UK candidates to international organisations which then make their own shortlist from candidates submitted by all countries. Final selection is done by the government of the developing country concerned.

Main recruiting organisations are: the United Nations (UN); the United Nations Educational, Scientific and Cultural Organisation (UNESCO); the United Nations Industrial Development Organisation (UNIDO); the International Labour Office (ILO); Food and Agriculture Organisation (FAO); World Bank (IBRD) and its associated organisations; the International Finance Corporation (IFC); the International Development Association (IDA); the Organisation for Economic Co-operation and Development (OECD); and the International Atomic Energy Agency (IAEA). The International Monetary Fund and the EEC are also occasionally assisted by the IRU.

Posts on the permanent staff of international organisations are allocated geographically and the IRU advises that career opportunities for British people are rare, except in the World Bank.

See also **Employment abroad; Employment abroad: developing countries; Employment abroad: voluntary service**.

Employment Abroad: Voluntary Service UK volunteers (only a few are not graduates or professionally or technically qualified) are sent at the request of overseas governments under the *British Volunteer Programme*. This is supported by the UK government, fund-raising organisations, foundations and industry and is operated by four voluntary organisations: the *Catholic Institute for International Relations*, the *International*

Voluntary Service, the *United Nations Association International Service* and *Voluntary Service Overseas*. Applications and enquiries direct to the organisations or to the BVP.
See also **Employment abroad**.

Employment Agencies These must be licensed annually (fee £72); apply to *Department of Employment Regional Offices*. Notices of application for a licence must be displayed on the premises concerned for three weeks, and advertised in a newspaper approved by the *Secretary of State for Employment*. To make representations against the granting of a licence write to the *DEm Regional Office*. In awarding a licence, the DEm considers the applicant, the premises and the conduct of the agency.

Employment: Complaints Individual conciliation in Great Britain is provided by the *Advisory, Conciliation and Arbitration Service* for complaints to **industrial tribunals**, even without an official complaint having been made concerning unfair dismissal, unequal pay, **sex discrimination, racial discrimination** and individual rights under the Employment Protection Act 1975.
See also **Dismissal**; **Employment: terms and conditions**.

Employment: Discipline Disciplinary practice and procedure in Great Britain is subject to a code of practice produced by the *Advisory, Conciliation and Arbitration Service*. Observance or otherwise of the code by employers is taken into account by **industrial tribunals** when adjudicating complaints against the employer. Code available from *Her Majesty's Stationery Office* or government bookshops.
See also **Employment: complaints**; **Employment: terms and conditions**.

Employment: Medical Suspension Employees suspended from work on medical grounds under health and safety regulations or codes of practice approved under the Health and Safety Work, etc., Act 1974 are entitled to receive normal pay for up to 26 weeks. In order to qualify, they must have worked for their employer continuously for at least four weeks and be physically capable of working. Details from *Department of Employment Unemployment Benefit Offices* or *Employment Service Agency Job Centres* or *Employment Service Agency Employment Offices* (explanatory leaflet ITL1 and application form IT1 also available); complaints to the *Industrial Tribunals' Central Office*; appeals against **industrial tribunal** findings, on a point of law only, to the *Employment Appeal Tribunal*.
See also **Employment: terms and conditions**; **Work: health and safety**.

Employment: Government Services The *Department of Employment* is the government department responsible for UK employment policy. *DEm Unemployment Benefit Offices* are responsible for the payment of **unemployment benefit** on behalf of the Department of Health and Social Security. *DEm Regional Offices* co-ordinate the work of local offices and administer the Wages Inspectorate and the Race Relations Advisory Service, and are also responsible for the supervision and inspection of the *Careers Service* provided by *local education authorities*. Manpower policy, public employment and training services are the responsibility of the *Manpower Services Commission* which operates through the *Employment Services Agency* (which runs employment offices, Job Centres and professional and executive recruitment to assist those seeking new employment), and the *Training Service Agency* (which runs Skill centres and various training schemes). Careers Offices are run by **local authorities** in association with the DEm to help school leavers.
See also **Jobs**; **Social security benefits**; **Unemployment: young people**; **Vacancies**.

Employment Research The *Department of Employment, Work Research Unit* assists organisations to take practical steps to increase the quality of working life for the mutual advantage of both employees and employers. Services are free.

See also **Employment: terms and conditions**.

Employment Rights: International Safeguards An industrial association of employers or of workers may make a representation to the International Labour Office, under Article 24 of its constitution, that any government has failed to secure in any respect the effective observance within its jurisdiction of any convention to which it is a party. The ILO may refer the representation to the government concerned asking for comments; and if none are received or they are unsatisfactory, may publish the representation and comments, if any. A delegate to the ILO Conference, who may be an individual worker or the representative of a workers' or employers' organisation, can file a complaint on the same grounds (Article 26) and the Governing Body may then appoint a Commission of Enquiry to consider the complaint. Enquiries to *Department of Employment, Overseas Division (ILO)*.
See also **Trade unions**.

Employment: Terms and Conditions An employer must normally give an employee written particulars of the terms of employment (i.e. names of employer and employee; date of commencement; job title; rate of pay or its basis of calculation; intervals of payment; hours of work; holiday entitlement; conditions relating to sickness or injury and pensions; minimum notice of termination; and disciplinary and grievance procedures). From 6 April 1978 he must inform employee whether a contracting-out certificate under the Social Security Pensions Act 1975 is in force for the employment in question.
He must also give an itemised pay statement giving amounts of gross and net wages, of deductions, and of net pay by each method of payment if more than one; certain payments for workless days (trade disputes excepted); special leave and pay for **maternity**, medical suspension, and **trade union** activities; time off for public duties (e.g. **jury service**); paid notice of termination of employment in accordance with a scale based on the length of employment.
Employees who think their employer disregards any of these provisions may complain to the *Industrial Tribunals Central Office* generally within three months; explanatory leaflet ITL1 and application form IT1 are available from *Employment Service Agency Job Centres*; *Employment Service Agency Employment Offices*; and *Department of Employment Unemployment Benefit Offices*. Appeals against industrial tribunal findings on a point of law only, should be made to the *Employment Appeal Tribunal*. Complaints that an employer is providing terms and conditions less favourable than those recognised as the general level of such terms may be made to the *Advisory, Conciliation and Arbitration Service*. If the complaint is not settled it may be referred to the *Central Arbitration Committee*.
See also **Dismissal; Employment: complaints; Industrial tribunals; Wages**.

Endangered Species Wildlife conservation licences are required for the import and export of certain wild animals and plants threatened with extinction as a result of commercial exploitation. This also applies to certain of their parts and derivatives. Licences are not normally granted for the import for commercial purposes of the very rare species, but may be given for other purposes such as breeding and exhibition. For the less endangered species, licences are granted readily, subject to certain conditions, the aim being to monitor the trade in case a more serious threat should develop. Licences are issued by the *Department of the Environment* and *Northern Ireland Department of Agriculture*, on the advice of three scientific authorities: the *Scientific Authority for Animals*; the *Royal Botanic Gardens, Kew*, which acts as a scientific authority for plants; and the *Nature Conservancy Council* which advises on general policy.
See also **Wild animals; Wild birds; Wild plants**.

Energy Conservation Programmes and projects are promoted regionally in

England by the *Department of Industry Regional Conservation Offices* and in Wales by the Industry Department of the *Welsh Office*; and for Great Britain as a whole by the Energy Conservation Unit at the *Department of Energy*, the aim of which is to stimulate, co-ordinate and review action on energy conservation policy in public and private sectors.

Quick advice to industrial and commercial businesses on energy economising from experts working under government contract is available (letter or telephone) through the *Department of Energy* (Energy Quick Advice Service).

Loans of up to £100,000 for repayment over a period of up to five years to finance industrial and commercial organisations' invesment in improvements in energy use, are available from the *Department of Energy* (Energy Saving Loan Scheme).

One-day surveys by fuel economy consultants are subsidised (50% up to a maximum of £30) by the *Department of Energy* (Energy Survey Scheme). Only non-domestic organisations qualify.

Energy Research Advice on the content of and on the opportunities to obtain contracts for participation in the research and development programmes of the European Communities and the International Energy Agency can be obtained from Chief Scientist Branch at the *Department of Energy*. The same Branch can also advise on domestic research and development work (except in atomic energy which is the responsibility of the *UK Atomic Energy Authority*).
See also **EEC**; **Research grants**.

Engineers There is no statutory registration of engineers in the UK governing the right to practise, but certain statutorily defined activities may only be undertaken by qualified engineers (e.g. management of mines and quarries, design and construction of high dams, operation and maintenance of ships and aircraft).

Professional standards are set by the *Council of Engineering Institutions* and its fifteen constituent institutions: *Royal Aeronautical Society*; *Institution of Chemical Engineers*; *Institution of Civil Engineers*; *Institution of Electrical Engineers*; *Institution of Electronic and Radio Engineers*; *Institute of Fuel*; *Institution of Gas Engineers*; *Institute of Marine Engineers*; *Institution of Mechanical Engineers*; *Institution of Mining Engineers*; *Institution of Mining and Metallurgy*; *Institution of Municipal Engineers*; *Royal Institution of Naval Architects*; *Institution of Production Engineers*; *Institution of Structural Engineers*.

The CEI's Engineering Registration Board registers chartered engineers (C Eng), technician engineers (T Eng (CEI)) and technicians (Tech (CEI)). Members of the 15 institutions who have passed the CEI examination (or hold an approved exempting qualification) and who have completed a period of practical training and responsible experience acceptable to CEI, qualify for registration as chartered engineers. Some institutions have additional requirements for election to corporate membership (apply direct to the institution). Chartered engineers are required to conform to a code of conduct promulgated by the CEI. Complaints about professional misconduct are investigated initially by the constituent association.

English Language Teaching The *British Council* co-operates with overseas ministries and education authorities in the development of English language teaching programmes, including teacher training, curriculum improvement and materials production. The BC provides a service in Britain and overseas for assessing the English proficiency of foreign speakers of the language. The BC's English Teaching Division provides advice and information on language learning, publishes periodicals and produces audio-visual materials. It can provide consultancy services in English language teaching ranging from initial appraisal to the design and implementation of a complete instructional programme.

Enquiries to: English Teaching Information Centre, at the *British Council* or the *British Council Overseas Office* in the country concerned.

Estate Agents and Surveyors Estate agents, valuers, auctioneers, surveyors and developers may all practise in the UK without qualifications, but professional standards are set by the *Incorporated Society of Valuers and Auctioneers* and the *Royal Institution of Chartered Surveyors*.
Basic qualifications for estate agents, valuers, auctioneers, developers and surveyors are determined by the examinations of the ISVA and RICS. Once the examinations have been passed, election to fellowship or associateship comes after a specified number of years of practice (FSVA/ASVA or FRICS/ARICS). Members are bonded. Both societies publish lists of members, and investigate complaints about possible professional misconduct.

Ethanol: Remission of Duty Ethanol, marked and denatured before delivery, may be used duty-free in the manufacture of perfumes and toilet preparations; apply to *Her Majesty's Customs and Excise*.
See also **Customs duty**; **Excise duty**.

Ethiopia For **exchange control** is a non-scheduled territory outside the **overseas sterling area** and the EEC. UK nationals travelling direct from the UK normally need only the following (but check): **passports**; **visas**; international certificates of **vaccination** against smallpox and yellow fever; **work permits** (if taking a job).
The UK has no reciprocal health or social security arrangements.
Enquiries to *Ethiopian Embassy* in London.
British diplomatic missions to Ethiopia are *British Embassy* and *British Consulate* in Addis Ababa.

Ethyl Alcohol: Control of Sale The Commissioners of Customs and Excise may permit the delivery of spirits (ethyl alcohol) for use in any art or manufacture without payment of **excise duty** where it is proved to their satisfaction that the use of **methylated spirits** is unsuitable or detrimental. **Customs duty** may, however, be payable on imported spirits. Apply to *Her Majesty's Customs and Excise*; details in Notices 47 and 58.

European Court The term usually refers to the *Court of Justice of the European Communities*. This court is available, when Community law is relevant, to the member states, to the institutions of the Communities, and to firms and individuals who are parties to proceedings before a national court or a party directly and individually effected by a Community act. It is the final interpreter of the law arising under the treaties establishing the European Communities.
See also **Company law and EEC**; **EEC**.

Euthanasia Euthanasia is not legal at present in the UK, nor does the medical profession accept it as desirable. The ethical aspects of euthanasia were the subject of a report published by the British Medical Association in 1971. This report affirmed the fundamental object of the medical profession as being the relief of suffering and the preservation of life; and concluded that it was right that dying patients could be relieved of suffering but that euthanasia could not be accepted by the medical profession. General enquiries to: *Home Office*.

Exchange Control All transactions involving foreign assets, **foreign currency** or interests, or **gold** bullion and all payments to persons resident abroad, even if the transactions are in sterling, are subject to exchange control, which is exercised by the *Bank of England* under powers delegated to it by the Treasury. For the purpose of exchange control, the terms 'abroad' and 'foreign' mean outside the scheduled territories, which at present comprise the UK, Channel Islands and Isle of Man, the Republic of Ireland and Gibraltar. Non-resident and external are terms in use with the same meaning. The Treasury has power to determine residential status, but as a general guide the country of residence is the country in which a person is currently living and has lived or intends to live for at least three years.

The aims of exchange control are to conserve Britain's gold and foreign currency resources, and to assist the balance of payments by controlling certain types of payments and by ensuring that funds due from abroad are promptly and properly received and are not used for any unauthorised purpose. The restrictions currently in force are mainly on transactions of a capital nature. Current payments, e.g. in the course of business or for travel or holidays, are not usually restricted, although they are supervised and may be subject to conditions. There are special concessions to help migrants to and from the UK; some transactions involving countries which are members of the **EEC** are subject to less stringent rules than similar transactions involving other foreign countries, and there are a few remaining concessionary rules in regard to transactions involving countries in the **overseas sterling area**. On the other hand the exchange control regulations in respect of transactions involving Rhodesian residents or Rhodesian assets are very restrictive because of the illegal declaration of independence. The Treasury has authorised the UK offices of many British and foreign commercial banks to execute a wide range of exchange control transactions on its behalf and to act as **authorised depositaries** for foreign currency securities. Such offices are known as **authorised banks**. More limited powers have been delegated to other authorised depositaries, such as **stockbrokers** and **solicitors**, in connection with transactions in securities; to travel agents in connection with travel; to two bullion brokers for transactions in gold; and to the *Comnissioners of Customs and Excise*, who also have in their own right certain powers concerned with the movement of goods and currency.

See also **Emigration: exchange control; Exporting; Immigration: exchange control**.

Excise Duty A tax chargeable on both UK imports and UK production of spirits (including perfumed spirits, wine, made-wine, beer, cider, perry, matches, mechanical lighters and hydrocarbon oils). It is generally payable on or before delivery of the dutiable produce for home use. Manufacturing, processing and storage prior to payment of duty is provided for by arrangements for licensed or registered premises or bonded warehousing and storage (see **Bonded warehouses**). Reliefs from excise duty include repayment of duty on certain goods exported (termed 'drawback'); for other reliefs see **methylated spirits; ethyl alcohol; ethanol; cider and perry; brewers; fuel; Royal Navy supplies**. Enquiries to *Her Majesty's Customs and Excise local office*; rates of duty and general information in 'Customs and Excise Tariff' from *Her Majety's Stationery Office*.

A special surcharge or rebate, the economic regulator, may be applied to certain excise duties. It is used as a means of regulating the balance between demand and resources in the UK. It is applied by Treasury order, up to a maximum of 10% of the rate last established by a Finance Act. Enquiries to HMCE; details in Notice 320.

See also **Customs duty**.

Exhibits: Import Duty Museums and galleries may be approved for importing exhibits or specimens into the UK without payment of **customs duty**. Apply for approval to *Her Majesty's Treasury*; details in Notice 361, from *Her Majesty's Customs and Excise*.

See also **National museums and galleries**.

Exhumation Removal of human remains from one burial place to another is an offence unless it is carried out with the authority of a licence, or in certain circumstances a Bishop's faculty. Licences (fee payable) are issued by the *Home Office*; each application is considered on its merits. Particular conditions may be attached to the licence, but the removal must always be effected with 'due care and attention to decency', and the body must be conveyed to a properly designated place.

See also **Burial and cremation; Death registration**.

Explosives: Control No person, except an agent for the Crown or a licensed owner of an explosives factory or magazine may legally acquire gunpowder or fuse without a police licence. Licences for the manufacture, storing, carrying and importing of explosives are granted by the *Home Secretary* and local authorities.
See also **Firearms control; Fireworks.**

Explosives: Safety Control of explosive and other highly reactive substances to meet EEC standards, and development of government policy on their classification, manufacture, importation, use and storage, is the responsibility of Hazardous Substances Branch A of the *Health and Safety Executive, Head Office.*
The *Health and Safety Executive, HM Explosives Inspectorate* issues licences for explosives factories, magazines and manufacture of ANFO explosives (Ammonium Nitrate in Fuel Oil); importation licences; special packing authorities (written authorities issued by inspectors, authorising packing of particular explosives for conveyance); and approval of acetylene cylinders and of sites using high pressure acetylene. It is also responsible for accident enquiries and gives specialist advice on the manufacture, packing, storage and conveyance of explosives.
See also **Transport: dangerous substances.**

Export and Import Training Courses
The customs entry clerks course, the *Institute of Freight Forwarders* induction course and the import office procedure course are provided free of charge in **assisted areas** and for nominal charges in other areas by the *Training Services Agency.*
See also **Training: special grants.**

Exporting Export licensing controls apply only to a very limited range of goods, while many facilities and aids for exporters from the UK are provided by central government departments and British banks. They include market information; marketing advice; advice on compliance with technical and legal requirements, documentation procedures and customs regulations; introductions to contacts abroad; overseas publicity; relaxation of **exchange control**; insurance and finance; and advice on the export of rights and technical and managerial advice, and on arrangements for manufacture under licence abroad.

Exporting: Aids from Government
Of the wide range of government information and services, some are free while others involve a contribution to costs. Services for exporters are under the general direction of the *British Overseas Trade Board.* Advice, information and assistance is available in London and the South-East from the Export Services and Promotions Division of the *Department of Trade* headquarters (3), and to exporters in the rest of the country through the *Department of Industry regional offices*, the *Scottish Economic Planning Department* in Glasgow, the *Welsh Office Industry Department* in Cardiff and the Export Services Branch of the *Northern Ireland Department of Commerce* in Belfast. General information in 'Export Handbook' available from BOTB. Services include help in identifying potential markets and demand for products in particular areas; identifying possible buyers, representatives and agents; assistance prior to visits overseas; reports on the commercial standing of potential agents; help in resolving disputes with overseas buyers; advice on technical and legal requirements; and help and advice on participation in overseas trade fairs.
Other public authorities largely concerned include the *Export Credit Guarantee Department* (insurance and finance); the *Bank of England* (exchange control); the *Foreign and Commonwealth Office* (personal contacts abroad); and the *Central Office of Information* and the *BBC Overseas Services* (world-wide publicity).

Exporting: Commercial disputes
The *British Overseas Trade Board* (in conjunction with commercial officers at *British diplomatic missions* abroad) can help to bring about amicable solutions to disputes between British

firms and overseas buyers; disputes subject to legal proceedings are excluded. Assistance may also be available from the *London Court of Arbitration of the London Chamber of Commerce and Industry* and the *City Corporation*, or the Tribunal of Arbitration of the *Manchester Chamber of Commerce and Industry*, or the Arbitration Committee of the *Bradford Chamber of Commerce*. The London and Manchester bodies also give practical advice on arbitration clauses in contracts.

Exporting: Contacts abroad The commercial departments of *British diplomatic missions* (embassies, high commission offices and consulates) advise British businessmen travelling abroad on export business about local conditions and trading methods, and arrange introductions to local officials and businessmen. Advance notice of visits should be given either direct to the British diplomatic mission or through the *Department of Trade Export Services and Promotions Division* or the export section of one of the *Department of Industry* offices. A great deal of useful information is available in advance from the Export Services and Promotions Division of the Department of Trade. Businessmen may have mail addressed to them care of the commercial department of the British diplomatic mission of the country they are visiting, but prior notice is necessary to the Department of Trade or Industry offices above.

Exporting: Documentation Apply to the Overseas Tariffs and Regulations Section of the *Department of Trade headquarters (3)* for documentation requirements for imports into overseas countries. For information and advice on documentation for exports required by UK customs and the special procedures which apply within the **EEC** under the **EEC Community Transfer System** (customs notices 750 to 756) apply to the International Customs Division at *Her Majesty's Customs and Excise*. Advice on export documentation in general may be obtained from chambers of commerce, shipping and forwarding agents, and banks.

The *Simplification of International Trade Procedures Board* (Sitpro) which is funded by the DoI, exists to rationalise international trade procedures and associated documentation. Sitpro is responsible for the UK's aligned export documentation system which can bring exporters major economies and improved efficiency in the completion of the paperwork required for export. Enquiries on the aligned system to Sitpro.

Certificates of origin may be required of UK exporters by certain overseas countries for particular goods. They are available from chambers of commerce authorised by the DoT; apply to DoT headquarters for list.

The Technical Help to Exporters service, which is sponsored by the *British Overseas Trade Board* and administered by the *British Standards Institution*, provides information, advice and assistance to British exporters on complying with overseas technical requirements.

Exporting: Exchange control Under Exchange Control regulations, payment for goods exported from the UK must normally be received in full within six months of shipment either in foreign currency (not Rhodesian) or in sterling from an account of a person or business resident abroad. Payment for exports over six months after shipment is permitted when the export is suitably insured with the *Export Credits Guarantee Department*. Otherwise special permission for longer credit must be obtained before the goods are exported. Exporters should apply to their bank. Exporters must offer foreign currency from export sales to an **authorised bank** immediately on receipt and keep evidence that full payment has been properly received for Her Majesty's Customs and Excise. A detailed leaflet is available from any bank or Collector of Customs and Excise.

Diamonds are subject to special controls; apply *Her Majesty's Customs and Excise GCC4*.

See also **Exchange control**.

Exporting: Export licences The Export Licensing Branch at the *Depart-*

ment of Trade headquarters (1) licences the following categories of exports under the Export of Goods (Control) Order 1970; security (military equipment, atomic energy materials and equipment, strategic items); conservation of supplies (including scrap metal); live animals; diamonds; antiques; cocoa and cocoa products; documentary and photographic material; and goods that might be exported to Rhodesia. Control of specific commodities may also be imposed at short notice. For current schedule of controlled goods and applications for licences, contact DoT headquarters (1).

Exporting: Financial assistance This is also provided to exporters through the *British Overseas Trade Board*. Apply to Fairs and Promotions Branch at the *Department of Trade headquarters (4)* for support for outward trade missions, participation in overseas trade promotions, seminars and symposia, and group export educational visits. Support for inward trade missions of overseas buyers and others in a position to influence them, and for approved export marketing research projects comes from the Special Export Services Branch of the *Department of Trade headquarters (3)*. Contributions (repayable if contract secured) towards the cost of a wide range of activities (excluding tender preparation) preceding the letting of main contracts for large projects overseas may be made by the Overseas Projects Fund; apply to Overseas Project Group at DoT headquarters (1); export trade revenue drawback and **value-added tax** reliefs are available; enquiries to *Her Majesty's Customs and Excise*.

Exporting: Insurance and finance This can be obtained from UK banks, often under schemes involving guarantees by the *Export Credit Guarantee Department*. These ECGD schemes take five main forms. Firstly, supplier credit is available to holders of a basic credit insurance guarantee from the ECGD, who can obtain finance at low rates under an additional unconditional guarantee given by ECGD to the bank providing the finance.

Secondly, with buyer credit schemes the ECGS may support loans for major projects and capital goods business made by banks direct to an overseas borrower: the bank makes its payments from the loan to the UK supplier on behalf of the overseas customer as work progresses and shipments are made.

Thirdly, the ECGD may guarantee lines of credit set up by UK banks to overseas borrowers to facilitate the placing of orders for British capital goods.

Fourthly, the ECGD gives up to 95% insurance cover to exporters against the risk of non-payment by an overseas customer caused by such reason as default, insolvency and political and economic changes. The service covers consumer goods, capital goods, services and constructional works.

Lastly, partial insurance against unexpected increases in UK costs can be arranged for major capital goods export contracts in excess of £2m which have a manufacturing period of at least two years.

Enquiries to *EGCD Regional Offices*.

Exporting: Manufacture under licence The *British Overseas Trade Board* can provide details of regulations affecting local manufacture and, in collaboration with Diplomatic Service commercial officers abroad, can help to identify possible overseas customers for know-how, or partners for agreements to manufacture under licence.

Exporting: Market information Market intelligence and research is available through the Export Intelligence Service of the *Department of Trade headquarters (3)*, which also provides help with overseas business visits; foreign samples; and information about the commercial standing of overseas traders. The DoT's Statistics and Market Intelligence Library at *Department of Trade headquarters (1)* makes available statistical and other published information for enquirers' own research. Special services for invisible exporters are described in 'Guide to Government Help for Invisible Exporters' from the *Committee on*

Invisible Exports. The European Components Service at DoT headquarters (3) seeks out export opportunities for UK engineering components in Western Europe. The Overseas Projects Group at DoT headquarters (1) arranges special forms of government support for contractors, manufacturers and others pursuing major contracts in connection with large projects overseas. Participation in overseas trade fairs and promotions may be arranged by the Fairs and Promotions Branch at *Department of Trade headquarters (4).* The *British Overseas Trade Board*'s computerised Export Intelligence Service supplies, on a paid subscription basis, details of specific export opportunities; market points and reports; calls for tender; manufacture-under-licence opportunities; changes in overseas tariff and import regulations, and other information.

Exporting: Publicity abroad Publicity overseas for British exporters can often be obtained through the facilities of the *Central Office of Information,* who are concerned with collecting from industry items suitable for dissemination abroad by way of Government information services. The COI are interested in news items, feature articles, tape recordings for broadcasting and films for television and other screenings. Further information may be obtained from COI, London, or the nearest COI Regional Office.

The *BBC* External Services broadcast throughout the world in English and 39 other languages. An important part of their output deals with developments in British industry, science and technology. New products and processes developed by firms in this country are featured prominently in news and other programmes, with the name of the manufacturer mentioned where appropriate. All enquiries reaching the BBC as a result of the broadcasts are passed on to the firms concerned.

The BBC External Services welcomes as much information as possible from industry. They are interested in new processes and products, export successes, contracts and exhibits at trade fairs abroad. Information should be sent to the *Export Liaison Managers* in London, or to the nearest BBC External Services Producer at any of the *BBC Regional Offices.*

Exporting: Registration for customs Exporters may register with *Her Majesty's Customs and Excise* under arrangements to ensure documentation of exports for statistical purposes. Registered exporters receive an assigned number which enables them to submit documentation within 14 days after the goods have been exported. If no customs-assigned number can be quoted then the goods must be entered for customs purposes before shipment. Apply HMCE.

Exporting: Treaties, regulations and procedures Information about commercial law, treaties and trade restrictions is available for the use of UK exporters from the Commercial Relations and Exports Division of the *Department of Trade headquarters (1).* Advice is also available on exporting to Communist countries; lists of Communist state trading organisations are available from the Export Services and Promotions at the DoT headquarters (3). Advice on exports to Japan is available from the Exports to Japan Unit at the *British Overseas Trade Board.* The Overseas Tariff and Regulations Section at DoT headquarters (3) and the BOTB can also provide precise and up-to-date information on the tariff and customs regulations of overseas countries and other legislation which affects the entry of British goods to overseas countries.

Information includes tariffs and customs regulations; import duties, licences and quotas; health regulations for livestock, meat, animal products, plants and seeds; consular invoices and fees; labelling and marking requirements; regulations concerning foodstuffs, drugs and pharmaceuticals and import of samples.

Extradition from the UK The UK has extradition treaties with a number of foreign countries and participates in the Commonwealth Scheme for the return of fugitive offenders, which

is embodied in parallel legislation in each country. One of the basic requirements of UK extradition law (apart from that dealing with the return of offenders to Eire (Irish Republic)) is that a prima facie case must be established by the requesting country. Among other conditions and safeguards is the application of the double criminality rule, which means that the alleged offence must be a criminal offence in the requested as well as the requesting country. Fugitives may not be extradited from the UK for a political offence. There is no prohibition in UK law on the extradition of nationals. If the courts decide that a fugitive should be extradited to a foreign or Commonwealth country, the final decision on his extradition then rests with the *Home Secretary*. If, however, the courts discharge the fugitive the Home Secretary may not overrule the decision.
See also **Criminal courts; Criminal justice; Deportation from the UK.**

Eye Donations   Eye donations are used to restore sight to blind people. Eyes for this purpose need to be removed without delay and preferably within six hours of death. Forms for signing by donors are available from the *Royal National Institute for the Blind*.
See also **Blindness; Blindness: aids; Blood donors; Kidney donations.**

Eye Treatment   Under the **National Health Service,** family **doctors,** child health clinics and the school health service may make the initial examination and referral of eye problems (free); the general ophthalmic services provide free sight-testing and the subsidised supply, replacement and repair of **spectacles**; the hospital eye service provides free specialist diagnosis and treatment.
The NHS general ophthalmic services are administered by local *Family Practitioner Committees*. These include representatives of ophthalmic medical practitioners (doctors who are qualified to test sight and to prescribe spectacles), ophthalmic opticians (who are qualified to test sight and prescribe, supply, replace and repair spectacles), dispensing opticians (who do not test sight or prescribe but supply spectacles to a prescription and replace or repair them). Lists of NHS ophthalmic medical practitioners and ophthalmic opticians are available at FPC offices and main post offices.
People who wish to have their eyes tested can go straight to an NHS ophthalmic medical practitioner or ophthalmic optician without a letter from their NHS family doctor, but if a person under 18 is found to need spectacles, their doctor must be told. Sight testing is normally free under the NHS but if the tester has to visit the person tested, a charge is made. If the sight tester finds a need for spectacles, he makes out a prescription which can be taken to any ophthalmic optician or dispensing optician.
For re-testing the patient again applies direct to any NHS ophthalmic medical practitioner or ophthalmic optician. Normally the interval between tests should be at least six months.

F

Factories Premises may be provided by the government for projects creating additional employment or, in some parts of the country, for re-housing an operation in the same general area when existing premises are unsuitable. Premises may be built in advance or to customers' specifications. The factory may be rent-free for the first two years of occupation when this is warranted by the number of jobs provided, but rents are otherwise based on current local market values. Any factory may be available for the purchase of a 99-year leasehold interest. Repayment of capital and interest can usually be spread over a period of up to 15 years at a fixed rate of interest. Leases may also include an option to purchase. Apply to *Department of Industry regional offices*; *Scottish Economic Planning Department*; *Welsh Office, Industry Department*; *Northern Ireland Department of Commerce*.

The day-to-day management of government factories is – according to location – the responsibility of the *English Industrial Estates Corporation*, the *Scottish Development Agency* or the *Welsh Development Agency*. The *Scottish Highlands and Islands Development Board* builds factories for lease to developers and has a programme of advance factory buildings.

Families on Low Incomes Certain families can receive many **social security benefits**, including **supplementary benefit** and **family income supplement** (if the head of the family is in full-time employment). Families receiving these last two are also entitled to exemption from **National Health Service** charges for dentures, dental treatment, glasses and prescriptions, and to free milk and vitamins. Families on low incomes who do not qualify for family income supplement or supplementary benefit may still be entitled to help with NHS charges and to free milk and vitamins if their income is only just above their requirements, judged broadly by supplementary benefit standards. Apply to *Department of Health and Social Security local office*; details in DHSS leaflet M11, also available from post offices. Grants for school clothing may be available from **local education authorities**, and help with the installation of a telephone, radio or television.

See also **Dental treatment**; **Eye treatment**.

Family Income Supplement The supplement is paid to people who work 30 hours a week or more, who have at least one dependent child and whose gross weekly income is below a certain level. The income level varies according to the number of children in the family and is currently £43.80 for a one-child family, increasing by £4.00 for each additional child. The supplement is equal to half the difference between the family's gross income and the prescribed amount, subject to a minimum of 20p and a maximum of £9.50 a week for a one-child family,

increasing by £1.00 for each additional child. Family income supplement is payable also to self-employed persons and gainfully employed single parents. Department of Health and Social Security leaflet FIS1 is available from post offices or *Department of Health and Social Security local offices*; claims should be sent to *Department of Health and Social Security (Family Income Supplements)*.
See also **Families on low incomes**; **Social security benefits**.

Fellowship Party Membership is open to UK and Australian nationals who are over 16, are not members of other political parties and who subscribe to the parties objects and principles which include non-violence and social justice. To join contact the *Fellowship Party Head Office*.

Fencing Fencing is governed worldwide by the Fédération Internationale d'Escrime. International fencing licences are obligatory for all international and national competitions. They are issued by the FIE through national federations. In the UK the governing body is the *Amateur Fencing Association*. It works closely with the *British Academy of Fencing* (the professional fencing masters' organisation). AFA organises national competitions and the training of amateur coaches and fencers, selects UK teams, advises on safety, etc. The *Scottish Amateur Fencing Union*, the *Welsh Amateur Fencing Union* and the *Northern Ireland Fencing Union* are affiliated to the AFA but act autonomously in their own region.

Fertilisers and Feeding Stuffs: Sale Certain prescribed information (e.g. of nutrient content) must be given in a statement (printed on either the container, and attached label, or an accompanying document) by every UK seller of these products. Purchasers have a right to have a sample analysed and certificated by an appointed Trading Standards Inspector. Name and address of nearest Inspector from local authority.

Festivals: Financial Support The *Arts Council of Great Britain* may subsidise arts festivals where these are of more than local importance. The subsidy, a guarantee against loss rather than an outright grant, is normally only given to festivals already supported by a local authority. The aim is to finance the staging of high-quality professional performances. *Regional Arts Associations* in England and Wales can also provide assistance for arts festivals.
In Scotland, the *Scottish Arts Council* subsidises the Edinburgh International Festival and also a number of smaller festivals including community arts festivals. In Wales, the *Welsh Arts Council* subsidises the Cardiff, Llandaff, Swansea, Vale of Glamorgan, Fishguard and North Wales festivals, as well as the Llangollen International Musical Eisteddfod and the Royal National Eisteddfod of Wales. In Northern Ireland, the *Arts Council of Northern Ireland* supports the annual Queen's University of Belfast Festival and arts festivals in provincial towns.
See also **Fine Arts: Financial support**; **Royal Academy of Art**

Field Sports The term covers a wide range of activities, each of which has its own governing organisation (see **hunting, shooting, coursing, angling**). General assistance and representation is provided by the umbrella organisation, the *British Field Sports Society*.

Fiji **Commonwealth** member. For **exchange control** is a non-scheduled territory in the **overseas sterling area** but outside the **EEC**. UK nationals travelling direct from the UK normally need only the following (but check): **passports**; **work permits** (if taking a job).
The UK has no reciprocal health or social security arrangements.
Enquiries to *Fiji High Commission* in London.
British diplomatic mission to Fiji is *British High Commission* in Suva.

Film Any person or group wishing to make an original, independent film can apply for a production grant to the Production Board of the *British Film Institute*. Films which conform to con-

ventional models or which might be expected to find backing elsewhere are not supported; nor are films which are primarily an extension of social work, i.e. purely educational or simply visual aids.
Production loans for commercial British films are made by the *National Film Finance Corporation*.
Subsidies for activities designed to increase the enjoyment and understanding of film and television (e.g. film exhibition, film workshops) and grants towards the capital costs associated with film exhibitions (i.e. buildings and equipment) and film centres are also available. Advice is taken from *Regional Arts Associations* in England, the *Scottish Film Council* in Scotland and the *Welsh Arts Council* in Wales.
See also **Film: Financial support; Film censorship; Film education.**

Film Archive The *British Film Institute*'s National Film Archive holds over 25,000 titles, including British and foreign feature and fiction films, short documentaries, newsreels, amateur films and television programmes. Viewing is at the BFI for researchers only. The BFI also makes a range of films available for non-theatrical and private viewing through its Film Availability Service.

Film: Financial Support The *Arts Council of Great Britain* provides financial support for professionally made documentary films on all arts subjects; financial support for avant-garde films and video made by artist film-makers or video-artists; material costs for professional artists, artist film makers and video artists; and support for avant-garde film festivals.
Regional Arts Associations can assist independent film and video projects in England and Wales. They are also increasingly concerned with promoting regional film culture with funds partly provided by the *British Film Institute*.
In Scotland, the *Scottish Arts Council* has funds for making films on artists, musicians, writers, etc., or films by artists. In Wales, the *Welsh Arts Council* grant-aids both professionally made documentary films on art subjects, and film and video makers whose projects explore and investigate the nature of the medium. The WAC also assists in the development of technical facilities by providing capital items of film and video equipment. In Northern Ireland, the *Arts Council of Northern Ireland* promotes tours of film programmes and supports independent film makers by grants and guarantees. Community video groups are grant-aided and given free access to the ACNIs pool of video equipment.

Film Censorship Public cinemas are licensed by the local authorities, which have a legal duty to control the content of films to which children under 16 are admitted, and to prohibit their entry to films which are designated as unsuitable for them. Local authorities also have the power (but not the duty) to control the content of films for adults. In practice most authorities only permit the showing of films, trailers or cinema advertisements which have first been seen by the film industry's independent censorship body, the *British Board of Film Censors*. Most authorities accept the BBFC's certificates for national distribution, although these have no force in law.
Legal powers of censorship rest entirely with the local authorities; they may refuse permission for a film with a BBFC certificate to be shown in their area or sanction the showing of a film to which the BBFC has refused a certificate. Similarly the authority may require additional cuts to those made by the BBFC, or restore parts of the original film excised by the BBFC.
The BBFC judges films in the light of intelligent contemporary public attitudes, and by the standards currently observed by other mass media. It also keeps in touch with standards abroad, although British law is in many ways more restrictive than that of other western nations. The BBFC may grant one of four certificates: 'X' – no one under 18 admitted; 'AA' – no one under 14 admitted; 'A' – anyone admitted but parents are advised that the film contains material they might prefer children under 14 not to see; and 'U' –

suitable for general exhibition without restriction.

The BBFC may issue a certificate conditional on certain cuts being made or it may refuse a certificate altogether. Where possible it offers film-makers the option of a more restrictive certificate as an alternative to cutting. There is no written code of standards, but the BBFC issues monthly reports giving reasons for its decisions and the precise quantity of footage cut. If a film is rejected, the film-maker may submit it to the Film Viewing Committee of a local authority, whose certificate enables the film to be shown in cinemas licensed by that authority. Occasionally the BBFC suggests to distributors that films be submitted to authorities first, particularly where the film may not be acceptable on a national basis, or where the BBFC feels it wrong to cut it to conform to national standards. If an authority rejects the film, the film company may appeal to the courts.

If a member of the public wishes to object to the exhibition of specific films, the proper procedure is to complain to the local authority, which has the power, unlike the BBFC, to order the withdrawal of the film or to prevent it being shown. The Criminal Law Act 1977 will bring the exhibition of films within the scope of the Obscene Publications Act, on essentially the same basis as publications and the theatre, so that prosecutions may only be brought by, or with the consent of, the *Attorney General*.

The *Home Office* issues model rules for cinema licensing. Private showings in film societies, film festivals and clubs are not subject to censorship but may be vulnerable to **prosecution** (disorderly house, conspiracy, etc.).

See also **Obscene publications**.

Film Education   Advice and information on the study of film and television – including curriculum and examinations at school, college and university – is available from the *British Film Institute* and the *Regional Arts Associations*. The BFI also subsidises the *British Universities Film Council*, the *Society for Education in Film and TV* and the *British Federation of Film Societies*.

See also **Film: Financial support**.

Film Levy   A levy is payable in respect of payments for admission to a cinema where one or more cinematograph films of a width exceeding 16 mm are being shown to the public, including any mixed performance at which cinematograph films both exceeding and not exceeding 16 mm are shown. The rate of levy is one ninth of the amount by which the payment for admission exceeds 12½p (after total advance weekly takings exceed £900). Exhibitors of such films are required to keep records of daily payments for admission at each price and make returns weekly to *Her Majesty's Customs and Excise*, details in HMCE Notice 111. Educational and children's entertainments are exempt; there are special provisions for charitable entertainments and entertainments in rural areas.

Filming in Streets   It is advisable to consult local police in advance. They have no power to authorise filming in the streets but they may object. In London the *Metropolitan Police Force* issues guidelines (e.g. no staged crime or street disturbance).

Fine Arts: Financial Support   In the field of fine arts (painting, sculpture, etc.) the *Arts Council of Great Britain* is largely concerned with the direct promotion of temporary art exhibitions and organising touring exhibitions. Permanent collections, with a few exceptions, are funded elsewhere. The AC presents exhibitions in London at its own Hayward and Serpentine Galleries and at other galleries in England. The Serpentine provides a platform for young and relatively unknown artists. Galleries and individuals are supported for exhibitions and other projects. Schemes, mainly for England, include bursaries and awards to individual professional artists and assistance towards the conversion of accommodation for artists' studios, and some funds may also be available for commissioned works of art in public buildings. Works of art can also be purchased for circulation in touring exhibitions or for long-term loan to art institutions and galleries.

The *Scottish Arts Council*, the *Arts Council of Northern Ireland* and the

Welsh Arts Council, in their regions, give grants to organisations to enable them to run galleries or workshops or to promote temporary exhibitions; hold exhibitions in their own galleries in Edinburgh, Belfast and Cardiff devoted primarily to works of contemporary artists; and support resident artists in all fields through purchases, commissions, competitions and award schemes.
Regional Arts Associations have a number of awards and schemes to assist, in the main, professional artists.

Fingerprints and Police Photographs
The *police* may take fingerprints of anyone aged over 10 for certain designated offences provided the person or the parents of someone under 17 give consent. In the event of a person refusing police may obtain an order from a magistrate to have fingerprints taken, provided the person is over 14 years. Fingerprints and other records are destroyed if a person is found not guilty.
A similar procedure with some variations applies in the matter of photographing persons charged with certain offences.
See also **Arrest and questioning of suspects**.

Finland For **exchange control** is a non-scheduled territory outside the **overseas sterling area** and the EEC. UK nationals travelling direct from the UK normally need only the following (but check): **passports; work permits** (if taking a job).
UK reciprocal arrangements cover social security (see leaflet SA19 obtainable from *Department of Health and Social Security, Overseas Group*) but not health.
Enquiries to *Finnish Embassy* in London or *Finnish Travel Information Centre* in London.
British diplomatic missions to Finland are *British Embassy* in Helsinki and *British Consulates* in six provincial centres.

Fire and Flammables at Work
Under the Health and Safety at Work Act, general UK policy on fire matters in industrial and work premises, the storage, use and disposal of flammable substances and liquids, and the storage of petroleum spirit is the responsibility of the Hazardous Substances Branch B at the *Health and Safety Executive Head Office*.
Technical advice on safety precautions for the storage and use of flammable substances is available from the *Health and Safety Executive, HM Factory Inspectorate Area Offices*.
See also **Fire safety; Work: health and safety**.

Fire Safety Fire certification is required under various Acts of Parliament by proprietors of hotels or boarding houses providing sleeping accommodation for more than six persons either above the first-floor, or below ground-floor levels; factories; and offices, shops and railway premises. The certificates list means of escape from the premises and related fire precautions. Apply to the Fire Prevention Officer at the Fire Department of the local authority (county council or Greater London Council).
A code of guidance on fire protection measures for holiday centres is available from the Fire Department at the *Home Office*.

Firearms The Firearms Act 1968 contains a series of graded controls over the acquisition, possession and use of firearms. In general, certificates to acquire, possess, or use most types of firearms must be obtained in advance from the chief officer of the local police.
A special authority from the *Home Secretary* or the *Secretary of State for Scotland* is required for the possession, acquisition, manufacture or sale of weapons classed as 'prohibited weapons'. These are continuous fire weapons (e.g. machine guns) and weapons designed for the discharge of noxious substances or articles.
Proofing of firearms or the testing of every firearm, except air weapons, is compulsory to ensure its safety before being first offered for sale. Enquiries to a gunmaker, *Proof House*, or *Birmingham Gun Barrel Proof House*. It is generally a criminal offence to sell or hire firearms to young people.
See also **Firearms: certificates**.

Firearms Certificates A firearms certificate (valid three years) from the police is required for the acquisition, possession or use of rifles, pistols, revolvers, specially dangerous air weapons, shot guns with barrels less than 24 inches long and for ammunition for those weapons. It is not issued unless the police are satisfied that the applicant has good reason for having it, is fit to be trusted with a firearm, and that public safety wil not be endangered. Conditions may be attached to the certificate (e.g. ammunition to be kept in a secure place except when in actual use).
Exemptions provide for antique firearms; possession of a weapon (for which someone else holds a certificate) in a theatrical or film production; approved rifle clubs and cadet corps; on board ship; for signalling purposes in an aircraft or aerodrome; for use in starting races; or as a gun bearer for someone using firearms for sporting purposes.
A shotgun certificate (valid three years) or Northern Ireland firearms certificate is required for smooth-bore guns with a barrel not less than 24 inches long which are not air guns. The police may refuse to grant a certificate if they consider that public safety or the peace would be endangered or if the applicant is prohibited under the Firearms Act from possessing firearms of any kind. Exemptions are as above, with provision for borrowing and use on private premises; use for target practice under arrangements approved by the police; and for visitors to Great Britain from abroad for not more than 30 days in any 12 months.
Air weapons (apart from those classified as specially dangerous) are not subject to certificate control, although there are general restrictions on their purchase, possession and use by persons under 17.
Dealers in firearms require a dealer's certificate (renewable annually on 31 May).
Appeal against refusal of a certificate in England and Wales to the crown court, and in Scotland to the sheriff court. A leaflet on 'Firearms – what you need to know about the law' is available from the *Home Office*.

Fireworks The 'Firework Code' has been prepared by the Firework Makers' Guild with the co-operation of the National Society for the Prevention of Cruelty to Children, the Royal Society for the Prevention of Accidents and the Royal Society for the Prevention of Cruelty to Animals. Members of the Guild place a copy of the Code in every boxed set of fireworks they manufacture and further copies are available, free of charge, from any shop selling fireworks. Its main points are: keep fireworks in a closed box; follow the instructions on each firework carefully; light fireworks at arm's length; stand well back; never return to a firework once lit; never throw fireworks; never put fireworks in your pockets; keep pets indoors; never fool with fireworks.
The Explosives (Age of Purchase) Act 1976 prohibits the sale of fireworks to anyone apparently under the age of 16; maximum penalty for this and for letting off fireworks in the street or a public place is £200.
Under agreements between the *Department of Prices and Consumer Protection* and the firework trade (manufacturers, wholesalers and retailers) the more dangerous types of firework – helicopters and flyabouts – have been phased out of production, the production of bangers has been considerably reduced and most fireworks are sold in ready-boxed selections: fireworks are generally available in shops only three weeks before 5 November and for a few days afterwards.
A leaflet giving detailed guidance on the organisation of firework displays is available from local authorities or the DPCP.

Fish: Freshwater Importation into the UK of live fish of the salmon family (including trout) is prohibited. Importation of live freshwater fish, or live eggs of the salmon family or of freshwater fish (including tropical fish), must be licensed. A certificate of health, based on results of tests over a specified period, must be produced for all ova and certain species of coldwater fish before a licence can be issued. Information on imports into England and Wales from Fisheries Division I at the

Ministry of Agriculture, Fisheries and Food, Headquarters (2); for Scotland the *Department of Agriculture and Fisheries for Scotland*.
To prevent the spread of certain notifiable fish diseases, restrictions are placed on the movement of fish, fish eggs or foodstuffs for fish from any location in England and Wales where evidence of the diseases is established. Details in England and Wales from MAFF Fisheries Division I.
In all cases of disease the consent of MAFF and the approval of the regional *Water Authority* receiving the consignment must be obtained before the diseased fish is moved.
See also **Agriculture: Scotland; Agriculture: Northern Ireland.**

Fish Producers Under EEC regulations an EEC country can approve fish producers' organisations whose role is to ensure that fishing is carried out along rational lines and that conditions for the sale of members' produce are improved. There are currently nine such organisations in the UK. They are eligible for financial support in their first three years of operation, and may claim compensation for fish which was offered for sale for human consumption in accordance with EEC rules and which failed to find a buyer. Details from Fisheries Division II at the *Ministry of Agriculture, Fisheries and Food Headquarters (2)* in England and Wales, or the *Department of Agriculture and Fisheries for Scotland* or the *Department of Agriculture for Northern Ireland*.

Fish: Research and Development The main centres of research and development are the fisheries laboratories of the *Ministry of Agriculture, Fisheries and Food*, the *Department of Agriculture and Fisheries for Scotland*, the *White Fish Authority* and the *Herring Industry Board*. Details of research and development are in the MAFF *Torry Research Station*'s advisory note No. 70.
Licences to take immature (undersized) seafish for scientific investigation are issued by the Fisheries Division 111B at the *Ministry of Agriculture, Fisheries and Food, Headquarters (2)*.

Fishing Harbours Grants and loans for construction, improvement or repair are available from Fisheries Division IIA at the *Ministry of Agriculture, Fisheries and Food, Headquarters (2)* in England and Wales.
See also **Agriculture: Scotland; Agriculture: Northern Ireland.**

Fishing Vessels Government grants and loans for either construction or improvement of fishing vessels are administered by the *White Fish Authority* and *Herring Industry Board*. Rates of grant are currently 25% of approved cost; loans of up to 50% of approved cost are only available for fishing vessels not exceeding 100 gross registered tonnage.
Fishing vessels must be registered with the Registrars of *Her Majesty's Customs and Excise* or, in Scotland, with fishery officers of the *Department of Agriculture and Fisheries for Scotland*. Safety regulations cover construction, safety equipment, stability, etc. Enquiries to *Department of Trade* (Marine Division).
See also **Shipping registration.**

Flags The Blue Ensign is flown by government-owned ships. Merchant ships may fly it when the Master is an officer on the retired or emergency lists of the Royal Navy or of a Commonwealth navy, or on the active or retired lists of the reserves of these navies. The Master must have a warrant from the *Ministry of Defence, Naval Law Division*.
Certain **yachts** may wear the Ensign, but the owner must be a member of a yacht club listed in the Navy List and hold a Ministry of Defence warrant issued through the club.

Flooding and Land Drainage *Water authorities* exercise a general supervision over all matters relating to land drainage in their area, as well as controlling main rivers and maintaining defence works against flooding from the sea.
See also **Water services.**

Flower and Vegetable Trials Trials are held at the *Royal Horticultural*

Society's Garden, Wisley, to evaluate plants, compare stocks of different cultivars, facilitate the formation of classification systems based on horticultural characteristics such as habit, vigour, time of flowering, and also on botanical characteristics. Permanent trials include asters, michaelmas daisies, border carnations, dahlias, delphiniums, early-flowering chrysanthemums, hemerocallis, irises, narcissi, pinks and sweet peas. Invited trials are ones where RHS Fellows, horticultural traders and the public are invited to send specified seed or plants. The results of trials are published in the journal of the RHS.
See also **Horticultural crops; Royal Horticultural Society**.

Flying   Flying as a sport comes under the international control of the Fédération Aeronautique Internationale. The UK representative on the FAI is the *Royal Aero Club*, but the Club has delegated control of all powered flying activities to the *Aircraft Owners and Pilots Association*. AOPA's members are owners and operators of private light aircraft, flying clubs, schools and instructors. It is responsible on a delegated basis for aspects of training. AOPA also organises competitions and events, and issues competition licences to pilots for national and international aeronautical competitions.

Flying: Private Pilots' Licences People flying privately (i.e. not for hire or reward) as co-pilots or pilots-in-command in UK aircraft must hold a private pilot's licence from the *Civil Aviation Authority, Flight Crew Licensing*. The CAA sets standards and requirements for the basic licence and associated ratings (e.g. night rating, instrument rating, aircraft group rating); details of minimum hours flying experience, training, tests and examinations in CAP53 from the *Civil Aviation Authority, Printing and Publications Services*.
For private pilot's licences, aircraft are classed in three groups: group A – single engined aircraft up to 5,700 kg maximum total weight authorised; group B – multi-engined up to 5,700 kg; group C – any aircraft over 5,700 kg. Tests and ground examinations are conducted at flying schools and clubs by instructors who are CAA-authorised examiners. Tests and courses for instructor rating are delegated to the *Aircraft Owners and Pilots Association*.
See also **Air pilots and air navigators**.

Flying: Professional Licences   The *Civil Aviation Authority* issues all UK flight crew licences, which must be held by pilots, flight engineers and flight navigators of British-registered aircraft engaged in commercial operations. Licence holders must have an appropriate aircraft 'type rating' for every type of aeroplane, helicopter or gyroplane which they fly professionally. This is obtained by passing a flight test on the appropriate aircraft, conducted by a CAA-authorised examiner, and passing a technical examination, conducted by the *Civil Aviation Authority, Airworthiness Division*.
Details of general requirements for the grant of a licence, examinations, flight tests and flying schools from *Civil Aviation Authority, Printing and Publications Services*. If you have previous flying experience, apply to *Civil Aviation Authority, Flight Crew Licensing* which will notify you of the extra requirements you need to qualify (e.g. courses of further flying and ground training at CAA-approved schools).

Food Additives   All additives permitted for use in food are controlled either by specific regulations under the Food and Drugs Acts 1955, or by the general provisions of the Acts. The system of control is based on two criteria: need, and safety in use. Regulations are made by the Minister of Agriculture, Fisheries and Food acting jointly with the Secretary of State for Social Services. Enquiries to Food Additives Branch of the Food Standards Division at the *Ministry of Agriculture, Fisheries and Food, Headquarters (2)*.

Food: EEC Intervention   Under EEC agricultural policy, if the UK market price of certain agricultural commodities falls below a given level, the *Intervention Board for Agricultural*

Produce buys the commodity at the EEC intervention price and later sells the commodities at EEC release prices. Details of price levels and commodities within Europe from IBAP.
Certificates of entitlement to buy beef and butter at prices below current market rates are issued by IBAP to non profit-making bodies.
Mobilisation contracts for food from intervention stocks to go to overseas development assistance are awarded by IBAP.
See also **Agricultural produce: EEC subsidies; Food: import and export.**

Food: Import and Export The *Intervention Board for Agricultural Produce* is responsible, in collaboration with *Her Majesty's Customs and Excise*, for administering EEC regulations relating to the import and export of a wide range of agricultural products and goods manufactured therefrom. IBAP functions include the issue of licences, the payment of export refunds, the collection of export levies, and the application of Monetary Compensatory Amounts (resulting from the 'green pound' arrangements) which are levied on exports and granted on imports. HMCE collect levies on imports.
See also **Agricultural produce: EEC subsidies; Food: EEC intervention.**

Football Football is organised worldwide by the Fédération International de Football Association and in Europe by the subsidiary Union Européenne de Football Association. These bodies recognise in each country a football association as the governing body of the game in that country. In the UK there are four national associations: the *Football Association* (England), the *Football Association of Wales*, the *Scottish Football Association*, and the *Irish Football Association* (Northern Ireland). These associations have permanent representation on the International Board which lays down the laws of the game.
In England the FA is responsible for the administration of both the professional and amateur game. Its specific responsibilities include discipline, rule-making, organisation of the annual (knock-out) FA Challenge Cup Competition, sanction of leagues and competitions and selecting and running international and representative teams. The other British FAs carry out similar functions.
The most important league in England and Wales is the Football League, to which belong 92 clubs, with mainly professional players, organised into four divisions. The *Football League Ltd* controls the annual League Championship for the four divisions and the Football League Cup Competition; it organises fixtures, provides referees for matches, and insures players, club properties, etc. The FA and the FL work closely together. Although there are 37,000 clubs outside the League, the winners of the FA Cup and all international players are invariably drawn from League clubs. Both bodies negotiate with the *Professional Footballers' Association*.
There is a *Scottish Football League*, organised in three divisions with 38 clubs, and a Scottish League Cup competition.
Women's football is governed in England and Wales by the *Women's Football Association*, in Scotland by the *Scottish Women's Football Association* and in Northern Ireland by the *Northern Ireland Women's Football Association*. The women's associations are autonomous – controlling their own leagues, international teams, national competitions and discipline – but follow the rules and regulations of the FA, the FA of Wales and the Scottish and Irish FA, and so abide by the international rulings of FIFA and UEFA.
In England and Wales the women have joint consultative committees with the FAs, and all women's matches with foreign opponents are cleared by the FAs.

Football Pools The Betting, Gaming and Lotteries Act 1963 requires a pool promoter to register with appropriate local authority, which in turn is responsible for the appointment of an accountant to whom the promoters are required to submit their rules and detailed accounts.
See also **Betting businesses; Betting duty.**

Football Pools: Charity Pool competitions conducted for the benefit of charitable or other societies are promoted under the provisions of the Pool Competitions Act 1971 – as extended by the Pool Competitions Act (Continuance) Order 1977. In order to promote competitions under the Act registered pool promoters must satisfy the *Gaming Board for Great Britain* that, amongst other things, they had held at least nine pool competitions in the period of 12 months ending with 24 November 1970. Enquiries to GBGB.
See also **Pool betting duty; Pool betting permits.**

Footpaths, Bridleways and Rights of Way The creation, diversion or closure, and the maintenance and recording of public footpaths and other public rights of way is the responsibility of the Highways Departments of local authorities.
The *Countryside Commission* plans and finances continuous rights of way for long journeys on foot, or in some cases on horseback or bicycle, throughout England and Wales. Nine of these long distance routes are complete, the longest (250 miles) being the Pennine Way. The acorn symbol is the long distance route mark. The CC awards grants to private and public landowners for the expenditure involved in creating recreation paths out of existing rights of way in the countryside.
In Scotland a long distance route from Glasgow to Fort William (the West Highlands Way) has been approved but is not yet officially open; enquiries about this and other routes in Scotland under consideration to the *Countryside Commission for Scotland*. Many established paths are also being signposted by the *Scottish Rights of Way Society*.
See also **Commons and open spaces; Public rights of way.**

Foreign Borrowing UK residents, other than **authorised banks** (see **Exchange control**) require permission from the *Bank of England* to borrow foreign currency except from authorised banks, which are subject to Bank of England directions in regard to such lending. UK residents also require Bank of England permission to pay interest or repay capital in foreign currency. In practice permission for foreign currency borrowing is normally given if repayment is not called for within two years or is likely to be covered by the proceeds of exports and provided that the foreign currency, if not needed to meet payments to non-residents, for which permission has been given, is at once sold to an authorised bank at the official exchange rate. The payment of interest on such loans is allowed if the rate is reasonable.
Borrowing in sterling from a person resident abroad is also in practice subject to exchange control, because repayment and payment of interest are so subject, even though the loan itself may not always be. Criteria for permission are much the same as for foreign currency loans, though the definition of a reasonable rate of interest is somewhat stricter.
Special regulations apply to foreign currency borrowing for investment abroad and sterling borrowing by UK companies controlled by non-residents (see **Direct investment: exchange control**).
For further information, advice or help apply to an authorised bank.
See also **Emigration: exchange control; Exporting; Foreign currency and credit.**

Foreign Currency and Credit Residents of the UK may buy foreign currency only for purposes approved by the *Bank of England*, and in general only from an **authorised bank** and at the official exchange rate, although certain travel agents have been authorised to issue foreign currency for travel expenditure, and **authorised depositaries**, including authorised banks, may acquire '**investment currency**' for the purchase of foreign currency securities. Any foreign currency, including balances, notes and travellers cheques, owned or acquired by UK residents must be promptly offered to an authorised bank at the official exchange rate unless permission for its retention or use has been obtained.
UK residents cannot usually open or operate foreign currency accounts with banks or other organisations abroad.

Temporary accounts for travel funds, however, may be permitted on application to an authorised bank, while firms with trading interests abroad can normally obtain permission to operate retained accounts, as can persons with sources of income abroad and with regular commitments to meet of a type for which permission for a remittance from the UK would be granted.

Sterling funds held by non-UK residents are freely convertible into **gold** or foreign currencies. Only authorised banks may open or operate accounts for non-residents without permission from the Bank of England.

For further information or help, consult an authorised bank (see **Exchange control**).

See also **Direct investment: exchange control; Exporting; Foreign borrowing; Emigration: exchange control; Immigration: exchange control; Imports: exchange control; Investment: exchange control; Payments abroad.**

Foreign Currency Securities Such securities, if owned by UK residents (whether in bearer or registered form) are generally required to be deposited with or, if kept abroad, to be held under the control of, an **authorised depositary**. All such securities owned by non-residents, where the documents of title are kept in the UK, are required to be held by an authorised depositary. Purchases and sales, etc., of all foreign currency securities in the UK must be controlled by an authorised depositary. UK residents may not purchase foreign currency securities with currency purchased at the official market rate of exchange; payment must be made with '**investment currency**', i.e. with foreign currency originating mainly from the sale of foreign currency securities owned by other residents of the UK. This normally changes hands at a premium which accrues to the sellers.

The *Bank of England* considers applications from professional managers of securities to borrow foreign currency (or to arrange for such borrowing on behalf of resident clients) from UK banks or non-residents to finance portfolio investment in foreign currency securities. The conditions governing such borrowing and its repayment are complex but are specially favourable for the purchase of securities issued by EEC institutions. Foreign currency securities acquired by UK residents other than by purchase, e.g. by legacy or gift from non-resident sources, are required to be held by authorised depositaries in 'restricted deposit'. When sold, permission from the BE is required; this is normally given provided that the sale does not allow the owner to benefit from the investment currency premium. There are certain concessions for migrants, i.e. persons changing their residential status.

See also **Emigration: exchange control; Exchange control; Immigration: exchange control.**

Foreign Decorations and Medals British subjects must obtain the Queen's permission to accept or wear the insignia of any foreign order. Full and unrestricted permission is generally given only in the case of decorations earned by services in the salaried employment of the foreign government concerned, by distinguished service in saving life, or by certain honorary consular services. Crown servants are not generally eligible for permission. In other cirumstances restricted permission may be granted. Apply in first instance to the *Foreign and Commonwealth Office* (Protocol Department).

See also **Gallantry awards: civil; Gallantry awards: military.**

Foreign Exchange Market The London market is the largest in the world. It is operated by telephone and telex between some 265 **authorised banks** and 15 foreign exchange and deposit brokers. The market in Eurodollars (and other 'Euro' currencies), which now exists in a number of countries, is centred in London. The market operates within a framework of rules agreed between the *British Bankers' Association* and the *Foreign Exchange and Currency Deposit Bankers' Association*, and within the **exchange control** regulations which are administered by the *Bank of England*. To buy or sell foreign exchange, consult an authorised bank.

Foreshore and Seabed: Ownership
The foreshore is that part of the seashore which in England, Wales and Northern Ireland lies between mean high and mean low water; and in Scotland between mean high and mean low water of spring tides. Much of the forshore around the coasts of the UK and in tidal rivers is owned by the Crown. Exceptions are the foreshores of Cornwall and Lancashire which are owned by the *Duchy of Cornwall* and the *Duchy of Lancaster* respectively and in some major estuaries where grants have been made to certain individuals and bodies.
Leases and licences (e.g. yacht club jetty, dredging, etc.) are granted by the Duchies of Cornwall and Lancaster and by the *Crown Estate Office*. Most of the seabed lying below mean low water out to territorial water limits, including that off Cornwall and Lancashire, is Crown property. Rights exercisable in the UK continental shelf, other than those in respect of coal, oil and gas, are also vested in the Crown.
See also **Boundaries; Construction work in tidal waters.**

Forestry Planting: Grants Under the Forestry Commission Basis III Dedication Scheme, woodland owners receive £100 per hectare for approved planting or replanting of forest trees and for undertaking to manage the woodlands in accordance with agreed plans and regular inspections. Planting of broadleaved trees and of caledonia pine in approved areas attracts a grant of £225 per hectare.
Other FC grants are for rehabilitation of existing woodlands, particularly broadleaved; and a management grant of £3 per hectare payable quinquennially for conifers under 25 years of age and broadleaves under 50. Minimum area eligible is normally 10 hectares but under the Small Woods Scheme there are grants for planting 0.25 to 10 hectares of broadleaves in lowlands. The FC consults local planning authorities and agricultural departments about the woodland owner's proposals. Apply to *Forestry Commission, Conservator of Forests,* for grants and free advice.
In Northern Ireland, under the Planting and Maintenance of Woodlands Scheme, the *Department of Agriculture for Northern Ireland, Forest Service* aids landowners to grow plantations for the production of commercial timber. A maximum grant of £112.50 per hectare, payable in instalments, is available to landowners who plant or replant and maintain approved areas of at least one hectare. In conjunction with this is the Scrub Clearance Scheme: a grant of £25 per hectare is given when the net cost of clearing unproductive scrub, prior to planting, is at least £50. Under the 500 Tree Scheme a minimum of 500 plants per order can be purchased for planting of areas of less than one hectare.
Grants for tree planting for amenity purposes are available from the *Countryside Commission for England and Wales,* the *Countryside Commission for Scotland,* the *Department of Agriculture for Northern Ireland, Forest Service* and some local authorities and for shelterbelts from the *Ministry of Agriculture Fisheries and Food* under the Farm and Horticultural Capital Grant Scheme and development regulations.

Fostering: Local Authorities Fostering of children in the care of **local authorities** is the responsibility of the authority concerned. Authorities welcome applications from people wishing to become foster parents for children in their care and will discuss all the implications with them. The prior investigation of prospective foster parents, their home and their household, as well as the continuing supervision of the foster child when placed in a foster home, are governed by statutory regulations which also prescribe the frequency of visits by social workers, and medical examinations of the child according to the age of the child and length of stay in the foster home.
They also prescribe the fostering records to be kept by the local authority, which include the case record of the child and a register of all children boarded in the local authority's area whether by the authority, other authorities or voluntary organisations. Foster parents are required to sign an undertaking agreeing to care for the child as a

member of their own family and to allow the local authority to remove the child if and when this becomes necessary.
Allowances are payable to local authority foster parents. Most authorities pay basic rates according to the child's age and these either include or are supplemented by provision for clothing, pocket money for the child, holidays, etc. Many authorities pay enhanced allowances for the difficult or disruptive child whose care makes heavier than normal demands upon the foster parents and who could not otherwise be fostered.
See also **Child care and welfare; Child health services.**

Fostering: Private Local authorities (Social Services Departments) must be satisfied of the well-being of children in their area whose care and maintenance is undertaken for more than six days by persons who are not relatives or guardians (27 days in some cases), and have powers to prohibit, or impose conditions on, the keeping of such foster children. Prospective foster parents are required by law to notify local authorities (Social Services Departments) of their intention to foster a child privately. Before a child is boarded with them, a local authority officer must visit them to ensure that they, their home and other members of the household are all suitable.
Scotland has a different system; information from *Scottish Information Office.*
See also **Child care and welfare.**

Foundlings The birth in England or Wales of an abandoned child whose date and place of birth are unknown may be registered in the Abandoned Children Register of the *Registrar General of England and Wales* and an ordinary short birth certificate issued, provided that the child has not been adopted; that the RG is satisfied that the birth was not outside England or Wales; and the birth is not known to have been previously registered, other than as a foundling. Application for a certificate for abandoned children now over 18 must be made to the RG by the abandoned persons themselves.

In Scotland, unless the precise place of birth is known, the birth is registered in the register of births for the registration district in which the child is found with the Director of Social Work for the area as informant. The birth may be re-registered if later evidence makes possible an entry omitting that the child was a foundling.
Similarly in Northern Ireland where any living infant child is found exposed and the birth is not know to have been previously registered, the birth is registered in the ordinary birth register.
See **Birth Registration** for procedures.

France EEC member. For **exchange control** is a non-scheduled territory in the EEC but outside the overseas sterling area.
UK nationals travelling direct from the UK normally need only the following (but check): **passports** (British visitors' passports are acceptable).
EEC or bilateral social security arrangements are applicable; leaflets and EEC Guides obtainable from *Department of Health and Social Security, Overseas Branch.* Apply to local social security office for leaflet SA28 which explains who is entitled to reduced-cost medical treatment under EEC health arrangements and how to get a certificate of entitlement (form E111).
Enquiries to *French Embassy* in London, *French Government Tourist Office* in London, *French Consulates-General* in Edinburgh and Liverpool, *French Consulates* in Belfast, Cardiff and Jersey, *French Consular Agents* in Folkestone and Liverpool and a *French Commercial Section* in Manchester.
British diplomatic missions to France are *British Embassy* in Paris, *British Consulates-General* in Bordeaux, Lille, Lyons, Marseilles, Pau and Strasbourg, and *British Consulates* or *Vice-Consulates* in ten provincial centres, French Guiana and Martinique.

Franking Machines Authority to use a postal franking machine must be obtained in advance from the *Post Office, (Head Postmaster/District Postmaster).* Machines may be leased or purchased from PO-authorised suppliers. The **Post Office Guide** lists suppliers, etc.

Fuel Heavy oil (i.e. gas oil) used as a fuel for vehicles which are not used on public roads and are not licensed for road use qualifies for a rebate of **excise duty**. Such oil must be dyed red and chemically marked. Other vehicles which qualify are road rollers; road construction machinery; vehicles exempted from licence duty which use public roads for distances not exceeding six miles per calendar week; agricultural machines, including snow ploughs; trench digging and excavating machines; mobile cranes; mowing machines; and work trucks. Further details from section RDD3 at *Her Majesty's Customs and Excise* and in HMCE Notice 75.

Other reliefs from excise duty on hydrocarbon oil (petrol and diesel) are available for growers of horticultural produce (HMCE Notice 183); use on **fishing vessels** and lifeboats (Notice 248); use as fuel in ships and **hovercraft** in home waters (Notice 263); use in certain industrial processes (Notice 184A); light oil for use as furnace fuel (Notice 184A); drawback on export (Notice 172).

See also **Motor vehicle excise licences**.

Funfares There is provision for the independent inspection and certification of all fairground devices, covering structural, mechanical and electrical safety. Enquiries to the *Home Office*.

A guide to safety at pleasure fairs is published by *Her Majesty's Stationery Office*.

Further Education Further education is the term used to cover all post-school education outside the **universities**. In the state education system it covers full- and part-time education for people over 16 (including cultural training and recreational activities). It thus comprises a wide range of institutions, including **polytechnics**, colleges of technology, technical colleges, colleges of art, agriculture or commerce and evening institutes, and an even wider range of courses, from **General Certificate of Education 'O'** levels to *Council for National Academic Awards* research degrees.

Students should apply direct to the institution; there is no central clearing house. Enquiries throughout most of the year to the *local education authority* (Further Education Department) in England and Wales. During August, September and October the *Further Education Information Service*, run by the *Department of Education and Science* (England and Wales) provides up-to-date information on vacancies in further education institutions, especially for those whose GCE 'A' levels were better or worse than expected and who are thus seeking a new place at a late date. The FEIS will also advise students about re-taking examinations etc. To locate a FEIS local advisory officer, ask a careers teacher, careers officer, student adviser or local education authority.

Independent further education establishments may apply to the DES for recognition as efficient. To obtain recognition involves an inspection by Her Majesty's inspectors, who concentrate on standards of education of full-time work, student welfare and premises. Courses must be broadly comparable with local education authority courses and the institution must have had a stable existence for not less than two to three years. After recognition the institution must be open to inspection by HMIs at all times.

Arrangements in Scotland and Northern Ireland are similar in principle but differ administratively.

See also **Education: Scotland; Education: Northern Ireland; Student grants**.

G

Gabon For **exchange control** is a non-scheduled territory outside the **overseas sterling area** and the **EEC**. UK nationals travelling direct from the UK normally need only the following (but check): **passports; visas;** international certificates of **vaccination** against smallpox; **work permits** (if taking a job); green cards for motor insurance (if bringing a car); international driving permits (if intending to drive: see **Motoring abroad**).
The UK has no reciprocal health or social security arrangements.
Enquiries to *Gabon Embassy* in London.
British diplomatic mission to Gabon is *British Embassy* in Libreville.

Gallantry Awards: Civil Civil awards for gallantry are recommended to the Sovereign by the *Prime Minister*. Anyone may recommend awards such as the George Cross, the George Medal, the Queen's Gallantry Medal, or the Queen's Commendation for brave conduct, by writing to the PM's Principal Private Secretary or by contacting an appropriate government department (e.g. the *Home Office* in the case of police and firemen, the *Department of Health and Social Security* in the case of doctors and nurses). Awards for gallantry are published from time to time but are not normally included in the half-yearly **honours** lists.
See also **Foreign decorations and medals**; **Gallantry awards: military**.

Gallantry Awards: Military Members of the Armed Services are recommended to the Sovereign for military awards by the *Secretary of State for Defence*.
See also **Foreign decorations and medals**; **Gallantry awards: civil**.

Gambia, The Commonwealth member. For **exchange control** is a non-scheduled territory in the **overseas sterling area** but outside the EEC. UK nationals travelling direct from the UK normally need only the following (but check): **passports;** international certificates of **vaccination** against smallpox; **work permits** (if taking a job).
The UK has no reciprocal health or social security arrangements.
Enquiries to *The Gambia High Commission* in London and *The Gambian Consulate-General* in Glasgow.
British diplomatic mission to The Gambia is *British High Commission* in Banjul.

Gambling Clubs Clubs, including both gaming and **bingo**, are regulated under procedures contained in the Gaming Act 1968. Schedule 2 to the Act sets out the procedures for licensing clubs. All licences are granted annually by the local (gaming) licensing authority. Initial licence application requires a 'certificate of consent to apply for licence' issued by the *Gaming Board of Great Britain*; this certificate is not renewable but remains valid until revoked by the GBGB.
Gaming clubs are restricted to certain areas, whereas there are no such restrictions on bingo clubs. There are no statutory restrictions on membership, except that no person under 18 may be present in any room in which gaming takes place; for bingo clubs this is relaxed to allow people under 18 to be present but not to take part. A member may not take part in gaming until 48 hours after application has been made in writing in person on the premises. In the case of bingo clubs there is only a 24 hour waiting period and no requirement for notice of intent to game.

All staff employed in actual gaming need to be certificated by the GBGB; for bingo clubs at present only the managers need to be certificated. Enquiries to GBGB or local (gaming) licensing committee.

Certain gaming may be carried on, among other activities, at clubs or miner's welfare institutes registered for the purpose under Part 11 of the Act. Registration is with the local (gaming) licensing authority. The procedures are set out in schedules 3 and 4 of the Act.
See also **Betting businesses; Gaming licences; Lotteries; Pool betting permits.**

Game Licences, Game Dealer Licences and Gamekeeper Licences These may be obtained from many post offices. They are issued on behalf of the local authority. In Scotland game dealer licences are only available from district councils and island area authorities. In Northern Ireland, from the Excise Duties Branch at the *Department of Finance, Northern Ireland.*

Gaming Licences Licences, valid for six months ending 31 March or 30 April each year, must be held for and displayed on any premises (including any means of transport) for which a licence is required under the Gaming Act 1968, i.e. any premises in Great Britain or its territorial waters on which any of the following games, or games esentially similar, are played: baccarat, punto banco, blackjack, chemin de fer, craps, French roulette, American roulette, big six, boule, chuck-a-luck, crown and anchor, faro, faro bank, hazard, poker dice, pontoon, trente et quarante, vingt-et-un, wheel of fortune. Duty is calculated on the rateable value of the premises and the number of gaming tables provided, which is specified on the licences when issued. The provider of the premises or any person concerned with the organisation or management of the gaming should apply for a licence to the local office of *Her Majesty's Customs and Excise local office.*
See also **Gambling clubs; Gaming premises; Lotteries; Pool betting permits.**

Gaming Machine Licences Licences must be held for and displayed on any premises in the UK (including the territorial waters of the UK adjacent to Great Britain) on which a gaming machine is provided for gaming, except at specified charitable entertainments and pleasure fairs. Ordinary licences are valid for either a whole year or half a year. Duty is payable upon licence application and depends upon the number of machines authorised, the cost to play once (over 1.25p being higher rate), and whether the premises have local authority approval under the Gaming Acts (see **Gaming premises**). Holiday season licences are valid from 1 March to 31 October inclusive for any year and apply only to machines where the cost to play once is a penny or less, and on premises satisfying prescribed conditions. Apply to *Her Majesty's Customs and Excise local office*; details in HMCE Notice 454. **Value-added tax** is also chargeable on the full net take of gaming machines. General enquiries to *Gaming Board of Great Britain.*
See also **Gaming machines; Pool betting duty.**

Gaming Premises The approval of the appropriate local authority is required for any premises where gaming by way of amusement with prizes is provided, under the provisions of the Gaming Acts. For the purposes of ordinary **gaming machine licences**, premises have local authority approval if there is in force for the premises a permit granted by the local authority under the Lotteries and Amusements Act 1976 Schedule 3 for the purposes of Section 34 of that Act or a licence under the Gaming Act 1968 and a direction giving by the licensing authority under Section 32 of that Act whereby Section 34 of the Act has no effect.

There are certain exceptions: premises licensed or registered under the Gaming Act 1968 Part II are not eligible for either of the first two permits; premises of a club or miners' welfare institute registered under the Gaming Act 1968 Part III cannot be treated as having local authority approval for the purpose of gaming machine licence duty, even if one of the first two permits is in force in respect of the premises; and for the purposes of the gaming licence, premises are treated as having local authority approval only when the number of machines for play is equal to, or less than, the number of machines specified in the direction. See also **Gambling clubs; Lotteries.**

Garden Plants International registration of a new variety both records it and ensures that no two plants have the same name and no one plant has two names. Forms, obtainable from the relevant authority, have to be completed giving such details as variety's proposed name, parentage, description, photograph (sometimes), name of raiser and registrant. International registration authorities are appointed by the *International Society for Horticultural Science*.
Authority for acacia is the *Los Angeles State and County Arboretum*; for achimenes, columnea, episcia, gesneriaceae, (bar saintpaulia), gloxinia and kohleria the *American Gloxinia and Gesneriad Society*; for aloe the *South African Aloe Breeders Association*; for amaryllidaceae (nerine and crindonna but not narcissus) the *American Plant Life Society*; for apple the *National Fruit Trials*; for azalea, garden conifers (including dwarf), daffodil, dahlia, delphinium, dianthus, lily, orchid and rhododendron the *Royal Horticultural Society*; for begonia the *American Begonia Society*; for bougainvillea the Division of Vegetable Crops and Floriculture at the *Indian Agricultural Research Institute*; for buxus the *American Boxwood Society*; for callistephus, petunia, and tagetes the *Institut für Zierpflanzenbau der TU*; for camellia the *International Camellia Society*; for carissa, chaenomeles, fagus, forsythia, gleditsia, lantana, malus, philadelphus, pieris, ulmus, weigela and woody plants without separate authorities the *Arnold Arboretum*; for perennial chrysanthemum the *National Chrysanthemum Society*; for coprosma, hebe, leptospermum, phormium and pittosporum the *Royal New Zealand Institute of Horticulture*; for escallonia and hydrangea *Golden Gate Park*: for fuchsia the *American Fuchsia Society*; for gladiolus the *North American Gladiolus Society*; for heather (andromeda, bruckenthalia, calluna, daboecia and erica) the *Heather Society*; for hedera the *American Ivy Society*; for hemerocallis the *American Hemerocallis Society*; for hosta the *American Hosta Society*; for hyacinths, tulips and bulbous plants without separate authorities the *Royal General Bulbgrowers' Society*; for ilex the Holly Society of America at the *US National Arboretum*; for iris (bar bulbous) *American Iris Society*; for magnolia the *Barnes Foundation Arboretum*; for mango the Division of Horticulture and Fruit Technology of the *Indian Agricultural Research Institute*; for paeonia the *American Paeony Society*; for pelargonium the *Nyndee Nomenclature Committee*; for penstemon the *American Penstemon Society*; for populus the *International Poplar Commission*; for pyracantha and viburnum the *US National Arboretum*; for rosa the *American Rose Society*; for saintpaulia the *African Violet Society of America*; and for syringa the *Royal Botanical Gardens, Hamilton*.
See also **Flower and vegetable trials; Plant Breeding; Royal Horticultural Society.**

Gas Bills   See **Electricity and gas bills.**

Gas and Electricity Disconnections Before disconnection the *Electricity Board* or *British Gas Corporation Region* reminds the consumer that supplies will be continued if arrangements can be made to ensure regular payments and clearance of arrears within a reasonable period. In cases of hardship contact appropriate welfare service (see **Social security benefits**).

Gas Leaks   If you smell gas in your home, immediately extinguish all naked flames; do not operate electrical switches; open doors and windows for ventilation; check if a cooker tap has been left on or if a pilot light has gone out; then turn off the supply at the meter and call the local gas service centre for your *British Gas Corporation Region*. Any leak must be repaired by a competent person and the gas supply must not be turned on until the repair has been completed. Checking a suspected leak will usually be free: the first 30 minutes of work on equipment owned by the *British Gas Corporation* is free, including parts and materials up to the value of £1. Work on non-BGC equipment taking more than 30 minutes will usually be charged for. If you smell gas outside report it at once to the nearest *gas service centre*.

Gas Regulations Safety regulations are administered by the *Department of Energy, Gas Standards Branch*. By law consumers, gas installers and the *British Gas Corporation* must observe its code; failure to do so could result in a fine of up to £400. Under the regulations, you must not let anyone use suspect appliances; only let competent people install or service appliances; turn off your main gas supply if you suspect a leak and inform the local gas service centre; and not turn the gas on again until the leak has been repaired. Only gas meters of a type approved and certified by the DEn Gas Standards Branch can be installed and used on consumers' premises. Accuracy of individual meters is checked by the Branch on request from the BGC or from consumers. Details are set out in 'Gas Meter Regulations' available from the Gas Standards Branch, *Her Majesty's Stationery Office* and government bookshops.
Gas quality regulations are also administered by the Branch. All natural and manufactured gas distributed to gas consumers is checked by gas examiners for standards of quality. For **EEC** directives concerning the manufacture and sale of gas meters and gas appliances, which are being issued to remove trade barriers, the Branch is again the UK government authority.
See also **Gas leaks**.

Gas Supply Supply to domestic and industrial consumers is arranged on application to the relevant *British Gas Corporation Region*. If the property owner or occupier requires, the BGC must give a supply of gas to premises situated within 25 yards of a gas main in normal current use. The BGC can charge the consumer for the cost of providing and laying pipes on his property or from the main to a property which is more than 30 feet away. The BGC is not normally obliged to supply gas where more than 25,000 therms of gas is demanded.
See also **Electricity and gas bills**; **Gas leaks**; **Gas regulations**.

General Certificate of Education Examinations are set by *Oxford and Cambridge Schools Examination Board*; *Oxford Delegacy of Local Examinations*; *Cambridge University Local Examinations Syndicate*; *London University Examination Board*; *Southern Universities' Joint Board*; *University Entrance and Schools Examinations Council*; *Welsh Joint Education Committee*; *Associated Examining Board*; *Joint Matriculation Board*; and *Northern Ireland Schools Examination Council*.
'O' level is normally taken after five years secondary school education (in year in which candidate is 16 on September 1st; earlier if headteacher certifies that it is educationally desirable); 'A' level is normally taken after two years in a sixth form.
'O' level results are graded A to E, or ungraded; A, B, C, are regarded as passes; grade D indicates a lower level of attainment; grade E is the lowest level of attainment judged by the board to be of sufficient standard to be recorded. 'A' level candidates may be awarded one of five pass grades – A to E; or be awarded an 'O' level pass; or be ungraded. 'O' and 'A' levels have no upper age limit and can be entered directly (i.e. not necessarily via an educational institution) by applying to the examination board.
Candidates attending schools in Wales tend to be restricted on the whole to taking WJEC exams, otherwise candidates can enter for any board's examinations. The corresponding system in Scotland is different; see **Education: Scotland**.

German Democratic Republic For **exchange control** is a non-scheduled

territory outside the **overseas sterling area** and the **EEC**. UK nationals travelling direct from the UK normally need only the following (but check): **passports**; **visas**; **work permits** (if taking a job); international driving permits (if intending to drive: see **Motoring abroad**). Reduced price petrol coupons are available at all main frontier posts. The UK has no reciprocal health or social security arrangements.
Enquiries to *German Democratic Republic Embassy* in London and Berolina Travel Ltd in London.
British diplomatic mission to the German Democratic Republic is *British Embassy* in East Berlin.

German Federal Republic EEC member. For **exchange control** is a non-scheduled territory in the EEC but outside the **overseas sterling area**. UK nationals travelling direct from the UK normally need only the following (but check): **passports** (British visitors' passports are acceptable).
EEC or bilateral social security arrangements are applicable; leaflets and EEC Guides obtainable from *Department of Health and Social Security, Overseas Branch*. Apply to the local social security office for leaflet SA28 which explains how to get free or reduced-cost medical treatment under EEC health arrangements and where to apply for the certificate of entitlement (form E111).
Enquiries to *German Federal Republic Embassy* in London, *German Tourist Information Bureau* in London, and *German Federal Republic Consulates-General* in Edinburgh and Liverpool.
British diplomatic missions to German Federal Republic are *British Embassy* in Bonn and *British Consulates* in Berlin, Bremerhaven, Dusseldorf, Frankfurt, Hamburg, Hanover, Munich and Stuttgart.

Ghana Commonwealth member. For **exchange control** is a non-scheduled territory in the **overseas sterling area** but outside the EEC.
UK nationals travelling direct from the UK normally need only the following (but check): **passports**; **visas**; international certificates of **vaccination** against smallpox and yellow fever; **work permits** (if taking a job). The UK has no reciprocal health or social security arrangments.
Enquiries to *Ghanaian High Commission* in London.
British diplomatic mission to Ghana is *British High Commission* in Accra.

Gibraltar UK Dependency. For **exchange control** is a scheduled territory.
UK nationals travelling direct from the UK normally need only the following (but check): **passports**; **work permits** (if taking a job).
UK reciprocal arrangements cover health and social security. Advice from *Department of Health and Social Security, Overseas Branch*. Free medical treatment at the General Practice Health Centre (charges for small proportion of hospital costs) for those normally resident in the UK, on production of UK passport. Charges for medicines.
Enquiries to *Gibraltar Tourist Office* in London.
The Queen's representative in Gibraltar is the *Governor and Commander in Chief* in Gibraltar.

Gifts and Loans Abroad Personal loans, gifts and payments to dependants, whether in money or kind, require **exchange control** permission, if they are made by UK residents to people abroad. Permissions are usually granted to a resident up to certain prescribed annual limits. These are: a total of £1,500 in gifts or loans to persons or charitable organisations resident anywhere outside the scheduled territories and in addition a total of £1,500 to persons or charitable organisations in countries of the **EEC** outside the scheduled territories; £2,000 to dependants abroad; and £100 in gifts in kind (excluding diamonds). Gifts and loans within the limits can be directly and immediately arranged by an **authorised bank**. Otherwise express permission must be sought from the *Bank of England*, which may give permission for the prescribed limits to be exceeded in special circumstances.
Gifts and loans may be transmitted through a bank or the *Post Office* and gifts may also take the form of **National**

Saving Certificates and **Premium Bonds**. Gifts taking the form of other securities, however, require the express permission of the BE, even if of a value within the permitted limits. All bequests under wills are allowed freely.
Apply to an **authorised bank**, which can arrange an application to the BE, if necessary.
See also **Direct investment: exchange control; Exporting**.

Gliding Gliding is governed internationally by the *Fédération Aeronautique Internationale*. The British member is the Royal Aero Club, which in turn has delegated responsibility for UK gliding to the *British Gliding Association*. The BGA controls glider registration, certificates of airworthiness, training and registration of pilots, certificates of achievement, safety, laws for pilots, national and regional championships and selection of British teams.

Gold Bullion and coin transactions are subject to **exchange control** restrictions. UK residents may not normally hold or deal in bullion either in the UK or abroad and any bullion which they own or acquire must normally be sold to an authorised dealer in gold, i.e. an officer of a bank or firm which is authorised by an Order of HM Treasury to act for all purposes of the Exchange Control Act 1947 as an authorised dealer in relation to gold (i.e. they are permitted to hold and deal in gold bullion). These include the *Bank of England*, **authorised banks** and two firms of bullion brokers. Users of gold for industrial purposes must have the approval of the Bank of England to purchase crude gold for their industrial requirements.
UK residents may hold gold coins without restriction. They may buy and sell gold coins minted in or before 1937 but, except for authorised dealers in gold, may not buy or sell gold coins minted after 1937 unless the coins are already held in the UK and are being sold by a resident who is not selling on behalf of a person living abroad. Gold coins minted after 1937 may be imported only be authorised dealers in gold who hold an open individual import licence issued by the *Department of Trade*. To export bullion or coin, apply to an authorised dealer.
See also **Exporting; Importing**.

Gold and Silver Mining Most deposits in the UK belong to the Crown. Applications for prospecting (and production/extraction) licences to *Crown Estate Office*.

Golf The two governing authorities which jointly determine and administer the rules for both amateur and professional golf are the *Royal and Ancient Golf Club of St Andrews*, Scotland (to which about 60 countries are affiliated) and the United States Golf Association. The R & A also adjudicates on amateur status, runs the British Open and various amateur championships and international team events, and selects British teams.
Professional golf in the UK is handled by the *Professional Golfer's Association*; handicapping by the *Council of National Golf Unions*; coaching by the *Golf Foundation*; and new golf courses by the *Golf Development Council*.
Men's amateur golf in the UK is controlled by the *English Golf Union*, the *Welsh Golfing Union*, the *Scottish Golf Union* and the *Golfing Union of Ireland*. They are co-ordinated by the CNGU and recognise the overall authority of the R & A. For women's amateur golf, the *Ladies Golf Union* co-ordinates the *English Ladies' Golf Association*, the *Welsh Ladies' Golf Union*, the *Scottish Ladies' Golfing Association* and the *Irish Ladies' Golf Union*.

Goods: Unsolicited Under the Unsolicited Goods and Services Act 1971 it is an offence in Great Britain for a trader, provided he has no reasonable cause to believe there is a right to payment, to demand such payment or make certain threats with a view to obtaining payment for goods (e.g. records, books, Christmas cards) which people have not ordered. If you receive goods which you did not ask for and do not want, you are not obliged to pay for or return them; and after 30 days if you write to the sender giving your name and address and saying the goods were unsolicited, or after 6 months even if you do not, the goods become your property as long as the sender has been given reasonable access for collection. Complaints should be made to the police or to the trading standards department of your local authority.

Government Ministers: Appointment The *Prime Minister* is appointed by the Sovereign; all other government ministers are appointed by the Sovereign on the advice of the PM. Parliamentary Private Secretaries are appointed by the minister concerned.

Government Stock: Purchase and Sale Purchase and sale of government stock can be registered on the *National Savings Stock Register* up to a maximum holding of £5,000 on any one stock on any one day for a commission which is generally less than a **stockbroker's**. Application forms from post offices; send with remittance to *Department for National Savings, Bonds and Stock Office*.
See also **National Savings bank accounts; National Savings certificates**

Grass and Heather Burning Licences are required in England and Wales from 1 April (16 April in Northumberland and Durham) to 31 October inclusive. Apply to *Ministry of Agriculture Fisheries and Food, Divisional Offices* 28 days before date for burning. Precautions are always required (e.g. 48 hours' notice to neighbours and anyone having an interest in the land; commencement only between sunrise and sunset; adequate supervision and safety equipment). Advice from MAFF (Divisional Offices).
See also **Agriculture: Scotland; Agriculture: Northern Ireland.**

Greece For **exchange control** is a non-scheduled territory outside the **overseas sterling area** and the **EEC**. UK nationals travelling direct from the UK normally need only the following (but check): **passports; work permits** (if taking a job); green cards for motor insurance (if bringing a car). Petrol coupon cards are available from all Greek land border customs offices. On presentation of the card, coupons may be purchased from any branch in Greece of the National Bank of Greece. **(See also Motoring abroad.)**
The UK has no reciprocal health or social security arrangements.
Enquiries to *Greek Embassy* in London and *Greek State Tourist Office* in London.
British diplomatic missions to Greece are *British Embassy* in Athens and *British Consulates* in Corfu, Crete, Kavalla, Patras, Rhodes, Salonika and Samos.

Grenada **Commonwealth** member. For **exchange control** is a non-scheduled territory in the **overseas sterling area** but outside the **EEC**. UK nationals travelling direct from the UK normally need only the following (but check): **passports; visas; work permits** (if taking a job).
The UK has no reciprocal health or social security arrangements.
Enquiries to *Grenada High Commission* in London.
British diplomatic mission to Grenada is based on *British High Commission* in Port of Spain, Trinidad.

Greyhound Racing The worldwide representative and consultative body is the World Greyhound Racing Federation. The UK authority is the *National Greyhound Racing Club Ltd*. It is responsible for rules and discipline at 50 large UK racecourses; another 59 'flapping' racecourses do not subscribe to any national set of rules. Organisation and administration of greyhound racing is the responsibility of the *British Greyhound Racing Federation* which comprises representatives from owners, trainers, breeders, veterinarians, racecourse managements etc.
Track Betting Licences are issued by local authorities (District Councils), but the *Home Secretary* sets the maximum percentage for operating expenses on the totalisators owned by racecourse managements. Racecourses can stage a maximum of 8 races a day on 130 days a year, with 16 races on four Special Betting Days, but no more than 14 betting days in one month.
See also **Betting businesses.**

Grievances Grievances concerning matters of public interest may be taken up with a **Member of Parliament** with a view to his tabling a Parliamentary question or motion on the matter or writing to the responsible government minister or referring it to the Parliamentary Commissioner for Administration.
See also **Disputes with public authorities; Injustice: government.**

Guard Dogs Under the Guard Dogs Act 1975, a handler must be present at all times when a guard dog is used, except in a dwelling house or on agricultural land. Warning notices must be exhibited. Enquiries to the *Home Office.*

Guardianship The *Home Office* has a general responsibility for the law relating to guardianship, as administered by the magistrates' courts.

Guatemala For **exchange control** is a non-scheduled territory outside the **overseas sterling area** and the **EEC.** UK nationals travelling direct from the UK normally need only the following (but check): **passports; visas; work permits** (if taking a job).
The UK has no reciprocal health or social security arrangements.
Enquiries to *Guatemala Embassy* in Paris, France.
British diplomatic missions to Guatemala are *British Consulates* in Guatemala City and Puerto Barrios.

Guides: London Tourist guides operating in London should be registered with the *London Tourist Board.* The LTB awards its Blue Badge of recognition after an examination; it provides a six month part-time training course.
See also **Tourist industry.**

Guinea For **exchange control** is a non-scheduled territory outside the **overseas sterling area** and the **EEC.** UK nationals travelling direct from the UK normally need only the following (but check): **passports; visas;** international certificates of **vaccination** against smallpox and yellow fever; **work permits** (if taking a job); green cards for motor insurance (if bringing a car); international driving permits (if intending to drive: see **Motoring abroad).**
The UK has no reciprocal health or social security arrangements.
Enquiries to *Guinea Embassy* in Paris, France or *Guinea Visa Office* in Rome, Italy.
British diplomatic mission to Guinea is *British Consulate* in Conakry. The main British mission responsible is *British Embassy* in Dakar, Senegal.

Guinea-Bissau For **exchange control** is a non-scheduled territory outside the **overseas sterling area** and the **EEC.** UK nationals travelling direct from the UK normally need only the following (but check): **passports; visas**/entry permits; international certificates of **vaccination** against smallpox; **work permits** (if taking a job).
The UK has no reciprocal health or social security arrangements.
There is no Guinea-Bissau mission accredited to the UK.
British diplomatic mission to Guinea-Bissau is *British Embassy* in Bissau (Ambassador himself resides in Dakar, Senegal).

Guyana **Commonwealth** member. For **exchange control** is a non-scheduled territory in the **overseas sterling area** but outside the **EEC.** UK nationals travelling direct from the UK normally need only the following (but check): **passports;** international certificates of **vaccination** against smallpox; **work permits** (if taking a job), green cards for motor insurance (if bringing a car), international driving permits are recommended (if intending to drive: see **Motoring abroad).**
The UK has no reciprocal health or social security arrangements.
Enquiries to *Guyana High Commission* in London.
British diplomatic mission to Guyana is *British High Commission* in Georgetown.

Gymnastics and Sports Acrobatics Gymnastics is controlled internationally by the Fédération Internationale de Gymnastique, and sports acrobatics by the International Federation of Sports Acrobatics. In the UK the

British Amateur Gymnastics Association represents all gymnastics – artistic, modern and rhythmic – and sports acrobatics, and controls all competitions, judging, coaching, selection of UK teams, etc. The BAGA has branches in nine English regions and in Scotland, Wales and Northern Ireland. Many affiliated bodies represent schools, prison services, armed forces, etc.

H

Haiti For **exchange control** is a non-scheduled territory outside the **overseas sterling area** and the **EEC**. UK nationals travelling direct from the UK normally need only the following (but check): **passports**; international certificates of **vaccination** against smallpox; **work permits** (if taking a job); green cards for motor insurance (if bringing a car); international driving permits (if intending to drive: see **Motoring abroad**). Tourists must obtain tourist cards on arrival.
The UK has no reciprocal health or social security arrangements.
Enquiries to *Haiti Embassy* in London. *British diplomatic mission to Haiti* is the *British Embassy* in Port-au-Prince.

Hallmarking Hallmarking is overseen by the *Department of Prices and Consumer Protection*. Under the Hallmarking Act 1973, it is an offence for a trader in the UK to describe an article as being made of gold, silver or platinum, unless it has been assayed and hallmarked by an authorised UK assay office. Imported articles have to be hallmarked before they can be sold in the UK.
Certain marks applied by assay offices overseas in accordance with international convention or treaty have been designated approved UK hallmarks and UK assay offices are authorised to apply such marks. They are a responsibility mark indicating the name of the sponsor; a number in Arabic numerals indicating the standard of fineness in parts per thousand; the mark of the authorised assay office; and a common control mark indicating the precious metal of which the article is made and its standard of fineness. These marks may appear alongside traditional UK hallmarks, except on articles of 800 and 830 silver which is not recognised under UK law.
Certain articles made from one or more precious metals are exempted from hallmarking, following a recommendation by the *British Hallmarking Council*. The exemptions include certain small articles; articles made before 1900; battered articles fit only to be re-manufactured; articles containing gold and platinum but not silver when the total weight of the precious metal parts is less than one gram and the gold parts weigh more than the platinum; articles containing silver and other precious metals when the total weight of the precious metal parts is less than 7.78 grams and the silver parts weigh more than the other precious metal parts.

Handball International control, world championships, etc., are the responsibility of the International Handball Federation. In the UK the *British Handball Association* is the governing authority. The *Scottish Handball Association*, the *Welsh Handball Association* and the *Irish Olympic Handball Association* (Northern Ireland) control development of the sport in Scotland, Wales and Northern Ireland.

Hang Gliding Controlled internationally by the Commission Internationale de Vol Libre (part of the Fédération Aeronautique Internationale). In the UK the governing body is the *British Hang Gliding Association*. It selects British teams, administers observers, grades pilots, vets commercial training schools and negotiates with national land-owning bodies over use of sites. There is no division between amateur and professional in this new sport. In Wales, Scotland and Northern Ireland, the sport is controlled respectively by the *Welsh Hang Gliding Club*, the *Scottish Sailwing Association* and the *Ulster Hang Gliding Club*, all affiliated to the BHGA.

Health Authorities The health ministers – the Secretary of State for Social Services in England and the Secretaries of State for Scotland, Wales and Northern Ireland – are responsible for all aspects of the health services in their respective countries.

The organisation responsible for administering these health services is three-tier in England and two-tier in Scotland, Wales and Northern Ireland. Within each of the four countries the health departments (the *Department of Health and Social Security* in England, the *Scottish Home and Health Department*, the *Welsh Office*, and the *Department of Health and Social Services in Northern Ireland*) are responsible for strategic planning. *Area health authorities* in England and Wales, *health boards* in Scotland and *health and social services boards* in Northern Ireland are responsible for area planning and operational control of all health services in their area.

In England only, because of its greater size and population, there is an additional tier of regional authorities. There are 14 regional health authorities (RHAs), each with one or more University Medical Schools within its boundaries. The RHA forms part of the chain of responsibility running from the Secretary of State, through the Department of Health and Social Security to each RHA and area health authority (AHAs). The function of the RHA is to develop strategic plans, policies and priorities according to the health service needs identified by the AHAs and on its assessment of individual areas' resource requirements. The RHA also provides services which require supra-area co-ordination.

There are 90 area health authorities (AHAs) in England and 8 in Wales. The AHA is the operational authority responsible for assessing needs and priorities and for planning, organising and providing services in its area in collaboration with local authorities. The AHA's boundaries, generally, match those of local government. Within each area, there are between one and six health districts, which whilst not statutorily established, carry out the day-to-day functions of health service provision at the local level. Health District Management Teams are accountable to AHAs.

In Scotland the Scottish Home and Health Department embraces hospitals, the general practitioner services (doctors, dentists, chemists and opticians) and the provision of community health services. Management and local planning responsibility rests with 15 health boards, financed by the Exchequer, through the Department and working under its general oversight. Certain services, such as supplies, ambulance and blood transfusion, are administered on a national basis by a Common Services Agency. Broad policy advice is provided by the Scottish Health Service Planning Council.

See also **Doctors; National Health Service.**

Health Education The *Health Education Council* is a semi-independent government-sponsored body set up in 1968 with responsibilities for the promotion and development of health education at a national level in England, Wales and Northern Ireland. Its functions are to promote and encourage education and research into healthy living and to assist government departments, health and local authorities and other statutory bodies. The Council publishes a wide range of health education material and

carries out national health education campaigns. In recent years the Council's campaigns have concentrated on smoking, alcoholism, sexually-transmitted diseases and family planning. In 1977–8 the Council proposes to undertake a major campaign to instil more positive public attitudes to healthy living. Further information can be obtained from the Council. In Scotland, similar functions are exercised by the *Scottish Health Education Unit*.
See also **Health authorities; National Health Service**.

Health Visitors Health visitors make regular visits to children at home and give advice to parents. They also visit handicapped people who are suffering from long-term illness to assess their health needs, and to give help and advice on health matters or nursing aids and equipment. Further information from NHS family **doctor** or child health clinic. Health visitors are employed by *area health authorities*.
See also **Child health services; Disablement; National Health Service**.

Hearing Aids Hearing aids are available on free loan to hard of hearing patients through the **National Health Service**. Apply first to NHS family **doctor** (you will be referred for examination to a special clinic in the local hospital and then to a hearing aid centre where a suitable NHS hearing aid will be fitted and supplied). NHS aids are serviced, maintained and supplied with batteries and other accessories without charge. Both body-worn and behind-the-ear aids are available; the latter to patients within the eligible categories only.
See also **Deafness; Disablement**.

Heavy Goods Vehicle Drivers' Licences Licences are required by all drivers of goods vehicles with a permissible maximum weight exceeding 7.5 tonnes (except for visitors from overseas driving vehicles which are temporarily in the UK and which they are authorised to drive by a licence issued in their home country). Drivers must be over 21; have passed a medical test; and have obtained a provisional heavy goods vehicle driver's licence and have driven subject to its conditions before passing a HGV driving test. Instruction for the test is available commercially. Apply for licence to *Department of Transport Traffic Area Office*. Appeal against refusal to issue a licence to the licensing authorities or to a magistrate's court (or the sheriff in Scotland). HGV drivers' hours of work and rest periods are prescribed and drivers are required to keep a record of hours worked and goods carried above $3\frac{1}{2}$ tons in an official logbook.
See also **Heavy goods vehicle operators' licences**.

Heavy Goods Vehicle Operators' Licences Licences must normally be held by operators of goods vehicles over $3\frac{1}{2}$ tonnes plated weight, operating for hire and reward or on their own account (exceptions are listed in Schedule 1 of the Goods Vehicle (Operators' Licences) Regulations 1969). Apply to the licensing authority at the *Department of Transport Traffic Area Office* for the area in which the applicant has an operating centre. Do not purchase vehicles or enter into contracts before the outcome of the application is known. A helpful booklet 'Guide to Operators' Licensing' is available from DoT Traffic Area Offices.
Prior to 1978 only one type of licence was issued. Now, following **EEC** regulations, there are three types of operator's licence. Standard licences are for operators carrying goods for hire and reward on domestic journeys. Proof is required of the applicant's good repute, financial standing and the professional competence of the person in charge of the applicant's transport operations. This last may be demonstrated by experience in the industry before 1 January 1975; by holding certain prescribed professional qualifications; or by passing an examination held by the *Royal Society of Arts*. Holders of standard licences may also carry goods on their own account.
Restricted licences are for 'own account' operators in both the domestic and international fields. Proof is required of good repute and

financial standing but not of professional competence. If an own account operator occasionally operates for hire and reward, he must hold a standard licence. International licences are for operators carrying goods for hire and reward on international journeys. In addition to the requirements for a standard licence, applicants have to furnish proof of the competence of the person in charge of international operations. Licences issued before 1978 do not discriminate between the three classes.

Certain **trade unions** and associations, any chief officer of police or any **local authority** may object to the grant of an operator's licence on the grounds that the applicant does not fulfill the requirements; burden of proof lies with the objector. If necessary, an application and objections may be considered at a public enquiry. Maximum duration of a licence is five years. Appeal against refusal or grant of a licence to the *Transport Tribunal*.

Applicants for a licence undertake to the licensing authority to meet certain requirements for the proper maintenance and safe operation of their vehicles. Goods vehicles are subject to spot checks for roadworthiness and safety standards by DoT inspectors.

Both employee and owner-drivers of goods vehicles exceeding 3½ tonnes plated weight must keep a record of their driving, other work and rest periods in an EEC-type record book (details in guides to domestic and international goods vehicle drivers' hours and records, from DoT Information Division). Drivers are subject to checks by DoT Traffic examiners on whether such records are being kept. See also **Heavy goods vehicle drivers' licences**.

Henley Royal Regatta Held annually on the Thames, Henley was founded in 1839 and its general control is vested in 51 stewards. Detailed management is in the control of a committee of management consisting of 12 stewards elected annually. Anyone may watch the racing from the regatta enclosure but entry to the stewards' enclosure is restricted to members and their guests. Details of membership, admission prices and other information (e.g. annual records of racing) from the secretary, *Henley Royal Regatta*.

Heralds Heraldic duties include granting arms (see **Armorial bearings, Pedigrees**); officiating at the major state ceremonies (e.g. coronations, state openings of Parliament, annual services of the Order of the Garter); making proclamations (e.g. of peace, war, accession); and introducing new peers into the **House of Lords**. The chief ceremonial officer of the Crown and the judge in the High Court of Chivalry, with jurisdiction over the English heralds, is the Earl Marshal, a hereditary post nominally financed by the Sovereign. He is responsible for most state ceremonies in England, Wales and Northern Ireland, assisted by the official heralds of the College of Arms (three Kings, six Heralds, and four Pursuivants of Arms) who are also members of the royal household.

In Scotland, the Lord Lyon King at Arms at the Court of Lord Lyon, assisted by three Heralds and three Pursuivants, is responsible for all state and public ceremonies and royal proclamations.

Hereditary Titles Creation of new hereditary UK titles (i.e. dukes, marquesses, earls, viscounts, barons and baronets) following recommendation to the Sovereign by the *Prime Minister* is still possible but is not a regular practice. **Life peerages** and other **honours** are bestowed.

Herrings UK **fishing vessels**, owners and traders in herring must be licensed by the *Herring Industry Board*. To finance its operations, the HIB imposes a levy, payable on first sales of fresh herring and on fresh herring landed in the UK and not sold on first sale. The HIB answers enquiries on any aspect of herring catching and utilisation. See also **White fish**.

Hill Livestock: Allowances Compensatory allowances are payable annually under **EEC** regulations to UK farmers who maintain cattle in a regular

breeding herd, or ewes in a qualfied flock on three or more hectares of eligible land as defined in the regulations. Claim in England and Wales from *Ministry of Agriculture, Fisheries and Food, Divisional Offices.*
See also **Agricultural produce: EEC subsidies; Agriculture produce: support; Agriculture: Scotland; Agriculture: Northern Ireland; Cattle and beef: subsidies.**

Hockey The world authority for men's hockey is the International Hockey Federation. UK control of the men's game, matches, coaching and umpires, etc., rests with the *Hockey Association* (England), the *Scottish Hockey Association* (Scotland), the *Welsh Hockey Association* (Wales) and the *Irish Hockey Union* (Northern Ireland and Eire). The *Great Britain Hockey Board* selects the men's British Olympic teams.
International women's hockey, which is played to the same rules book as men's, is governed for the greater part by the International Federation of Women's Hockey Associations, though the International Hockey Federation is also responsible for the women's sections of its member associations.
National teams, trials, coaching, administration, etc., are controlled by the *All England Women's Hockey Association*, the *Scottish Women's Hockey Association*, the *Welsh Women's Hockey Association* and the *Irish Ladies' Hockey Union*. All these are members of the *Women's Hockey Board of Great Britain and Ireland* under whose authority any Great Britain and Ireland team is selected.

Home Help Home help may be provided by local authorities (Social Services Departments) to assist with housework and other duties those who are handicapped through age or disability or have a handicapped person in the household. A charge may be made, based on the number of hours' help given each week, to those who can afford it.
In most areas, voluntary organisations also help families or individuals in a general way or by doing specific jobs (e.g. lighting fires, collecting library books or pensions, or helping with shopping). Further information from local authority Social Services Departments and any local voluntary organisations.
See also **Disablement.**

Homelessness It is the responsibility of local authorities (housing departments) to provide accommodation for homeless people who have not made themselves homeless intentionally and who have a priority need: i.e. those with at least one dependant under 16 (or others who are under 19 and either receiving full-time education or training or are otherwise unable to support themselves); those above normal retirement age; the chronically sick and disabled; battered women with children who have fled the marital home; pregnant women; those losing their homes as a result of an emergency such as fire, flood or other disaster.
Three conditions must be met before a local authority can decide that an applicant is intentionally homeless: the applicant must have deliberately done, or failed to do, something that has either made him homeless or is likely to force him to leave accommodation; it must have been reasonable for him to continue to occupy that accommodation; and he must have been aware of all the relevant facts. The onus is not on the applicant to satisfy the authority that he did not leave accommodation intentionally, and where there is doubt authorities should give the benefit of the doubt to the applicant. Accommodation provided should be such that families are not split apart.
Local authorities' duty to other homeless people is to furnish them with such advice and assistance as the authorities consider appropriate; they will also supply information about voluntary agencies who may help or provide refuge – these include *Shelter, SHAC,* and the *Salvation Army.* In addition the Supplementary Benefits Commission is responsible under the Supplementary Benefits Act 1976 (Part III, Section 30) for maintaining reception centres where temporary board and lodging may be provided for

'persons without a settled way of living', and are designed to 'make provision whereby persons without a settled way of living may be influenced to lead a more settled life'; apply to *Department of Health and Social Security local office*. Those homeless at night may seek immediate shelter at a police station. For permanent housing see **Housing**.
See also **Local authorities**; **Supplementary benefit**.

Honduras For **exchange control** is a non-scheduled territory outside the **overseas sterling area** and the **EEC**. UK nationals travelling direct from the UK normally need only the following (but check): **passports**; **work permits** (if taking a job).
The UK has no reciprocal health or social security arrangements.
Enquiries to *Honduras Embassy* in London.
British diplomatic missions to Honduras are *British Embassy* in Tegucigalpa and *British Consulate* in Puerto Cortes.

Honours Awards in the Order of the Garter, the Thistle, the Order of Merit and the Royal Victorian Order are in the Sovereign's own gift (see **Royal honours**). The *Prime Minister* is responsible for recommending to the Sovereign the award of civil honours; military honours are recommended by the *Secretary of State for Defence*. Awards for foreigners are honorary and are recommended by the *Secretary of State for Foreign and Commonwealth Affairs*. Lists of honours are published half-yearly at the New Year and on the Queen's Birthday. They include both military and civil awards.
The Most Honourable Order of the Bath has three classes: Knight Grand Cross (limited to 85 military and 30 civil), Knight Commander (205 military, 123 civil), and Companion (1,095 military, 730 civil). The Most Distinguished Order of St Michael and St George, which has three classes (GCMG, KCMG, CMG), is mainly for diplomats and others with distinguished service overseas. The Order of the Companions of Honour has 65 members. The Most Excellent Order of the British Empire has five classes (GBE, KBE, CBE, and Officer OBE and Member MBE and a Medal).
Names of individuals come up for consideration for official selection either by nomination by government ministers to the PM or by direct nomination to the PM from many differing sources (e.g. lord-lieutenants, Members of Parliament, organisations, and members of the general public). Ministers make recommendations to the PM every six months; their departments have their own procedures for obtaining nominations (e.g. consulting authorities within their sectors, firms, organisations, etc.).
Private nominations – by individuals or by representatives of organisations – can be made direct to the Principal Private Secretary at the *Prime Minister's Office*. Whatever the form of nomination, he passes the names to the Ceremonial Officer at the *Civil Service Department Ceremonial Branch*, who acts as secretary of the various honours and awards committees. A selected list of recommendations is sent subsequently by the head of the Home Civil Service to the PM.
The total number of names in any half-yearly honours list is limited, the numbers being reviewed every five years by the Committee on the Grant of Honours, Decorations and Medals at the CSD Ceremonial Branch. Political honours for political services as such have not been recommended by the PM of the day for inclusion in the half-yearly honours lists since the Birthday 1974.
See also **Gallantry: civil awards**; **Gallantry: military awards**; **Life peerages**; **Royal honours**.

Hops British producers must register with the *Hops Marketing Board* through which all their hops must be sold. The HMB adjusts the supply each year by the allocation of quotas. Under **EEC** regulations a subsidy is payable to hop growers on an acreage basis; payment, which is restrospective on rates decided annually after each harvest, is by the *Intervention Board for Agricultural Produce*.
See also **Brewers**.

Horseracing Horseracing is regulated by the *Jockey Club* which makes and enforces the rules, directs the proper conduct of racing, race meetings and racehorse training, and encourages the breeding of bloodstock. It is responsible for granting and withdrawing licences to racecourses, trainers, jockeys, officials, etc.; for advising on racing programmes; helping compile the fixture list; overseeing distribution of prize-money.

The *Horserace Betting Levy Board*, a government-appointed body responsible to the Home Office, assesses and collects a tax from **bookmakers** and the Tote Board and uses the fund to improve breeds of horses and horseracing. Its responsibilities include prize-money, racing security (including the prevention of doping), racecourse improvements, training of apprentices, technical services (the photo finish, starting stalls, etc.) and the National Stud.

Weatherbys serves as the racing secretariat, dealing with day-to-day administration and implementing the decisions of the Jockey Club.

All UK racecourses belong to the *Racecourse Association* which is concerned with admission prices, catering, provision of betting facilities, etc. See also **Ascot**.

Public enquiries about racing administration are answered by the *Racing Information Bureau*. Punters can apply to *Tattersalls Committee* for a decision in betting disputes.

Trainers, jockeys, officials, breeders, bookmakers, stable staff, etc., have their own associations which collectively make their views known to the Jockey Club and the Horserace Betting Levy Board through the *Racing Industry Liaison Committee*.

See also **Betting businesses; Betting duty**.

Horses All stallions over two years' old in England and Wales must be licensed. Exceptions are thoroughbred and pony stallions of prescribed breeds in certain areas. Apply to *Ministry of Agriculture, Fisheries and Food, Animal Health Division IIIC*.

See also **Agriculture: Scotland; Agriculture: Northern Ireland**.

Horticultural Crops In England and Wales the Plant Health Branch at the *Ministry of Agriculture, Fisheries and Food headquarters (2)* certifies crops of seed potatoes, blackcurrant bushes, strawberry plants, raspberry canes, hop plants, fruit trees (including finished trees, mother trees and rootstocks) and carnations. The certificates relate to the health and, except for hops and carnations, the purity of growing stocks. Fees are payable for inspection and certification.

A horticultural crop intelligence report is issued twice monthly by the Statistics Division 1 of MAFF on the condition of home-grown fruit and vegetable crops. End of the month reports also give estimates of production.

See also **Agriculture: Scotland; Agriculture: Northern Ireland; Fruit and vegetable trials; Garden plants; Plant breeding**.

Hosepipes and Garden Sprinklers A licence is almost always required from the local *water authority* or *water company*.

See also **Water services**.

Hospital Treatment Under the National Health Service, hospital treatment is completely free whether you are an in-patient, a day-patient or an out-patient. Out-patients (including day patients) pay a charge for drugs, elastic hosiery, wigs and fabric supports supplied by hospitals. People who are exempt from payment of prescription charges (see **Medicines and appliances: prescription charges**) are also exempt from the charges for drugs and elastic hosiery supplied by hospitals. In addition a person over 16 but in full-time attendance at school is exempt from the charge for elastic hosiery supplied by hospitals.

The following are exempt from the charges for wigs and fabric supports: anyone who is under 16 or in full-time attendance at school; anyone who is in receipt of **supplementary benefit** or **family income supplement**, or who is a dependant of a person in receipt of either of these; a war pensioner needing the appliance for his accepted disability; people and their dependants who are exempt from prescription charges on income grounds; people in a family getting milk and vitamins free on income grounds (see **Families on low incomes**). Anyone who does not fall into one of these categories can obtain help if his income is below a certain level. Entitlement to help on income grounds is calculated by *Department of Health and Social Security local offices*; claim forms are available from NHS hospitals.

Hospital casualty departments will accept emergency cases (see **Medical treatment: emergency**). Otherwise NHS patients should go first to their NHS family **doctor** for diagnosis and treatment. If hospital treatment is needed, he will refer them to a hospital consultant who will decide what form of hospital treatment is needed and the time of admission. There is no formal procedure for disputing a doctor's decision not to refer a patient to a consultant, but if a patient is dissatisfied, he can ask the *Family Practitioner Committee* to remove his name from the relevant doctor's list and to be placed on the list of another doctor (see **Doctors: complaints**).

Clinical decisions on admission to hospital and priority for admission are for the responsible hospital doctor to make. Again there is no formal appeal system against those decisions, but a patient who is worried about having to wait for admission can approach his family doctor, who will discuss the matter with the consultant if he thinks it necessary to do so.

In hospital the staff aim to help the patient resume independent life through medical and nursing care, and by remedial therapy from **physiotherapists, occupational therapists** and **remedial gymnasts**. Treatment may continue on an out-patient basis after leaving hospital. Hospital social workers, the local authority (Social Services Department), and the *Employment Service Agency* are available to assist with problems arising from hospital treatment at home or at work. Ambulance transport is available for people attending hospital as out-patients or day-patients who cannot use public transport; apply to your family doctor. People with low incomes attending hospital may obtain help with their travelling expenses; apply to DHSS local offices; form available at NHS hospitals. See also **Disablement**.

Hospitals Abroad UK nationals detained in hospital who do not have friends or relatives locally will, if possible, be visited by a British consular officer or a local British resident acting on his behalf, especially in case of language difficulties. Next-of-kin may also be contacted by the consulate. Contact the nearest British consular office or the *Foreign and Commonwealth Office, Consular Department.*

Hounds' Licences Licences may be obtained from specially authorised post offices in Great Britain; and from any *Clerk of Petty Sessions* in Northern Ireland.

House of Lords The House of Lords consists of the Lords Spiritual and the Lords Temporal. The Lords Spiritual are the Archbishops of Canterbury and York, the Bishops of London, Durham and Winchester, and 21 other bishops of the Church of England, according to their seniority as diocesan bishops. The Lords Temporal may be sub-divided into (1) all hereditary peers and peeresses of England, Scotland, Great Britain and the United Kingdom who have not disclaimed their peerages under the Peerage Act 1963, (2) all life peers and peeresses created by the Crown under the Life Peerages Act 1958, and (3) those Lords of Appeal in Ordinary who are appointed to assist the House in the performance of its judicial duties and who remain members of the House after their retirement. Hereditary peerages carry with them a right to sit in the House of Lords (subject to certain statutory disqualifications), provided the holder is 21 years of age or over, but anyone succeeding to a peerage may, within 12 months of succession, disclaim that peerage for his or her lifetime. Disclaimants lose their right to sit in the House of Lords but they gain the right to vote at parliamentary elections and to offer themselves for election to the House of Commons. No hereditary peerage has been conferred since 1965.

Hereditary peers of Ireland have the right to elect 28 of their number to sit in the House of Lords for life, but no elections have been held since 1921 and there are no representative peers for Ireland in the House.

Not all peers with a right to sit in the House of Lords attend the sittings of that House. Those who do not wish to attend may apply for leave of absence for the duration of a Parliament. Peers receive no salary for their parliamentary work, but they are entitled to travelling expenses from their homes to the Houses of Parliament and within specified limits they may claim payments for expenses incurred in attending the House (except for judicial sittings).

The House of Lords is presided over by the Lord Chancellor, who takes his place on the woolsack as ex officio Speaker of the House. In the absence of the Lord Chancellor his place may be taken by a deputy speaker appointed by the Crown or a deputy chairman appointed by the House or, if neither a deputy speaker nor a deputy chairman is present, by a speaker chosen by the Lords present.

See also **Hereditary titles**; **Life peerages**; **Peerage**.

House Renovation Grants Four types of house renovation grant are available through **local authorities**: improvement grants for improving existing dwellings to a high standard or for converting properties into flats; intermediate grants for providing certain standard amenities in existing dwellings together with essential repairs, which the council are obliged to pay if certain conditions are fulfilled; special grants for providing basic amenities for the overall benefit of houses in multiple occupation; repairs grants for repairs to dwellings in 'housing action areas' and 'general improvement areas' payable in cases of hardship at the discretion of the local authority.

The amount of the grant is normally half the eligible expense (i.e. half the approved cost of modernisation), but up to 60% is payable in general improvement areas and up to 75% (or even 90% in special hardship cases) in housing action areas. Loans may also be available in respect of the remaining expenditure which the applicant has to meet. The eligible expense limits are:

Improvement grant: Improvements and conversions – £5,000 per dwelling; Conversions of houses or other buildings having three storeys or more –£5,800 per dwelling; Intermediate grant: Up to £1,200 for amenities; £1,500 for repairs; Special grant: Depends on number of amenities provided; Repairs grant: £1,500.

Improvement grants are paid at local authorities' discretion. They must normally be satisfied that the house is likely to have a useful life of at least thirty years after the work has been done. While up to half the cost may relate to repairs and replacements they do not by themselves qualify for grant. Owner-occupiers are not eligible for improvement grants for improving dwellings or converting houses above specified rateable value limits (for improvements £400 in Greater London and £225 elsewhere in England and Wales, for conversions £600 in London and £350 elsewhere). Applicants must be freeholders or have a lease with at least five years to run. This includes both owner-occupiers and landlords. Grants are paid subject to conditions restricting occupation to owner-occupation or letting for a period of five years, in accordance with the applicant's certified intention when applying for grant. If the conditions are breached the applicant is liable to have to refund the grant with interest, if demanded by the local authority. A tenant cannot apply for grants but if the landlord is unwilling to carry out improvements, the tenant can ask the local authority to require him to instal any standard amenities that are missing. In housing action areas and general improvement areas local authorities may do so without being requested by the tenant.

Apply for grants to the local authority. Plans, specifications and an estimate will be required. Work should not be started until the local authority has approved the application, or the applicant may be disqualified from assistance. Approval for building regulation or planning purposes is not the same as grant approval. For general information see 'Your guide to house renovation grants', available from local authorities. Advice may be obtained from local authority environmental health officers or housing officers.

For details of the improvement grants scheme in Scotland see 'Improve your house, grants available' from local authorities. Advice from local authority environmental health officer.

House Sharing Houses occupied by more than one household ('houses in multiple occupation') are liable to registration by some local authorities; enquiries to authority. The authority may fix the maximum number of people who may live in a shared house, depending on the facilities; have a right of inspection; may require the house to be managed properly (i.e. maintained in a good and clean condition) and work to be carried out to improve living conditions. If the authority considers that the health, safety or welfare of residents is threatened, a control order may be made enabling the authority to take over control of the house for up to five years, paying the owner a fixed rate of compensation. Appeal against an authority's action lies with the courts.

Houseboats Houseboats on rivers and canals of the British Waterways Board require a houseboat certificate from the *British Waterways Board*.
See also **Canals and rivers**.

Housebuilders: VAT Do-it-yourself housebuilders who have built a complete new dwelling may reclaim **value-added tax** on certain goods purchased by them on or after 13 November 1974. The dwelling must not have been built in the course of business, nor be the conversion, reconstruction, alteration or enlargement of any existing building. People not registered for VAT, or registered other than for business as a builder or building contractor, should apply to *Her Majesty's Customs and Excise local offices*; details in HMCE notices 701 and 719.
See also **House renovation grants**.

Housing Associations are non-profit making voluntary housing bodies: under the Housing Act 1974 all Housing Associations, to be eligible for public loans and subsidy, must be registered with the *Housing Corporation*. The HC is a government-financed body set up in 1964 to promote the development of housing societies and to stimulate the building of new houses either for occupation on a co-ownership basis or for letting at fair rents. Government grant is available to meet the gap between fair rents and cost for new housing association schemes. Details available from *National Federation of Housing Associations*. The Register of Housing Associations can be inspected at the HC.
See also **Housing co-operatives**.

Housing Co-operatives These provide a means of improving housing management through collective control and ownership of their homes by the people who live in them. The Housing Rents and Subsidies Act 1975 enables the government to finance and aid co-operative management and ownership schemes including **housing associations** and local authority shared equity schemes. Information on public sector housing co-operative schemes from local authorities; on private sector housing association co-operatives from the *Co-operative Housing Agency* set up by the *Housing Corporation* to provide advice and support to those wishing to set up co-operatives; or from the *Scottish Federation of Housing Associations*.
See also **Housing associations**.

Housing Co-ownership Schemes Schemes provide for groups of not less than seven people to build or convert housing on a non-profit basis. The rent paid by members enables the ownership society to service the joint mortgage, upon which option mortgage subsidy is available. Loan finance

may be provided by the *Housing Corporation*.
See also **Housing associations; Housing co-operatives; Mortgages**.

Housing: Leasehold Persons occupying a house under a long lease at a ground rent have the right to buy the freehold or extend the lease for another 50 years if the lease was originally granted for a term of more than 21 years, is of the whole house, and is at a low rent (i.e. annual rent is less than two-thirds of the rateable value of the house, as assessed on 23 March 1965). In addition the house must have been the occupier's only or main residence, either for the whole of the last five years, or for a total of five years during the last ten years under the lease and on 23 March 1965 the house must have had a rateable value of not more than £400 if it is in the Greater London Area, or £200 anywhere else in the country (or if the house first entered the valuation list on or after 1 April 1973 and had a rateable value of not more than £1,000 in Greater London or £500 elsewhere). These arrangements do not apply to leased flats or maisonettes, nor to **rent charges** or freehold property. If the lease is extended rather than redeemed, the rent during the extension will be a modern ground rent, that is, a rent based on the value of the site in its present use, and this will usually be more than the original rent. After 25 years the rent will be reviewed and if necessary altered.

The freehold may be bought at any time during the original term of the lease (i.e. not once it has been extended); the market value of the land must be paid plus the value of the lease's extension for 50 years at a modern ground rent if it has not already been extended. Apply in first instance to a **solicitor**. In the event of dispute about the price apply to *Lands Tribunal*. Building societies and **local authorities** may lend money for the purchase of freehold.

Housing: Local Authority Housing for letting is provided by most local authorities. Conditions of eligibility vary considerably from area to area, e.g. some authorities require a set period of residence in the area before an application will be considered; others will not accept applications from people who do not meet certain criteria. The first step in obtaining such housing is to contact the local authority housing department to establish eligibility.

Once eligibility has been established a formal application to the authority is normally necessary, which may have to be renewed from time to time. The speed with which individual applicants are allocated accommodation varies from area to area and will normally depend on the availability of suitable property, the number of other applicants on the list, and (probably) on the applicant's existing housing situation and personal circumstances. Some authorities still allocate their housing on a date order basis; offers are made first to those who have been on the list longest. Most authorities, however, allocate at least partially on the basis of housing needs. The applicant's existing housing conditions and personal circumstances are assessed, and a weighting is given to each applicant for such factors as the physical condition of existing accommodation, lack of basic amenities, overcrowding, sharing accommodation with another family and medical history.

In areas where the demand for council housing exceeds the supply it may be some considerable time before accommodation is offered. Applicants willing to move to a **New Town** may obtain accommodation more quickly – advice from local authority or appropriate *New Town Development Corporation*.

To transfer from one local authority property to another, in either the same or a different area, apply to the local authority housing department concerned; transfer usually takes some time, unless priority is given on grounds of a medical condition aggravated by the state or nature of the existing property. Alternatively a mutual transfer may be arranged by advertising for a swap with other authority tenants and obtaining the approval of the authorities concerned to any subsequent transfer.
See also **Local authorities**.

Housing: Private Rented Tenancies
Tenancies in respect of privately-owned rented housing (as opposed to **Housing: local authorities** or by a registered **Housing association**) may be decided primarily by contract between landlord and tenant, but statutory provisions are available upon application by either tenant or landlord (or in some circumstances by the local authority) with the general objects of fixing rents and protecting tenure. The existence of a contractual tenancy agreement does not prohibit application for the imposition of the statutory provisions.

Tenancies from non-resident landlords, in general whether furnished or unfurnished, may be regulated tenancies, in which 'fair rents' are fixed by *Rent Officers* or, on objection, by *Rent Assessment Committees*; or controlled tenancies (which must have started before 6 July 1957), in which rents are fixed in relation to 1956 gross rateable values and a proportion of the costs of certain subsequent repairs and improvements. Either tenancy under a non-resident landlord has full protection (security of tenure) under the Rent Acts: a notice to quit, or the expiry of a fixed term protected tenancy (e.g. a 12-month lease) merely brings to an end the contract which created the tenancy, the protected tenant continuing in occupation as a statutory tenant. A statutory tenancy lasts as long as the tenant continues to live in the property and may be passed on to a statutory successor. (See 'Regulated tenancies – rents, rights and responsibilities: a guide for private landlords and tenants' from *Department of the Environment* or *Welsh Office*.)

A statutory tenant may be evicted only by the landlord obtaining a court order for possession – apply county court. This will be granted only if one of certain grounds can be shown: rent arrears, serious breaches of a tenancy agreement, damage to premises or furniture, causing a nuisance to adjoining occupiers, an offer of suitable accommodation unreasonably refused, danger to public health (see **House sharing**), or need by the landlord for his own or family's use. A court order for possession usually gives a tenant 28 days further tenure before expiry, at which time the landlord is entitled to obtain a Bailiff's Warrant from the court. Court bailiffs will execute an eviction a few days later. (A court must, however, make an order where an owner-occupier has let his own home, or where a person has let the home he means to occupy on retirement and, in either case, needs the dwelling for his own use, generally provided that written notice has been served at the beginning of the tenancy that possession may be recovered on the relevant grounds). Special provisions apply to owner-occupiers who intend letting their homes, e.g. during a temporary absence – see 'Letting your own home', from the *Department of the Environment* or *Welsh Office*.

In tenancies from resident landlords, reasonable rents can be fixed on application to *Rent Tribunals*. A resident landlord must live in the same building as the tenant, the building not being a purpose-built block of flats (see also **House sharing**). Tenants of resident landlords normally have only restricted protection against repossession by the landlord. Even so, a tenant of a resident landlord served with a notice to quit may apply to *Rent Tribunal* for a suspension of up to 6 months, and possibly reapply for further periods thereafter; only when these have expired may a landlord obtain a court order for repossession if the tenant does not leave of his own accord. A resident landlord need not supply grounds for repossession. Once a court order is granted the procedure for eviction is as above. (See 'Rooms to let' and Booklet FRI, both from *DOE* or *Welsh Office*.) Fixed-term tenancies from resident landlords are protected tenancies until the expiry of the term. Rents assessed by a *Rent Officer* or *Rent Assessment Committee* are registered and are open to free inspection at the Rent Office. Landlords may apply to the *Rent Officer* in advance of a first letting for a Certificate of Fair Rent establishing the fair rent for the dwelling. Similar arrangements apply to *Rent Tribunals*, rents being registered with local authority. Weekly tenants must be given a rent book in prescribed form. Premiums in addition to rent before granting a tenancy (e.g. by way of key money or excessive costs of fixtures and fittings, but not deposits returnable at the end of the tenancy) are generally illegal.

Tenancy contracts may provide that the rent under the tenancy shall be that registered by the rent officer, or may specify a contractual rent which is higher than the registered rent (although a landlord cannot generally enforce payment of such a contractual rent). A registered rent can be cancelled only by a joint application by a landlord and tenant to *Rent Officer*. Unless the terms of the contract permit rent increases a landlord wishing to increase the rent must serve a notice of increase in prescribed form (available from law stationers). Rent increases must generally be phased in equally over a period of three years. There is special provision for adjusting rents following increases in rates or in the costs of furniture or services, or following repairs and improvements to the property (subject to any local authority House improvement grant which has been used: see **House renovation**). Landlords are obliged to carry out certain repairs if the tenancy agreement is for less than seven years.

A controlled tenancy is passed on to members of the immediate family provided they have been living in the property for at least six months previously; the tenancy can be passed on once more under the same conditions, but then becomes a regulated tenancy. A landlord may change a controlled tenancy to a regulated tenancy (which normally enables the rent to be increased to at least the regulated fair rent) by providing the property with statutory standard amenities and then obtaining a Qualification Certificate from the local authority; a certificate of provisional approval can be issued by the authority to a landlord intending to carry out such improvements at the same time as he applies for a House improvement grant. Copies of these certificates, if granted, must be sent by the authority to the controlled tenant. Dwellings declared statutorily unfit cannot be decontrolled. Controlled tenancies with a rateable value of £70 or more on 31 March 1972 have been automatically decontrolled. It is a criminal offence for either a resident or non-resident landlord to harass a tenant with the object of possession or to evict him without a court order. Tenants may complain of harassment to local authority (usually the Town Clerk's Department), who have power to prosecute, or apply to county court for an injunction to restrain the landlord and for reinstatement, followed by a civil action for damages. See also **Homelessness**.

Those in rented accommodation tied to employment are licensees often paying only a nominal rent or no rent at all, and are not eligible for the full security available to tenants unless agricultural workers covered by the Rent (Agriculture) Act 1976.

Special provisions apply to tenancy agreements beginning before 16 August 1974, to formerly controlled tenancies where the first registered rent has been determined (see 'Controlled rents to fair rents', from *DOE* or *Welsh Office*) to ground rent tenancies, and to business or mixed business residential tenancies (see 'Security of tenure of business premises' – *HMSO*).

Rent regulation and protected tenancies do not apply to arrangements where a substantial part of the rent payments are in respect of board or attendance, to tenancies granted to students by specified educational institutions, to holiday lettings, to out-of-season lettings of student and holiday accommodation, to tenancies whose annual rent is less than two-thirds of the rateable value of the dwelling, or to tenancies of a dwelling whose rateable value exceeds £1,500 in Greater London or £750 elsewhere in England and Wales (usually as at 1 April 1973). For general information see 'Regulated tenancies – rents, rights and responsibilities, a guide for private landlords and tenants', and 'Landlords and the law' both from *DOE* or *Welsh Office*. For general position in Scotland see 'Regulated tenancies in Scotland', leaflet from Scottish *Rent Registration Offices* and local authorities. Advice from *Rent*

Officers, Citizens Advice Bureaux, local authorities, Housing Advisory or Aid Centres, or **solicitors** (see **Legal advice scheme**).
See also **Rate charges; Rent rebates and allowances.**

Hovercraft Hovercraft should generally be registered with the *Department of Trade* (Marine Division). Permits for commercial operation are also issued by the DoT, subject to safety certification by the *Civil Aviation Authority, Hovercraft Department.*

Human Rights: Amnesty International
Amnesty International believes that everyone has the right to hold and express convictions and has an obligation to extend the same freedom to others. It is a worldwide human rights movement which is independent of any government, or political, ideological or religious grouping. It campaigns for the release of men and women who are imprisoned anywhere for their religious or political beliefs or for their colour, language or ethnic origin, provided they have not used or advocated violence. These are termed 'prisoners of conscience'. Enquiries and membership information from *Amnesty International, British Section.*

Human Rights: European Convention
Any person, non-governmental organisation or group of individuals claiming to be the victim of a violation by one of the high contracting parties (including the UK) to the rights set forth in the European Convention for the Protection of Human Rights and Fundamental Freedoms may apply to the *European Commission of Human Rights*, provided the state has accepted the right of individual petition. The UK has accepted this right. The application should be made in writing; be signed by the applicant or his representative; and mention the applicant's name; the name of the high contracting party against which the claim is made; the object of the claim; as far as possible the provisions of the convention alleged to have been violated; a statement of the facts and arguments; any attached documents.

The applicant should also provide information to show that all domestic remedies have been exhausted and that the petition is made within six months from the date on which the final decision was taken in the matter by the court or authority of the state concerned. The application should be sent to the Secretary General at the Commission.

Under the Convention, the Commission must consider certain petitions inadmissible (e.g. those incompatible with the provisions of the convention, manifestly ill-founded, or an abuse of the right of petition). If the application is admissible, the Commission ascertains the facts and tries to reach a friendly settlement, and, failing this, it draws up a report containing both a statement of the facts and an opinion as to whether the facts found disclose a breach by the respondent state of its obligations under the convention.

The report is transmitted to the Committee of Ministers of the *Council of Europe*, whereupon the case may be brought before the *European Court of Human Rights* within three months by the Commission and/or by the contracting state concerned. If this does not occur, the Committee of Ministers decides whether or not there has been a violation of the Convention.

The Convention does not give individual applicants a right to refer a case to the court or to appear before it as parties. It is, however, open to the Commission to 'take into account' on its own authority any 'view' the applicant may make known to it on the Commission's report or on any other matter arising in the course of the proceedings. The court, by a majority vote, gives final judgments which are binding on the states concerned. The Court may, in certain circumstances, afford 'just satisfaction' to the victim of a violation and consider requests for interpretation or revision of its judgments. Further information from the Secretary to the Commission.

Human Rights: International Commission of Jurists The Commission defends the rule of law throughout the world, and works towards the full observance of the provisions in the Universal Declaration of Human Rights. It is a strictly non-political, independent and impartial, non-governmental organisation, having consultative status with the Economic and Social Council of the United Nations, UNESCO, and the Council of Europe. It is on the International Labour Organisation's Special List of Non-governmental Organisations. Enquiries to the *International Commission of Jurists* in Geneva.

Human Rights: International Defence and Aid Fund for Southern Africa The fund aids victims of the political situation in Southern Africa through legal defence costs; relief; and research and publications. It is one of the non-governmental organisations enjoying consultative status with the Economic and Social Council of the United Nations and with UNESCO. Its funds come from the United Nations Trust Fund, some 25 governments, affiliated committees in a number of countries, and from private donations.

Human Rights: National Council for Civil Liberties The *National Council for Civil Liberties* is an independent non-party organisation which defends civil liberties and human rights in England, Wales and Northern Ireland. Major concerns are the administration of justice; **sex** and **race discrimination**; emergency legislation; individual privacy and official secrecy; rights of prisoners; rights of homosexuals. In Scotland there is an affiliated but separate institution, the *Scottish Council for Civil Liberties*.
See also **Disputes with public authorities; Injustice.**

Humanities Grants for postgraduate study and research in the humanities (archaeology, architecture, art, classics, English, history, law, linguistics, modern languages, music, philosophy and theology) are available from the *Department of Education and Science, Higher and Further Education 1V*; the *Scottish Education Department*; and the *Department of Education, Northern Ireland, Scholarship and Student Awards Branch.*
If the subject for study borders between the humanities and sciences, the grant may be the responsibility of one of the research councils (see **Research grants**). Enquiries concerning students' eligibility and grant levels, etc., should be addressed direct to the most appropriate Department or research council.
Postgraduate student awards take two forms, state studentships and state bursaries. State studentships (one year) and major state studentships (three years) are awarded directly on merit by the DES and the DENI; apply through the university awarding the first degree, or through the university where the post graduate study is to take place. State bursaries (which are of less value to the holder and are equivalent to first degree awards) are awarded directly by the universities themselves. Universities obtain a quota of bursaries from the DES or the DENI and these are available to students taking designated full-time postgraduate courses. Enquire in England and Wales direct to the proposed place of study (not to the DES) which must nominate the student for an award before 15 July of the year in which the course begins. The DES informs students direct of their success or failure in obtaining a bursary. Northern Ireland students should apply to DENI only if wishing to study in Great Britain, otherwise to the Northern Ireland institution (see also **Education: Scotland; Education: Northern Ireland**).
Outside the universities, the *British Academy* is the recognised channel for government support of advanced research projects in the humanities and, to a lesser extent, in the social sciences. From its government grant it offers awards in aid of specific research projects or programmes to individuals, scholarly institutions or learned societies for original research at post-doctoral level. Work directed towards academic or professional qualifications is not eligible. Apply to the secretary at the BA.
See also **Student grants; Universities.**

Hungary For **exchange control** is a non-scheduled territory outside the **overseas sterling area** and the EEC. UK nationals travelling direct from the UK normally need only the following (but check): **passports**; **visas**; **work permits** (if taking a job); green cards for motor insurance (if bringing a car); international driving permits (if intending to drive: see **Motoring abroad**). The UK has no reciprocal health or social security arrangements.
Enquiries to *Hungarian Embassy* in London or *Hungarian Tourist Office 'Ibusz'* in London.
British diplomatic mission to Hungary is *British Embassy* in Budapest.

Hunting The different branches of hunting are represented by separate organisations, including the *Masters of Foxhounds Association*, the *Masters of Otterhounds Association*, the *Masters of Deerhounds Association*, the *Association of Masters of Harriers and Beagles*, the *Association of Masters of Basset Hounds* and the *British Falconers Club*. These organisations are affiliated to the *British Field Sports Society*.
See also **Field sports**.

Hygiene at Work Policy on lighting, thermal environment, ventilation, cleanliness, sanitary conveniences, washing facilities, drinking water and other welfare facilities in workplaces is the responsibility of Hazardous Substances Branch D at the *Health and Safety Executive Head Office*. Technical advice on hygiene in the workplace from the *Health and Safety Executive, HM Factory Inspectorate Area Offices*.
See also **Work: health and safety**.

Hypnosis Hypnotherapists can practise in the UK without any qualifications or training, but the professional association, the *British Hypnotherapy Association*, maintains a register of fully-trained therapists, recommends therapists and handles complaints about professional misconduct. A number of independent organisations, including the BHA and some university departments, provide training courses in hypnotheraphy. No public exhibition, demonstration or performance of hypnotism may be given unless authorised by the relevant authority under the provision of the Hypnotism Act 1952; apply to the local authority.

I

Ice Hockey is governed internationally by the International Ice Hockey Federation and in the UK by the *British Ice Hockey Association*. Rules, selection of British teams, administration, and international relations are the reponsibility of the BIHA. For the purpose of fixtures and routine activities the UK is divided into the *Northern Ice Hockey Association* (10 clubs) and the *Southern Ice Hockey Association* (14 clubs). All UK players affiliated to BIHA are male amateurs.

Iceland For **exchange control** is a non-scheduled territory in the **overseas sterling area** but outside the **EEC**. UK nationals travelling direct from the UK normally need only the following (but check): **passports; work permits** (if taking a job); green cards for motor insurance (if bringing a car); international driving permits (if intending to drive: see **Motoring abroad**).
The UK has no reciprocal health or social security arrangements.
Enquiries to *Icelandic Embassy* in London or *Icelandic Tourist Information Bureau* in London.
British diplomatic missions to Iceland are *British Embassy* in Reykjavik and *British Consulates* in Akureyri and Isafjord.

Illegitimate Children: England and Wales The father of an illegitimate child may be entered in the birth register either originally or (where no father's name was originally recorded) at a later date, provided either the father attends with the mother to effect a joint registration; the mother produces a statutory declaration made by him acknowledging his paternity; or the mother produces a certified copy of an affiliation order naming him as the father (in this case the child's written consent is required if over 16).
Where the natural parents of an illegitimate child marry one another and at the time of the marriage the father is domiciled in England or Wales, the child is made legitimate by the parents' marriage. In this case, the parents have a duty to apply for the birth to be re-registered. If at the time of the marriage the father is domiciled in another country the question whether the child is made legitimate depends on the law of that country.
Apply to re-register births of illegitimate children or children made legitimate to local *Registrar of Births, Deaths and Marriages* or direct to the *Registrar General of England and Wales*.
See also **Birth registration: England and Wales; Foundlings; Records of births, marriages and deaths.**

Illegitimate Children: Northern Ireland
The father of an illegitimate child may be entered in the birth register either originally or (where no father's name was originally recorded) at a later date, provided either the father attends with the mother to effect a joint registration; or the mother produces a statutory declaration made by him acknowledging his paternity.
Where the natural parents of an illegi-

timate child marry one another and at the time of the marriage the father is domiciled in Northern Ireland, the child is made legitimate by the parents' marriage. In this case, the parents have a duty to apply for the birth to be re-registered. If at the time of the marriage the father is domiciled in another country the question whether the child is made legitimate depends on the law of that country. Where the marriage takes place prior to the registration of the birth, the *Registrar General for Northern Ireland* may authorise registration in legitimate form at the outset.

Apply to re-register births of illegitimate children or children made legitimate to the *Registrar General for Northern Ireland*.

See also **Birth registration: Northern Ireland; Records of births, marriages and deaths.**

Illegitimate Children: Scotland The name and occupation of the father of an illegitimate child can be entered in the register of births at the time of registration only if he attends along with the mother to act as joint informant; or if the mother produces to the registrar a statutory declaration made by the father admitting paternity and herself signs a confirmatory declaration in the registrar's presence.

The father's name may be added to the birth entry later either on the authority of a statutory declaration by the father within one year of the date of birth and a confirmatory declaration made by the mother in the presence of a registrar; or, if the mother is deceased, on application by the father, within one year of the birth, to the sheriff to have his name added to the birth entry; or if the import of a decree of paternity has been recorded against the birth entry (Clerks of courts in Scotland have to send details of such decrees to the *Registrar General for Scotland*); or where the natural parents of a living illegitimate child marry each other and the father is domiciled in Scotland; the child is made legitimate by the marriage and the parents, surviving parent, person himself or his agent may apply to have the original birth entry re-registered.

For re-registration apply to *General Register Office (Scotland)*.

If at the time of the marriage, the father is domiciled in another country, whether the child is made legitimate depends on the law of that country.

See also **Birth registration: Scotland.**

Illness Abroad Treatment under the **National Health Service** is not available outside the UK, but under EEC social security regulations, those currently or formerly insured under Class 1 contributions to the UK National Insurance Scheme (see **National insurance contributions**) can receive immediately necessary medical treatment in any EEC country on the same basis as insured citizens of that country. In all EEC countries except Denmark, Gibraltar and Eire a form E111 is required, which should be obtained from the *Department of Health and Social Security* local offices well before departure from the UK. These arrangements do not normally apply to self-employed or unemployed people (exceptions are Denmark and the Federal Republic of Germany) nor do they apply to those travelling to an EEC country especially for medical treatment; they cover only emergency care. Detailed information from DHSS local offices and most travel agents. See also entry for each country.

Health arrangements with Austria, Bulgaria, Channel Islands, Czechoslovakia, German Democratic Republic, Gibraltar, Malta, New Zealand, Norway, Poland, Romania, Sweden, USSR and Yugoslavia allow people resident in the UK, on presentation of a British **passport** and/or **NHS medical card** to receive certain forms of emergency treatment either free of charge or at reduced costs.

Unless covered by these arrangements, UK nationals must pay the full cost of all medical expenses abroad. Insurance against this can be arranged through most travel agents or insurers. See also **Travel: health protection.**

Immigration Immigration into the UK is governed by the Immigration Act 1971. Everyone entering the UK, for whatever reason or length of stay, needs a **passport** or other identity document. Nationals of EEC members states may travel on their national identity cards.

The UK, the Channel Islands, the Isle of Man and the Irish Republic collectively form a common travel area. Passengers examined for immigration on control at their point of entry to the area are free to enter any other part without further examination. But passengers arriving in the UK may be refused leave to enter if there is reason to believe that they intend to enter any other part of the common travel area where they are not acceptable to the immigration authorities.

Certain groups of people are free from immigration control (see **Immigration: patrials**); generally everyone else requires formal leave to enter the UK (see **Immigration: non-patrials**). General advice from *Home Office Immigration and Nationality Department* and the *UK Immigrants Advisory Service*. Separate guides to the Immigration Act 1971 for **Commonwealth** citizens, for EEC and other non-Commonwealth nationals, and on rights of appeal against immigration decisions, available from the Home Office.

Immigration: Employment People who are neither **EEC** nationals nor **British subjects** with a grandparent born in the UK, and who wish to take or seek employment in the UK need (with some occupational exceptions) a **work permit** issued by the *Department of Employment*; first enquiry to the nearest *British diplomatic mission* overseas.

EEC nationals entering for employment will be admitted initially for six months and, if staying beyond that time, are required to obtain a residence permit valid for five years from the *Home Office Immigration and Nationality Department*.

Work permit holders may be admitted for a period of up to 12 months in the first instance, and their stay may be extended for a further three years, after which they may be accepted for permanent settlement. Foreign nationals given limited leave to enter for employment for more than three months are required to register with the *police* within seven days of arrival (fee payable). Limited leave may be extended or varied; apply to HO IND.

Immigration: Exchange Control Non-residents who become UK residents for exchange control purposes may be given exemption from exchange control requirements concerning foreign currency balances and securities held at the time they became residents of the UK, and income and capital deriving from these. Consult an **authorised bank**.

See also **Exchange control**; **Foreign currency and credit**; **Foreign currency securities**.

Immigration: Non-Patrials Generally everyone who is not patrial (see **Immigration: patrials**) requires formal leave to enter the UK. Some foreign nationals (mainly from Eastern Europe and the Near and Middle East) need a current **visa**; apply to nearest *British diplomatic mission*. People seeking admission as the wife, child or dependant of a person settled or employed in the UK, or as the husband or fiancé of a woman settled in the UK, must hold a current entry clearance (i.e. a visa if a national or citizen of Pakistan; an entry certificate if a **Commonwealth** citizen; or a Home Office letter of consent; apply to *British diplomatic mission*). People not required to have entry clearance who nevertheless wish to ascertain in advance whether they are eligible for admission may similarly apply for a visa, entry certificate or letter of consent.

Entry may be refused to non-patrials who do not qualify in the capacity in which they wish to enter; or on grounds of criminal record, medical incapacity or restricted returnability (i.e. where the Immigration Officer is satisfied that the person will not be admitted to another country after a stay in the UK); or if they are the subject of a deportation order (see **Deportation from the UK**); or if their exclusion is deemed conducive to the public good. A passenger may also be refused entry if false representations were made to obtain the entry clearance certificate, or if a change of circumstances since its issue has removed the basis of the person's claim to admission.

Appeal may be made against refusal of leave to enter; against a decision that formal leave to enter is required; or against a refusal to issue a certificate of patriality or an entry clearance. Give notice of appeal to the officer responsible for the decision. The appeal is heard in the first instance by an adjudicator.

Limited leave to enter the UK for a prescribed time is given on various terms to visitors, students (and their dependants), au pair girls (see **Au pair arrangements**), business visitors, people of independent means and those entering for employment. Foreign nationals given limited leave to enter for more than three months for employment, or in other cases for more than six months, must register with the *police* within seven days of arrival (fee payable). Limited leave may be extended or varied on application to the *Home Office Immigration and Nationality Department*.

If the application was made in time and was refused, the person normally has the right of appeal. A person whose leave is varied on the initiative of the Home Office also has a right of appeal. Give notice of appeal to the HO IND; it will be heard in the first instance by an adjudicator.

Indefinite leave to enter for an indefinite period is given only to those already accepted for permanent settlement, to dependants of such people or of those already settled in the UK, or to returning residents.

See also **Overseas students in the UK**.

Immigration: Patrials Certain groups of people have the right of abode in the UK and are free from immigration control. Broadly, citizens of the UK and colonies or of other **Commonwealth** countries connected with the UK by birth, descent, residence or marriage have this right and are 'patrial'. Citizens of the UK and colonies who are patrial by virtue of their UK residence, Commonwealth citizens who have the right of abode by descent, and women who are commonwealth citizens and who are married to men in either of those two categories must hold certificates of patriality in proof of that right. Obtain them from a *British diplomatic mission* overseas or from the *Home Office*.

Note that Commonwealth citizens from overseas, including citizens of the UK and colonies who hold passports issued by or on behalf of the government of any part of the Commonwealth outside the UK are subject to immigration control. Citizens of the UK and colonies who hold passports issued by British High Commissions or other British diplomatic posts outside the UK and the Republic of Ireland are also subject to control unless they have one of the accepted connections with the UK (by birth, descent, naturalisation, registration or adoption).

See also **British subjects; Citizenship of the UK and colonies; Naturalisation**.

Import Licences UK trade restrictions cover potatoes from all sources; fresh vegetables and a range of consumer goods from state trading countries; bananas from Latin America; and textiles from developing countries. In addition the *Department of Trade* maintains restrictions on imports, from all sources, of **radioactive materials** (for public health reasons); of **firearms** (for public safety reasons); and of **gold** coins, medals, etc. (for balance of payment reasons). The UK also operates import licensing surveillance (i.e. where licences are issued freely on demand without restriction as to quantity or value) on all textiles; colour television sets and tubes and portable monochrome television sets; zip fasteners; electronic calculators; and certain phosphate fertilisers. In the main surveillance licensing applies to imports of such goods consigned to the UK from non-EEC sources.

Enquiries about import licensing requirements and applications for licences to the *Department of Trade Import Licensing Branch*.

See also **Imports: exchange control**.

Imports: Exchange Control An **import licence** carries the right to pay for goods. The remittance of funds to the foreign supplier is, however, subject to **exchange control**. Generally any **authorised bank** can effect payment for imports provided that they are given appropriate documentary evidence to show that payment is properly due both as regards amount and timing. Special rules apply to advance payments for imports; any authorised bank should be able to advise and application must be made to the *Bank of England*. Cases of doubt are referred to *Her Majesty's Customs* or the *Bank of England*, as appropriate. A leaflet about importing formalities is available from banks.

There are no restrictions on the import of banknotes into the UK (in sterling or other currency) and of documents such as assurance policies, bills of exchange, travellers' cheques and postal orders.

To pay for goods ordered from an advertisement in a foreign magazine, the appropriate documentary evidence (e.g. a cutting from the magazine or an invoice together with evidence of shipment to the UK) should be presented to an authorised bank. Funds authorised for travel must not be used for any other purpose. Any person wishing to pay for goods (apart from keepsakes and small items for personal use) while abroad should apply to the BE.

See also **Foreign currency and credit**.

Imprisonment and Detention Abroad
In countries with which the UK has diplomatic relations British consular officers (see **Consuls**) are responsible for protecting UK nationals; this includes attempting to ensure that they receive fair treatment within the framework of the local law and civilised standards. They visit detainees whenever practicable. In the few countries with which the UK has no diplomatic relations the diplomatic mission of another country normally looks after the affairs of UK nationals. The *Foreign and Commonwealth Office Consular Department* should be consulted before departure for such countries.

Income Tax Income tax is applicable to individuals (see **Corporation tax** for companies) and is a tax on income, i.e. on earnings, profits from a trade or profession, rents, interest, dividends and other annual receipts. Bonuses, tips and fringe benefits can also be taxable.

Income tax is charged for the year beginning on 6 April. The gross income from all sources is 'aggregated'; deduction may then be made for personal allowances according to the taxpayer's personal and family circumstances and for certain charges (e.g. interest on a **mortgage** on the taxpayer's home). This produces the 'net taxable income', on which tax is charged in accordance with a scale laid down by Parliament year by year. There is usually an initial broad band of taxable income chargeable at the 'basic rate' of income tax. Above that, succeeding bands are chargeable at (rising) higher rates.

Income tax assessment in the UK is dealt with by the *Inland Revenue, HM Inspectors of Taxes*, in district tax offices throughout the UK; self-employed people deal with the office covering the area where their business address is; most employees deal with the same office as their employer (generally the tax office for the area where the employer's head or paying office is). Tax collection is dealt with by the *Inland Revenue, HM Collector of Taxes*. To find out which office is appropriate to you, enquire either of your employer or of the nearest *Inland Revenue, HM Inspector of Taxes*. Where Pay As You Earn work has been transferred to non-localised areas, enquiries are dealt with by local *Inland Revenue PAYE Enquiry Offices*. Most people make a return of income to their Inspector and, on the same form, claim for allowances, etc. If you think full allowances are not being given you, get in touch with your Inspector or, if that is not convenient, with any other Inspector or one of the *Inland Revenue PAYE Enquiry Officers*.

If you cannot agree with the Inspector as to whether you are entitled to a particular allowance or about the amount of tax he has assessed you have the right – and so does he – of having the matter brought before the Appeal Commissioners. If you wish to appeal, notify your Inspector. From there it is possible to appeal further, to the High Court, but only on a point of law.

Independent Schools In England, Wales and Northern Ireland anyone (without professional qualifications) can open an independent school and anyone can teach at it, provided that they have not been barred from teaching through their own misconduct (see **Teachers**). This is true of all independent branches of education (e.g. nursery schools, institutions of higher education, free schools, preparatory schools, public schools, schools for autistic children, schools for children with outstanding musical gifts, law schools, film schools, etc.).

Independent schools for pupils up to the age of 18 are, however, subject to inspection by Her Majesty's inspectors. They must register with the *Department of Education and Science* or the *Department of Education, Northern Ireland* (the registers are open to public inspection) and they must be open to inspection by the inspectors of the relevant education authority. Inspection concentrates on standards of education, quality of teaching and professional staff.

Independent schools may apply for membership of the *Headmasters' Conference* or the *Association of Head Mistresses*, which confers the status of public school. These schools usually accept pupils at about 12 or 13 years of age on the basis of a fairly demanding examination called the **Common entrance**. They may also offer scholarships on the basis of separate scholarship examinations. Many of the schools are still single sex (about half of them for girls) and at least partly boarding. But there are also day schools and co-educational schools, and certain boys' public schools now admit some girls direct to their top forms. Preparatory schools are schools preparing for public schools.

Information on independent schools for girls or boys from 5-18 (or help with their educational problems) is available from the *Independent Schools Information Service*, which recommends for a child three or four schools which parents are urged to visit to make their own choice. ISIS is controlled by the four main bodies which deal with public and preparatory schools, and its range of information covers the whole independent sector from 5-18. There are also scholastic agencies which find a place for a child, e.g. *Gabitas-Thring Educational Trust*.

See also **Education: Scotland; Education: Northern Ireland**; entries on **Schools**.

Index-Linked National Savings These are issued by *Her Majesty's Treasury* and administered by the *Department for National Savings*. Repayments on certain National Savings schemes are related to changes from the date of purchase in the retail price index. Index-linked bonuses are free of UK **income tax** and **capital gains tax**. Save As You Earn (Third Issue) contracts can be opened by people over 16 who agree to make 60 monthly payments of £4–£20 during five years. Application forms from post offices, banks and some employers; send form to *Department for National Savings Save As You Earn Office*. Retirement Issue **National Savings Certificates** are purchasable by men over 65 and women over 60, in units of £10 up to a maximum holding of £500. Buy them from POs and Trustee Savings Banks. In Northern Ireland purchase indexed Retirement Issue Ulster Savings Certificates at POs, banks and from the *Stock Exchange, Belfast*, and the *Ulster Savings Branch*.

See also **National Savings bank accounts**.

India **Commonwealth** member. For **exchange control** is a non-scheduled territory in the **overseas sterling area** but outside the EEC. UK nationals travelling direct from the UK normally need only the following (but check): **passports**; **work permits** (if taking a job).

The UK has no reciprocal health or social security arrangements.

Enquiries to *Indian High Commission* in London and *Indian Assistant High Commissioner's Offices* in Birmingham, Glasgow and Liverpool, and *Indian Consulate-General* in Manchester.

British diplomatic missions to India are *British High Commission* in New Delhi and *British Deputy High Commissions* in Bombay, Calcutta and Madras.

Indonesia For **exchange control** is a non-scheduled territory outside the **overseas sterling area** and the **EEC**. UK nationals travelling direct from the UK normally need only the following (but check): **passports**; **visas**; international certificates of **vaccination** against smallpox; **work permits** (if taking a job); green cards for motor insurance (if bringing a car); international driving permits (if intending to drive: see **Motoring abroad**).
The UK has no reciprocal health or social security arrangements.
Enquiries to *Indonesian Embassy* in London.
British diplomatic missions to Indonesia are *British Embassy* in Jakarta and *British Consulates* in Medan and Surabaya.

Industrial Accidents Employers of 10 or more people must have a book (or books) readily accessible to employees, in which an accident at work can be recorded by an injured person or by some other person acting on his behalf. The official Accident Book (form BI 510) is obtainable from *Her Majesty's Stationery Office*. Where the employer prefers to use an alternative form of Accident Book, this has to be approved by the *Secretary of State for Social Services*. Failure by an employee to report promptly an industrial accident can affect entitlement to Injury benefit.
See **Industrial injury and disease**; **Work: health and safety**.

Industrial Design The *Design Council* is the government grant-aided body set up to promote improved design in British products. It operates a range of services for industry and the general public (see **Design: consumer products**; **Design awards**). Other organisations are: the *Society of Industrial Artists and Designers*, the *Institution of Engineering Designers*, the *Council of Engineering Institutions* and the *Royal Society of Arts*.

Advice on design policy, and technical and design problems, is available to British companies from the industrial and engineering field officers of the Design Council who provide a diagnosis and referral service. They are supported by the DC's register of UK sources of technical advice (e.g. consultants, manufacturers, universities and research organisations). These and other services are available to all companies, but are free or cheaper for members of the DC's Design Advisory Service.

Industrial Designers and Artists These can practise legally without qualifications but professional standards are set by the *Society of Industrial Artists and Designers*. Licentiates (LSIAD) and diploma members (no affix) have completed a full-time course at a UK polytechnic or college of art and design; members (MSIAD) have a minimum of three years' in practice and their work has passed the Society's examination; associates (no affix) are non-practitioners engaged in design administration or education; fellows (FSIAD) normally have a minimum of seven years in practice and their work shows a 'high level of competence'. Complaints against members' professional conduct are investigated by the SIAD.
To contact a designer, go through the Design Information Service of the SIAD (it covers SIAD members, staff vacancies and freelance commissions) or the Designer Selection Service of the *Design Council*.

Industrial Development Certificates Application for **planning permission** for industrial development must usually be supported by an industrial development certificate. Certificates are not required in **assisted areas** (except intermediate areas). Apply to *Department of Industry regional offices*.

Industrial Development: Northern Ireland All Northern Ireland is an **assisted area** and all the schemes of assistance available in Assisted Areas in Great Britain are paralleled in Northern Ireland. There are also other schemes. For example, industrial advice grants towards the cost of engaging independent consultants to increase the efficiency of an undertaking are available to firms establishing factories in Northern Ireland. For expenditure up to £5,000, 50% is paid, and over £5,000 33¼%. Again, rates on industrial buildings in Northern Ireland may be reduced by 75% for firms establishing factories. Regional employment premium is payable to any employer with a manufacturing establishment in Northern Ireland which is registered in respect of employees at that establishment. The regional employment premium is payable at weekly rates for each full and part-time employee.

A flexible range of financial assistance may also be available from the *Northern Ireland Finance Corporation*, a government-sponsored financial institution empowered not only to assist existing undertakings but also to stimulate new investment by way of equity shareholdings, loans and loan guarantees to suitable applicants.

Information. about capital and industrial development grant schemes and incentives available in Northern Ireland is obtainable from *Northern Ireland Department of Commerce*. See also **Regional development grants**.

Industrial Disputes Disputes may be referred by the parties to the *Advisory, Conciliation and Arbitration Service* for conciliation (i.e. assisting the parties to reach a settlement by agreement) or mediation (i.e. a recommendation by a mediator or a board of mediation on the content of a settlement) or arbitration (i.e. a decision on a settlement by an arbitrator, a board of arbitration or the *Central Arbitration Committee*).

Apply to *Advisory, Conciliation and Arbitration Service, Regional Offices*. See also **Industrial relations; Industrial tribunals; Trade unions**.

Industrial Engineering Projects Projects may be inspected for compliance with any recognised national or international code or specification by *Lloyd's Register of Shipping*. Such projects may include nuclear, thermal and hydro-electric power stations, oil refineries and general engineering.

Industrial Expansion Advice The Department of Industry offers a free confidential advisory service on locations with favourable conditions, with particular reference to governent **assisted areas**. Enquiries to *Department of Industry* (headquarters (2)), or *Department of Industry* (regional offices), the *Scottish Economic Planning Department*, the *Welsh Office Industry Department* or the *Northern Ireland Department of Commerce*.

Industrial Injury and Disease Social **security benefits** are paid to employees injured or disabled by an accident at work or by certain industrial diseases; they do not depend on payment of **national insurance contributions**. An accident should be notified to the employer as soon as possible after it happens (see **Industrial accidents**). Injury Benefit is paid for a maximum period of 26 weeks from the date of an accident or of the development of the disease, for incapacity for work due to the accident or disease. Benefit may be increased for people with dependants and by **earnings-related supplement** if appropriate. It is paid instead of (not as well as) sickness benefit (see **Sickness**). Apply to *Department of Health and Social Security* (local offices). See leaflets NI5 (Injury benefit), NI2 (Prescribed diseases), NI3 (Pneumoconiosis and byssinosis), from DHSS.

When Injury benefit ceases Disablement Benefit may be paid to those suffering from physical or mental **disablement** (including occupational **deafness**) as a result of industrial accident or disease, whether they are working or not; apply to DHSS local offices. The amount of disablement benefit depends on the degree of disablement as assessed by a medical board; it is paid either as a weekly pension or as a lump sum depending on degree of disablement. See leaflet NI6 (Disablement benefit), NI207 (Occupational deafness).

Those still unable to work after the 26 weeks injury benefit period may be eligible for sickness or invalidity benefit (see **Sickness** and **Invalidity**). Allowances payable in addition to disablement benefit are special hardship allowance, unemployability supplement, hospital treatment allowance, constant attendance allowance, and exceptionally severe disablement allowance.

Disablement before 1948: if disablement results from employment before 5 July 1948, a special scheme of Workmen's Compensation provides benefit, including death benefit, to widows, etc., for pneumoconiosis and certain other slowly-developing diseases acquired in the course of specified occupations at that time (see leaflet PNI (pneumoconiosis related to employment before 1948). This can be supplemented by weekly payments – see leaflet WSI (Supplements to Workmen's Compensation). Apply to the *Department of Health and Social Security* (local offices).

Industrial Death Benefit may be paid to the widow or other dependant of an employee who dies as a result of industrial accident or disease. Apply to DHSS local offices (see leaflet NI10 (Death), from DHSS).

Industrial Installations Advice to local planning authorities on the technical implications of developments involving or near 'major hazard installations' is given by the Major Hazards Branch of the *Health and Safety Executive* (head office). Major hazard installations are industrial installations where, if any accident occurred, there might be substantial loss of life or serious injury outside the confines of the workplace.

To make representations about such planning applications, the public should contact the local authority (Planning Department). Leaflets (e.g. 'After Flixborough') are available from the HSE.

See also **Industrial accident**; **Industrial injury and disease**.

Industrial Planning Enquiries about government policy on planning agreements and also about matters concerning the *National Enterprise Board* to the Industrial Planning Division at *Department of Industry* (headquarters (2)).

Industrial Relations Advisory services are available in Great Britain from the *Advisory, Conciliation and Arbitration Service*, e.g. on legislation; negotiation and consultative machinery; communications; grievance, disciplinary, dismissal and redundancy procedures; trade union recognition; payment systems.

See also **Industrial disputes**; **Trade unions**.

Industrial Research and Development The Research and Development Requirements Boards of the *Department of Industry* (headquarters (3)) consider financial support of suitable R and D proposals from UK companies, research establishments, research associations, universities and similar bodies. Boards operate in the following technology areas: chemicals and minerals; computers, systems and electronics; engineering materials; garment and allied industries; mechanical engineering and machine tools; metrology and standards; ship and marine technology; technology transfer; and a Chief Scientist's Board deals with areas not covered by other Boards (but not aerospace). The Boards' criteria for R and D proposals include cost-effectiveness, competitiveness, need and exploitation. The DoI is prepared to support projects promoting better use of existing technology.

Industrial Training Boards Employers in certain industries are required to pay a levy to the appropriate *Industrial Training Board*, although employers with satisfactory training standards may be exempt. The ITBs give grants to employers to encourage training and advisory services are available. Enquiries to the *Training Services Agency*, or the ITB for the industry concerned. Appeals against the requirement to pay the levy (though not about the amount of the levy) may be made to an **industrial tribunal** through the *Industrial Tribunals Central Office*; appeals on decisions of ITBs about certificates of exemption to the Levy Exemption Referees.

Special grants from public funds to maintain training in industry during the economic recession include premium grants for employers who recruit additional young people for apprenticeships or other forms of extended training; training awards, enabling an *Industrial Training Board* to provide young people with apprenticeship or other extended training prior to placement with employers (used where an ITB anticipates that total recruitment by employers will fall short of an industry's long-term economic needs); recruitment and adoptions grants, used by ITBs to secure places with employers for former training-award trainees and redundant apprentices respectively; sandwich course grants for employers providing additional places to give college-based students industrial experience; miscellaneous grants to employers for re-grading training, retraining redundant workers and preserving temporarily under-utilised training facilities. Apply to the appropriate *Industrial Training Board* or to the *Training Services Agency*.
See also **Training: services and grants**.

Industrial Tribunals These are independent statutory bodies for the UK which judge cases and appeals under employment legislation (e.g. about industrial training levies, **redundancy** payments, contracts of employment, equal pay, race relations). They sit at the *Industrial Tribunal* regional offices. Application for decisions can be made by employers, employees or government bodies, **trade unions**, etc., depending on the legislation. Expenses incurred by attendance at hearings, loss of earnings or loss of **national insurance** benefits will be reimbursed. Records of all decisions may be inspected; some are published. Further information from the Industrial Tribunals' central office.
See also **Dismissal; Employment: terms and conditions; Industrial disputes.**

Industry and Commerce The principal focal point for the British business community's views is the *Confederation of British Industry*, an independent, non-party-political body financed entirely by industry and commerce. It exists primarily to ensure that governments of all political complexions understand the needs, intentions and problems of British business. It is widely consulted by government but has no regulatory role. Although completely independent, CBI nominees sit on such tripartite government bodies as the *Advisory Conciliation and Arbitration Service* and the *Manpower Services Commission*; staff tasks include preparation of policy, economic forecasting and advice to members. CBI membership includes more than 13,000 individual companies, of every size and from all sectors of business – manufacturing, banking, insurance, retailing, agriculture, and most of the nationalised industries. Enquiries to *Confederation of British Industry, Headquarters* or one of its regional offices.

Industry: EEC Finance The European Investment Bank will lend up to 40% of the fixed capital costs of projects which are for the development of the less-developed regions of the EEC (similar to UK **assisted areas**); or for the development of fresh activities called for by the progressive establishment of the EEC; or of common interest to several member states. Loans are available in a mixture of foreign currencies at low interest rates; minimum loan is approximately £650,000.
The *European Coal and Steel Community* lends at favourable interest rates for projects both in the coal and steel industries and in any industry which re-employs redundant coal or steel workers. Loans for small and medium-sized undertakings are available through a financial intermediary, the *Industrial Commercial Finance Corporation*. Further details available from RIF Division at the *Department of Industry*.

Industry: Mortgage and Amortisation Finance Finance may be available from local authorities and *New Town Development Corporations*. Apply to appropriate authority.

Injustice: Appeal to Privy Council
The Privy Council is the body on whose advice and through which the Sovereign exercises his or her statutory and a number of prerogative powers. It also has its own statutory powers, independent of the power of the Sovereign in Council.

The Judicial Committee of the Privy Council derives its appellate jurisdiction from the right of all the Queen's subjects to appeal for redress to the Sovereign in Council if they believe that the courts of law have failed to do them justice. It is the final court of appeal from the courts of United Kingdom dependencies and from the courts of those independent members of the **Commonwealth** (including some in which the Queen is not Sovereign) who have not elected to discontinue the appeal. The Judicial Committee is also the final court of appeal from the **Channel Islands** and the **Isle of Man** (which are Crown dependencies and not part of the United Kingdom), from prize courts in the United Kingdom and dependencies, and from certain professional disciplinary committees. It also has jurisdiction in a limited class of ecclesiastical appeals (see **Ecclesiastical law**).

Appeals come to the judicial committee either where a right of appeal has been specially created – for instance, by statute, order in council or letters patent – or by special leave of the Sovereign in Council on the advice of the judicial committee. They are heard by a board of the committee, whose members are usually selected from the Lord Chancellor, ex-Lord Chancellors and Lords of Appeal in Ordinary, although Lords Justices of Appeal and other members of the Privy Council who have held high judicial office (including Chief Justices and certain other judges from other Commonwealth countries who have been sworn of the Privy Council) may be asked to sit from time to time. The judicial committee does not, in theory, deliver judgment. It advises the Sovereign, who acts on its report and approves an order in council to give effect thereto. Its decisions, though not binding on the English courts, are treated with great respect by them.

Enquiries to a **solicitor** or the *Privy Council Office*.

Injustice: Criminal If fresh evidence appears that was not available at the time of the trial of a convicted offender, the *Home Secretary* may refer a case back to the Courts of Appeal. Advice from a **solicitor**.

Injustice: Government Injustice arising from maladministration in government departments in the UK is investigated by the *Parliamentary Commissioner for Administration* and, in departments of the Northern Ireland government, by the *Northern Ireland Parliamentary Commissioner for Administration*. A complaint must first be made to a member of the *House of Commons* who then decides whether to refer it to the Commissioner. Complaints may be made by individuals or bodies (including incorporated ones, but excluding local authorities and certain others).

Nearly all government departments are subject to investigation including, in the UK, the following:

Ministry of Agriculture, Fisheries and Food
Intervention Board for Agricultural Produce
Charity Commission
Civil Service Commission
Civil Service Department
Crown Estate Office
Customs and Excise
Ministry of Defence
Department of Education and Science
Department of Employment
Employment Service Agency
Department of Energy
Department of the Environment
Export Credits Guarantee Department
Office of the Director General of Fair Trading
Foreign and Commonwealth Office
Department of Health and Social Security
Health and Safety Commission
Health and Safety Executive
Home Office
Central Office of Information
Department of Industry
Inland Revenue
Land Registry
Lord Chancellor's Department

Lord President of the Council's Office
National Debt Office
Department for National Savings
Northern Ireland Office
Office of Population Censuses and Surveys
Manpower Services Commission
Ministry of Overseas Development
Department of Prices and Consumer Protection
Public Record Office
Public Trustee
Department of the Registers of Scotland
General Register Office, Scotland
Registry of Friendly Societies
Royal Mint
Scottish Office
Scottish Record Office
Stationery Office
Board ot Trade
Department of Trade
Department of Transport
Training Services Agency
Treasury
Treasury Solicitor
Welsh Office
And in Northern Ireland:
Department of Agriculture
Department of the Civil Service for Northern Ireland
Department of Commerce
Department of Education
Department of the Environment for Northern Ireland
Department of Finance
Department of Health and Social Services
Department of Manpower Services
Civil Service Commission
Office of Information Services

Injustice and maladministration are not defined in the Parliamentary Commissioner Act but most investigations concern delay; mishandling of correspondence; failure to take the correct action; mis-application of rules and regulations; or inadequate, incorrect or misleading advice or information. In general, departments attempt to remedy any injustice which the Commissioner considers has resulted from maladministration, but they are not legally bound to do so. A remedy may consist of an apology; the carrying out of action previously delayed; or be financial (e.g. an ex gratia payment). Many matters are outside the Commissioner's jurisdiction; over 60% of complaints received are rejected.

Injustice: Health Service Complaints by individuals and organisations about injustice and hardship arising from **National Health Service** failures and maladministration are investigated by the *Health Service Commissioner for England*, the *Health Service Commissioner for Scotland* or the *Health Service Commissioner for Wales*. The Commissioners are empowered to investigate failures in a service which a **health authority** had a duty to provide and any maladministration which affected action taken by or for a health authority, e.g. failures in accommodation and catering; failures or delays in ambulance services; long waits for admission to hospital or in outpatient clinics; inadequate nursing care and supervision of patients; use without warning of patients for teaching; unsympathetic attitude of staff towards patients and their relatives; inadequate explanations by medical staff to patients or relatives; loss of hospital or family practitioner records or delay in their production; treatment without consent; the way in which complaints are dealt with by health authorities. They do not investigate personnel matters; actions stemming from clinical judgment (e.g. faulty diagnosis and treatment); actions of general practitioners (**doctors**), **dentists, opticians** and **pharmacists** under contract with Family Practitioner Committees (see entry under each profession for the statutory procedures for complaints).

Before the Commissioners can investigate, the health authority concerned must have been notified of the complaint and allowed an adequate time for investigation and reply. If a complaint is upheld the most common remedies are an apology by the health authority and an improvement in procedures to minimise the likelihood of repetition.

The health authorities concerned are the Health Service Board and its Scottish and Welsh committees and, in England, regional health authorities, area health authorities, Family Practitioner Committees, Boards of Governors of post-graduate teaching hospitals and the Public Health Laboratory Service Board; in Scotland, Health Boards and the Common Services Agency for the Scottish Health Service; in Wales, area health authorities, Family Practitioner Committees. But complaints concerning certain special hospitals (e.g. Broadmoor) can only be investigated by the *Parliamentary Commissioner for Administration.*

There is no Health Service Commissioner for Northern Ireland but the *Northern Ireland Commissioner for Complaints* can look at complaints against health and social services boards.

Injustice: Local Local injustice can be investigated by the *Commission for Local Administration in England*; in Wales by the *Commission for Local Administration in Wales*; in Scotland by the *Commissioner for Local Administration (Scotland)*; and in Northern Ireland by the *Northern Ireland Commissioner for Complaints.* Their terms of reference are similar, although the Northern Ireland Commissioner can investigate a wider range of bodies and has powers to conciliate as well as to investigate; free leaflet available from each office.

The English, Welsh and Scottish Commissions are entitled to investigate complaints against all county, district and borough councils (including London and Scilly councils), all local authorities joint boards (e.g. national park boards), regional water authorities, and police authorities (other than the Metropolitan Police which is a Home Office responsibility). Authorities which the Northern Ireland Commissioner may investigate include the Milk, Seed Potatoes, and Pigs Marketing Boards; the Northern Ireland Certificate of Secondary Examinations Boards; the Northern Ireland Council for Nurses and Midwives, etc. Maladministration and injustice are not statutorily defined but the local commissioners (or Ombudsmen) have developed a working definition of maladministration which refers, for example, to the way in which an authority's decision has been taken and any administrative action (or inaction) based on or influenced by improper considerations (e.g. arbitrariness, malice or bias, including unfair discrimination) or improper conduct (e.g. neglect; unjustifiable delay; incompetence; failure to observe relevant rules or procedures). Injustice is considered more difficult to define since personal feelings and reactions vary enormously and the precise impact on the individual is therefore taken into account.

The three main areas of investigation have been in planning (e.g. failures in consultation, bias, neglect and misleading information); housing (e.g. maladministration of rent allowances, improvement grants and compulsory purchase orders); and education (complaints about the allocation of children to schools, wrongful reduction of student grants, etc.).

Certain matters cannot be investigated by the English, Welsh and Scottish commissioners, i.e. events which occurred before the legislation came into force; commercial transactions except those relating to land and buildings; job grievances and other personal matters; the general level of rates or water charges; internal educational matters (e.g. curricula, teaching methods and organisation and discipline within schools); complaints about police action, as distinct from maladministration by police authorities (see **Police: complaints**).

If a complaint is upheld, the two basic kinds of remedy by the responsible authority are action to ensure that similar maladministration does not happen again (e.g. revising procedures, improving communication with the public or disciplinary action) and action to remove the grievance (e.g. remedying a planning error, reallocating a school-child, arranging a house transfer). In Northern Ireland there is, in addition, provision, in a case of proved maladministration, for application to be made to the courts for damages.

Complaints must always be brought to the attention of the authority involved first, either to the department actually responsible or to the chief executive and then, if after a reasonable period the grievance still remains, to any member of the authority. If he does not remedy the matter the member should be asked to forward the complaint to the Commissioner. If the member refuses or fails to forward the complaint a direct approach to the Commissioner can be made.

Inland Revenue The *Inland Revenue* is responsible by statute for the administration of UK direct taxes; *Her Majesty's Customs and Excise* is responsible for indirect taxes.
Taxes dealt with by the IR include **income tax, capital gains tax, corporation tax, capital transfer tax** and other lesser known taxes, e.g. **development land tax**. The *Inland Revenue Valuation Offices* carry out valuations for rating purposes in England and Wales.
Inland Revenue Headquarters are in London. There are central IR offices for specialised matters (e.g. estate duty, capital transfer tax and some blocks of Pay As You Earn work); and IR local offices deal with taxes on matters arising in their allotted geographical area throughout the UK.
Income tax assessment is dealt with by *Inland Revenue, HM Inspectors of Taxes* in district tax offices. Tax collection is dealt with by *Inland Revenue, HM Collectors of Taxes* in collection offices. These are distinct from the tax offices of the Inspectors even though they may be under the same roof; one collection office may deal with matters arising from several tax offices.
To find out which office is appropriate to your need, enquire either of your employer (for income tax queries) or of the nearest *Inland Revenue HM Inspector of Taxes*. Where Pay As You Earn work has been transferred to non-localised areas, enquiries are dealt with by local *Inland Revenue PAYE Enquiry Offices*. Appeals against Inland Revenue assessments are made to the Appeal Commissioners; apply through the office which made the assessment.

Insurance Brokers Brokers can at present practise in the UK without qualifications but professional standards are upheld and are being strengthened by the *British Insurance Brokers' Association*, which is composed of the *Association of Insurance Brokers*, the *Corporation of Insurance Brokers, Federation of Insurance Brokers* and *Lloyd's Insurance Brokers Association*. Each constituent association imposes conditions for membership involving financial controls, qualifications and disciplinary requirements.
To find an accredited insurance broker, contact BIBA or one of its constituent associations. Complaints about professional misconduct should be made either to BIBA, or to the association of which the broker is a member.

Insurance Companies Companies must be authorised by the Department of Trade under the Insurance Companies Act 1972; enquiries and applications to *Department of Trade*.

International Publications Her *Majesty's Stationery Office* is the UK agent for the publications of most international organisations, such as the European Communities, United Nations, UNESCO, FAO, WHO, OECD, etc. They may be purchased over the counter or by post from any government bookshop or ordered from most other booksellers.
See also **Official publications**.

Interpol Interpol is the international police organisation, with headquarters in Paris. It acts as a contact between its members (about 120 countries) and circulates information about crime and criminals. Contact through local *police*.

Invalidity Pension People who have received social security **sickness benefit** for 28 weeks and remain unable to work owing to illness automatically receive an invalidity pension from *Department of Health and Social Security* (local office) (see leaflets NI16A (Invalidity Benefit) and NI196 (current benefit rates), from DHSS local offices). There are no separate contribution conditions for an invalidity pension, entitlement to 28 weeks of sickness benefit being the only condition. Men under 60 and women under 55 receiving an invalidity pension may also receive an invalidity allowance. Benefits may also be increased for people with dependants. Invalidity benefits are not treated as part of income for tax purposes. From 1 April 1978 invalidity pension is earnings-related (for details see **Retirement pension**).

Invalidity pension can be paid up to 5 years beyond 65 (60 for women) if there is entitlement to retirement pension. It is then payable at the rate at which the pension would be paid if the claimant retired; invalidity allowance can be paid in addition only if the invalidity pension became payable before pension age. Invalidity allowance can be paid in addition to retirement pension if it was payable for any day within the period of 13 weeks and one day before pension age (65 for men, 60 for women).

Men and single women who have not qualified for 26 weeks of sickness benefit are entitled to a non-contributory invalidity pension if they are of working age and have been incapacitated for 28 weeks. (See leaflet NI210, non-contributory invalidity pension, from DHSS local offices.) Married women are also entitled to a non-contributory invalidity pension from 17 November 1977 provided they have also been incapable of performing their normal household duties for at least 28 weeks. The non-contributory invalidity pension is tax-free, not subject to a means test and may be increased for dependants. Apply to *Department of Health and Social Security* (local offices).

Holidays may be provided for people who have been seriously ill; apply to local authority (Social Services Department).

Re-establishment centres run by the *Supplementary Benefits Commission* cater for those who because of long unemployment or irregular work need special help before being capable of returning to a regular job; apply to DHSS local office.

Invalid care allowance provides a benefit to those unable to work because they are caring for a disabled relative (see **Disablement: social security benefits**).

See also **Disablement; Industrial injury and disease; Social security benefits; War disablement**.

Inventions: Development The *National Research Development Corporation* is a public corporation which operates like a merchant bank in backing its technical judgment of UK innovations with finance, principally in joint-venture projects with industrial companies, developing products or processes where there is an element of technical risk; or by arranging commercial exploitation by licensing. Its principal sources of inventions are research organisations and universities but it also backs inventions by private individuals. Apply to the Head of Public Relations NRDC.

Investment Abroad: Insurance Capital and interest on new British equity or loan investment overseas may be insured for up to 15 years against political risks (e.g. war, expropriation and restrictions on remittances) with the *Export Credits Guarantee Department Headquarters*.

See also **Direct investment: exchange control; Exporting**.

Investment Currency Investment currency is **foreign currency**, originating mainly from the sale or redemption of **foreign currency securities** owned by UK residents, which they may use to purchase foreign currency securities and for certain other purposes, including direct investment and the purchase of property outside the scheduled territories. Permission is required from the *Bank of England* for such transactions. Investment currency normally changes hands at a premium which accrues to the seller. Investment currency owned by residents of the Republic of Ireland and of Gibraltar may be similarly used, with BE permission and local control approval.

See also **Direct investment: exchange control; Foreign borrowing; Property abroad: exchange control**.

Investment: Exchange Control The objects of **exchange control** over investment are to protect the balance of payments and to prevent any unauthorised transfer of UK assets to persons resident abroad or undertakings controlled by them. The underlying policy is to encourage investment into and out of the UK subject to certain safeguards. Accordingly, investment by UK residents in property or undertakings abroad or in **foreign currency securities**, investment by persons resident abroad and foreign interests in undertakings in the UK or sterling securities, and most other capital transactions between UK residents and persons resident abroad are subject to exchange control, which is administered by the *Bank of England* and by **authorised banks** and other **authorised depositories** on its behalf.

For further information, advice or help consult an authorised bank or other authorised depository.

See also **Direct investment: exchange control**; **Property abroad: exchange control**; **Sterling securities**.

Iran For **exchange control** is a non-scheduled territory outside the **overseas sterling area** and the EEC. UK nationals travelling direct from the UK normally need only the following (but check): **passports**; international certificates of **vaccination** against smallpox; **work permits** (if taking a job); green cards for motor insurance (if bringing a car); international driving permits are recommended (if intending to drive: see **Motoring abroad**).

The UK has no reciprocal health or social security arrangements.

Enquiries to *Iranian Embassy* in London.

British diplomatic mission to Iran is *British Embassy* in Tehran.

Iraq For **exchange control** is a non-scheduled territory outside the **overseas sterling area** and the EEC. UK nationals travelling direct from the UK normally need only the following (but check): **passports** without Israeli stamp; **visas**; international certificates of **vaccination** against smallpox; **work permits** (if taking a job); green cards for motor insurance (if bringing a car); international driving permits (if intending to drive: see **Motoring abroad**). They may also require internal travel permits and exit permits.

The UK has no reciprocal health or social security arrangements.

Enquiries to *Iraq Embassy* in London.

British diplomatic mission to Iraq is *British Embassy* in Baghdad.

Irish Traditional Arts These are supported and encouraged by the *Arts Council of Northern Ireland*. Traditional arts cover music, dancing, story-telling and recitation, folk drama and crafts such as instrument making, weaving and straw-work. Emphasis has been placed on the preservation of traditional music and the ACNI has provided grants and guarantees to organisations and individuals engaged in teaching or research in this area, and for musical events and seminars.

Ironstone Land Grants for the restoration of worked ironstone land to a good state of cultivation and fertility are made from the Ironstone Restoration Fund. Apply: *Ministry of Agriculture Fisheries and Food, Regional Office, Nottingham.*

Isle of Man The Isle of Man is subject to the English Crown but is not part of the UK. The Lieutenant Governor, the Queen's personal representative, presides over the island's legislative assembly (the Court of Tynwald) and retains some executive functions. Other Crown offices include those of First and Second Deemster (judges) and Attorney General; the latter is the legal adviser both to the Crown and to the island government. Other constitutional relationships with the UK are as in the **Channel Islands**.

Enquiries to *Home Office*.

Israel For **exchange control** is a non-scheduled territory outside the **overseas sterling area** and the EEC. UK nationals travelling direct from the UK normally need only the following (but check): **passports** (consult *Passport Office* stating which country to be visited); **work permits** (if taking a job); green cards for motor insurance (if bringing a car); international driving permits are recommended (if intending to drive: see **Motoring abroad**).

UK reciprocal arrangements cover

social security (see leaflet SA14 obtainable from *Department of Health and Social Security, Overseas Branch*), but not health.
Enquiries to *Israeli Embassy* in London.
British diplomatic mission to Israel is *British Embassy* in Tel Aviv.

Italy EEC member. For **exchange control** is a non-scheduled territory in the EEC but outside the **overseas sterling area**.
UK nationals travelling from the UK normally need only the following (but check): **passports** (British visitors' passports are acceptable); Italian translation of British driving licence (if intending to drive). Reduced price petrol coupons for visiting private cars are obtainable from Royal Automobile Club offices on personal application and also from Italian National Tourist Offices in Italy and most frontier posts, on production of a passport and payment in currency other than Italian. (See also **Motoring abroad**.)
EEC or bilateral social security arrangements are applicable; leaflets and EEC Guides obtainable from *Department of Health and Social Security, Overseas Branch*. Apply to local social security office for a leaflet SA28 which explains who is entitled to free medical treatment under EEC health arrangements and how to get a certificate of entitlement (form E111).
Enquiries to *Italian Embassy* in London, *Italian Consulate-General* in Edinburgh, *Italian Consulate* in Manchester, *Italian Vice Consulates* in Glasgow and Bedford, *Italian Consular Agent* in Cardiff and *Italian State Tourist Office* in London.
British diplomatic missions to Italy are *British Embassy* in Rome, *British Consulates* in Florence, Genoa, Milan, Naples, Palermo, Trieste, Turin, Venice, Cagliari and Messina.

Ivory Coast For **exchange control** is a non-scheduled territory outside the **overseas sterling area** and the **EEC**.
UK nationals travelling direct from the UK normally need only the following (but check): **passports**; international certificates of **vaccination** against smallpox and yellow fever; **work permits** (if taking a job); green cards for motor insurance (if bringing a car); international driving permits (if intending to drive: see **Motoring abroad**).
The UK has no reciprocal health or social security arrangements.
Enquiries to *Ivory Coast Embassy* in London.
British diplomatic mission to Ivory Coast is *British Embassy* in Abidjan.

J

Jamaica **Commonwealth** member. For **exchange control** is a non-scheduled territory in the **overseas sterling area** but outside the EEC.
UK nationals travelling direct from the UK normally need only the following (but check): **passports**; **work permits** (if taking a job).
UK reciprocal arrangements cover social security (see leaflet SA27 obtainable from *Department of Health and Social Security, Overseas Branch*) but not health.
Enquiries to *Jamaican High Commission* in London and *Jamaican Consulates* in Birmingham and Manchester.
British diplomatic mission to Jamaica is *British High Commission* in Kingston.

Japan For **exchange control** is a non-scheduled territory outside the **overseas sterling area** and the EEC.
UK nationals travelling direct from the UK normally need only the following (but check): **passports**; **work permits** (if taking a job); green cards for motor insurance (if bringing a car); international driving permits (if intending to drive: see **Motoring abroad**).
The UK has no reciprocal health or social security arrangements.
Enquiries to *Japanese Embassy* in London.
British diplomatic missions to Japan are *British Embassy* in Tokyo and *British Consulates* in Osaka and Kita Kyushu (Moji).

Jobs The *Employment Service Agency* finds jobs for both the unemployed and the employed, with special service for **nurses**, disabled people (see **Disablement: employment and training**), **armed forces recruitment** and professional and executive recruitment. In some circumstances fares and living expenses are provided for the unemployed seeking work beyond easy travelling distance from home. **Removal expenses** and other payments may be made to people obtaining such work; apply to local *Employment Service Agency employment office* or *Employment Service Agency Job Centre*.
Three-day courses in self-presentation for job-finding are run by the *ESA Professional and Executive Recruitment* (out-of-pocket expenses provided).
Temporary work for unemployed people under 24 and over 50 is provided by the job creation scheme of the *Manpower Services Commission*. Schemes are run by local communities to benefit the community (e.g. environmental improvements, clerical activity, social work, workshop activities); apply to the *Careers Office*, ESA Job Centre or ESA Employment Office.
See also **Occupational guidance**; **Unemployment: young people**; **Vacancies**.

Jordan For **exchange control** is a non-scheduled territory in the **overseas sterling area** but outside the EEC. UK nationals travelling direct from the UK

Judicial

normally need only the following (but check): **passports** without Israeli stamp; **visas**; international certificates of **vaccination** against smallpox; **work permits** (if taking a job); green cards for motor insurance (if bringing a car); international driving permits are recommended (if intending to drive: see **Motoring abroad**).
The UK has no reciprocal health or social security arrangements.
Enquiries to *Jordanian Embassy* in London.
British diplomatic mission to Jordan is *British Embassy* in Amman.

Judicial Appointments In England, Wales and Northern Ireland, the most important judicial appointments are made by the Crown on the advice of the Prime Minister or the Lord Chancellor, while a number of other judicial and related appointments are made by the Lord Chancellor.

Appointments made by the Crown include: Lord of Appeal in Ordinary; Lord Chief Justice; Lord Chief Justice of Northern Ireland; Master of the Rolls; President, Family Division; Lord Chief Justice of Appeal and Lord Chief Justice of Appeal, Northern Ireland. Judicial appointments made by the Crown on the advice of the *Lord Chancellor* include: High Court Judge; Circuit Judge; County Court Judge, Northern Ireland; Recorder; Resident Magistrate, Northern Ireland; Judge Advocate General; Judge Advocate of the Fleet; Employment Appeal Tribunal; Secretary of State for Employment; National Insurance Commissioners; National Insurance Commissioners, Northern Ireland; Queen's Counsel; Restrictive Practices Court; Transport Tribunal (President and Members – joint recommendation with Minister of Transport).

Appointments made by the Lord Chancellor include: Agricultural Land Tribunals (Chairman, Members and Land Drainage Panels); Aircraft Accident Inquiries (Commissioners and Assessors); Betting Levy Appeal Tribunal (Chairman); Commons Commissioners; Coroners (Northern Ireland only); Council on Tribunals; County Court Registrars; Foreign Compensation Commission; General Commissioners of Income Tax; Immigration Appeal Tribunals (President and Legal Members); Independent Schools Tribunal (Chairman); Industrial Tribunals (President and panel of Chairmen); Assistants to the Judge Advocate General; Justices of the Peace; Keeper of the Public Records; Chief Land Registrar; Lands Tribunal (President and Legal Members); Lands Tribunal for Northern Ireland (President and Legal Members); Law Commissioners; Lay Observer; Lord Chancellor's Visitors; Masters and Registrars of the Supreme Court; Medical Appeal Tribunals (Legal Chairmen); Mental Health Review Tribunals (Chairmen and Members); National Insurance Local Tribunals (Panel of Chairmen); Official Solicitor; Pensions Appeal Tribunals (President and Members); Performing Right Tribunal (Chairman); Plant Varieties and Seeds Tribunal (Chairman); Prevention of Fraud (Investments) Act 1958 Tribunal (Chairman and Legal Member); Public Trustee; Race Relations Assessors; Rent Tribunals and Rent Assessment Committees (Panel of Chairmen); Supplementary Benefit Appeal Tribunal (Chairmen); Value Added Tax Tribunals (President and Chairman); Wreck Commissioners.
See also **Ministerial appointments**.

Judo Judo is governed internationally by the European Judo Union and the International Judo Federation. In the UK the *British Judo Association* is the controlling body, responsible for administration, the code of conduct at national events, referees, coaching schemes, rules, etc. Within this structure, the *Welsh Judo Association*, the *Scottish Judo Federation* and the *Northern Ireland Judo Federation* are responsible for their own regions.

Jury Service People summoned to attend for jury service in a criminal or civil trial in England, Wales and Northern Ireland are selected at random from the electoral register. Each one is asked to complete a form attached to the jury summons and to return it to the Jury Summoning Officer; he then notifies people who are not qualified or who are excused from jury service. All others must attend court at the appointed time, and constitute the panel from which individual jurors are selected by ballot. In England and Wales a jury consists of 12 people; in Scotland 15 people; in Northern Ireland 12 people.

Before the hearing takes place the prospective jury is assembled in court and each member is called by name into the jury box and required to take an oath (or to affirm). At this stage it is open to the defendant to challenge up to three jurors without stating the reason. Any juror so challenged is automatically replaced for that case, although he or she will remain on the panel and will be liable for service in another trial.

For the procedure in Scotland, consult 'The legal system in Scotland', obtainable from *Her Majesty's Stationery Office*.

See also **Civil law disputes; Criminal courts.**

K

Kampuchea For **exchange control** is a non-scheduled territory outside the overseas sterling area and the **EEC**. Kampuchea does not admit visitors from Britain.
British diplomatic mission to Kampuchea has been withdrawn.

Keep Fit The *Keep Fit Association* promotes keep fit classes for women in the UK (with the *Keep Fit Association of Wales*, *Scottish Women's Keep Fit Association* and the *Keep Fit Association of Northern Ireland*) and organises teacher training, co-operating with local education authorities and the Sports Council.

Kenya Commonwealth member. For **exchange control** is a non-scheduled territory in the **overseas sterling area** but outside the **EEC**. UK nationals travelling direct from the UK normally need only the following (but check): **passports**; international certificates of **vaccination** against smallpox; **work permits** (if taking a job).
The UK has no reciprocal health or social security arrangements.
Enquiries to *Kenyan High Commission* in London.
British diplomatic mission to Kenya is *British High Commission* in Nairobi.

Kidney Donations Donations after death are needed by the **National Health Service**. Transplants are made to people suffering kidney failure who can then resume a full and active life. Kidneys for transplant need to be removed within half-an-hour of death. Kidney Donor Cards are available from *Department of Health and Social Security* (Leaflets Unit). These are for signature by donor and next of kin, to be carried subsequently at all times by the donor.

Korea Republic For **exchange control** is a non-scheduled territory outside the **overseas sterling area** and the **EEC**. UK nationals travelling direct from the UK normally need only the following (but check): **passports**; international certificates of **vaccination** against smallpox; **work permits** (if taking a job); green cards for motor insurance (if bringing a car); international driving permits (if intending to drive: see **Motoring abroad**).
The UK has no reciprocal health or social security arrangements.
Enquiries to *Korean Embassy* in London.
British diplomatic missions to Korea are *British Embassy* in Seoul and *British Consulate* in Busan.

Kuwait For **exchange control** is a non-scheduled territory in the **overseas sterling area** but outside the **EEC**. UK nationals travelling direct from the UK normally need only the following (but check): **passports** without Israeli stamp; international certificates of **vaccination** against smallpox; **work permits** (if taking a job); green cards for motor insurance (if bringing a car);

international driving permits (if intending to drive: see **Motoring abroad**).
The UK has no reciprocal health or social security arrangements.

Enquiries to *Kuwait Embassy* in London.
British diplomatic mission to Kuwait is *British Embassy* in Kuwait.

L

Labour Party Membership is open to any individual over 15 who is a **British subject**, or has lived in the UK for over a year, and is not a member of any political party or organisation which has separate policies and propaganda, or has its own branches or promotes parliamentary or local government candidates, or which owes allegiance to any foreign political organisation. Affiliated members are TUC-approved **trade unions**, co-operative societies, socialist societies and other organisations approved by the Party's National Executive Committee and constituency Labour Parties. Conditions are that the organisation accepts the Party's principles, etc., agrees to conform to its constitution and submits its political rules to the Party's NEC. Individuals wishing to join should contact their constituency association (see Labour Party in telephone directory) or the *Labour Party Headquarters*.

The party's ideology has been summarised as: 'to bring about a fundamental and irreversible shift in the balance of wealth and power in favour of working people and their families'.

The annual conference – about 1,100 delegates from constitutency parties and affiliated organisations – has the final say on party policy. Election manifestos are decided jointly by the Parliamentary Committee of the Parliamentary Labour Party and the NEC. The Parliamentary Labour Party consists of every Labour MP and the peers who take the Labour whip. The NEC is responsible for the day-to-day running of the party.

Lacrosse Lacrosse is governed internationally by the International Federation of Lacrosse. Men's amateur lacrosse is controlled in England by the *English Lacrosse Union*. It authorises the rules, promotes indoor and outdoor lacrosse, organises international matches and selects national teams. There are no men's clubs in Scotland, Wales or Ireland.

Women's lacrosse, which follows different rules from men's, is governed internationally by the International Federation of Women's Lacrosse Associations and nationally by the *All England Women's Lacrosse Association*, the *Scottish Ladies Lacrosse Association* and the *All Wales Ladies' Lacrosse Association*. The national bodies jointly determine British rules and select British teams.

Land Charges on Unregistered Land Land charges such as second **mortgages** in England and Wales have to be registered by the person having the benefit (e.g. the second mortgagee) against the name of the owner of the property on a central computerised register kept by *Her Majesty's Land Registry, Land Charges Department*. The aim of registration is to warn an intending purchaser of the third party interest, when it is of such a nature as will not be apparent from an inspection of the title deeds. Any person can make a search of the register against the name of the property owner and so a purchaser cannot in law plead ignorance of the registered third party interest and buys the property subject to it. *Her Majesty's Stationery Office* and law booksellers and printers sell printed forms for registration of land charges and for postal searches of the register. In urgent cases, you can make a search by means of a telephone call and get an immediate reply from the computer.

Many types of land charge can be registered. Most common are second mortgages which are not found among the title deeds (because the first mortgagee holds them and second and subsequent mortgagees will merely hold their own mortgage deed) and contracts for purchase (held by the intending purchaser). The register relating to unregistered land has four further sections in addition to land charges: these record pending court actions; writs and orders of the courts; deeds of arrangement; and annuities secured on land. Fees are payable for registrations and searches (telephone searches extra), but there is free enquiry service. See also subsequent entries on **Land**.

Land, Houses and Other Buildings: Buying Buying is normally done through an **estate agent**, who helps find property and transmits offers, a **solicitor**, who establishes legal ownership, and a **surveyor**, who inspects the property. The first stage, before contract, involves finding the property; making an acceptable offer; inspecting the property; searching the local authority register for any planning proposals or liabilities they may have recorded against the property; enquiring about boundaries and what fixtures and furnishings are included in the sale; approving the draft contract; fixing completion date; signing the contract and paying the deposit.

The second stage, after contract, covers checking the terms of the contract with the land register or title deeds; preparing a form of transfer (registered land) or conveyance (unregistered land); and completion, i.e. exchange of money for property. In the final stage the form stamps L(A) must be sent with the conveyance or transfer for stamping to the Inland Revenue stamp office, **stamp duty** must be paid if necessary and, where requisite, the purchase registered at the appropriate *Her Majesty's Land Registry District Land Registry* (see **Land ownership: registered title**). There can be complications, particularly with **mortgages**, ownership rights and security interests.

Land, Houses and Other Buildings: Selling Selling is normally done through an **estate agent**, who finds a buyer, and a **solicitor**, who transfers legal ownership, but there is no need in law for a seller to use these agents. The stages in the sale up to contract encompass an offer of property for sale and an acceptance of that offer at an agreed price; answering purchasers' queries; fixing a completion date (date of legal purchase); signing of contract (normally prepared by vendor), including payment of deposit by purchaser.

After contract the stages cover authorising the purchaser to check the land register (see **Land ownership: registered title**) or inspect the title deeds (see **Land ownership: unregistered title**) and exchange of money for property on completion date. There can be complications, particularly in establishing boundaries, ownership rights and security interests. A solicitor or any other professional agent who is negligent in acting for his client can be sued in the courts.

Land Ownership: Registered Title
Title to land, houses and other buildings must be registered with *Her Majesty's Land Registry* in many parts of England and Wales, particularly built-up areas (different laws and administrative arrangements apply in Scotland and Northern Ireland; enquiries to the *Department of Registers of Scotland* and the *Registrar of Titles* in Northern Ireland). The land certificate, which the Registry issues to the landowner after first registration, is the only proof of ownership of registered land recognised in law. It replaces the title deeds, which constitute proof of ownership of unregistered land, with the aim of making land transfer and other transactions (e.g. leasing and mortgaging) simpler, cheaper and more reliable.

Prior to issuing the land certificate, HMLR examines the title deeds and creates the register for the property, with a description of it in map terms, the owner's name and address, and limitations as to his ownership, with particulars of any **mortgage** lease, rights (e.g. **rights of way** or drainage) and any restrictive stipulations (e.g. as to building and use) to which the property is subject. After first registration, subsequent transactions affecting the property are registered simply by sending the transfer, mortgage and similar forms to HMLR, which examines them and updates the entry in the register and, when necessary, the map. The registers of title are private and open to inspection only by the owner or someone holding his written authority. The index maps on which every registration is plotted are open to public inspection at the appropriate *HMLR District Land Registry*, or a search of a particular property can be made by post. There are 10 district land registries or regional offices, each covering a separate geographical area. At each office there is a free enquiry service.
See also **Land charges on unregistered land**.

Land Ownership: Unregistered Title
Proof of ownership is evidenced by the title deeds, which are kept in the private custody of the owner or, if the land or houses or other buildings are in **mortgage**, of his mortgagee. Unregistered title exists throughout the UK, side by side with various systems of land registration or registration of deeds (see **Land ownership: registered title**). For any transaction with an unregistered title, the purchaser, etc., or his **solicitor** must examine the title deeds to determine whether the owner has the legal power to carry out the transaction and under what conditions he can do so. Where he does not appear to have a good title generally, or where there appears to be a particular flaw, it may be necessary to obtain the legal opinion of counsel as to what can be done to put the title to rights. On other occasions, insurance can be taken out to cover third party claims in respect of the defect. Most unregistered titles are, however, safe holding ones that give no difficulty. In cases of exceptional difficulty it may be necessary to go to court to establish title.

Landscape Architects There is no statutory qualification, but the professional body is the *Landscape Institute incorporating the Institute of Landscape Architects*. Admission to full (associate) membership is obtained by passing the Institute's professional practice examination, after completing (or being exempted from) all three parts of its technical examinations, coupled with a minimum of two years' relevant experience. On written request, the Institute will direct you to practitioners experienced in a particular aspect of landscape architecture. Enquiries to the registrar of the Institute.

Language Schools Anyone may start, run and teach at an independent language school, without a qualification, but the *Association of Recognised English Language Schools* works to bring together recognised schools with the common aim of improving the standards of English language teaching; a list of recognised schools is available from the ARELS.
See also **Education: Scotland; Education: Northern Ireland**.

Laos For **exchange control** is a non-scheduled territory outside the **overseas sterling area** and the **EEC**. UK nationals travelling direct from the UK normally need only the following (but check): **passports; visas**; international certificates of **vaccination** against smallpox; **work permits** (if taking a job); green cards for motor insurance (if bringing a car); international driving permits (if intending to drive: see **Motoring abroad**).
The UK has no reciprocal health or social security arrangements.
Enquiries to *Laoatian Embassy* in London.
British diplomatic mission to Laos is *British Embassy* in Vientiane.

Launderettes Water supplied to a launderette is metered and charged for by volume by the local *water authority* or *water company*.
See also **Water services**.

Law Centres Law Centres are independent agencies staffed by salaried lawyers and social workers. Each centre has its own management committee and most are funded substantially by central or local government. Their purpose is to satisfy the need for legal advice in deprived, mainly urban, areas of the community. Their work varies from centre to centre according to local needs: some operate an 'open door' policy and encourage the passer-by to call in; others accept clients only on referral from other agencies. Most centres concentrate on housing problems, social security and employment matters and juvenile crime. Most centres will represent their clients in court or at tribunals in addition to giving advice. In general centres do not operate a means test, but people who can obviously afford to pay for legal advice are usually referred to a **solicitor** in private practice.
See also **Legal aid**.

Law: European Economic Community
The United Kingdom became a member of the European Community on 1 January 1973. The European Communities Act 1972 gives legal effect in the UK to directly applicable rights and duties under Community law; it enables the government to make orders and regulations to give effect to the country's obligations as a member of the Community; and it alters existing UK law to take account of specific Community obligations.

Community law is the body of law arising out of treaties setting up the European Economic Community, the European Coal and Steel Community and the European Atomic Energy Community. 'Primary' Community law is to be found in the treaties; 'secondary' law comprises the instruments — regulations, directives and decisions — made under the authority of the treaties by Community institutions. These are the Council of Ministers, a body composed either of the foreign ministers of the nine member countries or of the ministers of those countries responsible for the subject under discussion, and the *European Commission*, a primarily executive body comprising Community officials. The law is normally applied by the domestic courts of the member countries, but the most authoritative rulings are given by the *Court of Justice of the European Community*.

The English, Scottish and Northern Ireland legal systems remain intact, and their courts continue to operate as before. In the event of conflict, however, Community law prevails over domestic law.

The most commonly used instrument of secondary Community law is the regulation, which is binding in its entirety and has the force of law in each member country without further action by the national parliament. Directives are binding as to the result to be achieved while leaving each member country to decide the method of implementation. This means that each country amends as necessary its own domestic laws or administrative practices to bring them into line with Community law. Decisions are usually concerned with specific problems, and are only binding on those to whom they are directed. They may, for example, enjoin a member country to stop an infringement of a treaty, or authorise a particular course of action. The Council of Ministers and the Commissions are also empowered to make recommendations or to give opinions; neither has binding force.

The main areas covered by the rules of Community law include: agriculture and fisheries; the movement of goods, labour, services and capital; transport; monopolies and restrictive practices; state aid for industry; and the coal, steel and nuclear energy industries.

Under the Community treaties the Court of Justice of the European Community interprets and adjudicates on the meaning of the treaties and of any measures taken under them by the Council of Ministers and the Commission. It hears complaints and appeals brought by or against Community institutions, member states or individuals, and it gives preliminary rulings on questions referred to it by courts in the member states. Thus questions of the validity and interpretation of Community law may be referred to the court by UK courts, and they must be so referred when the question arises in a court or tribunal from which there is no appeal. In a case of this kind the Court of Justice makes a preliminary ruling on the question referred, and this is binding on the national court on that particular point; it remains with the national court to apply the law thus interpreted and to decide the case. The Court of Justice consists of nine judges assisted by four advocates-general. See also **Human rights.**

Law: England and Wales The main sources of English law are legislation, 'unwritten' law and European Community law. Legislation consists of laws made by, or under the authority of, Parliament and may comprise statutes (Acts of Parliament) or delegated (or subordinate) legislation. Delegated legislation falls into two main groups. The first comprises Orders in Council (made by the Queen in Council) and orders, rules and regulations made by a government minister. These almost invariably take the form of 'statutory instruments' which are published and are subject to parliamentary scrutiny. The second consists of **byelaws** which have local effect and are made by local government or other public authorities by virtue of powers delegated by Parliament.

Unwritten law consists of the common law and equity. European Community law, which arises out of the UK's membership of the European Community, is largely confined in impact to economic and some social matters; it stands alongside both legislation and the unwritten law, and, in the event of conflict, takes precedence over them. The law today is contained in about 3,000 Acts of Parliament, some thousands of statutory instruments and statutory rules and orders, and over 300,000 reported cases. The *Law Commission* is responsible for codifying certain branches of English law.

Common law has evolved from spontaneously observed rules and practices, shaped and formalised by decisions made over many years by judges pronouncing the law in relation to the particular facts before them.

Under the doctrine of the sovereignty of Parliament, Acts of Parliament are binding on all courts, and take precedence over other sources of law such as rights conferred by the common law. The doctrine also holds that any Act of the UK Parliament can repeal or amend former statutes and that the courts cannot challenge Parliament's power.

English law is the historical source of the Anglo-American or 'common law' group of legal systems. It is quite distinct from the Romano-Germanic or 'civilian' systems common in Western Europe and South America which derive from Roman law – the law of the Roman Republic and Empire which was codified in the sixth century by the Emperor Justinian. Scots law (see **Law: Scotland**) belongs to a small group of 'mixed' legal systems which have legal principles, rules and concepts modelled on both Romanistic and English law.

Devolution in Wales is a major constitutional change being proposed by the government, which envisages the establishment of separate elected assemblies for Wales (and Scotland). The assemblies would have certain common characteristics and relationships to the central government, but are also intended to reflect the existing differences in governmental structure. The Welsh assembly would have certain powers of delegated legislation and some executive functions.

See also **Civil law disputes.**

Law: Northern Ireland In 1801 the Irish Parliament joined that of Great Britain, establishing the United Kingdom of Great Britain and Ireland; in 1922 Southern Ireland (now the Irish Republic) became a self-governing country outside the UK. Meanwhile the Government of Ireland Act 1920 had enacted a constitution for Northern Ireland which, while preserving the supreme authority of the UK Parliament in London and reserving certain matters to that Parliament, provided Northern Ireland with its own subordinate legislature and executive to deal with many domestic matters, such as agriculture, commerce, development, education, health and social services. Modern Northern Ireland legislation therefore derives from a source different from that of corresponding English or Scottish statutes, and may differ in substance. The Northern Ireland Parliament had jurisdiction over all matters relating to the inferior courts, but all Supreme Court matters remained the responsibility of the UK Parliament.

This continued until 1972 when, as a result of political instability and violence, a period of direct rule from London was introduced. The UK Parliament assumed responsibility for the government of Northern Ireland and brought the Northern Ireland Parliament to an end. In January 1974 a new type of constitution came into force providing for the devolution of domestic powers to a new legislative assembly and a power-sharing executive. Widespread opposition, however, led to the prorogation of the assembly in May 1974 and its dissolution in March 1975. In July 1974 direct rule was reintroduced under the Northern Ireland Act, and provision was made for the election of a constitutional convention to consider what arrangements for the government of Northern Ireland would be likely to command most widespread acceptance throughout the community. The convention met in 1975 and early 1976 but failed to agree. It was dissolved in March 1976.

The UK Parliament and government are responsible for law and order, electoral matters and business of national importance such as foreign policy, defence and certain aspects of taxation. The Secretary of State for Northern Ireland, a senior UK government minister, is responsible to the UK Parliament for the previously devolved services. Laws for Northern Ireland on matters formerly within the competence of the assembly are made by Order in Council. Northern Ireland departments, which have executive responsibility for the devolved matters, are the responsibility of ministers in the *Northern Ireland Office.*
See also **Civil law disputes.**

Law Reform Official proposals for law reform, in the sense of changing the law for the better, are in the first instance the responsibility of the appropriate government department, e.g. the Department of Trade (commercial law), Department of the Environment (housing). The *Law Commission* and the *Scottish Law Commission* are responsible for taking and keeping under review all the law with which they are respectively concerned, with a view to its systematic development and reform. The responsibilities of the LC extend to Northern Ireland only in respect of those areas of the law which the authorities there are not empowered to change. General law reform matters in Northern Ireland are handled by the *Office of Law Reform.*

The Criminal Law Revision Committee, a standing body of judges and lawyers appointed by the *Home Secretary*, examines aspects of English criminal law referred to it by him.

Law: Scotland The main sources of Scots law are judge-made law, certain legal treatises having 'institutional' authority, legislation and European Community law. The first two sources are sometimes referred to as the common law of Scotland. Legislation, as in the rest of the United Kingdom, consists of statutes (Acts of Parliament) or delegated (or subordinate) legislation authorised by Parliament (see **Law: England and Wales**). Many procedural rules of the Scottish courts are contained in statutory instruments: 'acts of sederunt' made by the Court of Session to regulate civil procedure in that court or the sheriff court, and 'acts of adjournal' made by the High Court of Justiciary to regulate criminal procedure in that court, the sheriff court or the district courts.

As an independent state before 1707, Scotland possessed a Parliament of its own which had developed in the late Middle Ages. In 1707, the United Kingdom of Great Britain was created by the Acts of Union; in law the Scottish and English Parliaments ceased to exist, and the UK Parliament, having English and Scottish members and peers, was constituted as a new legal institution. The Acts include certain safeguards for, among other things, Scots law and the Scottish courts. The special position of Scotland and its legal system is recognised within the UK Parliament by the establishment of a Scottish Grand Committee and Scottish Standing Committees of the House of Commons for the more

important stages of consideration of Bills applying only to Scotland. Scottish departments of government are responsible for certain executive functions in Scotland, and are the responsibility of ministers in the *Scottish Office.*
Devolution in Scotland is a major constitutional change being proposed by the government, which envisages the establishment of separate elected assemblies for Scotland (and Wales). The assemblies would have certain common characteristics and relationships with the central government, but are also intended to reflect the existing differences in governmental structure, particularly the fact that Scotland has its own distinctive legal system. The Scottish assembly would assume primary law-making powers in certain devolved domestic subjects, and there would be a Scottish executive with powers to make delegated legislation and carry out certain executive functions.
See also **Civil law disputes.**

Leader of the Opposition The leader of the opposition is invariably the leader of the party in the House of Commons which holds the greatest number of seats other than the government party, and is elected by that party.

Lebanon For **exchange control** is a non-scheduled territory outside the **overseas sterling area** and the **EEC.** UK nationals travelling direct from the UK normally need only the following (but check): **passports** without Israeli stamp; international certificates of **vaccination** against smallpox; **work permits** (if taking a job).
The UK has no reciprocal health or social security arrangements.
Enquiries to *Lebanese Embassy* in London.
British diplomatic mission to Lebanon is *British Embassy* in Beirut.

Legacies Subject to certain conditions, UK customs and excise and value-added tax are not charged on goods (other than consumable goods such as tobacco goods and alcoholic drinks) bequeathed as legacies from overseas. Claims to *Her Majesty's Customs and Excise*; details in HMCE Notice 468.
See also **Alcohol; Customs duty; Excise duty; Tobacco products; Value-added tax.**

Legal Aid Legal aid is intended to ensure the supply of legal services to those who need but cannot afford such services, by reimbursing out of public funds the lawyers who provide them. To be granted legal aid a person must satisfy the appropriate local committee of the *Law Society* that he is financially eligible and that he has reasonable grounds for being a party to the proceedings. The financial eligibility of legal aid applicants is assessed by the *Supplementary Benefits Commission* and an applicant must normally be interviewed at one of the SBC's legal aid assessment offices or at a local supplementary benefit office. When legal aid is urgently required it is possible for an emergency legal aid certificate to be granted before financial eligibility has been determined. Legal aid is granted in the form of a certificate which states how much, if anything, a person must pay as his contribution towards the costs. A person may appeal against the decision of a local committee refusing aid on grounds other than financial ineligibility to an Area Committee. There is no appeal against the decision of an AC.
The names and addresses of **solicitors** prepared to undertake legal aid work are published in the Solicitors Legal Aid Referral Lists, available in most public libraries and from any *Citizens' Advice Bureau.* Information about the legal aid scheme in England, Wales and Northern Ireland is in the booklet 'Guide to legal aid' and the leaflet 'Legal aid could help you', both available (free) from the LS and CABs. For information on Scotland, consult 'The legal system of Scotland', obtainable from *Her Majesty's Stationery Office.*

Legal Aid: Advice and Assistance Under the legal advice and assistance scheme (often known as the 'green form scheme') anyone financially eligible may obtain advice from a **solicitor** and if necessary from counsel, who will take appropriate steps on his behalf short of court proceedings (e.g. a solicitor may prepare contracts, wills or transfers of property, and advise and assist a person taking proceedings in a court or tribunal himself). The solicitor will assess whether a person is eligible for advice and assistance and the contribution, if any, payable. People receiving **supplementary benefit** or **family income supplement** are entitled to free legal advice and assistance. The *Lord Chancellor* is responsible for this scheme which is administered by the *Law Society* in England, Wales and Northern Ireland.

Legal Aid: Civil Court Proceedings Legal aid is available for most civil proceedings in most courts in England, Wales and Northern Ireland, including the House of Lords, the Court of Appeal, the High Court, county courts and magistrates' courts. It can also be used for proceedings before Land Tribunals, the Commons Commissioners and the Employment Appeal Tribunal, but no other tribunals. Legal aid is not available in the Judicial Committee of the Privy Council nor in any court for defamation proceedings or relator actions. Legal aid in civil proceedings is the responsibility of the *Lord Chancellor* and administered by the *Law Society*.

Legal Aid: Criminal Court Proceedings Applications for legal aid in criminal cases is made to, and decided by, the court concerned. Applications are considered in the first instance by the justices' clerk or, in the crown court, a member of the staff, who may grant aid unconditionally or subject to a down payment. Only the court may refuse legal aid. Aid is not available for a prosecutor, but any person charged with a criminal offence wishing to be legally represented may apply. There are no prescribed financial conditions governing eligibility, the decision being left to the court's discretion. A court must (subject to financial eligibility) grant legal aid to anyone charged with murder and to the respondent where the prosecutor appeals to the House of Lords. At the conclusion of criminal proceedings a person may be required to contribute towards his defence costs whether or not he is acquitted. The amount of the contribution is assessed on the basis of the defendant's means, declared in the form he must complete. The court may request the *Supplementary Benefits Commission* to investigate a defendant's means either as a routine check or because it has doubts about the statement's authenticity. The *Home Secretary* is responsible for legal aid in criminal court proceedings in England, Wales and Northern Ireland.

Legal Problems Overseas Legal problems arising from the implementation of bilateral and multilateral conventions to which the UK government is a party, and including all consular services (see **Consuls**) dealing with civil, criminal, family and private international law, are the responsibility of the Legal Procedures Section at the *Foreign and Commonwealth Office, Nationality and Treaty Department.* It will give advice to the general public on how to proceed in legal actions in civil and commercial matters requiring the service and enforcement of judgments; the enforcement of maintenance orders overseas; and extradition of fugitive criminals.

The Nationality and Treaty Department is not the chief government department in these matters but acts as the link between UK departments (e.g. the Home Office, the Lord Chancellor's Office, their Scottish and Northern Ireland equivalents, the supreme courts of judicature, the county courts, and the Department of Health and Social Security) and overseas governments either through British post overseas or their embassies/high commissions in the UK.

Legislation Private bills may be promoted in either the House of Commons or House of Lords by individuals or organisations; **parliamentary agents** give professional assistance. Individuals or organisations may petition (within strict time limits) against a private bill which affects their interests, to seek either its amendment or rejection. A list of private bills under debate is available from the

Legitimacy

Private Bill Officer of the two Houses. Petitioners may petition through a parliamentary agent or appeal in person. Bills against which petitions have been presented are referred to a select committee, before which petitioners may appear and call evidence. Advice from Private Bill Office at *House of Commons* or *House of Lords* as appropriate.

For public bills individuals and organisations can only directly influence progress in rare cases when bills are committed to a select committee (see **Parliamentary committees**). Otherwise it is necessary to contact the appropriate government minister or a member of the appropriate House (see **Members of Parliament**) asking them to move an amendment.

Proposals for European legislation made by the Commission of the European Communities, and other EEC proposals, are scrutinised by the European Communities Committee of the *House of Lords*; to make written or oral submissions to the Committee first write to the Committee Clerk. The Select Committee on European Legislation of the *House of Commons* is confined to scrutiny of EEC legislation, etc., with the object of determining the legal and/or political importance of instruments and their worthiness for debate by the House. Address submissions in writing to the Committee Clerk. See **EEC: legislative process**.

Statutory Instruments and other legislation delegated by Parliament to government ministers cannot be amended or petitioned against by members of the public directly. It is necessary to approach a Member of Parliament and invite him to take up a particular matter.

Legitimacy People born out of wedlock and not made legitimate by the subsequent marriage of their father and mother to each other are now in almost the same position in law as people born legitimate. However, where a question of legitimacy does arise, for example, over nationality or a claim for an interest in property, they may petition the High Court or a county court for a declaration of legitimacy. There is no power to declare anyone illegitimate. The law on legitimacy is among the responsibilities of the *Home Secretary*, but questions in a particular case are for the courts alone to decide. Consult a **solicitor**.

See also **Illegitimate children**.

Lesotho **Commonwealth** member. For **exchange control** is a non-scheduled territory in the **overseas sterling area** but outside the **EEC**. UK nationals travelling direct from the UK normally need only the following (but check): **passports**; international certificates of **vaccination** against smallpox; **work permits** (if taking a job); green cards for motor insurance (if bringing a car); international driving permits (if intending to drive: see **Motoring abroad**).

The UK has no reciprocal health or social security arrangements.

Enquiries to *Lesotho High Commission* in London.

British diplomatic mission to Lesotho is *British High Commission* in Maseru.

Liberal Party Membership is open to anyone who supports the aims and objects of the party and who is not an active member of another political party. All members have a vote in electing the party leader. There are 15 separate organisations, reflecting the party's commitment to a federal structure for the UK, but members join a local constituency association (for address see Liberal Party in telephone directory, ask at local library or contact the *Scottish Liberal Party*, the *Welsh Liberal Party*, the *Ulster Liberal Party*, or one of the 12 English Regional *Liberal Parties* or the *Liberal Party Organisation*).

The party's official aims are: 'to build a Liberal Society in which every citizen shall possess liberty, property and security, and none shall be enslaved by poverty, ignorance or conformity. Its chief care is for the rights and opportunities of the individual, and in all spheres it sets freedom first.' It believes that electoral and political reforms are needed to restore representative government.

Liberal policy is determined by the Assembly (which meets annually), Party Council (four times a year) and

the Standing Committee (monthly). The National Executive Committee is responsible for party organisations and relations between recognised units such as the Parliamentary Liberal Party, the Women's Liberal Federation, the National League of Young Liberals, the Association of Liberal Councillors, the Association of Liberal Trade Unionists and the Liberal Candidates' Association.
The Finance and Administrations Board administers the organisation and is responsible for raising and spending money.

Liberia For **exchange control** is a non-scheduled territory outside the **overseas sterling area** and the **EEC**. UK nationals travelling direct from the UK normally need only the following (but check): **passports**; **visas**; international certificates of **vaccination** against smallpox and yellow fever; **work permits** (if taking a job).
The UK has no reciprocal health or social security arrangements.
Enquiries to *Liberian Embassy* in London.
British diplomatic mission to Liberia is *British Embassy* in Monrovia.

Librarianship Senior librarian posts are open only to qualified librarians although in some libraries junior assistants can work without qualifications. The basic professional qualification is associateship of the *Library Association* which is gained by successfully completing examinations and a period of supervised work in a library. The LA is the professional body for librarians in the UK, maintaining under royal charter a register of associates and fellows. There are provisions under the byelaws for investigation of professional misconduct of members.

Libraries Anyone may use local authority public libraries free of charge; there are 5,000 service points and mobile libraries in England and Wales. Many libraries loan books, records, tape cassettes, pictures, special materials for adults learning to read and publications in languages such as Urdu, Gujerati and Hindi. In addition many of them have reference libraries and provide reference services.
They also provide special individual services for the housebound elderly or handicapped (e.g. books – and sometimes records, cassettes and jigsaw puzzles – brought to the home on a regular basis; special books with large print for the partially sighted; and a special 'talking book' service for the blind). For information ring the local central library (under your local authority in the telephone directory). There are also library collections in prisons, hospitals, factories and youth clubs. See also **Blindness: books**; **Disablement**.
The $2\frac{1}{4}$ million books and periodicals and the million documents in micro form held by the *British Library, Lending Division*, are available to the public by inter-library loan through any registered institutional borrower such as a public library, university library or professional industrial library. If the Lending Division does not have an item requested in stock it will try to obtain it from another library or suggest an alternative.
Under a provision in the Copyright Act 1911, publishers must normally deliver (free of charge) an entire copy of any work (including periodicals, journals and newspapers) published in the UK to the *British Library, Copyright Receipt Office*; the *Bodleian Library* (Oxford); the *University Library* (Cambridge); the *National Library of Wales*; the *National Library of Scotland*; and *Trinity College* (Dublin). This is not for copyright reasons, but for the maintenance of records of material published in the UK.
See also **Records and cassettes: loans**.

Libraries Overseas The British Council runs some 130 libraries overseas and is associated with 40 others. They vary from small branch libraries and reference collections to major libraries containing 100,000 volumes and audio-visual materials and offering lending, reference and information services. As part of the BC's training and exchange programmes, senior librarians from many countries come to Britain and British experts lecture overseas.

As agent for the *Ministry of Overseas Development*, the BC administers the Library Development Scheme and the Books Presentation Programme, which assist developing countries with books and periodicals, buildings, equipment, mobile libraries and advisory visits. The BC also administers the Ministry's Low-Priced Books Scheme, subsidising selected books to help the teaching and learning of English in certain developing countries.

The BC also purchases 16 mm films which are available on loan outside the UK by application to the relevant *British Council Overseas Office*. Subjects range from short films on educational topics, through films on art and artists, to full-length feature films; they may be shown only to invited non-paying audiences. The BC is the main point of contact in Britain for overseas festivals of short films, and submits many of the British short films entered for such festivals.

Enquiries to Libraries Department, Low-Priced Books Department, or Films Department at the *British Council, Headquarters*, or to the *British Council Overseas Office* in the country concerned.

Libya For **exchange control** is a non-scheduled territory outside the **overseas sterling area** and the **EEC**. UK nationals travelling direct from the UK normally need only the following (but check): **passports** without Israeli stamp; **visas**; international certificates of **vaccination** against smallpox; **work permits** (if taking a job).

The UK has no reciprocal health or social security arrangements.

Enquiries to *Libyan Embassy* in London.

British diplomatic mission to Libya is *British Embassy* in Tripoli.

Licensing hours Permitted opening hours in England and Wales for 'off licences' (see **Liquor licences**) are 8.30 a.m. to 10.30 p.m. on Monday to Saturday; 12.00 p.m. to 2.00 p.m. and 7.00 p.m. to 10.30 p.m. on Sunday, Christmas Day and Good Friday.

Permitted opening times for 'on licences' are on weekdays 11.00 a.m. to 10.30 p.m. with a break of 2½ hours beginning at 3.00 p.m. (in the London metropolitan area and other areas where it is deemed suitable evening hours can be extended until 11.00); on public holidays and Sundays 12.00 p.m. to 10.30 p.m. with a break of five hours from 2.00 p.m. Licensing justices have discretion to vary weekday opening hours in their district, provided that the total number of hours in any day does not exceed nine, ending at 10.30 p.m. (or where the terminal hour of 11.00 p.m. is adopted, nine and a half) with a minimum afternoon break of two hours in both cases.

Special provisions cover 'drinking-up time'; seasonal licences; six-day and early closing licences; Sunday closing in Wales and Monmouthshire; extensions of permitted hours in licensed premises and clubs; the award of special hours certificates to licensed premises also holding a music and dance licence; clubs used for music, dancing and refreshment to which the supply of liquor is ancillary (see **Clubs: liquor licences; Music and dance premises**); certification by the licensing authorities of the suitability of such club premises; and occasional licences permitting the holder of an 'on licence' temporarily to sell intoxicating liquor on premises other than those covered by the 'on licence'. Prohibition of the sale of intoxicating liquor outside permitted hours does not apply to licensed premises within the area of *Her Majesty's Customs and Excise* examination station at UK international airports.

For exemption from normal permitted hours in order to supply people who are either frequenting a public market, following a lawful trade or calling in the immediate vicinity, or on a special occasion, licensees should apply to the *police*.

See also **Shop opening hours**.

Lichtenstein For **exchange control** is a non-scheduled territory outside the **overseas sterling area** and the **EEC**. UK nationals travelling direct from the UK normally need only the following (but check): **passports**; **work permits** (if taking a job).

The UK has no reciprocal health or social security arrangements.

Enquiries to *Liechtenstein Diplomatic Mission to UK* at *Swiss Embassy* in London.
British diplomatic mission to Liechtenstein is based on *British Consulate-General* in Zurich, Switzerland.

Life Peerages Life peerages may be included in half-yearly honours lists (see **Honours**) or in the Prime Minister's Dissolution or Resignation lists, or may be gazetted from time to time (published in special supplements to the 'London Gazette'). Life peerages are mainly political; nominations are scrutinised by the Political Honours Scrutiny Committee, which is composed of three Privy Councillors, at the *Civil Service Department Ceremonial Branch*.

Lifts and Lifting Gear General UK policy on the safety of lifts and hoists, lifting gear and lifting machinery and industrial trucks; the preparation of new legislation; and advice on the administration of existing relevant legislation is the responsibility of the General Branch B at the *Health and Safety Executive Head Office*.
The Health and Safety Executive, HM Factory Inspectorate (Consultant Section F17B), is responsible for determining technical standards for the design and safe operation of lifting machinery and lifting gear, and preparing technical codes of practice, guidance notes and advisory literature. Advice at local level on the safe use of lifts, lifting machinery, lifting gear and industrial trucks from *Health and Safety Executive, HM Factory Inspectorate Area Offices*.
See also **Work: health and safety**.

Lighters: Cigarette Manufacturers must be licensed under arrangements for the payment of **excise duty**; apply to *Her Majesty's Customs and Excise*.

Lip Reading Lip reading can help both the slightly and severely deaf and particularly those who become deaf in adult life. Classes are run by many *local education authorities*, by some voluntary organisations and local clubs, by some local authority Social Service Departments and by a few Hearing Aid Centres. Details of local classes can be obtained from any of these.
See also **Deafness**.

Liquor Licences Generally in England and Wales, retail sales of intoxicating liquor are permitted only under the authority of a licence issued by the local licensing justices (a committee of justices acting for a given area).
Licences may be 'on licences' (i.e. allowing sale for consumption either on or off the premises for which the licence is granted) or 'off licences' (i.e. authorising sales for consumption off the premises only). On licences specify their application either to intoxicating liquor of all descriptions or to beer, cider and wine only, or in combination. Off licences specify, similarly, either intoxicating liquor of all kinds or beer, cider and wine only. Licences are granted subject to the fitness of the applicant and the suitability of the premises for which the licence is required.
Anyone can object to the grant of a licence or the required annual renewal in writing to the licensing justices. Applications and objections should go to the clerk to the licensing justices at the magistrates' court, also to the local authority and *Chief Officer of Police*.
Appeal against refusal to grant or renew a licence or against conditions attached to its award is to the crown court.
Removal of a licence to different premises, or its transfer for any premises to a different person, requires the specific consent of the licensing justices. Certain alterations on licensed premises also require consent.
A public register of the justices' licences granted in a licensing district (and of registration certificates) is maintained by the clerk to the justices; the register must include the name of the owner of the licensed premises. Special provisions cover restaurant licences and residential licences, which generally restrict the sale of liquor to those taking a table meal on the premises or to hotel residents and their bona fide guests, and canteen licences relating to seamen's canteens

run under the approval of the *Minister of Transport*.

Special renewal provisions relate to 'old on licences' in force as at August 1904 and subsequently declared final, and 'old beerhouse licences' for which a corresponding excise licence was in force on 1 May 1869.

A different law controls liquor licensing in Scotland, where applications for licences are heard by licensing boards appointed by islands and district councils.

See also **Alcohol; Clubs: liquor licensing; Excise duty; Licensing hours.**

Literature: Financial Support The *Arts Council of Great Britain* provides financial support for professional writers, translators and publishers. In England this includes grants to writers of fiction, poetry, criticism and biography, who have already published at least one volume or have had work published in literary magazines, and who need to buy time to complete a project already in hand. It also subsidises translation into English of foreign works; awards grants for a limited number of non-commercial presses and literary magazines; supports visits by creative writers to schools and colleges; gives financial guarantees against loss to publishers of new fiction, poetry, biography, autobiography, translations and children's books; gives assistance to a limited number of universities to establish creative writing fellowships; and publishes anthologies of poetry and stories to which both professional and amateur writers may contribute.

In Scotland, the *Scottish Arts Council* supports writers through a bursary scheme for professional writers, book awards to authors of published books; and writers' fellowships at the Universities of Dundee, Glasgow and Edinburgh and at *Colaisde Gaidhlig*. Grants may be awarded to literary magazines and to the publishers of books of Scottish cultural interest which are considered to be commercial risks. As well as supporting a number of public readings and poetry festivals the SAC operates a writers-in-schools scheme in association with the *Scottish Education Department*.

In Wales, the *Welsh Arts Council* subsidises translations into Welsh; grant-aids literary magazines; funds creative writing fellowships; and supports writers and publishers through awards, bursaries and grants. The WAC also publishes anthologies of poetry, and organises competitions and other events of literary interest.

In Northern Ireland, the *Arts Council of Northern Ireland* supports local magazines; organises readings by distinguished authors; grant-aids publishers of books of Northern Irish cultural interest; and funds two writers-in-residence fellowships.

Regional Arts Associations in England primarily assist professional writers with grants and bursaries, or through specific projects. The WAC helps the three Welsh RAAs to organise visits by writers to schools, colleges, etc.

Livestock: Exports Livestock and horses for export must comply with British export requirements and the import requirements of the importing country. Bovine animals and swine for inter-EEC trade must, with certain exceptions, comply with EEC directives. Advice on overseas import requirements from *Ministry of Agriculture, Fisheries and Food*, (Animal Health Division ID) in England and Wales.

British export requirements cover horses, cattle, sheep and pigs; licences and information from MAFF Animal Health Division 11 for England and Wales. Special provisions apply to thoroughbred **horses** intended for breeding or racing, which may be exempted on a *Jockey Club* licence.

Pre-export quarantine may be at official stations or approved private stations. Apply for approval of station for quarantine to MAFF Animal Health Division 1D.

See also **Agriculture: Scotland; Agriculture: Northern Ireland.**

Livestock Feeding EEC subsidies are paid to creameries supplying liquid skimmed milk and/or butter milk to farmers for stockfeeding and to farmers who produce and sell butter

or cream and use the liquid skimmed milk and/or buttermilk by-products for feeding to their own animals on their own farm. Claim from *Intervention Board for Agricultural Produce*.
See also **Agricultural produce: EEC subsidies**.

Livestock: Imports Import of livestock and horses for breeding is subject to special control; enquire in England and Wales to *Ministry of Agriculture, Fisheries and Food* (Animal Health Division IIIC).
See also **Agriculture: Scotland; Agriculture: Northern Ireland**.

Livestock: Welfare on Farms Government recommendations have been published for the welfare of cattle, pigs, domestic fowls and turkeys. These prohibit tail docking of cattle; surgical castration of poultry; operations on birds (other than feather clipping) to impede flight; and fitting of blinkers to birds by a method involving mutilation of the nasal septum. Other regulations control the method of pig docking and prohibit the docking of pigs more than seven days old, except by a veterinary surgeon on health grounds or to prevent injury from tail-biting. Details from *Ministry of Agriculture, Fisheries and Food* (divisional offices) for England and Wales.
See also **Agriculture: Scotland; Agriculture: Northern Ireland**.

Lloyd's List The List is an international daily newspaper covering marine, aviation, transport and insurance, published by *Lloyd's of London Press Ltd*. Much of the news comes from the world network of Lloyd's agents who also survey damaged ships and cargoes and settle local insurance claims for *Lloyd's of London*.

Lloyd's of London *Lloyd's of London* is an international insurance market in which most risks can be insured, e.g. marine, aviation, motor, household, fire, theft, earthquake, livestock and professional indemnity insurance.
Members of Lloyd's (over 10,000 men and women of all nationalities) are underwriters who set their personal fortunes at risk in return for a share of insurances offered at Lloyds. Their liability is both individual and unlimited. Each member belongs to a syndicate and his underwriting is conducted by the syndicate underwriter in the Underwriting Room at Lloyds.
New members must satisfy the Committee of Lloyds as to their integrity and financial standing and furnish securities which are held in trust against their underwriting liabilities by the Corporation of Lloyd's.
All business with Lloyd's underwriters must be placed through a Lloyd's broker. Over 260 firms of **insurance brokers** meet the standards set by the Committee of Lloyd's and they have offices or correspondents throughout the world. A list of broking firms is available from the Information Department at *Lloyd's of London*. Complaints about brokers should go to the Advisory Department.
To query Lloyd's insurance policies go first to the broker and, failing that, consult the Advisory Department. Other information on Lloyd's matters is available from the Information Department and *Lloyd's Publications and Shipping Intelligence*.

Lobbying Parliament Mass lobbies of Parliament should be arranged in advance through a Member of the House of Commons (see **Members of Parliament**) who can reserve the Grand Committee Room, off Westminster Hall. If the lobby is to be preceded by a procession or a meeting outside the precincts, inform the *police*.
See also **Petitions to Parliament**.

Local Authorities Local authorities are independent bodies with separately elected councils. Within the framework of national policies they take their own decisions, for which they are accountable to their electors and to the relevant central government minister. Council meetings and council committees are open to the public.
Local authorities' major functions and powers are conferred by general Acts of Parliament, usually promoted by central government, although local authorities may promote local or

private bills. Some powers are duties mandatory (i.e. the authority must provide services); others are purely permissive, enabling the authority to provide services. Authorities may spend annually up to a 2p rate for the benefit of their areas and inhabitants, but their expenditure is limited to the exercise of functions conveyed by Parliament, and action incidental to the exercise of those functions.

England and Wales have two main levels of local authority: county councils (54 authorities in all, including six 'metropolitan counties' and the Greater London Council) are responsible for local government services which need to be planned or conducted over a wide area; district councils (402 authorities, including London borough councils and the *City of London*) are generally responsible for more local services. Parish councils (community councils in Wales) form a third level which is responsible for immediately local services, but whose duties are generally exercisable concurrently by district councils. The allocation of functions between different levels is illustrated in the table below.

Scotland is divided into nine regions,

Broad allocations of main local government functions

Function	England: metropolitan areas		England: non-metropolitan areas Wales and Scotland		England: Greater London	Northern Ireland		
	County council	District council	County council	District council	GLC	Borough council	District council	Central govt.
Planning								
structure plans	*		*		*			
local plans		*		*		*		
development control		*		*		*		
country parks	*	*	*	*				
national parks	*		*					
derelict land	*	*	*	*	*	*		
Transport								
transport planning	*		*		*			
highways	*		*		*	*		
traffic regulation	*		*		*			
road safety	*		*		*			
parking	*		*		*	*		
public transport	*		*		*			
Education		*		*	*		*	*
Social Services		*		*			*	*
Housing		*		*	*		*	*
Fire services	*		*		*			*
Police service	*		*					
Consumer protection	*		*			*	*	
Environmental health								
building regulations		*		*	*		*	
clean air		*		*			*	
control of disease		*		*			*	
food hygiene		*		*			*	
refuse collection		*		*			*	
refuse deposit	*		*		*		*	
street cleaning		*		*			*	
Libraries		*	*	*		*		*
Museums and Arts	*	*	*	*	*	*	*	
Recreational facilities	*	*	*	*	*	*	*	
Tourism	*	*	*	*	*	*		
Cemeteries and Crematoria		*		*			*	
Footpaths	*	*	*	*		*	*	
Smallholdings			*		*			
Allotments		*		*	*			

within which are 53 districts, and three islands areas covering respectively Orkney, Shetland and the Western Isles; each has its own council. Large-scale services such as transportation, education, police and fire services, and strategic planning are the responsibility of regional councils; local planning, housing and amenity services are among those carried out at district level. Islands authorities have an all-purpose function.

Northern Ireland has had a single-tier structure of 26 district authorities since October 1973, when responsibility for administering many of the more important services formerly provided by local government was transferred to central departments – their administration is now carried out either through local offices of the departments concerned or through area boards responsible to them. District councils also have a responsibility to represent local views, and are consulted by the Department of Housing, Local Government and Planning on its regional functions.

Local authorities are financed by **rates**, **rate support grant**, other central government grants towards the cost of specific services, and loans (for capital expenditure). Details of each local authority's spending are shown on rate accounts sent to ratepayers; over the country as a whole the main pattern of expenditure is:

Education	55%
Highways	8%
Personal social services	6%*
Police	5%
Refuse disposal and collection	3%
Fire service	2%

No other service accounts for as much as 2% of local government expenditure. County and district councils consist of directly elected councillors. On average, county councils have between 60 and 100 members, metropolitan district councils 50 to 80 members and non-metropolitan district councils 30 to 60 members. The size of the councils is not controlled by legislation, nor is there a statutory ratio between members and electors, although electoral areas (known as wards in the case of districts or electoral divisions in respect of counties) of any one local authority have, as far as practicable, the same ratio of electors to councillors.

Councillors receive no salary but they receive an allowance and travelling expenses when they attend council meetings.

The council is headed by the chairman – who is elected annually by the councillors from their number. In a district which has been granted city or borough status (see **Cities**; **Boroughs**), the chairman is styled 'mayor' (or exceptionally, lord mayor) and the vice-chairman 'deputy mayor'.

The office of alderman has been abolished (it was phased out later in London than in the rest of England and Wales but ceased to exist there by May 1978). Former councillors may be given the title 'honorary alderman' but this title does not carry the right to sit on the council.

The most senior full-time paid official of the principal councils is normally known as the Chief Executive (formerly called the Clerk).

Parish and community councillors are also directly elected. In the case of a parish council there is a minimum size of five councillors. Where a parish or community council has resolved to adopt town status for their area, the council may be styled 'town council' and the chairman and vice-chairman are entitled to be called town mayor and deputy town mayor. The senior official of the council is normally known as the Clerk.

Each year there is one local government election day, on a Thursday, but not all councils are re-elected each year.

County councils: the whole council is elected once every four years – the next election being in 1981.

Metropolitan district councils: one third of the council is elected every year other than in a year of county council elections.

Non-metropolitan district councils: these may be elections of the whole council or of one third of the council depending on which system the

* This figure does not include social services payments made by central government.

district council has chosen. Whole council elections will in future be held every four years, the next year of election being 1979. Where the district council has opted to have elections by thirds, one third of the council will be elected every year, other than in a year of county council elections. The first year in which such arrangements may come into effect is 1979.

Parish and community councils: electoral arrangements will normally coincide with the arrangements made for the elections of district councillors for the same area, elections being held every four years.

Each councillor represents his own particular area and takes up problems affecting individuals or groups of people in that area.

Complaints concerning local authorities should be made to the relevant council office or to your own councillor (whose address may be obtained from the district council offices) or, concerning injustice arising from local authority maladministration, to the relevant *Commissioner for Local Administration*.

See also **Injustice: local; Disputes with public authorities.**

Local Government: Boundaries and Electoral Arrangements These are reviewed by the *Local Government Boundary Commissions*. In England, local government electoral arrangements are now under review. Changes are affected by orders made by the *Home Secretary*, on the basis of reports by the *Local Government Boundary Commission for England*. The LGBC first invites local authorities to prepare schemes, after consultation with local interests; then publishes proposals, and hears objections before making and publishing its recommendations to the HS. While criteria for electoral reviews are specified in the Local Government Act 1972, the HS has set limits to the number of councillors on each authority (county councils 60–100; metropolitan district councils 50–80; non-metropolitan district councils 30–60). The 1972 Act requires the LGBC to start reviews of boundaries of counties, metropolitan districts and London boroughs in 1984. Changes will be effected by orders of the *Secretary of State for the Environment*, on the basis of proposals made by the LGBC which will follow the same consultation procedures as in preparing reports for the HS.

Local Government Election Candidates To qualify to be elected to a **local authority**, it is necessary to be a **British subject, Commonwealth** citizen or citizen of Eire (Irish Republic) and to be at least 21 years of age on the relevant day. Candidates must also on the relevant day be and continue to be a local government elector for the area of the authority (see **Electoral registration**); or have during the whole of the preceding 12 months occupied as owner or tenant land or other premises in that area; or have had during those 12 months their principal or only place of work in that area; have resided in that area for those 12 months or (for members of a parish or community council) have resided either in the parish or community or within three miles of it during the last 12 months.

A person is disqualified if he holds any paid office or employment under the local authority for which the election is being held; or is a bankrupt; or has within five years before the election been surcharged by a district auditor to an amount exceeding £500 under Part X of the Local Government Act 1933; or has within five years before the day of election, or since his election, been convicted of any offence and had passed on him a sentence of imprisonment (whether suspended or not) for a period of not less than three months without the option of a fine; or is disqualified under Part 111 of the Representation of the People Act 1949 (which relates to corrupt or illegal practices); or is disqualified from membership for a specific period by order of the court because of his involvement in expenditure contrary to the law.

Nomination procedure is as for **Parliamentary election candidates**; no deposit is required.

In Northern Ireland, each candidate must be nominated on a form supplied by the deputy returning officer which has been signed by a proposer and seconder and two witnesses, all of whom must be registered in the district electoral area for which the candidate is being nominated. A deposit of £15 must be paid by each candidate.

A person is qualified to be elected to a local authority if he is a British subject or a person who was entered in the Northern Ireland Register of Electors in force on 29 March 1962 and if on the relevant day he is at least 21 years of age. Other qualifications and disqualifications are similar to those in England and Wales.

See also **Election agents**; **Election expenses**.

Local Government Elections For all local government areas in England and Wales elections are conducted in accordance with rules made by the *Home Secretary*. Ordinary election of councillors for all local government areas in England and Wales takes place on the first Thursday in May but the frequency and electoral arrangements vary for the different types of councils.

County council ordinary elections take place every fourth year after 1973; term of office is four years; all councillors retire together.

Metropolitan district council ordinary elections take place every year after 1975 other than a year of election of county councillors; term of office is four years; a third of the councillors in each ward retire in every ordinary year of election.

Non-metropolitan district councils may request the HS to provide either for a system of whole council elections (i.e. all councillors elected simultaneously) or for a system of elections by thirds (i.e. only a third elected at one election); ordinary elections take place in the case of whole council elections, in 1979 and every fourth year thereafter, and in the case of elections by thirds, in the year when such an order comes into force, and every year thereafter other than a year of election of county councillors; term of office is four years.

For parish councils (community councils in Wales), the district council fixes the number of parish councillors for each parish; they are elected by the local government electors for the parish. Ordinary election of parish councillors will take place in 1979 and every fourth year thereafter. Term of office of parish councillors elected after 1976 is four years.

The *Secretary of State for Scotland* makes the Scottish local election rules. In ordinary election years the day of election is the first Tuesday in May. Term of office of regional and islands area councillors is four years; elections take place in 1978. District councillors are at present serving a three-year term of office but after the district council elections in 1980, their term will also be four years.

Local elections in Northern Ireland are conducted in accordance with the Electoral Law Act (Northern Ireland) 1962 and with rules made by the Secretary of State for Northern Ireland. These elections take place on the third Wednesday of May every fourth year, i.e. 1977, 1981, etc., all councillors retiring at the same time. The elections are by the single transferable vote system of proportional representation.

See also **Election agents**; **Election expenses**; **Electoral registration**; **Local elections: candidates**.

Local History General guidance on the available UK records can be obtained from *Public Record Office*, and from the *Scottish Record Office* for Scotland, and the *Public Record Office of Northern Ireland* for Ulster.

See also **Records: public and historical**.

Lodging Houses Houses for the purpose of 'accommodating by night poor persons, not being members of the same family, who resort thereto, and are allowed to occupy one common room for the purpose of sleeping and eating' must be registered with the local authority.

London Buses and Underground *London Transport Executive* is responsible for the management and day-to-day operation of London's underground and red bus services. The *Greater London Council*, which has overall policy and financial control of

London Transport, receives a grant from central government annually for public transport, and decides how much of the remaining revenue necessary is to come from fares and how much, by way of subsidy, from the rates paid by Londoners. Proposals to increase fares to raise an agreed additional amount of revenue are submitted to the GLC by the LTE and a decision is reached following consideration by the GLC in public. Increases also have to be approved by the *Price Commission*, and, for London Transport bus services operating outside Greater London, by the Metropolitan Traffic Commissioners. See **Bus services and subsidies; Public service vehicles.**

Lost or Found Property Property lost or found should be reported to the local police station, including property found in cabs. Property lost or found in buses, coaches, etc., should be reported to the firm running the service. In London lost property is dealt with by the *Metropolitan Police Lost Property Offices* (open to the public Monday to Friday 9.00 a.m. to 4.00 p.m.) and *London Transport Lost Property Offices.*

Lotteries Certain charitable, sporting, cultural or other societies may promote lotteries within prescribed financial limits provided that they are registered with the local authority within whose area the office or head office is situated (in England, a London borough council, a district council, the Common Council of the City of London or the Council of the Isles of Scilly; in Wales a district council; in Scotland an islands or district council). If a society intends to promote a lottery where the total value of the tickets or chances to be sold exceeds £5,000, a scheme for the lottery approved by the society must also be registered with the *Gaming Board of Great Britain.* **Local authorities** themselves may promote lotteries for any purpose for which they have power to incur expenditure under any enactment, provided such lotteries are approved by the full council and registered with the GBGB.

Lotteries are subject to the following limitations: the price of tickets may not exceed 25p; the amount or value of a single prize must not exceed £1,000 for lotteries held at intervals of less than a month (a 'short-term' lottery), £1,500 for lotteries held more frequently than once every three months but not more frequently than once a month (a 'medium-term' lottery) or £2,000 for any other lottery; and the total value of tickets or chances sold should not exceed £10,000 for a short-term lottery, £20,000 for a medium-term lottery, or £40,000 for any other lottery.

With certain exceptions, lotteries must not be held more frequently than once a week and there must be not more than 52 in any period of 12 months. Not more than one half of the whole proceeds of a lottery may be appropriated for the provision of prizes and, in the case of a lottery with proceeds of £5,000 or less, not more than 25% may be appropriated on account of expenses (exclusive of prizes). Where the whole proceeds of a lottery exceeds £5,000, not more than 15% of those proceeds may be appropriated on account of expenses unless the GBGB authorises otherwise. In such cases the GBGB's authority should be sought before lotteries are promoted.

Under the Lotteries Regulations 1977, sales of lottery tickets are prohibited in licensed betting offices, licensed bingo or other gaming clubs, or in any premises used wholly or mainly for providing amusements with prizes, amusements by means of slot machines, or both. Sales of lottery tickets by means of vending machines are also prohibited, as are sales in the street, subject to an exception for sales from kiosks. Although the Lotteries Regulations do not prohibit door-to-door sales of lottery tickets, the provisions of the House-to-House Collections Act 1939 and the House-to-House Regulations 1947 may apply to such sales. Advice from the district council for the area concerned. Advertising is permitted subject to the limitations on the total amount that may be appropriated on account of expenses from the proceeds. Detailed notes on lotteries and model schemes are available from the GBGB. See also **Bingo registration; Gambling clubs; Gaming licences; Gaming premises.**

Luxembourg EEC member. For **exchange control** is a non-scheduled territory within the EEC but outside the **overseas sterling area.** UK nationals travelling direct from the UK normally need only the following (but check): **passports** (British visitors' passports acceptable).
EEC or bilateral social security arrangements are applicable; leaflets and EEC Guides obtainable from *Department of Health and Social Security, Overseas Branch.* Apply to local social security office for leaflet SA28 which explains who is entitled to reduced-cost medical treatment under EEC health arrangements, and how to get the certificate of entitlement (form E111).
Enquiries to *Luxembourg Embassy* in London.
British diplomatic mission to Luxembourg is *British Embassy* in Luxembourg.

M

Machine Safety General UK policy on the safe use at work of machinery (especially the guarding of machinery) including the preparation of legislation and codes of practice, is the responsibility of the Safety and General Branch A at the *Health and Safety Executive Head Office*. The *Health and Safety Executive, HM Factory Inspectorate* (Consultant Section 7) is responsible for determining practicable standards for guarding machinery to meet policy objectives and the preparation of technical codes of practice, guidance notes and advisory leaflets with technical content.
Advice at a local level on machinery safety is available from the *Health and Safety Executive, HM Factory Inspectorate* (area offices).
A permanent display of methods of machinery guarding can be seen at the *Health and Safety Executive Health and Safety Centre*.
See also **Clothing at work; Industrial accidents; Work: health and safety**.

Machinery Certification Certification for batch and line-produced machinery is conducted by *Lloyd's Register of Shipping*. Inspection includes manufacturers' quality control procedures; works receive continuing surveillance after the issue of certificates of approval.

Madagascar For **exchange control** is a non-scheduled territory outside the **overseas sterling area** and the **EEC**. UK nationals travelling direct from the UK normally need only the following (but check): **passports; visas;** international certificates of **vaccination** against smallpox; **work permits** (if taking a job).
The UK has no reciprocal health or social security arrangements.
Enquiries to *Madagascar Embassy* in Paris, France.
The *British diplomatic missions* to Madagascar are the *British Embassy* and *British Consulate* in Tananarive.

Malawi Commonwealth member. For **exchange control** is a non-scheduled territory in the **overseas sterling area** but outside the EEC. UK nationals travelling direct from the UK normally need only the following (but check): **passports;** international certificates of **vaccination** against smallpox; **work permits** (if taking a job).
The UK has no reciprocal health or social security arrangements.
Enquiries to *Malawi High Commission* in London.
British diplomatic missions to Malawi are *British High Commissions* in Lilongwe and Blantyre.

Malaysia Commonwealth member. For **exchange control** is a non-scheduled territory in the **overseas sterling area** but outside the EEC. UK nationals travelling direct from the UK normally need only the following (but check): **passports;** international certificates of **vaccination** against smallpox; **work permits** (if taking a job).

The UK has no reciprocal health or social security arrangements.
Enquiries to *Malaysia High Commission* in London.
British diplomatic missions to Malaysia are *British High Commission* in Kuala Lumpur and *Hon. British Representatives* in Kuching, Kota Kinabalu and Penang.

Mali For **exchange control** is a non-scheduled territory outside the **overseas sterling area** and the **EEC**. UK nationals travelling direct from the UK normally need only the following (but check): **passports**; **visas**; international certificates of **vaccination** against smallpox and yellow fever; **work permits** (if taking a job); green cards for motor insurance (if bringing a car); international driving permits (if intending to drive: see **Motoring abroad**).
The UK has no reciprocal health or social security arrangements.
Enquiries to *Mali Embassy* in Brussels, Belgium.
British diplomatic mission to Mali is based on *British Embassy* in Dakar, Senegal.

Malta **Commonwealth** member. For **exchange control** is a non-scheduled territory in the **overseas sterling area** but outside the **EEC**. UK nationals travelling direct from the UK normally need only the following (but check): **passports**; **work permits** (if taking a job); green cards for motor insurance (if bringing a car: see **Motoring abroad**).
UK reciprocal arrangements cover social security (see leaflet SA11 obtainable from *Department of Health and Social Security, Overseas Group*) and health. Outpatient treatment at casualty clinics free; small charge for inpatients; surgical operations charged.
Enquiries to *Maltese High Commission* in London, and *Malta Government Office* in London.
British diplomatic mission to Malta is *British High Commission* in Valetta.

Maps and Photographs: Environmental Maps and photographs are available from the *Department of the Environment Library*. It holds 500,000 maps, atlases, reports and books on cartography, and provides an intelligence service. It is available for reference, by appointment, to the general public as well as to government departments; certain maps are for sale. The Atlas of the Environment, together with its predecessor the Desk Atlas of Planning Maps of England and Wales, provides maps on a wide range of social and economic subjects.
The *Department of the Environment Slide Library* holds 35,000 35 mm slides mostly in colour, photographs covering housing, planning, architecture, conservation, pollution and the new towns, and 700 map slides. Slides are available on loan to any recognised organisation, including educational groups, as well as to central and local government departments.
The *Department of the Environment Air Photograph Unit*'s library of photographs, available to the general public and local authorities, holds both prints and film of all Royal Air Force photography, and negatives of all but current Ordnance Survey photography. Prints may be inspected by appointment and copies supplied to order. The Unit also has a central register of air photography of England which contains information on the coverage and scale of current commercial photography, in addition to the information available about all RAF and Ordnance Survey photography.
See also **Ordnance Survey maps and services.**

Marathon Races If marathon races are to be held on public highways, the *police* should be consulted in advance.
See also **Olympic Games.**

Maritime Arbitration Arbitration in all manner of maritime disputes is undertaken by the *London Maritime Arbitrators' Association.*

Marriage: England and Wales Unless you are to be married in a Church of England or a Church of Wales church (see below) you must give notice of intention to marry to a district's *Superintendent Registrar of Births, Deaths and Marriages* (in certain circumstances, a *Registrar of*

Births, Deaths and Marriages). The authority for a marriage to take place is either a SR's certificate or his certificate and licence.

For marriage by certificate each partner must give notice to the SR for the district in which he or she has lived for the seven days preceding the giving of the notice. If they both live in the same district only one notice is required. The notice must be displayed in the register office for 21 days. Then the SR can issue a certificate for the marriage to proceed, if no impediment to the marriage has been shown to exist.

For marriage by certificate and licence, only one notice is required. This must be given to the SR for the district in which one of the parties has resided for the preceding 15 days. The notice is not displayed and the SR can issue a certificate and licence after one clear day (excluding Sunday, Christmas Day or Good Friday) if no impediment has been shown to exist.

People giving notice of marriage are asked for evidence of age, identity and of the termination of any previous marriage.

All notices are entered in a marriage notice book and are valid for three months from the date of entry.

These preliminaries are the same whether the marriage is to be a civil one in a register office or a religious one in a registered building (i.e. certified to the *Registrar General of England and Wales* for worship and registered as a place where marriages may lawfully be solemnised). Anyone may perform the ceremonies in registered buildings but these must take place in the presence of a registrar or a person authorised by the RG to register marriages (an 'authorised person'). All marriages must usually be attended by at least two witnesses. Marriages outside a register office where no registrar is present are registered in duplicate registers, one of which is passed to the SR.

Marriages in Anglican churches: Clergymen in all churches of the Church of England and the Church of Wales can legally conduct weddings. They register the marriage in registers provided by the *Registrar General of England and Wales*; the original register is eventually forwarded to the RG and duplicate registers are retained by the parish. The marriage can take place by the publication of banns, common licence or Archbishop's special licence. To arrange a church marriage, the first step is to consult the local vicar.

For publication of banns the vicar is entitled to one week's notice prior to the first calling of the banns; one of the parties must be resident in the parish where the marriage is to take place or have their name entered upon the church electoral roll, having worshipped in that church for six months. Banns should be called in the parish church of both bride and bridegroom and if they are on the electoral roll of another church then the banns must also be published in the third church. The vicar of the church where the marriage is to take place must be given certificates from the other churches that the banns have been called in those churches.

Common licences can be obtained from the Diocesan Registrar (address from vicar) or from the *Archbishop of Canterbury's Faculty Office*. To obtain a common licence one of the parties must be able to swear an affidavit to the effect that one party has resided in the particular parish for 15 days or, if they are on a church electoral roll, produce a certificate to that effect. Marriage may take place immediately the licence has been issued.

Archbishop's special licences are obtained from the Archbishop of Canterbury's Faculty Office to which application should be made for the appropriate form and instructions. An Archbishop's special licence allows parties to marry outside their own parish without having any residential qualification; it also allows for marriage in school or college chapels and unlicensed buildings. Special licences are also necessary for emergency marriages in hospitals. Both special licences and common licences are valid for three months.

See also **Records of births, marriages and deaths.**

Marriage: Northern Ireland There are separate procedures for Church of

Ireland, Presbyterian, Roman Catholic and all other marriages. All civil marriages and marriages of other denominations and religions than those below must take place in a registrar's office or a church or building which has been registered by the *Registrar General for Northern Ireland* as a place where marriages may lawfully be solemnised, and a licence or certificate is normally necessary from the *Registrar of Births, Deaths and Marriages* in whose district or office the marriage is to take place. For certain denominations, however, the marriage may take place by special licence issued by the head of the denomination, provided one of the parties belongs to that denomination, e.g. Society of Friends' marriages may take place by registrar's certificate or by special licence. Jewish marriages can take place only by registrar's certificate.

For marriage by certificate, notice must be given to the registrar of the district in which the parties have resided for seven days preceding the giving of the notice. If the parties reside in different districts, notice must be served on the registrar of each district. A copy of the notice must be displayed in the registrar's office for 21 days after which the registrar can issue his certificate for the marriage to proceed, if no impediment to the marriage has been shown to exist.

For marriage by licence, one of the parties must have resided in the registrar's district for 15 days and the other for seven days immediately preceding the service of notice. If the parties reside in different districts, notice must be served on the registrar of each district and a residence of 15 days immediately before giving notice is necessary for each party. The registrar within whose district the marriage is to take place requires the certificate of the registrar of the other district before he issues his licence. A copy of the notice must be displayed in the registrar's office for seven days after which the licence may be issued, if the other preliminaries have been observed and no impediment to the marriage has been shown to exist.

All notices are entered in a marriage notice book and are valid for three months from the date of entry. In certain instances involving marriages in a registrar's office it is necessary to advertise the notice in a newspaper circulating in the district in two consecutive weeks.

Registration of marriages which take place in a registrar's office, or in the registrar's presence in a registered building not supplied with registers, is done by the registrar. For Roman Catholic marriages and marriages by special licences, a certificate is completed after the marriage and forwarded to the registrar for registration. In all other cases the marriages are registered in duplicate registers and when these are filled one is retained by the church or building and the other passed to the registrar of the district.

Church of Ireland: One or both parties must be Protestant Episcopalians. Marriage can take place on the authority of a licence; special licence; certificate from the *Registrar of Births, Deaths and Marriages*; or, if both parties are PEs after banns have been published. In all cases apply first to your local minister.

Licences are obtainable from a Church of Ireland licenser for a marriage in a church within his district. One of the parties must have resided for at least seven days in the licenser's district immediately before giving notice of the intended marriage. The licence is not issued for seven days after notice has been given. Before the licence is issued, one of the parties must make a declaration, which includes a clause to the effect that one of them has been resident in the district attached to the church in which the marriage is to take place for at least the preceding 14 days. The marriage must take place within three months from the date of notice.

Special licences may be granted by a bishop of the Church of Ireland when one or both parties are PEs. It authorises the marriage for any time and at any place within the bishop's episcopal superintendence.

Procedure for obtaining a certificate of marriage from a registrar is the same as for civil marriages. However, one of the couple must have been living for at least 14 days prior to the marriage within the

district attached to the church in which the marriage is to take place.
Publication of banns is regulated by the Church; apply to the local minister.
Presbyterian Church: Marriages may take place by licence, special licence or banns; for all of these apply to your local minister in the first instance.
To be married by licence or special licence, one at least of the parties must belong to the Presbyterian body concerned. A licence is obtainable from a licensing minister for marriage in a church within his Presbytery. But at least seven days before issuing a licence, the LM must have a certificate from the minister of the church where one of the parties has for a month preceding been a member, to the effect that notice of the intended marriage has been given. Immediately before the grant of the licence the party who gave notice must make an oath or declaration which includes a clause to the effect that one of the parties has had his or her usual residence within the presbytery for the preceding 15 days. The marriage must take place within three months from the date of entry of notice in the LM's notice book and within one month from the date of the licence.
A special licence may be granted by the Moderator of the Presbyterian body concerned, which authorises marriage at any time and at any place.
Banns may be published where both parties are Presbyterians, in the presence of the congregations of which they are members. Six days' notice to the minister is required and publication must be made on three Sundays preceding the marriage which must take place in the church (or in one of the churches) in which the banns have been published.
Roman Catholic Church: Procedure for marriage where both parties are Roman Catholics is in general regulated by the law of the Roman Catholic Church; apply for information to a RC clergyman. If only one of the parties is a RC, a licence from a licenser appointed by a RC bishop may be issued. Notice may be given to the licenser seven days before the issue of the licence. Alternatively a certificate, as for civil marriages, may be obtained from a *Registrar of Births, Deaths and Marriages*.
See also **Records of births, marriages and deaths**.

Marriage Overseas British **consuls** in a small number of foreign countries hold marriage warrants and can solemnise marriage in certain circumstances. Enquiries to the appropriate consul or to the *Foreign and Commonwealth Office, Nationality and Treaty Department*. Consuls no longer register local marriages, but local law marriage certificates (with translation if not issued in English) can be accepted by them for certification and deposit at the appropriate *Registrar General's* office in the UK, which can then issue certified copies on request.

Marriage: Scotland Marriage in Scotland is regulated by the Marriage (Scotland) Act 1977. A religious marriage (whether Christian or non-Christian) may take place in a church or elsewhere and may be solemnised by any minister, clergyman, pastor, priest or other person so entitled under the Act. A civil marriage may be solemnised in a registration office by any authorised *Registrar of Births, Deaths and Marriages* (or an assistant registrar).
Each party to a marriage (religious or civil) must submit a completed notice of intention to marry to the registrar for the registration district in which the marriage is to take place. The forms, obtainable from any registrar of births, deaths and marriages in Scotland, should be submitted preferably about four weeks; or, if either party has previously been married, about six weeks; and in any event, not more than three months or less than 14 clear days before the date of the marriage.
Each marriage notice must be accompanied by the appropriate fee; by the person's birth certificate; and by evidence of termination of any previous marriage. A person belonging to a country outside the UK must, with certain exceptions, also produce, if practicable, a certificate issued by a competent authority in his/her own

country to the effect that no impediment to his/her marrying is known.

The registrar enters particulars in a marriage notice book; publicly displays on a list the parties' names and the marriage date, normally for at least 14 days; and if satisfied that there is no legal impediment to the marriage he prepares a marriage schedule from information provided by the parties. For a religious marriage, he issues this schedule to the parties, who must produce it before the marriage ceremony to the person solemnising the marriage; otherwise the marriage will be void. Immediately after the ceremony the schedule is completed by the signatures of the parties, the witnesses and the celebrant, and then is returned within three days to the issuing registrar: it forms the basis of the entry which the registrar makes in the register of marriages.

For a civil marriage the schedule is not issued to the parties but is held available by the registrar at the ceremony and is signed thereafter as above. A fee for the civil marriage is payable in advance to the registrar.

Copies of the entry in the register of marriages (the marriage certificate) may be obtained from the registrar on payment of the appropriate fee.

See also **Records of births, marriages and deaths.**

Martial Arts Karate, kung fu, ju jitsu, aikido, kendo and the Korean martial arts are controlled centrally in the UK by the *Martial Arts Commission*, which keeps a register of clubs and individuals. The governing association or board of each martial art is responsible for its own technical standards and for organising tournaments, championships, referees, squad selection, etc. All the governing bodies are members of MAC.

Matches Manufacturers must be licensed under arrangements for the payment of **excise duty**; apply to *Her Majesty's Customs and Excise.*

Maternity Benefits Benefits consist of a lump sum Maternity Grant and a weekly Maternity Allowance. The grant must be claimed from between 14 weeks before and up to three months after the birth; either the husband or wife must have paid sufficient **national insurance contributions** in the relevant tax year. The allowance (with **earnings related supplement** in some cases) is paid for 18 weeks starting 11 weeks before the baby's expected birth date, where the relevant contribution conditions are satisfied. It is not paid while the woman is working, and must be claimed between 14 and 11 weeks before the expected date of birth. Apply to *Department of Health and Social Security* (local office); explanatory leaflets NI17A and NI196.

See also **Social security benefits.**

Maternity Leave A woman who has been employed by one employer continuously for at least two years is entitled to be absent from work from the 11th week before confinement and to return to the same job within 29 weeks after the birth. The employer must be notified at least three weeks before leave starts of her intention to return and given at least one week's notice of return. Complaints of unfair dismissal to the *Industrial Tribunals Central Office* – an explanatory leaflet ITL1 and application form IT1 are available from *Employment Service Agency Employment Offices*; *Employment Service Agency Job Centres* and *Department of Employment Unemployment Benefit Offices*. Appeals against industrial tribunal findings, on a point of law only, should be made to the *Employment Appeal Tribunal.*

See also **Industrial tribunals.**

Maternity Pay In addition to **maternity leave,** pregnant women may also claim pay from their employer for the first six weeks of absence. Qualifying conditions are as for maternity leave. Employers are reimbursed from the Maternity Pay Fund. Complaints of non-payment by employers or by the Fund to the *Industrial Tribunals' Central Office*. An explanatory leaflet ITL1 and application form IT1 are available from *Employment Service Agency Job Centres, Employment Service Agency Employment Offices* or *Department of Employment Unemployment Benefit Offices*. Appeals against industrial tribunal findings, on a point of law only, should be made to the *Employment Appeal Tribunal*. See also **Industrial tribunals**.

Mauritania For **exchange control** is a non-scheduled territory outside the **overseas sterling area** and the **EEC**. UK nationals travelling direct from the UK normally need only the following (but check): **passports**; **visas**; international certificates of **vaccination** against smallpox; **work permits** (if taking a job); green cards for motor insurance (if bringing a car); international driving permits (if intending to drive: see **Motoring abroad**).
The UK has no reciprocal health or social security arrangements.
Enquiries to *Mauritanian diplomatic mission for UK*, *Mauritanian Embassy* in Paris, France.
British diplomatic mission to Mauritania is the *British Consulate* at Nouakchott. The ambassador resides in Dakar, Senegal.

Mauritius Commonwealth member. For **exchange control** is a non-scheduled territory in the **overseas sterling area** but outside the **EEC**. UK nationals travelling direct from the UK normally need only the following (but check): **passports**; international certificates of **vaccination** against smallpox; **work permits** (if taking a job).
The UK has no reciprocal health or social security arrangements.
Enquiries to *Mauritius High Commission* in London.
British diplomatic mission to Mauritius is *British High Commission* in Port Louis.

Meals on Wheels A hot midday meal may be delivered at home to those who are unable to prepare one for themselves through age or disability; a small charge is generally made. In some areas meals are provided outside the home in lunch clubs or **day centres**. Further information from local authority (Social Service Department).
See also **Disablement**.

Meat Exports Animals whose meat is for export to Sweden, Switzerland or the **EEC** must be slaughtered at approved **abattoirs** in the UK and accompanied by required health certification. Lists of approved abattoirs in England and Wales are obtainable from the *Ministry of Agriculture, Fisheries and Food* (Animal Health Division IVB); from the *Department of Agriculture and Fisheries for Scotland*; or from the *Department of Agriculture for Northern Ireland*.

Medals: Armed Forces Medals for previous military service are dealt with by the *Royal Navy, Director General of Defence Accounts*; the *Royal Marines, Drafting and Records Office*; the *Army Medal Office*; and the *Royal Air Force Personnel Management Centre*. If you think you are entitled to a medal, write with details of the medal and full personal details including service number, rank, dates of service and regiment or branch of service.
See also **Gallantry awards: military**.

Medals, Seals and Dies These, e.g. prize medals, can be made to order by the *Royal Mint*. Enquiries to the marketing manager at the RM, Llantrisant.

Medical Information Service: British Library Computer searches are undertaken for a fee by the Medical Literature Analysis and Retrieval System of the *British Library, Lending Division*.

Medical Specialists Overseas *British Council Overseas Offices* initiate proposals for visits by British medical specialists, sponsored visits to the UK and awards for postgraduate medical studies. These are implemented by the BC staff at BC headquarters in consultation with the BC Medical Department. The BC supplies overseas countries with information about British medical education. Enquiries to Medical Department, *British Council* or the BC Overseas Office in the country concerned.
See also **Overseas professional visits and academic exchanges**; **Overseas students in the UK**; **Sponsored visits to the UK**; **Research grants**.

Medical Treatment: Emergency In an emergency a patient should visit or telephone his own **National Health Service** or private **doctor** if possible, or other nearby family doctor who can be reached without delay. NHS hospital accident emergency departments are available to deal with injuries and emergencies which require immediate hospital treatment; go to the nearest hospital which has an accident and emergency department (not every hospital has one but any local hospital will give directions). Alternatively telephone for an ambulance (telephone number 999) if unable to make the journey independently.

Medical Treatment: Overseas Visitors As a long-established UK policy, visitors whose need for treatment arises in the UK may be provided with treatment, if immediately necessary, under the **National Health Service**. Visitors must explain to a NHS family **doctor** that they wish to be treated under the NHS and give their home address instead of a NHS number.
People living overseas who come to this country for medical treatment must pay for it as private patients, unless they are covered by **EEC** Social Security Regulations and have come with the written authorisation of their Social Security Authority or Institution. Reciprocal arrangements with the Channel Islands, Gibraltar, Malta and the USSR also allow patients to be referred to the UK for NHS treatment under certain conditions.
See also **Illness abroad**.

Medicines Medicines, including sutures and certain other surgical materials, biological products, antibiotics, dental fillings, contact lenses and associated fluids, and intra-uterine contraceptives, must generally be licensed or certificated under the Medicines Act 1968 for administration to human beings or animals in the UK.
The manufacture, importation, and marketing of medicines must be in accordance with a product licence held either by the person responsible for the composition of the product (usually the manufacturer), or by the importer. Manufacture or packaging of medicinal products must be authorised by a manufacturer's licence, and the supply of a medicinal product for the purpose of a clinical trial in human beings must be covered by a clinical trial certificate. 'Biological' products, where purity or potency cannot be tested adequately by chemical means, are subject to special arrangements, for which in some cases Batch Release Certificates are issued on the advice of the *National Institute for Biological Standards and Control*. Special transitional provisions generally applied from the commencement of licensing in 1971. The issue of licences may be subject to particular labelling requirements, and the Medicines Act requires labelling and advertising to conform to certain standards; any advertisement or representation to a doctor or dentist concerning medicinal products must be preceded or accompanied by a date sheet delivered not longer than 15 months earlier. Certain special groups – medical, dental and veterinary practitioners, herbalists, etc. – and certain special classes of product – e.g. herbal medicines – are exempt from licensing.
The sale of medicines to anyone other than the ultimate user requires a Wholesale Dealers Licence. For retail sale, medicines will be divided under the Medicines Act into those supplied on prescription only, and those on the General Sale List, which need not be sold under the supervision of a pharmacist. All premises from which retail sales of medicines not on the General Sale List are made must be registered with the *Pharmaceutical Society of Great Britain*, which maintains an inspectorate (see **Pharmacists**).
Apply for licences to *Department of Health and Social Security*.
The Department is advised on the issuing of licences by the Medicines Inspectorate and by appropriate committees of independent experts, including the Committee on Safety of Medicines (which has six specialist sub-committees), the Committee on Review of Medicines (concerned with products already on the market), and the Committee on Dental and Surgical Products. Appointments to these committees are on the advice of the *Medicines Commission*. Applicants for licences are generally given an opportunity to make special representations

if the refusal of a licence appears likely, and further representations may be made to the Medicines Commission if the relevant Committee advises against issue. There are also further appeal procedures in special cases. 'British Pharmacopoeia', which lists all medicines available, is prepared by the *British Pharmacopoeia Commission* under the direction of the *Medicines Commission.*
See also **Dentists; Doctors; National Health Service.**

Medicines and Appliances: Prescription Charges Under the **National Health Service** there is normally a charge of 20p per item supplied against a prescription from a family **doctor.** Supplies are free to children under 16; men over 65; women over 60; those who hold an exemption certificate issued by a *Family Practitioner Committee* (i.e. expectant mothers, mothers of a child under one, and people with certain medical conditions); and people (and their dependants) who have an exemption certificate from the *Department of Health and Social Security* (these are recipients of **supplementary benefit** or **family income supplement,** people who cannot afford the charge, and people being treated for war or service disablement).
If you intend to claim a refund of prescription charges, complete the declaration on the back of the prescription form and ask the chemist for an official receipt (Form FP57/EC57). If you do not qualify for exemption but use more than 10 prescriptions in six months you save money by buying a prepayment certificate: this is a 'season ticket' covering all NHS prescription charges for six months (cost £2) or 12 months (£3.50); apply for leaflets and forms to post offices.
People receiving private (i.e. not NHS) treatment from a doctor have to pay the full cost of medicines and appliances (i.e. not the NHS subsidised rate).

Medicines and Appliances: Supply Under the **National Health Service** everyone is entitled to receive medicines and certain appliances prescribed by their NHS family **doctor** and certain medicines prescribed by their NHS **dentist.** (Some surgical appliances can be prescribed only by a NHS hospital consultant.)
A patient who receives a prescription from a doctor or dentist normally takes it to a chemist for dispensing. (Some doctors occasionally dispense medicines and appliances, e.g. in remote rural areas.) Most chemists in England dispense NHS medicines and appliances and display notices to this effect in their windows: lists for local areas are available at local *Family Practitioner Committee* offices and usually at main post offices. Individuals or firms which deal in special appliances prescribed by family doctors, including trusses, elastic hosiery, etc., which require measuring and fitting, are also on these lists.
Chemists are open during normal shop-opening hours and (for extra payment) take part in a rota so that one or more chemists in a district are open for one hour in the evening on early-closing days, one hour on Sundays and public holidays, and one hour after 6 p.m. on other days (half an hour in districts with very few chemists). Most areas also have a list of chemists (available at the local police station) who will dispense urgently required drugs or appliances outside normal opening hours provided the doctor has marked the prescription 'urgent'.
The FPC is responsible in each area for testing the quality and amount of medicines and appliances supplied, and for arranging that one or more places of business in each district are open at all reasonable times.

Members of Parliament Names and addresses of the Members of Parliament for local constituencies are available from public libraries. You can write to them at the Houses of Parliament and, when the Houses are sitting, anyone can ask at St Stephen's entrance to see a peer or MP without prior appointment; visitors are directed to the central lobby and given a card to complete; this is taken to the peer or MP if he can be found, who will say whether he is willing to see the visitor. But if possible appointments should be made in advance.

See also **Lobbying Parliament; Parliamentary elections.**

Mental Disability: Children Arrangements exist for the notification of congenital malformations including Down's syndrome (frequently called mongolism) which are apparent at birth. The care and progress of children notified under these arrangements is kept under special review by *area health authorities*. Not all mentally handicapping conditions are, however, apparent at birth. Regular developmental screening of young children, particularly those at risk, is carried out by **doctors, health visitors** and **social workers** to detect as early as possible any deviant mental development. Parents who suspect that their child is mentally handicapped should consult their **National Health Service** family **doctor** for advice.

Assistance available from local authorities include: **home helps**; home nursing; laundry services for the incontinent; sitters-in; play centres; **day nurseries**; nursery schools (see **Nursery education**); youth clubs; and residential care either permanently or temporarily, during emergencies or holidays. Arrangements vary with different authorities, but all authorities have a statutory duty to provide community services for the mentally handicapped.

Education of mentally handicapped children is the responsibility of local education authorities.

See also **Disablement: handicapped children's education; Disablement: social services.**

Mental Disability: Services Services for mentally handicapped people are provided by both the *area health authority* and the local authority (Social Services Department). Where mentally handicapped people and their families need help and advice their **National Health Service** family **doctor** will put them in touch with the relevant hospital specialist services or local authority social services department. Mentally handicapped adults may live at home, in hostels, in special residential accommodation or in hospital, depending on the degree of handicap and the type of care needed.

On reaching 16 many mildly handicapped adolescents go directly into open or sheltered employment; local authority Careers Offices can help them find work. The more severely handicapped can go either temporarily (for pre-work training) or permanently to an adult training centre run by the local authority social services department. Training is designed to develop good working habits, increase social competence and help each handicapped person to live a more independent life. Trainees usually receive a small payment for the work they do. There are also **day centres** run by authorities for severely handicapped or multiple handicapped people living at home. Hospital patients may do occupational therapy, gardening, simple maintenance work or help in the kitchens or laundries. People living in hospital can go daily to an adult training centre and those living at home to a hospital unit if appropriate.

In addition the Disablement Resettlement Officer of the *Department of Employment* can help capable people find paid work either in ordinary employment or in a sheltered workshop. Mentally handicapped people may also attend an Industrial Therapy Organisation and use further and adult education services provided by local education authorities.

See also **Adult education; Disablement; Further education.**

Mental Illness Those suffering from mental ill health are normally treated in the first instance by their **National Health Service** family **doctor** or as hospital out-patients. Where hospital admission is necessary, it may be to a mental illness hospital or to the psychiatric department of a general hospital near to the patient's home (see **Hospital treatment**). Most admissions are temporary, lasting only for a few days or weeks.

95% of mentally ill and mentally handicapped patients in hospital are there 'informally'. Their legal position is broadly that of any other hospital patient; for example they are regarded as having the right to refuse a particular form of treatment. They may discharge themselves at any time, subject to certain statutory powers which exist only to enable an informal patient to be prevented from leaving hospital for up to three days whilst a formal application is made for detention.

The Mental Health Act 1959 provides in respect of England and Wales, however, that in certain circumstances a mentally disordered person can be admitted to hospital without his or her consent as a 'detained patient'. If a person has committed a criminal offence, the court can decide, on the advice of two doctors, to make a hospital order, which places the person in hospital rather than passing a penal sentence. In serious cases, a crown court may make a hospital order and impose restrictions on discharge (restricted patients). For compulsory admission other than via the courts or prison the person must be suffering from mental disorder of a degree warranting detention in hospital, which must be necessary either in the interests of the patient's health or safety, or for the protection of others. Normally two medical recommendations are needed; application must be made by the nearest relative of the patient or by a mental welfare officer – in the first instance to NHS family doctor.

In an emergency, the recommendation of a single doctor (preferably one who knows the patient) is needed, and the application must be made by a relative or by a mental welfare officer; a second medical recommendation must be obtained within 72 hours if the patient is to continue to be detained in hospital. For detention for more than 28 days the patient (if over 21) must be suffering from mental illness or severe subnormality, and the consent of the nearest relative is required (Section 26 of the Mental Health Act). If the patient is detained under Section 26, the nearest relative has the right to discharge the patient unless this is barred on safety grounds.

It is considered that a doctor does not need to obtain the consent of the detained patient before giving treatment he considers necessary. A mentally disordered person found in a public place may be taken by a police constable to a place of safety so that he or she can be medically examined and interviewed by a mental welfare officer. All detained patients have the right to apply to the managers of the hospital for their discharge. In addition, those detained under Section 26 or under a hospital order made by a court without restrictions on discharge have the right to apply for discharge to a *Mental Health Review Tribunal*. They may do so once during the first six months, and then once during each period for which their detention is renewed (which can be for one year after the first and for periods of two years thereafter). The nearest relative of the patient may also apply, for example where the patient is detained under a hospital order made by a court or where the relative has been barred from discharging the patient.

Application forms and advice can be obtained either from the hospital or from the Clerk to the *Mental Health Review Tribunal* (mental health leaflets available from hospitals on admission). In the case of restricted patients, there is no right of direct access to a Tribunal, but the patient is entitled to ask for his case to be referred to a Tribunal by writing to the *Home Office*; the Home Secretary is not, however, obliged to accept the Tribunal's advice.

Occasionally mentally ill or severely subnormal people may be incapable of looking after themselves, or be in need of control but not in need of hospital care. Guardianship is intended for such cases and conditions are similar to an application for admission to hospital under Section 26; apply to local authority (Social Services Department). Either the authority or any individual can be made the guardian, but the authority must agree. A court can make a guardianship order as an alternative to a hospital order. Rights of application to a *Mental Health Review Tribunal* are similar to those for a patient detained in hospital. (See also **Wards of court**.)

Where a mentally disordered person is incapable of managing his or her financial affairs, advice should be sought from the **official solicitor** at the *Court of Protection*.

Services for the mentally ill include

direct help from field social workers, and community activities through day centres which may provide a range of recreational and occupational activities, and through hostels which may have a resident warden and other staff, or in which a group share the management of their own home. A number of voluntary organisations also run hostels providing accommodation. Information from local authorities (Social Services Department), *MIND* (national Association for Mental Health) and *National Schizophrenia Fellowship*. Specialist help in finding employment is available from *Employment Service Agency*, disablement resettlement officer.

Mentally Disordered Offenders Courts may make orders committing mentally disordered offenders to hospital or guardianship on a compulsory basis. Release procedures are the same as for civil patients who are compulsorily committed, except that offenders who are made subject to a restriction order by the crown court may only be released on the approval of the Home Secretary.
See also **Criminal courts; Hospital treatment; Mental Illness.**

Merchant Navy Examination and certification of seagoing officers and ratings is the responsibility of the *Department of Trade* (Marine Division).
Masters and navigating officers of British foreign-going ships and home-trade passenger ships must hold certificates of competency issued or recognised by the DoT. Grades of certificates granted on examinations (and sight test) are: second mate, first mate, master (foreign-going ships); mate, master (home-trade passenger ships). Aliens are only eligible to qualify for DoT certificate of competency as second mate (foreign-going). Details in DoT 'Examinations for certificates of competency in the Merchant Navy: masters and mates: regulations'.
Engineer officers in British foreign-going ships and home-trade passenger ships must hold certificates of competency issued by or recognised by the DoT. There are two grades of certificates – first class engineer (UK nationals only) and second class engineer – and three kinds of each grade of certificate: steam certificate; motor certificate; combined steam and motor certificate. Details in 'Regulations for the examination of engineers in the Merchant Navy' from the DoT.
Radio officers must normally be **British subjects, British protected persons,** or citizens of the Irish Republic, and must possess the Maritime Radiocommunications General Certificate of the *Home Office*, from which full details of nationality rules may be obtained. Examinations are administered by the *Post Office International and Maritime Telecommunications Region, Wireless Telegraph Section.*
Deck ratings qualify for the rating of Able Seaman (after a period of seagoing experience as a junior deck rating) with a certificate of competency from the DoT. Details in 'Merchant Shipping Notice M780' from the DoT. Seamen must be registered with the *Registrar General of Shipping and Seamen* (DoT).
Ship's cooks in a British foreign-going ship of 1,000 gross tons or above, which goes to sea from any place in the UK or the (near) continent of Europe, must hold a DoT's certificate of competency as ship's cook, obtainable by examination. Details in 'Merchant Shipping Notice M742', from the DoT. The shipping industry also has its own qualification requirements for cooks in ships for which possession of the DoT certificate is not a statutory requirement. (See **Merchant Navy: employment.**)
Merchant Shipping Notices may be obtained free from any Mercantile Marine Office at main ports, from the *Registrar-General of Shipping and Seamen,* or from the *Department of Trade, Marine Library.*

Merchant Navy: Employment Employment in the Merchant Navy is regulated by the shipping industry itself under the terms of an industrial agreement. General enquiries to the *General Council of British Shipping;* detailed information on careers, types of employment, pay and training from the *British Shipping Careers Service* in London or *British Shipping Careers Offices* of the GCBS in major ports.

Methylated Spirits A methylated spirits retailer's licence is required by anyone selling methylated spirits retail; apply to *Her Majesty's Customs and Excise*. Receipt and use of methylated spirits on which **excise duty** has not been paid (e.g. for preparation of medical articles for general sale and in dispensing on prescription) require authority from HMCE; details in HMCE notices 58, 54. Wholesale or dispensing chemists may obtain special authority to receive industrial methylated spirits for onward sale (maximum four gallons) to a person authorised by HMCE to receive such spirits; or to customers abroad, or (on presentation of a written order signed by a medical practitioner, dentist or veterinary surgeon) to a medical practitioner, dentist, veterinary surgeon or a responsible person on behalf of a hospital or nursing home (maximum ½ gallon); apply to HMCE, details in Notice 53.

Metrication The metric and imperial systems of measurement are both lawful in the UK for all purposes except where legislation is explicitly drawn up in one or the other, for example the Road Traffic Act which sets road speed limits in m.p.h.; and the Weights and Measures (equivalents for dealing with drugs) Regulations which provide for the dispensing of drugs and medicines to be conducted in metric only.
National co-ordination, publicity, advice and information regarding changeover is the responsibility of the *Metrication Board*. Overall responsibility for amending legislation to encompass metrication lies with the *Department of Prices and Consumer Protection* but each government department deals with legislative changes in its specific fields (e.g. Department of the Environment with building regulations).
Britain, like other countries, is adopting the International System of Units (SI units) which is governed by the International Bureau of Weights and Measures. Each UK industry works out its own metrication programme through its organisations (e.g. National Consultative Committee for the Construction Industry) and in consultation with the Metrication Board.

Mexico For **exchange control** is a non-scheduled territory outside the **overseas sterling area** and the EEC. UK nationals travelling direct from the UK normally need only the following (but check): **passports**; **visas**; international certificates of **vaccination** against smallpox; **work permits** (if taking a job).
The UK has no reciprocal health or social security arrangements.
Enquiries to *Mexican Embassy* in London.
British diplomatic missions to Mexico are *British Embassy* in Mexico City, *British Consulates* in Guadalajara and Monterrey, and *British Vice-Consulates* in Acapulco, Merida and Vera Cruz.

Midwives Midwives must be enrolled with the *Central Midwives Board* to practise in England and Wales; by the *Central Midwives Board for Scotland* in Scotland; and by the *Northern Ireland Council for Nurses and Midwives* in Northern Ireland. All these are statutory bodies.
The basic qualification is the SCM (State Certified Midwife) which is awarded by each of the statutory bodies to registered nurses after a one-year training and, by the CMB and CHB in Scotland, to others after a two-year training. Men, debarred before 1976, are now admitted to the profession, but at present training is limited to one course in England and one in Scotland for a transitional period as provided under the Sex Discrimination Act.
To find a midwife, contact the *regional health authority* or *area health authority* in England and Wales, the *Health Board* in Scotland, and the *Health and Social Services Board* in Northern Ireland.
Complaints about midwives should normally be made to the employing authority (see **Health authorities**) but complaints about grave professional misconduct can be made to the relevant national council or board.

See also **Disputes with public authorities; Nurses.**

Military Assistance The armed services put skills, manpower and equipment at the service of the civilian community at time of disaster, e.g. floods, air or rail accidents, mountain rescue. Application in emergencies should be made to the nearest police station, Service unit or local Army district headquarters (under Police, Army, etc., in telephone directory).
The Services also sometimes give routine assistance, e.g. simple land reclamation, nature conservation, well drilling. This aid is usually given to operations sponsored by non-profit-making bodies, e.g. local authorities or charities; only exceptionally is aid given to civilian firms or individuals. Service volunteers can also be attached full-time to social service organisations for set periods.
The Services make no charge when attempting to save lives; otherwise costs are borne by the sponsors. Application for routine aid should be made to local Army district headquarters by the sponsoring body direct or via your local authority.

Military Surplus Military equipment and stores become surplus occasionally and are made available for sale to the public. This is usually done by auctions, which are advertised in the press. Enquire about sales or particular items to *Ministry of Defence Procurement Executive, Sales Supply.*
See also **Arms: sale and purchase.**

Milk: Free Milk is supplied free to expectant mothers; children under five in large families or in families with low incomes; handicapped children between the ages of 5 and 16 who are not registered pupils at a school or special school; children with registered **child minders, day nurseries** and **playgroups.**
Details in *Department of Health and Social Security* leaflets from DHSS about how to apply.
See also **Child health services; Disablement: handicapped children; Families on low incomes; Vitamins.**

Milk: Production and Marketing Farmers intending to produce milk or milk products for sale for human consumption in the UK must register with the *Milk Marketing Board* and, in England and Wales, the *Ministry of Agriculture, Fisheries and Food*, in Northern Ireland the *Department of Agriculture for Northern Ireland* and in Scotland the *Department of Agriculture and Fisheries for Scotland.* There are legal requirements for buildings, water supplies and methods of production; advice on these from MAFF divisional offices, DANI and DAFS.
Milk produced for wholesale must be sold to the MMB in accordance with the wholesale milk contract. A producer intending to retail his own milk untreated must obtain a retail licence from the MMB and a producer's licence from MAFF divisional offices, DANI or DAFS. Farmers wishing to sell untreated milk not of their own production or heat-treated milk require a licence from the local authority. MMB approval is also required for cheese manufacture (farmhouse cheesemakers' scheme).
Services offered to farmers by MMB on a fee-paying basis include milk recording, milk-machine testing, costing and consultancy, **artificial insemination** and mastitis (monthly cell count service). Capital loans and a rental scheme are available to producers to encourage the installation of farm tanks (vats); apply to MMB.
See also **Agricultural finance.**

Mineral Exploration Financial assistance is available for certain projects under the Mineral Exploration and Investment Grants Act 1972. Apply to Minerals, Metals, Electrical Engineering, Process Plant and Industrial Technologies Division at the *Department of Industry* (headquarters 2); details in DoI booklet 'Financial assistance for mineral exploration in Great Britain: A guide for industry'.

Mines and Quarries The *Health and Safety Executive, HM Mines and Quarries Inspectorate*, is responsible for all matters relating to the enforcement of safety legislation in mines and quarries (e.g. control of dust; support

and ventilation of mine workings; security of mine waste tips; provision of information and advice on technical matters).
See also **Dust: health hazards; Work: health and safety.**

Mining Subsidence If your property is damaged as a result of coal mining subsidence, you can claim compensation from the *National Coal Board*. Within two months of the appearance of the damage you must send the NCB a 'damage notice'. Advice and the necessary forms can be obtained from the estates manager at any office of the NCB.
See also **Disputes with public authorities.**

Ministerial Appointments Paid posts (other than **judicial appointments**) to which the holder has been appointed by a UK government minister are listed in 'A Directory of Paid Public Appointments made by Ministers', available from *Her Majesty's Stationery Office*; it also gives sources for enquiries about appointments to particular public bodies. The Public Appointments Unit at the *Civil Service Department* answers general enquiries. It also maintains the central list of possible candidates for such appointments.
See also **Judicial appointments.**

Mink, Coypus, Musk-rats and Non-indigenous Rabbits These animals may only be kept under licence from the *Ministry of Agriculture, Fisheries and Food Divisional Offices* in England and Wales. The MAFF must be notified of any animals found at large. The keeping of grey squirrels also requires a licence.
See also **Agriculture: Scotland; Agriculture: Northern Ireland; Animals: dangerous.**

Missing Persons Missing persons should be reported first to the *police*. The *Salvation Army* may help in tracing missing persons.

Moles Control and poisoning of moles is undertaken in England and Wales by the *Ministry of Agriculture, Fisheries and Food Divisional Offices*, which also issue permits for the purchase of strychnine to destroy moles.
See also **Agriculture: Scotland; Agriculture: Northern Ireland.**

Monaco For **exchange control** is a non-scheduled territory in the EEC but outside the **overseas sterling area.**
UK nationals travelling direct from the UK normally need only the following (but check): **passports; work permits** (if taking a job); green cards for motor insurance (if bringing a car: see **Motoring abroad**).
The UK has no reciprocal health or social security arrangements.
Enquiries to *Monaco Consulate-General* in London and *Monaco Information Centre* in London.
British diplomatic mission to Monaco is *British Consulate* in Marseilles, France.

Moneylenders and Pawnbrokers Moneylenders and pawnbrokers must obtain a licence for consumer credit business from the *Office of Fair Trading*.
See also **Consumer credit.**

Mongolia For **exchange control** is a non-scheduled territory outside the **overseas sterling area** and the EEC.
UK nationals travelling direct from the UK normally need only the following (but check): **passports; visas; work permits** (if taking a job).
The UK has no reciprocal health or social security arrangements.
Enquiries to *Mongolian Embassy* in London.
British diplomatic mission to Mongolia is *British Embassy* in Ulan Bator.

Monopolies and Mergers Under the Fair Trading Act 1973, the *Monopolies and Mergers Commission* may investigate and report on monopoly situations and actual or proposed mergers (including newspapers mergers). It deals only with references made to it by the *Director General of Fair Trading* or the appropriate government minister (in the case of monopolies) or by the *Secretary of State for Prices and Consumer Protection* (in the case of mergers).

In certain circumstances following a MMC report the government has power to make orders with respect to the MMC's findings, regulating the conduct of the firms or bodies concerned. More commonly, undertakings are sought to avoid the use of such powers.

Reports of MMC investigations are published by *Her Majesty's Stationery Office*. Recent reports have covered such subjects as cat and dog foods, flour and bread, copying machines, glass manufacturing, restrictions on advertising by professional bodies, and frozen foods.

Morocco (including Tangier) For **exchange control** is a non-scheduled territory outside the **overseas sterling area** and the **EEC**. UK nationals travelling direct from the UK normally need only the following (but check): **passports** without Israeli stamp; **work permits** (if taking a job); green cards for motor insurance (if bringing a car); international driving permits (if intending to drive). Petrol coupons for private cars are available from Moroccan Bank for Foreign Trade in Casablanca and throughout Morocco. See **Motoring abroad**.

The UK has no reciprocal health or social security arrangements.

Enquiries to *Moroccan Embassy* in London and *Moroccan National Tourist Office* in London.

British diplomatic missions to Morocco are *British Embassy* in Rabat and *British Consulates-General* in Casablanca and Tangier.

Mortgages Mortgages for the purchase, development or improvement of private dwellings are available from building societies, life assurance companies and local authorities. Names and addresses of building societies and general information about their mortgage service can be obtained from the *Building Societies Association*. The Building Societies Year Book is available in many public libraries. The *Life Offices' Association* will give names and addresses of life assurance companies. (For local authority mortgages see **Mortgages: local authority**.)

The rate of interest charged on a mortgage is nearly always flexible, i.e. it can be varied by the lender on giving from one to three months' notice. Changes in the building society mortgage rate are recommended from time to time by the Council of the BSA; these changes are publicised through the media.

See also **Land, houses and other buildings: buying**.

Mortgages: Local Authority Loans for house purchase may be available from **local authorities**. These funds are limited and lending is currently restricted to certain priority categories. To supplement 'down market' lending authorities may nominate applicants to building societies with whom they are linked under the Building Society Support Scheme. In general local authority mortgages are likely to attract a higher percentage of the cost of the property than a building society mortgage; their interest rates can be higher. Advice on mortgages may be available from the Housing Advisory Service operated by some local authorities.

See also **Mortgages; Mortgages: option**.

Mortgages: Option Option mortgages are designed to help people with moderate incomes to buy their own homes, by giving benefits equivalent to those available to people with higher incomes. Ordinary mortgages attract relief from **income tax** on interest payments on loans up to £23,000, which produces a greater benefit to those paying tax on higher rates. Under an option mortgage a government subsidy is paid towards the mortgage interest in place of income tax relief at the basic rate. Apply for an option mortgage to suppliers of mortgages. Under the option guarantee scheme higher percentage loans are obtainable, up to 100% of the valuation on houses costing up to £14,000; building societies taking part in the scheme are prepared subject to the availability of funds to increase their usual percentage limit for a loan by up to 25% of the purchase price of a home, or to the valuation if this is lower. The government and insurance companies jointly guarantee the risk to the building societies. Apply under the guarantee scheme to the building society making the loan.

See 'Buying a home with an option mortgage' from the *Department of the Environment, Scottish Development Department* or *Welsh Office*.

Motor Car Racing and Rallying Racing and rallying are governed internationally by the Sporting Commission of the Fédération Internationale Automobile. In the UK the Motor Sport Division at the *Royal Automobile Club* governs all sport for motor vehicles with four or more wheels, such as circuit racing, rallying, autocross, trials and grass track, stock car and kart racing. The Rally Authorisation Department at the Royal Automobile Club is the official controller of all motor sport events on public roads. The RAC annually stages the British Grand Prix, the RAC International Rally and the London to Brighton Commemoration Run for veteran cars. In Scotland, the *Royal Scottish Automobile Club* and in Northern Ireland, the *Ulster Automobile Club* control the sports, subject to RAC authorisation.

Motor Vehicle Excise Licences Licences are required with few exceptions for mechanically propelled vehicles used on British public roads. Vehicle owners receive a reminder and application form from *Department of Transport Driving and Vehicle Licensing Centre*; this can be used to obtain a licence by personal application at a licence-issuing post office or a Vehicle Licensing Office of local authorities. If it is not received, or if there is any change in the vehicle or keeper's particulars, use application form V10 from post offices. Send the form to the local VLO enclosing licence fee; a certificate of insurance against third party liabilities (required under Road Traffic Act (Part VI) 1972 – other insurance cover is optional); and if necessary, a valid vehicle test certificate (see **Motor vehicle test certificates**). If any particulars about the vehicle differ from those in the registration document (see **Motor vehicle registration**), changes must be notified separately on Form V10 (from post offices and local VLOs). Rate of duty depends on the taxation class of the vehicle. Advice on the appropriate taxation class for a vehicle can be obtained from any local VLO. Information leaflet V100 is available from post offices and local VLOs. Goods vehicle licences are determined by the unladen weight of the vehicle, with lower scales for farmers' goods vehicles and showmen's goods vehicles (for fairs, etc.). Articulated vehicles are weighed and treated as an entity.
See also **Excise duty**.

Motor Vehicle Registration All mechanically propelled vehicles used on British public roads must be registered. Most new vehicles are in practice registered for the first time by the dealer; otherwise, apply to a local Vehicle Licensing Office of the local authority. The VLO will also advise about the need for inspection of a home-built or kit-constructed vehicle. A registration document (V5) will be sent from the *Department of Transport Driving and Vehicle Licensing Centre*. Changes in ownership and changes in the vehicle registration particulars must be notified immediately to the DVLC.
See also **Heavy goods vehicle operators' licences; Number plates**.

Motor Vehicle Test Certificates Certificates are required for most motor vehicles and must be renewed annually. Motor cars, motor cycles, motor caravans and light goods vehicles must be tested when they are three years old; apply to any Department of Transport approved Vehicle Testing Station (garages display signs if they are approved VTSs). Large passenger carrying vehicles (i.e. those with more than 12 seats excluding the driver's seat) must also be tested when three years old. Tests are carried out at Department of Transport Heavy Goods Vehicle Testing Stations; apply to *Department of Transport Traffic Area Offices*. Heavy goods vehicles and their trailers must be tested when one year old; apply to *Department of Transport Goods Vehicle Centre* on forms obtainable at main post offices. A statutory fee is chargeable for the test; if a vehicle fails to pass a certificate of failure must be issued. The standards to be met by most vehicles are contained in the Motor Vehicles (Tests) Regulations 1976; those for heavy goods vehicles and their trailers are in the Heavy Goods Vehicles (Plating and Testing) Regulations 1971 (as amended); both are available from *Her Majesty's Stationery Office*. Appeal against a certificate of failure may be made to the appropriate DoTTAO on payment of a further fee. Re-test of failed vehicles is carried out without further fee if repairs are completed without the removal of the vehicle from the testing station or, in the case of heavy goods vehicles or their trailers, they are submitted for re-test of a limited range of failed items on the same day or the day after. In a few other cases a reduced fee may be payable. Complaints about the conduct of a test by an approved examiner may be made to the appropriate DoTTAO.

Motorcycle Speedway Racing Speedway racing is controlled internationally by the Fédération Internationale Motocycliste. In England, Scotland, Wales, the Channel Islands and the Isle of Man, the *Auto-Cycle Union* represents the sport at international level but delegates national control of speedway regulations, licensing, meetings and international events to the *Speedway Control Board*. Licences are essential for riders (who are professionals), tracks, promoters and other officials; women are not eligible as riders. The *British Speedway Promoters Association* represents the commercial interests.

Motorcycling All sport on motor cycles and mechanically propelled three-wheelers is controlled internationally by the Fédération Internationale Motocycliste. The governing body affiliated to the FIM for all the UK except Northern Ireland is the *Auto-Cycle Union*. In Northern Ireland and Eire the controlling body is the *Motorcycle Union of Ireland*. ACU has delegated responsibility for speedway (the professional commercial branch – see **Motorcycle speedway**) but controls road racing and sprints, moto cross, grass track racing and trials. It is responsible for competition rules, organisers permits, insurance, British teams and the British rounds of the World Championship. It makes no division between professional and amateur. Some aspects of control in Scotland are delegated to the *Scottish Auto-Cycle Union*.

Motoring Abroad There is no central official advisory body on documentation and formalities for the movement overseas of private and commercial vehicles. In principle you can take a UK motor vehicle to almost any country, but in practice you must be governed by local regulations for vehicle insurance and validity of British driving licence, and political considerations. Touring information can be obtained from the *National Tourist Offices* in London.
The *Automobile Association* and the *Royal Automobile Club* provide information on formalities (e.g. green cards, international driving permits) for particular journeys to members touring in private vehicles to most countries in the world. International driving permits are issued by the AA and RAC to both members and non-members.
The *Department of Transport, International Road Freight Office* and the *Freight Transport Association* provide information concerning goods carrying vehicles; the *Confederation of British Road Passenger Vehicle Operators* provides information about passenger carrying vehicles.
Many Eastern European countries, including Russia, restrict the movement of vehicles and a route has to be agreed beforehand with the government travel agency of the country concerned.

Motoring Abroad: Petrol Concessions Concessions are sometimes available to UK nationals touring overseas in private cars only (not in commercial vehicles or on motor cycles). See separate entries on **Bulgaria; German Democratic Republic; Greece; Italy; Morocco; Poland; Yugoslavia.**

Mountaineering In the UK the sport is represented jointly by the *British Mountaineering Council* and the *Mountaineering Council of Scotland*. They administer the Mountain Leadership Training Schemes and the Mountain Guide qualification, and cooperate with the *Mount Everest Foundation* and the *Alpine Club* to help expeditions overseas.

Mozambique For **exchange control** is a non-scheduled territory outside the **overseas sterling area** and the **EEC**. UK nationals travelling direct from the UK normally need only the following (but check): **passports**; **visas**; international certificates of **vaccination** against smallpox and cholera; **work permits** (if taking a job); green cards for motor insurance (if bringing a car); international driving permits (if intending to drive: see **Motoring abroad**).
The UK has no reciprocal health or social security arrangements.
Enquiries to *Ministry of Foreign Affairs* in Maputo which handles diplomatic relations directly.
British diplomatic mission to Mozambique is *British Embassy* in Maputo.

Museums: Armed Forces Among the official museums of the armed forces are the *National Army Museum*, the *Royal Armoured Tank Museum*, the *Royal Air Force Museum*, the *Portsmouth Royal Naval Museum*, the *Fleet Air Arm Museum*, the *Submarine Museum*, the *Royal Marines Museum*. There are also 100 regimental and corps museums throughout the country.

Music and Dancing Premises Before public premises may be used for music and dancing it may be necessary to obtain a licence; enquiries to the local authority or clerk to the licensing justices at the local magistrates' court. Private dancing schools do not require a licence for their classes.

Music, Opera, Dance: Arts Council Support The *Arts Council of Great Britain* in England and the *Scottish Arts Council* subsidise professional orchestras, dance and opera companies and provide financial support for professional creative artists, e.g. composers, choreographers and lyric theatre designers. They commission musical scores; subsidise jazz recordings, commission choreography, design (for décor and costumes) and dance scores. They also co-ordinate and subsidise tours of large and small opera and dance groups and arrange tours of contemporary music and jazz ensembles. They can make a contribution towards the cost of building new concert halls or adapting existing ones. Limited guarantees are available to amateur societies towards the cost of engaging professional performers through the *National Federation of Music Societies*.
Regional Arts Associations assist, in the main, professional musicians, dancers and singers in England and Wales through specific projects or by way of grants and bursaries.
In Wales, the *Welsh Arts Council* subsidises the Welsh National Opera, the BBC Welsh Symphony Orchestra, the Welsh Amateur Music Federation and the Welsh Music Archive. It offers commissions to composers; awards for advanced study; and co-ordinates and subsidises tours by symphony and chamber orchestras as well as concerts of contemporary music. The WAC also sponsors recordings of contemporary Welsh music, a triennial competition for young singers and various music journals.
In Northern Ireland, the *Arts Council of Northern Ireland* supports two opera groups and an orchestra; provides bursaries for young instrumentalists and singers; promotes and subsidises tours by national and international chamber music groups and solo artists and by local societies and art committees.
See also **Arts: support**.

Music Scores Scores, including unpublished works, and recordings from any composer of reasonable ability are accepted by the *British Music Information Centre*. Radio and television producers, concert promoters, teachers, conductors and film background producers can hear or read new material free of charge.

N

Names In the UK any name and surname may be given to a child at registration of birth (see **Birth registration**). British subjects and residents may later assume new surnames without formally recording the change. In England and Wales no amendment can be made to the entry in the register of births to show a change of surname but the change can be evidenced by statutory declaration before a Justice of the Peace or a solicitor (apply to a **solicitor**); advertisement in local or national press; royal licence through the *College of Arms* (if change is needed for a will, settlement or change or arms); Act of Parliament through a private bill (not used since 1907); or (in Scotland) by an entry in the registers of the *Court of Lord Lyon*; or by drawing up a deed poll (apply to a **solicitor**). The deed poll can for greater authority be sworn by affidavit before a JP or solicitor, and then for greater permanence be enrolled at the *Supreme Court of Judicature, central office*, or at the College of Arms.

Aliens can change their surname only by royal licence or by special permission of the *Home Secretary* (except for women on marriage).

Change of forename may be evidenced as for surnames, but changing a name given in baptism has to be effected by Act of Parliament or by a bishop at confirmation to be legally valid. In England and Wales a new forename given within a year after birth registration may be added to the birth entry, whether given in baptism or not, provided that the child has not already been baptised in some other name. Apply to make additions to a local *Registrar of Births, Deaths and Marriages* or to the *Registrar General of England and Wales*.

In Scotland, a new forename or surname can be recorded against the birth entry if the person's birth was registered in Scotland and provided certain conditions are fulfilled. The original names continue to appear in any extract or certificate of the birth entry except where the new name is given to the child within a year after birth. Apply for recording a change to the *Registrar General for Scotland*.

In Northern Ireland if the forename is changed in baptism or if the child has not been baptised but the name is changed, the changed name may be added within two years from the date of birth. It is also possible to have a change of forename or surname recorded by means of a marginal note to the birth entry where the name as changed has been in use for a period of at least two years. Apply to the *Registrar General for Northern Ireland*. Fees are payable.

On **adoption** the change of forename or surname is recorded in the Adopted Children's Register of each Registrar General.

National Front Membership is open to all 'persons of a wholly European racial origin who are citizens either of the UK or of former Dominion lands of the British Commonwealth'.

Its official ideology is 'British nationalism and racialism'. Membership enquiries to the *National Front*.

National Giro The National Giro provides a current account banking and money transfer service for firms and private individuals. Accounts are held centrally at the *National Giro Centre*. Application forms for personal accounts (minimum deposit £1 and minimum age 15) and cards for business applications (G1026) are available from post offices.
See also **Bank accounts; National savings bank accounts.**

National Health Service Under the National Health Service all civilians are entitled free of charge to the services of a general medical practitioner (i.e. a family **doctor**). It is necessary to register as the patient of a doctor with a practice in the area of residence. Parents and guardians register for children under 16. The family doctor is the general link between patients and all NHS benefits and **Hospital treatment** (see also **Child health services; Medicines; Nursing at home**).
To register, first choose a doctor. Each *Family Practitioner Committee* publishes a list of NHS general medical practitioners in its area; copies of these lists are available from the FPC offices or at main post offices. The doctor chosen must then be asked if he or she will accept the applicant as a patient; if so, it is necessary to produce the **National Health Service medical card.** If no NHS medical card is available, a registration form will be completed and a card issued later. If acceptance is refused, as many doctors' NHS patients lists are full, the FPC may be asked for help in finding a doctor.
Once registered, patients may change their doctors immediately on moving address. To change doctors at an existing address it is necessary either to obtain the present doctor's consent or to apply to the FPC, in which case the change takes at least 14 days to effect.
Anyone who is away from home for three months can obtain treatment from any NHS doctor in the area in which he is staying as a 'temporary resident'; it helps to be able to produce the NHS medical card. Children at boarding school who are registered with the school doctor are treated as temporary residents at home; similarly students who are registered in the place where they study are treated as temporary residents during the vacations.
Emergency treatment can be obtained from any NHS doctor when you are away from home or your own doctor is not available (see **Medical treatment: emergency**).
See also **Dentists; Dentists: complaints; Doctors; Doctors: complaints; Eye treatment; Midwives; Nurses.**

National Health Service Medical Cards If you are a permanent resident in the UK or have come here with the intention of staying permanently or for a reasonable period of time (i.e. one or two years) you may register with a NHS family **doctor**. You will subsequently be issued with a NHS medical card by the local *Family Practitioner Committee*. Parents or guardians may register children under 16.
Medical cards are issued to patients for the purpose of obtaining general medical services other than **contraception** and **maternity services**. The cards are also used in the procedure for transferring a patient from the list of one doctor to that of another. The card should always be produced if the doctor asks to see it. If you decide not to register with a NHS doctor, the FPC will issue you with a medical card for dental and ophthalmic use only. Your medical card should always be kept in a safe place and its loss reported immediately to your doctor or FPC so that it can be replaced.
If you leave the UK for more than three months (e.g. for emigration, travel, employment) you should surrender your NHS medical card to the FPC (address also on card) or hand it to UK immigration officials at the point of departure; otherwise you will remain as a patient on your doctor's register. When you return you can be treated by any NHS doctor.
See also **Medical treatment**.

National Insurance: Contributions
Generally all people aged over 16 and under pension age (65 men, 60 women) are liable to pay national insurance contributions if they are gainfully employed in Great Britain (either as an employee or in self-employment). Those over pension age but not retired or treated as retired for national insurance purposes, are also liable for contributions if under 70 (men) or 65 (women).

There are four 'classes' of contribution: Employees and their employers pay Class 1 contributions, assessed as a percentage of employees' earnings subject to lower and upper earnings limits. Earnings below the lower earnings limit (£15 a week for the 1977–78 tax year) are not liable for contributions by either employee or employer. Earnings equal to or above the lower earnings limit are liable to contributions on all earnings up to the upper earnings limit (£105 for 1977–78) including those earnings below the lower earnings limit (see leaflets NI40 and NI39, from *Department of Health and Social Security* local offices). Employees' contributions are deducted from pay by the employer, normally at the time earnings are paid. Both employees' and employers' contributions are collected on behalf of DHSS by the Board of Inland Revenue with PAYE income tax (leaflet NP15 for employers).

Self-employed people are liable to Class 2 contributions (flat rate) and Class 4 contributions. Class 2 contributions are payable unless net earnings are expected to be below a specified level (£875 for the 1977–78 tax year), in which case application may be made to be excepted from liability (leaflets NI41, NI27A). Class 2 contributions are paid either by stamping a national insurance contribution card (see **National insurance stamps**), or by direct debit of a **bank account** or **National Giro** account. Class 4 contributions are payable in addition to Class 2 contributions as a percentage of profits or gains chargeable to income tax under Cases I and II of Schedule D. They are generally calculated and collected by the Inland Revenue. For 1977–78 the rate payable was 8% of profits on gains between £1,750 and £5,500.

People working both for an employer and on their own account may have to pay Class 1, 2 and 4 contributions subject to an overall maximum contribution liability, any excess contributions being refundable. To avoid paying excess contributions, people with high Class 1 earnings can apply to have their liability for Class 4 (and Class 2) contributions deferred (see leaflet NP18).

Voluntary contributions (Class 3, flat-rate) may be paid by those not paying either Class 1 or Class 2 contributions, or who wish to improve their record of Class 1 or 2 contributions paid during the year; there are strict time limits within which Class 1, 2 or 3 contributions have to be paid to count for benefits (see leaflets NI42, NI48). Class 3 contributions can be paid in the same way as Class 2 contributions or alternatively by cash or cheque to any DHSS local office.

Where insufficient contributions have been paid for **retirement pension** and **widows' benefit** purposes contributions may be credited for the tax years containing a person's 16th, 17th and 18th birthdays. Contributions may also be credited for weeks throughout which it is accepted that a person was incapable of work, or unemployed and available for employment, or when a person was following a course of training approved for credits (see leaflet NI125).

Special contribution arrangements apply to employees aged 70 or over (men) or 65 or over (women) (see leaflets NI39, NI40), married women (NI1), widows (NI51), employees with more than one job (NP28), women whose marriage ends by divorce or annulment (NI95), school leavers (NP12), people abroad (NI38, 132), mariners (NI24), share fishermen (NI47), airmen (NP5), war pensioners NI50), people working in the UK for overseas employers (NP16), domestic workers (NI11), company directors (NI35), nurses and midwives (NI46), agency staff (NI192), examiners and part-time lecturers, teachers and instructors (NI222), and ministers of religion (NP21). The effect of unpaid and late

paid contributions is given in NI148, and current contribution rates in the latest edition of NI208. Leaflets, information and advice from *Department of Health and Social Security* (local offices).
For national insurance benefits see **Social security benefits.**

National Insurance: Registration Everyone resident in Great Britain and over age 16 who takes up employment or self-employment or who wishes to contribute voluntarily is required to have a national insurance number so that a record can be kept of contributions. School children are registered automatically during the academic year in which they attain age 16 and are informed of their national insurance numbers; they do not normally need to apply. Any person not registered at 16 (e.g. owing to residence abroad at the time) can apply for a national insurance number to *Department of Health and Social Security* (local offices), or to local authority careers office if under 18. Forgotten or mislaid national insurance numbers will be traced by DHSS local offices.
In return for regular weekly or monthly contributions the national insurance scheme pays cash benefits (e.g. to those who are sick or unemployed, have a baby, retire or die leaving a widow). There are four classes of contributions carrying entitlement to different benefits. (See **National insurance contributions** and **Social security benefits.**)

National Insurance Stamps Stamps for self-employed people are sold at all post offices. For a refund for unused or spoiled stamps send form P2844 G, obtainable at any principal post office, to *Department of Health and Social Security*, Newcastle-upon-Tyne, or, in Northern Ireland to *Department of Health and Social Services, Northern Ireland.*
See also **National insurance contributions.**

National Museums and Galleries Trustees of the National Gallery, National Portrait Gallery, Tate Gallery, Wallace Collection, National Maritime Museum and some trustees of the *British Museum*, British Museum (Natural History) and the Imperial War Museum are appointed by the *Prime Minister,* following soundings by the Secretary for Appointments at the *Prime Minister's Office.*

National Parks The *Countryside Commission* can designate exceptionally fine stretches of relatively wild countryside as national parks. There are ten such parks in England and Wales: Peak District, Lake District, Snowdonia, Dartmoor, Pembrokeshire Coast, North York Moors, Yorkshire Dales, Exmoor, Northumberland, Brecon Beacons. Enquiries to *National Park Information Centres.*
If the Secretary of State for the Environment or for Wales confirms the CC's designation of a national park, no change occurs in the ownership of land. It does not become public property; nor do walkers, climbers or picnickers gain automatic right of access.
Having selected and designated a park, the CC advises on its planning and management. The parks, although administered locally by national park boards (in the Peak District and Lake District) or county council committees (in the other eight), exist for the benefit of the whole nation.
Scotland has no national parks, although proposals for a parks system are under consideration; enquiries to *Countryside Commission for Scotland.*
See also **Country parks; Countryside conservation and recreation grants; National Trust; Nature conservation.**

National Savings Bank Accounts Accounts can be opened by anyone over seven (if under, by relatives or friends). Ordinary accounts can be started with a minimum deposit of 25 pence; the maximum holding is £10,000. The interest rate is 5% and the first £70 is free of UK **income tax** and **capital gains tax.** To open an investment account a minimum deposit of £1 is needed; the maximum holding is £50,000. These accounts have a 10% interest rate which is

taxable. Accounts may be opened and deposits paid in at post offices, acting as agencies for the *National Savings Bank*.
See also **Bank accounts**; **National Giro**.

National Savings Certificates These are issued by *Her Majesty's Treasury* and administered by the *Department for National Savings*. The 14th Issue can be purchased from post offices and banks by individuals over seven (if under, by relatives or friends), jointly and by certain organisations, in £1 units (minimum purchase £5) up to a maximum holding of £1,000. The interest on national savings certificates is free of UK **income tax** and **capital gains tax**.
See also **Index-linked national savings**.

National Security The Security Service, covering internal national security, is responsible to the *Home Secretary*. The Foreign Security Service, which covers external national security, reports to the *Secretary of State for Foreign and Commonwealth Affairs*. The *Prime Minister* has overall responsibility for the two services, which have no specific legal powers and work in collaboration with the **police** forces (Special Branch). Where a breach of security is known to have occurred in the public service, the PM can convene the Standing Security Commission (three individuals appointed by the PM) to investigate, and to recommend changes in security arrangements. The Leader of the Opposition is always consulted about changes. The Commission usually reports to the PM but exceptionally, if sitting as a tribunal of inquiry, may do so to the Home Secretary.
See also **Attack on the UK**.

National Trust The *National Trust* in England, Wales and Northern Ireland, and the *National Trust for Scotland* exist to ensure that places of historic interest or natural beauty are held permanently for the nation. Both are independent charities holding land and buildings. By Act of Parliament, both can declare their property inalienable and appeal direct to a joint committee of both Houses of Parliament if a public authority or anybody else proposes to take their land by **compulsory purchase**. Under their country house schemes, a house and its contents may be presented with an endowment fund adequate to maintain it in perpetuity subject to public access. Under the Enterprise Neptune scheme, the NT acquires coast-line which is beautiful and unspoilt by development. The National Trust for Scotland also buys, restores and resells (under safeguard) little houses under its Little Houses Improvement Scheme. Enquiries about membership, visits and access, to the NI and NTS head offices.
See also **Conservation: beauty spots**; **Conservation: coasts**; **Country parks**; **National Parks**.

Naturalisation An alien or **British protected person** with necessary qualifications may be naturalised as a citizen of the UK and colonies at the discretion of the Home Secretary or a colonial governor. Qualifications include five years' residence or crown service; good character; sufficient knowledge of English; certain intentions as to future residence or service. Details in *Home Office* leaflet N315.
See also **Citizenship of the UK and colonies**.

Nature Conservation The *Nature Conservancy Council* is responsible for the conservation of flora, fauna and geological and physiographical features throughout Great Britain. It is appointed and financed by the *Department of the Environment* but it is free to express independent views.
It establishes and manages National **Nature Reserves** (e.g. Moor House, Cumbria; Isle of Rhum, Western Highlands; Snowdon, Gwynedd); advises the government on nature conservation policies; disseminates information to the general public; and commissions and undertakes research. Grants are available to further specific projects. Applications to the NCC Grants Officer.
There are separate NCC advisory committees and headquarters for England, Scotland, Wales and Great

Britain. In Northern Ireland nature conservation is the responsibility of the Conservation Branch at the *Department of the Environment for Northern Ireland*, advised by the Nature Reserves Committee.
See also **Country parks; National parks.**

Nature Reserves and Sites of Special Scientific Interest The *Nature Conservancy Council*'s 145 National Nature Reserves (NNRs), covering 300,000 acres, exemplify either different types of countryside, unusual communities of wild plants and animals, or special natural features, e.g. rock exposure, gorges and landslips. They are either owned/leased by the NCC, or established through nature reserve agreements with the owner and occupiers of the land.
Visitors are welcome to most reserves but access to areas with particularly sensitive plants or animals is restricted to holders of permits, issued by the NCC's 15 regional offices (apply in the first instance to the NCC national office). The NCC has designated over 3,000 additional areas as Sites of Special Scientific Interest (SSIs); landowners and local planning authorities are notified. Local planning authorities must consult the NCC before granting permission for development in these areas.
Advice and grants for local authorities, voluntary bodies and others who set up and maintain non-statutory nature reserves are available from the NCC. Local nature reserves are established by county and district councils.
Byelaws for nature reserves are made either by NCC (for national nature reserves), or **local authorities** (local nature reserves), and confirmed by the *Secretary of State for the Environment* (or the Secretaries of State for Scotland or Wales as appropriate). Appeals against proposed byelaws are to the Secretary of State, with possible subsequent public inquiry.
See also **Wild animals; Wild birds; Wild plants.**

Naval Architects   Naval architects may legally practice in the UK without qualifications, although there are exceptions for posts in certain government departments. The *Royal Institution of Naval Architects* is the qualifying authority which also investigates complaints about professional misconduct; the *Council of Engineering Institutions* (see **Engineers**) is the registering authority. Qualified naval architects are chartered engineers and corporate members of RINA, i.e. FRINA or MRINA; to find one, contact RINA.
See also **Architects.**

Nepal   For **exchange control** is a non-scheduled territory outside the **overseas sterling area** and the **EEC**. UK nationals travelling direct from the UK normally need only the following (but check): **passports; visas;** international certificates of **vaccination** against smallpox and cholera; **work permits** (if taking a job); green cards for motor insurance (if bringing a car); international driving permits (if intending to drive: see **Motoring abroad**).
The UK has no reciprocal health or social security arrangements.
Enquiries to *Royal Nepalese Embassy* in London.
British diplomatic mission to Nepal is *British Embassy* in Kathmandu.

Netball   Netball is controlled internationally by the International Federation of Netball Associations. In the UK the *All England Netball Association*, the *Scottish Netball Association*, the *Welsh Netball Association* and the *Northern Ireland Netball Association* control administration, coaching, umpiring, proficiency awards and tournaments, and select national teams autonomously in their own regions. Each association is represented on the British Isles Committee (on which Eire, the Irish Republic, is also represented) and the British Isles Rules Board.

Netherlands   **EEC** member. For **exchange control** is a non-scheduled territory in the **EEC** but outside the **overseas sterling area**. UK nationals travelling direct from the UK normally need only the following (but check):

passports (British visitors' passports acceptable).

EEC or bilateral social security arrangements are applicable; leaflets and EEC Guides obtainable from *Department of Health and Social Security, Overseas Branch.* Apply to the local social security office for leaflet SA28 which explains who is entitled to free or reduced cost medical treatment within EEC health arrangements, and how to get a certificate of entitlement (form E111).

Enquiries to *Netherlands Embassy* in London and *Netherlands National Touring Office* in London.

British diplomatic missions to the Netherlands are *British Embassy* in The Hague, *British Consulate-General* in Amsterdam and Rotterdam and *British Consulate* in Curaçao.

New Towns New towns are planned and built by their own *New Town Development Corporation*, appointed and financed by the government. They are later taken over by the *Commission for New Towns* in England and Wales, which is responsible for the maintenance and administration of land and property.

Lists of currently designated new towns, and details of the framework/master plan for a particular new town from the *Department of the Environment*. Information on houses, house design, estate roads, siting of new industry and commerce, public amenities, meeting places, land purchase and planning permission, and public participation in the planning stages from the NTDC. Hospitals are the responsibility of the *regional health authority*.

New towns in Scotland and Wales are the responsibility respectively of the Secretary of State for Scotland and for Wales. Enquiries to *Scottish Office*, *Scottish Economic Planning Department*, or the *Welsh Office*.

New Zealand **Commonwealth** member. For **exchange control** is a non-scheduled territory in the **overseas sterling area** but outside the EEC. UK nationals travelling direct from the UK normally need only the following (but check): **passports**; **work permits** (if taking a job); green cards for motor insurance (if bringing a car: see **Motoring abroad**).

UK reciprocal arrangements cover social security (see leaflet SA8 obtainable from *Department of Health and Social Security, Overseas Group*) and health. Hospital treatment free; small consultation fee to general practitioners.

Enquiries to *New Zealand High Commission* in London.

British diplomatic missions to New Zealand are *British High Commissions* in Auckland and Wellington and *Office of the British Representative* in Christchurch.

News Media and Government There is no censorship of news in the UK, but the government seeks to prevent or delay indiscretions contrary to the national interest by means of D notices and news embargos.

The D notice system is entirely voluntary and has no legal authority; it is agreed between the government and the media; the system provides editors with advice on those categories of information which the government regards as being secret for reasons of national security and asks editors to refrain from publishing such information.

D notices are issued to editors of national and provincial newspapers, news editors in television and radio, editors of journals of opinion and technical journals particularly concerned with defence matters, and selected publishers who publish books on defence and related subjects. D notices may only be issued on the authority of the *Defence, Press and Broadcasting Committee* which is composed of officials from government departments concerned with defence and national security and representatives of all the press and broadcasting organisations.

A news embargo is no more than an invitation to adhere to the conditions contained in it; the *Press Council* approves the embargo system when its purpose is to enable the press to have more adequate time to prepare reports.

Nicaragua For **exchange control** is a non-scheduled territory outside the **overseas sterling area** and the **EEC**. UK nationals travelling direct from the UK normally need only the following (but check): **passports**; international certificates of **vaccination** against smallpox; **work permits** (if taking a job).
The UK has no reciprocal health or social security arrangements.
Enquiries to *Nicaraguan Embassy* in London.
British diplomatic mission to Nicaragua is the *British Consulate* in Managua. The British Embassy in Managua was closed in 1976 and the ambassador lives in San José, Costa Rica.

Niger For **exchange control** is a non-scheduled territory outside the **overseas sterling area** and the **EEC**. UK nationals travelling direct from the UK normally need only the following (but check): **passports**; international certificates of **vaccination** against smallpox and yellow fever; **work permits** (if taking a job).
The UK has no reciprocal health or social security arrangements.
Enquiries to *Niger diplomatic mission to UK* at *Niger Embassy* in Paris, France.
The *British diplomatic mission* to Niger is the *British Embassy* in Niamey (Ambassador resides at Abidjan, Ivory Coast).

Nigeria **Commonwealth** member. For **exchange control** is a non-scheduled territory in the **overseas sterling area** but outside the **EEC**. UK nationals travelling direct from the UK normally need only the following (but check): **passports**; international certificates of **vaccination** against smallpox and yellow fever; **work permits** (if taking a job); green cards for motor insurance (if bringing a car); international driving permits (if intending to drive: see **Motoring abroad**).
The UK has no reciprocal health or social security arrangements.
Enquiries to *Nigerian High Commission* in London.
British diplomatic missions to Nigeria are *British High Commission* in Lagos and *British Deputy High Commissions* in Ibadan and Kaduna.

Night Refreshment Houses Refreshment houses kept open for the public at any time between 10.00 p.m. and 5.00 a.m. the following morning require a licence, renewable annually, if a justices' 'on licence' (see **Liquor licensing**) is not already held for the premises. In some cases, including that of the Greater London Council, local provisions also apply.
Applications to local authority (district council); details in 'Late Night Refreshment Houses Act 1969' from *Her Majesty's Stationery Office*.

Nobel Prizes Nobel prizes are awarded annually from a trust fund administered by the *Nobel Foundation* to people of any nationality, race, ideology or religion who have contributed most to chemistry, literature, peace, physics and physiology or medicine. A prize in economic sciences, in memory of Alfred Nobel, has been funded by the Sveriges Riksbank (Central Bank of Sweden) and is for all practical purposes administered within the Nobel Prize rules. The prizes are awarded by the *Academy of Sciences, Stockholm* (chemistry, economic sciences, physics); by the *Karolinska Institute, Stockholm* (physiology and medicine); the *Nobel Committee of the Norwegian Storting (Parliament)* (peace); and by the *Swedish Academy* (literature).
Anyone proposing himself for a Nobel Prize is ruled out of consideration. Those competent to propose candidates include: previous Nobel laureates; members of the prize-awarding bodies and of the Nobel Committees; professors in the various prize fields either at specified universities or by special invitation; presidents of representative authors' organisations (literature); members of certain international parliamentary or legal organisations (peace); members of parliaments and governments (peace).
The Swedish and Norwegian governments have no influence; any official representation or support in favour of

a certain candidate – whether diplomatic or otherwise – is of no avail.

Noise Abatement Zones These may be designated by local authorities, who may specify the classes of premises to which the noise abatement zone order applies. Confirmation is required by the *Secretary of State for the Environment.* The aim is long-term control of noise from fixed premises, particularly industrial premises. The local authority is required to measure the noise emanating from classified premises within a noise abatement zone and to keep a public register of the recorded noise levels. These levels then become the maximum which may emanate from those premises and, except with the written consent of the authority, it is an offence for them to be exceeded. Authorities may require a reduction in existing noise levels, having regard to the acceptability of the existing level of noise, to the practicability of reduction at reasonable cost, and to the public benefit that would result.

Noise: Aircraft Complaints about noise from civil aircraft taking off and landing at civil aerodromes should be directed to the aerodrome operator or to the airport consultative committee (see **Airports and aerodromes**); complaints about military aircraft should be addressed to the *Ministry of Defence, Provost and Security Services UK,* or to the station commanding officer.
Complaints about noise from flying aircraft should go to the *Civil Aviation Policy Division 5, Department of Trade.* State, if possible, whether the aircraft was flying outward or inward, the exact time it passed overhead, and whether it had any identifying characteristics or markings. Complaints about the ground running of aircraft engines should go to the aircraft owner or operator.
Certain areas around the busier UK airports have been designated by the Department of Trade as eligible for soundproofing grants. These are normally administered by the local authority. The *British Airports Authority* finances grants for those near Glasgow, Edinburgh, Prestwick and Aberdeen airports, even though these airports have not been designated by the DoT.
A free insurance scheme to compensate for damage caused by aircraft turbulence in specific areas around London, Heathrow, is operated by the Airport Support Department of the BAA.

Noise and Planning The *Department of the Environment* and the Welsh Office have drawn the attention of **local authorities** to the need to take noise into account when preparing structure or local plans and when considering applications for **planning permission**. Local authorities are required to publicise some applications for noisy developments. In other cases where new development will substantially affect neighbouring property, local authorities have been asked to notify neighbours of the application either individually or by posting of site notices. Those who wish to object to a proposed development on noise or any other grounds, should notify the local planning department. If permission for the development is refused and the applicant then appeals to the appropriate Secretary of State against the refusal, the local authority will advise on how to make objections known to the Secretary of State.
See also **Compulsory purchase: compensation.**

Noise at Work Responsibility for UK policy on the control of noise in places of work lies with the Hazardous Substances Branch B at the *Health and Safety Executive Head Office.* Technical advice and publications on noise control in workplaces are available from the *Health and Safety Executive, HM Factory Inspectorate Area Offices.*
See also **Work: health and safety.**

Noise: Construction Sites Local authorities have the powers to impose requirements on the way in which construction, demolition and similar works are to be carried out so as to minimise noise. Requirements may be specified before work commences or remedial action can be taken where work has already begun. Control may be exercised by the issue of a notice which may include specifications as to the plant or machinery which is, or is not, to be used, and the hours of operation and permitted noise levels from particular types of machinery. Contractors may apply to the **local authority** to make its requirements known; the authority has a duty to reply to an application within 28 days. A code of practice on construction site noise has been issued by the *British Standards Institution*. Complain about noise from an individual building site to the relevant local authority.

Noise: Loudspeakers Loudspeakers and ice cream chimes are banned in the streets between the hours of 9 p.m. and 8 a.m. There are a few exemptions from this rule, notably for the public services such as police, ambulance and fire brigades. During the daytime it is also illegal to use loudspeakers in streets for advertising entertainments, trade or business. There is an exemption for vehicles from which perishable foodstuffs (for example, ice cream) are sold, but loudspeakers on these vehicles may only be used between the hours of noon and 7 p.m. Offences should be reported to the *police* or to local authority environmental health department.

Noise Nuisance Local authorities have powers to deal with existing and potential general noise nuisances. If the local authority health department is satisfied that a noise does constitute a nuisance it normally attempts to resolve the matter by informal discussions with those responsible for the noise. If this fails, it normally serves an abatement notice on the person causing the noise or on the owner or occupier of the premises where the nuisance arises. If the recipient of the notice fails to comply with it, he can be proceeded against in the magistrates' court. Where the authority considers that summary proceedings would not afford an adequate remedy, it may seek an injunction in the High Court. Apply to local authority.

Occupiers of premises affected by noise may complain direct to a magistrates' court which, if satisfied that the noise amounts to a nuisance, will serve an abatement notice. Complaints to the clerk of the court. Alternatively, a civil action for noise nuisance can be taken at common law but, to succeed, it must be shown that the nuisance substantially affects the plaintiff's health, comfort or convenience. The remedy is by way of an action for an injunction to restrain the defendant from continuing the nuisance; it is sometimes possible to claim damages. Advice from a **solicitor**.

Controls of many minor noise nuisances are often contained in **byelaws**; consult local authorities. Noise sources included are music near houses, churches and hospitals; radios, televisions and record players; noisy street trading; noisy animals; noisy conduct at night; acoustic bird-scarers; seaside pleasure boats; model aircraft; fireworks. Where any of these noise nuisances is covered by a byelaw, enforcement is primarily a matter for the local authority, although there is no restriction on the individual's right to prosecute.

The *Secretary of State for the Environment* has powers to issue and approve codes of practice for the minimisation of noise. There are likely to be several of these, dealing with such noise nuisances as burglar alarms, bird-scarers, chain-saws and noisy sports. See also **Local authorities**.

Noise Nuisance: Vehicles Complaints about noisy vehicles should be addressed to the *police*. Measurement of the noise emissions from individual vehicles on busy public roads presents many technical problems for the police and there may be circumstances in which they find it difficult to help. Illegal use of motor horns should be reported to the police.

Complaints or suggestions about traffic routeing or regulation to local authorities. Changes in traffic patterns can have repercussions over a wide area and it is not always possible for complaints or suggestions to be met. Most authorities welcome constructive ideas.

Northern Ireland Labour Party The sister party in Northern Ireland of the Labour Party in Great Britain, it was founded in 1923. Membership is open to all who accept the party's constitution and aims. It has constituency branches and its ruling body is a 20-strong Executive Committee, elected at each annual conference. The party is non-sectarian and pursues democratic socialist policies. It is a member of the Socialist International.
Enquiries to: *Northern Ireland Labour Party*.

Norway For **exchange control** is a non-scheduled territory outside the **overseas sterling area** and the **EEC**. UK nationals travelling direct from the UK normally need only the following (but check): **passports; work permits** (if taking a job).
UK reciprocal arrangements cover social security (see leaflet SA16 obtainable from *Department of Health and Social Security, Overseas Group*) and health. In-patient treatment free. Out-patient and general practitioners' charges – 80% refunded on production of receipts and UK passport at local social insurance office.
Enquiries to *Norwegian Embassy* in London.
British diplomatic missions to Norway are *British Embassy* in Oslo and *British Consulates* in Bergen and nine other provincial centres.

Nuclear Installations Enforcement of the provisions for nuclear installations in the Health and Safety at Work, etc. Act (e.g. the licensing of nuclear sites and the implementation of the Nuclear Installations Act) and of provisions for radiological safety in the Factory Acts is the responsibility of the *Health and Safety Executive, HM Nuclear Installation Inspectorate*.
At nuclear sites the inspectorate imposes and enforces the safety conditions of the licence. Conditions may be varied and the licence revoked at any time. Before a licence is granted **local authorities** and others can make representations to the Health and Safety Executive or, in the case of power stations, to the minister, under the appropriate legislation. For matters of nuclear safety the Health and Safety Executive is ultimately responsible to the Secretary of State for Energy.

Number Plates If you own a motor vehicle with a registration mark you particularly want to keep when you change the vehicle, this is possible for a fee of £50, subject to certain conditions. Full details and application form can be obtained from Local Vehicle Licensing Office of local authority.
See also **Motor vehicle registration**.

Nursery Education Provision of nursery education is at the discretion of the *local education authority*; children are admitted to nursery school or nursery classes at the discretion of the head teacher.
See also **Education: Scotland; Education: Northern Ireland; Playgroups**.

Nurses By law the title registered or enrolled nurse is restricted to those who are on the register or roll of either the *General Nursing Council for England and Wales*, the *General Nursing Council for Scotland* or the *Northern Ireland Council for Nursing and Midwives*.
Registered nurses (SRN – general; RMN – psychiatric; RSCN – children; or RNMS – mental subnormality) have trained to a higher standard than enrolled nurses (SEN). The Councils do not control nursing practice, but control the qualifications and keep records of all who qualify, which are available to the public.
Complaints about nurses should normally be made to the employing authority, the *area health authority* in England and Wales, the *Health Board* in Scotland and the *Health and Social Services Board* in Northern Ireland. Complaints of grave professional misconduct can be made to the relevant Council, which may remove a nurse's name from the register or roll.
See also **Disputes with public authorities; Midwives**.

Nursing at Home Nursing at home is undertaken by district nurses, largely for the handicapped or chronically sick. Apply to NHS family

doctor. The *Department of Health and Social Security* (local offices) have a duty to provide nursing equipment for the care and after-care of patients who are nursed at home, e.g. ripple beds, airbeds, hoists, walking aids.

See also **Disablement: services; National Health Service.**

O

Oaths Oaths can be sworn before a Justice of the Peace or any practising **solicitor** or, exceptionally in cases of high court litigation, before certain officers of the *Supreme Court of Judicature*.

Obscene Publications There is no pre-censorship of published material in the UK, but it is an offence under the Obscene Publications Acts 1959 and 1964 to publish, or to possess for publication for gain, an obscene article. Obscenity is defined in terms of the article's tendency to deprave and corrupt people likely to see it, given the circumstances of publication. The courts decide whether a particular article is obscene; for criminal proceedings this may be either a magistrates' court or a jury in a crown court, while for proceedings for forfeiture of obscene articles kept for publication for gain, the decision rests with the local magistrates. Advice on complaining against obscenity from a **solicitor** and/or pressure group; complaints may be made direct to the *police*.
The Obscene Publications Acts 1959 and 1964 do not apply to Northern Ireland, where reliance is placed on the common law under which it is an offence to publish obscene material.
See also **Adult publications; Film: censorship.**

Obscene Telephone Calls Put the receiver down immediately; if this does not deter the caller and you receive a series of calls ring the General Manager (Service Division) at your local *Telephone Area Office*. He may suggest that your number is changed, or that incoming calls are intercepted by the operator for a while so that only bona fide calls come through. If you are seriously affected by offensive calls notify the *police*.

Occupational Guidance Advice about choosing or changing a job is available free to anyone from the *Employment Service Agency, Occupational Guidance Units*. The service is based on interviews with specially trained staff, supported by occupational psychologists. People still in full-time education or recent leavers can obtain advice from the Careers Service which also distributes literature to schools. The *Training Services Agency* provides industrial courses, occupational selection courses and wider opportunities courses for unemployed young people. General information: *Careers and Occupational Information Centre*.
See also **Employment: policy and services; Jobs; Vacancies.**

Occupational Pension Schemes Employers may contract out of the new scheme for **retirement pensions** operative from 1 May 1978 if they offer an alternative occupational pension scheme approved by the *Occupational Pensions Board*. The OPB will issue a contracting-out certificate if prescribed conditions are satisfied. For employees in contracted-out schemes, the state provides the basic pension and the occupational pension replaces the state's additional pension with a guaranteed minimum pension.

People in contracted-out schemes pay lower contributions to the state scheme; other **national insurance** benefits are unaffected. The guaranteed minimum part of an occupational pension must be inflation-proofed by the pension scheme before it is awarded and by the state after it is awarded. Employees' occupational pension rights must be transferable or retainable when changing to other employment. Women and men must have the same rights to belong. Details in leaflet NP23 from *Department of Health and Social Security* (local offices). Employees aged 26 or over with at least five years membership of an occupational pension scheme, whether contracted out or not, are entitled, on changing their job, to have their benefits in the scheme preserved for them, or possibly to have their rights transferred to a new employer's scheme. Details in leaflet OPB1 from *Occupational Pensions Board*.

Occupational Therapists Those practising in the UK **National Health Service** must be state registered by the Occupational Therapists' Board of the *Council for Professions Supplementary to Medicine*. Those in private practice or working for **local authorities** need not register. Basic qualification for registration is the three-year diploma course of the *British Association of Occupational Therapists*.

To find an occupational therapist contact the BAOT; the Occupational Therapists' Board publishes an annual register which is available at most public libraries. NHS occupational therapists treat only people who have been referred to them by a **doctor**.

Complaints about professional misconduct of state registered occupational therapists are investigated by the Occupational Therapists' Board of the CPSM. Complaints about disciplinary matters concerning NHS employees are investigated by the employing *area health authority* or Board of Governors in England and Wales, the *Health Board* in Scotland; or the *Department of Health and Social Services* in Northern Ireland; complaints should be addressed to the appropriate body.

See also **Disputes with public authorities**.

Office Development Permits Permits exercise a form of control on the creation of office space in certain conurbations (see Town and Country Planning Act 1971, sections 73–86). The restrictions at present apply only to the South-east economic planning region. Throughout the controlled area, all applications for **planning permission** for office developments above the exemption limit of 30,000 sq ft gross must be accompanied by an office development permit. Apply to *Department of the Environment* (Division CP2B).

Office Location Information and advice on office locations in the UK are available free to British and foreign companies from the *Location of Offices Bureau*. Information includes data on government and local authority plans, controls on office development, government incentives, office rentals, rates, communications developments and details of local amenities.

Official Publications *Her Majesty's Stationery Office* publishes UK Acts of Parliament, Bills, Statutory Instruments and other publications. They can be purchased over the counter or by post from any government bookshop. In addition, HMSO has agents in the main centres and in most large overseas countries, and publications can also be ordered through any bookseller.

Publications are, generally, sponsored by Parliament or by which ever government department is responsible for the text. It is exceptional for HMSO to commission publications; it does not consider manuscripts submitted by authors.

Official Solicitor The Official Solicitor is available to assist in legal proceedings where there might otherwise be a denial or miscarriage of justice. His functions include being responsible for the liberty of contempt prisoners and for bail applicants to a judge in chambers; being called upon by the *Court of Protection* to conduct enquiries into the property of mentally disabled persons and acting as receiver to manage the property of such people if it is not practicable for a relative or friend to do so; acting on behalf of children or mentally disabled persons who are involved in proceedings in any division of the High Court and sometimes in a county court (e.g. property disputes, damages claims, disputes over wardship, custody of children or adoption proceedings in the High Court); representing in High Court proceedings the estates of deceased people where no personal representatives have been appointed or classes of persons when no one else is available to represent them; acting as a judicial trustee, an ordinary trustee or an administrator of estates of deceased people where no one else with a proper interest is available to do so. The *Official Solicitor* does not act for private clients nor is he empowered to intervene in proceedings except to pursue an order or direction of a court or under the provisions of the rules.

Offshore Operations: Seaworthiness
Offshore services operating in the UK sector of the European continental shelf are surveyed (this includes inspection during manufacture) and certified by *Lloyd's Register of Shipping* acting for the British government. All types of fixed and mobile drilling and production platforms, submersibles and underwater habitats and equipment are covered.
See also **Oil and gas offshore operations; Shipping: registration; Ships and yachts: seaworthiness.**

Oil and Gas Exploration and Production Exploration and production of oil and gas in Great Britain and the UK continental shelf may only be carried out under licences issued by the *Department of Energy*. There are two types of licence, an Exploration Licence and a Production Licence. Offshore Exploration Licences are non-exclusive and permit the holders to search for, but not get, petroleum, and are valid for three years initially. Onshore Exploration Licences are also valid for three years initially but are exclusive; rights of entry onto land must be negotiated between the licensee and the landowner or occupier.
Offshore and Onshore Production Licences are exclusive and permit the holders to search, bore for and get petroleum. These licences are valid initially for four years but may be continued provided the licensees observe all the terms and conditions attached to the licences. Again, as with exploration licences, rights of entry onto land must be negotiated with the landowner or occupier.
Licences are awarded at ministerial discretion and there is no right of appeal against decisions.
See also **Oil and gas fields: finance; Oil and gas offshore operations.**

Oil and Gas Fields: Finance **Bank loans** for oil field development commonly make a charge on the licence and the oil to be produced, to increase the bank's security and to limit, both in duration and amount, the extent of their recourse to the borrower. For this charge, and any other action making the licence rights exercisable for the benefit of someone other than the licence-holder, consent is required under the Petroleum and Submarine Pipelines Act. Contact the Continental Shelf (Participation) Division at the *Department of Energy.*
As a last resort, and subject to Treasury approval, government guarantees or loans are available to oil companies on commercial terms. Contact the Continental Shelf (Participation) Division at the DEn.
EEC oil and gas research and development subsidies are available annually for payments of 30–40% of cost of production, exploration, storage, and transport projects. Application to the DEn.

Oil and Gas Offshore Operations
Drilling rigs and fixed production platforms in UK waters must be registered with the *Department of Energy* and be covered by a certificate of fitness. They

must also conform to various other regulations, copies of which are obtainable from *Her Majesty's Stationery Office*; queries to the Petroleum Engineering Division at the *Department of Energy*. Anyone planning to work on an installation in UK waters should refer to the regulations for guidance about their legal position, e.g. there is a minimum age limit of 18 for employees, and employees must either be experienced or receive supervision. (See also **Oil and gas: offshore safety**.) The *Department of Energy, Offshore Supplies Office* advises UK industry on home and foreign market opportunities in the supply of goods and services to offshore oil companies. The office administers an Interest Relief Grant Scheme for the UK content of contracts for fixed installations on the UK continental shelf and offers other selective financial assistance to offshore-related companies.
See also **Oil and gas fields: finance**; **Oil and gas: exploration and production**.

Oil and Gas: Offshore Safety The Safety and General Branch B at the *Health and Safety Executive Head Office* has responsibility for general policy in UK waters on occupational health and safety (as opposed to technical aspects of structural safety and 'blow-out' risks involved in producing oil and gas) which are covered by the *Department of Energy*); general policy on diving; preparation of relevant new legislation; and liaison with other government departments concerned with offshore industries.
Responsibility for inspection is divided between the Petroleum Engineering Division at the *Department of Energy* for offshore installations and the *Health and Safety Executive, HM Factory Inspectorate* for pipeline operations.
See also **Work: health and safety**.

Oil Dispersants The issue of licences for the use and/or manufacture of approved dispersants is by Fisheries Division IC at the *Ministry of Agriculture, Fisheries and Food, Headquarters (2)*.
See also **Pollution at sea**.

Oil Mixing Hydrocarbon oils of different **excise duty** categories may not be mixed without a general or individual licence; apply to *Her Majesty's Customs and Excise*.

Oil Storage and Delivery Refineries and producers' premises must be approved for bonded storage of hydrocarbon oils (e.g. petrol and diesel) which are liable to **excise duty** and **customs duty**; apply to *Her Majesty's Customs and Excise* (details in Notice 171). Duty must have been paid or accounted for on delivery of oil for any use other than operations permitted to be carried out in **bonded warehouses** and installations. Approved flow meters for recording delivery may be installed; approval from HMCE (details in Notice 179M). Construction or extension of oil refineries of over one million tons per annum crude oil distillation capacity, or extension of an existing refinery by over half a million tons needs authorisation by the *Secretary of State for Energy* before an application can be made for **planning permission**.

Old People Local authorities have a duty to provide residential accommodation for people in need of care and attention where this is not otherwise available to them and to provide domestic help for the elderly at home where necessary. They have powers to help with boarding the elderly in households to provide meals and recreation, arrange visiting and social work services, adapt buildings, and provide wardens and laundry services. Charges are made at each authority's discretion, but only for work done. Voluntary bodies may be used as agents. Apply to **local authority** (Social Services Department).
See also **Day centres**; **Social security benefits**.

Olympic Games Both Summer and Winter Games are controlled overall by the International Olympic Committee, but it delegates responsibility for competitions to the International Sports Federations of the individual sports. The IOC also works through National Olympic Committees (there are about 134 in the world; one for each country). They are responsible for developing the Olympic movement in their country and for sending teams (amateurs only) to compete at the Games. UK teams, which are drawn from England, Scotland, Wales and Northern Ireland, are organised by the *British Olympic Association* which raises funds to send its teams to the Games, and to pay their expenses while participating.

Oman For **exchange control** is a non-scheduled territory in the **overseas sterling area** but outside the EEC. UK nationals travelling direct from the UK normally need only the following (but check): **passports** without Israeli stamp; **visas**; international certificates of **vaccination** against smallpox and cholera; **work permits** (if taking a job). The UK has no reciprocal health or social security arrangements.
Enquiries to *Embassy of Sultanate of Oman* in London.
British diplomatic mission to Oman is British Embassy in Muscat.

Opticians Opticians practising in the UK must be registered by the *General Optical Council*. Basic qualifications for registration as both an ophthalmic optician and a dispensing optician are: Fellowship Diploma of the *British Optical Association*, Fellowship in Ophthalmic Optics of the *Worshipful Company of Spectacle Makers*, and Fellowship Diploma of the *Scottish Association of Opticians*. Basic qualifications for dispensing opticians only are: Fellowship Diploma of the *Association of Dispensing Opticians*; the Dispensing Certificate of the BOA and the Diploma in Dispensing Optics of the WCSM.
To find an ophthalmic optician or dispensing optician, consult the Opticians Register of the GOC (available in public libraries), the National Health Service Ophthalmic List (available at post offices) or the telephone directory yellow pages. In Northern Ireland a list of ophthalmic medical practitioners or ophthalmic opticians may be consulted at main post offices, offices of the *Health and Social Services Board*, or the Central Services Agency.

Complaints about professional misconduct of ophthalmic opticians and dispensing opticians are investigated by the GOC, and should be addressed to the Registrar. To complain about a NHS ophthalmic or dispensing optician, write to your local *Family Practitioner Committee* or, in Northern Ireland, the *Health and Social Services Board*, within eight weeks after the event about which you are complaining. Late complaints are investigated only if certain conditions are met. Formal investigations are made by the FPC's ophthalmic services committee. There is a right of appeal to the appropriate health minister.
See also **Eye treatment; Health authorities; Spectacles.**

Ordinary National Certificates and Higher National Certificates ONC and HNC courses (usually two-year, part-time) are available in a wide range of subjects (e.g. chemistry, engineering, business studies, computer studies). Entry requirements for ONCs are four **General Certificate of Education** 'O' levels (A, B or C) or **Certificate of Secondary Education** grade one passes, and the same plus one GCE 'A' level or ONC pass for HNC courses. Students should apply to particular colleges for details of subjects required for their courses.
The standard of ONC is roughly equivalent to 'A' level. ONC may be accepted as appropriate for entry to HNC courses and sometimes to courses leading to professional qualifications. HNC holders may be partially exempted from the examinations of professional bodies. (See also **Ordinary National Diplomas and Higher National Diplomas** for new developments.)
See also **Education: Scotland; Education: Northern Ireland.**

Ordinary National Diplomas and Higher National Diplomas OND courses (usually two-year, full-time) and HND courses (usually three-year, sandwich courses) are offered in a wide range of subjects (e.g. business studies, computer studies, sciences and a number of industrial technologies). Normal entry requirements for admission to an OND course are four General Certificate of Education 'O' levels (A, B or C) or Certificate of Secondary Education grade one passes. For HND courses, requirements are the same plus one GCE 'A' level or ONC or OND. However, some colleges may have additional requirements. Students should enquire at particular colleges for details of subjects required for their courses.

The standard of OND is roughly equal to GCE 'A' level. HND is nearer a pass degree. A student with an OND may be admitted to an HND course and sometimes to courses leading to professional qualifications. HND holders may be partially exempted from the examinations of professional bodies. Full details of all courses in college prospectuses.

Grants may be available for OND courses at the discretion of *local education authorities*. Grants for HND courses are paid by education authorities under the national grant regulations (see **Student grants**). The *Technician Education Council* has the general responsibility for developing a unified system of courses for technicians in England, Wales and Northern Ireland. The *Business Education Council* has been set up with similar responsibilities to TEC but in the field of business education. The two councils are currently working on the development of their policies; and their unified system of courses and qualifications will increasingly replace existing qualifications such as Ordinary National Certificates and Diplomas and Higher National Certificates and Diplomas; mandatory student grants are available for TEC and BEC diploma courses.

See also **Education: Scotland**; **Education: Northern Ireland**.

Ordnance Survey Maps and Services For Great Britain these are the responsibility of the *Ordnance Survey*, Southampton. Northern Ireland is the responsibility of *Ordnance Survey Northern Ireland*. Normally, small scale maps (1:25 000 and smaller) are distributed through retailers; large scale maps (1:1250, 1:2500, 1:10 000) and 35 mm microfilm copycards and map transparencies are supplied through OS agents. Main agents in England and Wales are *Cook Hammond and Kell* and in Scotland, *Thomas Nelson and Sons*. Full list of agents available from OS Southampton.

Services available at OS Southampton include map transparencies, enlargements, reductions, map mounting, air photographs and, for selected areas, topographic data on digital tape. Map catalogues and leaflets explaining the services are sent free on request.

Copies of recently revised maps, which are kept up to date by local surveyors, are available through OS agents or direct from local OS field offices (see local telephone directory).

Crown copyright exists on all OS maps and publications. Terms for reproduction must be settled in writing with OS Southampton.

See also **Maps and Photographs: environmental**.

Orienteering Orienteering is controlled internationally by the International Orienteering Federation and in the UK by the *British Orienteering Federation*. The Federation, whose members are 10 autonomous regional associations in England, the *Scottish Orienteering Association*, the *Welsh Orienteering Association* and the *Northern Ireland Orienteering Association*, is centrally responsible for rules, maintaining event standards, sponsorship, coaching award scheme, development, publicity, British teams and national negotiations with bodies such as the Forestry Commission.

Orphans Anyone, not necessarily the legal guardian, who takes an orphan child into their family and who is entitled to Child Benefit (see **Child social security benefits**) for the child may also be entitled to Guardian's Allowance, paid weekly. Usually both parents of the child must be dead but in some cases the allowance is payable when one parent is still alive. Apply *Department of Health and Social Security* (local offices); details in DHSS leaflet NI14. Guardian's allowance is paid in addition to child benefit, but a person with guardian's allowance who is the head of a one-parent family is not entitled to the 50p increase of child benefit for a first child.

Orthoptists Orthoptists practising in the UK **National Health Service** must be state registered by the Orthoptists' Board of the *Council for Professions Supplementary to Medicine*. Basic qualification for registration is the diploma awarded by the *British Orthoptic Council*.
The Orthoptists' Board publishes an annual register which is available at public libraries, and maintains and distributes annually a register of orthoptists - to ophthalmologists, orthoptists and hospitals. An orthoptist may only treat patients who are referred by an ophthalmologist.
Complaints about professional misconduct are investigated by the Orthoptists Board of the CPSM (if state registered) and the BOC. Complaints about disciplinary matters concerning NHS employees are investigated by the employing authority, the *area health authority* or Board of Governors in England and Wales, the *Health Board* in Scotland, and the *Health and Social Services Board* in Northern Ireland. Complaints should be addressed to the appropriate body.

Osteopaths Osteopaths may practise in the UK without qualifications but the *General Council and Register of Osteopaths Ltd*, set up following Ministry of Health recommendations in 1936, registers osteopaths from two sources, the *British School of Osteopathy* (after a four-year course) and the *London College of Osteopathy* (after a one-year course for medical practitioners). Registration legally entitles osteopaths to use the designation 'Registered Osteopath' and 'MRO' (Member of the Register of Osteopaths) and is a guarantee of standards of training.
To find a registered osteopath, contact the General Council or ask for the 'Annual Directory of registered Osteopaths' at a public library or *Citizens Advice Bureau*.
Complaints about professional misconduct of registered members are investigated by the preliminary Investigation Sub-Committee and then, if a prima facie case is made, by the Professional Ethics Committee of the General Council. Registered Osteopaths are bound by the Register's Code of Ethics.
Osteopathic treatment is not available under the **National Health Service**.

Overseas Agents The *Crown Agents for Oversea Governments and Administrations* are sponsored by the *Ministry of Overseas Development*. They provide appraisal and certification to overseas governments who are embarking on major development plans or multi-input construction projects which involve prime cost or cost plus contracting or turnkey bids. They also procure supplies for overseas public sector organisations including buying, shipping, technical inspection and insurance, and specialised services, e.g. provisions of security printing, currency, coinage, stamps and passports; and provide engineering and project management services overseas, including consultancy and advice and special provision for rural development. They offer financial services including management of medium and longer term funds in international money markets; arranging terms of trade and credit facilities; planning of foreign exchange availability; assisting the management of overseas obligations including World Bank and inter-governmental loans; and maintaining accounts in support of procurement or other services where Crown Agents are obliged to make disbursements on their principals' behalf. The Crown Agents have offices in the UK and overseas.
See also **Development aid; Disasters and emergencies overseas.**

Overseas Awards to British Students These are offered annually by overseas governments and institutions for studies abroad. Over 300 scholarships (usually for graduates) tenable for a full academic year are available as well as a number of bursaries for shorter periods. In 1976–77 awards were offered in the following countries: Belgium, Brazil, Bulgaria,

Chile, China, Czechoslovakia, Denmark, Federal Republic of Germany, Finland, France, Greece, Hungary, Iceland, Italy, Japan, Mexico, Mongolia, the Netherlands, Norway, Poland, Romania, Spain, Sweden, the Soviet Union and Yugoslavia.
The *British Council* publishes the awards and in some cases helps with the selection arrangements. Details from Scholarships Department at the *British Council*, or at the *British Council Overseas Office* in the country concerned.

Overseas Companies Companies incorporated outside Great Britain which have established a place of business in GB are obliged to register certain documents with the *Registrar of Companies*. Details of requirements can be obtained on request from the RC. The Secretary of State for Trade is empowered to regulate corporate names of overseas companies which have established a place of business in GB.
See also **Companies: formation and registration**.

Overseas Estate Administration The Legal Procedures Section of the *Foreign and Commonwealth Office, Nationality and Treaty Department* can give advice and in some cases assistance with the administration of estates of deceased persons situated overseas in which there is a British interest.
See also **Death abroad; Legacies: exemption from duty**.

Overseas Food Aid Donations of EEC food are obligatory under the Food Aid Convention of 1971 and in the UK are under the direction of the *Intervention Board for Agricultural Produce*.
See also **Food: EEC intervention**.

Overseas Professional Visits and Academic Exchange Those for British specialists in education, science, the professions and the arts are sponsored by the *British Council*. Hundreds of short tours and advisory visits are arranged annually enabling specialists to meet their opposite numbers, discuss common problems, advise or conduct courses and sometimes to lecture. Some visits are made under Cultural Exchange Agreements with East European countries. Travel grants are available on a restricted scale for attendance at certain overseas conferences.
Enquiries to the Specialist Tours Department at the *British Council, Headquarters*. Schemes administered by the BC for interchange between academic staff include the Commonwealth University Interchange Scheme (visits between all Commonwealth countries); the Academic Interchange with Europe Scheme; the Younger Research Workers Interchange Scheme; and the Academic Links Scheme. Enquiries to the Education and Science Division at the *British Council*, or the *British Council Overseas Office* in the country concerned.
See also **Medical specialists: overseas visits**.

Overseas Qualifications and British Equivalence In its capacity as National Equivalence Centre, the *British Council* will provide information and guidance on upper secondary and post 'A' level qualifications gained overseas. Although established specifically by the Council of Europe to answer enquiries on European qualifications, the Centre is also able to offer information on non-European qualifications, since the BC is represented in some 80 countries throughout the world. Enquiries to the National Equivalence Information Centre at the British Council.
The *Schools Council* offers guidance to students, employers and colleges on the equivalence to General Certificate of Education 'O' and 'A' levels of overseas qualifications (and of some UK qualifications, e.g. City and Guilds, RSA). The SC's assessments are made through consultation with members of its subject committees and with specialist school inspectors, to whom are submitted syllabuses and specimen examination papers obtained from overseas. About 120 countries are covered.

Overseas Sterling Area The overseas sterling area is composed of those countries which, immediately prior to 23 June 1972, were treated as scheduled territories for the purposes of **exchange control**. They are: Australia, Bahamas, Bahrain, Bangladesh, Barbados, Belize (British Honduras), Bermuda, Botswana, British Indian Ocean Territory, British Solomon Islands Protectorate, British Virgin Islands, Brunei, Cayman Islands, Cyprus, Falkland Islands and Dependencies, Fiji, Gambia, Ghana, Gilbert and Ellice Islands Colony, Guyana, Hong Kong, Iceland, India and Sikkim, Jamaica, Jordan, Kenya, Kuwait, Leeward Islands, Lesotho, Malawi, Malaysia, Maldive Islands, Malta, Mauritius and Dependency, Nauru, New Zealand, Nigeria, Oman, Pakistan, Papua New Guinea, Pitcairn Islands, Qatar, St Helena and Dependencies, Seychelles, Sierra Leone, Singapore, South Africa, South West Africa, Sri Lanka (Ceylon), Swaziland, Tanzania, Tonga, Trinidad and Tobago, Turks and Caicos Islands, Uganda, United Arab Emirates, Western Samoa, Windward Islands, Yemen: the People's Democratic Republic of, Zambia.

Overseas Students in UK Children from abroad aged 5–16 must attend school in the UK. Overseas students above school-leaving age may apply to attend UK educational institutions but the charges differ from those of UK students on non-advanced **further education** courses. There is an upper limit to the number of overseas students in British **universities** and publicly funded further education institutions.
See also **Education: Scotland; Education: Northern Ireland**.

P

Pakistan For **exchange control** is a non-scheduled territory in the **overseas sterling area** but outside the EEC. UK nationals travelling direct from the UK normally need only the following (but check): **passports; visas** (consult embassy); **work permits** (if taking a job); green cards for motor insurance (if bringing a car); international driving permits (if intending to drive: see **Motoring abroad**).
The UK has no reciprocal health or social security arrangements.
Enquiries to *Pakistani Embassy* in London, *Pakistani Consulate* in Bradford and *Pakistani Vice-Consulates* in Birmingham Glasgow and Manchester.
British diplomatic missions to Pakistan are *British Embassy* in Islamabad and *British Consulate-General* in Karachi.

Panama For **exchange control** is a non-scheduled territory outside the **overseas sterling area** and the **EEC**. UK nationals travelling direct from the UK normally need only the following (but check): **passports; visas** (except for tourists staying less than three months); **work permits** (if taking a job). The UK has no reciprocal health or social security arrangements.
Enquiries to *Panamanian Embassy* in London.
British diplomatic missions to Panama are *British Embassy* in Panama City and *British Consulate* in Colon.

Papua New Guinea Commonwealth member. For **exchange control** is a non-scheduled territory in the **overseas sterling area** and outside the **EEC**. UK nationals travelling direct from the UK normally need only the following (but check): **passports; visas;** international certificates of **vaccination** against smallpox and cholera; **work permits** (if taking a job). The UK has no reciprocal health or social security arrangements.
Enquiries to *Papua New Guinea High Commission* in London.
The *British diplomatic mission* to Papua New Guinea is the *British High Commission* in Port Moresby.

Parachuting Parachuting is governed internationally by the Fédération Aéronautique Internationale which runs the world championships through the International Parachuting Commission. The UK governing body, which is recognised by the Royal Aero Club, the Sports Council and the Civil Aviation Authority, is the *British Parachute Association*. It is responsible for UK teams, rules, tournaments, instructor training, safety and equipment. Affiliated to it is the *Scottish Sport Parachute Association* which controls clubs, championships and basic training in Scotland.

Paraguay For **exchange control** is a non-scheduled territory outside the **overseas sterling area** and the **EEC**. UK nationals travelling direct from the UK normally need only the following (but check): **passports; visas** (unless

holding Tourist Cards); international certificates of **vaccination** against smallpox; **work permits** (if taking a job); green cards for motor insurance (if bringing a car); international driving permits (if intending to drive: see **Motoring abroad**).
The UK has no reciprocal health or social security arrangements.
Enquiries to *Paraguayan Embassy* in London.
British diplomatic mission to Paraguay is *British Embassy* in Asuncion.

Pardons The right to pardon offences against the law is vested in the Crown, the Royal Prerogative of Mercy being in its origins an act of Royal Grace extending mercy to a subject. The *Home Secretary* recommends the use of the Royal Prerogative which can take two forms. If new considerations of substance arise which were not put before the court (e.g. inadmissible, hearsay) and which show a conviction to be clearly wrong, a free pardon can be granted. If such grave and positive doubts arise about a conviction that it would not be right to allow the sentence to stand, then the sentence, or the remainder of it, may be remitted.
See also **Criminal courts**; **Parole**.

Parking Restrictions Parking, loading and unloading vehicles may be restricted on roads where there is heavy traffic or in congested areas (e.g. town centres). In Great Britain **local authorities** are directly responsible for these regulations, although in their policies and procedures they are normally guided by principles set out by the *Department of Transport*. Local authorities are responsible for taking the initiative on matters involving planning, including special parking areas; car parks; closing off areas from traffic; creating cycleways; and creating walkways or other forms of pedestrianisation. Regulations are enforced by the police or traffic wardens. Restrictions and designated parking areas are indicated by signs and yellow line markings (described in the 'Highway Code'). Some authorities have parking meters, parking discs and residents' parking schemes; the rules are shown on road signs, on parking meters, etc. Further details from local authorities, the *police* and *Citizens Advice Bureaux*.
In Northern Ireland parking plans are the responsibility of the *Department of the Environment (Northern Ireland) Roads Service*, while pedestrianisation is the responsibility of the *DoE (Northern Ireland) Comprehensive Development Branch*.

Parliament: Access to Debates Anyone is admitted to the Strangers Gallery of either *House of Parliament* to listen to debates and question time, if they queue outside St Stephen's entrance. Guests of peers or of **Members of Parliament** can have seats booked in advance in the Lords. If you write in advance to an MP he may be able to let you have an admission order (no queuing) to the Strangers Gallery of the Commons, but he receives only a limited number — not more than two at a time.
Questions and motions cannot be initiated directly by members of the public. It is necessary to contact an MP and ask him to take up a particular matter. Parliament is in session from the latter half of January up to the end of July (with a recess of a week or fortnight at Easter and the Spring Bank Holiday) and from the latter half of October up to a few days before Christmas. The Commons sit from 2.30 p.m. Monday to Thursday and from 11 a.m. on Friday; oral questions to Ministers are answered 2.35–3.30 p.m. on Monday to Thursday. The Lords sit from 2.30 p.m. Tuesday and Wednesday (and sometimes Monday) from 3 p.m. Thursdays, and occasionally from 11 a.m. Fridays.
See also **Parliamentary committees**.

Parliament: Press Galleries Access to the press galleries of the two Houses is granted to representatives of the national and provincial daily press, national news agencies, broadcasting and television authorities and certain national weeklies on an annual basis; and to specialist periodicals, local newspapers and members of the overseas press when matters of interest to them are debated. Applications from newspapers, agencies, etc., for representation in the Members' Lobby should be made in writing, signed by the Editor, to the Sergeant at Arms at the *House of Commons* or to the Gentleman Usher of the Black Rod at the *House of Lords*.

Parliament: Publications and Records
A full report of parliamentary question-time and debates is published daily, on the morning after each sitting, in the official report (known as 'Hansard') of each House. 'Weekly Hansards' – comprising the daily parts bound up together – are also available. Formal records of the proceedings appear in the 'Minutes of Proceedings' of the House of Lords and the 'Votes and Proceedings' of the House of Commons, both of which appear daily and include the order paper for the next sitting. Amendments to be moved to bills are printed separately in the Lords, but are published together with the 'Votes and Proceedings' in the Commons. All these publications, as well as copies of bills being debated in Parliament, are published by *Her Majesty's Stationery Office*, and may be purchased from government bookshops or ordered through booksellers. 'Hansard' is usually available in larger public libraries.
The Records of both Houses of Parliament since 1497, including master copies of Acts of Parliament, are preserved in the *House of Lords Record Office*. The Record Office Search Room is open to members of the public; intending searchers are asked to contact the clerk of the records at the Lords Record Office.
Enquiries about the Lords' business, procedure and composition to *House of Lords, Information Office*; about administration and admission to *House of Lords, Black Rod's Office*; and about historical matters to Lords' Record Office.

Parliament: Tourists The Houses of Parliament are normally open for public viewing from 10.00 a.m. to 5.00 p.m. on Saturdays (except immediately preceding the State Opening); each **bank holiday** and the day following; Mondays, Tuesdays and Thursdays in August; Thursdays in September. Admission at the Norman Porch, House of Lords. In addition Westminster Hall is normally open from 10.00 a.m. to 5.00 p.m. on Saturdays and, during the Parliamentary recess, 10.00 a.m. to 4.00 p.m. on weekdays. The Houses are closed to visitors on Christmas Day and Boxing Day. On all other days parties must be arranged direct with a **Peer** or **Member of Parliament**. Enquiries to the Sergeant at Arms Office at the *House of Commons* and Black Rod's Office, *House of Lords*.

Parliamentary Agents Agents promote private parliamentary bills and conduct proceedings upon petitions to Parliament against such bills. They are registered (list available) in the Private Bill Offices at the *House of Lords* and *House of Commons*. Parliamentary agents regard themselves as part of the legal profession. To become one, it is necessary to serve an apprenticeship with a firm of parliamentary agents.
See also **Lobbying Parliament**; **Members of Parliament**.

Parliamentary Committees A limited number of seats (no reservations; first come first served) are available for the public to listen to committees of the *Houses of Parliament*; admission at St Stephen's entrance.
House of Commons standing and select committees comprise standing order committees (Public Accounts Committee, Expenditure, Standing Orders, Selections); committees set up regularly for a session or parliament (e.g. European Legislation, Nationalised Industries, Race Relations and Immigration, Science and Technology); and other committees set up for a specific matter (e.g. Vehicle Tax, Wealth Tax and Members' Interests). These committees receive evidence from government departments, individuals and organisations; notice of sittings and subjects of enquiry are in the press on Mondays.
Submissions should be sent to the Clerk to the (relevant) Committee, Committee Office at the *House of*

Commons. Regular sessional select committees of the *House of Lords* do not generally hear evidence from outside individuals or organisations and select committees on private bills normally hear evidence only from the promoters and petitioners and witnesses called by them. Individuals and organisations wishing to make submissions to a House of Lords select committee should write to the Clerk of the appropriate committee, *House of Lords*.
See also **Lobbying Parliament; Parliament: access to debates.**

Parliamentary Election Candidates British subjects, Commonwealth citizens and citizens of Eire (Irish Republic) who are over 21 years old may stand for election to the House of Commons, unless they are incapacitated through physical or mental disability, circumstances, character or conduct (e.g. peers, bankrupts); or hold certain offices (e.g. clergymen of the Church of England, members of the police or armed forces). Enquiries about national status to *Home Office Immigration and Nationality Department*; all other enquiries about personal eligibility to acting returning officer.
Each candidate must be nominated on a separate nomination paper, obtainable from the returning officer, which must be signed by a proposer, seconder and eight others (all registered electors of the constituency). The paper must be delivered to the returning officer at a time and place appointed by him with a deposit of £150, which is forfeited if the candidate obtains less than one eighth of the votes cast. Candidates may spend any amount of personal expenses but may only themselves pay up to £100; any further personal expense must be met by the election agent and fall within the permitted election expenses. Enquiries concerning nomination and expenses to acting returning officer.
Candidates may post one election address to each registered elector in their constituency free. Within set times before the date of the poll they may also hold parliamentary election meetings in a room either in a county or voluntary school situated in the constituency or an adjoining constituency in certain circumstances, or in a meeting room maintained by public funds situated within the constituency.
See also **Election agents; Election expenses; Elections: returning officers.**

Parliamentary Elections General elections for the House of Commons (all seats) are held either when a Parliament has run its full term of five years or when it is dissolved by the Queen on the advice of the Prime Minister. The PM normally determines the timing of a general election. A vacancy for individual seats is filled by a by-election; its date is customarily determined by the party which controlled the seat; writs for by-elections are issued by the Speaker of the *House of Commons* on an order motion of the House.

Parliamentary Entertaining Dinners, receptions, etc., may be held in the *Houses of Parliament* only if hosted by a member of the appropriate House who is to be present at the function and in whose name the invitations must be issued. Advertisement of such functions is prohibited. Apply to a **Member of Parliament** or a member of the **House of Lords**.

Parole Prisoners serving a fixed sentence totalling more than 18 months may be released on licence after serving 12 months or a third of their sentence, whichever expires later. Parole licences are granted in England and Wales by the *Home Secretary* and in Scotland by the *Secretary of State for Scotland*, on the recommendation of the Local Review Committee at each of Her Majesty's prisons and/or (depending on the case) the *Parole Board for England and Wales* or the *Parole Board for Scotland*. Licences may be revoked (and the prisoner recalled to jail) by the HS or the SS for Scotland.
Prisoners are automatically considered for parole unless they request otherwise. The licence contains specific conditions (e.g. reporting to a named probation officer, good behaviour, and work) and lasts, unless revoked, until

the prisoner would normally have been released with full remission.
A system of parole for Northern Ireland is under consideration. See also **Probation orders**.

Parole: Life Licences Prisoners serving life sentences are not eligible for parole as such but are released on a life licence; under its terms they may be recalled to prison at any time during the remainder of their lives should their conduct make it necessary. In England and Wales each case is considered by the *Home Secretary* but he cannot order the release of a life sentence prisoner unless he is recommended to do so by the *Parole Board for England and Wales* (though he is not bound to accept their recommendation) and after he has consulted the Lord Chief Justice and, if he is available, the trial judge. At a time fixed in consultation with the PB (usually after seven years but it may be shorter or longer according to the circumstances of the case), the prisoner's case is referred to the local review committee at the prison in which the prisoner is detained. The committee's recommendation is considered by the HS and forwarded to the PB; the PB may either recommend that the prisoner should be released or ask for the case to be reviewed again after a specified period (when it would be referred to the local review committee as the first stage in a further formal review).

Partnerships Partnership is the relation which subsists between persons carrying on a business in common with a view to profit (Partnership Act 1890). Such persons may be individuals, or corporate bodies such as limited companies. In England and Wales a partnership has no separate existence distinct from the partners of whom it consists, but in Scotland a partnership is a legal entity separate and distinct from its partners.
Any partnership which is carried on under a name other than the personal or corporate names of the partners should be registered under the Registration of Business Names Act 1916 with the *Registrar of Business Names*. Partners who wish to limit their personal financial liability may register under the Limited Partnerships Act 1907; enquiries for registration to *Registrar of Companies*.
See also **Business names; Companies: formation and registration**.

Party Political Broadcasts The *British Broadcasting Corporation* and the *Independent Broadcasting Authority* provide free air time for party political broadcasts; detailed allocation of time is agreed between them and representatives of the eligible parties – currently Labour, Conservative, Liberal, Scottish National and Plaid Cymru. The last two broadcast only in Scotland and Wales respectively.
Certain general rules help to determine qualification (e.g. size of general election vote, for broadcasts each year; or seats contested, for broadcasts before a general election) but actual allocation depends on negotiations between all qualifying parties. Traditionally the governing party gets the last broadcast before a general election. Parties can introduce different programmes for broadcasts in Scotland and Wales.

Passenger Ships Any ship carrying more than 12 passengers must hold a passenger certificate from the *Department of Trade* (Marine Division). Passengers do not include those employed or engaged in any capacity on board with the business of the ship. Certain small pleasure craft may also require to be licensed by local authorities.

Passports Passports are internationally recognised documents of nationality and identity. **British subjects** receive their passports normally from the authorities of the **Commonwealth** country of which they are citizens. UK passports are issued by the UK government (and by the govenments of colonial territories) to citizens of the UK and colonies (see **Citizenship of the UK and colonies**); British subjects without citizenship; citizens of the Irish Republic who have claimed to remain British subjects; and

British protected persons. They are not normally issued to other British subjects. Similarly foreigners receive their passports from the authorities of their own country, but stateless persons and foreigners unable to get passports from their own government may be able to obtain travel documents from the *Home Office Immigration and Nationality Department*.

UK passports are controlled by the *Foreign and Commonwealth Office*, and are the property of the government not of the holder. They are issued to facilitate travel abroad and re-entry to the UK. Passport holders must comply with the immigration requirements of other countries and obtain **visas** or permits as necessary (see entries for each country). UK travellers to countries that are incompatible (e.g. Arab states and Israel) should make enquiries to the nearest *Passport Office* or, in Northern Ireland, *Passport Agency*.

There are three different types of British passport: British standard passports, British visitors passports and British collective passports.

Passports: British Standard All citizens of the UK and colonies (as defined by the British Nationality Act 1948 and the various amending Acts) and certain **British subjects** without citizenship and **British protected persons** are eligible for British standard passports. They are normally issued for ten years, valid for all countries. At the time of issue the holder's spouse may be included enabling both parties to travel together or the holder (but not the spouse) to travel alone; children under 16 may, if they have a British national status as mentioned above, be included in their parent's passport. Separate passports for children under 16 are issued initially for five years and extended free for a further five years on production of a recent photograph. Standard passports normally have 30 pages but there is a 94-page version for businessmen and other frequent travellers.

In England, Scotland and Wales, standard passports are issued by any of the five *Passport Offices* and, in Northern Ireland, by the *Passport Agency*. Application forms are obtainable from the Passport Offices and Agency and from main post offices, banks and travel agents. Completed forms should be submitted to the appropriate office together with two identical photographs, the fee and relevant documents (e.g. **birth certificates**, adoption certificates, naturalisation certificates, documentary evidence confirming national status and evidence of change of name by marriage or deed poll). Photocopies of documents are unacceptable. Applications should normally be made at least four weeks before the passport is needed.

Standard passports are also issued and serviced overseas. Apply to nearest British consulate in foreign countries, the British High Commission in Commonwealth countries or the appropriate passport-issuing office in dependant territories (see separate entries for each country); addresses given under *British diplomatic missions*. Application should normally be made well before the proposed date of travel.

Passports: British Visitors' These are issued solely to citizens of the UK and colonies and are a simplified form of the standard passport, valid for one year and not renewable. They may not be used on business but merely for short holidays or similar private journeys to the following countries: Andorra, Austria, Belgium, France (including Corsica), Gibraltar, Italy (including Sicily, Sardinia, Elba), Liechtenstein, Luxembourg, Malta, Monaco, Netherlands, Portugal (including Madeira and the Azores), San Marino, Spain (including the Balearic and Canary Islands), Switzerland, Denmark (including Faroe Islands and Greenland), Finland, Iceland, Norway, Sweden, Greece, Turkey, Federal Republic of Germany, Western sectors of Berlin (for air travellers only), Bermuda, Canada.

In England, Scotland and Wales, visitors' passports are issued on personal application while you wait at main post offices, and in Belfast on personal or postal application to the *Passport Agency*. The completed application form must be accompanied by two identical photographs, the fee and identity documents (e.g. **National Health Service medical card, a birth certificate** or a Department of Health and Social Security retirement pensioner's order book). No **visas** are required. Visitors' passports cannot be issued overseas.

Passports: British Collective These are issued in lieu of separate passports to approved parties of British students or of Guides or Scouts who are UK nationals under 18 travelling in charge of a responsible leader. The leader must be over 21 and hold a valid individual standard passport. Not less than five and not more than 50 persons may be included. In England, Scotland and Wales, collective passports are issued by any of the five *Passport Offices* and, in Northern Ireland, by the *Passport Agency*. Application forms are available from any of these offices and applications should be made at least four weeks in advance.

Patent Agents Patent agents practising in the UK must by law be registered on the Register of Patent Agents, which is maintained by and available from the *Chartered Institute of Patent Agents*. Essential requirement for registration is success in the final examination of the CIPA; nearly all registered patent agents are also members of the CIPA.
Enquiries or complaints about patent agents should be addressed to the Secretary, CIPA.

Payments Abroad Payments by residents of the UK to or on behalf of persons resident abroad are subject to **exchange control**, whether or not money is actually sent abroad or whether payment is in sterling, foreign currency, goods, services, securities, rights or interests. The controls cover exports (see **Exporting**); imports (see **Imports; exchange control**); **gifts and loans abroad**; borrowing from abroad and repaying (see **Foreign borrowing**); all forms of investment abroad (see **Education abroad: exchange control**); sterling securities (see **Sterling securities: exchange control**); foreign currency securities; direct investment; property abroad; and settlement of any assets which give an interest to a person resident abroad except by legacy or inheritance. Assets due to persons abroad under **wills** or intestacies of persons resident in the UK are freely distributable.
For special concessions for immigrants and emigrants, see **Emigration: exchange control** and **Immigration: exchange control**. For the special position of Rhodesia, see **Exchange control**. For further information, help or advice, apply to an **authorised bank**.

Pedigrees Thousands of English, Welsh and Irish families of all classes are recorded in the registers of the *College of Arms*, together with many from America, Australia, New Zealand and other Commonwealth countries. The College produces copies of recorded pedigrees for a fee, which varies according to the complexity of the search. The College's heralds also undertake genealogical (and heraldic) research for people on a private professional basis. In Scotland and Eire similar functions are carried out by the *Court of Lord Lyon* and the *Chief Herald of Ireland*.
Debrett's Peerage in London and New York and *Burke's Peerage* in London provide information on a wide cross-section of pedigrees: e.g. royal, titled and landed families, and peerages. *Burke's Family History Bureau* and *Debrett's Ancestry Research* undertake genealogical research.
See also **Armorial bearings; Heralds**.

Peerage: Conflicting Claims In the case of dispute the Crown ultimately decides who is a peer. The Attorney-General advises the Crown, but the question is then normally referred to the Committee for Privileges of the *House of Lords*, which will ultimately tender its advice to the Sovereign.
See also **House of Lords**.

Pentathlon Modern pentathlon (a five-event sport for men and women comprising riding, fencing, swimming, shooting and running) which is governed internationally by the Union

Internationale de Pentathlon Moderne, and in the UK by the *Modern Pentathlon Association of Great Britain*. MPAGB selects British junior and senior teams, organises home competitions and national Championships. A biathlon run/swim badge scheme is also in operation to appeal to schools, colleges and sports and leisure centres.

Performing Animals The Performing Animals Regulation Act 1925 requires the exhibitors or trainers or performing animals to register details of the animals and their performances with the local authority. The register is open to public inspection. The Act specifically excludes from registration the training of animals for bona fide military, police, agricultural or sporting purposes.

Personal Problems Local authorities (Social Services Departments) provide advice on how to use the official and voluntary services in your area and general help from social workers. Apply to local authority (Social Services Departments) in the first instance for help if you or your family are in distress from physical or mental illness or handicap; or have difficulties stemming from blindness or deafness. **Local authorities** also give assistance to the parents of a handicapped or disturbed child and to the elderly who have particular problems arising from illness or handicap, and can help in many other situations arising from illness or disability.
See also **Advice; Blindness; Deafness; Disablement; Mental disability; Social security benefits**.

Peru For **exchange control** is a non-scheduled territory outside the **overseas sterling area** and the **EEC**. UK nationals travelling direct from the UK normally need only the following (but check): **passports; visas** (not always obligatory); international certificates of **vaccination** against smallpox; **work permits** (if taking a job).
The UK has no reciprocal health or social security arrangements.
Enquiries to *Peruvian Embassy* in London.

British diplomatic missions to Peru are *British Embassy* in Lima, *British Consulate* in Arequipa and *British Vice-Consulate* in Callao.

Pest Control The *Ministry of Agriculture, Fisheries and Food* (divisional offices) in England and Wales issue licences to **local authorities**, pest control servicing companies and research scientists for the use of stupefying bait to control certain bird pests; and to local authorities and pest control servicing companies for the use of the rodenticide thallium sulphate to control rats and mice. For such pest control apply to local authorities.
Advice on control of insect and mite infestation is available from the Pests Officer at the MAFF regional offices and Agricultural Advisory Officers at MAFF divisional offices.
See also **Agriculture: Scotland; Agriculture: Northern Ireland**.

Pesticides: Safe Use Under the UK government's Pesticides Safety Precautions Scheme, manufacturers do not market a product containing any new chemical for use in agriculture or recommend a new use for an existing product until recommendations for safe use have been agreed with the government; current recommendations for any particular chemical available from the *Ministry of Agriculture, Fisheries and Food* (Publications Branch).
After clearance under the PSPS, a product can be submitted for approval under the voluntary Agricultural Chemical Approvals Scheme. This enables users to select and advisers to recommend efficient and appropriate crop protection chemicals; and discourages the use of unsatisfactory and inefficient products; see latest booklet on the scheme available from *Her Majesty's Stationery Office*.
Under the Health and Safety (Agriculture) (Poisonous Substances) Regulations 1975, precautions must be taken when using the more toxic pesticides in agriculture; regulations available from HMSO.

Pet Shops Pet shops must be licensed annually by the local authority.

Petitions to Parliament Petitions submitted to either the *House of Commons* or the *House of Lords* must be in the prescribed form and presented by a member of the House concerned. Petitions to the Commons are printed as a supplement to 'Votes and Proceedings of the House'; they are transmitted by the Clerk of the House to a government minister whose observations in reply are also printed. Petitions to the Lords (rare) do not attract a government reply; they are recorded in the Minutes but are not printed unless a peer moves a debate on a petition. Apply for advice to your **Member of Parliament**. Helpful publication: 'House of Commons – rules concerning public petitions' from the Table Office of the House of Commons.
See also **Lobbying Parliament**.

Petrol Storage The local authority or harbour authority (for harbours) grants licences to keep petroleum spirit, e.g. on farms, garages and marinas. A licence is essential except when the total amount is no more than three gallons and it is kept in separate vessels containing no more than one pint; or when the amount is no more than 60 gallons and it is for use in motor vehicles, motor boats, aircraft and certain kinds of engines; to store petrol in this way you must comply with the Petroleum Spirit (Motor Vehicles, etc.) Regulations 1929. The licensor may attach such conditions to the licence as are expedient or necessary in the interest of safety.

Pharmacists Pharmacists practising in Great Britain must be registered with and a member of the *Pharmaceutical Society of Great Britain* (MPS). In Northern Ireland the corresponding body is the Pharmaceutical Society of Northern Ireland. Basic qualification is a degree which has been approved for registration purposes by the Council of the Society, followed by 12 months' pre-registration experience.

Names and addresses of pharmacists in Great Britain are available from the annual Register of Pharmaceutical Chemists, which is printed and published under the direction of the PSGB. The *Family Practitioner Committee* in each area has a list of chemists and appliance suppliers who have contacted to provide **National Health Service** pharmaceutical services (see **Medicines and appliances: supply**). In Northern Ireland the annual register is published by the *Department of Health and Social Services*, while the list of chemists and appliance suppliers is held by the *Central Services Agency*.

Complaints about professional misconduct can be investigated by the PSGB's statutory committee. To complain about services provided under the National Health Service, write to local FPC promptly (preferably within eight weeks) for investigation by its pharmaceutical services committee. Appeal against an adverse decision is to the appropriate health minister (see **Health authorities**). Complaints about hospital practice should go to the relevant *area health authority* (*Health Board* in Scotland). In Northern Ireland complaints should be addressed in the first instance to the area *Health and Social Services Board*. There is a right of appeal to the Department of Health and Social Services.
See also **Disputes with public authorities**.

Philippines For **exchange control** is a non-scheduled territory outside the **overseas sterling area** and the **EEC**. UK nationals travelling direct from the UK normally need only the following (but check): **passports; visas** (unless staying for less than three weeks and possessing an outward ticket and reservation); international certificates of **vaccination** against smallpox; **work permits** (if taking a job).
The UK has no reciprocal health or social security arrangements.
Enquiries to *Philippines Embassy* in London, *Philippines Consulate-General* in Glasgow and *Philippines Consulate* in Cardiff.

British diplomatic mission to Philippines is *British Embassy* in Manila.

Photography: Financial Support The *Arts Council of Great Britain* provides financial support for professional photography. In England recipients of its grants are professional photographers, especially those wishing to produce new work for exhibition or publication; exhibition organisers; publishers of British photographs; researchers in the social and aesthetic history of photography; and universities, colleges or communities wishing to establish a photographer in residence. Grants are also available for purchase of photographs for tours or long-term exhibitions and for communal dark rooms or studios.
In Scotland, the *Scottish Arts Council* supports the *Scottish Photography Group* which exhibits work by professional photographers. Photographers are eligible for grants.
In Wales, the *Welsh Arts Council* and in Northern Ireland, the *Arts Council of Northern Ireland*, provide grants, bursaries and commissions for photographers.
Regional Arts Associations may assist professional photographers in England through specific projects or awards.

Physiotherapists Physiotherapists practising in the **National Health Service** must be state registered by the Physiotherapists' Board of the *Council for Professions Supplementary to Medicine*; physiotherapists in private practice need not be registered. Basic qualification for registration is the three-year diploma course of the *Chartered Society of Physiotherapists*.
The Physiotherapists' Board publishes an annual register which is available at public libraries. Some private practitioners are listed in the telephone directory. NHS physiotherapists treat only people who have been referred to them by a **doctor**.
Complaints about professional misconduct of state registered physiotherapists are investigated by the Physiotherapists' Board of the CPSM or the CSP. Complaints about disciplinary matters concerning NHS employees are investigated by the employing authority (e.g. the *area health authority* or Board of Governors in England and Wales, the *Health Board* in Scotland or the *Department of Health and Social Services* in Northern Ireland). Address complaints to the appropriate body.
See also **Disputes with public authorities**.

Pig Health Scheme In England and Wales the Pig Health Scheme is administered by the *Ministry of Agriculture, Fisheries and Food*. Its purpose is to reduce the effects of disease on production so as to gain advantage from genetic improvements, and to make breeding stock of known health status available to the industry. Membership of the *Meat and Livestock Commission*'s Pig Improvement Scheme is obligatory to members of MAFF's Pig Health Scheme. Apply to veterinary officer at MAFF divisional offices.
See also **Agriculture: Scotland; Agricultural: Northern Ireland**.

Pilotage Pilotage services into UK ports are provided by local pilotage authorities. General enquiries to *Department of Trade* (Marine Division). See also **Trinity House**.

Pipelines Authorisation by the *Department of Energy* is necessary to construct a commercial cross-country pipeline longer than 10 miles. The DEn must give interested and affected parties the opportunity to register objections. For local pipelines (less than 10 miles in length) authorisation is by the local planning authority, but at least 16 weeks notice must be given to the DEn before construction work begins.
Before construction or use of submarine pipelines, authorisation is necessary from the DEn. Consent under the Coast Protection Act is also required from the *Department of Trade*, but application for this should be made first to the DEn. Consent may also be needed from the *Crown Estate Commissioners*.

See also **Foreshore and seabed: ownership; Oil and gas operations; Oil and gas offshore safety.**

Plaid Cymru The term means the party of Wales. Membership is open to all people who support its aims, regardless of their nationality, race or religion, provided that they are not members of other political parties contesting elections in Wales. Its governing body is the annual conference. The party's official aims are 'to win self-government for Wales, and membership of the United Nations, and to restore the Welsh language and culture'. Founded in 1925, the party won its first parliamentary constituency in 1966. To join apply to one of the 300 branches (see Plaid Cymru in telephone directories) or write to *Plaid Cymru Headquarters.*

Planning Land Use Existing development plans covering England and Wales are being replaced by a new system of structure plans (prepared by county councils) and local plans (normally prepared by district councils).

Structure plans are written statements, illustrated by a key diagram, which set out the main planning policies for the area and the most important general proposals for change. Individual properties and the effect of proposals on particular areas of land are not shown. Information on particular structure plans from the appropriate county council. General information from the *Department of the Environment* or (Wales) *Welsh Office*. When the plan has been approved by the *Secretary of State for the Environment* or in Wales, the *Secretary of State for Wales*, it provides the framework for local plans.

Local plans comprise a proposal map and a written statement. They show the ways in which the structure plan applies to particular areas and are a guide to development and conservation. There are three kinds of local plan: district plans are designed for areas where the factors affecting the development or other use of land need to be set out as a whole; action area plans are for areas indicated in the structure plan as areas where comprehensive change (development, redevelopment or improvement) is intended to start within ten years of submission of the structure plan, e.g. they might, typically, cover the part of a town centre which is to be redeveloped; subject plans set out in detail an authority's policy and proposals for some particular type of development or use of land (e.g. policy on mineral working).

See also **Local authorities.**

Local planning authorities are required by law to publicise matters they propose to include in structure and local plans; to provide opportunities for the public to put forward their views before becoming committed to particular planning policies and proposals; to send the Secretary of State a statement of the way in which they arranged for the participation of the public and the way in which the public responded. A copy of this statement is put on deposit with the plan for public inspection. The Secretary of State must be satisfied that participation and consultation on a plan has been adequate. Information on current plan from local authority.

Public participation at the preparatory stage in no way affects the right of organisations or individuals to object to structure and local plans at the formal stages. The appropriate Secretary of State must consider all objections to structure plans and hold an examination in public of selected matters affecting his consideration of the plan. This examination is conducted by a panel, under an independent chairman. Those invited to take part in the examination in public are organisations and individuals who can contribute to the discussion (see 'Structure plans – The examination in public', from local authority). Local planning authorities must consider all relevant objections to a local plan and all such objectors have the right to be heard at a public local inquiry. The inquiry is conducted for the local planning authority by an Inspector appointed by the Secretary of State.

For Scotland, see fact sheet 'Planning for development', from *Scottish Information Office.*

Planning Permission Permission is needed for all development, which is defined for planning purposes as including building and construction work; operations other than building (e.g. excavations); material changes of use (e.g. running a business from home or dividing a house into flats). See also **Building**. Application forms from the planning department of the relevant local authority in England and Wales (district council or London borough council). Applications are recorded in the local planning register which is open to public inspection. Although all applications have to be made to the district council or London borough council, the applications are, in certain circumstances, dealt with and decided by the county council or the Greater London Council.

If planning permission is refused by the local planning authority or granted subject to unacceptable conditions, there is a right of appeal to the *Secretary of State for the Environment* (in Wales the *Secretary of State for Wales* and in Scotland the *Secretary of State for Scotland*) within six months of receipt of the decision. Before the appeal is determined, an inquiry will be held under an Inspector appointed by the appropriate Secretary of State if either the appellant or the local planning authority requests it or if it is considered necessary for other reasons, for example where it is considered that matters of wide public interest are involved. In many cases, however, all the information needed to decide on appeal can be obtained in writing from the parties and by exchanging their representations without the formality of an inquiry.

If development is carried out without permission or conditions are not complied with, the local planning authority may serve an enforcement notice (against which there is a right of appeal to the Secretary of State) on the developer, specifying the steps which they require to be taken for the purpose of remedying the breach of development control. The authority may prosecute a developer who fails to comply with an enforcement notice once it has become effective.

Enquiries to planning departments of district councils or London borough councils, the *Department of the Environment* or the *Welsh Office*. Scottish position is outlined in factsheet 'Planning for Development' available from *Scottish Information Office*.

Some minor developments are given planning permission automatically and therefore no application is necessary. These include house extensions up to 50 cubic metres or one tenth of the volume of the original house, whichever is the greater up to a maximum of 115 cubic metres; fences up to one metre high adjoining a highway used by vehicular traffic, or up to two metres high elsewhere, provided that they do not obstruct the view in such a way as to cause danger. The Town and Country Planning General Development Order is subject to periodic amendment, however, and it is advisable to consult it before starting any development, however minor.

Plant Breeding The breeder of a new variety of certain species may be given the right to licence his variety for certain uses (e.g. sale of seed and other reproductive material; commercial production of seed) and demand royalties. Apply for a Grant of Rights and for information about varieties on which such rights have been granted to the *Plant Variety Rights Office*.

Anybody who considers that the holder of Plant Breeders' Rights has unreasonably refused to grant him a licence or has imposed unreasonable terms in granting one may apply to the PVRO for a compulsory licence.

See also **Garden plants; Horticultural crops; Royal Horticultural Society**.

Plant Pests and Diseases: Notification Colorado beetle, wart disease of potatoes, progressive wilt disease of hops, red core disease of strawberries, fireblight disease and plum pox (sharka disease) of certain fruit and ornamental trees must be notified if suspected in England and Wales to the Plant Health Branch at the *Ministry of Agriculture, Fisheries and Food* (Headquarters (2)).

See also **Agriculture: Scotland; Agriculture: Northern Ireland**.

Playgroups These provide sessional care for children between the ages of about 3½ and 5 years and are organised mainly by voluntary organisations, including parents. Playgroups are required to be registered with **local authorities** (Social Services Departments) who have powers of supervision and inspection to ensure that conditions are satisfactory, and may make grants to suitable playgroups. The *Pre-School Playgroups Association* gives help and advice on forming and running playgroups. Enquiries to PSPA headquarters in London, to PSPA regional offices; or to PSPA county associations or local branches (see telephone directories) and to the local authority (Social Services Department) which can provide a list of registered playgroups.
See also **Child day care; Child minders; Education: Scotland; Education: Northern Ireland; Nursery education.**

Poisons and Drugs Sales of poisons and **drugs** may be made only by a person lawfully conducting a retail pharmacy business. The retail sale or supply of all medicines which fail to meet the criterion of reasonable safety to qualify for general sale is lawful only if sold or supplied by a person lawfully conducting a retail pharmacy business from a registered pharmacy, and if the transaction is carried out or supervised by a **pharmacist**.
See also **Medicine and appliances: supply.**

Poland For **exchange control** is a non-scheduled territory outside the **overseas sterling area** and the **EEC**. UK nationals travelling direct from the UK normally need only the following (but check): **passports; visas; work permits** (if taking a job); green cards for motor insurance (if bringing a car); international driving permits (if intending to drive). Petrol coupons for private cars are available at frontier posts or branches of Polish Tourist Office (Orbis) in Poland, also from *Fregata Travel Ltd* and *Gdynia-America Shipping Lines* in London. See also **Motoring abroad.**
UK reciprocal arrangements cover health but not social security. Treatment free (doctors' visits charged); 30% charge on cost of prescribed medicines from public pharmacy to those normally resident in UK on production of **National Health Service medical card.**
Enquiries to *Polish Embassy* in London and *Polish Travel Office 'Orbis'* in London.
British diplomatic mission to Poland is *British Embassy* in Warsaw.

Police There is no national UK force. The police service in Great Britain is organised into 53 large police forces, each responsible for a separate area and subject to the eventual control of the *Home Secretary* or the *Secretary of State for Scotland*. All except one are linked to local government. In Northern Ireland there is a single force. In England and Wales there are 43 forces, each commanded by a chief officer who is chosen by the police authority. For the *Metropolitan Police Force* (the largest, covering most of London) the authority is the Home Secretary; for other forces the authority is a committee of elected local government representatives and magistrates. The HS has wide powers over both chief officers and police authorities. Appointments to senior posts are subject to his approval and he decides on appeals against disciplinary punishments.
Regional crime squads provide a national detective network directed against professional criminals, and work in close collaboration with the police, from which they are drawn.
Telephone emergency calls (999) are channelled through a local operator to the headquarters of the force, where action is taken. In London this is New Scotland Yard. For non-urgent calls, look under 'Police' in the telephone directory.
Police officers can be hired in certain circumstances in the interest of public order or security (e.g. for football matches, greyhound races, etc.). Contact local *police*.

Police: Complaints Complaints about the conduct of a police officer should be made in writing to the chief officer of the police force concerned

Who Decides What **Political**

(Commissioner of Police for the *Metropolitan Police Force* and for the *City of London Police*, otherwise Chief Constable) or by calling at any police station. An investigation, carried out by a senior officer who may come from a different police force, is normally started at once (unless the complaint is associated with criminal proceedings when it usually waits until court proceedings are completed). The complainant is asked to make a full statement; the police seek information from anyone else who can help to establish the facts; the police officer who is complained about can also make a statement. At the end of the investigation a report is sent to the deputy chief constable; unless he is satisfied that no criminal offence has been committed he sends the report to the *Director of Public Prosecutions*, who decides whether criminal proceedings should be brought. If there is a prosecution, the complainant can be called upon to give evidence.

The deputy chief constable also considers whether the evidence from the investigation justifies bringing a disciplinary charge. If not, he must send a report to the Police Complaints Board which either accepts his decision or recommends that disciplinary charges should be brought. Even with a complaint of substance a disciplinary charge may not be thought appropriate.

If disciplinary charges are brought, there is a formal hearing, normally before the chief officer alone or exceptionally, on PCB direction, before a tribunal consisting of the chief officer and two members of the PCB. The hearing is private but, unless the officer has admitted the charges, the complainant has a right to attend and normally is expected to give evidence.

The complainant and deputy chief constable are informed whether charges are to be brought and of decisions of the DPP and PCB. A complainant may also have separate remedy at civil law; advice from a **solicitor**.

The police officer concerned normally receives a copy of the original complaint or an account of an unwritten complaint. If he is charged with a disciplinary offence, he receives a copy automatically: if not charged, he can ask for a copy when the case is closed. He can bring legal proceedings for defamation after a false and malicious complaint. General information from the *Home Office* or any police station.

Police Recruitment Recruitment is open to people of British nationality or citizens of Eire (Irish Republic) who are intelligent, physically fit, $18\frac{1}{2}$ years of age (16 for cadet entrants) and not less than 172 cm (men) or 162 cm (women) in height. Enquiries to the area's *Police Force Headquarters* or to local police station.

Police Recruitment: Special Constables
Special constables are unpaid volunteers who support the regular police forces. Only persons of British nationality are eligible to join. Members of police forces; security organisations; the hospital, fire and ambulance services; and regular or certain reserve members of the armed services are all excluded. Enquiries to local *police*.

Political Asylum Political asylum in the UK is granted by the *Home Office Immigration and Nationality Department*. It is accorded to a person who does not otherwise qualify to have his stay in the UK extended, and who claims that if the extension were not granted he would have to go to a country to which he is unwilling to go due to a well-founded fear of being persecuted for reasons of race, religion, nationality, membership of a particular social group, or political opinion. Claims are carefully considered in the light of all the relevant circumstances. See also **Refugees**.

Political Levies These are made voluntarily by some **trade union** members. They are collected with membership dues by the trade union and are paid to the party specified by the members. By no means all trade unions collect a political levy, but income from this source provides the major source of *Labour Party* funds.

Polling Stations and Polling Districts
The local authority appoints the registration officer, and is responsible for dividing the constituency into polling districts and approving polling places. If 30 or more electors in a constituency make representation to the *Home Secretary* that the polling districts or polling places do not meet the reasonable requirements of the electors, the HS may direct the authority to make alternative arrangements.

In Northern Ireland it is the duty of the Chief Electoral Officer to designate polling stations in each polling district. He is required to publish a draft polling station scheme every four years and to take into account any objections received; he may also hold local enquiries in relation to the scheme. When the polling station scheme is finally approved it is published; copies are also available for inspection in the Chief Electoral Officer's office.

See also **Local government elections; Parliamentary elections.**

Pollution at Sea Pollution at sea is primarily the responsibility of the *Department of Trade* (Marine Division), which has an organisation for reporting and dealing with oil spills and incidents involving hazardous cargoes. It is responsible for enforcing the parts of the Prevention of Oil Pollution Act 1971 which relate to ships, and the Merchant Shipping (Oil Pollution) Act 1971 relating to compulsory insurance against liability for oil pollution.

Oil operators in British offshore waters pay compensation for damage caused by an escape of oil from any of their offshore installations, up to a total amount per incident of $25m; and there is no need to establish fault on the part of the operator. The scheme is administered by the *Offshore Pollution Liability Association Ltd*.

The scheme is now being replaced by the Convention on Civil Liability for Oil Pollution Damage Resulting from Exploration for and Exploitation of Sea-bed Mineral Resources. This Convention, likely to come into effect in 1978–79, imposes strict liability and a wide measure of compulsory insurance on offshore operators for oil pollution damage resulting from their activities; and provides that pollution victims have access to compensation through the courts of a member country. The Convention has been signed by Norway, Sweden, the Netherlands and the UK, which are passing enabling legislation.

Tanker owners are liable for oil damage from tankers around the UK to compensation at £74 per ton of the ship's tonnage up to a maximum of nearly £8m for any one incident. Governments and local authorities may claim compensation under the Tanker Owners Voluntary Agreement Concerning Liability for Oil Pollution which is administered by the *International Tanker Owners Pollution Federation Ltd*. Further compensation is obtainable under the Contract Regarding An Interim Supplement to Tanker Liability for Oil Pollution, administered in London by *Marine Pollution Compensation Services Ltd*.

Inshore and beach pollution is the responsibility of **local authorities** or the *Department of the Environment (Northern Ireland)* for Northern Ireland. Report oil spills to Her Majesty's Coastguard (telephone 999 and ask for coastguard).

See also **Oil dispersants.**

Pollution: Waste on Land The Control of Pollution Act 1974 set up comprehensive controls for the disposal of waste on land. When fully implemented, the Act will lay a duty on **local authorities** to ensure that in their area satisfactory arrangements are made for the disposal of all 'controlled waste', i.e. household, commercial and industrial waste. They are already responsible under the Act for operating a licensing system for waste disposal facilities which is designed to eliminate the worst disposal sites, while standards of operation at others can now be controlled through conditions attached to a licence. These conditions are designed to safeguard the environment generally and water supplies in particular, and anyone who disposes of waste covered by the licensing system without a licence or in breach of licence

Who Decides What **Population**

conditions is liable to heavy penalties. The objectives of site licensing together with other aspects of waste disposal policy and practice are discussed in the Waste Management Paper series which is available from *Her Majesty's Stationery Office*.

Local authorities are also responsible for the collection of domestic and commercial waste. This is currently carried out under the Public Health Act 1936, under which authorities (mainly district councils) may collect household refuse free of charge except for bulky or awkward household waste for which they may make a charge as they think fit. They may also collect trade refuse but must make a reasonable charge.

It is intended that these provisions will eventually be replaced by provisions in the Control of Pollution Act 1974. When these are implemented local authorities will have a duty to collect household waste free of charge except where it is isolated or inaccessible. They will also have a duty to collect commercial waste on request and to make a reasonable charge for the service. They will, however, be able to waive the charge if they feel this to be appropriate. The implementation of these sections has been delayed for financial reasons and it is not yet known when they will be brought into force.

See also **Local authorities**; **Water services**.

Pollution: Water Water authorities are responsible for administering the law relating to water pollution. Consent for the discharge of trade effluents must be obtained from the relevant authority which may fix charges.

See also **Water services**.

Polytechnics Polytechnics are part of the state system of education and responsible to the *local education authority* in England and Wales and to the *Department of Education, Northern Ireland*. Applications direct to each institution for all courses (see **Further education**).

See also **Education: Scotland**.

Pool Betting Duty Pool betting duty applies in Great Britain mainly to **football pool** betting, but can apply to bets on other contingencies, when the terms are such that the punter is unable to calculate in advance his exact winnings if successful. Exceptions are bets at starting price or tote odds with a bookmaker; bets with the totalisator at horse or greyhound racing; or bets whose winnings cannot be calculated in advance solely by reason of reduction in the event of certain outcomes (e.g. a tie).

Fixed-odds coupon betting is liable to pool betting duty where the bookmaker has invited the bet, and the invitation offers the punter a choice of bets and states the odds; bets commonly made without invitation and totalisator bets are excluded. Payments made for the chance of winning money or money's worth where those paying have a power of selection which may directly or indirectly determine the winner, and transactions which would be bets but for the fact that no stake money is paid, although other payments are made, are both liable to duty. The rate of duty is generally 40% of stake money (or equivalent). Special relief is granted for payments for the benefit of charity or sport (see **Football pools: charity**). Enquiries to *Her Majesty's Customs and Excise* (local offices); details in HMCE Notice 147.

See also **Betting duty**.

Pool Betting Permits Anyone intending to carry on a pool betting or fixed-odds coupon betting business (e.g. **football pools**) must have a permit for each of the premises used for that business. The permit is free and does not require renewal; apply to *Her Majesty's Customs and Excise*.

For pools competitions for the benefit of charitable or other societies see **Football pools: charity**.

Population Statistics UK government responsibilities for population policy matters are co-ordinated by the Lord Privy Seal. The *Office of Population Censuses and Surveys* and the *General Register Office* (Scotland) collect and provide UK population

statistics derived mainly from census and registration data and also analyse, interpret and disseminate them. Forward projections of the population in future years, based on assumptions about births, deaths and migration, are made annually.
See also **Censuses; Records of births, marriages and deaths.**

Ports Ports are run by four main types of harbour authority: nationalised bodies (e.g. the *British Transport Docks Board);* public trusts (e.g. the Port of London Authority); local authorities (e.g. Bristol); and statutory companies (e.g. the Manchester Ship Canal). Under the Harbours Act 1964, all major new harbour developments costing more than £1m must be authorised by the *Department of Transport.* The DTp gives loans to harbour authorities to assist new capital investment; makes orders affecting harbour authorities' duties, constitutions or amalgamation schemes; and appoints harbour authorities' board members
The DTp is advised by the *National Ports Council,* a statutory body. General enquiries about ports to the NPC; enquiries or complaints about port charges to the harbour authority concerned. Appeal against the imposition of ship, passenger or goods dues to NPC.

Portugal For **exchange control** is a non-scheduled territory outside the **overseas sterling area** and the **EEC**. UK nationals travelling direct from the UK normally need only the following (but check): **passports; work permits** (if taking a job); green cards for motor insurance (if bringing a car: see **Motoring abroad**).
The UK has no reciprocal health or social security arrangements.
Enquiries to *Portuguese Embassy* in London and *Portuguese State Information and Tourist Office* in London.
British diplomatic missions to Portugal are *British Embassy* in Lisbon and *British Consulates* in Figueira da Foz, Madeira (Funchal), Oporto, Portimao, Vila Real de S. Antonio.

Post: Customs Controls All letters and parcels sent to and from the UK are liable to examination by customs authorities here and abroad. Addressees (UK and abroad) are liable to be charged a fee on delivery for customs clearance.
Except for letters, invoices and similar correspondence, all private and trade articles sent abroad must be accompanied by a customs declaration form, available at post offices.
In some countries gifts of small value may be admitted free of customs charges. To obtain this concession, fill in the customs declaration form fully, writing 'gift' in the space provided. Some countries do not admit dutiable goods in the letter mail at all; some confine them to the registered letter service. Details in **Post Office Guide.**
See also **Customs: airmail parcels; Customs control; Postal imports: customs clearance.**

Post Mortems If a death is reported to the coroner, he decides whether or not to hold a post mortem. If someone dies in hospital but there is no reason to report the case to the coroner, the medical authorities decide. There is no appeal against the coroner's decision, but a post mortem carried out by a hospital requires the consent of the deceased's relatives.
If a relative insists on a post mortem, the coroner uses his discretion, but would be unlikely to refuse. Relatives can, at their own expense, be represented at the post mortem by their **doctor**. Post mortems can also be arranged privately; contact a specialist pathologist through the *Royal College of Pathologists.*
See also **Death registration; Death registration: coroners.**

Post Office Boxes and Bags Boxes and bags may be rented for a minimum period of twelve months at principal post offices. For boxes the annual charge for letters is £20; for parcels £20; for letters and parcels £40. The annual fee for a private bag is £20; £40 if used for letters and parcels. At some offices correspondence is placed inside a locked box and a key is provided free of charge. In rural districts mail may be called for at the normal delivery office for an annual fee of £20. This also covers use of a private bag. Enquiries to Head Postmaster.

Post Office: Complaints and Suggestions Complaints and suggestions about Post Office services can often be dealt with by the local post office or by the supervisor at the local telephone exchange. Otherwise telephone or write to the Post Office, Head Postmaster in your area for postal and counter services, or to the General Manager at your *Telephone Area Office* for tele-communications services. If you still have difficulty consult the *Post Office Advisory Committee* if there is one in your area. If you are still not satisfied, phone or write to the *Post Office Users' National Council* (England), *Post Office Users' Council for Scotland, Post Office Users' Council for Wales,* or *Post Office Users' Council for Northern Ireland*. These Councils, created to help the public, are independent bodies.

Post Office Guide Published annually, this details all Post Office services. Ask to see a copy at any post office or from *Her Majesty's Stationery Office*.

Post Office Sub-Postmasters Sub-postmasters are agents of the Post Office who often run a sub-post office in conjunction with a small retail business in areas where it would be uneconomical to maintain premises handling purely PO business. For vacancies contact the Post Office Head Postmaster of the area in which you want to be a sub-postmaster; ask him to inform you of any. You will need to satisfy him that you are competent to run a business, are financially stable, and have secure premises. If you meet these requirements but have no experience of post office work the PO provides training.

Post Offices Post Offices sell postage stamps, and issue and cash postal orders and money orders; accept parcels, registered and recorded delivery items for posting; accept inland and overseas telegrams for transmission, and provide Giro Banking services. They also, as agents for government departments, pay pensions, allowances and other **social security benefits**; issue motor vehicle licences, British Visitors' **passports, dog** and **hound licences, game licences** and **television licences**; sell **national insurance**, inland revenue, land registry, insolvency and television licence savings stamps and deal with National Savings (bank deposits and withdrawals, certificates, save as you earn, stocks and bonds).
See also **Motor vehicle excise licences; National Giro; National Savings bank accounts; Retirement pensions.**

Postal Imports: Customs Clearance Goods liable to a UK customs charge but which are of relatively small value are not normally required to be entered (see **Customs controls**) if the sender of the package has given a full and satisfactory declaration of the contents. UK customs officers then assess any charges when the package is presented to them at a postal depot, and the package is released for delivery by the postman, who normally collects any charges due. Delays and difficulties are most often caused by inadequate declaration of the goods by the sender. For consignments of higher value, a declaration has to be completed and returned to customs, together with payment or a claim for deferment under conditions in customs notice 101. Relief from **customs duty** and **value-added tax** is given in certain circumstances for some gifts from abroad. Other details in Notice 461. Apply for notices, forms and further information to *Her Majesty's Customs and Excise.*
See also **Customs: airmail parcels.**

Potatoes Under the government's Potato Marketing Scheme, producers in Great Britain who grow more than $\frac{4}{10}$ hectare must, if they sell any potatoes, register with the *Potato Marketing Board* and pay an annual contribution towards its costs. Registered producers must normally make their sales through merchants licensed by the PMB and conversely licensed merchants are normally required to buy potatoes only from registered producers. The PMB also lays down quality and grading standards for potatoes. Similar arrangements apply in Northern Ireland through the *Department of Agriculture for Northern Ireland.*

A guaranteed UK price is determined annually by the government, and applies to potatoes of that year's crop marketed from 1 August onwards. If average prices do not reach this level, a deficiency payment is made by the government to the PMB and DANI. In years of surplus production the PMB may contract with growers to buy up unwanted potatoes which may either be sold as stockfeed or left on farms. Similar arrangements apply in Northern Ireland.

Each summer the government and the PMB, in consultation with the Farmer's Union, determine a target area for the following season's crop. Quotas are allocated to registered producers, and growers exceeding their quota have to pay an excess levy to the PMB.

Seed potatoes for sale must be grown on land officially tested and certified as being free from potato cyst eelworm. Apply for soil sampling in England and Wales to the Plant Health Branch at the *Ministry of Agriculture, Fisheries and Food* by 15 February in the year of planting.

Poultry A health scheme is administered in England and Wales by the *Ministry of Agriculture, Fisheries and Food* to establish and maintain healthy sources of poultry for the benefit of both egg and meat producing flocks. Members of the scheme receive free advice on disease control from MAFF's veterinary staff and a postmortem service is available. Members must maintain acceptable standards of management and hygiene. Apply to Divisional Veterinary Officer at Ministry of Agriculture, Fisheries and Food (divisional offices).
See also **Agriculture: Scotland; Agriculture: Northern Ireland.**

Powerboat Racing Powerboat racing is controlled internationally by the Union Internationale Motonautique. In the UK the sport is managed by the *Royal Yachting Association.*

Pregnancy Under the National Health Service, expectant mothers can obtain treatment from a hospital or health clinic, their own NHS family **doctor**, or another general practitioner who has special training in maternity work. The latter are recognised by the local Obstetric Committee (a purely professional body); they are recorded in the obstetric list of the local *Family Practitioner Committee*, which is available from the FPC. A pregnancy test is given two weeks after the date of the last missed menstrual period; enquiries to NHS family doctor.
See also **Birth; Maternity benefits; National Health Service.**

Premium Bonds These are issued by *Her Majesty's Treasury* and administered by the *Department for National Savings.* £1 units (minimum purchase £5) can be bought in multiples of £5 up to a maximum holding of £2,000 by anyone over 16 (if under, by parents or guardians) from post offices and banks. Instead of paying interest, each unit is included in weekly and monthly draws for cash prizes which are free from UK **income tax** and **capital gains tax.** Winners are notified by post. Serial numbers of winning bonds are published in the 'London Gazette' and usually in the national press.

Prescription Charge Refunds Made at all post offices.
See **Medicine and appliances: prescription charges.**

Press: Malpractice Complaints against breaches of the (unwritten) ethical code of press practice are investigated by the *Press Council*, which aims not only to preserve the freedom of the Press but to maintain high standards of professional conduct. Anyone may complain free of charge about any newspaper, magazine, or periodical that is published in the UK, or about the behaviour of journalists employed. Complaints must be specific, not general. The remedy offered is an impartial and thorough investigation and the publication of an adjudication in the newspaper or magazine complained of. Further publicity can be avoided in special cases. The Council's investigations cover amongst other things: methods of obtaining **news** and photographs, culpable inaccuracy, privacy of individuals, race relations, chequebook journalism, harassment, unbalanced news reporting, the right of reply. Leaflet available.

Price and Profit controls Current prices policy in the UK is contained in the Price Commission Act and the Price Code. Official watchdog to both the Act and the Code is the *Price Commission*. Under the Act the PC may carry out on its own initiative in depth investigations into individual prices or charges, or at the request of the *Secretary of State for Prices and Consumer Protection* conduct an examination into the level of prices in a particular sector of the economy. If the PC concludes that the level of prices or charges is unjustified, price restrictions may be imposed.

The Code's main principles are to restrain prices by control on profit margins whilst safeguarding and encouraging investment; and to reinforce the effects of competition and to secure its full benefit in general price levels. Exports are excluded from price controls but prices of most goods and services supplied to the home market are covered. Exceptions include fresh food prices but the Commission monitors and reports on these. Consumers dissatisfied with a supplier's explanation of the price charged for a product or service should consult the PC. See also **Price reports**.

Large manufacturers and providers of services must notify the *Price Commission* at least 28 days in advance of their intention to increase prices. In addition, these enterprises and large distributors have to report their profit margins regularly to the PC. Other smaller concerns are required to keep records.

Action required depends on the type of business and its UK sales – see table.

Manufacturers and service firms must notify price increases according to the Prices and Charges (Notification of Increases and Information) Order 1977. During the 28-day notification period the PC can decide to investigate intended price increases according to the critera set out in the Price Commission Act 1977, but such investigations must be completed within three months. During an investigation the PC may in some circumstances 'freeze' a price or permit an interim increase; 'safeguard' provisions protect an enterprise's profits from falling below specified minimum levels. Arising from the investigations, PC recommendations may include restricting prices for up to 12 months from the date of the original notification, which can be enforced by orders made by the *Secretary of State for Prices and Consumer Protection*. Such orders are subject to parliamentary consent and must not be more severe than the PC's recommendations. Orders enforcing restrictions lasting more than 12 months require an affirmative resolution from both Houses of Parliament.

Type of business	Notify price increases, Report profit margins	Report profit margins only	Keep record of profit margins and price increases
Manufacturers	over £12m	—	£2.4–12m
Services	Over £9m	—	£0.6–9m
Distributors	—	over £18m	£0.6–18m
Construction	—	over £9m	£2.4–9m
Professions	—	over £0.9m	£0.24–0.9m

figures represent UK sales

Alternatively, the Secretary of State may accept undertakings instead of making an order.

The PC can also investigate prices that do not have to be notified in advance and the margins of distributors which, following an investigation, can be required to be reduced. The PC exercises control over net profit margins and also, in the case of distributors, gross percentage margins. If a firm exceeds its permitted level (based on previous years' profits) in any period of 12 months, the PC can require it to reduce its prices.

Retailers should not increase the price of goods that have been displayed for sale, but there are certain exceptions, e.g. when goods have a very slow stockturn; where items have been on special offer; where goods are exempted from restrictions on resale price maintenance under the Resale Prices Act; and when repricing would be contrary to the consumer's interests.

Price Maintenance The Resale Prices Act 1976 makes it unlawful for UK manufacturers and other suppliers to impose minimum prices at which goods are to be resold or to enforce such prices by withholding supplies or supplying on discriminatory terms dealers who do not cooperate. Aggrieved parties or the *Office of Fair Trading* may take proceedings in the courts against such offenders. The Act does not affect maximum prices or advertising or recommending a resale price.

The Act provides for the *Restrictive Practices Court* to exempt particular classes of goods from this general ban if the court is satisfied that the public interest would suffer more by banning resale price maintenance (e.g. because there would be a reduction in the variety or quality of the goods or in the number of retail outlets) than by allowing it to continue. The *Director General of Fair Trading* keeps a register of exempted goods, but only books and proprietary medicines have so far been exempted.

Price Reports *The Secretary of State for Prices and Consumer Protection* can required the *Price Commission* to conduct examinations into prices and profits in particular sectors of industry and trade. These examinations can take into account such questions as costs, efficiency, product quality, plans for activities and use of resources. Such questions must not specify an individual firm unless the Secretary of State considers that the enterprise is an absolute monopolist in its particular field. (See **Monopolies and mergers**.)

Arising from these examinations, the PC's recommendations can include restrictions on prices (see **Price and profit controls**).

The PC has undertaken studies of eggs, motor fuel, bananas, meat, diabetic foods, sanitary protection, food prices in outlying areas, poultry, coal, fish, raw material prices, small electrical goods, spectacles, small packs, television rentals, funeral charges, intruder alarms, hearing aids, coffee prices and margins, recommended retail prices, beer prices and margins, soft drinks in licensed premises, prescribed school clothing and call-out charges for visits to repair household equipment. In addition, quarterly reports are issued of 14,000 fresh food prices collected fortnightly from UK towns. All reports are available from *Her Majesty's Stationery Office*. Reports on alcoholic drink, tobacco products and bread prices in Northern Ireland are available free from the *Price Commission*.

Prison Discharge Prisoners may be released before serving their full sentence on the authority of the *Home Secretary* in England and Wales or the *Secretary of State for Scotland* in Scotland. All prisoners serving a prison sentence of more than one month are allowed remission of one-third of their sentence; this cannot reduce their sentence to below 31 days (30 days in Scotland). Remission may be lost for serious misconduct in prison.

As a preparation for release, selected prisoners may be allowed to work (and perhaps live) outside the prison and receive the normal pay and responsibilities of any employee. (See also **Parole; Parole: life licences; Prison: pre-release employment scheme**.) On discharge the prisoner receives necessary clothing; a small discharge grant (only if his sentence has lasted more than 14 days) or subsistence for his journeys and his fare paid to his destination. Subsequently, the *Department of Health and Social Security* has general responsibility for helping discharged prisoners and their dependants in need: it can also meet special requirements (e.g. working clothes, tools). Failing this, the probation and after-care service may offer aid from funds provided equally by the *Home Office* and **local authorities**. Voluntary societies (most are members of the *National Association for the Care and Resettlement of Offenders*) may also provide after-care (e.g. befriending prisoners; helping find work and lodgings; providing club rooms; befriending families).

On release most prisoners are completely free but some people (e.g. trainees, people under 21 when sentenced, people released from detention centres and people whose parole licence or life licence so specify) receive compulsory after-care supervision from the **probation and after-care** service.

See also **Rehabilitation of offenders**.

Prison: Pre-Release Employment Scheme This allows a prisoner to be employed in an ordinary civilian job outside prison for about six months before discharge. Most prisoners serving a sentence of four years or more are eligible for consideration for the scheme. Those selected live either in a prison hostel or a separate part of the prison, receive normal wages, meet their own expenses and support their own families. Enquiries to *Home Office*.

Prison Sentences The mandatory penalty for murder in the UK is imprisonment for life. A life sentence is also the maximum penalty which may be imposed for manslaughter and certain other offences, including rape, some robbery and arson.

In England and Wales a person who has not previously served a custodial sentence of a particular kind may not be sentenced to custodial treatment of that kind unless he is legally represented or has chosen not to be, and unless the court is satisfied that no other sentence will suffice. On the other hand, special sentences of somewhat longer duration (extended sentences) may be imposed on persistent offenders.

The Criminal Law Act 1977 includes a provision, likely to be brought into force in 1978, that a prison sentence of not less than six months and not more than two years may be divided into a part to be suspended and only served if the offender is reconvicted of an imprisonable offence within the total period of the original sentence. The provision will apply only to adult offenders, and not less than one quarter, nor more than three quarters of the sentence may be suspended.

Prisons to which offenders may be committed directly by a court are known as 'local prisons'; all are closed establishments. Other prisons, which may be 'open' or closed, receive prisoners on transfer from local prisons.

See also **Criminal sentences: non-custodial; Young offenders: custodial sentences**.

Prison Sentences: Suspended The courts may impose suspended prison sentences in England, Wales and Northern Ireland: offenders do not serve their prison sentences unless they commit a further offence punishable with imprisonment within a specified period (maximum two years). If a crime is committed within the period of a suspended sentence, the sentence will normally take effect and a further sentence may be imposed for the new offence. An offender who is given a suspended sentence of over six months may, in England and Wales, be made subject to a supervision order for all or part of the period during which the sentence is suspended.

Prison Visitors Prisoners receive visits from specially appointed prison visitors, whose work is voluntary and in England and Wales is co-ordinated and guided by the *National Association of Prison Visitors*.

Probate An applicant for a grant of Probate or Letters of Administration not intending to employ a solicitor should contact the Personal Application Department at the *Probate Registry* in London for form 48. This provides information on what applicants have to do to obtain a grant and the locations of the Probate Registries and Probate Offices where application for a grant may be made. See also **Wills**.

Probation and Prison After-Care The *Home Office Probation and After-Care Department* includes an inspectorate which reviews and advises chief probation officers on the administration of the service at local level, and encourages the service in the promotion of good practice and development. Periodic reports are published by the *Home Office* describing the work of the department. In Northern Ireland the Secretary of State for Northern Ireland has responsibility for the probation and after-care service. There is no separate Scottish probation service; local authorities' social work departments provide the services and offices required by the **criminal courts** in their areas.

Probation Orders Criminal courts can make a probation order for any offender (in England and Wales, of at least 17 years of age) found guilty of any offence (other than an offence for which there is a fixed penalty). Since co-operation between the offender and the probation officer is a cardinal feature of the system, the offender's consent to an order must be obtained. The court must explain in ordinary language exactly what is involved, and must be sure that the offender understands that if he fails to comply with the terms of the order he may be dealt with for the original offence, or (if the order is allowed to continue) fined up to £50 or ordered to undertake some form of **community service**. Probation is not, in the legal sense, a sentence in England and Wales, and cannot be made the subject of an appeal against sentence. An order normally requires the offender to be supervised by a probation officer for a specified period of one year to three years; to be of good behaviour; and to lead an industrious life. It may also require him to submit to treatment for his mental condition, or to live in a specified place such as an approved hostel.

To help more immature or inadequate offenders to respond to probation in an initially stable and supportive environment, courts in England and Wales can include in a probation order a requirement for residence in a special 'probation hostel'. The resident is expected to find employment outside the hostel, and from his earnings contributes towards his keep. Under the code name Impact, experiments in various forms of intensive supervision of offenders on probation with particularly difficult problems in their families, work or leisure are being carried out in five areas.

Under experimental schemes set up to test new provisions introduced in the Criminal Justice Act 1972, courts in four areas of England and Wales have power, with an offender's consent, to attach to his probation order a requirement that he attend, for up to 60 days, a day training centre providing social education linked with intensive probation supervision.

To help to ensure that a fine or other money owed to a magistrates' court is paid properly, an offender can be placed under the supervision of a probation officer (or other suitable person). No offender under 21 years of age can be sent to prison for the non-payment of a fine unless such an order has been made or the court feels that an order is undesirable or impracticable.

See also **Criminal courts**.

Professions Supplementary to Medicine Professions for which state registration with the *Council for Professions Supplementary to Medicine* is required are: chiropody; dietetics; medical laboratory technology; occupational therapy; orthoptics; physiotherapy; radiography; remedial gymnastics. The appropriate registration board of the CPSM approves courses, qualifications and training institutes. See separate entry for each profession. See also **Student grants: professions supplementary to medicine.**

Property Abroad: Compensation UK nationals who have been deprived of property in a foreign country may be eligible for compensation if an Order in Council has been published by Her Majesty's Government following upon an agreement with the government of the country concerned. In some instances a Registration Order is issued prior to negotiations with the foreign government. This is to obtain details of losses from UK nationals for use during such negotiations.

All such orders are brought to the notice of the public by an insertion under public notices of the main daily papers. There is always a closing date for submission of claims and it is vital for claims to be made within the time laid down.

Applicants under such orders do not need to be legally represented and may call upon the *Foreign Compensation Commission's* staff for advice. There is no charge for such services.

Property Abroad: Exchange Control UK residents wishing to buy property abroad (see **Exchange control**) for private use must obtain permission from an **authorised bank** or the *Bank of England* even if the vendor is a UK resident. No payment should be made in any currency before such permission has been given, nor should **foreign currency** which has been made available for other purposes (e.g. travel) be used towards settling property purchases. Seek guidance at an early stage from an authorised bank or authorised depository. Approval is limited to one property per family. Payment for property by private individuals to non-residents must be made with **Investment currency.** Special rules apply to the purchase of property by UK residents temporarily employed in the **EEC** (see **Employment abroad**) and to certain purchases abroad by migrants (see **Emigration: exchange control** and **Immigration: exchange control**).

Incidental expenses of property purchase (e.g. legal fees, cost of improvements, household furnishing and equipment) must normally be met with investment currency. Expenditure to preserve the property or arising directly from its ownership (e.g. rates, insurance, fuel and water charges) may, with permission (apply to an authorised bank) be met with foreign currency bought at current market rate in the official foreign exchange market. Foreign currency from property abroad sold by UK residents to non-residents may qualify either in whole or in part as investment currency. Enquiries to: BE or an authorised bank.

Property Valuations Section 35 of the Land Compensation Act 1961 provides for any person to ask the *Lands Tribunal* to certify that the value of land being sold by him to an authority possessing **compulsory purchase** powers is the best price that can reasonably be obtained. The provision, which is given effect by the Lands Tribunal Rules, allows trustees and others with limited powers of sale who negotiate a price to protect themselves. A fee is payable.

Prosecutions In England, Wales and Northern Ireland prosecutions are mostly brought by the **police** who have power to investigate and charge. In such cases the Law Officers (i.e. the Attorney General and Solicitor General) have no part in the decision to prosecute. For information on Scotland, consult 'The Legal System for Scotland' obtainable from *Her Majesty's Stationery Office.*

A private citizen can bring his own prosecution but, in practice, such cases are usually confined to the less serious offences, e.g. common assault. All prosecutions on indictment, whether private or not, are brought in the form of a written accusation of a crime made at the suit of the Crown. Accordingly, all cases on indictment are under the title of Regina v. the name of the defendant. This does not mean that the Crown takes over responsibility for the proceedings in a private prosecution; this remains with the private prosecutor.

For certain offences neither a private nor a **police** prosecution can be started (or continued if charges had already been brought) without the Law Officers' consent.
The *Director of Public Prosecutions* is appointed by the *Home Secretary* but is responsible to the Law Officers. His department is not a 'public office' within the normally accepted meaning of this term: matters referred to the DPP are confidential; they normally originate from chief officers of police, the courts and government departments. In the field of criminal law he exercises advisory and prosecuting functions and is empowered to take over the conduct of criminal proceedings at any stage. The DPP must undertake the prosecution of all offences punishable by death (treason) and any case whose importance or difficulty requires his intervention. His consent to prosecute is also needed for numerous separate statutory offences. Many offences must be reported to him by the police and he then decides whether to intervene in the public interest.
Other examples where the DPP's consent to prosecute is required include underwater pipelines; water resources; trading with the enemy; aiding and abetting suicide; oil pollution; radioactive substances; reservoirs; football pools; and the National Health Service. Under the Police Acts 1964, reports of investigations of complaints by members of the public alleging criminal offences by the police must be referred to the DPP. The DPP is responsible for the prosecution of cases committed for trial upon a coroner's warrant and in certain cases for the conduct of extradition proceedings. He is also the official petitioner in cases in which the court has made criminal bankruptcy orders. There are a number of acts which authorise special prosecutors to bring criminal proceedings, e.g. inspectors under the Weights and Measure Act 1963.
See also **Criminal courts**; **Criminal proceedings**.

Psychoanalysts   Psychoanalysts are legally permitted to practice in the UK without qualifications but the qualification held by most reputable UK psychoanalysts is training at the *Institute of Psycho-Analysis*. Most Institute members also hold qualifications in medicine, social work, teaching, etc. To find an analyst contact the Institute.
Complaints about professional misconduct are investigated by the Institute (and by the *General Medical Council*) where the psychoanalyst is a doctor). Complaints against psychoanalysts working in the **National Health Service** should be taken up with the appropriate **health authority**.
See also **Disputes with public authorities**.

Psychotherapists   Psychotherapists can practise in the UK without training or registration, though a number of independent organisations, such as the *British Association of Psychotherapists*, and some university departments, provide training courses in psychotherapy.

Public Analysts   Public analysts' statutory duties include the analysis of foods, drugs and agricultural products; provision of scientific advisory and analytical services to local authorities in relation to the Consumer Protection Act, the Trade Description Act, the Road Traffic Act and the Control of Pollution Act; and supply of unbiased, scientific reports to local authorities where required. Anybody can obtain similar services from public analysts on request to the nearest local authority; in particular any private purchaser has the legal right to complain to the PA in connection with the nature, substance and quality of food, etc.
Every UK 'food and drugs authority' (i.e. most large local authorities) is required to appoint a public analyst under the Food and Drugs Act, 1955. High scientific qualifications are required. Enquiries to the *Royal Institute of Chemistry* or to the President of the *Association of Public Analysts*.

Public Contracts: EEC   Public undertakings in the EEC are required to publish details of calls for tender for public works contracts of an estimated value of not less than one million units of account (a unit is equivalent to a US dollar). The 'Official Journal of the European Communities' publishes calls for tender (English language edition available from *Her Majesty's Stationery Office*). The Export Intelligence Service of the *British Overseas Trade Board* extracts details of calls for tender published in the 'Official Journal' (apart from those originating in the UK) for circulation to interested subscribers. Further details of EEC legislation on public works contracts are in the Department of the Environment circular 59/73, from HMSO.

Public Contracts: Preference Where price, quality, delivery date and other considerations are equal, government departments, nationalised industries and other public bodies place contracts with firms in special development areas in preference to those elsewhere. In appropriate cases, government departments operate a scheme under which firms in these areas which have been unsuccessful with their first tender may be given an opportunity to tender again for up to 25% of the requirement, at a price that will not increase the total cost. Apply for details of purchasing authorities operating this arrangement to *Department of Industry* (regional offices); *Scottish Economic Planning Department*; *Welsh Office* (Industry Department); *Northern Ireland Department of Commerce*.

Public Performances The Copyright Act 1956 grants authors and composers the control of public performances of their works. The owners of performing rights in musical works and in gramophone records generally exercise the right collectively in the UK through societies (e.g. *Performing Right Society Ltd*). The *Performing Right Tribunal* is empowered by the Act to settle disputes between these societies and individuals requiring licences to perform music in public or to broadcast.
See also **Copyright**.

Public Rights of Way Footpaths, bridleways, roads used as a public path and byways open to all traffic shown on Ordnance Survey 1:25000 second series and 1:50000 maps of England and Wales (not applicable in Scotland) are derived from definitive maps prepared by **local authorities**. The maps can be amended by later legal enactments. Enquiries about public rights of way should be made first to the local authority.
See also **Footpaths, bridleways and rights of way**.

Public Servants: Top Salaries Salaries including those of chairmen and board members of nationalised industries; judges and senior members of the judiciary (masters, registrars, and above); senior civil servants (under-secretary and above); and senior officers of the armed services (major-general or equivalent and above) are reviewed by the Review Body on Top Salaries at the *Office of Manpower Economics*. It makes its recommendations to the Prime Minister. If accepted, they are implemented by government departments responsible for individual nationalised industries; the *Lord Chancellor's Office* (and the *Scottish Courts Administration* and the *Northern Ireland Office*); the *Civil Service Department*; and the *Ministry of Defence*. The government has undertaken to accept the recommendations unless there are clear and compelling reasons for not doing so.

Public Service Vehicle Driving Licences Licences are required in addition to ordinary **driving licences** by all drivers of motor vehicles (other than tramcars or trolleys) carrying passengers for hire or reward when separate fares are paid (with certain exceptions) or when the vehicle is adapted to carry eight or more passengers. Apply *Traffic Commissioners* or, in London, to Commissioner of Police at the *Public Carriage Office*. Drivers must pass a PSV driving test, be over 21 years of age, of good character and medically fit. Training courses are run by the *Road Transport Industry Training*

Board; by certain bus undertakings for their employees; and by independent driving schools. General guidance in memorandum PSV/A from *Department of Transport Traffic Area Office*; appeal against refusal of a licence to magistrate's court (to the sheriff in Scotland). PSV drivers' hours of work and rest periods are prescribed – see DTp leaflet PSV147.
See also **Bus conductors**; **Public service vehicles**.

Public Service Vehicle Operators An operator must hold a road service licence or a permit for each service to be operated by a public service vehicle carrying passengers at separate fares. Applications for road service licences and objections and other representations from interested parties are heard by the *Traffic Commissioners* at a public sitting.
Applications must reach the TCs at least eight weeks before the service is designed to begin. Special provision is made for short-term licences, when the service is for some special purpose or occasion for a restricted period not exceeding eight weeks, and the need for it could not reasonably have been foreseen. In the Greater London Council area, road services other than excursions and tours require the agreement of the *London Transport Executive*.
A licence is valid only in the traffic area of the TCs who issue it. If the service is to run into other traffic areas, the licence needs to be backed by the TCs for each such area. Procedure for applications for backings is the same as for licence applications. No backing is needed for any area through which a service passes if passengers are not taken up, set down, or allowed to alight for any purpose requiring a halt of more than 15 minutes in the area. Such an area is known as a corridor area.
Permits are granted by the TCs in lieu of licences for stage services where the passengers are carried in vehicles with 12 seats or less, or for stage or express services where spare capacity on school contract buses is used for ordinary fare-payers with the education authority's consent. The TCs must be satisfied that no other transport facilities meet the reasonable needs of the proposed route. Procedure for permits is simpler than for licences, and formalities such as public sittings may be dispensed with.
For regulations concerning services to other European countries, see 'Journeys to Europe by coach or minibus', available from *Department of Transport* (Information Division).
See also **Bus services and subsidies**.

Public Service Vehicles A public service vehicle licence is required in addition to a vehicle excise licence (see **Motor vehicle excise licences**) for any motor vehicle used for carrying passengers for hire or reward. This includes both those normally charging separate fares and those adapted to carry eight or more passengers. Licences are granted by *Traffic Commissioners*. A certificate of fitness, issued by the *Department of Transport Traffic Area Offices*, has to be in force for the vehicle and the TCs must be satisfied as to the applicant's financial resources and vehicle maintenance arrangements. Full maintenance, inspection and repair records should be kept.

Public Service Vehicles: Complaints Complaints about operations may be made to the operator concerned and thereafter to the appropriate *Traffic Commissioners*. Where a consumers' council exists (e.g. *London Transport Passengers' Committee*) complaints can be taken up by that body. County councils have a duty to secure a co-ordinated and efficient transport system and deal with complaints on these two aspects. The TCs are statutorily independent bodies but in certain circumstances there is a right of appeal against their decision to the *Secretary of State for Transport*.

Public Trustee The *Public Trustee Office* (a non profit-making organisation covered by a state guarantee) is empowered to act as executor or administrator of the estate of a deceased person dying domiciled in England and Wales or as trustee of a **will** or settlement (either by original appointment or by transfer at a later stage alone or jointly with others) in the same way as a private individual or commercial trust corporation. Although the Public Trustee cannot accept a trust which is foreign, exclusively charitable, or for the benefit of creditors, nor an insolvent estate, he can act as trustee for and manage pension funds, disaster funds and funds of private individuals or institutions. He also administers unit trusts for money in court. The PT is always willing to give general advice about his powers and duties to anyone who proposes to appoint him as executor or trustee. Pamphlets giving details of the services offered and the current fees are provided on request.

Q

Qatar For **exchange control** purposes is a non-scheduled territory in the **overseas sterling area** and outside the **EEC**. UK nationals travelling direct from the UK normally need only the following (but check): **passports** (without Israeli stamp); **work permit** (if taking a job); international certificate of **vaccination** against smallpox; green card for motor insurance (if bringing a car: see **Motoring abroad**). The UK has no reciprocal health and social security arrangements.
Enquiries to *Qatar Embassy* in London.
British diplomatic mission in Qatar is the British Embassy in Doha.

Queen's Awards The Queen's awards for export and technology are made to organisations which have achieved either a substantial and sustained increase in export earnings, to a level which is outstanding for the products or services concerned and for the size of the applicant unit's operations, in the application of technology to a production or development process in British industry; or the production for sale of goods which incorporate new and advanced technological qualities.
Recipients of the award are entitled to display the emblem for five years. Apply by 31 October each year on forms available from the *Queen's Awards Office*.

Queen's Counsel QCs are the senior rank of **barristers**. They comprise about one tenth of the profession and are appointed, in England and Wales, by the Queen on the recommendation of the *Lord Chancellor*. In Northern Ireland QCs are appointed by the *Secretary of State for Northern Ireland* on the recommendation of the Lord Chief Justice of Northern Ireland; in Scotland, by the *Secretary of State for Scotland* on advice from the Lord Justice-General.
See also **Solicitors**.

R

Racecourse Betting Under the terms of the Betting, Gaming and Lotteries Act 1963 and the Horserace Totalisator and Betting Levy Boards' Act 1972, the *Horserace Betting Levy Board* grants certificates of approval of a ground as a horserace course. It is a condition of the grant of such a certificate that a place shall be provided for bookmakers to carry on their business. Pool betting on horseracing can only be conducted on an approved racecourse; the exclusive right to do this is vested in *Horserace Totalisator Board*.
See also **Bookmakers Levy; Horseracing; Pool betting permits.**

Racial Discrimination Racial discrimination in employment, housing and the provision of services is unlawful. A person who experiences discrimination, either directly or indirectly, in England, Wales and Scotland can complain to an **industrial tribunal** in employment matters, and bring a case before a county court (a sheriff court in Scotland) in non-employment matters. Northern Ireland has its *Fair Employment Agency* to ensure that the terms of the Fair Employment Act (Northern Ireland) are adhered to by employers. Direct discrimination occurs, for example, where an employer refuses an applicant because of his colour. It includes segregation.
Indirect discrimination occurs when rules and regulations, which cannot be justified on non-racial grounds, have the effect of putting a particular racial group at a disadvantage, e.g. to require a high standard of English from a labourer might be considered unlawful if the result is to exclude members of any racial group which had limited English but could do the job.
Forms for making a complaint to an industrial tribunal are available from *Employment Service Agency employment offices*; *Employment Service Agency Job Centres*; and *Department of Employment unemployment benefit offices*. Normally complaints must be made within three months of the action complained of. Before the hearing the *Advisory Conciliation and Arbitration Service* is available to attempt to bring about a settlement.
Cases other than employment cases are dealt with by county courts (sheriff courts in Scotland). Proceedings must be started normally within six months of the action complained of. If the complaint concerns education in the public sector, it must be referred, first, to the *Department of Education and Science* who are allowed two months to deal with it.
The *Commission for Racial Equality*, set up by the Race Relations Act 1976, works towards the elimination of discrimination and promotes equality of opportunity and good relations between different racial groups. It helps people who believe they have been discriminated against by giving general advice on the case; by advising on procedures and how best to present a case; or by putting the com-

plainant in touch with somebody else who can help. In special circumstances the CRE may be able to represent complainants and pay any costs.
Other sources of help include **trade unions**, professional bodies, local community relations councils, ethnic minority organisations, legal advice centres and *citizens' advice bureaux*. Free legal advice and aid may be available from a **solicitor**.
See also **Legal aid**.

Radio Licences Under the Wireless Telegraphy Act, 1949, licences are required for the use and installation of all types of radio apparatus with the exception of equipment designed only for the reception of messages sent by telephony from authorised broadcast stations broadcasting for general reception, and messages sent by telephony or telegraphy from licensed amateur stations. The majority of licences are issued for private mobile radio systems (taxis, ambulances, gas and electricity boards, building contractors, etc.), maritime and aeronautical uses, amateur transmissions and metal detectors.
All applications and enquiries should be addressed to the Licensing Branch, R1 Division at the *Home Office Radio Regulating Department*.
Licences for the reception of television broadcasts are issued under the authority of the Broadcasting Department at the *Home Office* (see **Television licences**).

Radio Telephones Radio telephones in vehicles operate through the Post Office in Greater London, Birmingham, East Pennines, Severnside and South East Wales, South Lancashire and Tyne, Wear and Tees. Subscribers can take incoming calls from any UK telephone and make calls to all UK and many overseas numbers. Equipment must be supplied by a PO-approved manufacturer. Charges are higher than for ordinary **telephones**. Details from General Manager, local *Telephone area office*.
Radio telephones are also installed in many ships, yachts and small craft, but rarely in aircraft. Operating on VHF, each set has at least three separate channels for distress calls, inter-ship communication and for speaking to the shore. Services from ship to shore include making calls to subscribers in the UK and most other countries – personal call, credit card and transfer charge facilities are available; sending spoken radio telegrams; being linked, without charge, to a doctor or hospital. Radio telephone calls can be made by any phone subscriber to suitably equipped vessels by calling the Post Office Coast Radio Station nearest the ship (if she is close to the UK) or by asking the operator for Portishead Radio, stating 'Ships Telephone Service' in either case. Radio telegrams can be sent by telex direct to a radio station for relaying to a ship; by phone – find number in dialling code booklet under 'Maritime Services'; or by filling in the appropriate form at any post office. Enquiries to Maritime Radio Services Division of the *Post Office External Telecommunications Executive*.
A ship licence for sending and receiving radio telephone calls costs £5.50 p.a.; for receiving only, £4.40 p.a.; and for emergency use only, £3.20 for five years. Enquiries about licences and the installation of suitable equipment on vessels to Licensing Branch of the *Home Office Radio Regulatory Division*.

Radio-active Materials Treatment of irradiated matter involving the extraction of plutonium or uranium, or the enrichment of uranium, may be undertaken only under permit from the *UK Atomic Energy Authority* (for purposes of research and development only) or the *Secretary of State for Energy* or (in Scotland) the *Secretary of State for Scotland*. The approval of the authority which issued the permit is also required for the disposal of fissile material obtained from either of these processes. Requests for permits to the UK Atomic Energy Authority, the Atomic Energy Division at the *Department of Energy*, and the *Scottish Economic Planning Department*.
Use of radioactive materials in schools or other educational establish-

Radiographers Radiographers practising in the **National Health Service** must be state registered by the Radiographers' Board of the *Council for Professions Supplementary to Medicine*. Basic qualification for registration is the diploma course of the *College of Radiographers*.

The Radiographers' Board publishes an annual register which is available from public libraries. NHS radiographers treat only those people who have been referred to them by a **doctor**.

Complaints about professional misconduct are investigated by the Radiographers' Board of the CPSM and/or the College. Complaints about disciplinary matters concerning NHS employees are investigated by the employing authority (i.e. the *area health authority* or Board of Governors in England and Wales, the *Health Board* in Scotland or the *Health and Social Services Department* in Northern Ireland). Address complaints to the appropriate investigating body.

Rail Freight Grants are payable towards the cost of facilities for loading and unloading rail-borne freight where otherwise road transport would be used because of the inadequacy of existing rail facilities. Their purpose is to contribute to reducing local environmental damage caused by heavy lorries. Apply to FC Division at the *Department of Transport headquarters*.

Rail Travel: Complaints and Suggestions Complaints should be addressed in the first instance to the relevant Area Manager, *British Rail*, or at a higher level to the BR Divisional Manager. Further complaints, if you are still dissatisfied, may be made to the *British Railways Board* or to the relevant Transport Users Consultative Committee (address from local railway station).

Complaints or suggestions about the provision or timetabling of rail passenger services should be made directly to the BRB.

Complaints or suggestions about rail travel in Northern Ireland should be made in the first instance to the *Northern Ireland Railways Co. Ltd*; thereafter communications may be addressed to the *Transport Users Committee*, Belfast.

See also **Travel concessions**.

Railways: Private Statutory authority is required to operate private railways (e.g. by preservation groups, railway enthusiasts, industrialists) if they cross public thoroughfares. They must also be run so as to comply with certain safety regulations. Write for details of how to apply for the requisite 'Light Railway Order' and general information to the Railways Division at *Department of Transport headquarters*.

Rambling Rambling and the public's right of access to the British countryside is fostered by the *Ramblers Association*, the *Long Distance Walkers Association*, the *Commons, Open Spaces and Footpaths Preservation Society* (legal advice), the *Youth Hostels Association*, the *Scottish Youth Hostels Association*, the *Holiday Fellowship* and *Countrywide Holidays Association*. The last four provide accommodation for ramblers. See also **Footpaths, bridleways and rights of way**.

Rate Rebates Rebates are available to residential 'occupiers' on a scale according to size of family, including people who live alone; income; and general rates payable (excluding water rates and sewerage charges). Occupiers include not only owner-occupiers and council tenants but also tenants and sub-tenants in either furnished or unfurnished property, whether they pay rates directly to the council or whether rates are included in their rent to the landlord. There are no income limits for rebates. They may be payable either as a grant or as a rent credit (to council tenants); they are also available to those in receipt of **supplementary benefit** which covers rates in full. Apply to: local authority.

In special circumstances claims for rate rebates can be backdated to 1 April of the financial year in which the claim was made. See 'How to pay the rates' from **local authorities,** *Department of the Environment,* or in Scotland from the *Scottish Information Office* and in Wales, where the pamphlet is also available in Welsh, from the *Welsh Office.*
See also **Rent rebates and allowances.**

Rate Support Grant Rate support grant is paid by central government to supplement local authority income from **rates.** About 60% of local authority spending (excluding housing subsidies, rate rebates and mandatory **students' grants**) is covered by rate support grant. The grant comprises firstly the domestic element, paid according to the number of ratepayers to compensate **local authorities** for statutory reductions in rates for all domestic rate payers (domestic rate relief); secondly, a grant based on each local authority's rateable resources, to compensate those unable to provide satisfactory services at reasonable rates by comparison with richer areas; thirdly, a needs grant compensating for variations in the amount different authorities need to spend to provide a comparable level of service.
Rate support grant is fixed by the Secretary of State for the Environment after discussion with local authority associations. Enquiries to the *Department of the Environment.*

Rates Rates are a tax on the beneficial occupation of property. They are levied by **local authorities.**
Rates are calculated on the basis of rateable values for each property (called an hereditament) in each local authority area, except for agricultural land which is exempt. Rateable values are assessed independently of local authorities by the *Inland Revenue Valuation offices* on the basis of the rent that might reasonably be charged for the property on the open market. (In Scotland independent assessors are appointed by local authorities to perform similar functions.) Rateable value is a fixed proportion of the gross value, which represents one year's accrued rent including rates and assuming repairs and insurance paid by the landlord at the time of a valuation. All properties were last revalued in 1973: a 'rent return' is sent to properties in the area to obtain an indication of the general level of rents; properties are then classified according to size and age, and gross values estimated. These estimates are then adjusted according to individual characteristics of each property: upwards for favourable position, extensions, central heating, built-in furniture, double glazing; downwards for unfavourable position, liability to noise and nuisance, space in the property of limited use, or adaptation for use by a disabled person. The gross value may be reassessed by the valuation officer if alterations are carried out which would increase the rateable value of the property by more than £30, in which case there is a right of objection within 28 days by the occupier. The rateable values of similar properties may be seen in the Valuation List open for inspection at the local authority.
Occupiers may also register objections to rateable value at any time on application to local *Inland Revenue Valuation offices*; this may lead to a hearing at a local Valuation Court (see 'How to appeal', from *Greater London Council Valuation Panel*) or 'Which' magazine May 1975.
The rates actually payable each year are calculated on the basis of a declared 'rate in the pound' per pound of rateable value. The rate in the pound is usually fixed annually in respect of financial years ending 31 March by each rating authority. There is no appeal against this. Rates on dwelling houses are then required to be reduced by Domestic Rate Relief of 18.5p in the £, or on 'mixed' (i.e. business/residential) hereditaments of 9p in the £. Local authorities may also collect water charges on behalf of some *water authorities.* Rates are often payable biannually, in April and October, in advance; or by agreement in advance domestic ratepayers may opt to pay in 10 monthly instalments

(March and April usually being the 'free' months). Failure to pay rates leads to a court summons, but this may be dropped upon agreement to pay by instalments.
See also **Rate rebates; Sewerage; Water supply.**

Record Sales Charts are compiled of the top 50 selling singles in Great Britain each week by the *British Market Research Bureau* from diaries recording over the counter sales in a sample of 300 record shops. The *British Broadcasting Corporation*, the British phonographic industry and *Music Week* provide finance. Enquiries to the BMRB.

Records and Cassettes: Loans Records and cassettes are available on loan (either free or with a small subscription) from major public libraries, and may be available on application from some other libraries. Apply to nearest public library.
See also **Libraries.**

Records and Documents: Certification The *Public Record Office* certifies the authenticity of copies of public records and they then become acceptable as evidence in a court of law. The *Scottish Record Office* has power to issue extracts or certified copies of any records transmitted to the Keeper of the Records of Scotland.
See also **UK documents abroad: verification.**

Records: Births, Marriages and Deaths Records of births, marriages and deaths are preserved at the *General Register Office* for England and Wales since 1 July 1837; at the *General Register Office (Scotland)* for Scotland since 1855; and at the *General Register Office (Dublin)* for Northern Ireland from 1864 to 1921 and the *General Register Office (Belfast)* since 1922. (See also **Registers of births, marriages and deaths**).
Records of Church of England births, marriages and deaths since the 16th century are held in parish registers and bishops' transcripts; apply in the first instance to the record office of the appropriate diocese, usually the county record office. Diocesan records of the Church of Wales are in the *National Library of Wales*; parish registers of the Church of Scotland from 1553 onwards are preserved in the General Register Office (Scotland), which also holds decennial census records for Scotland from 1841 to 1891. Roman Catholic registers are generally in the custody of priests-in-charge of local churches. There are no Jewish registers.
Since the mid-19th century, earlier non-parochial registers (i.e. records of births, marriages and deaths solemnised outside the C of E and not necessarily notified to parish officials despite the Registration Act of 1695) were deposited centrally in England and Wales and are now held at the *Pubic Record Office*. The PRO also houses the register of the Independent Church of St Petersburg 1818–40; **censuses** of population since 1841; British military service records, militia musters with records of immigrants and emigrants and records of seamen; tithe records; enclosure awards; and records relating to America and the colonies, and the American Revolution. Records of baptisms, marriages and burials abroad (1706–1739) which have been returned to the UK are preserved in the *Guildhall Library*, London, or *Lambeth Palace Library*, London, or, for India and Burma, the *India Office Library and Records*.
See also **Birth registration; Death registration; Marriage.**

Records: Public and Historical UK official documents over 30 years old are generally open to public inspection and are called public records; they extend back to the 11th century. Most are housed by the *Public Record Office*. To inspect them obtain a reader's ticket (corporate tickets available to organisations) from the PRO by sending an application form and a recommendation from a recognised institution or person.
It is advisable to find out whether the records to be searched are at Kew or Chancery Lane. 'British National Archives' (government sectional list 24 from *Her Majesty's Stationery Office*) lists indexes and guides to the pub-

lished documents and published facsimiles, and gives transcripts and précis of certain original documents. Photocopying, typewriting and tape-recording facilities are available.

Government records normally become open for inspection 30 years after their creation; exceptions (earlier or later) may be prescribed by the Lord Chancellor. Records of parliament since 1487 are housed in the *House of Lords Record Office* (some from before 1487 are in the PRO); births, marriages and deaths in England and Wales in the *General Register Office* and the *General Register Office (Scotland)*; Northern Ireland records in the *Public Record Office of Northern Ireland* and the office of the *Registrar General for Northern Ireland*.

Some government departments maintain their own records and provide facilities for inspection, e.g. the *Probate Registry* (principal office) holds wills since 1858, and the *India Office Libary and Records* holds records of the former India Office, the East India Company and the Indian Army. The Lord Chancellor is advised in maintaining the services of the PRO by the *Advisory Council on Public Records*. The *National Register of Archives* catalogues privately-owned records which may be consulted by historical researchers, and is compiled by the *Royal Commission on Historical Manuscripts*.

The *National Register of Archives (Scotland)* is a branch of the Scottish Record Office. The Secretary of State for Scotland is advised by the *Scottish Records Advisory Council* on questions relating to the public records of Scotland.

See also **Records: births, marriages and deaths; Royal archives.**

Recreational Facilities Facilities for physical recreation such as adventure playgrounds, youth clubs, holiday camps, school camps, playing fields and play centres must be provided (in a manner at their own discretion) by *local education authorities*.

See also **Education: Scotland; Education: Northern Ireland.**

Red Deer Red deer are controlled by the *Red Deer Commission*.

Redundancy Employers are required to make a lump-sum compensation payment to male employees under 65 and female employees under 60 who are dismissed because of redundancy, or in certain circumstances laid off or kept on short-time, after serving at least 104 weeks reckonable service since the age of 18.

Employees must claim payment within six months of termination of employment. If they cannot secure payment from the employer (e.g. he is insolvent) payment may be claimed from the Redundancy Fund on application to the *Department of Employment Unemployment Benefit Office*. (See **Employer's insolvency.**)

Employers must notify the DE about redundancies in advance and may reclaim 41% of the redundancy payment from the Redundancy Fund up to six months after the payment. Certain types of redundancies must be notified 60 or 90 days before the first dismissals.

Employers are required by law to consult in advance any **trade union** which they may recognise as representing the group or category of employees they are proposing to dismiss as redundant.

Disputes about entitlement to redundancy payments or about rebates from the Fund are referred to **industrial tribunals** for arbitration. Application should be made within six months of the effective date of termination of employment to DEm Unemployment Benefit Office; appeals (on points of law only) to the *Employment Appeal Tribunal*.

While serving notice, redundant employees with a minimum of two years' service with their employer are entitled to reasonable time off with pay to look for new employment or make arrangements for training for future employment. Complaints of non-compliance are referred to industrial tribunals via DEm offices.

See also **Employment: terms and conditions.**

Refugees The UK government department responsible for refugees is the *Home Office* (public enquiry office open from 9.00 a.m. to 4.00 p.m. Monday to Friday; telephone enquiries

bureau 01-686-0688). Applications to enter the UK as a refugee are considered individually and on their merits. Where an international operation is mounted, a share of the refugees may be accepted by the UK alongside other participating countries, as determined by the United Nations.
See also **Political asylum**.

Regional Development Grants Grants at 20% (22% in the special development areas) are available in England, Scotland and Wales towards capital expenditure incurred in providing new buildings or works (other than mining works) and adaptations of existing buildings on premises used wholly or mainly for qualifying activities in special development areas, development areas and intermediate areas (see **Assisted areas**); and new machinery or plant for use in premises used wholly or mainly for qualifying activities in those areas.

Qualifying activities mainly encompass manufacturing, processing of scrap and certain repair activities, together with scientific research and training of staff relating to any other qualifying activity. Mining and construction were qualifying activities up to 1 November 1976 and grants may be available on expenditure defrayed before 6 August 1976 or on assets provided before 1 April 1977.

Grants apply to capital expenditure defrayed on or after 22 March 1972 provided that, for buildings, construction was not begun before that date. Applications are subject to time limits and should be made not later than two years after the end of the quarter during which the asset was provided.

Application forms and full details of the scheme from *Department of Industry Regional Development Grants Committee*.

For assistance to industry in Northern Ireland, see **Industry: Northern Ireland**.

Register of Births, Deaths and Marriages In England and Wales statutory records of all births, deaths and marriages since 1837 are contained in the registers of the Registrar General for England and Wales. An alphabetical index to the registers can be consulted free of charge in the Public Search Room at the *General Register Office*. The registers are not open to the public but certificates of certified copies of any reference selected from the index can be bought.

In Scotland statutory registers of all births, deaths and marriages since 1855 are in the custody of the Registrar General for Scotland; alphabetical indexes may be consulted at the *General Register Office (Scotland)*, from which information about charges for access and extracts is available.

In Northern Ireland the registers of the *Registrar General for Northern Ireland* contain records of all births, deaths and Roman Catholic marriages in Northern Ireland since 1 January 1864 and other marriages since 1 April 1845. Births and deaths registers from 1864 and certified copies of marriages from 1 January 1922 are held in the *General Register Office (Belfast)*. Original registers of Northern Ireland marriages from 1845 are in the custody of the 26 registrars of births, deaths and marriages (situated mainly in district council offices in principal towns) and of the clergy. Searches may be made and certificates issued for requisite fees.
See also **Records of births, marriages and deaths**.

Registration of Births and Deaths Overseas British **consuls** in foreign countries can register the births and deaths of citizens of the UK and colonies within their consular districts; apply to the appropriate British Consulate (see separate entries on individual countries) or to the *Foreign and Commonwealth Office, Nationality and Treaty Department*. Full documentary evidence of UK citizenship must be produced.

A child of the second or subsequent generation born abroad will normally only become a UK citizen if and when its birth is entered in the consular register; this should be done within a year of birth, otherwise permission of the Secretary of State, FCO, must be obtained. It is only granted in exceptional circumstances.

British High Commissioners in Commonwealth countries (addresses under

British diplomatic missions) also maintain registers for recording the births and deaths of citizens of the UK and colonies and certain other categories of **British subjects**.

All births and deaths registered by British officials abroad are recorded centrally in the *General Register Office* in London, from which certificates can be obtained.

See also **Birth registration; Death registration; Citizenship of the UK and colonies**.

Regius Professors Regius professors and certain academic appointments (e.g. the Master of Trinity College, Cambridge) are made by the Sovereign on the advice of the *Prime Minister*, following soundings by the Secretary for Appointments at the Prime Minister's Office.

Rehabilitation of Offenders Criminal convictions carrying sentences of less than two and half years become 'spent' under the Rehabilitation of Offenders Act 1974 if no further conviction occurs during the rehabilitation period, which varies according to the sentence for the original offence. Once a conviction has become spent the convicted person does not have to reveal or admit its existence in most circumstances. An employer cannot generally refuse to employ, or act to dismiss, someone because they have a spent conviction. Convictions carrying sentences of more than two and a half years, however, can never become spent.

Police records are kept of spent convictions, but these cannot be disclosed to anyone unless there is an official reason. Spent convictions can be disclosed in subsequent criminal proceedings or in any proceedings to do with children, but not in any other civil proceedings unless the judge is satisfied that justice cannot otherwise be done.

Failure by an employer to observe the requirements of the Act is an offence; complain to the *police*.

See also **Criminal court proceedings; Criminal sentences**.

Remedial Gymnasts Remedial gymnasts practising in the **National Health Service** must be state registered by the Remedial Gymnasts' Board of the *Council for Professions Supplementary to Medicine*. Basic qualification for registration is the certificate of the *Society of Remedial Gymnasts* following a three-year training (or a shortened training of 18 months for those holding a Diploma in Physical Education, and members of HM Forces attaining the Advanced Course Certificate in Physical Training Instruction).

The Remedial Gymnasts' Board publishes an annual register, which is available at public libraries. NHS remedial gymnasts treat only those people who are referred to them by a **doctor**.

Complaints about professional misconduct are investigated by the Remedial Gymnasts Board of the CPSM. Complaints about disciplinary matters concerning NHS employees are investigated by the employing authority (the *area health authority* or Board of Governors in England and Wales, the *Health Board* in Scotland or the *Department of Health and Social Services* in Northern Ireland). Address complaints to the relevant body.

Removal Expenses Removal expenses are paid under the employment transfer scheme to people unemployed or threatened with redundancy who obtain new work beyond normal travelling distance from home; under the key workers scheme to employees transferred beyond daily travelling distance of home to key posts (i.e. accepted as such by the *Employment Service Agency*) in new establishments in special development, development or intermediate areas; and under the nucleus labour force scheme to previously unemployed workers recruited by firms establishing new units in areas of high unemployment who are temporarily transferred for training. Under the last scheme the assistance is limited, as the workers will return to the home area, but otherwise removal expenses include travel, settling-in, support for dependants and up to 75% of legal and agents' fees in buying and selling houses. Apply to *Employment*

Service Agency Employment Office or *Employment Service Agency Job Centre*.
See also **Assisted areas; Employment**.

Rent Charges Rent charges on freehold property, in the form of perpetual annual rent, ground rent or chief rent, may be redeemed. Apply to *Department of the Environment* in England, in Scotland to the Scottish Development Department, or in Wales to the Welsh Office.
See also **Housing: leasehold**.

Rent Rebates and Allowances Tenants of furnished and unfurnished accommodation may qualify for assistance towards paying the rent. Local authorities and *New Town Development Corporations* (see **New towns**) operate rent rebate schemes for their own tenants and local authorities also operate rent allowance schemes for private tenants in their areas. Three things are taken into account: size of family; gross income; and amount of rent (excluding **rates** and charges for furniture and most other services). See 'There's money off rent' from local authorities or *Department of the Environment* (in Scotland from *Scottish Information Office*). Apply to: the local authority rent rebate and allowance officer or, for new town tenants, to the rent rebate officer at the appropriate NTDC.
See also **Rate rebates; Housing**.

Repatriation from the UK People subject to UK **immigration** control who wish to leave the UK permanently may get financial assistance from UK public funds towards their travel costs, if this is thought to be in their best interests. Apply to *International Social Services of Great Britain*.

Repatriation to the UK If citizens of the UK and colonies, resident in the UK, run short of funds during a trip abroad, they should try to make their own arrangements (e.g. by contacting their family, bank or friends). If all other means fail, however, British **consuls** may, against the applicant's undertaking to pay the debt and the restriction of his **passport** for further travel, arrange his return to the UK at the cheapest rate. Apply to the nearest British consul (addresses given under *British diplomatic missions*). Full passport facilities are not normally restored until expenses and the consular fee are repaid. Consular officers are not empowered to settle debts incurred by UK nationals abroad.
See also **Citizenship of the UK and colonies**.

Rescue: Air, Land, Sea After receiving an emergency 999 telephone call, the police summon the nearest, quickest and most appropriate service available (e.g. lifeboat, military helicopter or civilian rescue team). Two Royal Air Force co-ordination centres exist, one in southern England and one in Scotland, to speed this process. Ministry of Defence policy is that Army, Navy and RAF rescue facilities (which include mountain rescue teams) primarily serve the Forces but will, if available, aid civilians in distress. Search and rescue at sea is the responsibility of *Her Majesty's Coasguard Service*, administered by the *Department of Trade*. The Coastguard initiate and co-ordinate civil marine search and rescue operations in liaison with the *Royal National Lifeboat Institution*, the Royal Navy, Royal Air Force through the Post Office, civil air traffic control centres and other vessels at sea and, if necessary, with the search and rescue services of other nations responsible for adjacent sea areas. To enquire about missing vessels at sea, ask the Coastguard.
Search and rescue operations for military personnel and also for civil aircraft in distress are the responsibility of the *Ministry of Defence*.
Under the Yacht and Boat Safety Scheme, a detailed description of small boats going to sea may be filed annually with the Coastguard on a special form (CG66) from coastguard stations, harbour masters, yacht clubs and marinas. Thereafter the Coastguard will record any information received about each craft by telephone before departure, from intermediate stops, or by sightings. Change of itinerary should be notified to the Coastguard. See 'Coastguard Yacht

and Boat Safety Scheme' leaflet from Coastguard or DoT.

Research Grants Grants for research work in the sciences and social sciences are available from the five independent research councils set up by the government and partially financed by the *Department of Education and Science*. (See also **Humanities**.)

Agricultural and veterinary research: Grants for work in all science relevant to agriculture are available from the *Agricultural Research Council*. They may be made to increase the effort on an established line of research or to facilitate the development of a new technique or new approach to a fundamental problem. Apply to the Research Grants Board at the ARC. The ARC is financed jointly by the DES, the *Ministry of Agriculture, Fisheries and Food* and the *Department of Agriculture and Fisheries* in Scotland. It also awards grants each year to 30 graduates in science or veterinary science to study for a PhD at one of the ARC's own institutes or one of the state-aided institutes. Apply to the Training section at the ARC.

Medical research: The *Medical Research Council* provides funds for research in all subjects related to the biomedical sciences, the main areas being neurobiology and mental health; cell biology and cell disorders; physiological systems and physiological disorders; tropical medicine; environmental, occupational and social medicine. These funds support projects and programmes of research; fellowships to be held in the UK and abroad; postgraduate studentships; block grants to designated research institutes; and the MRC's own research units and other laboratories. Details of the MRC's research programme are in the MRC Handbook and in its Annual Report.

Medical sciences postgraduate awards: Grants are available in all fields of biomedical research from the *Medical Research Council* to postgraduate and postdoctoral scientists as well as to clinicians. Postgraduate studentships' places are allocated annually on a quota basis to applicant departments; the heads of departments select eligible students for nomination to the MRC.

Eligibility includes an hons I or II degree and a period of normal residence in the UK. Training fellowships at postdoctoral and post-registration levels are awarded for research training at an annual competition; a small number of travelling fellowships is also available annually.

A Training Awards Panel is responsible both for allocations and awards. Closing dates are advertised in the scientific press and by notification to departments.

Natural environment research: Grants in the geological, terrestrial ecology, freshwater and marine biological sciences and also in physical oceanography, hydrology and atmospheric sciences are made by the *Natural Environment Research Council* to supplement the resources derived from the University Grants Committee or elsewhere which the institution (university, polytechnic or technical college) is already applying to the support of research. The Council's own research establishments also provide research facilities.

Natural science postgraduates: Grants for training in the geological, terrestrial, freshwater and marine biological sciences and also in physical oceanography, hydrology and atmospheric sciences are made to enable students to continue their training beyond a good honours first degree by the *Natural Environment Research Council*; enquiries to University Support Section at the NERC: The major awards are advanced course studentships lasting one year and research studentships tenable for up to three years. Applications for studentships must be submitted through the institution in which the student proposes to work by the head of department or research school. Applications are not accepted direct from individual students.

Science research: The *Science Research Council* supports basic research and postgraduate training in astronomy, the biological sciences, chemistry, engineering, mathematics and physics. Most of the SRC resources go to helping research workers in universities, colleges, and polytechnics carry out research (SRC research grants) and to enabling graduates in science and engineering to train further in methods of research (SRC studentships) or to do full-time original and independent research (SRC fellowships). Support and research facilities for university research are provided at the SRC's research establishments and through SRC membership of international organisations (e.g. the European Organisation for Nuclear Research, the European Space Agency, the 150-inch Anglo-Australian Telescope, the Institut Laue-Langevin and the European Incoherent Scatter Project).

The SRC awards its studentships through the heads of the departments or research schools where the awards are to be held. Details of all the special postgraduate, postdoctoral and industrially oriented schemes are in the SRC booklet 'Studentships and Fellowships'.

The *Royal Society of London*, the national academy of sciences in Great Britain, administers a parliamentary grant-in-aid for scientific investigations and publications, and represents Great Britain to the member-unions of the International Council of Scientific Unions (unions for astronomy, biochemistry, biology, biophysics, chemistry, crystallography, geodesy, and geophysics, geography, geology, mathematics, nutritional sciences, pharmacology, physics, physiological science, scientific radio, theoretical and applied mechanics and history of science, medicine and technology). The RSL, which has no UK institutes or laboratories of its own, usually makes its appointments to a university. Current appointments include 14 research professors and 30 research fellowships; visiting fellowships for research both in Britain and overseas are available. Details in the RSL's Yearbook; enquiries to the executive secretary at the RSL.

Social science research: The *Social Science Research Council* awards grants towards work at universities, polytechnics and institutions of higher education in economics, education, ethnic relations, industrial relations, management, planning, social administration, psychology, economic and social history, social anthropology, computing and linguistics. Further advice from the secretary of each subject committee at the SSRC. Project and programme grants are available.

Grants for postgraduate courses in economics, education, ethnic relations, industrial relations, management, planning, social administration, psychology, economic and social history, social anthropology and computing are available to students who have been accepted by a British university on a course of study approved by the *Social Science Research Council*. Enquiries to the Postgraduate Training Division at the SSRC; applications direct to the university.

Reserve and Auxiliary Forces The Territorial and Army Volunteer Reserve, a part-time army of civilians, becomes part of the regular army in time of national emergency. Volunteers have the same uniform, equipment and training standards as the regular army; are committed to at least two weeks' camp each year plus four or 12 days' training depending on the unit and receive pay during training. Apply to the local TAVR centre, Army Careers Information Office or TAVR Association (all in telephone directory under Army).

The Ulster Defence Regiment is a volunteer regiment which operates in Northern Ireland. It is officered by regular army officers and is under the command of the General Officer Commanding Northern Ireland. Apply to *Ulster Defence Regiment Headquarters*.

The Royal Auxiliary Air Force, largely composed of part-time civilians, mans the R.Aux.A.F. Maritime Headquarters Unit – mainly communications and signals. Enquiries to *Royal Auxiliary Air Force No. 1 Maritime Headquarters Unit*.

The Royal Observer Corps, a uniformed organisation responsible to the Ministry of Defence, is a key field force of the UK Warning and Monitoring Organisation against nuclear attack. It has special equipment and has been trained to plot and report nuclear

bursts and to monitor the travel of resultant nuclear fall-out. ROC recruits men and women from all walks of life aged between 16 and 55 to spend one evening a week and a few week-ends a year training for duty at Operations Rooms and Monitoring Posts throughout the UK. Apply to *Royal Observer Corps Headquarters* or the ROC local commandant (see telephone directory). The Royal Naval Reserve is a part-time volunteer force which buttresses the professional manpower of the Royal Navy; general enquiries to the *Royal Naval Reserve Sea Training Centres*; enquiries about specialist entry for mercantile marine officers to the nearest *Naval Liaison Officer* or the Admiral Commanding Reserves at the *Ministry of Defence (Navy)*; about entry for communications and headquarters units to the Commanding Officer at the *Royal Naval Reserve Communications Training Centre* or the *Royal Naval Reserve Shore Headquarters Unit*; and for the postal branch (post office employees only) through post offices.
The Royal Marines Reserve is a part-time force which now recruits people other than ex-Royal Marines; enquiries to *Royal Marines Reserve.*

Restrictive Covenants on Land These may be discharged or modified on application to *Land Tribunals.* Applications are advertised and the Tribunal hears objections before reaching a decision.

Retirement Pension A retirement pension is paid as a **social security benefit** to men (from age 65) and women (from age 60) who have retired from work, and to men over 70 and women over 65 whether retired or not; recipients must have paid **national insurance contributions** up to a qualifying level in about 90% of working life. Non-contributory retirement pension is payable to people over 80 who have not contributed but meet specific residence criteria. Retirement pension comprises: basic pension due to national insurance contributions; increase for a wife (or sometimes another adult dependant) who does not draw a retirement pension in her own right; increase for dependent children; graduated pension earned by graduated contributions; extra pension if pension deferred; and age addition for people aged 80 or over.
Invalidity allowance (see **Invalidity**), and Attendance allowance for severely disabled people (see **Disablement: social security benefits**) may also be paid with retirement pension. A pensioner may also qualify for a supplementary pension (see **Supplementary benefit**). Earnings during the first five years after the minimum pension age should not exceed the amount allowed under the 'earnings rule' if the rate of pension payable is not to be reduced; see leaflet NI196, from *Department of Health and Social Security* (local offices). Retirement pension may also be reduced after eight weeks as an in-patient in hospital; it forms part of income for tax purposes. The DHSS usually sends a claim form automatically about four months before retirement age; if not received enquire at DHSS local offices in good time before retirement. Pension is normally paid weekly in advance through post offices, or four-weekly or quarterly in arrears by crossed order on application (see DHSS leaflet NI105); it can generally be paid abroad if desired. See DHSS leaflets NI15 (retirement pension), and NI184 (over-80's).
Wives who are over 60 and retire receive a pension on their husband's national insurance contributions when the husband qualifies. They may qualify for a pension on their own contributions if satisfying the relevant conditions, but both the husband's and wife's pension cannot now be paid at the same time. (From April 1979 a wife will be able to combine her entitlement on her own contribution with that on her husband's contributions.) A wife may receive graduated pension for any graduated contributions she has paid herself. Wives under 60 do not get a pension, but the husband's pension may be increased for her as a dependant. Widows over 60 generally qualify for basic retirement pension or for Widows' benefit (see **Widow's benefits**). Wives must

claim separately to DHSS local offices for a pension on the husband's contributions; see leaflets NI15B (married women), and NI15A (pension for widows).
From April 1978 a new state pension scheme applies, the benefits of which will begin to be paid from April 1979. It comprises an inflation-proofed basic pension and an additional earnings-related pension. The basic pension is equivalent to the present flat-rate national insurance retirement pension and is subject to fulfilment of the present contribution conditions. The amount of the additional pension earned year by year will be $1\frac{1}{4}$ % of that part of earnings which lies between the lower and upper earnings limits for the payment of contributions. (The lower earnings limit about equals the single person's basic pension, and the upper limit is about seven times that amount.)
Once the scheme has been in operation for more than 20 years, the additional pension will be based on the best 20 years of earnings within the scheme; the maximum additional pension will then be 25% ($20 \times 1\frac{1}{4}$). People retiring within 20 years may receive full basic pension, but a proportionately reduced additional pension. Graduated pension for graduated contributions up to 6 April 1975 is paid in addition on retirement. Earnings-related contributions continue but the percentage of earnings contributions are reduced for those in a 'contracted out' occupational pension scheme (see **Occupational pensions**).
Women who contributed receive the same benefits as men and basic pension rights are preserved during a period away from work to bring up a family, or to care for a sick relative. But if a married woman or widow pays reduced rate contributions she will not benefit under these arrangements. A wife who is not eligible to a pension in her own right may qualify for a basic pension on her husband's contributions. A widow may add her husband's additional pension to any pension earned by her own contributions. See leaflet NP30 (New pensions), available from DHSS local offices. Invalidity pension and widows' benefit will also be based on the new pension scheme from 1 April 1978.

Rhodesia Following Rhodesia's illegal declaration of independence, there is no UK diplomatic mission in Rhodesia and no Rhodesian mission in London. Normal UK **exchange control** rules do not apply. UK residents are advised to consult their bankers before engaging in any business or effecting any transaction involving Rhodesian residents. The *Foreign and Commonwealth Office Consular Department* should be consulted before travel to Rhodesia.

Riding Internationally, all competitive riding, show jumping, combined training (or horse trials) dressage and combined driving, is governed by the Fédération Equestre Internationale. The UK affiliated federation is the *British Equestrian Federation* which represents both the *British Horse Society* and the *British Show Jumping Association* in international affairs.
The BHS, which incorporates the *Pony Club* (for young riders) and affiliated riding clubs, is the UK governing body for all aspects of riding other than show jumping. It administers an approved riding establishment scheme, employs an inspectorate to watch for cases of neglect and inefficiency, and organises internationally-recognised instructors' examinations.
The BSJA is responsible for UK show jumping and its rules and conditions. No rider can take part in official shows unless he is a member of BSJA and his horse is registered with BSJA. The BHS, BSJA and Pony Club have regional branches throughout the UK.

Riding Establishments These must be licensed annually by the local authority. Livery stables and private stables do not need licences.

Road Accidents Drivers of vehicles involved in road accidents in which injury is caused to someone else or damage is caused to another motor vehicle (or animal or other property on or near the road) must stop. They must give their names and addresses (and the owners') and the vehicles registration number to anyone with reasonable grounds for requiring them; if someone else is injured they must also produce a certificate of insurance. Drivers who do not give their names and addresses should report the accident to the *police* as soon as possible and in any case within 24 hours; insurance certificates (where necessary) should be produced within five days.

At the time of the accident it is useful for insurance and legal purposes to record the names and addresses of independent witnesses and other drivers, owners and **insurance companies** concerned; the number of all relevant certificates of insurance; the registration numbers and damage to other vehicles involved; damage or injury to people; date, time and exact location of the accident; the circumstances of the accident including speeds, road width, road signs, the weather, condition of road surface and tyre marks; the final position of vehicles in the accident (plus sketch map); and the identification of any police officers to whom particulars are given. Consult a **solicitor**.

Road Haulage: International Permits
The UK has concluded bilateral agreements with 22 European countries to ensure the freer movement of UK goods abroad, and to assure hauliers of consistent treatment at the hands of foreign authorities. Under 11 of the 22 agreements (those not marked 'liberal' in the table opposite) goods vehicles from one country must be authorised in advance by a permit when travelling to another country party to the agreement. On production of the permit at the border, the haulier is allowed to pass into or through the country. He may still have to pay some local taxes, depending on the terms of the agreement. Permits are allocated by the *Department of Transport International Road Freight Office*.

For road haulage to all other countries, hauliers must deal direct with that country's authorities to obtain permission to carry goods there. Such permission could involve payment of extra road or fuel tax on application for a temporary licence to operate in the country concerned. Permission to enter may also be withheld.

Apart from bilateral permits, small quotas of multilateral permits are issued to UK hauliers for use in the EEC (272 permits) and European Conference of Ministers of Transport countries (20 permits). These are normally valid for one year and authorise any number of journeys through any or all of the member states of each organisation. They and their accompanying journey record books are again allocated and issued by the DTpIRFO, which is also responsible for monitoring their usage.

Road Planning   Planning of trunk roads is the responsibility of the *Secretary of State for Transport* and is handled locally by the *Department of Transport Road Construction Units* or the *Department of Transport Regional Offices*. Other roads are the responsibility of **local authorities** (county councils or in London the *Greater London Council* or London borough councils); apply to the local authority concerned for details of procedures, or to local *Highway Authority* for details of current schemes.

For new trunk roads the procedure is that the practicable alternative routes are first investigated; then a consultation document (available from local authorities, local libraries and sometimes post offices) is published describing the alternative routes with general information on costs, broad environmental effects and other relevant factors; a public exhibition is held of maps and plans of the route; a questionnaire with the consultation document allows individuals to state their preferences and factors in their choice; comments are taken into account in deciding the route to be developed; and the decision is published with a summary of the response and reasons for the choice of the preferred route.

Schemes where there are no genuine alternatives and schemes which are urgently required and do not raise important environmental considera-

Bilateral road haulage agreements between UK and 22 European countries

Country	Types of permit	Size of quota
Austria	Quota	3,400 (approx.)
Belgium	Liberal	—
Bulgaria	Liberal	—
Czechoslovakia	Permits	No limit
Denmark	Liberal	—
Finland	Quota	1,500
France	General quota	38,000
	Co-op quota	8,500
Germany (East)		
GDR	Permits	No limit
Germany (West)	General quota	8,250
GFR	NATO	2,000
	Co-op quota	1,500
	Short distance transit	2,500
	West Berlin	180
Greece	Liberal	—
Hungary	Quota	2,500
Italy	General quota	4,450
Luxembourg	Liberal	—
Netherlands	Liberal	—
Norway	Liberal	—
Poland	Liberal at present	—
Portugal	General quota	325
	Unaccompanied trailer	440
	Co-op quota	125
Romania	Liberal	—
Spain	Quota	2,500
Sweden	Liberal	—
Switzerland	Liberal	—
Yugoslavia	Quota: Non-Taxable	1,000 terminating
	Non-Taxable	1,000 transit
	Taxable	3,000

tions, are not subject to public consultation on alternatives. But a full statement describing the scheme is still issued.

Once the preferred route is announced, the line of the new road is published as a formal proposal under the Highway Acts and given publicity, including advertisement in local newspapers and (normally) individual notification to occupiers of houses along or close to the line of the road; these notices say where the proposal, with plans and an explanatory statement, can be inspected during a specified period (never less than six weeks). Normally this is the *Department of Transport Headquarters* in London, the *DoT Regional Office* or the *DoT Road Construction Unit* concerned, the local authority office and local public libraries; and sometimes also post offices. Comments and objections at this stage can be sent to the DoT office named in the advertisement.

A public inquiry may be held, depending on the objections and the issues (details in 'Public inquiries into Road Proposals – what you will need to know' from *Department of Transport* (Information Division). The Secretary of State considers the objections and any Inspector's Report from a public inquiry. If the Secretary of State intends to modify the proposals substantially, he has to take into account the views of land-owners or tenants who may be newly or differently affected; these are consulted and given time to make their views known.

Objectors are finally notified individually of the decision and a notice appears in local newspapers. The land can then be acquired and work proceed. Rules for alterations to other roads, footpaths and private accesses are much the same; proposals are published and objections can be made.

Road Safety Advice on road safety in Great Britain is the responsibility of **local authorities**; enquiries to local authority road safety officers. In Northern Ireland advice is available from the *Department of the Environment (Northern Ireland)* road safety officers, who may be contacted through the local offices of the five *Education and Library Boards*.

Roads: Land Acquisition Acquisition of land for road development normally needs a **compulsory purchase** order, and all known owners and occupiers of property are notified when it is published. But before this the district valuer may ask landowners if they are willing to sell by agreement, and offer to negotiate on behalf of the Secretary of State for Transport.
Earlier still, a road proposal may make it difficult for someone wishing to move to get a fair price for his house. Once a decision about a preferred route is announced (see **Road planning**) and provided certain conditions laid down in the Town and Country Planning Act 1971 are met, the *Department of Transport* can be made to buy a property if it is on that route. Until that announcement is made the DTp cannot be made to buy blighted property, but may do so where there is hardship.
See also **Compulsory purchase: compensation**.

Romania For **exchange control** is a non-scheduled territory outside the **overseas sterling area** and the **EEC**. UK nationals travelling direct from the UK normally need only the following (but check): **passports**; **visas**; **work permits** (if taking a job); green cards for motor insurance (if bringing a car: see **Motoring abroad**).

UK reciprocal arrangements cover health but not social security. Medical treatment free (medicines charged) on production of UK passport and evidence of normal UK residence, e.g. **National Health Service medical card**.
Enquiries to *Romanian Embassy* in London and *Romanian Information Office* in London.
British diplomatic mission to Romania is *British Embassy* in Bucharest.

Rowing Rowing is governed internationally (standardisation of rules, international regattas, licensing of umpires) by the Fédération Internationale des Sociétés d'Aviron. In the UK the *Amateur Rowing Association* is the governing body which sets racing rules, qualifies coaches and selects UK teams.
Regattas are co-ordinated in England and Wales by the ARA, in Scotland by the *Scottish Amateur Rowing Association* and in Ireland by the *Irish Amateur Rowing Union*. Members of the associations are clubs, regattas and individuals. The *Hants and Dorset Amateur Rowing Association*, *West of England Amateur Rowing Association* and *Coast Rowing Association* control rowing on sea and estuary and have their own rules and national championships.

Royal The use of the title Royal requires the consent of the Sovereign. It is the duty of the Home Secretary to advise the Sovereign on this matter. It is granted very sparingly. Application should be made to the *Home Office*.

Royal Academy Summer Exhibition The *Royal Academy of Arts* accepts submissions for exhibition from living artists of any nationality. About 1,300 works are normally chosen from over 11,500 submissions. Dates and details are contained in the Notice to Artists available from the secretary every February. The exhibition is the UK's largest contemporary art show.
See also **Arts: Royal Academy of**; **Arts: support**.

Royal Archives Access to the Royal Archives is restricted. For access, apply to the Assistant Keeper of the *Royal Archives* at Windsor Castle.
See also **Records: public and historical**.

Royal Arms and Emblems The Home Secretary has a constitutional responsibility to advise the Queen on the granting of royal arms and emblems. Applications to the *Home Office*, which consults with the Garter-King-of-Arms at the *College of Arms* and then conveys Her Majesty's decision. The Lord Lyon King of Arms at the *Court of Lord Lyon* exercises the Crown's jurisdiction in armorial matters in Scotland.
See also **Armorial bearings; Heralds**.

Royal Charters Royal charters are granted by royal prerogative to bodies in Great Britain and the Commonwealth, mainly to benevolent institutions, learned societies, scientific and professional institutions, bodies promoting the arts or education and similar organisations which are not run for profit. They are generally conferred in recognition of outstanding achievement in a particular sphere. The first step is to send a petition and outline of the proposed charter to the *Privy Council Office*. The PCO then publishes notice of receipt of the petition in the 'London Gazette' (and the 'Edinburgh Gazette' in Scottish cases), inviting objections to or comments on the petition. The petition and charter, with any objections and the petitioners' answers, are referred, by an Order in Council, to the Privy Council, which will include representatives of the interested government departments.
If approved, the Order approving the charter is signed by the Clerk of the Privy Council and sent with the charter to the *Home Office, Scottish Office* or *Welsh Office*, as appropriate, for sealing. Subsequently the *Lord Chancellor's Office* (England and Wales) or the *Crown Office* (Scotland) arranges for the Queen's signature. Letters patent are then issued to the body concerned.

No prior indication can be given as to the possibility of an application being successful and, in cases where a petition is submitted and the application for the grant of a charter is rejected, in no circumstances can reasons be given for this rejection.

Royal Garden Parties These may be attended only by invitation issued on behalf of the Queen by the *Lord Chamberlain*. Lists of recommendations are submitted to the Lord Chamberlain by the armed services, professions and a very large number of societies, organisations and public bodies, in accordance with pre-arranged quotas; it is from these that invitation lists are compiled. Applications from individuals cannot be considered.

Royal Honours These (Order of the Garter, Order of the Thistle, Order of Merit, Royal Victorian Order, and Royal Victorian Chain) are entirely in the gift of the Queen and no ministerial recommendation is involved.
See also **Gallantry awards: civil; Gallantry awards: military; Honours**.

Royal Horticultural Society Advice is available from the *Royal Horticultural Society* to all its fellows. Fellowship (open to any individual interested in gardening for a modest subscription), entitles you to fellow's tickets for free admission to the RHS gardens at Wisley and to the RHS shows and meetings including the **Chelsea Flower Show**. Tickets are transferable. Other RHS services include a library, fruit identifications, garden inspections, soil, etc., analyses.
See also **Flower and vegetable trials; Horticultural crops**.

Royal Maundy The selection of recipients for the Royal Maundy ceremony is based on service to the church and community. Recipients should be aged 65 or over and should reside in the area or diocese in which the Royal Maundy service is held. It is customary for the names of likely candidates to be recommended by clergy or ministers from churches of varying denominations.

Royal Navy Supplies Delivery of duty-free food and drink, tobacco and matches for use on board HM Ships requires revenue authority; apply to *Her Majesty's Customs and Excise* (details in Notice 428).
See also **Customs duty; Excise duty.**

Royal Patronage Applications for patronage by the Queen should be addressed to the Keeper of the Privy Purse at *Buckingham Palace*. For other members of the royal family, write to their individual private secretaries at *Buckingham Palace* (Duke of Edinburgh, Prince of Wales, Princess Anne); *Clarence House* (Queen Mother); *Kensington Palace* (Princess Margaret, Princess Alice Duchess of Gloucester, Duke and Duchess of Gloucester, Prince Michael of Kent, Princess Alice Countess of Athlone); *St James's Palace* (Duke and Duchess of Kent, Princess Alexandra). Patronage is only given to institutions which have proved through time and results that they are firmly established and on a sound financial basis.

Royal Visits Members of the royal family accept invitations to attend a large variety of functions, e.g. opening a new building or celebrating a centenary. Invitations should be addressed to the private secretary of the member of the royal family invited at *Buckingham Palace* (The Queen, Duke of Edinburgh, the Prince of Wales, Princess Anne); *Clarence House* (Queen Mother); *Kensington Palace* (Princess Margaret, Princess Alice Duchess of Gloucester, Duke and Duchess of Gloucester, Prince Michael, Princess Alice Countess of Athlone); or *St James's Palace* (the Duke and Duchess of Kent, Princess Alexandra).

Royal Warrants of Appointment Warrants are granted to individual tradesmen by the Queen, the Duke of Edinburgh and (from 1980) the Prince of Wales. The tradesmen's firms must have provided supplies or services directly for a period of three years; indirect supplies through a government department do not qualify. Application forms from the appropriate royal household or the secretary, Royal Household Tradesmen's Warrants Committee at the *Lord Chamberlain's Office.*

Rugby Football Rugby Union Football (team of 15 men) is governed internationally by the International Rugby Football Board which has two representatives each from England, Scotland, Ireland, Wales, New Zealand, South Africa and Australia. Within England the *Rugby Football Union* controls the game (its members are 3,500 amateur clubs and schools). It is responsible for all matters concerning playing, refereeing, coaching and administration but delegates local responsibility to its 33 constituent bodies (27 county unions, Oxford and Cambridge Universities, the three services and the Rugby Football Schools Union). The *Welsh Rugby Union*, the *Scottish Rugby Union* and the *Irish Rugby Football Union* control the game in their countries.
Rugby Football League (teams of 13) has an international board controlling the game for the UK, France, Australia, New Zealand, Papua and New Guinea. Within the UK it is played by 30 professional clubs and is governed by the *Rugby Football League* which is responsible for UK teams, colts, rules, tournaments, referees and discipline. The amateur game of rugby league is organised by the *British Amateur Rugby League Association.*

Rural Development Aid Small manufacturing and servicing industries in rural areas can be provided with advice and loans by the *Council for Small Industries in Rural Areas* in England, the *Development Board for Rural Wales*, the *Scottish Development Agency*, and the *Local Enterprise Development Unit* in Northern Ireland. In England small rural industries are those normally employing not more than 20 skilled people in country towns of up to 10,000 inhabitants; in Scotland, those employing up to 100 people in towns of up to 15,000 inhabitants. Small tourism enterprises providing overnight accommodation in rural parts of development areas are eligible for assistance; agriculture, horticulture and the retail trades are excluded. CoSIRA acts as the agent of the *Development Commission* within a broad policy framework laid down by the Commissioners. The Development Board for Rural Wales similarly acts as agent for the Welsh Development Agency. The Development Commision is an independent Royal Commission set up under the Development and Road Improvement Funds Acts of 1909 and 1910 to assist schemes in England intended to benefit the rural economy, provided that no other statutory source of funds exists. The Development Fund is used to provide small factories in selected rural areas and offers grants to voluntary bodies in the social field (Rural Community Councils and National Council of Social Service) and such schemes put forward by non-profit-making bodies as are considered by the Commission to enhance the rural economy. The *National Council of Social Service* may provide grants or loans to rural voluntary organisations – e.g. for the building of a village hall. General advice from CoSIRA (Advisory Service Division).

Rural Development Grants The *National Council of Social Services* provides loans to rural voluntary organisations, e.g. for building a village hall. In England the *Development Commission* offers grants to voluntary bodies in the social field through local county councils or the NCSS.
See also **Rural development aid; Small businesses in Wales.**

Rwanda For **exchange control** is a non-scheduled territory outside the **overseas sterling area** and the **EEC**. UK nationals travelling direct from the UK normally need only the following (but check): **passports; visas; work permits** (if taking a job); green cards for motor insurance (if bringing a car); international driving permits (if intending to drive: see **Motoring abroad**).
The UK has no reciprocal health or social security arrangements.
Enquiries to *Rwanda diplomatic missions to UK* at *Rwanda Embassy* in Brussels, Belgium.
The *British diplomatic mission* to Rwanda is the *British Embassy* at Kigali.

S

Sales of Goods When a purchase is made in the UK the seller and buyer enter into a legally binding contract; this is made when goods displayed for sale attract what is legally an offer from a buyer, which is accepted by the seller. As part of the contract the seller must then ensure that the goods meet any description applied to them.

If the seller is acting in the normal course of his business (i.e. it is not a private sale) he is generally obliged also to ensure that goods sold are of merchantable quality (i.e. they are in a proper condition) and are fit for the particular purpose for which goods are being bought. (Sale of Goods Act 1893 as amended).

A seller of goods or services cannot evade his obligations by issue of any kind of guarantee, and a seller who fails to meet any of the obligations has broken the contract of sale and it is his responsibility in law to effect restitution; he cannot transfer responsibility to the manufacturer. Manufacturers may however accept responsibility for the first part of their products' life, and completion of a guarantee may provide a contract with the manufactuer in addition to legal rights with the seller.

A buyer may claim repair of faulty goods, or their exchange for sound goods, or reimbursement of the money paid; he is not obliged to accept a credit note. Claim first in person or in writing to the seller and/or manufactuer. If this fails to provide a settlement, general and/or more specific advice may be obtained from organisations listed under **Consumer protection**. If these approaches fail, the buyer may have a legal claim: general advice from **solicitor**. (see also **Small claims; Civil law disputes**.)

Under the Weights and Measures Act 1963, the weight or some other indication of quantity has to be shown on most prepacked goods; and certain prepacked foods may only be made up for sale in prescribed quantities, and when metric packs are introduced must be clearly marked 'metric pack' to distinguish them from existing imperial prescribed quantity packs.

These obligations are normally the responsibility of the packer although the seller has a duty to ensure that he does not offer for sale goods which do not comply with the law.

It is more generally an offence to give short weight or measure so the packer must ensure that the minimum weight statement he applies to his pack will still be accurate when the goods are finally sold.

The seller must use accurate weighing and measuring equipment and it is similarly an offence for him to supply less than the quantity agreed between the buyer and seller.

A seller is specifically required to indicate the price, including the unit price, where appropriate, of goods or services specified in any Order made under the Price Act 1974 (as amended by the Price Commission Act 1977). Under the Food and Drugs Act 1955 (or Food and Drugs Act Northern Ireland 1956) he is also obliged to observe specific

regulations covering food hygiene, food labelling and food composition; under the Consumer Protection Act 1961 (or Consumer Protection Act Northern Ireland 1965), to observe specific regulations concerning the sale of goods that may be unsafe or liable to cause death or serious injury (e.g. **electrical appliances**, toys, carrycot stands, oil heaters, domestic hardware); under the Trade Descriptions Act 1968, to have offered 'reduced-price' goods for sale at the higher price for at least 28 consecutive days in the previous six months; and under the Consumer Credit Act 1974, to be licensed if dealing with credit in any form (see **Consumer credit**).
For general advice, see 'Fair deal – a shoppers' guide', from *Office of Fair Trading*.

San Marino For **exchange control** is a non-scheduled territory in the EEC but outside the **overseas sterling area**. UK nationals travelling direct from the UK normally need only the following (but check): **passports**; **work permits** (if taking a job).
The UK has no reciprocal health or social security arrangements.
Enquiries to *San Marino Personal Representative* in London.
British diplomatic mission to San Marino is *British Consulate* in Florence, Italy.

Samaritans Volunteers aged 17 and over are always needed to help run the *Samaritans'* 24-hour, free-of-charge, confidential service of listening to and befriending the suicidal and despairing. There are 167 branches in the UK and Eire. Apply, preferably in writing, to your nearest branch. Applicants are carefully selected and given preparation.
See also **Personal problems; Suicide and despair**.

Sand and Land Yachting These sports are controlled internationally by the Fédération Internationale de Sand and Land Yachting and in the UK by the *British Federation of Sand and Land Yacht Clubs* which selects teams, implements standards, etc. There are three regional clubs in England: *Cotswold Land Yacht Club*, *Fylde International Sand Yacht Club* and *Anglia Land Yacht Club*, while in Scotland there is the *Scottish Association of Sand and Land Yacht Clubs*.

Saudi Arabia For **exchange control** is a non-scheduled territory outside the **overseas sterling area** and the **EEC**. UK nationals travelling direct from the UK normally need only the following (but check): **passports** without Israeli stamp; entry permits; international certificates of **vaccination** against smallpox; **work permits** (if taking a job).
The UK has no reciprocal health or social security arrangements.
Enquiries to *Saudi Arabian Embassy* in London.
British diplomatic mission to Saudi Arabia is *British Embassy* in Jedda.

School Attendance In England and Wales, it is the responsibility of parents to ensure that their children receive education between the ages of 5 and 16. (See also **Schools admission, exclusion and expulsion**.) In the majority of cases children attend a state or **independent school**. If children attend a state school they are expected to attend 400 sessions (i.e. 400 half days) annually. This can be reduced by up to 20 sessions each year (e.g. on account of polling in the school buildings) at the discretion of the *local education authority*. Holidays in state schools during school terms can be authorised by headteachers. Independent schools each fix their own terms and holidays and headteachers authorise pupils' absence at their discretion. Parents are responsible for ensuring that their children attend the school at which they are registered. The educational welfare officers of the local education authority may issue attendance orders to enforce attendance; if this is ignored, the authority may prosecute parents.
Children who become 16 between 1 September and 31 January may finish schooling at the end of the Easter term; those who become 16 between 1 February and 31 August may leave at the end of May (the Friday before the last Monday).

Nomadic children (gypsies, fairground children, canal boat children, vagrant children) are required to attend school for a minimum of 200 sessions a year. Children over 14 may be allowed to be absent from school to take part in theatre performances provided their parents have obtained a licence from the local education authority. It may prohibit the employment of children if it is prejudicial to their health or interferes with their education.

Children may be educated outside the state or independent school system but their education must be approved by the local education authority. Home teaching may be provided by parents, if they can show that the education provided is suitable for the children's age, aptitude and ability.

See also **Education: Scotland; Education: Northern Ireland**.

School Crossings Local authorities in England and Wales outside London may make arrangements for school-crossing patrols. Siting of these patrols is a local matter, and local *police* are involved in varying degrees in the training recruitment, equipment and supervision of patrols. In London the Commissioner of Police at *Metropolitan Police Headquarters* is responsible for making these arrangements and in the **City of London**, the Common Council of the City.

Schooling for Children in Special Categories In England and Wales the *local education authority* must make provision (e.g. special classes, lessons) for mentally and physically handicapped children (see **Disablement: handicapped children's education**); children with special aptitudes; gifted children; children with broken homes; children whose parents are abroad. It may also send these children to **independent schools**.

The local education authority has the power to decide whether a child needs special education. Parents who think their child needs special education should apply to special education section at the authority. They can appeal against the authority's decision to the Secretary of State for Education.

The authority usually agrees the education arrangements with the parents, who can visit the proposed special schools, units or classes. Children can transfer back to an ordinary school when indicated by one of the regular assessments of the child. When the authority decides upon a particular boarding school for a handicapped child it must pay the full cost of that provision; it may also help with the cost when boarding education is desirable (the help must be no more than sufficient to avoid hardship). For all children not able to travel to a suitable school everyday, the authority must pay the cost of lodgings near a school, or of a place at a boarding school. The authority may pay the cost of boarding education for other children (e.g. parents abroad, home circumstances prejudicial to the child, special aptitudes).

Home teaching may be provided by the local education authority in extraordinary circumstances (e.g. the last stages of a pupil's pregnancy, severe illness, etc.) for up to five sessions a week on application by the parent to the headteacher, the doctor or by the local authority social services department. Headteachers may refer a child to an educational psychologist.

In Northern Ireland, there are similar arrangements; but parents have the right of appeal to the *Department of Education, Northern Ireland*.

See also **Education: Scotland; Education: Northern Ireland**.

Schools: Admission, Exclusion and Expulsion In England and Wales, once a child is 5, it is the duty of parents to apply to the headteacher of a school (either a state primary school or an independent school) for a school place. Admission to state schools is generally delegated to the headteacher by the controlling body (i.e. the *local education authority* in county schools and the governors in voluntary schools – See **Schools: management**). If the headteacher is unable to accept the child, the local education authority will be informed and propose alternatives for the parent. Parents cannot contest a headteacher's refusal to accept a child.

Once in a primary school, arrangements

to transfer children to other state schools are made by the authority through the headteacher while the parents still live within the same local education area. If the parents move out of the neighbourhood, it is their duty to apply to the headteacher of an appropriate school in the new area. (Children may attend a school in a different area to the one in which they live at the discretion of the authorities concerned.) Parents have the preference of choice of state school for their child if there are vacancies at the school. But the local education authority may decide that the choice is unsuitable because of the child's age, ability and aptitude, or that it involves unreasonable expense. The authority can be overruled by the *Department of Education and Science.* Local education authorities may impose catchment areas on schools. Admission to a zoned school for a child outside the catchment area is at the discretion of the authority.

Admission to independent schools is controlled individually by each school. Application should be made directly to a school. (See **Independent schools**.)

Headteachers of state and independent schools usually have powers temporarily to suspend a child from school; suspension may have to be confirmed by the governors. A child may also be expelled from a state school by the local education authority or governors. The *Department of Education and Science* may reinstate an expelled pupil; procedures vary according to the articles of government of each school.

Through the authorised medical officer, the authority may exclude children from school because they are in a verminous or foul condition or on health grounds. Once a child is expelled, it is the parent's responsibility to see the head of the expelling school. The authority will then allocate a new school for the child. If the parents are dissatisfied with the allocation they can appeal to the DES which can overrule the authority.

See also **Education: Scotland; Education: Northern Ireland.**

Schools: Curricula and Language of Instruction   In England and Wales, curricula in state schools are legally controlled by the *local education authority* or the school governors but, in practice, they are usually determined by the headteacher. **Independent schools'** curricula are their own responsibility, subject to the comments of Her Majesty's inspectors who are responsible to the *Department of Education and Science.* The only exception to this is that there is a requirement for religious worship and instruction. In state schools this is normally Christian but non-denominational in character; in aided and special agreement schools it may be denominational (e.g. Catholic) but parents may then opt for children to receive non-denominational teaching. The language of instruction in schools is determined by the local education authority.

See also **Education: Scotland; Education: Northern Ireland.**

Schools: Discipline and Uniform   In England and Wales, discipline in state schools, including detention, is the responsibility of the headteacher, and of the teachers acting in loco parentis. The only exception is that the *local education authority* has power to issue regulations controlling corporal punishment in state schools. If this is not done, the headteacher can decide whether or not to allow corporal punishment in the school. Wearing a school uniform in state schools is at the discretion of the headteacher.

See also **Education: Scotland; Education: Northern Ireland.**

Schools: Management   In state schools in England and Wales, governors (secondary schools) and managers (primary schools) are appointed by the *local education authority.* The relationship between authority and governors and managers varies depending on the status of the school and its articles of government. Two-thirds of state (i.e. publicly-maintained) schools are county schools, established and maintained by the *local education authority*; one-third are voluntary schools, established by other bodies (often churches) but financially maintained by the authority.

In county schools, all the governors and managers are appointed by the authority. In voluntary 'controlled' schools governors and managers are two-thirds local authority and one-third voluntary interest appointments and the authority appoints the teachers; in voluntary 'aided' schools the voluntary body appoints two-thirds and the authority one third and the authority appoints the teachers on the basis of the governors' recommendations; in voluntary 'special agreement' schools (almost always secondary schools) the governors are again two-thirds/one-third but the governors appoint the teachers, subject to some authority control. Management of independent schools is their own affair, subject to inspection by Her Majesty's inspectors (see **Independent schools**).

In Northern Ireland, controlled schools are under the direct management of *education and library boards*, and are wholly financed from public funds; voluntary schools are grant-aided schools under the management of persons approved by the *Department of Education, Northern Ireland*, or of boards of governors established in accordance with approved schemes.

A school council may be set up, and its constitution and working determined, at the discretion of the headteacher.

State school buildings may be used for non-school purposes, such as orchestral rehearsals, theatrical performances, and sports on application to the headteacher or local education authority.

Lavatories and kitchen facilities are included in any inspection by Her Majesty's inspectors who may make appropriate recommendations. A school may be closed down by the *local education authority* (Environmental Health Inspector) where the lavatories, kitchens, etc., constitute a health hazard. In extreme cases the *local education authority* (Fire Officer) may close any educational premises which do not meet with fire regulations; the Architects and Building Branch at the *Department of Education and Science* advises on fire precautions and regulations.

See also **Education: Scotland; Education: Northern Ireland**.

Schools: Meals, Milk, Transport and Clothing In England and Wales *local education authorities* must provide school lunches (and meals in boarding schools) for children in state schools at charges set by the *Department of Education and Science*. The DES also sets the level of parental income below which children are entitled to free school meals; parents should apply to the local education authority. Headteachers decide whether children may eat packed lunches in state schools. Authorities must supply free milk to children in all state schools up to the age of 7; to individual children aged 7–12 if the school doctor certifies that it is necessary for their health; and to all children in special schools.

Authorities may sell milk to all other pupils in state schools.

Local education authorities and *Education and Library Boards* have discretionary powers to assist with the fares of any pupil. They must provide transport, or pay the cost of travel, to the nearest state school (grant-aided school in Northern Ireland) if it is more than three miles from a child's home (two miles for children under 8, England and Wales; under 11, Northern Ireland).

Clothing allowances for any school clothing (not just uniform except in Northern Ireland), may be paid to parents in case of hardship on application by parents to the authority.

See also **Education: Scotland; Education: Northern Ireland**.

Schools: Parents' Rights Apart from the right of choice of school parents in England and Wales have a limited number of educational rights in state schools. They have a general right to enter school premises but should seek the school's permission: the precise rights of entry to a school are determined by the individual headteacher. Parent-teacher associations are established at the discretion of headteachers who also determine terms of reference, normally in consultation and in agreement with the parties involved.

If schools do not provide instruction in a particular religion parents may request that their children receive religious instruction in another school in the locality, or failing that, special

instruction in their own school. Parents may withdraw their children from religious observance or instruction; they have no right to withdraw their children from any other classes, even sex education.
See also **Education: Scotland; Education: Northern Ireland; Schools: admission, exclusion and expulsion.**

Schools: Re-organisation of Secondary School System Local education authorities in England and Wales are required to put forward proposals for the abolition of selection in secondary schools and for the introduction of a fully comprehensive system in their area to the *Department of Education and Science.* They are under no legal obligation to consult locally, but are expected and encouraged to do so by the DES. Schemes of comprehensive re-organisation must be approved by the DES. In Northern Ireland, area *Education and Library Boards* have been invited to undertake the planning and restructuring of secondary education following the government's decision to introduce a comprehensive system.
See also **Education: Scotland; Education: Northern Ireland.**

Science, Technology and Agriculture Overseas The British Council provides information on a wide range of scientific subjects. Enquiries to: *British Council Headquarters* or *British Council Overseas Office* in the country concerned.

Scientific and Technical Reports Reports resulting from research work done by government departments, including the Ministry of Defence, can be obtained from the *Department of Industry, Technology Reports Centre.*

Scottish Conservative Party Membership is open to anyone over the age of 15 who supports the views of the party and subscribes to the local constituency associations.
To join, contact the constituency Conservative Association (under political organisations in Scottish telephone directories) or the *Scottish Conservative Party Headquarters.* There is a constituency association for each of the 71 Scottish constituencies, federated at national level in the *Scottish Conservative and Unionist Association,* and specialist bodies at national level, e.g. women's advisory council, Young Conservatives, local government advisory committee, trade unionists.
The party has strong links with the **Conservative party** in England and Wales, but maintains independence through the SCUA which holds its own conference. Scottish Conservative MPs and peers take the general Conservative whip.
The SCP officially claims that membership provides 'the opportunity to influence policy at local and national level, to help restrict increasing government interference in private and business life, and to put nation before nationalisation'.

Scottish Cup Final The Scottish Cup Competition is organised by the *Scottish Football Association.* Its 75 member clubs participate; those not in membership of the Scottish Football League play in a qualifying competition. The Cup Final, and usually the semi-finals also, are played at Hampden Park, Glasgow, which is rented for the occasion from Queen's Park Football Club. Tickets for the final are allocated by the SFA to the competing clubs, the ground club, other member clubs and the public. A public sale of tickets is held through ticket agencies throughout the country and postal applications are accepted by the SFA.
See also **Cup Final; Football.**

Scottish Highlands and Islands Individuals willing to live and work in the Scottish highlands and islands are recorded and listed by the *Scottish Highlands and Islands Development Board.* It includes graduates and semi-skilled workers interested in suitable opportunities. Enquiries to the Director of Industrial Development and Marketing of the SHIDB.
See also **Assisted areas.**

Scottish Labour Party The Scottish Labour Party (formed 1976) is a socialist party. It seeks a powerful Scottish parliament with control over domestic affairs including a decisive say over North Sea oil policy. Devolution is seen as a first step towards an independent Scotland within the EEC. The SLP constitution excludes block voting and internally the party practises proportional representation as well as supporting proportional representation for **parliamentary elections**. Membership application forms from the General Secretary, *Scottish Labour Party*.

Scottish Liberal Party The Scottish Liberal Party is part of the UK Liberal Party but has had a separate organisation since 1946. Membership is open to any Liberal in Scotland (or out of Scotland, if wished) and is achieved by joining either as a national member through *Scottish Liberal Headquarters* or as a member of a local Association. There is an active association in most of the 71 Scottish constituencies: the *Scottish Liberal Office* in Edinburgh can provide addresses, etc. Liberals aged between 16 and 28 are also eligible to join the Scottish Young Liberal Movement.

Scottish National Party Membership is open to individuals who support the aims of the party and who reside in the UK. Members overseas may join the SNP Association (particulars available from *Scottish National Party Headquarters* in Edinburgh). SNP aims are self-government for Scotland (i.e. national sovereignty) within the **Commonwealth**, and the furtherance of all Scottish interests. It wants a Scottish parliament elected by the citizens of Scotland. SNP's outlook is democratic and internationalist. To join apply to the national secretary at the Edinburgh headquarters.

Scrap Metal Dealers These must register with the local authority.

Securities: Ownership Anyone may own stocks, shares, gilt-edged and local/public authority loans. Ownership of shares is registered on the register of each individual company by its registrar; gifts are registered either at the *Post Office* (if bought through post offices) or at the *Bank of England* if bought elsewhere. Transfer from one owner to another by buying and selling, inheritance or gift can be arranged by a **stockbroker** who establishes a fair price (necessary for tax purposes) by showing the business to the market.

The Stock Exchange rules (available from the Membership Department of the *Stock Exchange*) regard the transaction to have taken place from the moment that the broker deals with the jobber. Thus all rights of ownership such as dividends or new shares must be transferred by the selling broker from that point even though the share concerned may not yet have been registered in the new owner's name.

Transfer of gilt-edged/local and public authority loans are effected by informing the official registrar for each authority, or the Bank of England as appropriate, by forwarding the certificate and the signed, stamped transfer.

Companies quoted on the SE have the right to require shareholders to disclose whether they are the beneficial owners of shares and, if not, who else has an interest in the shares. Anyone who holds $\frac{1}{10}$ or more of the shares in a company quoted on the SE which carry unrestricted voting rights must notify the company. The particulars are entered on the company's register of substantial interests.

See also **Companies; Stock Exchange listing**.

Securities: Prices Prices for all listed securities (see **Stock Exchange listing**) are collected by *Stock Exchange* officials and pubished in the 'Stock Exchange Daily Official List' daily at 5.30 p.m. and displayed on television screens in places that subscribe to the SE's market price display service (e.g. **stockbroker**' offices). The price of individual bargains is completely confidential to the client, the broker and the jobber.

Prices in the List represent the range within which business was conducted during the entire day. Prices in the morning newspapers are those at the close of business (i.e. the mid-market price of the final quotation of the day, irrespective of whether business was actually done). Thus the official quotation and the prices in the newspapers may differ dramatically.

The 'Financial Times' publishes the FT Index of Industrial Ordinary Shares, based on 30 industrial shares selected on 1 July 1935, which is calculated on mid-market prices (the difference between the average buying and selling prices quoted by the jobbers) at 10.00 a.m. and then hourly until 5.00 p.m. It also publishes the FT Actuaries Indices, covering a wider range of shares which can be analysed by industry. Both the FT Index and the FT Actuaries Indices are widely quoted (although not official SE indices of prices).

Securities: Sale and Purchase Sale and purchase of securities, including stocks, shares, gilt-edged, local authority loans and public authority loans, is largely concentrated in a single market, the *Stock Exchange*, which now includes all the British and Irish exchanges. In the UK there are *Stock Exchange trading floors* in Birmingham, Liverpool, London, Manchester, York, Glasgow, Edinburgh and Belfast. The public cannot buy or sell directly on the SE; dealings can only be conducted through a SE member, i.e. brokers who act as agents for investors, buying and selling from jobbers, who buy and sell on their own behalf (see **Stockbrokers and stockjobbers**).

Investors, whether buying or selling, must pay a commission to the broker for each transaction, except in certain circumstances, e.g. pre-sale or closing purchase during the same trading account. A minimum scale of charges is set by the SE Council, and is available from the Membership Department at the SE.

Special *Bank of England* regulations apply to the purchase of **foreign securities** by UK residents, and the sale of **sterling securities** to persons resident abroad (see **Exchange control**).

See also **Government stock: purchase and sale**; **Stock Exchange listing**.

Seeds Seeds of cereals, fodder plants, beet, oil and fibre plants, vegetables and seed potatoes must comply with marketing regulations and with prescribed standards for purity, germination and weed seed content; seed containers must be sealed and labelled with prescribed information, and under EEC regulations all varieties of marketed seed must be included on a national List of Varieties. Samples of seed may be tested at any of the UK Official Seed Testing Stations. Advice in England and Wales from the *Ministry of Agriculture Fisheries and Food, Seeds Branch* and for seed potatoes from the Plant Health Branch at the *Ministry of Agriculture Fisheries and Food, Headquarters (2)*. Advice on choice of seeds and crop varieties is available from the *National Institute of Agricultural Botany*.

See also **Agriculture: Scotland**; **Agriculture: Northern Ireland**; **Agricultural produce: grading**.

Senegal For **exchange control** is a non-scheduled territory outside the **overseas sterling area** and the **EEC**. UK nationals travelling direct from the UK normally need only the following (but check): **passports**; **visas**; international certificates of **vaccination** against smallpox and yellow fever; **work permits** (if taking a job); green cards for motor insurance (if bringing a car); international driving permits (if intending to drive: see **Motoring abroad**).

The UK has no reciprocal health or social security arrangements.

Enquiries to *Senegal Embassy* in London.

British diplomatic mission to Senegal is *British Embassy* in Dakar.

Sewerage In England and Wales the collection, treatment and disposal of sewage is the responsibility of the 10 *water authorities* (see **Water services**). For properties connected to the public sewer, a charge is made for collection, treatment and disposal of sewage based on the rateable value of the property and a very much smaller charge is also made to cover the cost of environmental services (i.e. pollution control, recreation, fisheries and navigation). Sewerage charges apply to all properties connected to the public sewer regardless of use. Properties not connected to the public sewer do not pay for sewage disposal but must pay

the environmental services' charge. Cesspits are emptied by the local authority which fixes charges for the service. In Scotland responsibility for sewerage and sewage disposal rests with the nine regional and three islands councils (see **Local authorities**). Changes are met mainly from general rating.
See also **Pollution: water; Rates.**

Sex Discrimination Sex discrimination in the fields of education and training, employment, and the provision of goods, credit and services to the public is illegal in England and Wales under the Sex Discrimination Act 1975; advertisements which indicate an intention to discriminate unlawfully are themselves unlawful (see **Sex discrimination: advertising**). Both men and women have rights under the Act. Exceptions include firms with five or fewer employees; private households; the armed forces; and jobs where a person's sex is a genuine occupational qualification, e.g. acting, modelling.
Under the Act, direct sex discrimination means treating a woman, on the grounds of her sex, less favourably than a man is or would be treated in similar circumstances; indirect sex discrimination means asking for a requirement which, although applied equally to both sexes, has the effect of ruling out members of one sex (e.g. if an employer unjustifiably demands a technical skill which few women may possess, this may well be indirect sex discrimination, as might discriminating against a person because he or she is married. The Act also protects individuals from being victimised because they have asserted or intend to assert their rights under it or under the Equal Pay Act.
For further details see entries immediately following. See also **Wages: equal pay.**

Sex Discrimination: Advertising
Advertisements which indicate an intention to discriminate unlawfully, are themselves unlawful. Advertisements with job descriptions such as 'waiter', 'salesgirl', 'postman' will be deemed to discriminate unless they show clearly that both sexes are eligible. Complaints should be made to the *Equal Opportunities Commission* or the *Equal Opportunities Commission for Northern Ireland* as they alone can bring a case.

Sex Discrimination: Education
Single-sex establishments are permissible, but co-educational establishments must not discriminate in admissions, access to courses, benefits, facilities or services. In respect of public sector education, first give notice of your complaint to the Secretary of State at the *Department of Education and Science* in England, the *Welsh Education Department* in Wales, the *Scottish Education Department* in Scotland, and allow him a period of two months in which to consider your complaint. Following this you have six months in which to complain to a county court. In all other education cases, where notice to the Secretary of State is not required, complaint should be made to a county court within six months of the act complained of. Advice from *Equal Opportunities Commission* or *Equal Opportunities Commission for Northern Ireland*.

Sex Discrimination: Employment
In **employment** there must be no discrimination in recruitment; training; transfer; promotion; the provision of benefits or services normally granted to employees; **dismissals** or other unfavourable treatment of employees. Contract workers and partners are covered by the Act and discrimination by **trade unions**, organisations of employers, professional associations, employment agencies and licensing bodies is also unlawful.
To complain about sex discrimination in employment, first see your trade union representative or *Advisory Conciliation and Arbitration Service*. The *Equal Opportunities Commission* and the *Equal Opportunities Commission for Northern Ireland* will always give advice. If an employment case goes to law it is heard by an **industrial tribunal**. A case must be registered with an industrial tribunal within three months of the deed you complain of, using

form IT1 – available from *Department of Employment unemployment benefit offices*; *Employment Service Agency Job Centres*; or the EOCs.

Sex Discrimination: Housing, Credit, Goods and Services With a few exceptions discrimination in the fields of housing, credit and provision of goods and services is unlawful (e.g. a bank, building society or finance house must offer you credit, a mortgage or a loan on no less favourable terms than those offered to a member of the opposite sex). Complain to your local county court within six months of the act complained about; advice from the *Equal Opportunities Commission* or the *Equal Opportunities Commission for Northern Ireland*.

Sex Discrimination: Legal Aid Advice and assistance to would-be complainants under either the Sex Discrimination Act or the Equal Pay Act is available from the *Equal Opportunities Commission*, which provides a form (the 'questions procedure') which the complainant can send to the alleged discriminator, asking for reasons for the treatment complained of. The EOC may also provide representation at a tribunal or county court.
Legal aid is available for cases under both Acts; it is not available for applications to individual tribunals, but may be applied for in respect of county court cases.
Northern Ireland has its own provisions under the Sex Discrimination (Northern Ireland) Order 1976 and a separate *Equal Opportunities Commission for Northern Ireland*.

Seychelles **Commonwealth** member. For **exchange control** is a non-scheduled territory in the **overseas sterling area** but outside the **EEC**. UK nationals travelling direct from the UK normally need only the following but check): **passports**; international certificates of **vaccination** against smallpox and cholera; **work permits** (if taking a job).
The UK has no reciprocal health or social security arrangements.
Enquiries to *Seychelles High Commission* in London.

British diplomatic mission to Seychelles is *British High Commission* in Victoria.

Sheep The government's Fat Sheep Guarantee Scheme makes up the average market price to the guaranteed price when necessary. To qualify, sheep or their carcasses have to be certified as meeting certain standards, minimum weights and other qualifications laid down by the *Ministry of Agriculture, Fisheries and Food*. Certification in England and Wales is carried out by fatstock staff of the *Meat and Livestock Commission* at approved liveweight and deadweight centres on behalf of MAFF.
See also **Agriculture: Scotland**; **Agriculture: Northern Ireland**; **Wool marketing**.

Ship Charter The chartering of tramp ships for single voyages throughout the world and on time charter is arranged daily at the *Baltic Exchange* by shipbrokers and shipowners' agents. Shipbroker members of the Exchange can be contacted through the *Institute of Chartered Shipbrokers* or through the secretary of the **Baltic Exchange**.

Shipbrokers Shipbrokers may be qualified by achieving membership of the *Institute of Chartered Shipbrokers* which exercises professional supervision over members and secures for them professional standing in the UK and Commonwealth to assist them in the discharge of their duties.
Complaints against the professional conduct of members are investigated by the ICS.

Shipbuilding and Docks: Safety The Safety and General Branch B at the *Health and Safety Executive* (head office) is responsible for general UK policy on safety in docks, shipbuilding, ship repairing and oil rig and production platform manufacture; the preparation of new legislation, codes of practice and EEC directives; and advice on the effects of the Health and Safety at Work etc Act 1974 in ports, harbours and coastal waters. Technical advice at local level on shipbuilding and docks

Shipping

safety and health from *Health and Safety Executive, HM Factory Inspectorate* (area offices).

Shipping Accidents Accidents affecting British registered vessels in UK territorial waters are investigated by the *Department of Trade,* to whom shipping accidents must be notified. To report an accident around UK shores, telephone 999 and ask for *Coastguard.* To enquire about missing vessels (at sea) or persons around UK shores, and regarding searches in progress, ask the Coastguard. If the accident occurs abroad, ask the *Foreign and Commonwealth Office.*

Shipping Notices Merchant shipping 'M' notices are prepared by the *Department of Trade* (Marine Division) to provide essential information for shipowners, shipbuilders and ships' crews. The notices contain information and advice on such matters as safety equipment and procedures, navigation, medical matters, cargo storage, examination regulations and manning requirements. M notices are available free of charge from *Department of Trade* (Marine Library) and *Department of Trade* (Mercantile Marine Office).
Admiralty notices for mariners contain navigational information and are issued by the *Ministry of Defence,* (Hydrographic Department), Taunton.

Shipping Registration British ships, sea-going yachts, sea fishing boats and **hovercraft** should be registered with *Her Majesty's Customs and Excise* (Chief Registrar of British Ships) under the Merchant Shipping Act 1894. The main exceptions are ships not exceeding 15 tons net employed solely on rivers or coasts.
The purpose of registration is to obtain the protection of British law, to establish the title of British owners and the identity and tonnage of ship. While registration is not compulsory, it greatly facilitates dealings such as transfers of ownership and mortgages, and customs clearance.
See also **Fishing vessels; Lloyd's of London; Yachts.**

Shipping: Registration and Approval Lloyd's Register of Shipping issues shipping tonnage certificates; undertakes load lines and safety certification in accordance with international standards; and conducts shipping instrumentation approval (including type-approved control and electrical equipment, loading instruments and individual ships loading indicators). Lists of approved equipment available from LRS.
The annual 'Register Book' of Lloyd's Register of Shipping is updated by monthly supplements and describes the world's merchant ships over 100 tons gross, whether classed with LRS or not (see **Ships and Yachts: seaworthiness**). It includes offshore drilling rigs; LRS-classed refrigerated cargo installations; refrigerated stores; container terminals. Supplementary volumes give details of builders, owners, docks. There is a separate statistical publication and a yacht register is issued annually by LRS covering British and foreign boats.

Ships and Yachts: Seaworthiness Ships and yachts are classified by Lloyd's Register of Shipping (see **Shipping: registration and approval**) and, on the basis of this classification, accepted by owners, underwriters, charterers and national authorities as of appropriate structural and mechanical efficiency. Ships of all types can be built to Lloyd's Register Class, which involves survey from plan approval stage to completion trials. Survey covers materials, hull construction, machinery, refrigeration, electrical systems and control equipment. Classification standards are published in the form of Rules. To maintain class, ships must be re-inspected periodically. An alternative to the LR Class scheme for yachts and motor boats is the four-part LR Building Certificate. This certifies standards of construction (for hull moulding, hull and superstructure construction, and machinery installation) without involving periodic re-inspection.
See also **Lloyd's of London; Yachts.**

Ships: Licensing Ships of less than 40 tons register weight, kept at or based on a place in the UK, must be licensed if it is intended that they will proceed beyond prescribed distances from the UK coast, unless they are exempt by virtue of the use to which they are being put. Apply to *Her Majesty's Custom and Excise.* **Yachts** are generally exempt.

Ships: Sale and Purchase The sale and purchase of ships is handled by shipbrokers specialising in this trade. They can be contacted through the *Institute of Chartered Shipbrokers* or the secretary of the *Baltic Exchange.*

Shipwork Goods Goods of any description imported into the UK for use in the construction, repair, maintenance or conversion of the ships, boats or other vessels listed in *Her Majesty's Customs and Excise* Tariff, Part 12A, are free of customs duty, subject to customs control. Details from HMCE notices 770 and 770A.

Shoeblacks: Licences In the Metropolitan Police District the Commissioner of Police at *Metropolitan Police Force Headquarters* is empowered to licence shoeblacks and assign them places to carry out their trade. Licences are in force for one year.

Shooting The sport covers both **field sport** and competitive shooting with shotgun, full-bore rifles and pistols, small-bore (.22) rifles and pistols, and .177 air rifles and pistols, over fixed distances.

For field sport, UK governing bodies are the *British Field Sports Society* and the *Wildfowlers Association of Great Britain and Ireland.* Full-bore target shooting is governed internationally by the International Shooting Union and in the UK by the *National Rifle Association* which is responsible for rules, technical advice, an annual Open Meeting, policing legislation and selecting and sponsoring British teams. Within this structure, the *Welsh Rifle Association*, the *Scottish National Rifle Association* and the *Ulster Rifle Association* control their countries.

Small-bore target shooting is governed internationally by the International Shooting Union and in the UK by the *National Small-bore Rifle Association* with functions as described for the NRA. National bodies affiliated to the NSRA are the *Welsh Smallbore Shooting Union*, the *Scottish Smallbore Rifle Association*, the *Scottish Pistol Association* and the *Ulster Counties Smallbore Shooting Association.* International air rifle and air pistol shooting at 10 metres distance also comes under the International Shooting Union and in the UK the NRSA.

Air rifle and air pistol shooting at six yards, which is unique to the UK, is governed by the *National Air Rifle and Pistol Association.* It is responsible for rules, annual postal competitions, and an annual Championship Meeting.

Competitive shotgun shooting at clays at various distances is governed by the *Clay Pigeon Shooting Association* (England), the *Welsh Clay Pigeon Shooting Association*, the *Scottish Clay Pigeon Association* and the *Ulster Clay Pigeon Shooting Association* which are responsible for advice on constructing ranges, national competitions in the UK, and selecting and sponsoring British shooters and teams in international events.

The *Muzzle Loaders Association of Great Britain* is the governing body for competitive shooting with muzzle-loading black powder rifles and pistols, and advises on the necessary licences and organises UK and international competitions. Great Britain shooting teams are selected by the Joint Shooting Committee of the NRA, the NSRA and the national clay pigeon shooting associations.

Shop Opening Hours Under the Shops Act 1950 every shop must be closed for the serving of customers not later than 8.00 p.m. (9.00 p.m. on one late day and 1.00 p.m. on one early day in every week) unless an order has been made by the local authority exempting all similar shops in the area from this provision. All shops must be closed for the serving of customers on Sunday except for certain transactions (specified in the Fifth Schedule to the Act).

Responsibility for administration and enforcement of the Act rests with the **local authorities** which are required to appoint inspectors for its enforcement and for instituting such proceedings as may be necessary for that purpose.

See also **Liquor licensing**.

Shop Stewards Shop stewards are members of a **trade union** who have been elected to be the union's workplace representative. They are normally elected by members of their own union, but some are elected by workers from several unions.

Responsibilities of shop stewards include trade union organisation; providing information to union members; acting as 'middle man' in negotiations and consultations between unions and management; and local membership, including recruitment and contributions. They also act as a channel of communication between the membership and the fulltime officials and the union's executive.

Sickness Benefit Social Security Sickness Benefit is paid for up to 28 weeks to people incapable of work because of illness or disablement and who have paid sufficient **National insurance contributions**. Benefit may be increased for dependants and **Earnings-related supplement** may also be payable. Benefit may be withheld if the claimant's own conduct has caused the incapacity.

Application for sickness benefit is normally by forwarding a doctor's statement (formerly a medical certificate) from family **doctor**, or other medical evidence from hospital, to *Department of Health and Social Security* (local office). Medical evidence of incapacity must continue to be submitted while incapacity for work lasts, a fresh doctor's statement being obtained as soon as the previous one expires.

People receiving sickness benefit may not work without consulting the DHSS, nor behave in a way that might delay recovery; they must leave a forwarding address with the DHSS if absent from home. Benefit is reduced after more than eight weeks in hospital. **Invalidity** pension replaces sickness benefit when illness persists for more than 28 weeks. See leaflets NI16 (sickness benefit), NI9 (stay in hospital), NI38 (absence abroad), from DHSS local offices.

See also **Social security benefits**.

Sierra Leone Commonwealth member. For **exchange control** is a non-scheduled territory in the **overseas sterling area** but outside the EEC. UK nationals travelling direct from the UK normally need only the following (but check): **passports**; entry permits; international certificates of **vaccination** against smallpox and yellow fever; **work permits** (if taking a job); green cards for motor insurance (if bringing a car), international driving permits (if intending to drive: see **Motoring abroad**).

The UK has no reciprocal health or social security arrangements.

Enquiries to *Sierra Leone High Commission* in London.

British diplomatic mission to Sierra Leone is *British High Commission* in Freetown.

Singapore Commonwealth member. For **exchange control** is a non-scheduled territory in the **overseas sterling area** but outside the EEC. UK nationals travelling direct from the UK normally need only the following (but check): **passports**; international certificates of **vaccination** against smallpox; **work permits** (if taking a job). The UK has no reciprocal health or social security arrangements.

Enquiries to *Singapore High Commission* in London.

British diplomatic mission to Singapore is *British High Commission* in Singapore.

Sinn Fein: the Workers' Party Membership is open to anyone over 16 who accepts the party's political programme, abides by the discipline of the organisation, supports the organisation financially and works in one of the units of the organisation under the direction of the leadership. Associate membership is open to people residing outside Ireland. The official support

group in Britain is Clann na hEireann. The objective of Sinn Fein the Workers' Party is the creation of a United Democratic Socialist Republic of Ireland, in which state power will lie in the hands of the working people of Ireland, and the means of production, distribution and exchange will be controlled democratically by the working people through public ownership.
Further details from *Sinn Fein the Workers' Party*.

Skateboarding The governing body of skateboarding is *The Skateboarding Association*. Its offices are at the *Sports Council* in London. Responsibilities of this new association include safety standards, competition structure, etc.

Skating Internationally, ice skating is governed by the International Skating Union and roller skating by the Fédération Internationale de Roller Skating. In the UK both amateur sports are governed by the *National Skating Association of Great Britain*. It supervises UK teams, rules, championships and competitions, amateur status, referees, judges, tests, etc. The professional skaters' association is the *International Professional Skating Association*. Ice hockey is governed separately by the *British Ice Hockey Association* and roller hockey by the *National Roller Hockey Association*.

Skiing Skiing has a number of different disciplines. Alpine (downhill skiing), Nordic (cross country) and Free Style competitions are governed worldwide by the Fédération Internationale de Ski. Biathalon skiing (cross country with shooting) is controlled internationally by the Union Internationale Moderne Pentathalon et Biathalon. In the UK the authorities are the *National Ski Federation of Great Britain*, the *Scottish National Ski Council*, the *Ski Council of Wales* and the *Ulster Ski Federation*. British teams are selected by the NSFGB which also administers rules, determines amateur/professional status, runs tournaments in the UK and abroad, and supervises qualifying examinations for coaches on snow and artificial slopes.
Grass skiing is organised in the UK on behalf of the NSFGB by the *Ski Club of Great Britain*. It co-ordinates European, British, regional and local race circuits; selects the British team; qualifies instructors and fixes UK meetings.

Skips For Waste Removal Skips may not be deposited in a public place without prior permission from the local authority. The local *police* should also be informed.

Small Businesses in Wales Small manufacturing and servicing industries in Wales can obtain advice on all aspects of establishing or expanding their business from the Small Business Unit of the *Welsh Development Agency*. The Unit provides guidance on management, marketing and technical services and, where appropriate, can provide loan capital up to £50,000. The WDA also has a variety of factory sites and premises available, many ideally suited for the smaller firm.

Small Claims The main tribunal in England and Wales for the determination of small claims is the county court. Apply to the *County Court Office* for a claim form; small fee payable.
The county court registrar can refer consumer claims and other cases involving £200 or less to informal private arbitration at the request of either party; for cases involving more than £200, arbitration is with both parties' consent, or it can be left to the registrar to decide whether the case should go to arbitration. Circuit judges can refer cases involving up to £2,000 to arbitration.
The registrar normally acts as arbitrator; legal representation is discouraged. For claims of up to £100 no legal costs can be recovered except when one of the parties has acted unreasonably or when damages over £5 are awarded for personal injury. Helpful leaflets available from *Lord Chancellor's Office* or county courts.

In Scotland claims up to £50 may be treated inexpensively in the sheriff's Small Debt Court. Apply to **solicitor** or sheriff clerk. New arrangements for claims up to £250 in preparation. Northern Ireland has different procedures; apply to **solicitor**.

Smallholdings Local authorities in England and Wales let smallholdings to people with some agricultural experience who want to be self-employed farmers. They sometimes make loans of working capital to tenants of these statutory holdings (not to smallholders generally). Details from any local authority.

Statutory smallholdings with organised services and for horticulture only are also provided for people with some experience of practical farm work, on estates in England managed for the Ministry of Agriculture, Fisheries and Food by the *Land Settlement Association*. Loans of working capital are sometimes made to the tenants of these smallholdings.

All smallholders may also be considered for the general schemes of **agricultural finance**.

This is not applicable in Ireland; for Scotland, see **Agriculture: Scotland**.

Smoke Control Areas may be declared smoke control areas by **local authorities** under the Clean Air Acts 1956 and 1968. The emission of smoke from the chimneys of buildings including dwelling houses is prohibited although specific buildings may be exempted. Factories are controlled by local authorities through other provisions of the Clean Air Acts, frequently by smoke control orders, or in certain cases by *Health and Safety Executive, HM Alkali and Clean Air Inspectorate*.

Local authorities are obliged to publicise proposed smoke control areas and make provision for objections. After taking account of any objections, smoke control orders establishing the areas must be confirmed by the *Secretary of State for the Environment* at least six months before taking effect. Grants are available in respect of houses built before 16 August 1964 towards the cost of replacing or converting any coal burning appliance in regular use to enable it to meet the requirement of the smoke control order. The grant is based on the expenditure which the local authority considers reasonably necessary, at a rate of 70p in the pound of the approved cost (more in hardship cases). Apply to local authority, in time to ensure that expenditure is incurred between the date of confirmation of the order and that when the order comes into operation. Complaint of nuisance arising from smoke and other **air pollution** should be made in the first instance to the person or organisation apparently causing the nuisance; if this is ineffective complain to local authority.

See also **Air pollution; Work: health and safety**.

Snooker See **Billiards**.

Social Democratic and Labour Party Membership is open to individuals who subscribe to the principles and objects of the party and are not members of any other party; also to corporate bodies (e.g. **trade unions** affiliated to the Irish Congress of Trade Unions, cooperative societies, socialist societies, professional associations and cultural organisations) which accept the principles and objects of the party. Membership applications are handled centrally, apply to: *Social Democratic and Labour Party* headquarters in Belfast.

The main principles and objects of the SDLP are: maintaining a socialist party in Northern Ireland; cooperating with the Irish Congress of Trade Unions; promoting Irish unity based on the consent of the majority of people in Northern Ireland; contesting elections with a view to forming a Northern Ireland government which will abolish all forms of religious, political, class or sex discriminations; promoting culture and the arts, especially native culture; implementing public ownership and democratic control of essential industries and services as the common good requires, and providing employment as necessary, by the establishment of publicly owned industries.

Social Security Benefits Certain social security benefits are available as of right to residents of Great Britain in specific circumstances. These are child benefit (see **Child social security benefits**); **family income supplement**; non-contributory **invalidity** pensions; invalid care allowance, attendance allowance and other benefits for handicapped people (see **Disablement**); and free family planning advice and treatment (see **Contraception**).

There are also **supplementary benefits**, which are contingent on financial circumstances, and **national insurance** benefits, which depend on the amount and class of **national insurance contributions** and include additional allowances for a dependent wife or children (see table for details).

receive help with, or exclusion from certain charges: prescriptions (see **Medicines and appliances: prescription charges**), **dental charges, spectacles, milk** and **vitamins** (for all of which see leaflet M11); hospital fares (see **Hospital treatment** and leaflet H11); drugs and appliances supplied by **hospitals**; social services (see **Disablement: social services**); school meals and milk, school clothing assistance, educational maintenance allowances (see **Child social security benefits**); special help for blind and deaf persons (see **Blindness; Deafness**); services for physically handicapped people and the mentally disordered (see **Disablement; Mental disability**); **rent rebates and allowances, rate rebates**, and **Legal aid** and advice. General

**National Insurance Benefits
from different classes of contributions**

Class 1 contributions†	*Class 2 contributions*	*Class 3 contributions*
Unemployment benefit*	Sickness and invalidity benefits	Maternity grant
Sickness* and invalidity benefits	Maternity benefits	Widows' benefits
Industrial injury and disablement benefits	Widows' benefits	Retirement pension
Maternity* benefits	Retirement pension	Child's special allowance
Widows'** benefits	Child's special allowance	Death grant
Retirement pension	Death grant	
Guardian's allowance		
Child's special allowance		
Death grant		

† Reduced rate contributions paid by certain married women and widows do not give title to benefits other than industrial injury and disablement benefits.
* May be increased by earnings related supplement.
** May be increased by widows' earnings-related addition (see **Earnings-related supplement**).

Apply for social security benefits to *Department of Health and Social Security* local offices, except for unemployment benefit, for which apply to *Department of Employment* local unemployment benefit offices.
In addition residents of Great Britain receiving **supplementary benefit** or **family income supplement**, or whose income is below a certain level or in some cases, solely on grounds of age, medical circumstances or need, may

enquiries to *Department of Health and Social Security* (local offices).
Claims for social security benefits other than supplementary benefits and those benefits at the discretion of **local authorities** are generally decided by statutorily independent insurance officers of the *National Insurance Commissioners*. Appeal against an insurance office decision on a claim to a social security benefit is to a national insurance local tribunal and finally to

the National Insurance Commissioner. Apply to appeal to DHSS local officer or to *Department of Employment* local unemployment benefit offices in cases of unemployment benefit. The insurance officer first considers whether there are grounds for review of his original decision; if he is unable to find any grounds he will prepare the appeal for submission to the local tribunal. Appeal against a decision of the Supplementary Benefit Commission on a claim for supplementary benefit is to the Supplementary Benefits Appeal Tribunal; apply to DHSS local offices.

Social Workers The body responsible for the promotion of training and the award of qualifications for social work in local authority Social Services Departments, the **National Health Service**, the probation and education services, and in related voluntary work, is the *Central Council for Education and Training in Social Work*. The Council is an independent statutory body, and its responsibilities cover training for the health and welfare services, child care, probation after-care and work in centres for the mentally handicapped. Complaint against professional misconduct of a social worker should be made in the first instance to the employing authority or organisation. See also **Injustice: local.**

Socialist Party of Great Britain Membership is open to all who accept its objects and principles, which are 'to abolish private and state ownership of the means of production and distribution; to establish a world-wide community where wealth is commonly owned, production commonly controlled, and where there are no wages, no money, and all have free access to what is produced'.
Founded in 1904, the party is independent and opposed to all other political organisations except its companion parties in Australia, Austria, Canada, Ireland, New Zealand and USA. Enquiries to the *Socialist Party* head office or to branches, which are listed in the monthly 'Socialist Standard'.

Socialist Workers Party Membership is open to anyone subscribing to its aims. Enquires to *Socialist Workers Party*, London office.

Solicitors Formal title is Solicitor of the Supreme Court. To practise in England and Wales a solicitor must hold a practising certificate issued by the *Law Society*; in Scotland, by the *Law Society of Scotland*; and in Northern Ireland, by the *Incorporated Law Society of Northern Ireland*. In the UK it is not possible to be both a solicitor and a **barrister**. The basic qualification is both passing the relevant Society's qualifying examination and serving a period of articles, at least two years with a practising solicitor. In Scotland a degree in law from a Scottish university is required.
To find a solicitor: in England and Wales consult either the Law List or the Legal Aid National Referral List (both available for reference in any public library), in Scotland the Law Directory and in Northern Ireland a legal or commercial directory; the yellow pages of the telephone directory; or contact any *Citizens Advice Bureau*.
Complaints alleging professional misconduct against a solicitor in England or Wales are investigated by the LS. The Solicitors' Disciplinary Tribunal (independent of the LS) hears such complaints; if it finds a complaint justified, it has powers to 'strike-off' a solicitor (i.e. deprive him of the right to practise), suspend him or impose certain other penalties. The Lay Observer, an independent lay person appointed by the Lord Chancellor to observe the way in which the LS investigates complaints, can, if he thinks necessary, refer matters decided by the LS back to it for reconsideration. A similar system operates in Scotland where complaints are investigated by the LSS, heard by the Scottish Solicitors' Disciplinary Tribunal, and overseen by a Lay Observer appointed by the *Secretary of State for Scotland*.
Complaints alleging professional misconduct against Northern Ireland solicitors should be made in writing to the ILSNI.

Somali Democratic Republic For **exchange control** is a non-scheduled territory outside the **overseas sterling area** and the EEC. UK nationals travelling direct from the UK normally need only the following (but check): **passports; visas;** international certificates of **vaccination** against smallpox and yellow fever; **work permits** (if taking a job).
The UK has no reciprocal health or social security arrangements.
Enquiries to *Somali Democratic Republic Embassy* in London.
British diplomatic mission to Somali Democratic Republic is *British Embassy* in Mogadishu.

SOS Messages SOS messages on television and radio can be arranged by personal call, by letter or by telephone to the *British Broadcasting Corporation*. Occasionally arrangements can be made with the independent television programme companies to insert messages within ITV's local programmes. Arrangements can also be made with the independent local radio programme companies for the insertion of messages. Normally messages for relatives of dangerously sick people are only accepted with a medical certificate; messages for missing persons or witnesses from the police, messages concerning the treatment of rare diseases from major hospitals. Messages abroad in cases of urgency follow the same rules and go through the *European Broadcasting Union*, which has, as active members, broadcasting organisations in 31 countries. In the UK, the BBC and the *Independent Broadcasting Authority* are members.

South Africa For **exchange control** is a non-scheduled territory in the **overseas sterling area** but outside the EEC. UK nationals travelling direct from the UK normally need only the following (but check): **passports; visas** (but consult South African Embassy); international certificates of **vaccination** against smallpox; **work permits** (if taking a job); green cards for motor insurance (if bringing a car); international driving permits (if intending to drive: see **Motoring abroad**).
The UK has no reciprocal health or social security arrangements.
Enquiries to *South African Embassy* in London.
British diplomatic missions to South Africa are *British Embassy* in Pretoria (Cape Town – January to June), *British Consulates-General* in Johannesburg, Cape Town and Durban and *British Consulates* in East London and Port Elizabeth.

Soviet Union For **exchange control** is a non-scheduled territory outside the **overseas sterling area** and the EEC. UK nationals travelling direct from the UK normally need only the following (but check): **passports; visas; work permits** (if taking a job); green cards for motor insurance (if bringing a car); international driving permits (if intending to drive: see **Motoring abroad**).
Enquiries to *Soviet Union Embassy* in London and *Intourist* in London.
British diplomatic mission to Soviet Union is *British Embassy* in Moscow.

Spain For **exchange control** is a non-scheduled territory outside the **overseas sterling area** and the EEC. UK nationals travelling direct from the UK normally need only the following (but check): **passports; work permits** (if taking a job); green cards for motor insurance (if bringing a car); international driving permits (if intending to drive: see **Motoring abroad**).
UK reciprocal arrangements cover social security (see leaflet SA34 obtainable from *Department of Health and Social Security, Overseas Branch*), but not health.
Enquiries to *Spanish Embassy* in London, *Spanish Consulates-General* in Liverpool and Southampton and *Spanish Tourist Office (SSTD)* in London.
British diplomatic missions to Spain are *British Embassy* in Madrid, *British Consulates-General* in Barcelona and Bilbao, *British Consulates* in Algeciras, Alicante, Las Palmas (Grand Canary), Malaga, Palma (Balearic Is.), Santa Cruz de Teneriffe (Canary Is.) and Seville and

British Vice Consulates in seven other provincial centres and Ceuta (Spanish Morocco).

Spectacles Spectacles are available under the **National Health Service** from ophthalmic **opticians** and dispensing opticians on production of a prescription (see **Eye treatment**). You do not have to get your spectacles from the same firm as the prescription. Spectacles in the NHS range (which include frames, single vision lenses, bifocals, toughened lenses, prism lenses and tinted lenses) are subsidised. You can choose to have your spectacles made up in NHS lenses and frames; NHS lenses and private frame; or both private lenses and frame. The optician must show you the NHS range of frames if requested.

Most people have to pay the standard NHS charges, but children (i.e. people under 16 or still at school) are supplied free with spectacles in a NHS frame designated suitable for children, and receive lenses free in other NHS spectacles if they are 10 or over. People receiving **supplementary benefit** or **family income supplement** and others with low incomes (and their dependents: see **Families on low incomes**) are exempt from the charges and may claim a refund if they have paid them from the *Department of Health and Society Security* (local office); leaflet M11 from the DHSS or from main post offices gives details of how to claim help with NHS charges.

Replacement to the same prescription and repair are normally free for children with NHS spectacles who attend a school receiving the benefits of the NHS school health service (see **Child health services**), but everyone else has normally to pay the full cost unless they show they were not responsible for causing the damage or unless payment would cause financial hardship.

Damaged spectacles may be taken to any ophthalmic optician or dispensing optician, but preferably to the original supplier, who decides whether they can be repaired or replaced without a further sight test.

Speech Disability Treatment by a qualified speech therapist is available through the **National Health Service**. **Speech therapists** are trained to assess, diagnose and treat all forms of speech disabilities such as stuttering, disorders of language and articulation in children, and lost or impaired speech in adults following illness or injury. In the first instance, advice should always be sought from your family **doctor**. Children can be referred to a speech therapist directly via the school health service or sometimes even by the parents themselves.

See also **Child health services**.

Speech Therapists Speech therapists practising in the **National Health Service** must have a qualification recognised by the *College of Speech Therapists*. The CST recognises a number of degree courses and courses awarding its own diploma. It produces an annual list of members which is available at public libraries, but not all speech therapists practising or eligible to practise in the UK are members. In the great majority of cases, patients are referred to a speech therapist by a doctor.

Complaints about professional misconduct are investigated by the CST. Complaints about disciplinary matters concerning NHS employees are investigated by the employing authority (i.e. the *area health authority* or Board of Governors in England and Wales, the *Health Board* in Scotland, or the *Area Health and Social Services Board* in Northern Ireland. Address complaints to the appropriate body.

See also **Disputes with public authorities**.

Spirits: Distillers' and Dealers' Licences
No person may manufacture spirits in the UK by distillation or any other process except under the authority of a distiller's licence; apply to *Her Majesty's Customs and Excise*. The sale of spirits (or the soliciting or taking of orders for spirits) in wholesale quantities (two gallons or one case) requires a spirits dealer's licence; apply to HMCE (details in Notice 26).

See also **Alcohol**.

Sponsored Visits to UK The *British Council* administers schemes for UK study and professional visits by overseas nationals. Its responsibilities vary but can cover selection, placing, travel to the UK, reception on arrival, accommodation, programming, payment of allowances, UK travel, general welfare and repatriation at the end of the visit. The BCs own programmes include specialist courses for groups from overseas; summer schools for overseas teachers of English; and symposia, conferences and seminars arranged on request from other countries. It also awards scholarships for one year's postgraduate study and fellowships for 2-3 years' postgraduate work; it places overseas scholars nominated and financed by their own countries in UK institutions; and finances short term professional and academic visits (e.g. by ministers and vice chancellors); it also arranges individual and group professional study programmes on a payment basis.

Schemes which the BC administers for other bodies include the Ministry of Overseas Development's bilateral Technical Cooperation Training Programme; the Commonwealth Education Fellowship Scheme; Indian Centres of Advanced Study Scheme; Tropical Medicine Awards; UK components of schemes of the United Nations and UN specialised agencies such as FAO, WHO, etc.; certain council of Europe Schemes; and the UK programme under the OECD Training Scheme. The BC is responsible to the *Commonwealth Scholarship Commission* for travel, payments and general welfare of award holders under the Commonwealth Scholarship and Fellowship Plan.

Application procedures for all these schemes vary: many awards are obtainable by a nomination only; some by a personal application through the *British Council Overseas office* or the *British diplomatic mission* in the applicant's country. General enquiries to Home Division Administration Unit, at the British Council or the British Council Overseas Office in the country concerned.

Sport For most individual sports there is a governing or representative body covering the UK or Great Britain as a whole, while for many sports there are also separate and subordinate bodies for some or all of the constituent countries, i.e. England, Wales, Scotland and Northern Ireland (all Ireland in some cases). (See entries for each sport.) Government finance for UK, British and English sport is administered by the *Sports Council*; for Scottish sport by the *Scottish Sports Council*; for Welsh by the *Sports Council for Wales*; and for Northern Ireland by the *Sports Council for Northern Ireland*.

The four Sports Councils are independent and separate bodies whose members are appointed by the Secretaries of State for the Environment, for Scotland, for Wales or for Northern Ireland as appropriate.

The Councils foster sport and physical recreation, encouraging both higher standards and wider participation. The three Councils in Great Britain give capital grants for providing or improving sports facilities, and each of the four UK Councils offer revenue grants to governing bodies of sport for administration, coaching, training, development and international events. They also support special projects, e.g. for the handicapped and in deprived urban areas.

All the Councils provide information for the public and technical advice to local authorities, governing bodies of sport, and other appropriate agencies. The *Sports Council National Documentation Centre* at Birmingham University provides a UK bibliographic service for sports research.

Each of the Councils operates one or more national sports centres with residential and training facilities. The *Sports Council Sports Centres* are at Bisham Abbey, Crystal Palace, Holme Pierrepoint (water sports only), Lilleshall Hall, Cowes (sailing), and Plas y Brenin (mountaineering). The *Scottish Sports Council Sports Centres* are Glenmore Lodge (outdoor training), Inverclyde, and Cumbrae (water sports).

The *Sports Council for Wales Sports Centre* is the National Sports

Centre in Cardiff. The Sports Council for Northern Ireland operates the *Northern Ireland Mountain Centre* at Tollymore.

Within England nine Sports Council Regional Councils – autonomous bodies working through local authorities, local sports organisations, etc. – are concerned with developing indoor and outdoor recreation; promoting public participation; long-term strategies for sports development; and setting up local sports councils.

Within Scotland local authorities and local sports organisations are encouraged to form jointly Islands, Regional or District Sports Councils to encourage the development of sport within the respective local authority area.

Within Northern Ireland district councils are encouraged to form District Sports Councils.

In each country there is a body representative of the governing bodies of sport for that country. The collective representative of English sporting and recreational organisations (and of some British governing bodies) is the *Central Council of Physical Recreation*. It advises the public on how to join a sports club, who to contact in a sports organisation, and gives information about participation in sport, sponsorship, press and television consulting. The *Scottish Standing Conference of Sport*; the *Welsh Sports and Games Association*; the *Northern Ireland Council of Physical Recreation* do similar work in their countries. Facilities for sport are available to local societies and clubs on application to the Recreation Department of the local authority.

Sport for the Disabled Sport for the disabled is governed worldwide by the International Sports Organisation for the Disabled and in the UK by the *British Sports Association for the Disabled*. BSAD selects international teams, organises national games at senior and junior level and arranges courses for those working with the disabled. Organisation is through BSAD branches in England and Northern Ireland and the *Scottish Sports Association for the Disabled* and the *Welsh Sports Association for the Disabled*. (Paraplegics in Ulster can also contact the *Northern Ireland Paraplegic Association*.) Sports in which the disabled officially participate include angling, archery, badminton, basket ball, canoeing, cricket, fencing, field events (shot putt, discus, javelin, medicine ball), football, golf, club throwing, pony riding, rambling, rifle shooting, rink bowls, sailing, shinty, slalom, snooker, swimming, ten pin bowling, table tennis, track events (walking, running, wheelchair races) and volley ball.

See also **Disablement**.

Sports Grounds Under the Safety of Sports Grounds Act 1975, regulations about the issue of safety certificates by **local authorities** in England and Wales; designation of grounds; determination of appeals in relation to certificates in England are the responsibility of the *Home Secretary*. A guide to the Act is available from *Her Majesty's Stationery Office*; enquiries initially to the local authority. The Act applies similarly in Scotland.

Squash The International Squash Rackets Federation governs world squash. The central British authority, the *Squash Rackets Association*, selects and coaches UK and English teams, administers the rules, controls professional and amateur status, sets standards for equipment and court specifications, co-ordinates fixtures, and also runs national and international tournaments, examinations for coaches, referees and marking, and a technical advisory service for clubs. The *Welsh Squash Rackets Association*, the *Scottish Squash Rackets Association* and the *Irish Squash Rackets Association* (all Ireland) govern the sport within their countries.

Separate bodies deal with professional coaches in clubs (*Squash Rackets Professionals' Association*), professional competitors (*International Squash Players Association*).

Women's squash is governed by the *Women's Squash Rackets Association* (UK and England), the *Irish Women's Squash Rackets Association* (Ulster and Eire) and the WSRA and SSRA women's sections.

Squatting Local authorities may license the use of houses awaiting demolition or renovation for the use of squatters – apply to local authority (housing or social services departments) Some housing associations have similar arrangements. Squatters may arrange for the supply of services to the premises.

Squatting without a licence is not a criminal offence unless damage or theft occurs or an offence is committed under Part II of the Criminal Law Act 1977 which provides five specific offences in relation to squatting: to use or threaten violence to secure entry to premises on which another is present; for a trespasser to fail to leave premises when required to do so by or on behalf of a displaced residential occupier or a protected intending occupier (a person intending to take up occupation who has purchased the property for that purpose or who has been allocated a tenancy by a **local authority, housing association, New Town** Development Corporation or the Commission for New Towns); for a trespasser to have a weapon of offence upon the premises which he entered as a trespasser; to enter or remain upon the premises of a diplomatic mission as a trespasser; to restrict or obstruct an officer of the court who is seeking to execute an order for possession against a trespasser.

Any house owner, including a landlord, may go to court for a possession order if his property is squatted: consult a **solicitor**.

Sri Lanka **Commonwealth** member. For **exchange control** is a non-scheduled territory in the **overseas sterling area** but outside the **EEC**. UK nationals travelling direct from the UK normally need only the following (but check): **passports**; **visas**; international certificates of **vaccination** against smallpox; **work permits** (if taking a job); green cards for motor insurance (if bringing a car); international driving permits recommended (if intending to drive: see **Motoring abroad**).

The UK has no reciprocal health or social security arrangements.
Enquires to *Sri Lanka High Commission* in London.
British diplomatic mission to Sri Lanka is *British High Commission* in Colombo.

Stamp Duty Stamp duty is the oldest extant UK tax, first imposed in 1694. Today by law many commercial and legal documents need to be stamped (e.g. conveyances of land and buildings; leases; share transers). The stamp is normally impressed on the document and shows the amount of duty, which can be fixed or variable depending for example on the type of transaction and the value or cost of the property.

Stamp duty is administered by the *Inland Revenue, Stamp Offices*. Disagreements between the payer of the duty and the IR can be resolved through the High Court; apply in first instance to the *Inland Revenue, Stamp Offices Adjudication Section* in Worthing.

See also **Land, houses and other buildings: buying**.

Stamps National insurance, inland revenue, land registry, insolvency, television licence and postage stamps are available at most post offices. If collectors deposit cash with the *Philatelic Bureau* in Edinburgh, new stamps and first day covers are sent automatically as they are issued by the Post Office. Specific orders are also taken. The 'Philatelic Bulletin', published monthly, gives details of all new stamp issues, first day cover services and postmarks. Philatelic services are also available at the *Post Office Chief Office* and at head post offices in London (Trafalgar Square), Belfast, Birmingham, Blackpool, Bournemouth, Brighton, Bristol, Cardiff, Edinburgh, Glasgow, Leeds, Liverpool, Manchester, Newcastle, Oxford, Sheffield, Southampton. See also **Post offices**.

Statistics Each government department prepares its own statistics, which are collected and co-ordinated by the *Central Statistical Office*. The

Key Statistics and Departmental Sources

Agriculture, fisheries and food	*Ministry of Agriculture, Fisheries and Food, Statistics*
Balance of payments	*Central Statistical Office*
Betting and liquor licensing	*Home Office, Statistics*
British aid	*Ministry of Overseas Development, Statistics*
Capital expenditure and stocks of industry	*Department of Industry, Statistics*
Civil Service Employment	*Civil Service Department, Statistics*
Company accounts	*Department of Industry, Statistics*
Construction industries	*Department of the Environment, General Statistics*
Criminal, Justice and Penal matters	*Home Office, Statistics*
Distribution, Census of	*Business Statistics Office*
Earnings, wage rates	*Department of Employment, Statistics*
Education	*Department of Education and Science, Statistics*
Electoral statistics	*Home Office, Statistics*
Employment, unemployment, unfilled vacancies	*Department of Employment, Statistics*
Financial statistics	*Central Statistical Office*
Health and social security	*Department of Health and Social Security, Statistics*
Hire purchase	*Department of Trade, Statistics*
Households	*Department of the Environment, Statistics*
Housing	*Department of the Environment, General Statistics*
Immigration	*Home Office, Statistics*
Industrial production, Index of	*Central Statistical Office*
Insurance	*Department of Industry, Statistics*
Local government financial statistics	*Department of the Environment, General Statistics*
National accounts, etc.	*Central Statistical Office*
Northern Ireland statistics	*Northern Ireland Office Statistics*
Population and vital statistics (England and Wales)	*Office of Population Censuses and Surveys, Statistics*
Price indices: retail	*Department of Employment, Statistics*
wholesale	*Department of Industry, Statistics*
Production, Census of	*Business Statistics Office, Production census*
Retail Trade	*Department of Trade, Statistics*
Road accidents	*Department of the Environment, General Statistics*
Roads, road traffic	*Department of the Environment, Road Statistics*
Seaport traffic	*Department of the Environment, General Statistics*
Taxes: direct	*Board of Inland Revenue, Statistics*
indirect (e.g. VAT)	*Her Majesty's Customs and Excise, Statistics*
Tourism	*Department of Trade, Statistics*
Trade statistics	*Department of Trade, Statistics*
Scottish statistics	*Scottish Office, Statistics*
Welsh statistics	*Welsh Office, Statistics*

main statistics and departmental sources are tabled below. A list of all major statistical publications and departmental contact points is available (free) from CSO Press and Information Service – 'Government Statistics: a brief guide to sources'. Much of the information is designed to be readily usable by people outside government (e.g. business management) and is published regularly by *Her Majesty's Stationery Office*. Other information is available on request from the CSO, the *Statistics and Market Intelligence Library* and the *Business Statistics Office*.

Steam Boiler and Pressure Plant Responsibility for UK policy on matters relating to the safety of pressure systems containing steam, air, water, vapour, gas or liquid lies with the Safety and General Branch at the *Health and Safety Executive* (head office). Responsibility for determining technical standards for the design and safe operation of steam boiler and other pressure plant, and preparing technical codes of practice, guidance notes and advisory literature lies with the *Health and Safety Executive, HM Factory Inspectorate, Consultant Section F17B*. Technical advice at a local level on pressure systems safety from *Health and Safety Executive, HM Factory Inspectorate* (area offices). See also **Work: health and safety**.

Sterilisation Sterilisation is available free of charge under the **National Health Service**. Apply to your **doctor** or to a family planning clinic; either will make the necessary arrangements where it is agreed that sterilisation is the appropriate form of birth control. The spouse or steady sex partner of the person concerned is usually counselled over the nature and implications of the operations; doctors may refuse to operate if they consider that sterilisation is not suitable in a particular case or if the spouse does not agree to the operation. The *Medical Defence Union* and the *Department of Health and Social Security* advise doctors not to carry out a sterilisation operation for birth control purposes if the spouse withholds consent.

Sterling Securities: Exchange Control Authorised depositaries can make freely and promptly the majority of purchases and sales of sterling securities quoted on the *Stock Exchange* (see **Stock Exchange**) on behalf of all persons, wherever resident. An **authorised depositary** must establish the residential status for exchange control purposes of both buyer and seller. If the buyer is resident outside the scheduled territories (see **exchange control**) payment in foreign currency or in sterling from an account of a person resident abroad must be obtained by the authorised depositary on or before the date of completion. If the seller is resident abroad, the authorised depositary may normally effect the deal and lodge the transfer, remitting the proceeds abroad or crediting them to external account, provided that certain conditions are met.

All issues of securities in the UK require approval but where the person acquiring the securities is resident in the scheduled territories (and is not acting as a nominee for a non-resident) the issue can generally be made without reference to the Bank of England. Permission is also required for the issue of sterling bearer securities and for any act which would result in a corporate body ceasing to be controlled by UK residents (see **Direct investment**). Enquiries to *Bank of England*. Certain sterling securities (chiefly bearer securities) must be kept in the custody of an authorised depositary if owned by UK residents or if held in the UK by non-residents. The import and export of registered sterling securities may generally be effected without formality but those sterling securities which are depositable may be exported by authorised depositaries only in accordance with the BE's rules.

Still-births Births of children who are still-born (i.e. born after the 28th week of pregnancy without breathing or showing any signs of life) must be registered much as for a live birth (see **Birth registration**). The information required by the Registrar of Births, Deaths and Marriages is the same as for a live birth, except that the still-born child is not given a name or surname.

A certificate of still-birth signed by a medical practitioner (see **Doctors**) or a certified **midwife** will normally be available and must be produced to the registrar at the time of registration (or, rarely, a coroner's certificate in England, Wales and Northern Ireland). No extracts or certificates of still-birth entries are issued except on the authority of the *Registrar General for England and Wales*, the *Registrar General for Scotland*, or the *Registrar General for Northern Ireland* as appropriate.

A still-birth may not be registered after three months (except in Northern Ireland after an inquest) and cannot be registered by a declaration made outside the sub-district where it occurred.

Stock Exchange Listing The right for a UK company's stocks or shares to be bought and sold on the *Stock Exchange* can only be obtained by satisfying the strict conditions laid down in the SE 'Yellow Book' (available from the Public Relations Department at the SE). Conditions include a minimum of five years' trading background with satisfactory accounts; a capital value of at least £500,000; and an agreement by the company to publish full and regular financial information (much more than is required by law: see **Companies**). The company must also sign an agreement before being admitted to listing. Listing is granted (and withdrawn if the terms of the listing agreement are broken) by the Quotations Committee of the SE. Any foreign company already listed on a stock exchange recognised by the SE may be freely dealt in (see also **Securities: sale and purchase**).

Unlisted (i.e. not quoted) shares may be bought and sold in the market with the prior consent of the Quotations Committee; advice from a **stockbroker**.

Stock Exchange Visits The public can watch the *Stock Exchange* at work from the public galleries in London, Glasgow, Manchester and Dublin. It is advisable to contact the Public Relations Department at the SE in advance.

Stockbrokers and Stockjobbers Stockbrokers and jobbers must be individually elected members of the *Stock Exchange* to deal on any of the *Stock Exchange trading floors* in Britain and Ireland. (See **Securities: sale and purchase**). It is not possible to be both a broker and a jobber.

Investors can obtain the names of three stockbroking firms willing to deal with new clients from the Public Relations Department at the SE; they can be introduced to brokers by banks and solicitors; or they can ask a bank to deal directly with a broking firm on their behalf.

To become a member of the SE involves working for three years in the office of a SE member firm (list available from the Education Department at the SE); passing the SE examination (brokers); nomination for election by two members; and election by the SE Council. Nationality restrictions have been abolished. All members' names and addresses (home and business) are entered on the SE Members Book (available for public purchase from the Membership Department of the SE and for reference in most business libraries).

New members must join one of the SE existing member firms. They must pay £1,000 to the SE Nomination Redemption Fund (which exists to compensate those members who, prior to 1965, purchased the right to apply for membership from an outgoing member) and the annual £300 subscription fee to the SE. Enquiries to the Membership Department at the SE.

Clients can complain about the professional conduct of a SE member firm (including its office management and financial analysis) and of individual brokers and jobbers to the Central Advisory Department at the SE which investigates complaints and may require the firm concerned to make reparation. If a SE member firm is 'hammered' (i.e. unable to meet its commitments) the SE Council will consider claims for losses by clients; these may be met out of the SE's discretionary compensation fund.

SE members who are principals in their firms have unlimited personal liability for the commitments of their firm; associate members (i.e. those employed by member firms) can assume voluntarily unlimited liability if they are employed by a limited corporate member. (A small number of firms are limited liability companies in order to be able to attract outside investment; each outside investor is limited to 10% liability.)

New firms are admitted to SE membership if all the partners are already members of the SE and the firm can comply with the minimum liquidity requirements. The SE Council sets these requirements and determines admission.

Dealers in securities who are not members of the SE must be licensed or otherwise exempted under the Prevention of Fraud (Investments) Act 1958; apply to Companies Administration Division, *Department of Trade* (headquarters). A list of licensed or exempted dealers is published annually in 'Particulars of Dealers in Securities and of Unit Trusts' available from *Her Majesty's Stationery Office*. Amendments to the list appear in 'Trade and Industry', in editions published on the second Friday of each month, available from Department of Industry headquarters (1).

See also **Securities: sale and purchase**; **Securities: prices**.

Stranded People   People who become stranded or destitute in the UK should seek advice from the local *police* who may be able to assist with immediate accommodation and travel problems (see also **Homelessness**).

Stray Animals   Strays should be reported or taken to the local *police*, who will place them in a pound pending recovery by the owner.

Street Collections   In the Metropolitan Police District of London no collection or sale of any article may be made in the street or a public place unless a permit has been obtained from the Commissioner of Police at the *Metropolitan Police Force Headquarters*; and then only on the day and between the hours and in the district stated in the permit. The position in other areas depends on local **byelaws** (see also **Street trading**).

Street Messengers   In the London Metropolitan Police District the Commissioner of Police at *Metropolitan Police Force Headquarters* is empowered to license messengers and assign them places at which to ply their trade. Licenses are in force for one year.

Street Musicians   The *police* in London streets will not normally intervene unless there is obstruction or an objection from a member of the public. Elsewhere there are sometimes **byelaws** forbidding musicians (e.g. covering transport authorities' areas).

Street Trading   Street trading is controlled only where local legislation is in force. Street trading licences are issued only for certain pitches in designated streets. Licences are issued by **local authorities** who can also charge for the removal of refuse and for administration; this is sometimes set out in **byelaws**. Information from the local authority.

Strikes: Supplementary Benefit
Supplementary benefit is available for a participant's family living with him, but not for a striker's own requirements. A single man or woman on strike cannot receive **supplementary benefit** unless he or she is able to prove 'urgent need'. In calculating income strike pay and **income tax** refunds, together with certain kinds of other income, are taken into account, though up to £4 per week may be ignored. Claims to *Department of Health and Social Security* (local offices) (who may, however, redirect claims during a strike).

The decision as to whether a person is involved in a trade dispute is made by the independent insurance officer specially appointed under the Social Security Act 1975 to consider claims for **unemployment benefit**; there is a right of appeal against his decision. The *Supplementary Benefits Com-*

mission, which is responsible for supplementary benefits although they are claimed through DHSS local offices, follows his decision in the claim for supplementary benefit and there is also a right of appeal against the Commission's decision.
In the first 15 days after return to work a striker can get benefit as a loan (if he does not receive sufficient wages or advance from his employer) which is subsequently deducted from his later earnings by the employer. Details in leaflet SB2 available from DHSS local offices.

Strikes, Work to Rule, etc. Official industrial action means that the action is supported by the unions to which those taking action belong; unofficial means it is not union-supported. Each **trade union** has its own decision procedure. The decision is made at national level.
See also **Industrial disputes**.

Student and Youth Exchanges
These are promoted internationally by the *British Council* through the administration of official funds on the advice of voluntary organisations and other interests. Enquiries to: Exchanges Department, at the *British Council Headquarters* or the *British Council Overseas Office* in the country concerned.

Student Grants Students attending full-time courses leading to a first degree or a comparable or nearly comparable qualification, and resident in England or Wales, may be entitled to a mandatory student grant. The *Department of Education and Science* designates the courses according to the local authority Awards Regulations 1977. Educational institutions wishing to offer a designated course, comparable to first degree courses, should enquire to DES.
In England and Wales, *local education authorities* are obliged by law to award grants to 'eligible' students who have been accepted on such designated courses. Authorities also have discretionary powers to make similar awards to students who have been accepted on other courses or who do not comply with all the conditions of eligibility. Use of these powers varies widely between authorities. Students must apply before the course starts to the authority of the area in which they are normally resident by 30 June/31 October/28 February for autumn/spring/summer/course starts respectively.
'Eligible' students normally must have lived in the UK for three years immediately preceding the course (unless student, spouse or parent has been temporarily employed abroad); have not previously attended any course of further education (however financed); have applied in writing to the authority before the start of the course; have passed 2 'A' levels or equivalent; and give a written undertaking to repay any excess payments.
'Designated courses' are all courses leading to a British university first degree; a Council for National Academic Awards first degree; a diploma of higher education; a higher national diploma; three-year university diploma courses; initial teacher training including postgraduate certificates in education or art teachers certificates or diploma. Some part-time teacher-training courses and a small number of individual courses are also designated. Individuals wishing to know which courses are designated in England and Wales may obtain the booklet 'Designated Courses' from the Information Division at the DES.
For the following non-designated courses grants are normally available, but at the local education authority's discretion: courses leading to 'A' levels; Ordinary National Diploma; Open University; Trinity College, Dublin; National University of Ireland; overseas universities; independent theological colleges and seminaries; vocational postgraduate courses (not research/training); British Council courses in Germany and British Institute courses in Paris before employment as 'assistants'; courses, where the employer is not paying, leading to the Law Society Qualifying Examinations; training courses for **social workers, health visitors,** youth officers and community

centre wardens; and some day-release courses. Local education authorities tend to support courses within their own area.
The level of grant for designated and non-designated courses is broadly similar, except for students under 19 attending a non-advanced course (e.g. 'A' level), where the grant is equivalent to that for staying on at school (e.g. books, travel, lunches, etc.).
Grants are normally calculated by assessing students' requirements in terms of maintenance, etc., and deducting the student's resources, which include student's income, spouse's contribution and, except where the student has been self-supporting for three years or is mature, i.e. over 25, parents' contribution based on parents' income.
Mature students' rates are higher and grants for two homes and dependents are available, subject to certain conditions. Students in receipt of mandatory awards will in future have their fees paid by the local education authority.
In Northern Ireland, the area *education and library boards* provide student grants under similar arrangements.
See also **Education: Scotland**; **Education: Northern Ireland**.

Student Grants: Professions Supplementary to Medicine Grants for trainee orthoptists, physiotherapists, occupational therapists, radiographers, remedial gymnasts, dental hygienists and dental auxiliaries are available from the *Department of Health and Social Security* (Awards Section), or the *Scottish Education Department*. The conditions of these grants are the same as other mandatory student grants (see **Student grants**).
See also entry on each profession, and **Professions supplementary to medicine**.

Sudan For **exchange control** is a non-scheduled territory outside the **overseas sterling area** and the **EEC**. UK nationals travelling direct from the UK normally need only the following (but check): **passports** without Israeli stamp; **visas**; international certificates of **vaccination** against smallpox; **work permits** (if taking a job).
The UK has no reciprocal health or social security arrangements.
Enquiries to *Sudanese Embassy* in London.
British diplomatic mission to Sudan is *British Embassy* in Khartoum.

Suez Canal Certificates These are issued in the UK by the *Department of Trade*.

Sugar Beet In the UK sugar beet is grown under contracts made annually between growers and the *British Sugar Corporation*. Minimum beet prices, related to sugar production within national quotas, are fixed each year under **EEC** regulations. Sugar beet growers and the BSC contribute equally to a levy for research and education.

Suicide and Despair If you are in trouble phone the *Samaritans* any time day or night. The Samaritans offer through their 167 branches in the UK and Eire a 24-hour absolutely confidential service (free of charge) of listening and befriending the suicidal and despairing.
See also **Samaritans**.

Supplementary Benefits Supplementary benefits are social security cash benefits payable to people in Great Britain who are not in full-time work or full time secondary education and whose income is not enough to meet their requirements. They are not generally available to single people unless in urgent need. Supplementary benefits comprise supplementary pension for those over pensionable age and supplementary allowance for other people aged 16 or over. They do not depend on **national insurance contributions**.
Requirements are assessed on 'scale rates' which are intended to provide for all normal day-to-day living expenses, including heating. They take account of dependants, housing costs (e.g. rent, mortgage interest for owner occupiers, rates) and special needs (e.g. extra heating allowance for poor health, or central heating for damp

rooms). Higher scale rates apply to pensioners and people under pensionable age other than the unemployed who have received supplementary benefit for two years or more. Entitlement of supplementary benefit depends on the income of husband, wife or dependants living in the same household. Husband and wife may earn up to £4 per week without entitlement being affected and the first £4 of any other income which the household may have is disregarded. Income from capital is taken into account by assuming capital of £1,250 or above to produce an income of 25p per week per £50 over £1,200 whatever the actual income from the capital may be. (Capital of less than £1,250 is ignored together with any income it may produce). The value of owner occupied houses is ignored.
Details in leaflet SB1 available from post offices or *Department of Health and Social Security* (local offices). People who are fit and under pension age are normally required to register for work as a condition of receiving supplementary benefit; apply to *Department of Employment* (local unemployment benefit offices).
Recipients of supplementary benefit are visited at intervals by DHSS officers. In certain circumstances disabled people may qualify even when in full-time work; students in higher education may qualify exceptionally during vacation if they are available for employment. Appeal against a decision on supplementary benefits to an independent Appeal Tribunal – apply DHSS local offices within 21 days of decision.
See also **Trade disputes; Strikes; Social security benefits.**

Surfing Surfing is governed internationally by the International (World) Surfing Federation and the European Surfing Association. In Great Britain and the Channel Isles, the *British Surfing Association* sets rules for contests, organises national championships and selects British and English teams. Welsh and Scottish teams are selected by the *Welsh Surfing Federation* and the *Scottish Surfing Federation*, which are affiliated to the BSA.

Surinam For **exchange control** is a non-scheduled territory outside the **overseas sterling area** and the **EEC**. UK nationals travelling direct from the UK normally need only the following (but check): **passports**; **work permits** (if taking a job); green cards for motor insurance (if bringing a car); international driving permits (if intending to drive: see **Motoring abroad**).
The UK has no reciprocal health or social security arrangements.
Enquiries to *Surinam Embassy* at The Hague, Netherlands.
The *British diplomatic mission* to Surinam is the *British Consulate* at Paramaribo. The ambassador resides at Georgetown, Guyana.

Survey Information Information on triangulation, levelling and conversion of rectangular and geographical co-ordinates is available from *Ordnance Survey*, Southampton. Permission must always be obtained from the land owner or tenant for access to any particular station or point located on private property.

Surveyors Surveyors can practise in the UK without qualifications, but the best qualified professionally are chartered surveyors, who are either Associates or Fellows of the *Royal Institution of Chartered Surveyors*. They qualify by passing the RICS examinations (or by obtaining a degree which affords exemption), and by completing a period of approved professional experience. Their professional functions include valuation and estate agency, quantity surveying, building surveying, land agency, land and mineral surveying and planning and development.
To find a chartered surveyor see the RICS yearbook which is available at most public libraries, or contact the information officer at RICS headquarters.
Complaints of professional misconduct are investigated by the RICS which has power to impose disciplinary sanctions upon members.

Swans Swans are royal birds, which by tradition belong to the Sovereign. There are exceptions; on the Thames certain birds also belong to the *Dyers Company* and the *Vintners Company*. Her Majesty and the companies only exercise their jurisdiction on the lower reaches of the Thames. In the ceremony of Swan Upping, the keeper of Her Majesty's Swans and the two companies identify the birds. The companies' swans are marked with nicks on their beaks; unmarked birds are the property of the Sovereign.

Swaziland Commonwealth member. For **exchange control** is a non-scheduled territory in the **overseas sterling area** but outside the **EEC**. UK nationals travelling direct from the UK normally need only the following (but check): **passports**; **work permits** (if taking a job); green cards for motor insurance (if bringing a car); international driving permits (if intending to drive: see **Motoring abroad**).
The UK has no reciprocal health or social security arrangements.
Enquiries to *Swaziland High Commission* in London.
British diplomatic mission to Swaziland is *British High Commission* in Mbabane.

Sweden For **exchange control** is a non-scheduled territory outside the **overseas sterling area** and the **EEC**. UK nationals travelling direct from the UK normally need only the following (but check): **passports**; **work permits** (if taking a job).
UK reciprocal arrangements cover social security (see leaflet SA9 obtainable from *Department of Health and Social Security, Overseas Group*), and health. In-patient treatment and certain prescribed medicines are free to those normally residing in UK; 75% of cost of general practitioner and out-patient treatment reimbursed on production of receipt and UK passport at local administration office.
Enquires to *Royal Swedish Embassy* in London.
British diplomatic missions to Sweden are *British Embassy* in Stockholm, *British Consulate-General* in Gothenburg and *British Consulates* in six other provincial centres.

Swimming Swimming is governed internationally by the Fédération Internationale de Natation Amateur, and overall in the UK by the *Amateur Swimming Federation of Great Britain*, which selects UK teams. In England the *Amateur Swimming Association*, via five regional districts, organises national championships, disabled swimming, education, diving, water polo, etc., sets standards for facilities and safety and selects English teams. Equivalent bodies in Wales, Scotland and Ireland (Northern Ireland and Eire) are the *Welsh Amateur Swimming Association*, the *Scottish Amateur Swimming Association* and the *Irish Amateur Swimming Association*.

Swimming Pools Planning permission from local authority is required for building a public swimming pool and a licence is required from the *water authority* or *water company* (see **Water services**) to fill it. Water is metered and charged for by volume.

Swiss Bank Accounts Swiss bank accounts, including those held by foreigners, are secret under criminal Swiss law, unless the Swiss Civil or Criminal Codes specifically require otherwise (e.g. actions involving inheritance, bankruptcy, debt collection and all criminal cases). Foreign governments can only obtain information under multilateral conventions and where the offence is a crime under Swiss law. Tax evasion – simple failure to declare or pay taxes – is not a crime in Switzerland. Swiss bank accounts may be numbered: only a few senior bank officials know the name which goes with the number, but it is not possible, under the law, to open a Swiss bank account unless the identity of the holder is known to the bank. UK nationals wishing to open a Swiss bank account come under the **exchange control** regulations for bank accounts

Switzerland

overseas. Enquiries in the UK to the London offices of the three largest Swiss banks: *Credit Suisse*; *Swiss Bank Corporation*; and *Union Bank of Switzerland*.

Switzerland For **exchange control** is a non-scheduled territory outside the **overseas sterling area** and the **EEC**. UK nationals travelling direct from the UK normally need only the following (but check): **passports**; **work permits** (if taking a job).

UK reciprocal arrangements cover special social security (see leaflet SA6 obtainable from *Department of Health and Social Security, Overseas Group*), but not health.

Enquires to *Swiss Embassy* in London and *Swiss National Tourist Office* in London.

British diplomatic missions to Switzerland are *British Embassy* in Berne, *British Consulates-General* in Geneva and Zurich, *British Consulates* in Basle and Lugano and *British Vice-Consulate* in Montreux.

Syria

Syria For **exchange control** is a non-scheduled territory outside the **overseas sterling area** and the **EEC**. UK nationals travelling direct from the UK normally need only the following (but check): **passports** without Israeli stamp; **visas**; international certificates of **vaccination** against smallpox; **work permits** (if taking a job); green cards for motor insurance (if bringing a car); international driving permits (if intending to drive: see **Motoring abroad**).

The UK has no reciprocal health or social security arrangements.

Enquiries to *Syrian Embassy* in London.

British diplomatic mission to Syria is *British Embassy* in Damascus.

T

Table Tennis Table tennis is controlled internationally by the International Table Tennis Federation, in Europe by the European Table Tennis Union, and in the UK by the *English Table Tennis Association* (England), the *Table Tennis Association of Wales* (Wales), the *Scottish Table Tennis Association* (Scotland) and the *Irish Table Tennis Association* (all Ireland). Each is responsible in its region for administering the laws, international tournaments, coaching, qualification of umpires and referees and selecting the national teams.

Take-over and Mergers The City Panel on Take-overs and Mergers administers and enforces the City Code, whose provisions must be followed in any take-over bid for a UK public company. The Code, which does not have the force of law, represents the collective opinion of those professionally concerned in the field of take-overs and mergers on a range of business standards. The Panel is a body representative of those using the securities markets and one of the cornerstones of the City's self-regulatory system.

Tanzania Commonwealth member. For **exchange control** is a non-scheduled territory in the **overseas sterling area** but outside the **EEC**. UK nationals travelling direct from the UK normally need only the following (but check): **passports**; international certificates of **vaccination** against smallpox; **work permits** (if taking a job); green cards for motor insurance (if bringing a car); international driving permits (if intending to drive: see **Motoring abroad**).
The UK has no reciprocal health or social security arrangements.
Enquiries to *Tanzanian High Commission* in London.
British diplomatic mission to Tanzania is *British High Commission* in Dar-es-Salaam.

Taxis The *Home Secretary* has power under the Metropolitan Public Carriage Act 1869 to prescribe fares in respect of journeys by cab within the Metropolitan Police district and the City of London. Under the London Cab Order 1934 (amended in 1955) the Assistant Commissioner of the *Metropolitan Police Force* has responsibility for granting driver's carriage licence having due regard to the fitness of the vehicle; enquiries to *Public Carriage Office*. Outside the London area, **local authorities** (district councils) can take powers under the Local Government Miscellaneous Provisions Act 1976 or the Town Police Clauses Act 1847 to control private hire cars and hackney cabs, including fares.

Teachers Teachers in state schools must normally be professionally qualified; teachers in **independent schools** need not. The basic professional qualification is a Certificate of Education, a Bachelor of Education or, for new graduates other than BEds, a postgraduate certificate of education. There is a multiplicity of specialist teaching qualifications in music and art. Enquiries about teachers' qualifications to *Department of Education and Science, Mowden Hall.*

There are, however, exceptions: mathematics and science graduates can teach in state secondary schools in England and Wales; those who graduated before the 1 January 1974 can teach in state secondary schools; those who graduated before 1 January 1970 can teach in secondary and primary schools.

There is no professional register of teachers but the DES keeps a list of teachers in England and Wales who are disbarred from teaching on account of their criminal convictions or misconduct – 'List 99'. This applies to all state and independent schools. The list is not open to public inspection. Teachers may apply to be taken off the list. Complaints against the professional conduct (excluding misconduct) can only be investigated by their employers as there is no professional disciplinary body. A parent wishing to complain about his child's teacher should contact the headteacher first, and then the *local education authority*. See also **Education: Scotland; Education: Northern Ireland.**

Teaching Overseas The *British Council* recruits British teachers and advisers (in all subjects but principally English language) on behalf of overseas employers such as schools, training colleges, universities and ministries of education.

Enquiries to Appointments Department, at the *British Council Headquarters.*

Other recruiting agencies are the *Ministry of Overseas Development*; the *Technical Education and Training Organisation for Overseas Countries*; *Christians Abroad*; the *Inter-University Council for Higher Education Overseas*; and the *British Volunteer Programme.*

Telecommunications The Post Office has the exclusive right to run the telegram system; private circuits for the transmission and reception of speech, data, alarm signals, music and pictures; telex; telephone services (see **Telephones**), including **radio telephones**; confravision – audio-visual conference facilities; and data transmission. Exceptions include those systems run solely for domestic purposes; business systems used only by employees of the business; and systems situated entirely in a single set of premises occupied by the person running the system. Private circuits can be rented from the PO. Details from General Manager, *Telephone Area Office.*

Telegraph Poles and Telephone Kiosks Post Office responsibility lies with the General Manager of each local *Telephone Area Office.* The written consent of the owner and occupier has to be obtained before telegraph poles, telephone kiosks or other equipment are put on private property. The PO usually agrees to make good any damage done while placing, maintaining or removing the item and cannot acquire any rights over the property, no matter how long the item remains. Most owners give consent free or for a nominal sum.

Telephone Attachments Written Post Office consent is necessary before attaching answering, recording, facsimile machines, etc., to a PO installation. Apply to General Manager, Sales Division, *Telephone Area Office.*

Before marketing a product for use with PO installations contact *Post Office Telecommunications Headquarters* for advice and technical data.

Telephone Directories Telephone subscribers are entitled to a free set of local directories and a free entry in them. Its form is usually agreed with the Post Office before a telephone is installed or connected. Women living alone are advised to publish only their surname and initials. There are charges for extra entries and ones in special type.

Prior to publication, new numbers can be found by phoning Directory Enquiries. If you wish, your number

can be ex-directory (i.e. deliberately not published in the directory); and Directory Enquiries will then either withhold or give out the number as the subscriber wishes, or will let the subscriber decide whether to accept each call.
Enquiries about directories to General Manager, Sales Division, local *Telephone Area Office*.

Telephone Disconnections The Post Office disconnects subscribers for non-payment of account. A final notice is sent 25 days after the first bill; customers then have seven days to pay before disconnection. There is a £3 reconnection charge and customers are liable for rental payment during a period of disconnection. Telephones are also disconnected on request (e.g. if the subscriber is going away for a period). Enquiries to General Manager, local *Telephone Area Office*.

Customers anticipating difficulties in paying their bills should contact the General Manager, Accounts Division, local TAO; **local authorities** or *Department of Health and Social Security* (local offices) may help in certain circumstances.

Telephone Tapping Telephone tapping must be authorised for each occasion by the Home Secretary. Warrants are applied for by the *police* or security services only in cases of suspected serious crime or subversive activities against the state.
See also **National security**.

Telephones Only telephones which are supplied and fitted by the Post Office can legally be connected to the public telephone system. Privately fitted instruments discovered by PO technicians will be disconnected. For telephone installation or removal contact the Sales Division at your local *Telephone Area Office*.
The maximum charge for installing a phone is £45; less in certain circumstances. Taking over an existing phone line can cost as little as £5. Rental charge for a telephone line is payable quarterly in advance. Extensions, etc., increase the rental. Businesses pay more than domestic users.

To stop your telephone service notify the Sales Division at least seven days in advance. You will be billed for outstanding charges and calls made since the last account.

PO aids for the handicapped include, for the hard of hearing, telephone instruments which amplify sound, telephone bells of varying loudness and pitch, loudspeaker telephones, phones which allow listening with both ears; for people with speech problems, telephones with faint-speech amplifiers; for the blind – Card Callmakers which automatically dial selected numbers and Keyphones which are operated by push-button instead of by dial; for people with mobility problems, Card Callmakers, Keyphones, loudspeaker telephones and special single-button phones which send a signal for help to the exchange operator. Details from General Manager, Sales Division, *Telephone Area Office*.

Television and Radio Broadcasting Contracts Contracts are awarded by the *Independent Broadcasting Authority* to independent television programme companies and independent local radio programme companies which derive their income from the sale of advertising time in their own transmission areas. Contracts are awarded to applicants 'likely to provide the greatest contribution to the quality of broadcasting'. TV contracts, to July 1979, are held by 15 programme companies. Local radio contracts, for three-year terms, are held by 19 companies.
Transmission facilities are owned and run by the IBA which charges rentals to the programme companies to meet the costs of discharging this and its other functions.

Television and Radio: Live Shows
To obtain free tickets to see a BBC radio or television show, write a month in advance to the *British Broadcasting Corporation, Ticket Unit*, enclosing a stamped addressed envelope and stating ages for children.
For tickets to shows on independent networks apply to the ticket office at the independent television programme company which produces the show

Television

(except for children's shows, everyone must be 16 or over); for radio shows write either to the appropriate independent local radio programme company or to the building where the show is held.

Television and Radio Programmes Programmes on UK commercial networks are the responsibility of each programme company (independent television programme companies and independent local radio programme companies) subject to approval by the *Independent Broadcasting Authority* which exercises strong central control. The *British Broadcasting Corporation* is responsible for programmes on its own networks.

Complaints against programme content or the processes by which they were produced (e.g. invasion of privacy) can be investigated, in the case of the BBC, by the (independent *BBC Programmes Complaints Commission* or in the case of commercial television and radio companies, by the *IBA Complaints Review Board*. Anyone who feels that they have been treated unfairly or unjustly in a programme may complain. In the case of the IBA, all complaints about programmes are reviewed; complaints are either upheld or dismissed. The BBCPCC reviews complaints subject to certain provisions and the BBC publishes adjudications in one or more of its journals.

Both the BBC and the programme companies welcome scripts and scores for broadcasting. To submit scripts and scores to the BBC, send radio plays to the Script Editor, *BBC Radio Drama*; radio light entertainment scripts to the Script Editor *BBC Light Entertainment (Radio)*; TV scripts to the Head of BBCTV Script Unit *BBC Television Centre*; scores of serious music for radio to the Chief Assistant, *BBC New Music*; and popular and light music to the Assistant Head of BBC Radio 2 at *BBC Headquarters*. Scripts and scores for independent TV and local radio should be sent direct to individual programme companies.

The BBC Community Programme Unit at the BBC Television Centre enables individuals or sections of the community to make their own television programmes for BBC2; technical assistance and advice are provided. Similarly ITV companies also carry 'access' programmes. Some *BBC regional television stations* provide similar facilities for issues of local concern.

Television and Radio: Public Services The British Broadcasting Company is responsible for a public service of broadcasting for general reception at home and overseas, as a body corporate set up by Royal Charter and operating under licence. It operates two television networks (BBC 1 and BBC 2), four domestic radio channels (BBC Radio 1, 2, 3, and 4), worldwide radio broadcasts (BBC External Services) and 20 BBC local radio stations. Enquiries to *BBC Headquarters*.
See also **Television and radio programmes**; **Television and radio: shows**.

Television Licences Licences are required by law for use of colour or black and white television receiving sets. One annual licence covers the use of all sets in a household; but if any of them receives television in colour the covering licence must be for a colour set. Lodgers, paying guests, etc., require separate licences. Application forms are available from all post offices, and licences can also be obtained for them and from the *National Television Licence Records Office* on payment of the appropriate fee.

No licences are required for radio sets (but see **Radio licences**). The *Home Office* is responsible for determining the licence fee and for policing evasion. You can save for a licence by buying television licence savings stamps, along with the cards to hold them, from all POs.

Tennis Proper name is lawn tennis. Amateur/professional status was abolished in 1968; everyone is now a 'player' and can play either for money or on an amateur basis. The game is governed internationally by the International Lawn Tennis Federation and in Great Britain by the *Lawn Tennis Association*. LTA selects teams, enforces rules, organises national squads, trains coaches, sanctions official championships and tournaments in England and Wales and recognises the *British Women's Tennis Association*, the *Professional Tennis Coaches' Association* and the *Lawn Tennis Umpires' Association of Great Britain*. The Lawn Tennis Championships at Wimbledon are organised jointly by the *All England Lawn Tennis and Croquet Club* and the LTA. See also **Wimbledon**.

Within the LTA, the *Welsh Lawn Tennis Association* and the *Scottish Lawn Tennis Association* control the sport in Wales and Scotland.

In Ulster and Eire, lawn tennis is governed by the entirely separate *Irish Lawn Tennis Association*.

Ten Pin Bowling Ten pin bowling is governed internationally by the Fédération Internationale des Quilleurs. The UK authority is the *British Ten Pin Bowling Association* which oversees rules, tournaments, awards, leagues, etc. It inspects bowling lanes annually to verify conformity to specification, and publishes a list of bowling centres.

Thailand For **exchange control** is a non-scheduled territory outside the **overseas sterling area** and the **EEC**. UK nationals travelling direct from the UK normally need only the following (but check): **passports**; **visas**; international certificates of **vaccination** against smallpox; **work permits** (if taking a job); green cards for motor insurance (if bringing a car); international driving permits (if intending to drive: see **Motoring abroad**).

The UK has no reciprocal health or social security arrangements.

Enquiries to *Thai Embassy* in London. British diplomatic missions to Thailand are *British Embassy* in Bangkok and *British Consulate* in Chiang Mai.

Theatre Licensing Premises used for the public performance of plays must be licensed under the Theatres Act 1968 by the local authority (in London the *Greater London Council* and elsewhere the district council). Plays are not subject to any pre-censorship and the licensing authority is forbidden by law to use its powers to control the nature of the plays which may be performed in the premises. The Act makes it a criminal offence to present certain kinds of play (e.g. those which are obscene); as with **obscene publications**; the courts decide what is obscene. Proceedings under the Act may be instituted only with the consent of the *Attorney General*. The Theatres Act does not apply to Northern Ireland where reliance is placed on the common law and section 4 of the Vagrancy Act 1824 under which it is an offence to expose wilfully to public view any obscene or indecent exhibition.

See also **Film censorship**.

Theatres: Financial Support The *Arts Council of Great Britain* provides subsidy for some 60 theatre companies in England; financial support for professionals working in the theatre; part of the cost of building new theatres or adapting existing ones; subsidies for large, medium and small-scale touring theatre companies. In England other schemes cover bursaries for writers working in temporary isolation from the theatre; increased fees for writers under contract to theatres; royalty supplements for new initiatives in creative writing; training attachments to theatres for young designers and directors; secondments and bursaries for experienced designers; in-service training, associate directorships and sabbaticals for experienced directors; secondment of actors from theatre companies to teach, direct or act with students at drama schools. Limited financial help may also be given to those working with puppets.

Regional Arts Associations can provide assistance for professional theatre companies and actors in England and some RAAs support peripatetic theatre companies which bring drama to areas often without purpose-built theatres.

In Scotland, the *Scottish Arts Council* grant-aids some ten professional drama companies; assists the programmes of theatres which receive touring companies; and supports theatre-in-education work. Encouragement is given to Scottish playwrights through commissions, bursaries and attachments to theatre companies. Bursaries are available for theatre directors and those training in other branches of theatre.

In Wales, the *Welsh Arts Council* supports 16 companies ranging from large touring companies to small experimental groups.

In Northern Ireland, the *Arts Council of Northern Ireland* supports two theatre companies; awards grants and guarantees to professional companies or to amateur societies employing professional assistance; subsidises certain productions; and directly promotes touring professional companies and puppet theatres.

Theatrical Agencies Anyone may start a theatrical staff employment agency but, under the Employment Agencies Act 1973, a licence is required from the *Department of Employment* (regional offices). After 12 consecutive months of practice, agents can become provisional members of the *International Agents Association*, and full members after six further months probationary period. EAA administers rules and regulations to establish a code of conduct and ethics, and holds a list of members.

See also **Employment agencies**.

Tobacco Manufacturers These must register premises used for the storage of tobacco products with *Her Majesty's Customs and Excise*.

See also **Customs duty; Excise duty**.

Tobacco Products Duty Duty is chargeable on cigarettes, cigars, hand-rolling tobacco, and other smoking and chewing tobaccos, whether or not containing any tobacco substitutes or additives. Herbal cigarettes, herbal smoking mixtures and snuff are excluded. The duty has completely replaced other customs revenue duty on tobacco. Special provision exists for the duty to be paid in arrears; apply to *Her Majesty's Customs and Excise*.

The tobacco products duty regulator is a power to vary any of the rates of tobacco products duty, applied by Treasury order, up to a maximum of 10% of the rate last established by a Finance Act. Enquiries to HMCE.

See also **Customs duty; Excise duty**.

Togo For **exchange control** is a non-scheduled territory outside the **overseas sterling area** and the EEC. UK nationals travelling direct from the UK normally need only the following (but check): **passports; visas;** international certificates of **vaccination** against smallpox; **work permits** (if taking a job); green cards for motor insurance (if bringing a car: see **Motoring abroad**).

The UK has no reciprocal health or social security arrangements.

Enquiries to *Togo diplomatic mission to UK* at *Togo Embassy* in Brussels, Belgium or *Togo Hon. Consulate* in London.

The *British diplomatic mission* to Togo is based on the *British Embassy* at Accra, Ghana.

Tonga **Commonwealth** member. For **exchange control** is a non-scheduled territory in the **overseas sterling area** but outside the EEC. UK nationals travelling direct from the UK normally need only the following (but check): **passports; visas** (over 30 days stay); **work permits** (if taking a job).

The UK has no reciprocal health or social security arrangements.

Enquiries to *Tonga High Commission* in London.

British diplomatic mission to Tonga is *British High Commission* in Nuku'alofa.

Tourist Industy Four independent government-financed statutory bodies are responsible for the promotion of tourism in Great Britain. The *British Tourist Authority* is responsible for overseas promotion and certain general matters affecting tourism in Great Britain as a whole. The *English Tourist Board, Scottish Tourist Board* and *Welsh Tourist Board* are responsible for encouraging the development and improvement of facilities and amenities for tourists in their respective areas, and for tourist promotions in Great Britain. They give financial assistance to selected tourist projects, including in some cases hotels, in special development areas and development areas (see also **Assisted areas; Regional development grants**). A separate statutory *Northern Ireland Tourist Board* is responsible under the *Northern Ireland Department of Commerce* for the promotion of tourism in Northern Ireland.

Town and Country Planning The planning system in this country is based on a framework of plans of differing scope and level of detail. Regional strategies are normally prepared by professional teams working jointly to central government, the **local authorities** and the *Regional Economic Planning Councils*. They set the broad framework of policies for a region.

Structure plans are prepared by the county councils and after an examination in public before an appointed panel with an independent chairman have to be approved (with or without modifications) by the Secretary of State for the Environment or for Scotland or Wales. These plans set out the county-wide policies for the development and other use of land (including measures for the improvement of the physical environment and the management of traffic).

Local plans are prepared normally by district councils but sometimes by county councils and show land use proposals in detail. The local planning authority must consider all objections to a local plan and all objectors have the right to be heard at a public local inquiry conducted by an Inspector appointed by the Secretary of State for the Environment.

Most development requires **planning permission**. Such development includes building and construction work, operations other than building such as excavations, and changes of use such as running a business from home, or dividing a house into flats. Apply to the planning department of the district council or London borough. Planning is not concerned with whether any new buildings are properly constructed. That is dealt with by Building Regulations (see **Building**).

If permission is refused by the local authority or granted subject to unacceptable conditions, the applicant has a right of appeal to the Secretary of State for the Environment (or Scotland or Wales). This often results in a public enquiry.

If development is carried out without permission or conditions are not complied with the local planning authority may serve an enforcement notice (against which there is a right of appeal to the Secretary of State) specifying the steps which they require to be taken for the purpose of remedying the breach of development control. The authority has a right to prosecute developers who fail to comply with an enforcement notice once it has become effective. See also **Planning land use**.

Town Twinning Twinning between British and European local authorities is promoted by the *British Council* by grants for visits of key people; by subsidising exhibitions and exchange programmes; by registering of links; by administering the Joint Twinning Committee made up of local authority associations and by publications. Enquiries to Joint Twinning Committee at the *British Council Headquarters* or at the *British Council Overseas Office* in the country concerned.

Toxic and Corrosive Materials General UK policy on the use at work of corrosives and toxic substances, including carcinogens and suspected carcinogens but excluding fibrogenic dusts, is the responsibility of Hazardous Substances Branch C at the *Health and Safety Executive*. Technical advide at a local level is available from *Health and Safety Executive, HM Factory Inspectorate* (area offices). Advice on medical aspects of handling toxic and corrosive substances is available from local offices of the *Health and Safety Executive, Employment Medical Advisory Service*. See also **Work: health and safety**.

Trade Union Membership and Activities
Employees may complain to an **industrial tribunal** if an employer dismisses an employee, or takes some action against him short of dismissal, either for being a member of an independent **trade union** or taking part in its activities, or for not becoming a member of a trade union which is *not* independent. Application forms and leaflets from any *Employment Office* or *Employment Service Agency Job Centre* or *Department of Employment*, (Unemployment Benefit Office).

Anyone dismissed or given notice of **dismissal** from his job as a result of being expelled from, or refused admission to, a trade union where trade union membership is a condition of employment may appeal to the Independent Review Committee at the *Trades Union Congress*.

Time off from work must be permitted by employers for trade union duties and activities under the Employment Protection Act. Guidance on the relevant sections of the Act is contained in a code of practice, 'Time Off for Trade Union Duties and Activities' produced by the *Advisory, Conciliation and Arbitration Service*. This Code will be taken into account by industrial tribunals hearing complaints under the Act.

Trade Union Recognition
A trade union which cannot secure recognition for collective bargaining purposes from an employer may refer a 'recognition issue' to the *Advisory, Conciliation and Arbitration Service*. ACAS will try to settle the issue by encouraging agreement between employer and trade union and failing that investigates, and publishes a written report containing its recommendation for recognition, if any, and its reasons. If an employer fails to comply with an ACAS recommendation, the union may apply to the *Central Arbitration Committee* for an award of terms and conditions of employment for the employees concerned, the award being binding on the employer. There are no statutory provisions for complaints of a refusal to allow a **closed shop**, nor, any longer, for complaints by conscientious objectors about enforcement of a closed shop.

Trade Unions
Anyone doing a job can join a trade union. There are unions for all skills and occupations from craftsmen to clerical workers. To learn which union is appropriate, first find out to which union other people in your workplace belong; if there is no union organisation, contact the local offices of one of the unions or write to the *Trades Union Congress*.

Some unions link membership qualifications with a training scheme; only on completion of training can the worker become a full member. Others admit untrained members. There is a problem in some industries in finding employment without union membership, and in industries with surplus labour union membership may be difficult to obtain.

Applications for membership are normally handled by the union's local branches, and general enquiries by the union's head office.

The TUC (and in Scotland the *Scottish Trades Union Congress*) represents a collective trade union view. Over 100 unions, representing 11m employees (or 90% of trade union members) are affiliated to the TUC. Policy is decided at Congress held in September each year, where delegates from all affiliated unions meet for a five-day conference. Congress elects a 38-strong General Council, which meets monthly and makes policy between Congresses.

The General Council in turn elects specialist committees from its members to consider questions on the economy, education, international affairs, social insurance, industrial welfare and trade union organisation. One function of the Council is to make representations to the government on behalf of the trade union movement. In the case of disputes between unions, there are procedures under which the TUC acts as arbitrator.

See also **Employment**.

Trade Unions: Disclosure of Information
Disclosure of information to trade unions for collective bargaining purposes is subject in Great Britain to a code of practice produced by the

Advisory, Conciliation and Arbitration Service. Observance or otherwise of the Code is taken into account by the *Central Arbitration Committee* when complaints against employers are made by **trade unions**. See also **Trade unions: independence.** Code from *Her Majesty's Stationery Office* or government bookshops.

Trade Unions: Independence A trade union must be independent if it is to make use of certain provisions of the Employment Protection Act 1975 (e.g., the provision that an employer must on request disclose information required by an independent trade union for collective bargaining purposes).

Any trade union may apply to the *Certification Officer for Trade Union and Employers' Associations* for a certificate that it is independent.

Trading Agreements In the UK agreements relating to the supply or acquisition of goods or to the supply or acquisition of commercial services must be registered with the *Office of Fair Trading*, if they contain restrictions about such matters as prices, terms and conditions, quantities or descriptions, persons or areas to be supplied. Certain agreements are exempt (e.g. those relating to the granting of **patent** licences, bilateral exlusive dealing agreements, agreements about terms of **employment**, certain professional services) and others can be exempted by Order (e.g. agreements of importance to the national economy, agreements to prevent or restrict increases or secure reductions in **prices**).

Agreements submitted are first considered by the OFT and if requiring registration placed on the public Register of Restrictive Agreements. (Copies of the Register are available for public inspection at the offices of the OFT in London, Edinburgh, Belfast.) The *Director General of Fair Trading* has a statutory duty to refer registered agreements to the *Restrictive Practices Court* and they are considered to be contrary to the public interest unless the parties to them can prove otherwise. If the Court finds that the restrictions are contrary to the public interest the restrictions become void and it is unlawful for the parties to continue to operate them. The Court may also make an order restraining the parties from making agreements to the like effect.

However, the Director General may ask the *Secretary of State for Prices and Consumer Protection* for a direction not to refer an agreement to the Court if he considers that the agreement is insignificant in its effect on competition. If a direction is made the agreement remains on the Register but is not referred to the Court and can continue to be operated.

If a registrable agreement is not submitted to the OFT within the time limits laid down by the Act (i.e. within three months of its being made or before the restrictions take effect, whichever is earlier) the restrictions are void, continued operation of them is illegal and the parties may become liable to legal proceedings by the OFT. In addition, anyone affected by the operation of a void agreement may seek damages in the civil courts. The OFT follows up complaints that restrictive agreements are being operated without registration.

Training: Grants and Services Managing and developing the training programme of British industry and commerce is the responsibility of the *Training Services Agency* of the *Manpower Services Commission.* Most vocational training is still carried out by employers, but the government has recently taken steps to help provide trained manpower. Exchequer funds are available to cover the operating expenses of **industrial training boards** and for grants for certain key training activities.

Services available to employers on application to the *Training Services Agency* comprise free places at TSA Skillcentres for people sponsored by employers; mobile instructors to assist employers with specific in-plant training projects; training of instructors; and training within industry courses. These last are provided at suitable venues and cover job relations, job instruction and communications, job methods, safety, office supervision, retail distribution and operator and clerical instruction; employees can also apply for them to the TSA. Individuals can train and improve their employment prospects under the Training Opportunities Scheme at Skillcentres (generally for engineering, construction or vehicle trades), colleges of **further education** (office training, catering and higher-level courses) and employers' establishments; apply to *Training Services Agency* or the *Employment Service Agency*. Trainees receive tax-free allowances and other benefits while attending; courses are free. (See also **Jobs**.)

Trampolining Trampolining is controlled internationally by the International Trampoline Association and in the UK by the *British Trampoline Federation Ltd*. Its Central Council selects British teams, etc. Within the BTF, the sport is governed in nine English divisions and the *Scottish Trampoline Association*, the *Northern Ireland Trampolining Association* and the *Welsh Trampolining Association*.

Translation Service: British Library Translation of Russian, Slavonic and Japanese articles, and more occasionally books, is undertaken free of charge by the *British Library, Lending Division*, at the request of any resident in the UK. Duplicates are made available for purchase or loan.

Transport: Dangerous Substances The *Health and Safety Executive, HM Explosives Inspectorate* gives specialist advice on the conveyance by road or air of dangerous substances. It is also responsible for approval of petroleum spirit tank wagons and gas cylinders, and specialist advice on transportable pressure vessels (see also **Steam boilers and pressure plant**).
The Hazardous Substances Branch A at the *Health and Safety Executive* (Head Office) is responsible for implementing **EEC** labelling directives, developing UK policy and advising government departments about the conveyance, nationally or internationally, by all forms of transport, of all hazardous substances apart from **radio-active materials**.
See also **Explosives: safety**; **Work: health and safety**.

Travel Concessions Concessionary fares for the elderly are available on *British Rail* and on buses in many parts of the country. In London and some other areas, free passes are available for use by the elderly outside rush hours. Enquiries to local authority or transport undertakings.

Travel: Exchange Control There is no restriction on the amount of money which UK residents may spend on travel within the scheduled territories (i.e. the UK, including the Channel Islands and the Isle of Man, the Republic of Ireland and Gibraltar) (see **Exchange control**). For travel expenditure for every journey outside the scheduled territories, UK residents are entitled, if travelling with a valid **passport**, to purchase, without formality, from banks or travel agents up to £500 per person per journey in foreign exchange (foreign currency notes, coin, travellers' cheques, sterling travellers' cheques, letters of credit, transfers to banks abroad); the limit of £500 is increased to £1,000 for journeys of two months or more. This money must be recorded in the travellers' passports. The £500 does not have to cover the cost of fares and travel services (including hotel and cruise accommodation) paid either in sterling to a UK travel agent or by remittance through an **authorised bank (Exchange control)**. All travellers may also take with them up to £100 in UK or other scheduled territory notes.
UK residents who possess cheque or **credit cards** issued by banks or companies in the UK with whom the *Bank of England* have made special arrangements may use them outside the scheduled territories for travel expenditure within specified limits and conditions notified to holders by the issuers.
Persons travelling to countries outside the scheduled territories for business or professional reasons who need more than £300 for the journey may apply to a bank or travel agent for an addi-

tional allowance of foreign currency; the highest allowance available is £100 a day up to a maximum of £3,000 for any one journey. Applications for sums in excess of these amounts for business or professional journeys, or excess of £500 (or £1,000) for any single private journey must go to the *Bank of England*. Special arrangements to meet the needs of companies and firms whose representatives require to make frequent business journeys outside the scheduled territories at short notice may be authorised. Apply to BE.

There are a limited number of excursions without **passports** from specific points in the UK to specific points abroad. On these the traveller is entitled to take with him only £100 in UK or other scheduled territory notes which may be changed into foreign currency during the excursion to meet personal travel expenditure. The conditions of operation are laid down by the *Home Office* and obtainable from the companies running the excursions.

See also **Foreign currency and credit**.

Travel: Health Protection Before departure check the **vaccination** requirements of countries which you intend to visit with the country's diplomatic mission in the UK (see entry for individual countries) or the *Department of Health and Social Security* (overseas travel enquiries). Some countries require international certificates of vaccination for smallpox and/or yellow fever and for others vaccination is advisable against cholera, typhoid, paratyphoid, poliomyelitis, and infectious hepatitis and anti-malarial tablets. Smallpox certificates are required for re-entry to the UK if you have visited an infected country within the last 14 days.

Other helpful measures include carrying details of your blood group, allergies, chronic diseases and regular drugs; consulting a **doctor** immediately if you are scratched or bitten by any animal abroad for fear of rabies (do *not* wait until return to the UK); avoiding certain foods; boiling water; informing your doctor of all countries visited if you feel ill on your return. Details in 'Notice to Travellers – Health Protection' from the *Department of Health and Social Security*.

Some countries have reciprocal health arrangements with the UK. Prior to visiting an EEC country you should get leaflet SA28 from a DHSS local office. This will explain whether you are entitled to free or reduced cost medical treatment in EEC countries and how, if necessary, to obtain an entitlement certificate (E111). When visiting Poland or Bulgaria take your **National Health Service medical card**. See also **Illness overseas**. If you are visiting countries without reciprocal health arrangements take out private insurance against medical expenses abroad; apply to travel agent. Treatment abroad can be very expensive.

See also **Hospitals abroad**.

Treasure Trove Treasure trove is 'any gold or silver, in coin, plate or bullion, found hidden in a house or in the earth or other private place, the owner thereof being unknown'. In the absence of an owner, treasure trove belongs to the Crown; the finder is usually rewarded to the value of the treasure.

Discovery of treasure trove should be notified to the *police* or the *British Museum*. A coroner will then conduct an inquest into the circumstances of the discovery, but will not adjudicate on title as between the Crown and other claimants.

Tree Felling Licences (valid two years) are required for the felling, or sale for felling, of growing trees beyond 825 cubic feet of timber (hoppus measure) per quarter of a calendar year for use on the owner's own property or (up to 150 cubic feet) for sale. Other exceptions for which a licence is not required (unless a **Tree Preservation Order** applies) include garden and fruit trees, underwood, thinnings, and certain 'dedicated woodlands' (see **Forestry planting: grants**). Apply to *Forestry Commission* (Conservator of Forests), who will arrange inspection of trees and may impose replanting conditions on the issue of a felling licence. Replacement may qualify for forestry planting grant. Agricultural Departments, local planning authorities and other appropriate interests have a right of objection to the issue of felling licences. Appeal to: *Minister for Agriculture, Fisheries and Food*, or Secretary of State for Scotland or Wales as appropriate in accordance with procedure in Forestry (Felling of Trees) Regulations 1951. If a tree preservation order applies and a felling licence is not otherwise required apply for permission to fell to: local authority; appeal against refusal of such permission to *Secretary of State for Environment* (in England and Wales) or *Secretary of State for Scotland*. 'Advice to Woodland Owners': *Forestry Commission*.

Tree Planting Grants Grants for amenity purposes may be obtained by private and public landowners. These grants are intended for planting areas of less than one hectare, where the *Countryside Commission* or the *Countryside Commission for Scotland* consider such planting conducive to countryside conservation or informal recreational enjoyment. **Local authorities** have their own tree planting schemes for private and public land. These range from a complete tree planting and maintenance service to grants. Tree planting grants for timber production on blocks of over one hectare are available from the *Forestry Commission*; tree planting grants for agricultural purposes from the *Ministry of Agriculture, Fisheries and Food* (see **Forestry planting: grants**).

Tree Preservation Orders Planning authorities are empowered to make tree preservation orders in the interests of amenity where they consider it expedient. The effect of such orders is to prohibit the cutting down, topping, lopping, uprooting, intentional damage or destruction of the trees concerned except with the consent of the local authority, and to enable the authority to require replanting where felling has been specifically permitted or an order contravened. Local authorities may confirm unopposed TPCs.
Where there are objections a decision is made by the *Secretary of State for the Environment*, the *Secretary of State for Scotland* or the *Secretary of State for Wales*, who also determine appeals against local authority decisions. Advice on planting and tree care and surgery may also be available from: local authority, or from *Tree Council* (c/o *Department of the Environment*). A consultants' register is maintained by the *Arboricultural Association*.

Tree Suppliers Nurserymen who market within the **EEC** the seed, young plants and parts of plants of the following species – European Silver Fir, European Larch, Japanese Larch, Norway Spruce, Sitka Spruce, Corsican Pine, Scots Pine, Weymouth Pine, Douglas Fir, Beech, Sessile Oak, Pedunculate Oak, Red Oak, Poplar – must issue a supplier's certificate to the buyer showing that the material conforms to EEC standards. A booklet 'The marketing of forest tree seed and plants within the EEC' is available free from *Forestry Commission, Publications Branch*.

Tribunals See **Administrative tribunals**.

Trichologists Basic qualification is associate membership of the *Institute of Trichologists (Incorporated)*. Written complaints about professional misconduct of members are investigated by the Institute.

Trinidad and Tobago Commonwealth member. For **exchange control** is a non-scheduled territory in the **overseas sterling area** but outside the EEC. UK nationals travelling direct from the UK normally need only the following (but check): **passports**; international certificates of **vaccination** against smallpox; **work permits** (if taking a job).
The UK has no reciprocal health or social security arrangements.
Enquiries to *Trinidad and Tobago High Commission* in London.
British diplomatic mission to Trinidad and Tobago is *British High Commission* in Port of Spain.

Trinity House Pilots These are licensed (but not employed) by

Trinity House Pilotage Service and answerable to it for their professional conduct. They must be masters or certified watch-keeping officers with considerable experience. The relevant experience depends on the pilotage district to which the pilot is appointed. See also **Pilotage**.

Tug of War International Championships, etc., are organised by the world governing body, the Tug-of-War International Federation. In the UK the *Tug-of-War Association* is the authority. It determines rules (indoor and outdoor events), arranges tournaments, judges, etc., and selects English teams. Welsh and Irish teams are selected by the independent *Welsh Tug-of-War Association* and the *Northern Ireland Tug-of-War Association* respectively. There is no Scottish Association.

Tunisia For **exchange control** is a non-scheduled territory outside the **overseas sterling area** and the **EEC**. UK nationals travelling direct from the UK normally need only the following (but check): **passports** without Israeli stamp; **work permits** (if taking a job); green cards for motor insurance (if bringing a car); international driving permits recommended (if intending to drive: see **Motoring abroad**).
The UK has no reciprocal health or social security arrangements.
Enquiries to *Tunisian Embassy* in London and *Tunisian Tourist Centre* in London.
British diplomatic mission to Tunisia in *British Embassy* in Tunis.

Turkey For **exchange control** is a non-scheduled territory outside the **overseas sterling area** and the **EEC**. UK nationals travelling direct from the UK normally need only the following (but check): **passports**; **work permits** (if taking a job); green cards for motor insurance (if bringing a car); international driving permits recommended (if intending to drive: see **Motoring abroad**).
UK reciprocal arrangements cover social security (see leaflet SA22 obtainable from *Department of Health and Social Security, Overseas Group*), but not health.
Enquiries to *Turkish Embassy* in London and *Turkish Tourism Information Office* in London.
British diplomatic missions to Turkey are *British Embassy* in Ankara, *British Consulate-General* in Istanbul and *British Consulate* in Izmir.

U

Uganda Commonwealth member. For **exchange control** is a non-scheduled territory in the **overseas sterling area** but outside the EEC. Diplomatic relations with UK have been broken off and citizens of the UK and colonies should consult *Foreign and Commonwealth Office* in London before going there.
UK interests in Uganda are handled by the *French Embassy* in Kampala.

UK Documents Abroad: Verification Documents required for presentation overseas (e.g. education qualifications, marriage certificates, contracts) are undertaken by the *Foreign and Commonwealth Office, Nationality and Treaty Department* in the UK, the British consulate in non-**Commonwealth** countries; and by local public notaries or other officials in Commonwealth countries. Enquiries about the authentification of documents for overseas students should be sent to the relevant university or embassy.

UK Education: Information for Foreigners The *British Council* is responsible for supplying individuals and institutions overseas with information on all aspects of the British education system. This includes giving information on courses, research and industrial training in science, technology, engineering and agriculture, the social sciences, law, management and business studies, the arts, humanities, English language teaching and English studies, medicine, librarianship, teacher education and educational technology.
See also **Arts tours overseas; Libraries abroad; Medical specialists: overseas visits; Teaching overseas.**

Ulster Liberal Party The party is part of the UK Liberal Party but has had a separate organisation since 1956. It is a totally non-sectarian party and membership is open to Liberals from Northern Ireland, whether resident there or not. To join contact the *Ulster Liberal Party*.

Ulster Unionist Party Membership is open to people who are eligible to register as electors in any of the Northern Ireland wards. No one is excluded on grounds of race, religion or creed but people are debarred from membership if they belong to a political or other movement whose objects are opposed to or detrimental to the Ulster Unionist Party.
To join contact the *Ulster Unionist Headquarters* or one of the 12 constituency associations (see Ulster Unionist in Northern Ireland telephone directories). Each association is based on a UK constituency and acts as a link between MPs, former members of the Northern Ireland Constitution Convention, local councillors and persons wishing to make contact with them.
The party's official aims are 'to maintain Northern Ireland under the Crown as an integral part of the UK and to uphold democratic institutions of

government for Northern Ireland and to safeguard the British citizenship of the people of Northern Ireland'. It is affiliated to the *National Union of Conservative and Unionist Associations* and is represented on its Central Council, Executive Committee and General Purposes Committee.

Underwater Swimming Underwater swimming is controlled internationally by the Confédération Mondiale des Activités Subaquatiques. The British governing body is the *British Sub-Aqua Club* which has branches in 28 countries. Its activities include running regional coaches, a national boat, youth schemes, and instructor training. Connected to it are the *Welsh Association of Sub-Aqua Clubs*, the *Northern Ireland Federation of Sub-Aqua Clubs* and the *British Sub-Aqua Club Scottish Federation*. In addition to the BSACSF in Scotland there is the separate *Scottish Sub-Aqua Club*.

Unemployment Benefit Benefit is paid to unemployed people who have paid or been credited with adequate **national insurance contributions** and who otherwise fulfil prescribed qualifying conditions. These include a requirement to register as available for employment with either an *Employment Service Agency Job Centre* or an *Employment Service Agency employment office* or (if under 20 and full-time education completed within the last two years) with local authority careers office.
Claim for unemployment benefit in person to *Department of Employment* (local unemployment benefit office) or by post if living more than 10 miles by road from such an office. Payment is normally made weekly in arrears. Unemployed people may also be entitled to increased benefit for dependants, **earnings-related supplement,** supplementary allowance (see **Supplementary benefits**), or a **redundancy** payment.
Benefit can be refused or diminished to those who do not attend interviews for new work; are receiving certain other **social security benefits**; have received payment in lieu of notice from the previous employment or of remuneration received had the previous employment not been left; go abroad (unless to EEC to seek work or occupation in seafaring); are imprisoned; go away on holiday; participate in or are directly interested in a strike or lockout; take up a part-time job; leave previous employment voluntarily without just cause or are dismissed for misconduct; refuse to take suitable employment when offered it; limit unduly the work acceptable. See leaflets NI12 (Unemployment Benefit), NI55 (Seasonal Workers), SL8 (Supplementary Allowance), NI155A (Earnings-related supplement), NI196 (Current benefit rates), and 'The Redundancy Payment Scheme' – all from *Department of Employment* (local unemployment benefit offices) or *Department of Health and Social Security* (local offices). Leaflet SA29 (Employment in EEC) is available from DHSS (Newcastle-upon-Tyne).
See also **Jobs; Occupational guidance.**

Unemployment: Young People Young people unable to find employment on leaving education may apply for training awards to the local authority *Careers Office* or the *Training Services Agency*. There are TSA preparatory courses for people whose standard of literacy or numeracy inhibits employability. Other TSA programmes for young people are short industrial courses (introducing a range of tasks in one occupation); occupational selection courses (which assess aptitude for a number of tasks); and wider opportunities courses (to help people identify activities they like and do well).
Work experience (and a standard weekly allowance) is provided under the *Manpower Services Commission*'s work experience programme. It places young people with individual firms (e.g. engineering, commercial, agricultural) to give them a realistic introduction to working life; apply to the *Careers Office* or *Employment Service Agency*.
Temporary work is provided under the MSC's job creation scheme and its community industry scheme (for

young people who are personally or socially disadvantaged). The latter scheme, which is sponsored by **local authorities** and voluntary organisations, provides work of social value but the main aim is to prepare the employees for normal employment; apply to *Careers Office*.

Unidentified Flying Objects The *Ministry of Defence, S4 (Air)* investigates UFO reports to see if there are defence implications. It does not investigate the scientific significance of the phenomena. From its experience over a number of years, sightings are considered to originate mostly from aircraft, or the lights of aircraft seen under unusual conditions, balloons, meteorological phenomena, astrological sightings, space satellites and space 'junk'. If you see something which you are sure is of defence interest, notify the MOD. Your letter will be acknowledged but you will not be told the result of any investigation. See also **National security**.

Union Movement A political party of which membership is open to all who share the ideals of the Movement. These include the establishment of a third force from a united Europe, the former Dominions and Southern Africa; a strong European central government for defence and economic matters; national and regional governments for internal affairs and the maintenance of traditional languages and cultures; and for Britain, a real government of national unity. Enquiries to the Secretary, *Union Movement*.

Unit Trusts Unit trusts promoted to the public require authorisation by the Secretary of State for Trade; enquiries to *Department of Trade* (Companies Administration Division). Under the Prevention of Fraud (Investments) Act 1958, only unit trusts investing in **securities** may be authorised. Safe custody of the assets and general safeguarding of unitholders' interests are the duties of the trustee. Details of authorised unit trusts (including the names and addresses of each trustee) are published annually in 'Particulars of Dealers in Securities and of Unit Trusts', available from *Her Majesty's Stationery Office*; amendments appear in 'Trade and Industry', in editions published on the second Friday in each month, from the *Department of Industry* (headquarters).

United Arab Emirates For **exchange control** is a non-scheduled territory in the **overseas sterling area** but outside the **EEC**. UK nationals travelling direct from the UK normally need only the following (but check): **passports** without Israeli stamp; **visas**; international certificates of **vaccination** against smallpox; **work permits** (if taking a job).
The UK has no reciprocal health or social security arrangements.
Enquires to *United Arab Emirates Embassy* in London.
British diplomatic missions to United Arab Emirates are *British Embassies* in Abu Dhabi and Dubai.

United Sates For **exchange control** is a non-scheduled territory outside the **overseas sterling area** and the **EEC**. UK nationals travelling direct from the UK normally need only the following (but check): **passports**; **visas**; **work permits** (if taking a job); green cards for motor insurance (if bringing a car); international driving permits recommended (if intending to drive: see **Motoring abroad**).
UK reciprocal arrangements cover social security pensions only (no leaflet).
Enquiries to *United States Embassy* in London and *United States Consulates-General* in Belfast and Edinburgh.
British diplomatic missions to United States are *British Embassy* in Washington, *British Consulates-General* in Atlanta, Boston, Chicago, Cleveland, Detroit, Houston, Los Angeles, New York, Philadelphia, St Louis, San Francisco and Seattle, *British Consulates* in five other provincial centres and in Anchorage (Alaska), San Juan (Puerto Rico) and St Thomas (US Virgin Is.).

Universities Universities are national educational institutions, established by

Royal Charter or Act of Parliament, receiving funds through the *University Grants Committee* (in Northern Ireland, funds are given direct by the *Department of Education, Northern Ireland* on advice from the UGC). Universities are separate from **polytechnics** and other institutions in the state system of **further education**; students from any part of the UK or from overseas may be admitted. Each university controls its own admissions, but in England and Wales student applications for first-degree courses (excepting the Open University) are submitted through the *Universities Central Council on Admissions*; candidates may apply to five universities. Most, but not all, applications for first-degree courses in Scotland and Northern Ireland are also submitted through UCCA. UK residents accepted for a fulltime university course are normally entitled to a grant (see **Student grants**).

The 'Compendium of University Entrance Requirements', published by the *Association of Commonwealth Universities* for the Committee of Vice Chancellors and available in public libraries, lists entrance requirements for all courses in all UK universities at first-degree level. For postgraduate courses, apply direct to the university. See also **Research grants**.

The *Open University* requires no formal academic qualifications at entry. It provides part-time courses leading to degrees; tuition is by a combination of television, radio, correspondence texts, personal tuition and residential summer schools. Applications direct to the OU.

There is one independent UK university, the University College at Buckingham.

See also **Education: Scotland**; **Education: Northern Ireland**.

Upper Volta For **exchange control** is a non-scheduled territory outside the **overseas sterling area** and the **EEC**. UK nationals travelling direct from the UK normally need only the following (but check): **passports**; **visas**; international certificates of **vaccination** against smallpox and yellow fever; **work permits** (if taking a job); green cards for motor insurance (if bringing a car); international driving permits (if intending to drive: see **Motoring abroad**).
The UK has no reciprocal health or social security arrangements.
Enquiries to *Upper Volta Hon. Consulate* in London.
The *British diplomatic mission* to Upper Volta is based on the *British Embassy* at Abidjan, Ivory Coast.

Uruguay For **exchange control** is a non-scheduled territory outside the **overseas sterling area** and the **EEC**. UK nationals travelling direct from the UK normally need only the following (but check): **passports**; international certificates of **vaccination** against smallpox; **work permits** (if taking a job); green cards for motor insurance (if bringing a car); international driving permits if staying for more than 90 days (if intending to drive: see **Motoring abroad**).
The UK has no reciprocal health or social security arrangements.
Enquiries to *Uruguayan Embassy* in London and *Uruguayan Consulate* in Liverpool.
British diplomatic mission is *British Embassy* in Montevideo.

V

Vacancies Vacancies can be notified by employers to three kinds of government agency. Through the network of *Employment Service Agency Employment Offices* and *Employment Service Agency Job centres*, vacancies are filled without charge to employer or candidate. The *Employment Service Agency Professional and Executive Recruitment* for professional, scientific, technical, managerial and overseas appointments (and, in London, executive secretaries) has optional advertising and interviewing services. It charges employers for successful placement on a scale from 5% to 18% of starting salary, but is free to candidates. The *Careers Service* (Department of Employment and local authority) for young people is free to employers and candidates.
See also **Employment agencies; Jobs; Occupational guidance.**

Vaccinations Many countries require travellers arriving from certain other countries to produce valid international certificates of vaccination. Separate certificates cover smallpox (valid three years) and yellow fever (valid ten years). Each country has its own requirements, but these may be varied at short notice. Before travel check for recent changes with the *Department of Health and Social Security* (overseas travel enquiries), who are likely to have the most up-to-date information, or with the relevant country's UK diplomatic mission (see country entries). Changes are notified internationally by the *World Health Organisation*.

For yellow fever vaccinations, attend a yellow fever vaccination centre, the international certificate (fee payable except in Northern Ireland) is supplied after vaccination. For smallpox, get a blank certificate from a travel agent or the DHSS in England, the *Welsh Office*, the Northern Ireland *Department of Health and Social Services* or the *Scottish Home and Health Department*. Take this to your NHS family **doctor**, who will vaccinate you and complete the certificate; a fee is sometimes payable for the completion of the certificate. The certificate must then be stamped by the local authority in whose area the doctor practises.

Other vaccinations may be advisable, e.g. cholera, typhoid, paratyphoid, poliomyelitis and infectious hepatitis: apply to your doctor. Antimalarial tablets are not available on NHS prescription.
See also **Medicines and appliances: supply; Travel: health protection.**

Value-Added Tax VAT is payable on goods and services within the UK in the course of a business. Suppliers of goods and services who are registered for VAT charge VAT as a percentage rate of the value of the supply to customers; customers who are themselves registered and who in turn supply goods and services charge VAT likewise to any further customers. Thus they remit to (or are repaid by) *Her Majesty's Customs and Excise* the difference between tax paid for 'input' supplies and that charged on 'output' supplies. This means that the tax is borne finally by consumers, who cannot charge it on to further customers. Details from HMCE in Notice 700 – 'VAT – General Guide'.

Goods and services may be exempt; zero-rated; or positively-rated at either the standard rate or higher rate (HMCE Notice 701); *Her Majesty's Treasury* has power by statutory instrument to amend the schedules containing those goods and services which are exempted, zero-rated or higher-rated. Imported goods (but not generally services) are liable for VAT; exports of goods and services are zero-rated (i.e. VAT is not chargeable on output supplies but VAT on input supplies is repayable by HMCE).

Transactions within the scope of VAT include sales; hirings; hire-purchase; performance of services and the granting of a right; production or acquisition of goods in the course of business but applied to personal use; and free gifts.

Businesses within its scope include any trade, profession or vocation, and facilities provided by a club or association for its members. Trade and professional associations, trade unions, and charities subsidising transactions from charitable funds are generally excluded. There are special schemes for retailers who cannot keep records of every transaction (HMCE notice 727). Taxable persons (i.e. those whose taxable turnover exceeds the present limit of £7,500) must register (apply to HMCE); keep specified records and accounts; have use of microfilm and computers approved (apply to HMCE at systems design stage or earlier); preserve records for at least three years unless prior agreement to a shorter period has been obtained from HMCE. Voluntary registration of those whose turnover is below the limit is permissible if a genuine, continuing need for it can be shown.

Registered persons receive a certificate of registration notifying them of a VAT registration number and tax period. There is special provision for advance registration; for those whose taxable supplies are all zero-rated; for groups of corporate bodies; and for businesses carried on by persons not resident in the UK. Appeal against the decision of HMCE on certain matters may be made to VAT tribunals; details in leaflets 1 and 2 from *VAT Tribunal Headquarters.*

Relevant HMCE notices are 701 (scope and coverage), 702 (imports), 703 (exports), 704 (retail export schemes), 705 (tax-free sales of motor vehicles to tourists, etc.), 706 (partial exemption, self supply – stationery), 708 and 715 (construction industry), 709 (hotels and catering and holiday services), 710 (supplies by or through agents), 714 (young children's clothing and footwear), 716 and 718 (changes in rate of tax), 719 (refund of VAT to do-it-yourself housebuilders) 364 (awards for distinction) and 728 (trading stamps issued with sales of petrol).

Certain second-hand goods are taxed only on the seller's margin (i.e. the amount by which the selling price exceeds the price at which he bought). Relevant HMCE notices are 711 (second-hand cars), 712 (second-hand works of art, antiques and scientific collections), 713 (second-hand caravans, motor-cycles), 720 (second-hand boats and outboard motors), 721 (second-hand aircraft), 722 (second-hand electronic organs).

Value-Added Tax Regulator This is a power to vary the positive rates of **value-added tax**, applied by Treasury Order, up to a maximum of 25% of the rate last established by a Finance Act. Enquiries to *Her Majesty's Customs and Excise* (details in VAT notice 716).

Vehicle Testing Stations These are operated by examiners authorised by the Department of Transport for the examination of specified classes of vehicle. Apply for authorisation to *Department of Transport Traffic Area Offices.*

Vehicles run on Gas Owners must pay **customs duty** and **excise duty** on the fuel, but it is the responsibility of the suppliers of the gas to charge the excise duty and to make correct returns to *Her Majesty's Customs and*

Excise for the tax received on gas for road use.

Venereal Disease If you think you may have VD you can consult your NHS family **doctor**. If he is not equipped to do the necessary accurate tests, you will be directed to a Special Clinic; or you can go direct to a Special Clinic for free advice and treatment. No introductory doctor's letter or appointment is necessary. Special Clinics are equipped and staffed to diagnose and treat sexually transmitted diseases quickly. If another type of condition is discovered you will be referred to the appropriate hospital department. People of all ages can attend. The locations and opening hours of special clinics are advertised on notices and posters in health centres, post offices and public lavatories; they are also given in the telephone directory under the heading 'venereal disease' or 'VD'. Some areas have a recorded telephone message which gives information about symptoms and clinics. Enquiries may also be made to the casualty department of your local hospital or at a Citizen's Advice Bureau.

At the clinic you will be given a number, but giving a correct name and address is essential in case a patient loses or forgets the clinic number. You must be prepared to undress and have an examination, which will include the genital area; to give a sample of urine; and to have a blood test. The doctor will also enquire about symptoms and (in some detail) recent sexual activity of any kind. Some people who are not sexually active may also develop conditions which can best be investigated at a Special Clinic. A doctor's certificate of attendance can be given if time has to be taken off work or education.

Whatever happens in the clinic is confidential and not told to anyone else, even if they should enquire.

Venezuela For **exchange control** is a non-scheduled territory outside the **overseas sterling area** and the EEC. UK nationals travelling direct from the UK normally need only the following (but check): **passports**; **visas**; international certificates of **vaccination** against smallpox; **work permits** (if taking a job); green cards for motor insurance (if bringing a car) international driving permits (if intending to drive: see **Motoring abroad**).

The UK has no reciprocal health or social security arrangements.

Enquiries to *Venezuelan Embassy* in London and *Venezuelan Consulate-General* in Liverpool.

British diplomatic missions to Venezuela are *British Embassy* in Caracas and *British Vice-Consulates* in Maracaibo, Puerto La Cruz and Valencia.

Veterinary Medicinal Products
The Medicines Act 1968 provides for the licensing of veterinary medicinal products for marketing, and for the issue of animal test certificates for trials of them. Products covered include medicines; sheep dips; teat dips; warble fly dressings; growth promotors; and medicinal products for incorporation in animal feeding stuffs. Before issuing a licence or certificate the licensing authority can seek advice from the Veterinary Products Committee, which advises on the safety, quality and efficacy of products. Explanatory leaflets on how to apply for a product licence or animal test certificate in England and Wales from *Ministry of Agriculture, Fisheries and Food, Animal Health Division III 'B'*.

See also **Agriculture: Scotland**; **Agriculture: Northern Ireland**.

Veterinary Surgeons Veterinary surgeons practising in the UK must be registered with, and be a member of, the *Royal College of Veterinary Surgeons*. Basic qualification is a veterinary degree from the universities of Bristol, Cambridge, Glasgow, Edinburgh, Liverpool or London or from Trinity College or University College, Dublin. Graduates of some overseas universities are also eligible for membership of the RCVS without extra examinations.

The RCVS publishes a register of members from which you can find the names and addresses of veterinary surgeons practising in your area.

Complaints about a member's professional behaviour are investigated first by the Preliminary Investigations Committee of the RCVS and then, if formal action is to be taken, by its Disciplinary Committee.

Vietnam, Socialist Republic of For **exchange control** is a non-scheduled territory outside the **overseas sterling area** and the EEC. UK nationals travelling direct from the UK normally need only the following (but check): **passports**; **visas**; international certificates of **vaccination** against smallpox and cholera; **work permits** (if taking a job); green cards for motor insurance (if bringing a car); international driving permits (if intending to drive: see **Motoring abroad**).
The UK has no reciprocal health or social security arrangements.
Enquiries to *Vietnamese Embassy* in London.
British diplomatic mission to Vietnam is *British Embassy* in Hanoi.

Visas Entry certificates and letters of consent for entry into the UK and UK dependent territories are issued by most British embassies, high commisions and consulates abroad. (See entry for each country). In some places these *British diplomatic missions* also act for **Commonwealth** countries. Visas and entry certificates to foreign countries are issued where required by the embassy or consulate of the country to be visited (see entry for each country).

Vitamins Vitamins are supplied free of charge to expectant and nursing mothers and children under five in large families or familes on low incomes. Details about how to apply in *Department of Health and Social Security* leaflets MV1 and M11 from DHSS local offices.
See also **Families on low incomes**; **Maternity benefits**.

Volleyball Volleyball is governed world-wide by the International Volleyball Federation and in the UK by the *English Volleyball Association*, *Scottish Volleyball Association*, *Welsh Volleyball Association* and *Northern Ireland Volleyball Association*. For the Republic of Ireland the *Eire Volleyball Association* is the authority.

Voluntary Services: Government Aid Financial assistance from the government to voluntary organisations whose interests span the responsibilities of several government departments, but which are not the specific responsibility of any given department, may be available through the Voluntary Services Unit of the *Home Office*.

W

Wages Most employees' pay is determined either by collective agreements between **trade unions** and employers or employers' associations, or by individual negotiation with the employers. However, minimum wage rates are established statutorily by Wages Councils in certain specified industries (e.g. most retail trades, part of catering, hairdressing, toys, laundries, garment manufacture). Notices of what these rates are must be displayed by employers. If you think you are being paid below the minimum fixed by a Wages Council, apply to the *Department of Employment Wages Inspectorate* (enquiries are confidential).

Government suppliers are obliged as part of their contract to maintain fair wages and conditions of employment for the trade concerned under the Fair Wages Resolution. Some local authorities and nationalised industries set similar terms for supply contracts. Employees with a grievance against such employers may complain to *Department of Employment*, which checks that the resolution applies. The complaint then goes to the *Advisory, Conciliation and Arbitration Service*, and if necessary, to the *Central Arbitration Committee* for a decision. Increases in wages should accord with prevailing government incomes policies. Information about current provisions from *Department of Employment regional offices*.

See also **Employment: terms and conditions**.

Wages: Equal Pay Under the Equal Pay Act 1970 anyone doing the same or broadly similar work for the same employer as a person of the opposite sex, or employed in a job which has been rated as equivalent under a job evaluation study, is entitled to the same rate of pay and terms of employment. Claims for equal pay to the *Industrial Tribunals' Central Office* (application forms (IT1) and leaflets from *Department of Employment* (Unemployment Benefit Offices); *Employment Service Agency Employment Offices*; or *Employment Service Agency Job Centres*); appeal against the finding on a point of law to *Employment Appeal Tribunal*. Trade unions and employers may also ask the *Central Arbitration Committee* to remedy the discriminatory aspects of a collective agreement which sets out conditions applying specifically to men only or women only. General advice from *Equal Opportunities Commission* or the *Advisory Conciliation and Arbitration Service*. In Northern Ireland the relevant bodies are the *NI Department of Manpower Services*; the *Equal Opportunities Commission for Northern Ireland*.

See also **Employment: terms and conditions; Sex discrimination: employment.**

Wages: Manual Workers A manual worker covered by the Truck Acts must be paid the whole of his wages in cash (less the statutory deductions, e.g. **income tax**) unless he requests payment by some other means. A worker not in the scope of the Acts may be paid by any method the employer chooses. Complaints about infringements to the *Department of Employment Wages Inspectorate*.

Walks Walks and similar events sponsored for charities are not controlled statutorily, but organisers are advised in the interests of safety to consult local *police*.
See also **Rambling**.

War Dead The dead of both World Wars were, by law, buried as close as possible to where they fell. Bodies may not be moved but a personal inscription can be added to the official headstone. To find out where someone who fell, or was posted missing, is buried or commemorated contact the *Commonwealth War Graves Commission*, which is responsible for war graves and memorials at home and abroad, including those of World War II civilian casualties. The dead and missing of other conflicts, from the Boer War onwards, are the responsibility of the *Ministry of Defence (Dept PS12)* for Army; *Naval Law Division* for Naval; and *AR9* for RAF). The Commission and the Ministry will tell you precisely how to locate a particular grave or memorial if you want to visit it.

War Disablement People disabled through service in either of the two World Wars, or through armed forces service since 1945, and civilian and mercantile marine casualties of the 1939–45 war, receive a tax free War Disablement Pension, regardless of earned income. It is either a weekly pension based on rank and the degree of disablement, or a lump sum if disablement is assessed at less than 20%. It is generally payable anywhere in the world. Extra allowances provide for unemployability; constant attendance; lowered standard of occupation; exceptionally severe disablement; comforts; age; wear and tear of clothing; and treatment. Apply to *Department of Health and Social Security* (local offices); details in leaflets MPL110, 149, 150.

War pensioners are entitled to special services through the DHSS War Pensioners Welfare Service (address from DHSS local offices); priority treatment for their pensioned disability at **National Health Service** hospitals and clinics (see **Hospital treatment**); and special arrangements for residential care. People blinded by war service are provided for by *St Dunstans*.
See also **Disablement**.

War Widows A widow can claim a war widow's pension if the husband's death resulted from service in the armed forces, from an injury as a civilian or Civil Defence Volunteer in the Second World War, or if the husband was entitled to a war pension constant attendance allowance at the full day rate or higher (see **War disablement**). It is paid weekly (monthly if the husband was an officer). The rate depends on the husband's rank, with special allowances for children, education, rent and older widows. Widows of severely disabled war pensioners receive a temporary allowance for 26 weeks if the husband was receiving constant attendance allowance or unemployability supplement (see **War disablement**), even if his death was not attributable directly to war injuries. Enquiries to *Department of Health and Social Security* local offices. Details in DHSS leaflets MPL147 (officers), MPL148 (other ranks and civilians).

Wards of Court Wards of court are people under 18 or legally incapable of managing their affairs, whose guardianship is overseen by a court, normally the High Court. They can either be under the care of a guardian appointed by the court, or, in cases where a child is brought under the court's care but no guardian is appointed, under the direct guardianship of the court.
To make someone a ward of court, apply first to the *Principal Registry of the Family Division* or to a Family Division district registry. Once formal application is made the person automatically becomes a ward, but this ceases after 21 days if no appointment has been obtained for a hearing.

Otherwise the person remains a ward until the determination of the application.

The 'Supreme Court Practice 1976' governs applications and appeals affecting minors. Appeals to the High Court are made to the divisional court of the Family Division.

The *Home Office* will, on request, try to prevent the unauthorised removal of a minor who is a ward of court from UK jurisdiction by alerting major sea and airports, if there is real and imminent danger that the child may be removed.

Waste Food Collectors and processors of waste foods in England and Wales must be licensed annually. Apply to veterinary officers at *Ministry of Agriculture, Fisheries and Food* (divisional offices).
See also **Agriculture: Scotland; Agriculture: Northern Ireland.**

Water Abstraction Abstraction of water from any inland source (e.g. wells, boreholes, rivers) for domestic, industrial and agricultural purposes generally requires a licence from a *water authority* which may fix charges. In Scotland a Water Order is made by the Secretary of State for Scotland at the request of the regional council.
See also **Water services.**

Water: Fluoridation Fluoride may be added to the public water supply by a *water authority* or *water company* at the request of the *area health authority* (*Health Board* in Scotland).
See also **Health authorities; Water services.**

Water: Plumbing Fittings must conform with the water byelaws in force in order to prevent waste, undue consumption, misuse or contamination of water. New fittings may be submitted for approval to the *National Water Council*. Domestic plumbing maintenance is normally the responsibility of the consumer. *Water authorities* and *water companies* will arrange for the water supply to be turned off to allow for domestic plumbing work. A few authorities and companies provide a limited service, e.g. free rewashering.
See also **Water services.**

Water Services River work, water supply and sewage disposal in England and Wales are the responsibility of 10 *water authorities* under the overall guidance of the *National Water Council*. The authorities are responsible to the Secretary of State for the Environment (the Secretary of State for Wales in the case of the *Welsh National Water Development Authority*). The Minister of Agriculture, Fisheries and Food has certain powers relating to land drainage and fisheries.

Water authorities provide directly most of the services for which they are responsible, except for two services. **Local authorities** are agents for the development and maintenance of the local **sewerage** systems (but not for sewage treatment); and statutory *water companies* supply water within certain areas under arrangements with the water authorities, and serve a fifth of the population of England and Wales. Your supplier is given under 'water' in local telephone directory.

The functions carried out in England and Wales by water authorities are, in Scotland, shared between the *Department of Agriculture and Fisheries* (fisheries), river purification boards (cleanliness of rivers) and regional councils (water supply and sewerage, etc.).
See also **Pollution: water.**

Water Skiing Water skiing is governed internationally by the World Water Ski Union and in the UK by the *British Water Ski Federation*. The BWSF selects British teams, sets safety standards, runs a gradings scheme (covering tricks, slalom and jump), and for its member clubs provides coaching courses, judges and technical advice. The BWSF has nine English and three national divisions – the *Welsh Water Ski Committee*, the *Scottish Water Ski Association* and the *British Water Ski Federation Northern Ireland Regional Group*.

Weather Services The recorded weather forecast, which can be obtained by dialling the number listed in the special services section of the telephone directory, is provided by the *Meteorological Office*. Further information about the climate and specialised forecasts (e.g. for pilots, farmers, ice-cream manufacturers) can be obtained direct from the MO or from local meteorological offices. The MO also runs weather centres, where personal callers are welcome, in London, Glasgow, Manchester, Newcastle and Southampton (see local telephone directory under Meteorological or Weather Office).

Weightlifting Weightlifting is governed in the UK by the *British Amateur Weight Lifters' Association* which controls all aspects of the sport, including weight training and power lifting. Internationally the sport is controlled by the International Weightlifting Federation and the International Powerlifting Federation.

Welsh Language Government policy is to foster the living Welsh language and to encourage its official use alongside English in Wales. The *Secretary of State for Wales* is entrusted with the 'guardianship' of the Welsh language and has appointed the *Council for the Welsh Language* (Cyngor yr Iaith Gymraeg) to examine and keep under review social and other factors affecting the language and to give guidance on the encouragement of its use.
The *Royal National Eisteddfod* is the main cultural institution devoted to Welsh. The *Welsh League of Youth* (Urdd Gobaith Cymru) is the government-supported youth movement which encourages the language. The *Welsh Arts Council* assists applicants writing Welsh literature. The two principal learned societies are the *Welsh Academy* (Yr Academi Gymreig) and the older, London-based *Honourable Society of Cymmrodorion*.
In schools, *local education authorities* have statutory responsibility for deciding the extent to which Welsh is taught as a first or second language or used as a medium of instruction. The Secretary of State encourages authorities to make bilingual provision that is in keeping with the needs and characteristics of their area; parental wishes are taken into account. The *Welsh Joint Education Committee* sponsors a standard form of spoken Welsh for learners and runs the *Welsh Books Scheme* which sponsors selected books for schools. Under this an author can be paid directly and be given editorial assistance; a publisher can have a guaranteed minimum sale and practical assistance with distribution.
In legal proceedings in Wales, under Section 1 (i) of the Welsh Language Act, 1967, the Welsh language may be spoken by any party, witness or other person who decides to use it. Similar arrangements exist for **industrial tribunals**.
Local government is encouraged to use Welsh by the Secretary of State but each local authority decides for itself. The *Welsh Office Translation Unit* provides a Welsh language translation service for all central government departments. The Unit is supported by the independent *Advisory Welsh Translation Panel* which was set up by the Secretary of State.
For traffic signs in Wales the general policy is to introduce both Welsh and English. The Secretary of State has decided that on safety grounds some signs must have English first; otherwise, the order of languages is determined by county councils.

Welsh Liberal Party The Welsh Liberal Party (Plaid Ryddfrydol Cymru) was formed in 1878. Its aim is to further the principles of Liberalism in Wales and to promote the well-being of Wales as a nation. Membership is open to any Liberal from Wales, whether living in Wales or not. Join through the constituency association or through the two *Welsh Liberal Offices* or as a national member through *Welsh Liberal Party Headquarters*.

White Fish The *White Fish Authority* assists the industry in making the best use of the resources of white fish available to the UK by providing technical advice on the capture, handling and processing of white fish; publicising white fish as a food; and giving financial aid to catchers and processors – e.g. making loans of up to 80% for processing and ice-making plants. The WFA is mainly financed from a levy on first-hand sales of white fish, but its research and development work is grant-aided by the government.

Who's Who Who's invited to be in 'Who's Who' is determined by a selection board chosen by the publishers, *A. & C. Black Ltd.* Peers, MPs, baronets, knights, judges, QCs, holders of certain chairs, senior officers of the armed services and senior civil servants are all invited. In the arts, most professions, commerce and industry, there is no rule of thumb but factors taken into account include the frequency and circumstances with which a name appears before the public; service to government, local government, and to professional institutions; the importance of a company or institution nationally or in its own field; leadership of a large body of people or opinion; serious critical attention, but not necessarily universal approval, of artist's productions. Youth and wealth are no bar. The selection board's prime aim is to provide a book of use to those likely to purchase or consult it.

Widowers No regular social security pension or allowance is paid to husbands upon their wife's death, but under the new state Pension scheme (see **Retirement pension**) effective from May 1978, a man's pension may be increased on his wife's earnings record if he is sick or they are both over pension age when she dies. Enquiries to *Department of Health and Social Security* (local office). See also **Social security benefits**.

Widow's Benefits Widows under 60 usually receive widow's allowance for the first six months of widowhood, with increases for any qualifying children, and with an earnings related addition (see **Earnings related supplement**) if the husband had paid class 1 contributions on earnings of more than 50 times the lower weekly earnings limit for contributions in the relevant **income tax** year (see **National insurance contributions**). Widows with qualifying children receive a widowed mother's allowance from the date widow's allowance ends. A widow's pension is paid to a widow who is 40 or over when her husband dies or when her widowed mother's allowance ends; between 40 and 49 the rate of pension is age-related.

From April 1978 the rate of widowed mother's allowance and widow's pension is related to the whole of the rights built up by the husband under the new earnings pension scheme (see **Retirement pension**). Entitlement to widow's benefits depends on the late husband's national insurance contributions, and gaps in contributions may diminish the benefit. A divorced wife is ineligible for widow's benefits. Apply to *Department of Health and Social Security* (local offices); for details see DHSS leaflets N113; N195 (for women whose marriage ends by divorce or anulment); IR23 (income tax); NI105 (methods of payment).
See also **Industrial injury and disease** (for industrial death benefit); **War widows** (for war widows' pensions); **Child social security benefits**.

Wild Animals Under the Conservation of Wild Creatures and Wild Plants Act 1975, certain native species, including **badgers**, seals and seven listed creatures (greater horse-shoe bat; mouse-eared bat; sand lizard; smooth snake; natterjack toad; large blue butterfly; common otter) are protected in Great Britain. Licences to take or kill these creatures for scientific or educational purposes, or to prevent the spread of disease, must generally be obtained in advance from the *Nature Conservancy Council* or from the *Ministry of Agriculture, Fisheries and Food* respectively. Licences for similar purposes in relation to seals must be obained from the *Home Office*.
See also **Endangered species; Nature conservation; Wild birds**.

Wild Birds All wild birds and their nests and eggs are protected in Great Britain under the Protection of Birds

Acts 1954 and 1967. With certain limited exceptions, licences to take, kill or capture birds, take or destroy eggs, or ring or mark birds are required from the *Department of the Environment* or the *Scottish Home and Health Department*. Applications for licences are referred to a Birds Advisory Committee.

The Protection of Birds Acts do not for the most part cover certain game birds. Under the Game Acts the close season for game birds are: pheasant (2 February to 30 September); partridge (2 February to 31 August); black grouse (11 December to 19 August); red grouse (11 December to 11 August); ptarmigan (11 December to 11 August in Scotland only; it is fully protected at all times in England and Wales).

Schedules to the Protection of Birds Acts list the degree of protection given to different species other than game birds; any species not mentioned in the schedules is fully protected throughout the year.

Second Schedule:
Wild birds which may be killed or taken by authorised persons, i.e. the owner or occupier of the land on which the action takes place or any person authorised by the owner or occupier; someone authorised by a local authority or one of certain other bodies such as *Nature Conservancy Council*, certain local fishery committees, conservators of various rivers, etc.,
 Bullfinch (only in certain areas)
 Cormorant
 Crow, carrion
 Crow, hooded
 Domestic pigeon (gone feral)
 Dove, collared
 Goosander (Scotland only)
 Gull, great black-backed
 Gull, lesser black-backed
 Gull, herring
 Jackdaw
 Jay
 Magpie
 Merganser, red-breasted (Scotland only)
 Oystercatcher (only in certain areas)
 Raven (Argyll and Skye only)
 Rock dove (Scotland only)
 Rook
 Shag
 Sparrow, house
 Starling
 Stock dove
 Woodpigeon

Third Schedule:
Wild birds which may be killed or taken outside the close season, 1 February to 31 August except where indicated otherwise.
Note that the close season for wild duck and geese when below high water mark is 21 February to 31 August.
Those birds in Part II of the First Schedule.
 Capercaillie – close season 1 February to 30 September
 Coot
 Curlew (other than stone curlew)
 Gannet (on Sula Sgeir only)
 Godwit, bar-tailed
 Moorhen
 Plover, golden
 Plover, grey
 Redshank, common
 Snipe, common – close season 1 February to 11 August
 Snipe, jack – close season 1 February to 11 August
 Wild duck of the following species (see note above):
  Common pochard
  Gadwall
  Mallard
  Shoveler
  Teal
  Tufted duck
  Wigeon
 Wild geese, including:
  Bean goose
  Canada goose
  Greylag goose
  Pink-footed goose
  White-fronted goose
 Woodcock – close season 1 February to 30 September except in Scotland, where 1 February to 31 August

Fourth Schedule:
Wild birds which may not be sold alive unless close-ringed and bred in captivity:
 Blackbird
 Blackcap
 Bluethroat
 Brambling
 Bullfinch
 Bunting (all species)
 Chaffinch

Chiffchaff
Chough
Crossbill (all species)
Cuckoo
Dipper
Fieldfare
Firecrest
Flycatcher (all species)
Goldcrest
Goldfinch
Greenfinch
Hawfinch
Hoopoe
Jay
Kingfisher
Lark (all species)
Linnet
Magpie
Martin (all species)
Nightingale
Nightjar
Nuthatch
Oriole, golden
Owl (all species except the little owl)
Pipit (all species)
Raven
Redpoll (all species)
Redstart (all species)
Redwing
Ring ouzel
Robin
Shrike (all species)
Siskin
Sparrow, hedge
Sparrow, house
Sparrow, tree
Starling
Stonechat
Swallow
Thrush (all species)
Tit (all species, including Bearded tit)
Treecreeper
Twite
Wagtail (all species)
Warbler (all species)
Waxwing
Wheatear
Whinchat
Whitethroat (all species)
Woodpecker (all species)
Wren
Wryneck
Yellowhammer

The Secretary of State may establish bird sanctuaries, to which access may be restricted, and in which all wild birds and eggs are protected at all times and may also be given protection against wilful disturbance. Sanctuary Orders apply in the following areas:

Abberton Reservoir, Essex
Brean Down, Somerset
Burry Estuary, West Glamorgan
Charlton's Pond, Billingham, Durham
Cleddau, Haverfordwest, Pembs.
Durleigh Reservoir, Somerset
Cley Marshes, Norfolk
Fairburn Ings and Newton Ings, Fairburn, Yorks, West Riding
Farne Islands, Northumberland
Fetlar Island, Shetlands
Gibraltar Point, Lincs.
Havergate Island, Suffolk
Horse Island, Ardrossan, Ayr
Humber Estuary, Yorks./Lincs.
Inchmickery
Lady Isle, Firth of Clyde
Loch Eye, Ross and Cromarty
Loch Garten, Inverness
Low Parks, Hamilton, Lanark
Porth Reservoir, Melancoose, Cornwall
Possil Marsh, Glasgow
Southport, Lancs.
Tamar Lake, Devon/Cornwall
Trethais Island, Cornwall
Walmsley, Cornwall
Wicken Sedge Fen, Cambs.
Wyre-Lune, Lancs.

This summarises the general position but see 'Wild Birds and the Law' published by the *Royal Society for the Protection of Birds*. Enquiries to RSPB.

See also **Swans**.

Wild Plants It is an offence for any unauthorised person to uproot any wild plant without reasonable excuse, under the Conservation of Wild Creatures and Wild Plants Act 1975, and the picking, uprooting or destruction of rare plants of species listed in schedule 2 of the Act is prohibited. Authorised persons are defined as owners and occupiers of land, their servants and anyone authorised by them.

The following species are protected at present: Alpine gentian, alpine sowthistle, alpine woodsia, blue heath, Cheddar pink, diapensia, drooping saxifrage, ghost orchid, Killarney fern, lady's-slipper, mezereon, military orchid, monkey orchid, oblong

woodsia, red helleborine, Snowdon lily, spiked speedwell, spring gentian, Teesdale sandwort, tufted saxifrage, wild gladiolus. Enquiries to *Nature Conservancy Council*.
The schedules can be varied by order; they provide a flexible means of protecting endangered species not protected under earlier legislation. The number and distribution of rare species may be expected to fluctuate over time; the Nature Conservancy Council monitors these changes and may, from time to time, recommend revisions of the schedules.

Wills Wills are documents whereby a person (the testator) disposes of his property on death. The testator must sign the will and his signature must be witnessed by two people who cannot benefit under the will. The advice of a **solicitor** should, however, always be sought.
The will should name one or more persons (the executors) to carry out the terms of the will and after the death of the testator the court will, assuming everything is in order, issue a grant of **probate** which will authorise the executors to administer the estate. Grants of probate are issued by the *Probate Registry* in England and Wales; by the Registrars at the *Royal Courts of Justice* (Belfast) in Northern Ireland; and by the sheriff in Scotland.

Wimbledon The Wimbledon Lawn Tennis Championships are held annually at the *All England Lawn Tennis and Croquet Club*. They are run by a committee consisting of the 12 members of the AELTCC and seven delegates from the *Lawn Tennis Association*. Centre court tickets are available as of right to Wimbledon debenture holders, members of the AELTC and councillors of the LTA; other people should write for application forms (available 1 January) to the secretary of the AELTC; some tickets are also available from theatre ticket agencies. No. 1 court tickets (covered stands) are handled by *Keith Prowse Ltd;* the secretary of the AELTC issues open stand tickets by ballot (application forms available 1 January).
See also **Tennis**.

Wine Wine and related products being transported within the **EEC** must under EEC regulations be accompanied by official documents certifying the description and origin of the consignment. Apply to *Wine Standards Board of the Vinters' Company*. The WSBVC also approves the marking of closing devices for wine in the UK and maintains an inspectorate. Marks may be a code number or name and address. Enquiries to WSBVC.

Wine: Production UK producers of wine or made-wine for sale must hold an excise licence for every premises concerned in the production under arrangements to secure payment of **excise duty**. Wine is liquor produced from the fermentation of fresh grapes or the must thereof; made-wine is liquor produced from the fermentation of any other substance or from mixing fermented products. Growers of grapes need not hold licences unless they wish to sell wine; but a concession allows the processing of grapes to take place at the premises of a co-operative for return of wine in bottled state free of excise duty, provided that a licence is obtained. Producers of wine may also claim an allowance of up to 240 gallons of wine a year for domestic consumption free of excise duty.
The fortification of wine of UK production must be carried out in an excise warehouse or winery; **customs duty** (if any) on **spirits** used for fortifying must be accounted for in advance. Apply for licence to *Her Majesty's Customs and Excise* (details in Notice 162).

Women and Government The *Women's National Commission* is an advisory committee to the UK government. Its terms of reference are 'to ensure by all possible means that the informed opinion of women is given its due weight in the deliberations of government on both national and international affairs'.

Wool Marketing Except in the Shetland Islands, UK producers with more than four adult **sheep** must register with the *British Wool Marketing Board*. It buys all their fleece wool at a guarantee price with an adjustment for the quality of the wool and the BWMB's marketing costs.

Work: Health and Safety The Health and Safety at Work Act imposes a general duty on employers, employees, suppliers, owners of premises and the self-employed to ensure that workplaces are made and kept safe and healthy. There are many other laws covering specific fields. The *Health and Safety Executive* enforces the laws and advises industry through inspectorates (separate ones exist for factories, mines and quarries, nuclear installations, explosives, alkali and clean air and agriculture), through its Employment Medical Advisory Service, and through two policy branches, the Safety and General Division and the Hazardous Substances Division. It is responsible to the *Health and Safety Commission* which in turn is responsible for most matters to the Secretary of State for Employment.
The Commission, which has a full-time chairman and nine part-time members drawn from both sides of industry and local authorities, supervises the enforcement of legislation and reviews the need for new legislation. It is aided by advisory committees. General leaflets and advice are available from the HSE head office and specific advice and leaflets from its branches and inspectorates.
Inspectors can issue employers with improvement or prohibition notices in respect of partial operations or activities. Employers can appeal against the terms of such notices to the *Industrial Tribunals Central Office*. The Employment Medical Advisory Service deals with government medical and nursing policy for all aspects of occupational health (e.g. advice on occupational health services at places of work; assessment of biochemical or biophysical hazards associated with work processes; medical surveys and researches; monitoring of reported cases of industrial disease).
Regional offices of the Service offer medical and nursing advice, and publications on occupational hazards to health, occupational rehabilitation and youth employment.
See also **Air pollution; Clothing at work; Dust; Industrial injury and disease; Machine safety; Smoke control.**

Work permits Work permits are governed by the Immigration Rules for the Control of Entry which stem from the Immigration Act 1971. In general, overseas nationals who do not have the right of abode in the UK must have a work permit before being employed in the UK. But certain specified categories (e.g. au pairs, see **Au pair arrangements**) do not need permits. In some cases (e.g. actors, singers), applications must be supported by the relevant **trade union** or the permit will be refused.
Only the person's future employer can apply for the permit; application forms and leaflets OW5 and OW6 from *Department of Employment* (Unemployment Benefit Offices) or *Employment Service Agency Job Centres* or *Employment Service Agency Employment Offices* or *Department of Employment, Overseas Labour Section*.
The DEm is responsible for the issue of work permits and for ensuring that the conditions for their issue are satisfied; the *Home Office Immigration and Nationality Department* is primarily responsible for enforcing the rules and investigates information about illegal working, instigating police action if appropriate.
Like UK nationals, overseas workers employed in the UK must pay **National insurance contributions;** apply to the nearest *Department of Health and Social Security* (local office) for an insurance number.
Further information from the *Department of Employment Overseas Labour Section*.
See also **Immigration.**

Wrecks Wrecks are the responsibility of a customs officer known as the Receiver of Wrecks. If the owner is unknown, he will establish ownership; if the owner is known but the salvage claim to the wreck is in dispute this can be settled in the county court. Enquiries to *Her Majesty's Customs and Excise.*

Wrestling Olympic-style amateur wrestling is governed internationally by the International Amateur Wrestling Federation. In Great Britain the *British Amateur Wrestling Association* selects UK teams while the *English Olympic Wrestling Association* and the *Scottish Amateur Wrestling Association* control their own regions. Professional wrestling is controlled by individual promoters.

Y

Yachting Yacht racing is controlled internationally by the International Yacht Racing Union. The UK authority for all aspects of yachting is the *Royal Yachting Association*. It represents UK yachtsmen's interests nationally and internationally; initiates training programmes (there are over 400 RYA-recognised teaching establishments); regulates UK yacht racing (e.g. is responsible for organising events, handicapping, racing appeals, registration and measurement); issues booklets (e.g. on international flag etiquette and collision regulations) and selects teams for the Olympics and other world championships.
A number of clubs organise offshore racing round and from the British Isles. The largest of these is the *Royal Ocean Racing Club* which is the senior club for this sport in Europe. It leads in controlling safety regulations, rating of boats, and other points particular to offshore sailing.

Yachts: Duty-free Stores Shipment of duty-free stores is normally restricted to vessels of 40 tons net register or more; but subject to certain conditions, such items may be shipped on yachts or other private craft of less than 40 tons register departing for a port beyond certain limits (i.e. south of Brest or north of the bank of the Elbe). Apply in advance to *Her Majesty's Customs and Excise*, which will also advise on the procedure for shipping stores; details in HMCE Notice 8.
See also **Customs duty; Excise duty**.

Yachts: Registration Yachts and other private craft which proceed abroad must be registered under the Merchant Shipping Act 1894. Apply to *Registrar of British Ships*; details in Notice 8, from *Her Majesty's Customs and Excise*.

Yacht Surveys Surveys and design appraisal are conducted by *Lloyd's Register of Shipping* for new craft, including the tonnage measurement survey required for British registration.
See also **Ships and yachts; seaworthiness; Shipping: registration and approval**.

Yemen Arab Republic For exchange control is a non-scheduled territory outside the **overseas sterling area** and the **EEC**. UK nationals travelling direct from the UK normally need only the following (but check): **passports** without Israeli stamp; **visas**; international certificates of **vaccination** against smallpox and cholera; **work permits** (if taking a job).
The UK has no reciprocal health or social security arrangements.
Enquiries to *Yemen Arab Republic Embassy* in London.
British diplomatic mission to Yemen Arab Republic is *British Embassy* in Sana'a.

Yemen, People's Democratic Republic For **exchange control** is a non-scheduled territory in the **overseas sterling area** but outside the EEC. UK nationals travelling direct from the UK normally need only the following (but check): **passports** without Israeli stamp; **visas**; international certificates of **vaccination** against smallpox and cholera; **work permits** (if taking a job).
The UK has no reciprocal health or social security arrangements.
Enquiries to *Yemen People's Democratic Republic Embassy* in London and *Yemen People's Democratic Republic Consulate* in Birmingham.
British diplomatic mission to Yemen People's Democratic Republic is *British Embassy* in Aden.

Young Adult Offenders Offenders aged from 17 to 20 years are recognised as a category distinct from child and adult offenders, and special forms of custodial treatment are devoted to them. The main non-custodial measures are generally the same as for adults, although in a few places an order to attend an **attendance centre** (see **Children and young peoples' orders**) may be made.
The custodial sentences available to the court are: detention in a **detention centre**; **borstal training**; and imprisonment (see **Prison sentences**). The first two are both also used for offenders under 17. For detention centres there are separate committal arrangements and separate centres for offenders aged 17 and over and for those aged under 17; there is no such distinction in the borstal system.
Special provisions within the penal system apply to young offenders. The responsible government departments are, in England and Wales, the *Home Office* and the *Department of Health and Social Security*; in Scotland, the *Home and Health* and the *Education Departments*; and in Northern Ireland, the *Northern Ireland Office*. **Local authorities** (Social Services Department) are responsible for many functions relating to children and young people (see **Child care and welfare**).
A person aged under 17 years cannot be sentenced to imprisonment, and no court may pass a sentence of imprisonment on an offender aged 17–20 years unless satisfied that no other method of dealing with him is appropriate. If imprisonment is imposed, the term must normally be of not more than six months or less than three years (or 18 months if the person has served a previous sentence of not less than six months' imprisonment or a sentence of borstal training). Sentences of up to two years may be ordered by a court, as in the case of adult offenders, to be suspended.
Prisoners under the age of 21 at the time of their sentence are classified as young prisoners and serve their sentence separately from older prisoners unless they are reclassified as adults and treated as such in an adult prison. Reclassification, which depends on their degree of maturity or criminal sophistication, may be effected when they reach the age of 18, but for many does not take place until they reach the age of 21. Most young prisoners serving medium- and long-term sentences go to one of eight young prisoners' centres – allocation is as far as possible on the basis of proximity to home – while those with short sentences mostly remain at their local prison in accommodation separate from older prisoners. A few go to remand centres as members of working parties providing domestic and maintenance services.
A person found guilty of murder who was under the age of 18 when the crime was committed must be sentenced to detention 'during Her Majesty's pleasure'. Offenders subject to this sentence, or to life imprisonment, may be released on licence.
In Scotland no offender under 21 years may be sent to prison. Where neither borstal nor detention centre training is suitable for an offender aged 16–20, detention in a special 'young offenders institution' may be ordered.
See also **Parole**; **Prison sentences**.

Yugoslavia For **exchange control** is a non-scheduled territory outside the **overseas sterling area** and the **EEC**. UK nationals travelling direct from the UK normally need only the following (but check): **passports; work permits** (if taking a job); green cards for motor insurance (if bringing a car). Petrol coupons for private cars, only obtainable at frontier posts from travel agents (Kompass or Putnik) and garages. Not available within Yugoslavia. See **Motoring abroad.**

UK reciprocal arrangements cover social security (see leaflet SA17 obtainable from *Department of Health and Social Security, Overseas Branch*), and health. Hospital and general medical treatment free on production of UK passport; a small charge for prescribed medicines.

Enquiries to *Yugoslav Embassy* in London and *Yugoslav National Tourist Office* in London.

British diplomatic missions to Yugoslavia are *British Embassy* in Belgrade, *British Consulate-General* in Zagreb and *British Consulate* in Split.

Z

Zaire For **exchange control** is a non-scheduled territory outside the **overseas sterling area** and the EEC. UK nationals travelling direct from the UK normally need only the following (but check): **passports**; **visas**; international certificates of **vaccination** against smallpox and yellow fever; **work permits** (if taking a job).
The UK has no reciprocal health or social security arrangements.
Enquiries to *Zaire Embassy* in London.
British diplomatic mission to Zaire is *British Embassy* in Kinshasa.

Zambia **Commonwealth** member. For **exchange control** is a non-scheduled territory in the **overseas sterling area** but outside the EEC. UK nationals travelling direct from the UK normally need only the following (but check): **passports**; entry permits; international certificates of **vaccination** against smallpox; **work permits** (if taking a job).
The UK has no reciprocal health or social security arrangements.
Enquiries to *Zambian High Commission* in London.
British diplomatic mission to Zambia is *British High Commission* in Lusaka.

Zoos To establish or operate a safari park, wildlife park, zoological garden or zoo park, etc., requires the permission of, or is subject to the control of, first the local authority and then various other bodies, e.g. for land use – local authority and *Department of the Environment*; animal welfare – *Home Office*; animal diseases, transport, import, quarantine – *Ministry of Agriculture, Fisheries and Food* and the *Northern Ireland Department of Agriculture*; conservation and import and export of endangered species – *Department of the Environment*.
There is no special legislation yet in force controlling zoos but private individuals keeping animals as pets are subject to the Dangerous Wild Animals Act 1976 and Home Office control.
The two UK zoo associations are the *Federation of Zoological Gardens of Great Britain and Ireland* (includes most zoological societies and trusts) and the *National Zoological Association of Great Britain* (includes most safari parks). The *Zoological Society of London* (founded as a scientific society in 1826) has on exhibition at Regent's Park, London, and at Whipsnade Zoo one of the largest and most comprehensive collections of animals in the world. Other 'Broad spectrum' collections are at the *North of England Zoological Society* in Chester, the *Royal Zoological Society of Scotland* in Edinburgh, the *Bristol, Clifton and West of England Zoological Society*, and *Bellevue Zoo*, Antrim Road, Belfast; specialist collections include *Twycross Zoo Park* (primates), the *Wildfowl Trust* at Slimbridge, Peakirk, etc. (waterfowl), *Marwell Zoological Park* (ungulates), and *Jersey Zoological Park* (primates and some rodents).

A

A & C Black Ltd, 35 Bedford Row, London WC1R 4JH (01–242–0946)
Academy of Sciences, Frescati, S–10405 Stockholm 50, Sweden
Accepting Houses Committee, 1 Crutched Friars, London EC3 (01–481–2120)
Access, 7 St Martin's Place, London WC2 (01–839–7090)
Acupuncture Association and Register Ltd, 34 Alderney St, London SW1V 4EU (01–834–1012)
Advertising Standards Authority, 15–17 Bridgemount St, London WC1E 7AW (01–580–0801)
Advisory, Conciliation and Arbitration Service, Head Office, Cleland House, Page St, London SW1P 4ND (01–222–4383)
Advisory, Conciliation and Arbitration Service Regional Offices
—— Midlands, Alpha Tower, Suffolk St Queensway, Birmingham B1 1TZ (021–643–9911)
—— North West, Boulton House, 17–21 Chorlton St, Manchester M1 3HY (061–228–3222)
—— Northern, Westgate House, Westgate Rd, Newcastle-upon-Tyne NE1 1TJ (0632–612191)
—— Scotland, 109 Waterloo St, Glasgow, G2 7BY (041–221–6832)
—— South East, Hanway House, Red Lion Sq, London WC1R 4NH (01–405–8454)
—— South West, 16 Park Place, Clifton, Bristol BS8 1JP (0272–211921)
—— Wales, 2–4 Park Grove, Cardiff CF1 3QY (0222–45231)
—— Yorkshire and Humberside, City House, Leeds LS1 4JH (0532–38232)
Advisory Council on Public Records, Public Record Office, Chancery Lane, London WC2A 1LR (01–405–0741)
Advisory Welsh Translations Panel, Oxford House, Cardiff (0222–44171)
Afghanistan, Embassy of the Republic of, 31 Prince's Gate, London SW7 1QQ (01–589–8891)
African Violet Society of America, 4988 Schollmeyer Ave, St Louis, Mo 63109, USA
Agricultural Credit Corporation Ltd, Agricultural House, 25–31 Knightsbridge, London SW1X 7NJ (01–235–6296)
Agricultural Land Tribunals,
—— Plas Crug, Aberystwyth, Dyfed SY23 1NG (0970–3162)
—— Block C, Government Buildings, Brooklands Ave, Cambridge CB2 2DR (0223–58911)
—— Block 2, Government Buildings, Lawnswood, Leeds LS16 5PY (0532–67–4411)
—— Government Buildings, Kenton Rd, Newcastle-upon-Tyne NE1 2YA (0630–869811)
—— Block 2, Government Buildings, Chalfont Drive, Nottingham NG8 3RH (0602–292251)
—— Block A, Government Office, Coley Park, Reading RG1 6DT (0734–581222)
—— Quantock House, Paul St, Taunton TR1 3NX (0823–87922)
—— Woodthorne, Wolverhampton WV6 8TQ (0902–754190)
Agricultural Mortgage Corporation Ltd, Bucklersbury House, 3 Queen Victoria St, London EC4 N8DU (01–248–6711)
Agricultural Research Council, 160 Great Portland St, London W1N 6DT (01–580–6635)
Agricultural Wages Board, Eagle House, 90–6 Cannon St, London EC4N 7MT (01–623–4266)
Air Taxi Operators Association, Stapleford Aerodrome, Stapleford Tawney, Nr Romford, Essex (01–599–1087)
Air Touring International, Elstree Aerodrome, Elstree, Herts (01–953–4870)
Air Travel Reserve Fund Agency
—— (administration) Space House, 43–59 Kingsway, London WC2B 6TE (01–379–7311)
—— (Chairman) 20 Manvers St, Bath BA1 1LX
Aircraft Owners and Pilots Association, Artillery Mansions, 50a Cambridge St, London SW1V 4QQ (01–834–5631)
Airline Users Committee, Space House 43–59 Kingsway, London WC2B 6TE (01–379–7311)
Airports
—— Aberdeen Airport, Dyce, Aberdeenshire AB2 0DU (0224–722331)
—— Ashford Airport, Nr Hythe, Kent (0703–66156)
—— Belfast/Aldergrove Airport, Belfast (0232–29271)
—— Birmingham Airport, Birmingham B26 8QJ (021–753–4272)
—— East Midlands Airport, Castle Donington, Derby DE7 2SA (0332–810621)
—— Edinburgh Airport, Edinburgh EH12 0AL (031–333–1000)

Airports—cont.
—— Gatwick Airport, Horley, Surrey RH6 0NP (01-668-4211)
—— Glasgow Airport, Paisley, Renfrewshire PA3 2ST (041-887-1111)
—— Guernsey Airport, Guernsey, Channel Islands (0481-37766)
—— Heathrow Airport, Hounslow, Middlesex TW6 1JH (01-759-4321)
—— Jersey Airport, Jersey, Channel Islands (0481-37766)
—— Liverpool Airport, Liverpool L24 8QQ (051-427-4101)
—— Luton Airport, Luton, Bedfordshire (0582-36061)
—— Manchester Airport, Wythenshawe, Manchester 22 (061-437-5200)
—— Prestwick Airport, Prestwick, Ayrshire KA9 2PL (0292-79822)
—— Southend-on-Sea Airport, Southend-on-Sea, Essex (0702-40201/6)
—— Stansted Airport, Stansted, Essex CH24 8QW (0279-502380)
Al-Anon, Family Group UK and Eire, 61 Great Dover St, London SE1 4YF
Albanian diplomatic mission, Albanian Embassy, 131 Rue de la Porte, 75116 Paris, France (553-5132, 553-8938)
Albtourist, Bld. Deshmoret e Kombit 8, Tirana, Albania
Alcohol Education Centre, Bethlem and Maudsley Hospital, 99 Denmark Hill, London SE5 8AZ
Alcoholics Anonymous, 11 Redcliffe Gardens, London SW10
Algerian Embassy, 6 Hyde Park Gate, London SW7 5EW (01-584-9502)
Algerian National Tourist Office, 35 St James's St, London SW1 (01-839-5315)
All England Lawn Tennis and Croquet Club, Church Rd, Wimbledon, London SW19 5AE (01-946-2244)
All England Netball Assocation, 70 Brompton Rd, London SW3 1HD (01-584-2578)
All England Women's Hockey Association, 160 Great Portland St, London W1N 5TB (01-636-0264)
All England Women's Lacrosse Association, 70 Brompton Rd, London SW1 1EQ (01-584-2508)
All Wales Ladies Lacrosse Association, 51 St Nicholas Rd, Barry, South Glamorgan (0446-3101)
Alliance Party of Northern Ireland Headquarters, 88 University St, Belfast BT7 1HE (0232-2474)
Allied Irish Banks Ltd, PO Box 512, 3–4 Foster Place, Dublin 2 (0001-760371)
Alpine Club, 74 Audley St, London W1 (01-499-1542)
Amateur Athletic Association, 70 Brompton Rd, London SW3 1EE (01-584-7715)
Amateur Basketball Association of Ireland, Castle Rd, Bulterstown, County Waterford, Eire
Amateur Basketball Association of Ireland, 3 Holmdene Gardens, Belfast BT14 7LJ (Ulster Council)
Amateur Basketball Association of Scotland, 8 Frederick St, Edinburgh EH2 2HB (031-225-7143)
Amateur Boxing Association, 70 Brompton Rd, London SW3 1HA (01-584-9187)
Amateur Fencing Association, 83 Perham Rd, London W14 9SP (01-385-7442)
Amateur Rowing Association
—— Headquarters, 6 Lower Mall, London W6 9DJ (01-748-3632)
—— Welsh Rowing Council, 74 Woolaston Ave, Lakeside, Cardiff (0222-754259)
Amateur Swimming Association, Harold Fern House, Derby Sq, Loughborough, Leics LE11 0AL
Amateur Swimming Federation of Great Britain, Harold Fern House, Derby Sq, Loughborough (0509-30431)
American Begonia Society, 1130 North Milpas St, Santa Barbara, Cal 93103, USA
American Boxwood Society, Blandy Experimental Farm, Boyce, Va 22620, USA
American Fuchsia Society, Hall of Flowers, Golden Gate Park, San Francisco, Cal 94122, USA
American Gloxinia and Gesneriad Society, 26 Hotchkiss St Sth, Binghampton, NY 13903, USA
American Haemerocallis Society, 2244 Cloverdale Ave, Baton Rouge, La 70808, USA
American Hosta Society, University of Minnesota Landscape Arboretum, Box 13201, Route 1, Chaska, Mn 55318, USA
American Iris Society, 2315 Tower Grove Ave, St Louis, Missouri 63110, USA
American Ivy Society, National Center for American Horticulture, Mt Vernon, Va 22121, USA
American Paeony Society, 1246 Donlea Crescent, Oakville, Ontario, Canada L6J IV7
American Penstemon Society, 711 Magnolia Ave, Mena, Ark 71953, USA
American Plant Life Society, 5804 Cemino de la Costa, La Jolla, Cal 92037, USA
American Rose Society, 4048 Roselea Place, Columbus, Ohio 43214, USA
Amnesty International, British Section, Tower House, 8–14 Southampton St, London WC2E 7HF (01-836-5621)
Andorran Delegation, 63 Western Rd, London SW18 (01-874-4806)
Anglia Land Yacht Club, 17 Taylors Close, Mepperhall, Beds

Anglia Television Ltd, Anglia House, Norwich NR1 3JG (0603-28366)
Appeal Tribunal, 231 The Strand, London WC2 (01-353-8060)
Apple and Pear Development Council, Union House, The Pantiles, Tunbridge Wells, Kent TN4 8HF (0892-20255)
Approved Coal Merchants' Scheme, Domestic Coal Consumers' Council, Thames House South, Millbank, London SW1P 4QJ (01-211-5820)
Arboricultural Association, 59 Blythwood Gardens, Stansted, Essex
Archbishops' Appointments Secretary, Fielden House, Little College St, London SW1
Archbishop of Canterbury's Faculty Office, 1 The Sanctuary, London SW1 (01-222-5381)
Architects Registration Council of the UK, 73 Hallam St, London W1N 6EE (01-580-5861)
Area Education Office, contact Local Education Authority
Area Electricity boards, see Electricity Boards
Area Health Authority, contact Department of Health and Social Security Local Office
Area Health and Social Services Boards (Northern Ireland)
—— Eastern, 65 University St, Belfast BT7 1HM (0232-44611)
—— Northern, County Hall, 182 Galgorm Rd, Ballymena, Co Antrim BT42 1QD (Ballymena 3333)
—— Southern, 20 Seagoe Industrial Area, Portadown, Craigavon, Co Armagh BT63 5QD (Portadown 36611)
—— Western, 50 Gransha Park, Clooney Rd, Londonderry BT47 1TG (Londonderry 860086)
Argentine, Embassy of the Republic of, 9 Wilton Crescent, London SW1X 8RP (01-235-3717)
Argentine, Consulate of the Republic of, 54 Castle St, Liverpool 1 (051-236-3939)
Army Careers, PO Box LEL, London W1A 1EL
Army Medal Office, Ministry of Defence, Block A, Government Buildings, Droitwich, Worcs WR9 8AU
Arnold Arboretum, Harvard University, Jamaica Plain, Mass 02130, USA
Artificial Limb and Appliance Centre, see in telephone directory
Arts Council of Great Britain, 105 Piccadilly, London W1 (01-629-9495)
Arts Council of Northern Ireland, Riddel Hall, 181A Strandmillis Rd, Belfast BT9 5DU (0232-663591)
Asbestos Information Committee, PO Box 4QS, London W1A 4QS
Ascot Office, St James's Palace, London SW1 (01-930-9882)
Associated Examining Board, Wellington House, Aldershot, Hants GU11 1BQ (0252-25551)
Associated Lancashire Schools Examining Board, 77 Whitworth St, Manchester M1 6HA (061-236-6020)
Associated Television Network Limited, ATV Centre, Birmingham B1 2JP (021-643-9898)
Association of British Launderers and Cleaners, Lancaster Gate House, 319 Pinner Rd, Harrow, Middlesex HA1 4HX (01-863-7755)
Association of British Travel Agents, 53-54 Newman St, London W1P 4AH (01-580-8281)
Association of Certified Accountants, Incorporated by Royal Charter, 22 Bedford Sq, London WC1B 3HS (01-636-2103)
Association of Commonwealth Literature and Language Studies, University of Queensland, St Lucia, Brisbane, Queensland, Australia
Association of Commonwealth Universities, 36 Gordon Sq, London WC1H 0PF (01-387-8572)
Association of Dispensing Opticians, 22 Nottingham Place, London W1M 4AT (01-935-7411)
Association of Head Mistresses, 29 Gordon Sq, London WC1H 0PU (01-387-1361)
Association of Head Mistresses of Preparatory Schools, Meadow Brook, Abbott's Drive, Virginia Water, Surrey GU25 4QS (099-04-3258)
Association of Insurance Brokers, 157 High St, Colchester, Essex CO1 1PG (0206-44343)
Association of Manufacturers of Domestic Electrical Appliances, Leicester House, 8 Leicester St, London WC2H 7BN (01-437-0678)
Association of Masters of Basset Hounds, The Estate Office, Hampden, Andoversford, Cheltenham (024-282-333)
Association of Masters of Harriers and Beagles, Rissington Manor, Cheltenham, Gloucestershire (0451-20255)
Association of Public Analysts, Dr L E Coles, President, Mid Glamorgan County Public Health Laboratory, The Parade, Cardiff CF2 3UJ (0222-28033)
Association of Recognised English Language Schools, Chalmers House, 43 Russell Sq, London WC1B 5DH
Atomic Energy Authority, 11 Charles II St, London SW1 (01-930-6262)

Attendance Allowance Board, Norcross, Blackpool FY5 3TA
Attorney General, Law Officers' Department, Royal Courts of Justice, London WC2A 2L (01–405–7641)
Australian High Commission, Australia House, Strand, London WC2B 4LA (01–438–8000)
Austrian Embassy, 18 Belgrave Mews West, London SW1X 8HU (01–235–3731)
Austrian National Tourist Department, 16 Conduit St, London W1 (01–629–0461)
Auto-Cycle Union, 31 Belgrave Sq, London SW1X 8CQ (01–235–7636)
Automobile Association, Head Office, Fanum House, Basingstoke, Hants RG21 2EA (0256–20123)

B

Badminton Association of England, 44–45 Palace Rd, Bromley, Kent BR1 3JU (01–464–0031)
Badminton Union of Ireland, 28 Ballymacash Rd, Lisburn, Co Antrim, N Ireland
Bahamas, High Commission for the Commonwealth of the, 39 Pall Mall, London SW1 5JG (01–930–6967–9)
Bahrain, Embassy of the State of, 98 Gloucester Rd, London SW7 4AU (01–370–5132–3)
Baltic Air Charter Association, Baltic Exchange Chambers, 14–20 St Mary Axe, London EC3A 8BU (01–283–8287)
Baltic Exchange, St Mary Axe, London EC3A 8BU (01–283–9300)
Bangladesh, Assistant Commissioner for the People's Republic of,
—— 31–33 Guildhall Buildings, 12 Navigation St, Birmingham B2 4BT (021–643–2386)
—— 20 Princes St (2nd floor), Manchester M1 4LU (061–236–4853)
Bangladesh, High Commission for the People's Republic of, 28 Queen's Gate, London SW7 5JA (01–584–0081, 01–589–4842)
Bank of England, Threadneedle St, London EC2R 8AH (01–601–4444)
Bank of Ireland, Lower Baggot St, Dublin 2 (0001–785744)
Bank of Scotland Ltd, Head Office, The Mound, Edinburgh EH1 1YZ (031–225–3431)
Barbados High Commission, 6 Upper Belgrave St, London SW1 8AZ (01–235–8686–9)
Barclaycard, Barclaycard Centre, Marefair, Northampton NN1 1SG (0604–21100)
Barclays Bank Ltd, Head Office, 54 Lombard St, London EC3 (01–626–1567)
Baring Bros & Co Ltd, Head Office, 88 Leadenhall St, London EC3 (01–588–2830)
Barnes Foundation Arboretum, Merion Station, Montgomery County, Penn 19066, USA
BBC, see British Broadcasting Association
Beacon Radio, PO Box 303, Wolverhampton WV6 0DQ (0902–757211)
Belgian Consulate-General, Television House, 5 Mount St, Manchester M2 5WS (061–834–0482, 061–832–5331)
Belgian Embassy, 103 Eaton Sq, London SW1W 9AB (01–235–5422)
Belgian National Tourist Department, 66 Haymarket, London SW1 (01–930–9618)
Belgian Trade Office, Rotunda Building, 150 New St, Birmingham (021–643–8496)
Bellevue Zoo, Antrim Rd, Belfast, Northern Ireland
Benin Diplomatic Mission to UK, Embassy of the People's Republic of Benin, 87 Ave Victor Hugo, Paris 16, France (553–5045)
Benin, Honorary Consulate of the People's Republic of (visas), 125–129 High St, Edgeware, Middx (01–951–1234)
Bermuda Department of Tourism, 84 Baker St, London W1 (01–487–4391)
Berolina Travel Ltd, 19 Dover St, London W1 (01–629–1664)
Billiards and Snooker Control Council, Alexandra Chambers, 32 John William St, Huddersfield (0484–35416)
Birmingham Gun Barrel Proof House, Banbury St, Birmingham 5 (021–643–3860)
Birmingham Broadcasting (BRMB Radio), Radio House, PO Box 555, Birmingham B6 4BX (021–359–4481)
Board of Inland Revenue, Statistics, Somerset House, Strand, London WC2R 1LB (01–438–6649)
Bodleian Library, Oxford OX1 3BG (0865–44675)
Bolivian Embassy, 106 Eaton Sq, London SW1W 9AD (01–235–4248)
Bookmakers' Committee, 17–23 Southampton Row, London WC1 (01–405–5346)
Border Television Ltd, Television Centre, Carlisle CA1 3NT (0228–25101)

Botswana High Commission, 162 Buckingham Palace Rd, London SW1W 9TJ (01–730–5216)
Boundary Commission for England, St Catherines House, 10 Kingsway, London WC2B 6JP (01–242–0262)
Boundary Commission for Northern Ireland, Dundonald House, Upper Newtownards Rd, Belfast BT4 3SU (023–121–4522)
Boundary Commission for Scotland, New St Andrew's House, Edinburgh EH1 3TF (031–556–8400)
Boundary Commission for Wales, St Catherines' House, 10 Kingsway, London WC2B 6JP (01–242–0262 ex 2071)
Bradford Chamber of Commerce, Commerce House, Cheapside, Bradford BD1 4JZ (0274–28166)
Brazilian Embassy, 32 Green St, Mayfair, London W1Y 4AT (01–629–0155)
Brazilian Consulate-General, 323–330 Corn Exchange, Fenwick St, Liverpool L2 7QH (051–236–6185)
Bristol Clifton and West of England Zoological Society, Clifton, Bristol BS8 3HA
British Academy, Burlington House, Piccadilly, London W1V 0NS (01–734–0457)
British Academy of Fencing, 3 Filey Close, Egmont Rd, Sutton, Surrey
British Actors' Equity Association, 8 Harley St, London W1
British Adult Publications Association Ltd, 3rd floor, 11 Soho Sq, London W1 (01–437–8834)
British Adult Publications Control Board, 3rd floor, 11 Soho Sq, London W1 (01–437–8834)
British Airports Authority, 2 Buckingham Gate, London SW1E 6JL (01–834–6621)
British Amateur Athletic Board, 70 Brompton Rd, London SW3 1EE (01–584–7715)
British Amateur Baseball Federation, 197 Newbridge Rd, Hull UH7 2LR (0482–76169)
British Amateur Boxing Association, 70 Brompton Rd, London SW3 1HA (01–584–9187)
British Amateur Dancers' Association, 2 Norfolk House, Brixton Oval, London SW2 1KX (01–733–2642)
British Amateur Gymnastics Assocation, 23A High St, Slough, Berks SL1 1DY (75–32763)
British Amateur Rugby League Association, Britannia Building, 3 Upperhead Row, Huddersfield (0484–44131)
British Amateur Weight Lifters' Association, 3 Iffley Turn, Oxford (0865–44630)
British Amateur Wrestling Association, 2 Huxley Drive, Bramhall, Cheshire (061–439–4187)
British and Irish Basketball Federation, Calomax House, Lupton Ave, Leeds 9 (0532–496045)
British Association of Concert Agents, 44 Catelnau Gardens, Arundel Terrace, London SW13 9DU (01–748–7361)
British Association of Occupational Therapists, 20 Rede Place, Bayswater, London W2 4TU (01–229–9758)
British Association of Psychotherapists, 121 Hendon Lane, London NW2
British Association of Ski Instructors, New Shopping Centre, Grampian Rd, Aviemore, Inverness-shire PH22 1RP
British Astronomical Association, Burlington House, Piccadilly, London W1V 0NL (01–734–4582)
British Balloon and Airship Club, Kimberley House, Vaughan Way, Leicester LE1 4SG (0533–51051)
British Bankers' Association, 10 Lombard St, London EC3 (01–623–4001)
British Board of Film Censors, 3 Soho Sq, London W1V 5DE (01–437–2677/8)
British Bobsleigh Association, 515 Watford Way, London NW7 (01–203–0055)
British Boxing Board of Control, Ramillies Buildings, Hill's Place, London W1R 2BS (01–437–1475)
British Broadcasting Corporation, Headquarters, Broadcasting House, London W1A 1AA (01–580–4468)
British Broadcasting Corporation Light Entertainment (Radio), Broadcasting House, London W1A 1AA (01–580–4468)
British Broadcasting Corporation Local Radio Stations
—— Birmingham, Pebble Mill Rd, Birmingham B5 7SA (021–472–5141)
—— Blackburn, King St, Blackburn, Lancs BB2 2EA (0254–62411)
—— Bristol, 3 Tyndalls Park Rd, Bristol BS8 1PP (0272–311111)
—— Brighton, Marlborough Place, Brighton, Sussex BN1 1TU (0273–680321)
—— Carlisle, Hilltop Heights, London Rd, Carlisle, Cumberland CA1 2NA (0228–31661)
—— Cleveland, 91–93 Linthorpe Rd, Middlesbrough, Cleveland TS1 5DG (0642–48491)
—— Derby, 56 St Helens St, Derby DE1 3HY (0332–361111)
—— Humberside, 9 Chapel St, Hull HU1 3NU (0482–23232)
—— Leeds, Merrion Centre, Leeds LS2 8NJ (0532–42131)
—— Leicester, Epic House, Charles St, Leicester LE1 3SH (0533–27113)

British Broadcasting Corporation Local Radio Stations—*cont.*
—— London, 35A Marylebone High St, London W1A 4LG (01–486–7611)
—— Manchester, PO Box 90, NBH, Oxford Rd, Manchester M60 1SJ (061–228–3434)
—— Medway, 30 High St, Chatham, Kent (0634–46284)
—— Merseyside, Commerce House, 13–17 Sir Thomas St, Liverpool L1 5BS (051–236–3355)
—— Newcastle, Crestina House, Archbold Terrace, Newcastle-upon-Tyne NE2 1DZ (0632–814243)
—— Nottingham, York House, York St, Nottingham NG1 3JB (0602–47643)
—— Oxford, 242–254 Banbury Rd, Oxford OX2 7DW (0865–53411)
—— Sheffield, Ashdell Grove, 60 Westbourne Rd, Sheffield S10 2QU (0742–686185)
—— Solent, South Western House, Canute Rd, Southampton SO9 4PJ (0703–31311)
—— Stoke-on-Trent, Conway House, Cheapside, Hanley, Stoke-on-Trent, Staffs ST1 1JJ (0782–24827)
British Broadcasting Corporation New Music, Yalding House, 156 Great Portland St, London W1N 6AJ (01–580–4468)
British Broadcasting Corporation Overseas Services, Bush House, PO Box 76, The Strand, London WC2B 4PH (01–240–3456)
British Broadcasting Corporation Programmes Complaints Commission, 31 Queen Anne's Gate, London SW1H 9BU (01–839–6894)
British Broadcasting Corporation Radio Drama, Broadcasting House, London W1A 1AA (01–580–4468)
British Broadcasting Corporation Regional Offices and Television Centres
—— East, St Catherine's Close, All Saints Green, Norwich NR1 3ND (0603–28841)
—— Midlands, Broadcasting Centre, Pebble Mill Rd, Birmingham B5 7QQ (021472–5353)
—— North, Broadcasting Centre, Woodhouse Lane, Leeds LS2 9PX (0532–41181/8)
—— North East, Broadcasting House, 54 New Bridge St, Newcastle-upon-Tyne NE1 8AA (0632–20961)
—— North West, New Broadcasting House, Oxford Rd, Manchester M60 1SJ (061–236–8444)
—— Northern Ireland, Broadcasting House, Ormland Ave, Belfast BT2 HQ (0232–44400)
—— Scotland, Broadcasting House, Queen Margaret Drive, Glasgow G12 (041–339–8844)
—— South, South Western House, Canute Rd, Southampton SO9 1PF (0703–26201)
—— South West, Broadcasting House, Seymoure Rd, Mannamead, Plymouth PL3 5BD (0752–62283)
—— Wales, Broadcasting House, Llantrifsant Rd, Llandaff, Cardiff CF5 2YQ (0222–564888)
—— West, Broadcasting House, 21–33b Whiteladies Rd, Clifton, Bristol BS8 2LR (0272–32211)
British Broadcasting Corporation Television Centre, Wood Lane, London W12 7RJ (01–743–8000)
British Broadcasting Corporation Ticket Unit, London W1A 4WW
British Calibration Service, National Physical Laboratory, Teddington, Middx TW11 0LW (01–977–3222)
British Canoe Union, 70 Brompton Rd, London SW3 1DT (01–584–9229)
British Commonwealth Games Federation, 12 Buckingham St, London WC2N 6DJ (01–930–1761)
British Consulates, see British diplomatic missions
British Consulates-General, see British diplomatic missions
British Council
—— Headquarters, 65 Davies St, London W1Y 2AA (01–499–8011)
—— 10 Spring Gardens, London SW1A 2BN (01–930–8466)
British Council Media Department, Tavistock House South, Tavistock Sq, London WC1 9LL (01–387–0166)
British Council Overseas Offices
—— (Afghanistan), 855/2 Shehabuddin Wat, PO Box 453, Kabul (31667)
—— (Algeria), 6 Ave Souidani Boudjenaa, Algiers (60–56–82, 60–56–83)
—— (Argentina), Marcelo T de Alveat 590–4°, Buenos Aires (31–4480, 31–7747, 32–2249)
—— (Australia), Edgecliff Centre, 203–233 New South Head Rd, Edgecliffe (Sydney), NSW 2027 (32–3773, 32–4100, 32–4597)
—— (Austria), Schenkenstrasse 4, A–1010 Vienna (63–26–16)
—— (Bahrain), Al Mathaf Sq, PO Box 452, Manama (51415)
—— (Bangladesh), 5–7 Fuller Rd, PO Box 161, Ramna, Dacca 2 (245271)
—— (Belgium and Luxembourg), Avenue Galilee-Faileilaan 5, Boite 10, 1030 Brussels (2–19–36–00)
—— (Botswana), Queens Rd, PO Box 439, Gaborone (2178)

British Council Overseas Offices—*cont.*
—— Brazil
CRN 708/9–B13–Nos 1–3 Caixa Postal 14–2336, 70,000 Brasilia DF (0612–72–3060)
c/o Sociedade Brasileira de Cultura Inglesa, Rua General Carneiro 679, 80,000 Curitiba (Pr), Caixa Postal 505 (0412–22–8606)
Rua Nicaragua 112, Espinheiro, Caixa Postal 860, 50,000 Recife PE, Pernambuco (0812–22–1835)
Avenida Portugal 360, Caixa Postal 2237–ZC–00, 20,000 Rio de Janeiro RJ ZC–82 (246–8133)
c/o Sociedade Brasileira de Cultura Inglesa, Caixa Postal 1604, Avenida Higienopolis 449, 01,000 Sao Paulo SP (01167–1007)
—— (Cameroon), Les Galeries, Rue de L'Intendance, Yaoundé (BP 818, Yaoundé) (22–16–96, 22–31–72)
—— (Canada), c/o British High Commission, 80 Elgin St, Ottawa, Ontario K2P 0K8 (613–237–1530)
—— (Chile), Eliodoro Yanez 832, Casilla 154–D, Santiago (234622, 234739)
—— (Colombia), Calle 11 No 5–16, Apartado Acreo 4682, Bogata 1 (43–81–81, 43–8–184)
—— (Cyprus), 3 Museum St, PO Box 1995, Nicosia (42152)
—— (Czechoslovakia), Jungmannova 30, Prague 1 (British Embassy, c/o FCO (Prague), King Charles St, London SW1) (244500)
—— (Denmark), British Embassy, Møntegrade 1, 1116 Copenhagen K (11–20–44)
—— (Egypt), 192 Sharia el Nil Agouza, Cairo (British Embassy, c/o FCO (Cairo), King Charles St, London SW1) (Cairo 808648)
—— (Ethiopia), Artistic Building, Adua Ave (PO Box 1043, Addis Ababa (Addis Ababa 11–00–22)
—— (Finland), Eteläsplanadi 22A, 00130 Helsinki 13/06 (640–505)
—— France
9 rue de Constantine, 75006 Paris (555–54–99; Telex: 0022 250912)
2 bis Allées Francois Verdier, Toulouse (62–76–17)
—— Federal Republic of Germany
Hardenbergstrasse 20, 1 Berlin–12 (31–01–76)
Hahnenstrasse 6, 5 Cologne–1 (23 66 77; Telex: 003–8881147)
Harvestehuder Weg 8a, 2 Hamburg 13 (44–79–51)
Giselastrasse 10/1, 8 Munich 40 (39–46–39)
—— Ghana
Liberia Rd, PO Box 771, Accra (21766)
Claude St, PO Box 1996, Kumasi (3462)
—— Greece
17 Philikis Etairias, PO Box 488, Athens 138 (36–33211)
13 King Constantine Ave, Salonica (235–236)
—— (Hong Kong), Easey Commercial Building, 20th floor, 253–261 Hennessy Rd, Wanchai, Hong Kong (5–724335)
—— (Hungary), British Embassy, Harmincad Utca 6, Budapest V (British Embassy, c/o FCO (Budapest), King Charles St, London SW1) (182–880)
—— India
British High Commission, British Council Division. French Bank Building, Homji St, Bombay 400001 (268921)
British High Commission, British Council Division, 5 Shakespeare Sarani, Calcutta 700016 (445370, 445378/9, 444804)
British High Commission, British Council Division, 150–A Anna Salai, Madra 600002 (86151)
British High Commission, British Council Division, 21 Jor Bagh, New Delhi 110003 (618341)
—— (Indonesia), Jalan Iman Bonjol 57–59, Jakarta (50589)
—— Iran
Kh, Chaharbagh Bala 171, PO Box 28, Isfahan (031–42124)
Kh, Kouhsangi 34, PO Box 13, Meshed (051–44771)
Kh, Zand 275, PO Box 65, Shiraz (0331–32737)
Keyanian House, Kuche Ahrab 148, 5th Quarter, PO Box 5, Tabriz (041–52096)
Kh, Ferdowsi 58 and 38, PO Box 1589, Tehran (303346, 392571, 392034)
—— (Iraq), 7/2/9 Waziriya, PO Box 298, Baghdad (20091)
—— (Israel), 140 Hayarkon St, PO Box 3302, Tel Aviv (222194; Telex: 0023–68417)

British Council Overseas Offices—*cont.*
—— Italy
   British Institute, Via Manzoni 38, 20121 Milan (782018)
   British Institute, Via Riviera di Chiaia 185, 80121 Naples (668046)
   Palazzo del Drago, Via delle Quattro Fontane 20, 00184 Rome (4750018; Telex: 0023-32084)
—— Japan
   77 Kitashirakawa, Nishimachi, Sakyo-ku, Kyoto 606 (075–791–7151)
   Iwanami Jimbo-Cho Building, 1 Jimbo-cho 2-chome, Kana, Chiyoda-ku, Tokyo 101 (c/o British Embassy, No. 1 Ichiban-cho, Chiyoda-ku, Tokyo 102) (03–264–3721)
—— (Jordan), Amman Centre, Jebel Amman, PO Box 634, Amman (36147)
—— Kenya
   Oginga Odinga Rd, PO Box 454, Kisumu (2957)
   City House, Nyerete Ave, PO Box 90590, Mombasa (23076)
   Kenya Cultural Centre, Harry Thuku Rd, PO Box 40751, Nairobi (334855)
—— (Korea), c/o British Embassy, No. 4 Jung-Dong, Sudaemoon-Ku, Seoul 120 (73–7157, 75–7341)
—— (Kuwait), Al Arabi St, Al Mansouriyah, PO Box 345, Safat (515512, 549376)
—— (Lesotho), Hobson's Sq, PO Box 429, Maseru (2609)
—— Malawi
   Victoria Ave, PO Box 456, Blantyre (36500)
   Taurus House, Capital City, PO Box 30222, Lilongwe 3 (30484)
—— Malaysia
   Jalan Bukit Aman, PO Box 539, Kuala Lumpur 01–02, Peninsular Malaysia (22601)
   Wing-Onn Life Building, 1st Floor, 1 Chester St, Kota Kinabalu, PO Box 746, Sabah, East Malaysia (54056)
   Bangunan Ang Cheng Ho, Jalan Tuanku Abdul Rahman, PO Box 615, Kuching, Sarawak (22632)
—— (Malta), Piazza Indipendenza, Valletta (25038, 29010, 24110)
—— (Mauritius), Royal Rd, Rose Hill (42034)
—— (Mexico), Maestro Antonio Caso 127, PO Box 30–588, Mexico 4 DF (566–61–44)
—— (Morocco), 22 Ave Moulay Youssef, BP 427, Rabat (203–14)
—— (Nepal), Kanti Path, PO Box 640, Kathmandu (11305)
—— (Netherlands), Keizersgracht 343, Amsterdam C (223644)
—— (New Zealand), c/o British High Commission, Reserve Bank Building, 2 The Terrace, PO Box 1812, Wellington 1 (726049)
—— Nigeria
   36 Ogui Rd, PO Box 330, Enugu (2005)
   Dugbe, PMB 5103, Ibadan (21354/5)
   Hospital Rd, PO Box 81, Kaduna (43484; Telex: 2000–71159)
   Kofar Nasarawa, Kano City, PMB 3003, Kano (2055, 2629)
   Western House, 8–10 Broad St, PO Box 3702, Lagos (56990)
—— (Norway), Fridtjof Nansens plass 5, Oslo 1 (42–68–48)
—— (Oman), Mutrah, PO Box 1090, Muscat, Oman (3494)
—— Pakistan
   23, 87th St G 6/3, PO Box 1135, Islamabad (22504, 22670)
   50 Abdullah Haroon Rd, PO Box 146, Karachi 0409 (90–51–2036–8)
   32 Mozang Rd, PO Box 88, Lahore (99–52755–6)
—— (Peru), Edificio Pacifico Washington, Piso 11, Natalio Sanchez 125 (Cuadra 6 Av Arequipa), Apartado 11114, Santa Beatriz, Lima (28–37–70)
—— (Poland), Al Jerozolimski 59, 00–697 Warsaw (286401–2, 287188; Telex: 0042-812555)
—— Portugal
   British Institute, Rua Alexandre Herculano 34, Coimbra (039–23–549)
   Rua de Luis Fernandes 3, Lisbon 2 (320173)
—— (Qatar), PO Box 2992, Doha, Qatar (27191, 26193)
—— (Romania), British Embassy, 24 Strada Jules Michelet, Bucharest (British Embassy, c/o FCO (Bucharest), King Charles St, London SW1) (11–16–34)
—— Saudi Arabia
   PO Box 3424, Jedda (22624)

British Council Overseas Offices—Saudi Arabia—*cont.*
Sharia Sitteen, Malaz, PO Box 2701, Riyadh (63109, 64676)
—— (Senegal), 38 Boulevard de la Republique, Dakar (c/o British Embassy, BP 6025, Dakar) (329–72)
—— (Sierra Leone), Tower Hill, PO Box 124, Freetown (22223)
—— (Singapore), 310 Cathay Building, Mount Sophia, Singapore 9 (26144)
—— South Africa
    91 Parliament St, Cape Town 8001 (22–7583)
    170 Pine St, Arcadia, Pretoria 0002 (74–6325)
—— (Soviet Union), British Embassy, Cultural Section, Ulista Repina 12, Moscow V–79 (c/o FCO Moscow, King Charles St, London SW1) (233–45–07)
—— Spain
    British Institute, Calle Amigo 83, Barcelona 6 (2480072)
    Almagro 5, Madrid 4 (4191266)
—— (Sri Lanka), 190 Galle Road, PO Box 753, Colombo 3 (27616)
—— (Sudan), 45 Sharia Gama'a, Khartoum (British Embassy, c/o FCO (Khartoum), King Charles St, London SW1) (80269, 70159)
—— (Sweden), c/o British Embassy, Skarpogatan 6–8, S–115–27 Stockholm (670–140)
—— (Syria), c/o British Embassy, Quarter Malki, 11 Mohammad Kurd Ali St, Imm, Kotob, Damascus (332–561)
—— (Tanzania), Independence Ave, PO Box 9100, Dar es Salaam (22726)
—— (Thailand), 428 Rama 1 RD, Siam Suare 2, Bangkok 5 (c/o British Embassy, Ploenchit Road, Bangkok) (2526136)
—— (Tunisia), c/o British Embassy, 5 Place de la Victoire, Tunis (245–100, 245–324)
—— Turkey
    27 Adakale Sokak, Yenisehir, Ankara Y10 (252340)
    c/o The British Consulate-General, Pera House, Beyoglu, Istanbul (PK 436 Beyoglu, Istanbul) (452298)
—— (United Arab Emirates), British Council Centre, Nr. Rashid Hospital, al Kamara, PO Box 1636, Dubai (70109)
—— (United States of America), British Embassy, 3100 Massachusetts Ave NW, Washington DC 20008 (202–462–1340)
—— (Venezuela), c/o British Embassy, Edificio La Estancia Piso 12, Avenida La Estancia No. 10, Cuidad Commercial Tamanaco, Apartado 1246, Caracas 101 (91–10–91, 91–13–91)
—— (Yemen Arab Republic), Sheikh Sinan Abu Luhum Building, Sana's, PO Box 2157 (023)
—— Yugoslavia
    Generala Zdanova 34, Post Fah 248, 11001 Belgrade (332441)
    Ilica 12/1, 41001 Zagreb (446244)
—— (Zaire), c/o British Embassy, Kinshasa (23483, 23280 and 22666)
—— (Zambia), Heroes Place, Cairo Rd, PO Box 3571, Lusaka (Lusaka 75341)
British Council Students Centre, 11 Portland Place, London W1N 4EJ (01–636–6888)
British Crafts Centre, 32 Earlham St, London WC2 (01–836–6993)
British Crown Green Bowling Association, 21 Beechwood Rd, Bedworth, Nuneaton, Warwickshire (0203–314417)
British Cycling Federation, 70 Brompton Rd, London SW3 1EN (01–584–6706)
British Cyclo-Cross Association, 8 Bellam Rd, Hampton Magna, Nr Warwick (0926–43116)
British Decorators' Association, 6 Haywra St, Harrogate, North Yorkshire HG1 5BL (0423–67292)
British Dental Association, 64 Wimpole St, London W1M 8AL
British Dietetic Association, 305 Daimler House, Paradise St, Birmingham B1 2BJ (021–643–5480)
British diplomatic missions
—— Afghanistan, British Embassy, Karte Parwan, Kabul (Kabul 30511)
—— Algeria, British Embassy, Résidence Cassiopée, Bâtiment B, 7 Chemin des Glycines (BP 43, Alger-Gare) (60–56–01)
—— Andorra, British Consulate-General, Edificio Torre de Barcelona, Avenida Generalisimo Franco 477 (13th Floor), Apartado de Correos 12111, Barcelona 11 (239–1300, 259–1601)
—— Angola (visa address), Servicos de Emigracao e Fronteiras, Rua Mouzinho de Alburqueque 11, Luanda (Telex 09913370)

British diplomatic missions—*cont.*
—— Argentine Republic
   British Embassy, Luis Agote 2412/52, Casillo de Correo 2050, Buenos Aires (80–7071, 80–7011)
   British Vice-Consulate, Roca 431–37 Cipolletti, Provincia de Rio Negro (71406)
   British Vice-Consulate, Casilla de Correo 82, San Martin 378, Comodoro Rivadavia (0961–2288)
   British Vice-Consulate, Casilla de Correo 65, Rio Gallegos (8–176)
   British Vice-Consulate, Estancia 'Viamonte', Rio Grande, Tierra del Fuego (Rural 4)
   British Consulate, Cordoba 1137, Casilla de Correo 325, Piso 7, Oficina 9, Rosario (041–25593)
—— Australia
   British High Commission, Commonwealth Ave, Canberra (73–0422)
   British Consulate-General, 8th Floor, 70 Pirie St, Adelaide, S Australia 5000 (2234572)
   British Consulate-General, BP House, 193 North Quay, Brisbane, Queensland 4000 (07–221–4933)
   British Consulate-General, CML Building, 330 Collins St, Melbourne, Victoria 3000 (602–1877)
   British Consulate-General, Prudential Building, 95 St George's Terrace, Perth, Western Australia 6000 (21–5611, 21–7891)
   British Consulate-General, Gold Fields House, 1 Alfred St, Sydney Cove, Sydney 2000, New South Wales (27–7521)
—— Austria
   British Embassy, Reisnerstrasse 40, 1030 Vienna (731575)
   British Embassy, Consular Section, Wallnerstrasse 8, 1010 Vienna (637502)
   British Consulate, Erlerstrasse 17/1, 6020 Innsbruck (28320)
—— Bahamas, British High Commission, Bitco Building (3rd Floor), East St, PO Box N7516, Nassau (57471)
—— Bahrain, British Embassy, PO Box 114, Al Mathaf Sq, Manama (54002)
—— Bangladesh, British High Commission, DIT Buildings Annexe, Dilkhusha, PO Box 90, Dacca 2 (243251, 244216, 246867)
—— Barbados, British High Commission, 147–9 Roebuck St, PO Box 676c, Bridgetown (63525)
—— Belgium
   British Embassy, Britannia House, Rue Joseph 11 28, 1040 Brussels (219–11–65)
   British Consulate-General, Van Schoonbekeplein 6, 2000 Antwerp (32–69–40, 32–88–29)
   British Consulate, Dok 58, 9000 Ghent (25–68–75)
   British Consulate, Rue Beeckman 45, 4000 Liège (23–58–31)
   British Consulate, Ijzerstraat 21, 8400 Ostend (70–16–15)
—— Benin, Ambassador and Consul-General resident at Lagos, Nigeria
—— Bolivia, British Embassy, Avenida Arce 2732–2754, Casilla 694, La Paz (29401, 51400)
—— Botswana, British High Commission, Private Bag 23, Gaborone (2483)
—— Brazil
   British Embassy, Avenida das Nacoes, Lote 8, Caixa Postal 07–0586, Brasilia DF (25–2710)
   British Consulate, Avenida Presidente Vargas 119, Caixa Postal 98, Belem (23–4613)
   British Vice-Consulate, Edificio Guimaraes 5, andar Avenida Alfonso Pena 952, Caixa Postal 576, Belo Horizonte, Minas Gerais (22–6318)
   British Vice-Consulate, Rua Dr Joao Moreira 163, Caixa Postal 663, Fortaleza (Ceara) (1–1143)
   British Vice-Consulate, Agencias Mundiais, Praca 15 de Novembro, 15 Altos, Caixa Postal 165, Manaus, Amazonas (2–7433)
   British Consulate, Edificio Banco Nacional do Norte, Avenida Marques de Olinda, Caixa Postal 184, Recife, Pernambuco (4–0650)
   British Consulate, Rua Uruguai 91 (5th Floor), Caixa Postal 737, Porto Alegre (24–0589)
   British Consulate-General, Praia do Flamengo 284, Rio de Janeiro (225–7252)
   British Vice-Consulate, Rua Marechal Floriano 133, Caixa Postal 52, Rio Grande (2–3842, 2–3843)
   British Vice-Consulate, Edificio Wildeberger, Caixa Postal 91 and 69, Salvador, Bahia (Bahia 2–0816)

British diplomatic missions—Brazil—cont.
British Consulate, Rua Visconde de Rio Branco 337, Caixa Postal 204, Estado de Sao Paulo, Sao Vicente, Santos (8–3068)
British Consulate-General, Avenida Paulista 1938 (17th Floor), Caixa Postal 846, Sao Paulo (287–7722)
British Vice-Consulate, Edificio Banco Mineiro da Producao, Avenida Governador Bley 186 Sala 808/9, Caixa Postal 812, Vitoria Espirito Santo (3–223, 3–0004)
—— Brunei, British High Commission, Jalan Residency, Bandar Seri Begawan (2231, 3121)
—— Bulgaria, British Embassy, Boulevard Marshal Tolbukhin 65–67, Sofia (885361)
—— Burma, British Embassy, 80 Strand Rd, Box 638, Rangoon (15700)
—— Burundi, British Consulate, BP 1344, Bujumbura (3206)
—— Cameroon
British Embassy, Le Concorde, Ave J F Kennedy, BP 547, Yaoundé (22–05–45, 22–07–96)
British Consulate, Soppo Priso Building, Rue Alfred Saker, Douala (42–21–77, 42–22–45)
—— Canada
British High Commission, 80 Elgin St, Ottawa K1P 5K7 (237–1530)
British Consulate-General, Suite 1404, 3 McCauley Plaza, 10025 Jasper Ave, Edmonton T5J 1S6, Alberta (424–0481)
British Consulate, Centennial Building, 10th Floor, 1645 Granville St, Halifax, Nova Scotia B3J 1X3 (422–7488)
British Consulate-General, Room 901, 635 Dorchester Boulevard West, Montreal H3B 1R6 (866–5863)
British Consulate, 500 Grande-Allée Est, Suite 707, Quebec, PQ G1R 2H5 (525–5187)
British Consulate-General, 8th Floor, 200 University Ave, Toronto, Ontario M5H 3E3 (864–1290)
British Consulate-General, 4th Floor, Bank of Nova Scotia Building, 602 West Hastings St, Vancouver, BC V6B 1P6 (683–4421)
British Consulate, 4th Floor, Monarch Life Building, 333 Broadway Ave, Winnipeg R3C 0S9 (942–3151)
—— Central African Empire, British Consulate, SCKN, PO Box 809, Bangui (21–66, 21–67)
—— Chad, British Consulate, Socopao du Tchad, Avenue de Brazza, BP751, Ndjamena (2932)
—— Chile
British Embassy, La Concepcion 177, Casilla 72–D, Santiago (239–166)
British Consulate, Baquedano 184, Casilla 30, Antofagasta (21709, 21982)
British Consulate, 18 de Septiembre, No. 153, Casilla 653, Arica (31098)
British Consulate, San Martin 949, Casilla 1087, Concepcion (25977)
British Consulate, Calle Regimiento Coquimbo 160, Casilla 97 (169)
British Consulate, Roca 858, Casilla 327, Punta Arenas, Magallanes (22740)
British Consulate, Blanco 737, Casilla 82–V Valparaiso (56117)
—— China, British Embassy, 11 Kuang Hua Lu, Chien Kuo Men Wai, Peking (52–1961)
—— Colombia
British Embassy, Calle 38 13 35, 11th Floor, Air Mail Box 4508, Bogota (698100)
British Consulate, Carrera 44, No. 45–57, Air Mail Box 706, Barranquilla (26936)
British Consulate, Edificio Garces No. 410, Air Mail Box 1326, Cali (721752, 721753)
—— Congo, British Ambassador resident at Kinshasa, Zaire
—— Costa Rica, British Embassy, 3202 Paseo Colon, Apartado 10056, San José (21–56–88)
—— Cuba, British Embassy, Edificio Bolivar, Capdevila 101–3, e Morro y Prado, Apartado 1069, Havana (61–5681)
—— Cyprus, British High Commission, Alexander Pallis St, PO Box 1978, Nicosia (73131)
—— Czechoslovakia, British Embassy, Prague 1, Thunovska 14 (533347, 533340, 533370)
—— Denmark
British Embassy, 36–40 Kastelsvej, DK–2100 Copenhagen (14–4600)
British Consulate, Hasserisvej 139, DK–9000 Aalborg (13–12–33)
British Consulate, Grenaavej 144, DK–8240, Risskov, Aarhus (06–176633)
British Consulate, Grimsbyvej DK–6700 Esbjerg (13–0811)
British Consulate, Gardavegur, DK–3870 Klaksvig, Faroe Islands (5489)
British Consulate, Frederiskgade 2–4, DK–5000 Odense (11–54–56)
British Consulate, Yviri ivd Strand 17, DK–3800 Thorshavn, PO Box 49, Faroe Islands (13510)

British diplomatic missions—*cont.*
—— Dominican Republic
    British Embassy, Avenida Independencia No. 84, Apartado 1352, Santo Domingo (682–3128, 682–3129)
    British Vice-Consulate, Calle John F Kennedy 61, Puerto Plata (363)
—— Ecuador
    British Embassy, Calle Gonzalez Suarez 111, Casilla 314, Quito (230070, 523124, 521755)
    British Consulate, Junin 105 y Malecon, Casilla 410, Guayaquil (3057000)
—— Egypt
    British Embassy, Ahmed Raghab St, Garden City, Cairo (20850)
    British Consulate-General, 3 Mina St, Roushdy, Ramleh, Alexandria (47166, 49458)
—— El Salvador
    British Embassy, ·11a Avenida Norte (BIS) No. 611, Colnia Duenas, Apartado 23–50, San Salvador (21–9106, 22–05–90, 22–39–45)
    British Vice-Consulate, Sala 10, Edificio Admin de la CEPA, Port Acajutla (52–3000)
—— Equatorial Guinea, British Ambassador resident at Yaoundé, Cameroon
—— Ethiopia
    British Embassy, Fikre Mariam Abatechan St, Addis Ababa (113055)
    British Consulate, Papassinos Building, Ras Desta Damtew Ave, Addis Ababa (151305)
    British Consulate, Gellatly Hankey Building, Haile Selassie 1 Ave, PO Box 254, Asmara, Eritrea (110131)
—— Fiji, British High Commission, Civic Centre, Stinson Parade, PO Box 1355, Suva (311033)
—— Finland
    British Embassy, 16–20 Uudenmaankatu, Helsinki 12 (Helsinki 12574)
    British Consulate, Enso-Gutzeit Osakeyhtio 48100, Kotka 10 (952–16160)
    British Consulate, Kajaani Oy, Toppilan, Tehdas, PO Box 9, 90101 Oulu 10 (981–343521)
    British Consulate, Oy Werner Hacklin, Stevedores, Mantyluoto, 28880 Pori 88, Bjorneborg (939–43122)
    British Consulate, Oy Tampella Ab, Textile Mills, 33100 Tampere 10, Tammerfors (931–32400)
    British Consulate, Huhtamaki Oy, PO Box 406, 20101 Turku 10, Abo (921–382322)
    British Consulate, Lennart Baackman, Strandgatan 3 Vaasa (961–12140)
—— France
    British Embassy, 35 Rue du Faubourg St Honoré, 75008 Paris (266–9142); Consular/Visa section 260–33–06)
    British Vice-Consulate, 2–4 Rue Rossi, 2000 Ajaccio, Corsica (21–01–26, 21–05–98)
    British Vice-Consulate, Société Basque Automobile, Allées Paulmay, 64–100 Bayonne (59–25–19–58)
    British Consulate-General, 15 Cours de Verdun, 33081 Bordeaux Cedex (522835, 528951, 524886)
    British Vice-Consulate, c/o British Railways, Gare Maritime, BP 327/1, 62201 Boulogne-sur-Mer (31–58–17)
    British Vice-Consulate, 9–11 Rue Felix Carras, 62100 Calais (344548)
    British Vice-Consulate, 8 Rue Louis-Philippe, 50100 Cherbourg (53–14–46)
    British Vice-Consulate, c/o Jules Roy, 6 Place de l'Yser, 59377 Dunkirk (66–78–12)
    British Vice-Consulate, 37 Avenue de Champagn, 51200 Epernay (51–31–02)
    British Consulate, 22 Rue l'Allouette, PO Box 664, Cayenne, French Guiana (1034)
    British Consulate, 9 Quai George V, 76600 Le Havre (42–27–47)
    British Consulate-General, PO Box 3477, 11 Square Dutilleul, 59019 Lille Cedex (57–35–49, 57–01–77, 54–52–38)
    British Consulate-General, 24 Rue Childebert, 69 288 Lyon Cedex 1 (375967, 424649)
    British Consulate-General, 24 Avenue du Prado, 13006 Marseille (53–43–32)
    British Vice-Consulate, 23 Rue du XXe Corps Americain, 57000 Metz (68–39–96)
    British Vice-Consulate, Westminster Foreign Bank Ltd, 6 Rue Lafayette, 44009 Nantes Cedex (71–08–50)
    British Consulate-General, 105–9 Rue du Faubourg St Honoré, 75008 Paris (260–33–06)
    British Vice-Consulate, c/o Raquer France, 1 Rue Buffon, 66000 Perpignan (34–94–04, 34–56–99)
    British Consulate-General, 10 Rue de General de Castelnau, 67007 Strasbourg Cedex (366491)

British diplomatic missions—*cont.*
—— Gabon, British Consulate, Luterma, SA BP24, Libreville (223–30, 207–04)
—— Gambia, The, British High Commission, 78b Wellington St, PO Box 507, Banjul (244)
—— German Democratic Republic, British Embassy, 108 Berlin, Unter den Linden 32 34 (220–2431)
—— Germany, Federal Republic of
    British Embassy, Friedrich Ebert Alle 77, 5300 Bonn (23–40–61)
    British Consulate-General, 1-Berlin 12, Uhlandstrasse 7/8 (309–52–93, 309–51–46)
    British Military Government, 1 Berlin 19, Olympia-Stadion, BFPO 45 (309–4497)
    British Consulate, Eiswerke Strasse, Postfach 6, 2850 Bremerhaven-F (Ostseite) (471–7–1084)
    British Consulate-General, 4 Dusseldorf, Nordsternhaus, 14 Georg-Glock-Strasse (434281, 434481)
    British Consulate-General, 6 Frankfurt, Bockenheimer Landstrasse 51–3 (720406, 720400)
    British Consulate-General, 2 Hamburg 13, Harvestehuder Weg 8a (431351)
    British Consulate-General, 8 Munich 40, Amalienstrasse 62 (39–40–15)
    British Counsulate-General, 7 Stuttgart 1, Kriegsbergstrasse 28 (293216, 224607)
—— Ghana, British High Commission, Barclays Bank Building, High St, PO Box 296, Accra (64651, 64123, 64134)
—— Greece
    British Embassy, I Ploutarchou St, Athens 139 (736–211)
    British Vice-Consulate, Zambeli 2, Corfu (28–055, 22–995)
    British Vice-Consulate, Plateia Eleftheriou Venizelou 13, Anothen Ionikis Heraklion, Crete, (224–012)
    British Vice-Consulate, 45 Thessalonikis St, Karalla (23–704)
    British Vice-Consulate, 2 Votsi St, Patras (277–329, 275–811)
    British Vice-Consulate, Polydorou 6, PO Box 47, Rhodes (27–247, 27–306)
    British Consulate, 11 King Constantine Ave, PO Box 332, Salonika (278006, 278169)
    British Vice-Consulate, St Theodore St, Port Vathy, Samos (27314)
—— Grenada, British High Commissioner resident at Port of Spain, Trinidad
—— Guatemala
    British Consulate, Edificio Maya, 8 Piso, Via 5, No. 4–50, PO Box 8, Zona 4, Guatemala City (61329, 64375)
    British Consulate, c/o Bandegua, Puerto Barrios (no telephone number – operator connects by name)
—— Guinea, British Consulate, La Torré Faction Guinéenne, BP 158, Conakry (621–65)
—— Guinea-Bissau, British Ambassador resident at Dakar, Senegal
—— Guyana, British High Commission, 44 Main St, PO Box 625, Georgetown (65881)
—— Haiti, British Consulate, 21 Avenue Marie-Jeanne, Cité de l'Exposition, PO Box 1302, Port-au-Prince (2–12–27, 2–22–25)
—— Holy See, British Legation, 91 Via Condotti, 1–00187, Rome (689–462, 687–479)
—— Honduras
    British Consulate, Hotel Marichal, 5 Calle, 5 Ave No. 407, Apartado Postal No. 15488, Tegucigalpa (22–00–69)
    British Consulate, Pasaje Porteno, Barrio El Centro, Puerto Cortes
—— Hong Kong
    British Trade Commission, PO Box 528, 9th Floor, Gammon House, 12 Harcourt Rd (5–230176)
    British Diplomatic Service Mail Office, Building No. 8, RAF Station, Kai Tak, Kowloon (3–837671, 3–828331)
—— Hungary, British Embassy, Harmincad Utca 6, Budapest V (182–888)
—— Iceland
    British Embassy, Laufasvegur, 49 Reykjavik (15883)
    British Vice-Consulate, Bygedaveg 118, 9, Akureyri (21400)
    British Vice-Consulate, Urdarveg 8, Isafjord (235)
—— India
    British High Commission, Chanakyapuri, New Delhi 21, 1100–21 (690371)
    British Deputy High Commissioner, Mercantile Bank Building, Mahatma Gandhi Rd, PO Box 815, Bombay 400 023 (25–99–81)

British diplomatic missions—*cont.*

British Deputy High Commissioner, 1 Ho Chi Minh Sarani, Calcutta 16, 700016 (44–5171)
British Deputy High Commissioner, 150a Anna Salai, Madras, 2, 600002 (83136)
—— Indonesia
British Embassy, Jalan Thamrin 75, Jakarta (41091–41098)
British Consulate, Jalan Imam Bonjol 18, PO Box 163, Medan (22250)
British Consulate, Jalan Ngagel 123, PO Box 21, Surabaya (Darmo 8852, 8853)
—— Iran, British Embassy, Avenue Ferdowsi, Tehran (645011, 646017)
—— Iraq, British Embassy, Sharia Salib Ud-Din, Karkh, Baghdad (32121, 30632)
—— Irish Republic, British Embassy, 33 Merrion Rd, Dublin 4 (695211)
—— Israel
British Embassy, 192 Rehov Hayarkon, Tel Aviv 63405 (249171)
British Consulate-General, Sahar House, 23 Rehov Ben Yehuda, Tel Aviv 63806 (54514)
—— Italy
British Embassy, Via XX Settembre 80a, I–00187 Roma (4755441, 4755551)
British Vice-Consulate, Via San Lucifero, 87, I–09100 Cagliari (62–755)
British Consulate, Palazzo Castelbarco, Lungarno Corsini 2, I–50123 Florence (212594, 284133, 287449)
British Consulate-General, Via XII Ottobre, 2 (13 Piano), I–16121 Genoa (564833)
British Consulate, Corso Garibaldi 267/A, I–98100 Messina (46977, 51012)
British Consulate-General, Via San Paolo 7, 20121 Milan (803–442)
British Consulate-General, Via Francesco Crispi 122, I–80122 Naples (663883, 682482, 663321)
British Consulate, Via Marchese di Villabianca, 9, I–90143 Palermo (253364)
British Consulate, 2 Via Rossini, I–34132 Trieste (69135)
British Consulate, Corso Vittorio Emanuele 1, I–10125 Turin (657676)
British Consulate, PO Box 679, 30100 Venice (27207)
—— Ivory Coast, British Embassy, 5th Floor, Immeuble Shell, Ave Lamblin, PO Box 2581, Abidjan (22–66–25, 32–27–76, 32–49–80)
—— Jamaica, British High Commission, 58 Duke St, PO Box 628, Kingston (93–21930)
—— Japan
British Embassy, 1 Ichiban-cho, Chiyoda-ku, Tokyo 102 (03–265–5511)
British Consulate, Holme Ringer and Co. Ltd, 9–9 Minamato-machi, Moji-ku, Kita-Kyushushi 801 (093–331–1311)
British Consulate-General, Hong Kong and Shanghai Bank Building, 45 Awaji-machi, 4-chome Higashi-ku, Osaka 541 (06–231–3355)
—— Jerusalem, British Consulate-General, 19 Nashashibi St, Sheikh Jarrah Quarter, East Jerusalem (282481)
—— Jordan, British Embassy, Third Circle, Jebel Amman, PO Box 87 (41261–66)
—— Kampuchea, British Embassy, 96 Moha Vithei 9 Tola, BP 150, Phnom Penh (2–3974). Staff temporarily withdrawn from post
—— Kenya, British High Commission, Bruce House, Standard St, Nairobi, PO Box 30465 (35944)
—— Korea
British Embassy, 4 Chung-Dong, Sudaemoon-ku, Seoul (75–7341, 73–7689, 70–4566)
British Vice-Consulate, President's Room, Hyopsung Shipping Corporation, 2nd Floor, Dong Bang, Life Insurance Building, 194–Ka Chungang-Dong, Chung-Ku, Busan (42–3316)
—— Kuwait, British Embassy, Arabian Gulf St, PO Box Safat 2 (432047)
—— Laos, British Embassy, Rue Pandit J Nehru, PO Box 224, Vientiane (2333, 2374)
—— Lebanon, British Embassy, Ave de Paris, Ras Beirut (36–25–00, 36–25–64)
—— Lesotho, British High Commission, PO Box 521, Maseru (3961)
—— Liberia, British Embassy, Mamba Point, PO Box 120, Monrovia (21055, 21107, 21491)
—— Libya, British Embassy, 30 Sharia Gamal Abdul Nasser, Tripoli (31191)
—— Liechtenstein, British Consul-General resident at Zurich, Switzerland
—— Luxembourg, British Embassy, 28 Boulevard Royal, Luxembourg (2–98–64, 2–98–66)
—— Madagascar, British Consulate, 5 Rue Robert Ducrocq, BP167, Behoririka Tananarive
—— Malawi
British High Commission, Lingadzi House, PO Box 300 42, Lilongwe 3 (31544)
British High Commission, Victoria Ave, Blantyre, PO Box 479 (33022)

British diplomatic missions—cont.
—— Malaysia
British High Commission, Wisma Damansara, Jalan Semantan, PO Box 1030, Kuala Lumpur 23–03 (741533, 28179)
Office of the British Representative, c/o Hong Kong and Shanghai Banking Corporation, Kota Kinabalu, Sabah, East Malaysia PO Box 1602 (53232)
Office of the British Representative, The Chartered Bank, Jalan Tun Haji Openg, PO Box 12, Kuching, Sarawak (21231)
Office of the British Representative, Datuk Keramat Holdings Building, 73 Jalan Datuk Keramat, Penang (63702, 63705)
—— Mali, British Ambassador resident at Dakar, Senegal
—— Malta, British High Commission, 7 St Anne St, Floriana (21285)
—— Mauritania, British Consulate, BP 629, Ecole Normale Supérieure, Nouakchott (528–39)
—— Mauritius, British High Commission, PO Box 586, Cerne House, Chausée, Port Louis (20201)
—— Mexico
British Embassy, Lerma 71, Col Cuauhtemoc, Mexico City 5, DF, PO Box 96 Bis (511–48–80, 514–33–27, 514–38–86, 514–36–86)
British Consulate, Hotel Las Brisas, PO Box 281 (46605)
British Consulate, Kerdo di Tejada 2264–102, Guadalajara (15–14–06)
British Consulate, Calle 58 No. 450, PO Box 89, Merida Yucatan (16799)
British Consulate, Ave Ruiz Cortines Al Pk, 2333 Monterrey, NL (5–11–800)
British Consulate, Avenida Morelos 145, Vera Cruz (2–43–23)
—— Monaco, British Consul-General is resident at 24 Avenue de Prado, 13006 Marseille, France (53–43–32)
—— Mongolia, British Embassy, 30 Enkh Taivny Gudamzh, PO Box 703, Ulan Bator (51033)
—— Morocco (including Tangier)
British Embassy, 28 bis Avenue Allal ben Abdallah, BP 45, Rabat (20905, 314–03, 329–96)
British Consulate-General, 60 Boulevard d'Anfa, PO Box 762, Casablanca (61440)
British Consulate-General, 52 Rue d'Angleterre, PO Box 2122 M'Sallah, Tangier (35895)
—— Mozambique, British Embassy, Avenue Augusto de Castilho 310, PO Box 55, Maputo (26011)
—— Nepal, British Embassy, Lainchaur Kathmandu, PO Box 106 (11081, 11588)
—— Netherlands
British Embassy, Lange Voorhout 10, The Hague (64–58–00)
British Consulate-General, Johannes Vermeerstraat 7, Amsterdam OZ (736128)
British Consulate-General, Parklaan 18, Rotterdam 2 (361555)
—— New Zealand
British High Commission, Reserve Bank of New Zealand Building, 9th Floor, 2 The Terrace, PO Box 1812, Wellington 1 (726–049)
British High Commission, 9th Floor, Norwich Union Building, Queen Anne St, Auckland 1 (32–973)
Office of the British Representative, c/o J Ballantyne and Co. Ltd, PO Box 1460, Christchurch (71819)
—— Nicaragua
British Consulate, Viages Griffith, Apartado 949, C8 Centro Comercial San Francisco, Carretera a Masaya, Managua (8785)
British Vice-Consulate, Apartado Postal 64, Calle Comercio, Bluefields
—— Niger, British Ambassador resident at Abidjan, Ivory Coast
—— Nigeria
British High Commission, Kajola House, 62–4 Campbell St (Private Mail Bag 12136), Lagos (51630)
British Deputy High Commission, Finance Corporation Building, Lebanon St (Private Mail Bag 5010), Ibadan (21551)
British Deputy High Commission, United Bank for Africa Building (Private Mail Bag 2096), Hospital Rd, Kaduna (22573)
—— Norway
British Embassy, Thomas Heftyesgate 8, Oslo 2 (56–38–90)
British Consulate, Skateflukaien, PO Box 130, 600 Alesund (071–24460)
British Consulate, Slottsgaten 1, 5015 Bergen (21–70–33, 21–09–90)
British Consulate, Strandgaten 151, PO Box 128, 550 Haugesund (047–24050)

British diplomatic missions—Norway—*cont.*
  British Consulate, Vageveien 7, PO Box 148, 6501 Kristiansund North (073–75333)
  British Consulate, Tollbodgt 2, Boks 71, 4600 Kristiansund South (24452)
  British Consulate, Kongensgt 50, 8500 Narvik (082–44036)
  British Consulate, Dusavik, PO Box 178, 4001 Stavanger 30 (045–42021)
  British Consulate, Prestegate 2, 3100 Tonsberg (033–11605)
  British Consulate, Sluppenveien 10, PO Box 684, 700 Trondheim (075–35590)
  British Consulate, Sjogate 17, 9000 Tromso (083–84050)
—— Oman, British Embassy, Muscat PO Box 300 (722411)
—— Pakistan
  British Embassy, Diplomatic Enclave, Ramna 5, PO Box 1122, Islamabad (22131)
  British Consulate-General, York Place, Runnymeade Lane, Port Trust Estate, Clifton, Karachi (532041)
—— Panama
  British Embassy, Via Espana 120, Apartado 889 Zona 1, Panama City (23–0451/2/3
  British Consulate, Edificio El Rey (room 9), PO Box 1108, Cristobal, Colon, Canal Zone (47–7060)
—— Papua New Guinea, British High Commission, United Church Building (3rd Floor), Douglas St, Port Moresby (243–331)
—— Paraguay, British Embassy, 25 de Mayo, 171 (PO Box 404), Asuncion (44–472, 49146)
—— Peru
  British Embassy, Edificio El Pacifico Washington (Piso 12), Plaza Washington, Avenida Arequipa, PO Box 854, Lima (283830, 283836)
  British Consulate, Andres Martinez 400, Casilla 265, Arequipa (25942, 22549)
  British Vice-Consulate, Saenz Pena 164, Callao (293330, 293695)
—— Philippines, British Embassy, Electra House, 115–17 Esteban St, Legaspi Village, Makati, Rizal, Manila (89–10–51)
—— Poland, British Embassy, Aleje Roz No. 1, Warsaw (281001)
—— Portugal
  British Embassy, 35–9 Rua S Domingos a Lapa, Lisbon (661191, 661122, 661147, 663181)
  British Consulate, Quinta de Santa Maria, Estrada de Tavarede, Figueira da Foz (22235)
  British Consulate, British Trade Commission, 707 Shell House, Queens Rd Central, Macao, Hong Kong PO Box 528 (H–230176)
  British Consulate, 30 Av Dr Manuel d'Arriaga, Funchal, Madeira (21221)
  British Consulate, Avenida da Boavista 3072, Oporto (684789)
  British Consulate, Rue Santa Isabel, 21–1 Esq Portimao (0082–23071)
  British Consulate, Rua General Humberto Delgado 4, Vila Real de S Antonio (29)
—— Qatar, British Embassy, PO Box 3, Doha (23991)
—— Rhodesia, British High Commision has been closed
—— Romania, British Embassy, 24 Strada Jules Michelet, Bucharest (11–16–35)
—— Rwanda, British Embassy, BP 320, Kigali (204)
—— San Marino, British Consul-General resident at Palazzo Castelbanco, Lungarno Corsene 2, 1–50123 Florence (212594)
—— Saudi Arabia, British Embassy, PO Box 393, Jedda (52544, 52628, 52849, 52974)
—— Senegal, British Embassy, 20 Rue du Doctuer Guillet, PO Box 6025, Dakar (22383)
—— Seychelles, British High Commission, Victoria House, Victoria (2000)
—— Sierra Leone, British High Commission, Standard Bank Sierra Leone Ltd Building, Wallace Johnson St, Freetown (23961)
—— Singapore, British High Commission, Tanglin Circus, Singapore 10 (639333)
—— Somali Democratic Republic, British Embassy, Waddada Xasan Geeddi Abtoow 7/8, PO Box 1036, Mogadishu (2288, 3472)
—— South Africa
  British Embassy, 91 Parliament St, Cape Town (2–7583)
  British Consulate-General, African Eagle Centre, 12th Floor, 2 St George's St, Cape Town 8000, PO Box 500 (43–7266)
  British Consulate-General, Barclays Bank Building, 7th Floor, Field St, Durban 4001, PO Box 1404 (313131)
  British Consulate-General, Watsons Shipping East London (Pty) Ltd, 5th Floor, Gasson Centre, Church St, East London, PO Box 4 (2–1971)

British diplomatic missions—South Africa—*cont.*

    British Consulate-General, 5th Floor Nedbank Mall, 145–7 Commissioner St, Johannesburg 2000, PO Box 10101 (21–8161)
    British Consulate, Lochhead White and Wommersley (Pty) Ltd, 18 Strand St, Port Elizabeth, PO Box 213 (041–522160)
    British Consulate-General, 6 Hill St, Pretoria 0002 (74–3121)
—— Soviet Union, British Embassy, Moscow 72, Naberezhnaya Morisa Toreza 14 (231–95–55)
—— Spain
    British Embassy, Calle de Fernando el Santo 16, Madrid 4 (419–0200)
    British Consulate, Avenida Francisco Franco 11, Algeciras (66–16–00)
    British Consulate, Canalejas No. 1, Apartado de Correos 564, Alicante (22–41–18)
    British Vice-Consulate, Calle Gerona 32, Almeria (214–403, 215–982)
    British Consulate-General, Edificio Torre de Barcelona, Avenida Generalissimo Franco 477, 13th Floor, Apartado de Correos 12111, Barcelona 11 (259–1601)
    British Consulate-General, Alameda de Urquiko 2–8, Bilbao 8 (4157600, 4157711, 4157722)
    British Vice-Consulate, Avenida Ramon de Carrenza 26/7–5B, Cadiz (211124)
    British Vice-Consulate, Queipo de Llano 2, Ceuta, Spanish Morocco (512522)
    British Vice-Consulate, Avenida Bartolome Rosello 24–9, Apartado 307, Ibiza (30–18–18)
    British Vice-Consulate, Avenida Alvaro Domecq 6, Jerez de la Frontera (33–13–00)
    British Consulate, Edificio Hocasa Piso 6, Calle Alfredo L Jones 33, Apartado 2020, Las Palmas, Grand Canary (262508)
    British Consulate-General, Embassy, Consular Section, Madrid (419–02–00)
    British Consulate, Edificio Duquesa Calle Duquesa de Parcent, Malaga (217–571)
    British Consulate, Avda Jaime 111, 5–1 Palma de Mallorca, Balearic Islands (212085, 212445)
    British Consulate, Edificio Marichal Suarez Guerra 40–5, Santa Cruz de Tenerife, Canary Islands (242000)
    British Consulate, Plaza Nueva 8 (Dpdo), Seville (228875)
    British Vice-Consulate, Santian 4, Tarragona (201815, 201246, 205268)
    British Vice-Consulate, Plaza de Compostela, 6th Floor, PO Box 49, Vigo (986–21–14–50, 986–21–14–87)
—— Sri Lanka, British High Commission, Galle Rd, Kollupitiya, PO Box 1433, Colombo 3 (27611)
—— Sudan, British Embassy, New Aboulela Building, Barlaman Ave, PO Box 801, Khartoum (70766, 70760)
—— Surinam, British Consulate, c/o VSH United Buildings, Vant, Hogechuysstraat, PO Box 1300, Paramaribo (72870)
—— Sweden
    British Embassy, Skarpogatan 6–8, 115 27 Stockholm (67–01–40)
    British Consulate, Drottninggatan 48, PO Box 604, 810 26 Gavle (180300)
    British Consulate-General, Gotgatan 15, S–411 05 Gothenburg (113830, 135915)
    British Consulate, Thore Shipping AB, Stagneliusgatan 3, S–252 39 Helsingborg (042–11–68–12, 142–11–76–12)
    British Consulate, Trysensgrand 2, 951 06 Lulea (16329)
    British Consulate, Lilla Nygatan 11, S–211 38 38 Malmo (126635, 30806)
    British Consulate, Tradgardsgatan 42, Fack, 601 01 Norrkoping 1 (10–00–40)
    British Consulate, Skepparplatsen 1, 851 88 Sundsvall (155500)
—— Swaziland, British High Commission, Allister Miller St, Mbabane, Private Bag (2581)
—— Switzerland
    British Embassy, Thunstrasse 50, 3005 Berne (44–50–21)
    British Consulate, 4001 Basle, Rittergasse 35 (235842)
    British Consulate-General, 37–9 Rue de Vermont, 6th Floor, 1211 Geneva 20 (343800, 332385)
    British Consulate, Via Maraini 14a, 6900 Lugano (091–54–54–44)
    British Vice-Consulate, 15 Bourg Dessous, 1814 La Tour de Peilz, Montreux, Vaud (54–12–07)
    British Consulate-General, Directorate of British Export Promotion in Switzerland, Dufourstrasse 56, 8008 Zurich (47–15–20)
—— Syria, British Embassy, Quarter Malki, 11 Mohammad Kurd Ali St, Damascus (332–561)

British diplomatic missions—*cont.*

—— Tanzania, British High Commission, Permanent House, Independence Ave, PO Box 9200, Dar-es-Salaam (29601)
—— Thailand
British Embassy, Wireless Road, Bangkok (2527161)
British Consulate, Charoen Prathet, Chiang Mai (36006)
—— Togo, British Ambassador resident at Accra, Ghana
—— Tonga, British High Commission, Nuku'alofa
—— Trinidad and Tobago, British High Commission, 4th Floor, Furness House, 90 Independence Sq, PO Box 778, Port of Spain (52861)
—— Tunisia, British Embassy, 5 Place de la Victoire, Tunis (245–100, 245–324, 245–649, 244–805)
—— Turkey
British Embassy, Sehit Ersan Caddesi 46/A, Cankaya, Ankara (274310)
British Consulate-General, Tepebasi Beyoglu, Istanbul (447540, 447545)
British Consulate, Necatibey Bulvari 19/4, Pk 300 Izmir (45470–45479, 32502)
—— Uganda, British Interests Section of the French Embassy, 10–12 Parliament Ave, PO Box 7070, Kampala (57054)
—— United Arab Emirates
British Embassy, PO Box 248, Abu Dhabi (41305, 42097, 43247)
British Embassy, PO Box 65, Dubai (31070)
—— United States
British Embassy, 3100 Massachusetts Ave, NW, Washington DC 20008 (202–462–1340)
British Consulate, 2216 Post Road, Anchorage, Alaska (907–272–1431)
British Consulate-General, Suite 912, 225 Peachtree Street, NE, Atlanta, Georgia 30303 (404–524–5856)
British Consulate-General, Suite 4740, Prudential Tower, Prudential Center, Boston, Mass 02199 (617–261–3060)
British Consulate-General, 33 North Dearborn St, Chicago, Illinois 60602 (312–346–1810)
British Consulate-General, 1828 The Illuminating Building, 55 Public Sq, Cleveland, Ohio 44113 (216–621–7674)
British Consulate, 813 Stemmons Tower West, 2730 Stemmons Freeway, Dallas, Texas 75207 (214–637–3600)
British Consulate-General, 2200 Detroit Bank and Trust Building, 211 Fort St West, Detroit, Michigan 48226 (313–962–4776)
British Consulate-General, Suite 2250, 601 Jefferson, Houston, Texas 77002 (713–659–6270)
British Consulate, c/o Greater Kansas City Foreign Trade Zone Inc, Crown Center, 2440 Pershing Rd, Kansas City, Missouri 64108 (816–421–7666)
British Consulate-General, 3701 Wiltshire Boulevard, Los Angeles, California 90010 (213–385–7381)
British Consulate, 10th Floor, 321 St Charles Ave, New Orleans, Louisiana 70130 (504–586–8300)
British Consulate-General, 845 Third Ave, New York, NY 10022 (212–593–2258)
British Consulate-General, 12 South 12th St, Philadelphia, Pennsylvania 19107 (215–52430)
British Consulate, 824 Bank of California Tower, Portland, Oregon 97205 (503–227–5669)
British Consulate-General, Gateway Tower, 1 Memorial Drive, St Louis, Missouri 63102 (314–621–4688)
British Consulate, PO Box 687, Charlotte Amalie, St Thomas, United States Virgin Islands 00801 (774–0033)
British Consulate-General, 9th Floor, Equitable Life Building, 120 Montgomery St, San Francisco, California 94104 (415–981–3030)
British Consulate, Room 1014, Banco Popular Center, Hato Rey, PO Box 2157, San Juan, Puerto Rico 00936 (809–767–4435)
British Consulate-General (Commercial), 1216 Norton Building, 801 Second Ave, Seattle, Washington 98104 (206–622–9253)
British Consulate, 932 Wainwright Building, 229 West Bute St, Norfolk, Virginia 23510 (804–627–1934)
—— Upper Volta, British Ambassador and Consul-General resident at Abidjan, Ivory Coast
—— Uruguay, British Embassy, Calle Marco Bruto 1073, Montevideo (79–10–33, 79–11–33, 79-91–73)

British diplomatic missions—cont.
—— Venezuela
British Embassy, Edificio La Estancia Piso 12, Avenida La Estancia No. 10, Ciudad Comercial, Tamanaco Apartado 1246, Caracas (91–10–91, 91–14–77)
British Vice-Consulate, Edificio Gomez Castro Piso 2, Avenida El Milagro, Apartado 285, Maracaibo, Estado Zulia (227151, 226751, 227311)
British Vice-Consulate, Campo Meneven, Casa No. 222 Guaraguao, Puerto La Cruz, Estado Anzoategui, Apartado 4104 (081–21816)
British Vice-Consulate, c/o Corporacion Mercantil Venezolana, Cruce Calle Cantaura Con Avenida Diaz, Moreno Valencia Edo, Carabobo (80285, 89091)
—— Vietnam, Socialist Republic of, British Embassy, 16 Pho Ly Thuong Kiet, Hanoi (2349, 2510)
—— West Indies Associated States
Office of the British Government Representative, George Gordon Building, PO Box 227, Castries, St Lucia (2484)
Office of Her Majesty's Commissioner in Anguilla, The Valley, Anguilla (451, 452)
Office of the Deputy British Government Representative, 28 St Mary's St, PO Box 483, St John's, Antigua (20342, 20008)
Office of the Deputy British Government Representative, Grenville St, PO Box 132, Kingstown, St Vincent (71701)
—— Western Samoa, British High Commission, Nuku'alofa, Apia
—— Yemen Arab Republic, British Embassy, 11–13 Qasr al Jumhuri St, PO Box 1287, Sana'a (2684, 5714)
—— Yemen, People's Democratic Republic, British Embassy, 28 Shara Ho Chi Minh, Khormaksar, Aden (24171)
—— Yugoslavia
British Embassy, 46 Generala Zdanova, Belgrade (645055, 645034, 645043, 645087)
British Consulate, Obala Marsala Tito 10, 58000 Split (058–41–464)
British Consulate-General, Ulica Ilica 12, PO Box 454, 41001 Zagreb (445–522, 446–333, 447–533)
—— Zaire, British Embassy, Avenue de l'Equateur, 5th Floor, PO Box 8049, Kinshasa (23483, 23280, 22666)
—— Zambia, British High Commission, Independence Ave, PO Box RW50, Lusaka (51122)
British Electrotechnical Approvals Board, The Green, 9–11 Queens Rd, Hersham, Walton-on-Thames KT12 5LU (01–984–4401)
British Embassy – see British Diplomatic Missions
British Equestrian Federation, National Equestrian Centre, Stoneleigh, Kenilworth, Warwickshire (0203–27192)
British Falconers Club, c/o The Management Centre, University of Aston, Gosta Green, Birmingham 4 6TE (021–3611)
British Federation of Film Societies, 72 Dean St, London W1V 6AA (01–437–4355)
British Federation of Sand and Land Yacht Clubs, The Flat, 51 Commonside, Ansdell, Lytham St Annes, Lancs
British Field Sports Society, 26 Caxton St, London SW1 0RG (01–222–5407)
British Film Institute, 81 Dean St, London W1V 6AA (01–437–4355); Production Board (01–437–3428)
British Gas Corporation Headquarters, 59 Bryanston St, London W1A 2AZ (01–723–7030)
British Gas Corporation, Regions
—— East Midlands Gas, PO Box 145, De Montfort St, Leicester LE1 9DB (0533–50022)
—— Eastern Gas, Star House, Potters Bar, Hertfordshire (77–51151)
—— North Eastern Gas, New York Rd, Leeds LS2 7PE (0532–36291)
—— North Thames Gas, North Thames House, London Rd, Staines, Middlesex TW18 4AE (81–61666)
—— North West Gas, Welman House, Altrincham, Cheshire WA15 8AE (061–928–6311)
—— Northern Gas, PO Box 1 GB, Newcastle-upon-Tyne, NE99 1GB (0632–683000)
—— Scottish Gas, Granton House, 340 West Granton Rd, Edinburgh EH5 1YB (031–552–6271)
—— South Eastern Gas, Katharine Street, Croydon, Surrey CR9 1JU (01–688–4466)
—— South West Gas, Riverside, Temple St, Keynsham, Bristol BS18 1EQ (027–56–61717)
—— Southern Gas, PO Box 104, 80 St Mary's Rd, Southampton SO9 7GJ (0703–824124)
—— Wales Gas, Snelling House, Bute Terrace, Cardiff CF1 2UF (0222–33131)

British Gas Corporation, Regions—*cont.*
—— West Midlands Gas, Wharf Lane, Solihull B91 2JP (021–705–6888)
British Gliding Association, Kimberley House, Vaughan Way, Leicester (0533–51051)
British Greyhound Racing Federation, St Martin's House, 140 Tottenham Court Rd, London W1P 0AS (01–387–0705)
British Hallmarking Council, 41 Church St, Birmingham B3 2DY (021–236–9021)
British Handball Association, 48 Stanley St, Liverpool 1 (051–236–4851)
British Hang Gliding Association, Monksilver, Taunton, Somerset
British High Commission – see British diplomatic missions
British Horse Society, National Equestrian Centre, Stoneleigh, Kenilworth, Warwickshire (0203–27192)
British Hypnotherapy Association, 67 Upper Berkeley St, London W1 (01–723–4443)
British Ice Hockey Association, 20 Bedford St, London WC2E 9HP (01–240–5222)
British Institute of Embalmers, 5 Greenfield Crescent, Edgbaston, Birmingham B15 3BE (021–454–2177)
British Insurance Association, Aldermary House, PO Box 538, Queen St, London EC4P 4JD (01–248–4477)
British Insurance Brokers' Association, Fountain House, Fenchurch St, London EC3 (01–623–7378)
British Judo Association, 70 Brompton Rd, London SW3 1DR (01–584–3273)
British Library
—— Copyright Receipt Office, Store St, London WC1E 7DG (01–636–1544)
—— Lending Division, Great Russell St, London WC1 3DG (01–636–1544)
—— Newspaper Library, Colindale Ave, London NW9 5HE (01–200–5515)
—— Readers Admissions Office, Great Russell St, London WC1B 3DG (01–636–1544)
—— Science Reference Library, Southampton Buildings, Chancery Lane, London WC2 (01–405–8721)
British Market Research Bureau Ltd, Saunders House, 53 The Mall, Ealing, London W5 3TE (01–567–3060)
British Mountaineering Council, Crawford House, Precinct Centre, Booth St East, Manchester M13 9RZ (061–273–5835)
British Museum, Bloomsbury, London WC1 (01–636–1555)
British Music Information Centre, 10 Stratford Place, London W1 (01–499–8567)
British Olympic Association, 12 Buckingham St, London WC2N 6DJ (01–930–1761)
British Optical Association, 65 Brook St, London W1Y 2DT (01–629–3382)
British Orienteering Federation, Lea Green, Matlock, Derbyshire DE4 5GH (062984–628)
British Orthoptic Council, Royal Eye Hospital, Oxford Rd, Manchester M13 9WH (061–273–1875)
British Orthoptics Society, Royal Eye Hospital, Oxford Rd, Manchester M13 9WH (061–273–3300)
British Overseas Trade Board, Hillgate House, 26 Old Bailey, London EC4M 7HU (01–248–5757)
British Overseas Trade Board Regional Offices
—— Northern Ireland Department of Commerce, Chichester House, 64 Chichester St, Belfast BT1 4JX (0232–34488)
—— Ladywood House, Stephenson St, Birmingham B2 4DT (021–632–4111)
—— The Pithay, Bristol BS1 2PB (0272–291071)
—— Government Buildings, Gabalfa, Cardiff CF4 4YL (0222–62131)
—— Alhambra House, 45 Waterloo St, Glasgow GL6AJ (041–248–2855)
—— Priestley House, Park Row, Leeds LS1 5LF (0532–443171)
—— Room G25 (London and South East), Export House, London (01–248–5757 and 01–2809–565)
—— Room G21 (Eastern), Export House, London (01–248–5757 and 01–2809–684)
—— Sunley Building, Piccadilly Plaza, Manchester M1 4BA (061–236–2171)
—— Stanegate House, 2 Groat Market, Newcastle-upon-Tyne NE1 1YN (0632–24722)
—— Severns House, 20 Middle Pavement, Nottingham NG1 7DW (0602–56181)
British Parachute Association, Kimberley House, 47 Vaughan Way, Leicester LE1 4SG (0533–59778/59635)
British Pharmacopeia Commission, 8 Bulstrode St, London W1 (01–487–2665)
British Phonographic Industry, 33 Thurloe Place, London SW7 (01–589–7439)
British Pregnancy Advisory Service Head Office, Austy Manor, Wooton Wawen, Solihull, West Midlands B95 6DA (Henley-in-Arden 3225)

British Pregnancy Advisory Service Branches
—— First Floor, Guildhall Buildings, Navigation St, Birmingham B2 4BT (021–643–1461)
—— Pelhams Clinic, Millhams Rd, Kinson, Bournemouth BH10 7LH (02016–77720)
—— 4 High Street Arcade Chambers, Cardiff CF1 2BE (0222–372389)
—— 26 Queen Street, Chester CH1 3LG (0244–27113)
—— 2nd Floor, 245 North St, Glasgow G3 7DL (041–204–1832)
—— 2nd Floor, 58 Petty France, Victoria, London SW1H 9EU (01–222–0985)
—— Suite F, Ground Floor, 57 Hilton St, Manchester M1 2EJ (061–236–7777)
—— Lower Ground Floor, Harley Buildings, 11 Old Hall St, Liverpool L2 1BB (051–227–3721)
—— 160 Charles St, Sheffeld S1 2NE (0742–738326)
—— Wistons Site, Chatsworth Rd, Brighton, Sussex BN1 5PA (0273–509726)
—— Second Floor, 8 The Headrow, Leeds, Yorkshire LS1 6PT (0532 443861)
British Professional Cycle Racing Association, 'Mingulay', Hebden Hall Park, Hebden, Nr Skipton, North Yorks (0756–752–730)
British Rail
—— London Midland Region, Euston Rd, London NW1 (01–387–9400)
—— Southern Region, Waterloo Station, London SE1 (01–928–5151)
—— Western Region, Paddington Station, London W2 (01–723–7000)
—— Eastern Region, King's Cross Station, London N1 (01–837–4200)
British Railways Board, 222 Marylebone Rd, London NW1 6JJ (01–262–3232)
British School of Osteopathy, 16 Buckingham Gate, London SW1E 6LB (01–828–9479)
British Shipping Careers Offices
—— 79 Regent Quay, Aberdeen AB1 2AR (0224–291367)
—— Gloucester Rd, Avonmouth BS11 9AQ (02752–2507/3039)
—— 76–8 Tomb St, Belfast BT1 3FL (0232–27426–7)
—— Daimler House, Paradise Circus, Queensway, Birmingham B1 2BJ (021–643–3272)
—— Roath Basin Docks, Cardiff CF1 5TG (0222–28411)
—— Ground Floor Suite, 6 Castle Hill Rd, Dover CT16 1QM (0304–202254)
—— 2 Midland House, High St, Dovercourt CO12 3PS (025–55–4472)
—— East Old Dock, Edinburgh EH6 6LS (031–554–5937/2327–8)
—— 186 Broomielaw, Glasgow G1 4RF (041–221–2443)
—— 14 Cleethorpe Rd, South Humberside, Grimsby DN31 3LD (0472–570545)
—— 35–59 Hyton St, Hull HU1 2PS (0482–28017)
—— Mann Island, Pier Rd, Liverpool L3 1DQ (051–236–6031)
—— 20–22 Prescot St, London E1 8BD (01–709–9221/5021)
—— Stock St, Middlesbrough, Cleveland TS2 1LU (0642–434245)
—— Cuthbert House, All Saints Office Centre, Newcastle NE1 2AH (0632–21031/2/3 and 26782)
—— Prudential Buildings, Armada Way, Plymouth PL1 1HW (0752–65942 and 64712)
—— 19–23 Canute Rd, Southampton SO1 1FJ (0703–23546)
—— AEU House, 34 Orchard St, Swansea SA1 5AW (0792–55267/8)
—— St Andrews Rd, Tilbury RM18 7EB (037–52–2352)
British Shipping Careers Service, 146–50 Minories, London EC3N 1ND (01–481–8731)
British Show Jumping Association, National Equestrian Centre, Stoneleigh, Kenilworth, Warwickshire (0203–27192)
British Speedway Promoters' Association, Cottrell House, 53–63 Wembley Hill Rd, Wembley, Middlesex (01–903–6155)
British Sports Association for the Disabled, Stoke Mandeville Sports Stadium, Harvey Rd, Aylesbury, Bucks (0296–84848)
British Standards Institution
—— Head Office, 2 Park St, London W1A 2BS (01–629–9000)
—— Testing Station, Maylands Ave, Hemel Hempstead, Herts HP2 4SQ (0442–3111)
British Sub-Aqau Club, 70 Brompton Rd, London SW3 1HA (01–584–7164)
British Sub-Aqua Club Scottish Federation, 55 Strathtay Rd, Perth (0738–20173)
British Sugar Corporation Ltd, Central Offices, Oundle Rd, Peterborough PE2 9QU (0733–63171)
British Surfing Association, 18 Bournemouth Rd, Parkstone, Poole, Dorset (0202–746154)
British Tenpin Bowling Association, 19 Canterbury Ave, Ilford, Essex (01–554–9173)
British Tourist Authority, 64 St James's St, London SW1 (01–629–9191)
British Toy Manufacturers Association Ltd, 6th Floor, Region House, 89 Kingsway, London WC2B 6RS (01–242–9158)

British Trampoline Federation Ltd, Headquarters, 152A College Rd, Harrow, Middx (01–863–7278)
British Transport Docks Board, Melbury House, Melbury Terrace, London NW1 6JY (01–486–6621)
British Universities Film Council, 72 Dean St, London W1V 6AA (01–437–4355)
British Vice-Consulates – see British diplomatic missions
British Volunteer Programme, 26 Bedford Sq, London WC1B 3HU (01–636–4066)
British Water Ski Federation, 70 Brompton Rd, London SW3 1EG (01–584–8262)
British Water Ski Federation, Northern Ireland Regional Group, Bloomfield, Strangmore, Dungannon (086–873–2662)
British Waterways Board, Melbury House, Melbury Terrace, London NW1 6JX (01–262–6711)
British Waterways Board Area Amenity Assistants,
—— Reservoir House, Icknield Port Rd, Birmingham B16 0AA (021–454–7091)
—— Lock Lane, Castleford WF10 2LH (0977–554351)
—— Dock Office, Gloucester GL1 2EJ (0452–25524)
—— (London), 43 Clarendon Rd, Watford WD1 1JE (92–31363)
—— Navigation Rd, Northwich, Cheshire (0606–74321)
—— 24 Meadow Lane, Nottingham NG2 3HL (0602–862411)
—— Swan Meadow Rd, Wigan WN3 5BB (0942–42239)
—— (Scottish Canals), Old Basin Works, Applecross St, Glasgow G4 9SP (041–332–6936)
—— (Caledonian Canal), Caledonian Canal Office, Clachnaharry, Inverness IV3 6RA (0463–33140)
British Waterways Board Craft Licensing Office, Willow Grange, Church Rd, Watford WD1 3QA (92–26422)
British Waterways Board Fisheries Officer, Willow Grange, Church Rd, Watford WD1 3QA (92–26422)
British Women's Tennis Association, Reddington House, Winnington Rd, London N2 (01–455–0304)
British Wool Confederation, Lloyds Bank Chambers, Hustler Gate, Bradford, BD1 1PH (0274–27103)
British Wool Marketing Board, Oak Mills, Station Rd, Clayton, Bradford, West Yorkshire BD14 6JD (0274–882091)
British Wool Marketing Board (Northern Ireland), 20 Tirgracey Rd, Muckamore, County Antrim BT41 4PS (084–941–3130)
Brunei High Commission, Government Agency, 35 Norfolk Square, London W2 (01–402–0045)
Buckingham Palace, London SW (01–930–4832)
Building and Design Centre, Hope St 1, Liverpool (051–709–9416)
Building Societies Association, 14 Park St, London W1Y 4AL (01–629–0515)
Bulgaria, Embassy of the People's Republic of, 12 Queen's Gate Gardens, London SW7 5NA (01–584– 9400, 9433)
Bulgarian National Tourist Office, 126 Regent St, London W1 (01–437– 2611)
Burke's Family History Bureau, 56 Walton St, London SW3 1RB (01–584–8134)
Burke's Peerage Ltd, 56 Walton St, London SW3 1RB (01–584–1106/8134)
Burmese Embassy, Embassy of the Socialist Republic of the Union of Burma, 19A Charles St, London W1X 8ER (01–499–8841)
Burundi Diplomatic Mission to UK, Burundi, Embassy of the Republic of, Square Marie Louise 46, Brussels 1040, Belgium (33–55–92/33–57–15)
Bus and Coach Service enquiries, 172 Buckingham Palace Rd, London SW1 (01–730–0202)
Business Education Council, 76 Portland Place, London W1N 4AA (01–580–3050)
Business Statistics Office, Cardiff Road, Newport, Gwent NPT 1XG (0633–56111)
Business Statistics Office Production Census, Lime Grove, Ruislip, Middx HA4 8RS (01–866–8771 ex 523)

C

CAM Education Foundation, 15 Wilton Rd, London SW1V 1NJ (01–828–7506)
Camanachd Association, 5 Park Terrace, Foyers, Inverness-shire
Cambridge University Local Examinations Syndicate, Syndicate Buildings, 17 Harvey Rd, Cambridge CB1 2EU (0223–61111)

Cameroon, Embassy of the United Republic of, 84 Holland Park, London W11 3SB (01-727-0771)
Camping Club of Great Britain and Ireland Ltd, 11 Lower Grosvenor Place, London SW1W 0EY (01-828-1012)
Canadian Consulates,
—— 22 North St, Belfast BT1 1LA (0232-27365)
—— Bristol and Westhouse, 2 St Philip's Place, Birmingham B3 2QJ (021-233-2127)
—— Ashley House (2nd Floor), 181-195 West George St, Glasgow G2 2HS (041-248-3026)
—— Barlow House (2nd Floor), Minshull St, Manchester (061-236-0682)
Canadian High Commission, Macdonald House, 1 Grosvenor Sq, London W1X 0AB (01-629-9492)
Canoe Association of Northern Ireland, 55 Carnreagh, Hillsborough, Co Down (0846-682354)
Capital Radio, Euston Tower, London NW1 3DR (01-388-1288)
Caravan Club, East Grinstead House, London Rd, East Grinstead (0342-26944)
Careers and Occupational Information Centre, 97 Tottenham Court Rd, London W1P 0ER
Careers Office – look in telephone directory under Careers Service
Careers Service – look in telephone directory under Careers Service
Catholic Institute for International Relations, Overseas Volunteer Department, 41 Holland Park, London W11 (01-727-3195)
Cedok (London) Ltd (Czechoslovak Tourist Bureau), 17-18 Old Bond St, London W1X 3DA (01-629-6058)
Central African Empire Diplomatic Mission to UK, French Consulate-General, 29 Boulevard Montmorency, 75016 Paris (224-42-56)
Central Arbitration Committee, 1 The Abbey Garden, Great College St, London SW1P 3SE (01-222-8571)
Central Council for Agricultural and Horticultural Co-operation
—— England and Wales, 301-344 Market Towers, New Covent Garden Market, 1 Nine Elms Lane, London SW8 5NQ (01-720-2144)
—— Northern Ireland, 20 High St, Portadown, Craigavon, Co Armagh BT62 1HU (0762-33144)
—— Scotland, 18 Claremont Crescent, Edinburgh EH7 4JW (031-556-6574)
Central Council for Education and Training in Social Work
—— Derbyshire House, St Chad's St, London WC14 8A3 (01-278-2455)
—— 9 South St David St, Edinburgh 2
Central Council of Physical Recreation, 70 Brompton Rd, London SW3 1HE (01-584-6651)
Central Electricity Generating Board, 15 Newgate St, London EC1A 7AU (01-248-1202)
Central Examining Board for Dental Hygienists, 37 Wimpole St, London W1M 8DQ (01-486-2171)
Central Midwives Board, 39 Harrington Gardens, London SW7 4JY (01-373-4801)
Central Midwives Board for Scotland, 24 Dublin St, Edinburgh EH1 3PU (031-556-1671)
Central Office of Information, Hercules Rd, London SE1 (01-928-2345)
Central Services' Agency, 27 Adelaide St, Belfast BTR 8TH (0232-24431)
Central Statistical Office, Great George St, London SW1P 3AQ (01-233-6135)
Certification Office for Trade Union and Employers' Associations, Vincent House Annexe, Hide Place, London SW1P 4NG (01-828-7603)
Chad Diplomatic Mission to UK, Avenue de Meise 75, 1200 Brussels (Brussels 2676639)
Channel Television, The Television Centre, Rouge Bouillon, St Helier, Jersey, Channel Islands (0534-23451)
Charities Aid Foundation, 48 Pembury Road, Tonbridge, Kent TN9 2JD (0732-356323)
Charity Commission, 14 Ryder St, St James's, London SW1Y 6AH (01-214-6000)
Chartered Institute of Patent Agents, Staple Inn Buildings, High Holborn, London WC1V 7PZ (01-405-9450)
Chartered Institute of Public Finance and Accountancy, 1 Buckingham Place, London SW1E 6HS (01-834-6433)
Chartered Society of Physiotherapy, 14 Bedford Row, London WC1R 4ED (01-242-1941)
Chief Electoral Officer's Office, Bedford House, Belfast (0232-45353)
Chief Herald of Ireland, Genealogical Office, Dublin Castle, Dublin, Eire (Dublin 751284)
Chief Officer of Police – contact local police station or police force headquarters
Child Guidance Clinics – contact local authority
Child Health Clinic – contact local authority
Chilean Embassy, 12 Devonshire St, London W1N 2DS (01-580-1023)
Chinese Embassy, Embassy of the People's Republic of China, 31 Portland Place, London W1N 3AG (01-636-5637)

Christians Abroad, 15 Tufton St, London SW1P 3Q (01–222–2165)
Citizens Advice Bureaux – look in local telephone directory under Citizens Advice Bureaux
City and Guilds of London Institute, 76 Portland Place, London W1N 4AA (01–580–3050)
City Corporation, Guildhall, London EC2P 2EJ (01–606–3030)
City of London, Guildhall, London EC2P 2EJ (01–606–3030)
City of London Police, Headquarters and CID, 26 Old Jewry, London EC2 (01–606–8866)
City University, St John St, London EC1 (01–253–4399)
Civil Aviation Authority, Space House, 43–59 Kingsway, London WC2B 6TE (01–379–7311)
Civil Aviation Authority, Airworthiness Division, Brabazon House, Redhill, Surrey RH1 1SQ (91–65966)
Civil Aviation Authority, Flight Crew Licensing, Aviation House, 129 Kingsway, London WC2B 6MM (01–405–6922)
Civil Aviation Authority, Hovercraft Department, Sunley House, 90 High Holborn, London WC1V 6LP (01–405–6911)
Civil Aviation Authority, Printing and Publications Services, Greville House, 37 Gratton Rd, Cheltenham, Glos GL50 2BN
Civil Aviation Authority, UK Registers of Civil Aircraft and of Aircraft Mortgages, Aviation House, 129 Kingsway, London WC2B 6NN (01–405–6922)
Civil Aviation Policy Division 5, Dept of Trade, The Adelphi, John Adam St, London WC2 (01–217–3000)
Civil Service Commission, Alencon Link, Basingstoke, Hants, RG21 1JB (0256–29222)
Civil Service Department, Whitehall, London SW1A 2AZ (01–839–7733)
Civil Service Department Ceremonial Branch, Standard House, Northumberland Ave, London WC2 (01–839–7733)
Civil Service Department Statistics, Whitehall, London SW1A 2AZ (01–839–7733)
Civil Service Motoring Association Ltd, 797 London Rd, Thornton Heath (01–684–8871)
Clarence House, London (01–930–3141)
Clay Pigeon Shooting Association, 107 Epping New Rd, Buckhurst Hill, Essex (01–505–6221)
Clerk of Petty Sessions – look under 'Petty Sessions Offices' in local telephone directory.
Clydesdale Bank Ltd, Head Office, 30 St Vincent Place, Glasgow G1 2HL (041–248–7070)
Coast Amateur Rowing Association, 6 Farm Ave, Horsham, Sussex (0403–2825 and 0444–50046)
Coastguard – in emergency dial 999. For other addresses see Her Majesty's Coastguard Service
Cocoa Association of London, Cereal House, 58 Mark Lane, London EC3R 7NE
Coffee Terminal Market Association, Cereal House, 58 Mark Lane, London EC3R 7NE (01–488–3736).
Coffee Trade Federation, 69 Cannon Street, London EC4 (01–248–4444)
Colaisde Gaidhlig, Sabhal Mor, Ostaig, Scotland
Coleg Harlech, Harlech, Gwynedd LL46 2PU (076–673–363)
College of Acupuncture, 118 Foley Rd, Claygate, Esher, Surrey (01–834–3353)
College of Arms, Queen Victoria St, London EC4V 4BT (01–248–2762)
College of Radiographers, 14 Upper Wimpole St, London W1M 8BN (01–935–5727)
College of Speech Therapists, Harold Poster House, 6 Lechmere Rd, London NW2 8BU (01–459–8521)
Colombian Embassy, Flat 3A, 3 Hans Crescent, London SW1X 0LR (01–589–9177)
Commission of the European Communities
—— UK Office, 20 Kensington Palace, London W84 QQ (01–727–8090)
—— Brussels, rue de la Loi 200, 1049 Brussels (Brussels 735–0040)
Commission for Local Administration in England, 21 Queen Anne's Gate, London SW1H 9BU (01–930–3333)
Commissioner for Local Administration, Scotland, 125 Princes St, Edinburgh EH2 4AD (031–226–2823)
Commission for Local Administration, Wales, Derwen House, Court Rd, Bridgend, Mid Glamorgan (0656–61325)
Commission for the New Towns, Glen House, Stag Place, Victoria, London SW1E 5AJ
Commission for Racial Equality, Elliot House, 10–12 Allington Street, London SW1E 5EH (01–828–7022)
Commissioners of Customs and Excise, King's Beam House, Mark Lane, London EC3R 7HE (01–626–1515)
Committee on Invisible Exports, 18th Floor, 23 Fenchurch St, London EC3 3DD (01–626–3641)

Common Entrance Examination for Girls' Schools, 2 Bankfield, Kendal, Westmorland LA9 5DS
Common Entrance Office, Ashley Lane, Lymington, Hants SO4 9YR (059–75947)
Commons, Open Spaces and Footpaths Preservation Society, 166 Shaftesbury Ave, London WC2 (01–836–7220)
Commonwealth Association of Architects, 17 Northumberland Ave, London WC2N 5AP
Commonwealth Association of Museums, c/o Museum of London, London Wall, London EC2Y 5HN
Commonwealth Association of Planners, 18 Northumberland Ave, London WC2N 5BJ
Commonwealth Association of Surveying and Land Economy, 12 Great George St, London SW1P 3AD
Commonwealth Council for Educational Administration, Faculty of Education, University of New England, Armidale, Australia 2351
Commonwealth Development Corporation, 33 Hill St, London W1A 3AR (01–629–8484)
Commonwealth Development Corporation, Mananga Agricultural Management Centre, PO Box 96, Tshaneni, Swaziland
Commonwealth Engineers Council, 2 Little Smith St, London SW1
Commonwealth Foundation, Marlborough House, Pall Mall, London SW1Y 5HX (01–930–3783)
Commonwealth Fund for Technical Co-operation, Commonwealth Secretariat, Marlborough House, Pall Mall, London SW1Y 5HX
Commonwealth Games Councils
—— England, 12 Buckingham St, London WC2N 6DJ (01–930–1761)
—— Isle of Man (Commonwealth Games Association), 10 Porte Chee Avenue, Douglas
—— Jersey (Commonwealth Games Association), 54 Mont Es Croix, St Brelade, Jersey
—— Guernsey, Janstars, Emrais Lane, Catel, Guernsey
—— Northern Ireland, 22 Mountcoole Park, Belfast BT14 8JR
—— Scotland, 1 Cockburn St, Edinburgh 1 (031–557–0606)
—— Wales, 9 Cathedral Rd, Cardiff
Commonwealth Geographical Bureau, School of Oriental and African Studies, Malet St, London WC1E 7HP
Commonwealth Human Ecology Council, 63 Cromwell Rd, London SW7 5BL (01–373–6761)
Commonwealth Institute, Kensington High St, London W8 (01–602–3252)
Commonwealth Legal Bureau, 807–265 Poulin Ave, Ottawa, Canada K2B 7Y8
Commonwealth Legal Educationists Association, Commonwealth Secretariat, Marlborough House, Pall Mall, London SW17 5HX (01–839–3411)
Commonwealth Library Association, PO Box 534, Kingston 10, Jamaica
Commonwealth Magistrates Association, 28 Fitzroy Sq, London W1P 6DD
Commonwealth Medical Association, BMA House, Tavistock Sq, London WC1H 9JP
Commonwealth Nurses Federation, 18 Northumberland Ave, London WC2N 5BJ
Commonwealth Pharmaceutical Association, Pharmaceutical Society of Great Britain, 1 Lambeth High St, London SE1 7JN
Commonwealth Scholarship Commission, 36 Gordon Sq, London WC1H 0PF (01–386–8572)
Commonwealth Secretariat, Marlborough House, Pall Mall, London SW1Y 5HX (01–839–3411)
Commonwealth Society for the Deaf, 83 Kinnerton St, London SW1 (01–235–8182)
Commonwealth Veterinary Association, 360 Bronson Ave, Ottawa, Ontario, Canada K1R 6J3
Commonwealth War Graves Commission, 2 Marlow Rd, Maidenhead, Berks SL6 7DM (0628–34221)
Communist Party of Great Britain, Communist Party Headquarters, 16 King St, London WC2 (01–836–2121)
Communist Party of Ireland Headquarters, 37 Pembroke Lane, Ballsbridge, Dublin 4 (Dublin–754968)
Companies Registration Office, Companies House, Crown Way, Maindy, Cardiff CF4 3UZ (0222–38858)
Companies Registration Office, London Search Room, Companies House 55–71 City Rd, London EC1Y 1BB (01–253–9393)
Companies Registration Office, Scotland, Exchequer Chambers, 102 George St, Edinburgh
Conciliation and Arbitration Services – see Advisory Conciliation and Arbitration Service
Confederation of British Industry, Headquarters, 21 Tothill St, London SW1H 9LP (01–930–6711)
Confederation of British Industry Regional Offices
—— 3 Botanic Ave, Belfast BT7 1JG (0232–26658)

Confederation of British Industry Regional Offices—*cont.*
—— Hagley House, Hagley Rd, Edgbaston, Birmingham B16 8PS (021-454-7991)
—— 8-10 Whiteladies Rd, Bristol BS8 1NZ (0272-37065)
—— Pearl Assurance House, Greyfriars Road, Cardiff CF1 3JR (0222-32536)
—— Beresford House, 5 Claremont Terrace, Glasgow G3 7XT (041-332-8661)
—— Arndale House, Crossgates, Leeds LS15 8EU (0532-644242)
—— Emerson House, Albert St, Eccles, Manchester M30 0LT (061-707-2190)
—— 1 St Nicholas Buildings, Newcastle-upon-Tyne NE1 1RF (0632-21644)
—— 17 St Wilfrid Sq, Claverton, Nottingham (0607-44-3311)
Confederation of British Road Passenger Vehicle Operators, Sardinia House, 52 Lincolns Inn Fields, London WC2A 3LZ (01-831-7546)
Congolese Embassy, 57 bis, Rue Scheffer, Paris 16, France (727-77-09)
Conservative and Unionist Central Office, 33 Smith Sq, London SW1P 3HH (01-222-9000)
Consular Department, Foreign and Commonwealth Office, Clive House, Petty France, London SW1H 9HD (01-213-3000)
Consumers Association, 14 Buckingham St, London WC2N 6DS (01-839-1222)
Consumers Committees
—— for Great Britain and for England and Wales, Great Westminster House, Horseferry Rd, London SW1P 2AE
—— for Scotland, Chesser House, Gorgie Rd, Edinburgh EH11 3AW
Cook Hammond and Kell Ltd, 22-24 Caxton St, London SW1H 0QU (01-222-4945)
Co-op Bank Ltd, Head Office, New Sentry House, Manchester M60 4EP
Co-operation Housing Agency, 180 Tottenham Court Rd, London W1 (01-636-2261)
Co-operative College, Loughborough (Eleake 2333)
Co-operative Party, 158 Buckingham Palace Rd, London SW1W 9UB (01-730-8187)
Corporation of Insurance Brokers, 15 St Helen's Place, London EC3A 6DS (01-588-4387)
Corporation of London, Guildhall, London EC2 (01-606-3030)
Costa Rican Embassy, 1 Culross St, London W1 (01-493-9761)
Cotswold Land Yacht Club, 57 Cotham Brow, Redland, Bristol
Council for National Academic Awards, Department of Education and Science, Elizabeth House, 39 York Rd, London SE1 7PH
Council for Professions Supplementary to Medicine, York House, Westminster Bridge Rd, London SE1 (01-928-2612)
Council for Small Industries in Rural Areas, Queen's House, Fish Row, Salisbury, Wilts SP1 1EX (0722-24411)
Council for Small Industries in Rural Areas, Credit Services Division, 11 Cowley St, London SW1P 3NA (01-930-7134)
Council for Vehicle Servicing and Repair, 94 Park Lane, London W1Y 3TA (01-491-7060)
Council for the Welsh Language, Cathays Park, Cardiff (0222-28066)
Council of Accreditation of Correspondence Colleges, 27 Marylebone Rd, London NW1 (01-935-5391)
Council of Engineering Institutions, 2 Little Smith St, London SW1P 3DL (01-799-3912/4)
Council of Europe, 67006 Strasbourg Cedex, France
Council of Legal Education, 4 Gray's Inn Place, London WC1R 5DX (01-405-4635)
Council of Legal Education (Northern Ireland), Institute of Professional Legal Studies, Queen's University, Belfast BT7 1NN (0232-45133)
Council of Ministers – see European Council of Ministers
Council of National Golf Unions, 7 College St, Nottingham NG1 5AS (0602-46377)
Country Landowners' Association, 16 Belgrave Sq, London SW1 (01-235-0511)
Countryside Commission, John Dower House, Crescent Place, Cheltenham, Glos GL50 3RA (0242-21381)
Countryside Commission for Scotland, Battleby, Redgorton, Perth PH1 3EW (0738-27921)
Countrywide Holidays Association, Birch Heys, Cromwell Range, Manchester 14 (061-224-2867)
County Court, county court offices – look in local telephone directory under courts
Court of Justice of the European Communities, Palais de la Cour de Justice, Kirchberg, Luxembourg
Court of Lord Lyon, Her Majesty's New Register House, Edinburgh EH1 3YT (031-556-7255)
Court of Protection, Staffordshire House, Store St, London WC1 (01-636-6877)
County Court Office, Small Claims – look in local telephone directory under courts
Court of Session, Parliament Square, Edinburgh (031-225-2595)

Courts Martial Appeal Court, Royal Courts of Justice, The Strand, London WC2 (01–405–7641)
Crafts Advisory Committee, 12 Waterloo Place, London SW1Y 4AU (01–839–1917)
Credit Suisse, 27 Austin Friars, London EC2N 2LB (01–628–7131)
Cricket Council, Lord's Cricket Ground, London NW8 8QN (01–289–1611)
Criminal Injuries Compensation Board, Russell Square House, 10 Russell Sq, London WC1B 5EN (01–636–2812)
Crown Agents for Overseas Governments and Administrations, Head Office, 4 Millbank, London SW1P 3JD (01–222–7730)
Crown Agents for Overseas Governments and Administrations, Overseas Offices
—— East Africa, 2nd Floor, IPS Building, Kimathi Street, PO Box 47246, Nairobi, Kenya (25524 & 26917)
—— West Africa, Western House, 8/10 Broad Street, PO Box 583, Lagos, Nigeria (21241)
—— North America, 3100 Massachusetts Avenue NW, Washington D.C. 20008, USA (202–402–1340)
—— Caribbean, Barclays Bank Building, Roebuck Street, PO Box 82, Bridgetown, Barbados (60458)
—— South East Asia, 6th Floor, Chartered Bank Building, 2 Jalan Ampang, Kuala Lumpur 01–16, Malaysia (21538 or 21545)
—— Singapore and Indonesia, Suite 707, Cathay Building, Mount Sophia, Singapore 9 (321167)
Pexamin Pacific inc., 2nd Floor, PPM Building, Jalan Menteng, Raya 9, PO Box 2169, Jakarta, Indonesia (357310 or 357275)
—— Australasia and the Western Pacific, 9th Floor, IAC Building, 54–62 Carrington St, Sydney, NSW 2000, Australia (290–2266)
—— Far East, 7th Floor, Tokyo Chamber of Commerce and Industry Building, No. 2–2 3-chome, Merut-ouchi, Chiyoda-ku, Tokyo 100, Japan
—— Middle East, 3rd Floor, Al Monayyed Building North, PO Box 531, Manama, Bahrain, Arabian Gulf (Bahrain 54672)
—— Iran, Millbank Technical Services (Iran) Limited, Abbasabad, Mir Emad Kh 13, Opposite No. 42, PO Box 33-487, Tehran, Iran (859671)
Crown Appointments Commission, Fielden House, Little College St, London SW1
Crown Estate Commissioners,
—— Crown Estate Office, 13–15 Carlton House Terrace, London SW1Y 5AH (01–214–6000)
—— New St Andrew's House, Edinburgh EH1 3YX
—— Crown Building, Cathays Park, Cardiff CF1 3NQ (0222–28066)
Crown Estate Office, 13–15 Carlton House Terrace, London SW1Y 5AH (01–214–6000)
Crown Office, 9 Parliament Sq, Edinburgh EH1 1RH (031–226–6831)
Croquet Association, Hurlingham Club, Ranelagh Gardens, London SW6 (01–736–3148)
Cuban Embassy, 57 Kensington Court, London W8 5DQ (01–937–8226)
Customs and Excise – see Her Majesty's Customs and Excise
Cycle Speedway Council, 67 St Francis Way, Chadwell St Mary, Grays, Essex RM16 4RB
Cyclists' Touring Club, Cotterell House, 69 Meadrow, Godalming, Surrey (048–68–7217)
Cyprus High Commission, 93 Park St, London W1Y 4ET (01–499–8272)
Cyprus Tourism Public Relations Office, Windsor House, 83 Kingsway, London WC2 (01–242–2522)
Czechoslovak Travel Bureau, 17–18 Old Bond St, London W1X 3DA (01–629–6058)
Czechoslovakia, Embassy of the Socialist Republic of, 28 Kensington Palace Gardens, London W8 4QY

D

Debrett's Ancestry Research, 67 Parchment St, Winchester, Hampshire (0962–67366)
Debrett's Peerage Ltd,
—— 23 Mossop St, London SW3 (01–581–0174/5)
—— 1675 York Ave, New York City, USA (212–831–1186)
Defence, Press and Broadcasting Committee, Ministry of Defence, Main Building, Whitehall, London SW1
Dental Estimates Board, Compton Place Rd, Eastbourne, Sussex EN20 8AD (0323–25552)

Dental Services Agency, Northern Ireland, Central Services Agency, 25/27 Adelaide St, Belfast 2 (0232–24431)
Department for National Savings, Blythe Rd, London W14 1SB (01–603–2000)
Department for National Savings, Bonds and Stock Office, Lytham St Annes, Lancs FY0 1YN (0253–721212)
Department for National Savings, Save As You Earn Office, Millburngate House, Durham DH99 1NS (0385–64900)
Department for National Savings, Savings Certificate Office, Millburngate House, Durham DH99 1NS (0385–64900)
Department of Agriculture and Fisheries for Scotland, Head Office, Chesser House, 500 Gorgie Rd, Edinburgh EH11 3AW (031–443–4020)
Department of Agriculture and Fisheries for Scotland Area Offices
—— Atholl House, 82–8 Guild St, Aberdeen AB9 2ZL (0224–574567)
—— Russell House, King St, Ayr, KA8 0BE (0292–66931)
—— 161 Brooms Rd, Dumfries, DG1 3ES (0387–3100)
—— 5 Cowgate, Dundee DD1 2HT (0382–26504)
—— 38–9 Drumsheugh Gardens, Edinburgh EH3 7SS (031–225–5191)
—— 71 Renfield St, Glasgow G2 1LW (041–332–9161)
—— Government Building, Longman Rd, Inverness IV1 1SF (0463–34141)
—— Cameron House, Albany St, Oban, PA34 4AE (061–3071)
—— Government Buildings, 2 St Ninians Rd, Stirling, FK8 2HR (0786–3181)
—— Strathbeg House, Clarence St, Thurso, KW14 7JJ (0847–3104)
Department of Agriculture for Northern Ireland, Dundonald House, Upper Newtownards Rd, Belfast BT 3SB (0232–650111)
Department of Agriculture Forest Service (Northern Ireland), Dundonald House, Upper Newtownards Rd, Belfast BT4 3SB (0232–650111)
Department of Education and Science
—— Head Office, Elizabeth House, 39 York Rd, London SE1 7PH (01–928–9222)
—— Higher and Further Education IV, Honeypot Lane, Canons Park, Stanmore, Middx (01–952–2366)
—— Statistics, Elizabeth House, 39 York Rd, London SE1 7PH (01–928–9222)
—— Welsh Office, Cathays Park, Cardiff CF1 3NQ (0222–28066)
Department of Education, Northern Ireland, Rathgael House, Balloo Rd, Bangor, Co Down (0247–66311)
Department of Employment, Head Office, St James's Sq, London SW1 (01–214–6000)
Department of Employment local offices – look under Employment Service Agency Employment Offices in local telephone directory
Department of Employment, Overseas Division (ILO), 11 Tothill St, London SW1H 9LN (01–214–6000)
Department of Employment, Overseas Labour Section, Ebury Bridge House, Ebury Bridge Rd, London SW1W 8PY (01–730–9661)
Department of Employment Regional Offices
—— 2 Duchess Place, Hagley Rd, Birmingham B16 8 (021–455–7111)
—— The Pithay, Bristol BS1 2NQ (0272–291071)
—— 4th Floor, Companies House, Crown Way, Maindy, Cardiff CF4 3UW (0222–388588)
—— 43 Jeffrey St, Edinburgh EH1 1UU (031–556–8433)
—— City House, Leeds LS1 4JH (0532–38232)
—— Hanway House, 27 Red Lion Sq, London WC1R 4NH (01–405–8454)
—— Sunley Building, Piccadilly Plaza, Manchester M60 7JS (061–832–9111)
—— Wellbar House, Gallowgate, Newcastle-upon-Tyne NE1 4TP (0632–27575)
Department of Employment, Statistics, Orphanage Rd, Watford, Herts WD1 1PJ (92–28500)
Department of Employment, Unemployment Benefit Office – for local offices, look in telephone directory under Employment, Department of
Department of Employment Wages Inspectorates
—— 2 Duchess Place, Hagley Rd, Birmingham B16 8NS (021–455–7111)
—— The Pithay, Bristol (0272–291071)
—— Companies House, Crown Way, Maindy, Cardiff CF4 3UW (0222–388–588)
—— 43 Jeffrey St, Edinburgh EH1 1UU (031–556–8433)
—— 109 Waterloo St, Glasgow G2 7BY (041–248–5427/9)

Department of Employment Wages Inspectorates—*cont.*
—— Hempstead House, Hemel Hempstead, Herts HP1 1DW (0442–3714)
—— St Clare House, Greyfriars, Ipswich IP1 1LY (0473–56731)
—— City House, Leeds LS1 4JH (0532–38232)
—— Hanway House, Red Lion Sq, London WC1R 4NH (01–405–8454)
—— Quay House, Quay St, Manchester M3 7JE (061–832–6506)
—— Newgate House, Newgate St, Newcastle-upon-Tyne NE1 5RJ (0632–27575)
—— Castlegate House, Castle Gate, Nottingham NG1 7BW (0602–51944)
Department of Employment, Work Research Unit, Steel House, 11 Tothill St, London SW1H 9LN (01–799–7777)
Department of Energy, Thames House South, Millbank, London SW1P 4QJ (01–211–7326)
Department of Energy, British Approvals Service for Electrical Equipment in Flammable Atmospheres, Harpur Hill, Buxton, Derbyshire SK17 9JM
Department of Energy, Gas Standards Branch, Government Buildings, Saffron Road, Wigston, Leicester LE8 2US (053378–5354)
Department of Energy, Offshore Supplies Office, Alhambra House, 45 Waterloo St, Glasgow G2 6AS (041–221–8777)
Department of the Environment
—— Head Office, 2 Marsham Street, London SW1 (01–212–3434)
—— Air Photograph Unit, 6th Floor, Prince Consort House, Albert Embankment, London SE1 7TF (01–211–4326)
—— Ancient Monuments and Historic Buildings, Fortress House, 23 Saville Row, London W1X 1AB (01–734–6010)
—— Commercial Property Division, Queen Anne's Chambers, 28 Broadway, London SW1H 9JU (01–273–3186)
—— Division CP2B, Queen Anne's Chambers, Tothill St, London SW1
—— General Statistics, 2 Marsham St, London SW1P 3EP (01–212–3434)
—— Library, RC3/01, 2 Marsham St, London SW1 (01–212–4847)
—— Redemption of Rent Charges, Housing Division 9, Becket House, 1 Lambeth Palace Rd, London SE1 7ER (01–928–7855 ex 574)
—— Road Statistics, St Christopher House, Southwark Street, London SE1 0TE (01–928–7999)
—— Slide Library, Rm 601, Prince Consort House, Albert Embankment, London SE1 7TF (01–211–6926)
Department of the Environment for Northern Ireland
—— Parliament Buildings, Stormont, Belfast BT4 3SS (0232–63210)
—— Comprehensive Development Branch, Parliament Buildings, Stormont, Belfast BT4 3SS
—— Roads Service, Headquarters Division, Stoney Rd, Belfast BT4 3TR
Department of Finance, Northern Ireland, 3–5 Frederick St, Belfast BT1 2NH
Department of Health and Social Security
—— Headquarters, Alexander Fleming House, Elephant and Castle, London SE1 6BY (01–407–5522)
—— Awards Section, Friars House, 157–68 Blackfriars Rd, London SE1 6EU (01–703–6380)
—— Family Income Supplements, Poulton-le-Fylde, Blackpool FY6 8NW
—— Invalid Care Allowance Unit, Norcross, Blackpool FY5 3TA
—— Local Offices – look in local telephone directory under Health and Social Security
—— Local Tribunals – contact local Health and Social Security Office
—— Medicines Division, Finsbury Square House, 33–7a Finsbury Sq, London EC2A 1PP (01–638–6020)
—— Overseas Branch (and Group), Newcastle-upon-Tyne NE9 1YX (0632–857111)
—— Overseas Travel Enquiries, Alexander Fleming House, Elephant and Castle, London SE1 6BY (01–407–5522)
—— Physical Handicap Branch, Alexander Fleming House, London SE1 6BY
—— Statistics, 10 John Adam St, London WC2N 6HD (01–217–4134)
Department of Health and Social Services, Northern Ireland, Dundonald House, Upper Newtownards Rd, Belfast BT4 3SF (0232–650111)
Department of Industry Headquarters
—— 1 Victoria St, London SW1H 0ET (01–215–7877)
—— Millbank Tower, Millbank, London SW1P 4QU (01–211–3000)
—— Abell House, John Islip St, London SW1P 4LN (01–211–3000)

Department of Industry Regional Conservation Offices
—— Ladywood House, Stephenson St, Birmingham B2 4DT (021–632–4111)
—— The Pithay, Bristol BS1 2PB (0272–291071)
—— Priestly House, 1 Park Row, Leeds LS1 5LF (0532–443171)
—— Concord House, 454–8 London Rd, Croydon, Surrey (01–684–9781)
—— Charles House, 375 High St, Kensington, London W14 8QH (01–603–2070)
—— Sunley Buildings, Piccadilly Plaza, Manchester M1 4BA (061–236–2171)
—— Stanegate House, 2 Groat Market, Newcastle-upon-Tyne NE1 1YN (063–247722)
—— Northern Ireland Director of Commerce, Chichester House, 64 Chichester St, Belfast (232–34488)
—— Severns House, 20 Middle Pavement, Nottingham NG1 7DW (0602–56181)
—— Market Place House, Reading, Berkshire RG1 2BN (0734–581261)
—— Scottish Economic Planning Dept, Alhambra House, 45 Waterloo St, Glasgow G2 6AT (041–248–2855)
—— Welsh Office, Government Buildings, Gabalfa, Cardiff CF4 4YL (0222–62131)
Department of Industry Regional Development Grants Committee, Regional Development and Investment Grants Offices
—— 24–6 Newport Rd, Cardiff CF2 1SY (0222–492611)
—— Queensway House, West Precinct, Billingham, Cleveland TS23 2NF (0642–553671)
—— Magnet House, 59 Waterloo St, Glasgow G2 7BT (041–221–9833)
—— Room 2722, Millbank Tower, Millbank, London SW1P 4QU (01–211–5518)
—— St Peter's House, Stanley Precinct, Bootle, Merseyside L20 3LZ (051–922–4030)
Department of Industry Regional Offices
—— Ladywood House, Stephenson St, Birmingham B2 4DT (021–632–4111)
—— The Pithay, Bristol BS1 2PB (0272–291071)
—— Priestley House, Park Row, Leeds LS1 5LF (0532–443171)
—— Charles House, 375 Kensington High St, London W14 8QH (01–603–2060)
—— Sunley Building, Piccadilly Plaza, Manchester M1 4BA (061–236–217)
—— Stanegate House, 2 Groat Market, Newcastle-upon-Tyne NE1 1YN (0632 24722)
—— Severns House, 20 Middle Pavement, Nottingham NG1 7DW (0602 50181)
Department of Industry Small Firms Information Centres
—— 53 Stephenson St, Birmingham B2 4DH (021–643–3344)
—— Colston Centre, Colston Ave, Bristol BS1 4UB (0272–294546)
—— 16 St David's House, Wood St, Cardiff CF1 1ER (0222–396116)
—— 57 Bothwell St, Glasgow G2 6TU (041–248–6014)
—— Royal Exchange House, Boar Lane, Leeds LS1 5NS (0532–445151)
—— 1 Old Hall St, Liverpool L3 9HT (051–236–5756)
—— 65 Buckingham Palace Rd, London SW1W 0QX (01–828–2384)
—— 35 Wellington St, Luton LU1 2SB (0582–29215)
—— Peter House, Oxford St, Manchester M1 5AN (061–832–5282)
—— 22 Newgate Shopping Centre, Newcastle-upon-Tyne NE1 5RH (0632–25353)
—— 48–50 Maid Marian Way, Nottingham NG1 6GF (0602–49791)
Department of Industry, Statistics, 1 Victoria St, London SW1H 0ET (01–215–7877) (capital expenditure statistics – 01–215–5705; insurance statistics – 01–215–5538; wholesale price indices – 01–215–3157)
Department of Industry Technology Reports Centre, Station Square House, St Mary Cray, Orpington, Kent BR9 3RF
Department of Prices and Consumer Protection, Millbank Tower, London SW1P 4QU (01–211–3000)
Department of the Registers of Scotland, Meadowbank House, 153 London Rd, Edinburgh EH8 7AU
Department of Trade Headquarters
—— (1) 1 Victoria St, London SW1H 0ET (01–215–7877)
—— (2) Sanctuary Buildings, 16–20 Great Smith St, London SW1P 3DB (01–215–7877)
—— (3) Export House, 50 Ludgate Hill, London EC4M 7HU (01–248–5757)
—— (4) Hillgate House, 26 Old Bailey, London EC4M 7HU (01–248–5757)
—— (5) Gavrelle House, 2–14 Bunhill Row, London EC1Y 8LL (01–606–4071)
Department of Trade Accidents Investigation Branch, Shell Mex House, Strand, London WC2R 0DP (01–217–3000)

Department of Trade, Companies Administration Division, 1 Victoria St, London SW1H 0ET (01-215-7877)
Department of Trade Export Services and Promotions Division, Export House, 50 Ludgate Hill, London EC4M 7HU (01-248-5757)
Department of Trade Import Licensing Branch, Charles House, 375 Kensington High St, London W14 8QH (01-603-4644)
Department of Trade Industrial Property and Copyright Department, 25 Southampton Buildings, London WC2A 1AY (01-405-8721)
Department of Trade—local Mercantile Marine Offices
—— 41¼ Union Street, Aberdeen AB1 2BN
—— Post Office Buildings, Avonmouth Rd, Avonmouth, Bristol BS11 9EX
—— Custom House, Belfast, BT1 3ET
—— 3 Bute Pl., Cardiff CF1 6ND
—— Snargate St, Dover CT17 9BZ
—— Imperial Buildings, Bar Rd, Falmouth, Cornwall
—— Clive House, 3 India St, Glasgow G2 4PW
—— Murray Street, Grimsby, Humberside
—— Posterngate, Hull HU1 2LW
—— 38 Museum St, Ipswich IP1 1JQ
—— 1 John's Pl., Leith, Edinburgh EH6 7EL
—— Graeme House, Derby Sq., Liverpool L2 7SH
—— 18 Ensign St, London E1 8LJ
—— 12-16 Woodlands Rd, Middlesbrough TS1 3BE
—— Ground Floor, Jubilee Buildings, Upper Hill St, Milford Haven SA78 3LY
—— Phoenix House, Notte St, Plymouth, Devon PL1 2HF
—— Canute Rd, Southampton SO9 3ST
—— 25 Market Pl., South Shields, NE33 1JH
—— Pier St, Swansea, SA1 1SP
—— Tilbury House, Calcutta Rd, Tilbury RM18 7NA
Department of Trade Marine Division, Sunley House, 90-3 High Holborn, London WC1V 6LP (01-405-6911)
Department of Trade Marine Library, Sunley House, 90-3 High Holborn, London WC1V 6LP (01-405-6911)
Department of Trade Official Receivers' Offices
—— Commercial Union House, Martineau Sq, Birmingham B2 4UP (021-236-8631)
—— Burlington Arcade, Bournemouth BH1 2JS (0202-28208)
—— West Riding House, Cheapside, Bradford BD1 4LJ (0274-33651)
—— Windsor House (East Entrance), 30-5 Edward St, Brighton BN2 2JZ (0273-64301, 688265)
—— Sun Alliance House, 4 Colston Ave, Bristol BS1 4BN (0272-290268)
—— 49 Bateman St, Cambridge CB2 1LT (0223-58911)
—— Lombard House, 12-17 Upper Bridge St, Canterbury CT1 2NQ (0227-62070, 65037)
—— 3rd Floor, Hayes House, The Hayes, Cardiff CF1 2UG (0222-30575)
—— Dee Hills Park, Chester CH3 5AR (0244-21471/2)
—— Park House, 22 Park St, Croydon CR9 1TX (01-681-2633)
—— Eastgate House, High St, Exeter EX4 3JU (0392-36886)
—— Grosvenor House, Station Rd, Gloucester GL1 1ST (0452-21658/9)
—— Beverley House, St Stephens Sq, Hull HU1 3XF (0482-23720, 23729)
—— St Clare House, Greyfriars, Ipswich IP1 1LX (0473-56731)
—— Pearl Chambers, East Parade, Leeds LS1 5BX (0532-448851)
—— Prospect House, 94 Regent Rd, Leicester LE1 7DE (0533-22251/3)
—— West Africa House, 25 Water St, Liverpool L2 0RQ (051-236-9131)
—— Petros House, St Andrews Rd North, Lytham St Annes FY8 2JD (0253-721271)
—— 3rd Floor, 4 St Nicholas Buildings, St Nicholas St, Newcastle-upon-Tyne NE1 1RF (0632-21104)
—— 90 Abington St, Northampton NN1 2BX (0604-37288)
—— Davey House, Castle Meadow, Norwich NOR 02D (0603-28983)
—— 1 Collin St, Nottingham NG1 7EP (10602-51596)
—— 63 New George St, Plymouth PL1 1RD (0752-68554)
—— PO Box No. 40, Monarch House, 75-9 Caversham Rd, Reading RG1 8AW (0734-581931)

Department of Trade Official Receivers' Offices—*cont.*
—— Gordon House, Star Hill, Rochester (0634–42603, 46906)
—— Townbury House, 11 Blackfriars St, Salford M3 5AB (061–832–2471)
—— 8–12 Furnival Gate, The Moor, Sheffield S1 4QN (0742–26691)
—— Western Range, 83–5 London Rd, Southampton SO9 1NQ (0703–23348/9, 23340)
—— 2nd Floor, Colman House, 61 Victoria Ave, Southend-on-Sea SS2 6EF (0702–41316)
—— 4 Bridge Rd, Stockton-on-Tees, Teesside TS18 3BP (0642–65598)
—— London House, Hide St, Stoke-on-Trent ST4 1QN (0732–45256)
—— 5th Floor, Sun Alliance Building, 166–7 St Helen's Rd, Swansea SA1 5DL (0792–42861)
—— 40 Clarendon Rd, Watford WD1 1HJ (0923–44288)
—— Bankruptcy (London), Thomas More Building, Royal Courts of Justice, Strand, London WC2A 2JY (01–405–7641)
—— Companies Winding-up (London), Atlantic House, Holborn Viaduct, London EC1N 2HD (01–583–8931)
Department of Trade Statistics, 1 Victoria St, London SW1H 0ET (01–215–7877) (Hire purchase statistics – 01–215–3162; retail trade statistics – 01–215–3220; Tourism statistics – 01–215–3164)
Department of Transport Headquarters, 2 Mersham St, London SW1
Department of Transport Driver and Vehicle Licensing Centre, Longview Road, Morriston, Swansea SA6 7JL (0792–782341)
Department of Transport Goods Vehicle Centre, 91–2 The Strand, Swansea SA1 2DH
Department of Transport Information Division, 2 Marsham St, London SW1P 3 EB (01–212–3434)
Department of Transport International Road Freight Office, 36–42 Low Friar St, Newcastle-upon-Tyne (0632–610031)
Department of Transport Map Library, 27–9 Albert Embankment, London SE1 7TF
Department of Transport Regional Offices
—— East Midlands, Cranbrook House, Cranbrook St, Nottingham NG1 1FB (0602–46121)
—— Eastern, Charles House, 375 Kensington High St, London W14 8QH (01–603–3444)
—— North West, Sunley Building, Piccadilly Plaza, Manchester M1 4BE (061–832–9111)
—— Northern, Wellbar House, Gallowgate, Newcastle-upon-Tyne NE1 4TD (0632–27575)
—— South Eastern, Charles House, 375 Kensington High St, London W14 8QH (01–603–3444)
—— South West, Froomsgate House, Rupert St, Bristol BS1 2QN (0272–297201)
—— West Midlands, Five Ways House, Islington Row, Middleway, Birmingham B15 1SR (021–643–8191)
—— Yorkshire and Humberside, City House, Leeds LS1 4JD (0532–38232)
Department of Transport Register of Approved Driving Instructors, 2 Marsham St, London SW1P 3EB (01–212–3434)
Department of Transport Road Construction Units
—— Fortman House, 59–63 Goldington Rd, Bedford MK40 (0234–63161)
—— Federated House, London Rd, Dorking, Surrey RH4 (0306–5922)
—— Windsor House, Cornwall Rd, Harrogate, North Yorks HG1 2PW (0423–68903)
—— Brandon House, 52–4 Holly Walk, Leamington Spa, Warwickshire CV32 4JE (0926–27041)
—— Crystal House, Birley St, Preston PR1 2AQ (0772–54701)
—— Victoria House, 26b Fore St, Taunton, Somerset (0823–85151)
Department of Transport Traffic Area Offices
—— Greyfriars House, Gallowgate, Aberdeen AB9 2ZS (0224–23411)
—— Cumberland House, 200 Broad St, Birmingham B15 1T9 (021–643–5011)
—— The Gaunts House, Denmark St, Bristol BS1 5DR (0272–297221)
—— Terrington House, 13–15 Hills Rd, Cambridge CB2 1NP (0223–58922)
—— Caradog House, 1–6 St Andrew's Place, Cardiff CF1 3PW (0222–24801/8)
—— Ivy House, 3 Ivy Terrace, Eastbourne, East Sussex BN4 QP (0323–21471)
—— 24 Torphichen St, Edinburgh EH5 8HD (031–229–9166)
—— Hillcrest House, 386 Harchills Lane, Leeds LS9 6NF (0532–38144)
—— Government Buildings, Bromyard Ave, Acton, London W3 7AY
—— Arkwright House, Parsonage Gardens, Deansgate, Manchester M60 9AN (061–832–8644)
—— Low Friar House, 36–42 Low Friar St, Newcastle-upon-Tyne NE1 5XR (0632–610031)
—— Birkbeck House, 14–16 Trinity Sq, Nottingham NG1 4BA (0602–45511)
Design Centres
—— Design Centre, 28 Haymarket, London SW1Y 4SU (01–839–8000)

Design Centres—*cont.*
—— Scottish Design Centre, 72 St Vincent St, Glasgow G2 5TN (041–222–6121)
—— Cardiff Design Council Centre, Pearl Assurance Building, Greyfriars Rd, Cardiff
Design Council, 28 Haymarket, London SW1Y 4SU (01–839–8000)
Development Board for Rural Wales, Ladywell House, Newtown, Powys SY16 1JB (0686–26965)
Development Commission, 11 Cowley St, London SW1P 3WA (01–222–9134)
Director General of Fair Trading, Field House, Bream's Buildings, London EC4A 1PR (01–242–2858)
Director of Public Prosecutions, 4–12 Queen Anne's Gate, London SW1H 9AZ (01–930–2188)
Disabled Living Foundation, 346 Kensington High St, London W14 8NS (01–602–2491)
District councils – see text article on local authorities
District Valuer, Office of the Chief Valuer
—— England and Wales, New Court, Carey St, London WC2A 2JE
—— Scotland, 43 Rose St, Edinburgh EH2 2NJ
Domestic Coal Consumers' Council, Thames House South, Millbank, London SW1P 4QJ (01–211–5820)
Dominican Republic, Embassy of the, 4 Braemar Mansions, Cornwall Gardens, London SW7 4AG (01–937–1921)
Downtown Radio, PO Box 293, Newtonwards, Co Down, Northern Ireland (0247–815555)
Duchy of Cornwall, 10 Buckingham Gate, London SW1 (01–834–7346)
Duchy of Lancaster, Lancaster Place, London WC2 (01–836–8277)
Duke of Edinburgh's Award, International Head Office, 5 Prince of Wales Terrace, London W8 5PG (01–937–5205)
Duke of Edinburgh's Award Regional Offices
—— 4 Abbey St, Bath BA1 1NH (0225–64141)
—— 55 Lisburn Road, Belfast BT9 7GS (0232–667123)
—— 81 High St, Bromley, Kent BR1 1JY (01–464–4273)
—— 9 Cathedral Rd, Cardiff CF1 9HA (0222–28570)
—— 10 Palmerston Place, Edinburgh EH12 5AA (031–225–2658)
—— Voluntary Organisations Centre, 263 Queensway, Bletchley, Milton Keynes, Bucks MK2 2BZ (0908–75874)
—— 14 Junction Lane, Burscough, Nr Ormskirk, Lancashire (070–489–3743)
—— Edinburgh House, Bagot St, Abbots Bromley, Rugeley, Staffs (0283–840279)
—— c/o Richardsons Westgarth & Co. Ltd, Wallsend, Tyne and Wear NE28 6QL (0632–625306)
Dyers Company, Dyers Hall, Dowgate Hill, London EC4 (01–236–7197)

E

East Anglian Examinations Board, The Lindens, Lexden Rd, Colchester, Essex CO3 3RL (0206–71244)
East Midlands Regional Examinations Board, Robins Wood House, Robins Wood Rd, Aspley, Nottingham NG8 3NH (0602–295367)
East of Scotland College of Agriculture, School of Agriculture, West Mains Rd, Edinburgh EH9 3JG (031–667–1041)
Ecuador, Embassy of, 3 Hans Crescent, London SW1X 0LS (01–584–1367)
Education and Library Boards, Northern Ireland
—— Belfast, 40 Academy St, Belfast BT1 2NQ (0232–29211)
—— North Eastern, County Hall, 182 Galgorm Rd, Ballymena, Co Antrim BT42 1HN (0266–3333)
—— South Eastern, 18 Windsor Ave, Belfast BT6 9EF (0232–661188)
—— Southern, 3 Charlemont Place, The Mall, Armagh (0861–523811)
—— Western, Headquarters Office, 1 Hospital Rd, Omagh BT79 0AW (0662–2611, 0662–44431)
EEC Information Unit, Department of Industry, 1 Victoria St, London SW1H 0ET (01–215–4301)
Eggs Authority, Union House, Eridge Rd, Tunbridge Wells, Kent TN4 8HF (0892–33987)
Egyptian Embassy, Embassy of the Arab Republic of Egypt, 26 South St, London W1Y 6DD (01–499–2401)
Eire Volleyball Association, 3 Ennafort Rd, Raheny, Dublin 5, Eire

El Salvador, Embassy of, 16 Edinburgh House, 98 Portland Place, London W1N 3AA (01–636–9563/4)
Electricity Boards
—— East Midlands: PO Box, North PDO, 398 Coppice Rd, Arnold, Nottingham NG5 7HX (0602–269711)
—— Eastern: PO Box 40, Wherstead, Ipswich, Suffolk IP9 2AQ (0473–55841)
—— London: 46 New Broad St, London EC2M 1LS (01–588–1280)
—— Merseyside and North Wales: Head Office, Sealand Rd, Chester CF1 4LR (0244–40133)
—— Midlands: PO Box 8, Mucklow Hill, Halesowen, West Midlands B62 8BP (021–422–4000)
—— North Eastern: PO Box 1 SE, Carliol House, Newcastle-upon-Tyne NE99 1SE (0632–27520)
—— North Western: Cheetwood Rd, Manchester M8 8BA (061–834–8161)
—— South Eastern: 10 Queen's Gardens, Hove, Sussex BN5 2LS (0273–739211)
—— South Western: Electricity House, Colston Ave., Bristol BS1 4TS (0272–26062)
—— Southern: Southern Electriticy House, Littlewick Green, Maidenhead, Berks SL6 3QB (0628082–2166)
—— Yorkshire: Wetherby Rd, Scarcroft, Leeds LS14 3HS (0532–892–123)
Electricity Consultative Council – address from your Electricity Board showroom or under electricity in local telephone directory
Electricity showrooms – see under electricity in the local telephone directory, or apply to the Electricity Board
Embassy of Sultanate of Oman, 64 Ennismore Gdns, London SW7 1NH (01–584–6782)
Employment Appeal Tribunal, 4 St James's Sq, London SW1 (01–214–6000)
Employment Office – look under Employment Service Agency Employment Offices in local telephone directory
Employment Service Agency, Head Office, 7 St Martin's Place, London WC2N 4JH (01–930–7833)
Employment Service Agency – for local offices (most queries) look in telephone directory under Employment Service Agency
Employment Service Agency Employment Offices – look in telephone directory under Employment Service Agency
Employment Service Agency Jobcentres – for local offices look in telephone directory under Employment Service Agency
Employment Service Agency Occupational Guidance Units – look in telephone directory under Employment Service Agency
Employment Service Agency, Professional and Executive Recuitment, Head Office, 4 Grosvenor Place, London SW1X 7SB
Engineers Registration Board, 2 Little Smith St, London SW1P 3DL (01–799–39124)
English Basket Ball Association, Calomax House, Lupton Ave, Leeds 9 (0532–496044)
English Bowling Association, 4 Lansdowne Crescent, Bournemouth BH1 1RX (0202–22233)
English Bowling Federation, 5 Milton St, Ipswich IP4 4PP (0473–75259)
English Curling Association, 233 Black Bull Lane, Fulwood, Preston (0772–718126)
English Folk Dance and Song Society, Cecil Sharp House, 2 Regents Park Rd, London NW1 7AY (01–485–2206)
English Golf Union, 12A Denmark St, Wokingham, Berkshire RG11 2BE (0734–781952)
English Indoor Bowling Association, 730 Romford Rd, London E12 (01–553–5539)
English Lacrosse Union, 64 Broad Walk, Hockley, Essex SS5 5DF (037–04–6415)
English Lawn Tennis and Croquet Club, Church Rd, London SW19 5AE (01–946–2244)
English Olympic Wrestling Association, 2 Huxley Drive, Bramhall, Cheshire (061–439–5749)
English Regional Liberal Parties
—— Devon and Cornwall: Tremethick, St Martin, Looe, Cornwall PL13 1PB (050–34–333)
—— East Midlands: 82 Burlington Rd, Sherwood, Nottingham NG5 2GS (0602–605327)
—— Eastern Region: Sheridan House, 4 Glisson Rd, Cambridge (0223–56935)
—— Greater Manchester: 3rd Floor, Danlee Buildings, 53 Spring Gardens, Manchester M2 2BY (061–236–8807)
—— Home Counties: 2A Station Rd, Egham, Surrey (389–7744)
—— London: 53 Victoria St, London SW1H 0EU (01–799–2263)
—— Merseyside: 59 Forefield Lane, Gt Crosby, Liverpool L23 9TQ (051–924–6853)
—— North Western: 98 Skeffington Rd, Preston, Lancs (0772–59684)
—— Northern Counties: 27 Earlswood Avenue, Low Fell, Gateshead NE9 6AH (0632–878782)
—— West Midlands: 31–33 Essex St, Birmingham 5 (021–622–2414)

English Regional Liberal Parties—*cont.*
—— Western Counties: 127 Mendip Road, Yatton, Avon BS19 4EX (0934–833504)
—— Yorkshire and Humberside: 15 Queen Sq, Leeds 2 (0532–452396)
English Table Tennis Association, 21 Claremont, Hastings, E Sussex TN34 1HA (0424–433121)
English Tourist Board, 4 Grosvenor Gardens, London SW1W 0DU (01–730–3400)
English Volleyball Association, 128 Melton Rd, West Bridgford, Nottingham NG2 6EP (0602–812669)
English Women's Bowling Association, 22 Bloomfield Park, Bath, Avon (0225–312560)
English Women's Bowling Federation, Devonia, 305 Dogsthrope Rd, Peterborough (0733–240336)
English Women's Indoor Bowling Association, 1 Whitehaven, Bayleys Caravan Park, Lent Rise, Burnham, Bucks (062–86–63687)
Entertainment Agents Association, 18 Charing Cross Rd, London WC2 (01–240–1724)
Equal Opportunities Commission, Overseas House, Quay St, Manchester M3 3HN (061–833–9244)
Equal Opportunities Commission for Northern Ireland, Lindsay House, Gallender St, Belfast BT1 5DT (0232–42752)
Ethiopia, Embassy of the Provisional Military Government of, 17 Prince's Gate, London SW7 1PZ (01–589–7212)
European Broadcasting Union, 1 Rue de Varembe, CH 1211, Geneva 20, Switzerland
European Coal and Steel Community, 20 Kensington Palace Gdns, London W8 (01–727–8090)
European Commission – see Commission of the European Communities
European Commission of Human Rights, Council of Europe, 67006 Strasbourg Cedex, France
European Council of Ministers, 170 rue de la Loi, 1040 Brussels (Brussels 736–7900)
European Court of Human Rights (Enquiries in UK), 25A St John's Wood High St, London NW8 7NH (01–722–3066)
European Court of Justice – see Court of Justice of the European Communities
European Investment Bank, 2 Place de Metz, Luxembourg
European Parliament, Centre Européen, Plateau de Kirchberg, PO Box 1601, Luxembourg (Luxembourg 43001)
European Patent Office, Motorama House, 8000 Munich 80, Rosenheimer Str 30/11 (010–4989–41211)
Export Credits Guarantee Department, Head Office, Aldermanbury House, Aldermanbury, London EC2P 2EL (01–606–6699)
Export Credits Guarantee Department Regional Offices
—— River House, High St, Belfast BT1 2BE (0232–31743)
—— Colmore Centre, 115 Colmore Row, Birmingham B3 3SB (021–233–1771)
—— 1 Redcliffe St, Bristol BS1 6NP (0272–299971)
—— 72–80 Hills Rd, Cambridge CB2 1NJ (0223–68801)
—— 320 Purley Way, Croydon, Surrey CR9 4HL (01–686–9921)
—— Fleming House, 134 Renfrew St, Glasgow G3 6TL (041–332–8707)
—— West Riding House, 67 Albion St, Leeds LS1 5AA (0532–450631)
—— Waverley House, 7–12 Noel St, London W1V 3PB (01–437–2292)
—— 593–9 High Rd, Tottenham, London N17 6SW (01–808–4570)
—— Elizabeth House, St Peter's Sq, Manchester M2 4AJ (061–228–3621)
Export Liaison Managers, Export Liaison Unit, South East Wing, Bush House, The Strand, WC2 B4PH (01–240–3456)

F

Faculty of Actuaries, 23 St Andrew Sq, Edinburgh EH12 1AQ
Faculty of Advocates, Advocates' Library, Parliament House, Edinburgh EH1 1RF (031–226–5071)
Faculty of Architects and Surveyors, 68 Gloucester Pl, London W1 (01–935–9966)
Fair Employment Agency, Lindsay House, Callender St, Belfast 1 (0232–42752)
Family Practitioner Committees – look in telephone directory either under Family Practitioner Committee or under the name of the area health authority; or ask at Department of Health and Social Security local office, or a principal post office
Family Welfare Association, 501–5 Kingsland Rd, Dalston, London E8 4AU

Federation of Alcoholics Residential Establishments (FARE), 45 Great Peter St, London SW1P 3LT
Federation of British Carpet Manufacturers, Dorland House, 14–16 Lower Regent St, London SW1Y 4PL (01–930–8711)
Federation of British Craft Societies, 80a Southampton Row, London WC1 (01–242–2209)
Federation of Commodity Associations, Plantation House, Mincing Lane, London EC3M 3HT (01–626–1745)
Federation of Insurance Brokers, 1 Queen Victoria Rd, Coventry CV1 3JG (0203–21999)
Federation of Oils, Seeds and Fats Associations, 24 St Mary Axe, London EC3A 8ER (01–283–5511)
Federation of Zoological Gardens of Great Britain and Ireland, Zoological Gardens, Regent's Park, London NW1 4RY (01–722–3333)
Fellowship Party Head Office, Woolacombe House, 141 Woolacombe Rd, London SE3 (01–856–6249)
Fiji High Commission, 34 Hyde Park Gate, London SW7 5DN (01–584–3661)
Financial Times, Bracken House, Cannon St, London EC4
Finnish Embassy, 38 Chesham Place, London SW1X 8HW (01–235–9531)
Finnish Travel Information Centre, Finland House, 56 Haymarket, London SW1 (01–839–4048)
Fircroft College, Selly Oak, Birmingham (021–472–0116)
Fleet Air Arm Museum, Royal Naval Air Station, Yeovilton, Somerset (Ilchester 551)
Food and Agriculture Organisation of the United Nations, Via delle Terme di Caracalla, 00100 Rome, Italy
Football Association, 16 Lancaster Gate, London W2 3LW (01–262–4542)
Football Association of Wales, 3 Fairy Rd, Wrexham, Clwyd (0978–2425)
Football League Ltd, Lytham St Annes, Lancashire FY8 1JG (0253–729421)
Footwear Distributors' Federation, 69 Cannon St, London EC4N 5AB (01–248–4444)
Foreign and Commonwealth Office
—— Headquarters, Downing St (West), London SW1A 2AH (01–233–3000)
—— Aircraft Accidents, Clive House, Petty France, London SW1 9HD (01–213–3666)
—— Claims Department, Charles House, 5–11 Regent St, London SW1Y 4LU (01–214–6000)
—— Consular Department, Clive House, Petty France, London SW1H 9HD (01–213–3000)
—— Nationality and Treaty Dept, Clive House, Petty France, London SW1H 9HD (01–213–3000)
Foreign Compensation Commission, Alexandra House, Kingway, London WC2B 6TT (01–836–0701)
Foreign Exchange and Currency Deposit Bankers' Association, Butler (International) Ltd, Adelaide House, London Bridge, London EC4R 9BU
Forestry Commission, Headquarters, 231 Corstorphine Rd, Edinburgh EH12 7AT (031–334–0303)
Forestry Commission, Conservator of Forests
—— 6 Queen's Gate, Aberdeen AB9 2NQ (0224–33361)
—— Victoria House, Victoria Terrace, Aberystwyth SY23 2DA (097–2367)
—— Flowers Hill, Brislington, Bristol BS4 5JY (027–27–78311)
—— Block D, Government Buildings, Brooklands Ave, Cambridge CB2 2DY (0223–54495)
—— Churchill House, Churchill Way, Cardiff CF1 4TU (0222–40661)
—— Dee Hills Park, Chester CH3 5AT (0244–24006)
—— Greystone Park, 55–57 Moffat Rd, Dumfries DG1 1NP (0387–2425)
—— Portcullis House, 21 India St, Glasgow G2 4PL (041–248–3931)
—— 21 Church St, Inverness IV1 1EL (0463–32811)
—— The Queen's House, Lyndhurst, Hants SO4 7NH (042–128–2801)
—— 1A Grosvenor Terrace, York YO3 7BD (0904–24684)
Forestry Commission, Publications Branch, Alice Holt Lodge, Wrecclesham, Farnham, Surrey (04204–2255)
Fregata Travel Ltd, 100 Dean St, London W1
Freight Transport Association, Hermes House, St John's Rd, Tunbridge Wells, Kent TN4 9UZ (0892–26171)
French Commercial Section, Canada House, 3 Chepstow St, Mahcnester M1
French Consular Agent's Office, 4 Church St, Folkestone CT20 2AR
French Consulates
—— 4 Wellington Park, Belfast BT9 6JD
—— 129 Queen St, Cardiff (0222–22742)
—— 2 Westway Chambers, 39 Don St, St Helier, Jersey (CEN 21741)

French Consulates-General
—— 27 Regent Terrace, Edinburgh 7 (031–556–6266)
—— Cunard Building, Pier Head, Liverpool 3 1ET
French Embassy, 58 Knightsbridge, London SW1X 7JT (01–235–8080)
French Government Tourist Office, 178 Piccadilly, London W1 (01–493–3171/6)
Further Education Information Service, Room 531, Elizabeth House, York Rd, London SE1 7PH (01–928–9222)
Fylde International Sand Yacht Club, 10 Chatsworth Rd, St Annes, Lytham St Annes, Lancs

G

Gabitas-Thring, Educational Trust Ltd, Advisory Service, 6 Sackville St, London W1 (01–734–0161)
Gabon, Embassy of the Republic of, 48 Kensington Court, London W8 5DB (01–937–5285)
Gaelic Athletic Association, Ulster Branch, Ballybay, Co Monaghan (Ballybay 84)
GAFTA Soya Bean Meal Futures Association, c/o Grain and Feed Trade Association, Baltic Exchange Chambers, 24/28 St Mary Axe, London EC3A 8EP (01–283–5146)
Gambian Consulate-General, (Hon), 4 Claremont Terrace, Glasgow G3 TXR (041–332–2474)
Gambian High Commission, 60 Ennismore Gardens, London SW7 1NH (01–584–1242)
Gaming Board of Great Britain, Berkshire House, High Holborn, London WC1 (01–240–0821)
Gas regions – see British Gas Corporation Regions
Gas Service Centre – look under gas in local telephone directory
Gas showrooms – look under gas in local telephone directory
Gdynia–America Shipping Lines, 104 Great Portland St, London W1
General Council and Register of Osteopaths Ltd, 16 Buckingham Gate, London SW1E 6LB (01–828–0601)
General Council of British Shipping, 30 St Mary Axe, London EC3 (01–283–2922)
General Dental Council, 37 Wimpole St, London W1M FDQ (01–486–2171)
General Medical Council, 44 Hallam St, London W1N 6AE (01–580–7642)
General Nursing Council for England and Wales, 23 Portland Pl., London W1A 1BA (01–580–8334)
General Nursing Council for Scotland, 5 Darnaway St, Edinburgh EE3 6DP
General Optical Council, 41 Harley St, London W1N 2DJ (01–580–3898)
General Register Office, St Catherine's House, 10 Kingsway, London WC2B 6JP (01–242–0262)
General Register Office, Belfast, Oxford House, 49–55 Chichester St, Belfast BT1 4HL (0232–35211)
General Register Office, Dublin, Registrar General, Custom House, Dublin 1 (Dublin 742961)
General Register Office, Scotland, New Register House, Edinburgh EH1 3YT
General Register Office, Adopted Children's Register, PO Box 7, Titchfield, Fareham, Hants PO15 5RU
German Democratic Republic, Embassy of the, 34 Belgrave Sq, London SW1X 8QB (01–235–9941)
German Federal Republic Consulates-General
—— 16 Eglinton Crescent, Edinburgh EH12 5DG (031–337–2323)
—— Norwich House, 8–12 Water St, Liverpool L2 8TA
German Federal Republic, Embassy of the, 23 Belgrave Sq, London SW1X 8PZ (01–235–5033)
German Tourist Information Bureau, 61 Conduit St, London W1 (01–734–2600)
Ghanaian High Commission, 13 Belgrave Sq, London SW1X 8PR (01–235–4142)
Gibraltar Tourist Office, 15 Grand Buildings, Trafalgar Sq, London WC2 (01–930–2284)
GLC District Surveyor – look in telephone directory under Greater London Council district surveyors
Golden Gate Park, San Francisco, Cal. 94122, USA
Golf Development Council, London Scottish Golf Club, Windmill Enclosure, Wimbledon Common, London SW19 5NQ (01–789–7517)
Golf Foundation, Allington House, 136–42 Victoria St, London SW1E 5LD
Golfing Union of Ireland, (Ulster Branch), 33 Victoria Ave, Newtownards, Co Down (0247–3345)
Good Housekeeping Institute, Chestergate House, Vauxhall Bridge Rd, London SW1V 1HF (01–834–2331)
Governing Bodies Association, 27 Church Rd, Steep, Petersfield, Hants (0730–4823)
Governing Bodies of Girls' Schools Association, 27 Church Rd, Steep, Petersfield, Hants (0730–4823)
Government Bookshops
—— 80 Chichester St, Belfast BT1 4JY
—— 258 Broad St, Birmingham B1 2HE

Government Bookshops—*cont.*
——— Southery House, Wine St, Bristol BS1 2BQ
——— 41 The Hayes, Cardiff CF1 1JW
——— 13A Castle St, Edinburgh EH2 3AR
——— PO Box 569, London SE1 9NH (01–928–1321) (trade and London mail order)
——— 49 High Holborn, London WC1V 6HB (callers only)
——— Brazenose St, Manchester M60 8AS
Governor and Commander-in-Chief, Government House, Hamilton, Bermuda (2–3600)
Grain and Feed Trade Association, Baltic Exchange Chambers, 24–28 St Mary Axe, London EC3A 8EP (01–283–5146)
Grampian Television Ltd, Queen's Cross, Aberdeen AB9 2XJ (0224–53553)
Granada Television Ltd, Granada Television Centre, Manchester M60 9EA (061–832–7211)
Grand National Archery Society, National Agricultural Centre, Stoneleigh, Kenilworth, Warwickshire CV8 2LZ (0203–23907)
Great Britain Hockey Board, 70 Brompton Rd, London SW3 1HB (01–584–2584)
Greater London Council, County Hall, London SE1 (01–633–5000)
Greater London Council Valuation Panel, Valuation Department, Central Office, County Hall, London SE1 (01–633–5000)
Greek Embassy, 1A Holland Park, London W11 3TP (01–727–8040)
Greek State Tourist Office, 195 Regent St, London W1 (01–734–5997)
Grenada, High Commission for, King's House, 10 Haymarket, London SW1Y 4DA (01–930–7902)
Guatemala, Embassy of, 73 Rue de Courcelles, Paris 8 France (227–78–63)
Guild of Air Pilots and Air Navigators, PO Box 13, Air Terminal, Buckingham Palace Rd, London SW1W 9SR (01–730–0471)
Guildhall Library, Guildhall, London EC2 (01–606–3030)
Guinea, Embassy of the Republic of, 62 Boulevard de Courcelles, BP 578, 75 Paris, 17eme (766–54–98, 766–55–19)
Guinea, Visa Office of the Republic of, Via Luigi Luciani 41, 00197 Rome, Italy (872007/804 505)
Gunmakers (Worshipful Company of), Proof House, 48 Commercial Rd, London E1 (01–481–2695)
Guyana, High Commission for, 3 Palace Court, Bayswater, London W2 4LP (01–229–7684)

H

Haiti, Embassy of the Republic of, 17 Queen's Gate, London SW7 5EU (01–581–0577)
Hambros Ltd, Head Office, 41 Bishopsgate, London EC2 (01–588–2851)
Hants and Dorset Amateur Rowing Association, Wardsworth, 14 Yeovil Close, Bitterne, Southampton
Harlech Television Ltd, Television Centre, Cardiff CF1 9XL (0222–21021)
Head Postmaster – his address is your nearest Principal Post Office, which is listed in local telephone directory under Post Office Services, Principal Post Offices
Head Post Offices – addresses available from Principal Post Offices which are listed under Post Office Services in local telephone directory
Headmasters' Conference (Incorporated), 29 Gordon Sq, London WC1H 0PS (01–388–1765)
Health and Safety Commission, Regina House, 259–69 Old Marylebone Rd, London NW1 5RR (01–723–1262)
Health and Safety Executive, Head Office, Baynards House, 1–13 Chepstow Place, London W2 4TF (01–229–3456)
Health and Safety Executive, Employment Medical Advisory Service
——— Head Office, Baynards House, 1–13 Chepstow Place, London W2 4TF (01–229–3456)
——— Regional Offices
    Eastern and South East Midlands, 4 Dunstable Rd, Luton, Beds LU1 1SX (0582–415722)
    London and South Eastern, Farringdon St, London EC4A 4BA (01–583–5020)
    North Eastern, 8 St Paul's St, Leeds LS1 2LE (0532–446191)
    North Western, Quay House, Quay St, Manchester M3 3JE (061–831–7111)

Health and Safety Executive, Employment Medical Advisory Service—Regional Offices—*cont.*
  Northern, Government Buildings, Kenton Bar, Newcastle-upon-Tyne NE1 2YN (0632–863411)
  Scotland, Meadowbank House, London Rd, Edinburgh EW8 7AU (031–661–6171)
  South Western, Beacon Tower, Fishponds Rd, Bristol BS16 3HA (0272–659573)
  Wales, St Davids House, Wood St, Cardiff CF1 1PB (0222–43984)
  West Midlands, Auchinleck House (5th Floor), Broad St, Birmingham B15 1DL (021–643–8441)
Health and Safety Executive, Health and Safety Centre, 97 Horseferry Rd, London SW1 (01–828–9255)
Health and Safety Executive, HM Agricultural Inspectorate
  —— Head Office, Eagle House, 90–6 Cannon St, London EC4N 6HT (01–623–4266)
  —— Regional Offices
    Tufton House, Tufton St, Ashford, Kent TN23 1RJ (0223–24658)
    Priestley House, Priestley Rd, Basingstoke RG24 9NW (0256–3181)
    Somerset House, 37 Temple St, Birmingham B2 5DT (021–643–3752, 021–632–6781)
    The Triad, Stanley Rd, Bootle L20 3PG (051–922–7211)
    Government Buildings, Burghill Rd, Westbury on Trym, Bristol BS10 6NJ (0272–50000)
    Brunel House, 2 Fitzalan Rd, Cardiff CF2 1SH (0222–497777)
    39–43 Baddow Rd, Chelmsford CM2 0HL (0245–84661)
    Meadowbank House, 153 London Rd, Edinburgh EH8 7AU (031–661–6171)
    314 St Vincent St, Glasgow G3 8XG (041–204–2646)
    Festival House, Jameson Rd, Hull HU1 3JR (0482–223487)
    8 St Paul's St, Leeds LS1 2LE (0532–446191)
    King House, George St West, Luton LU1 2DD (0582–34121)
    Government Building, Kenton Bar, Newcastle-upon-Tyne NE1 2YX (0632–869811)
    Government Building, Gladstone Rd, Northampton NN5 7QC (0604–52388)
    Birkbeck House, Trinity Sq, Nottingham NG1 4AU (0602–45511)
    Victoria House, Ormskirk Rd, Preston PR1 1HH (0772–59321)
    4 College Precincts, Worcester WR1 2LG
Health and Safety Executive HM Alkali and Clean Air Inspectorate,
  —— Main Office, Queen Anne's Chambers, 28 Broadway, London SW1H 9JU (01–273–3000)
  —— Regional Offices
    Priestley House, Basingstoke RC24 9NW (0256–3181)
    Government Buildings, Hamilton Rd, Cambridge CB4 1BS (0223–63287)
    Portcullis House, 21 Crowbridge Rd East, Cardiff CF1 9AZ (0222–388531)
    1 Hamilton Place, Chester CH1 2BH (0244–40939)
    Vincent House, 2 Woodland Rd, Darlington DL3 7PJ (0325–52177)
    3 Cable St, Lancaster LA1 1HE (0524–67583)
    5 North Hill Rd, Headingly, Leeds BS6 2XA (0532–759303)
    Mill House, Brayford Side North, Lincoln LN1 1YW (0522–54180)
    Quay House, Quay St, Manchester M3 3JB (061–831–7111)
    118a Banner Cross Rd, Sheffield S11 9HR (0742–35600)
    3rd Floor, Greyfriars House, Stafford (0785–54180)
    51 Vessey Rd, Sutton Coldfield, Warwickshire B73 5NR (021–354–9102)
    Spur 19, Government Buildings, Forest Road, Hawkenbury, Tunbridge Wells, Kent (0892–30347)
    Union House, High St, Weston-super-Mare (0934–20218)
    Charteris House, 2 Charteris Rd, Woodford, Essex (01–505–5226)
Health and Safety Executive HM Explosives Inspectorate, Baynards House, 1 Chepstow Place, London W2 4TF (01–229–3456)
Health and Safety Executive HM Factory Inspectorate
  —— Consultant Sections, 25 Chapel St, London NW1 5DT (01–262–3277)
  —— Area Offices
    East Anglia, 39–43 Baddow Rd, Chelmsford, Essex CM2 0HL (0245–84661)
    East Midlands, Belgrave House, 1 Greyfriars, Northampton NN1 2LQ (0604–2133)
    Greater Manchester, Quay House, Quay St, Manchester M3 3JE (061–831–7111)
    London Northeast Area, Royal London House, 18 Finsbury Sq, London EC2A 1DH (01–638–2841)

Health and Safety Executive HM Factory Inspectorate—Area Office—*cont.*
    London Northwest Area, Chancel House, Neasden Lane, London NW10 2UD (01–459–8844)
    London South, Wedge House, 36 Blackfriars Rd, London SE1 8PD (01–928–1374)
    The Marches, Norwich Union House, 40 Trinity St, Hanley, Stoke-on-Trent ST1 5LJ (0782–263492)
    Merseyside, The Triad, Stanley Rd, Bootle L20 3PG (051–922–7211)
    North East, Government Buildings, Kenton Bar, Newcastle-upon-Tyne NE1 2XY (0632–869811)
    North Midlands, Birkbeck House, Trinity Sq, Nottingham NG1 4AU (0602–45511)
    North West, Victoria House, Ormskirk Rd, Preston, Lancs (0772–59321)
    Northern Home Counties, King House, George St West, Luton, Beds LU1 2DD (0582–34121)
    Scotland East, Meadowbank House, London Rd, Edinburgh EH8 7AU (031–661–6171)
    Scotland West, Royal Exchange Assurance House, 314 St Vincent St, Glasgow G3 8AX (041–204–2646)
    South Area, Priestley House, Priestley Rd, Basingstoke RG24 9NW (0256–3181)
    South East Area, Paymaster General's Buildings, Russell Way, Three Bridges, Crawley, Sussex RH10 1UH (0293–511671)
    South West, Inter-city House, Victoria St, Bristol
    South Yorkshire and Humberside, Sovereign House, 40 Silver St, Sheffield S1 2ES (0742–739081)
    Wales, Brunel House, 5 Fitzalan Rd, Cardiff CF2 1SH (0222–497777)
    West and North Yorkshire, 8 St Paul's St, Leeds LS1 2LE (0532–446191)
    West Midlands, Somerset House, 37 Temple St, Birmingham B2 5DT (021–643–3752)
Health and Safety Executive HM Mines and Quarries Inspectorate, Regina House, 259–69 Old Marylebone Rd, London NE1 5RR (01–723–1262)
Health and Safety Executive HM Nuclear Installations Inspectorate, Thames House North, Millbank, London SW1P 4QL (01–211–3000)
Health and Social Services Boards – see Area Health and Social Services Boards, Northern Ireland
Health Board – look under Health Boards in local Scottish telephone directory
Health Education Council, 78 New Oxford St, London WC1A 1AH
Health Service Commissioner for England, Church House, Great Smith St, London SW1P 3BW (01–212–6271)
Health Service Commissioner for Scotland, 71 George St, Edinburgh EH2 3EE (031–225–7465)
Health Service Commissioner for Wales, 3rd Floor, Queens Court, Plymouth St, Cardiff CF1 4DA (0222–394621)
Hearing Aids Council, 40a Ludgate Hill, London EC4M 7DE (01–992–4320)
Heather Society, Yew Trees, Horley Row, Horley, Surrey RH6 8DF
Heathrow Airport, Hounslow, Middx TW6 1JH (01–759–4321)
Henley Royal Regatta, Regatta Headquarters, Henley-on-Thames, Oxon RG9 2LY (049–12–2153)
Her Majesty's Coastguard Service, Head Offices, Department of Trade, Sunley House, 90 High Holborn, London WC1 (01–405–6911)
Her Majesty's Coastguard Service, Regional Offices
—— Doverstrait, Deal, Kent (03045–61872)
—— South East, Shoreham-by-Sea, Sussex (07917–3882)
—— South, Brixham, Devon (08045–2191)
—— South West, St Ives, Cornwall (073670–5953)
—— East, Pier Gardens, Gorleston-on-Sea, Norfolk (0493–61432)
—— West, Mumbles, Swansea, Glamorgan (0792–68472)
—— North East, Tynemouth, North Shields, Northumberland (08945–70621)
—— North West, Formby, Liverpool L37 2HL (07048–72586)
—— East Scotland, 10 Linics Rd, Bridge of Don, Aberdeen (0224–702599)
—— West Scotland and N. Ireland, Bangor, Co. Down (0247–3069)
—— North Scotland, Wick, Caithness (02277–0955)
Her Majesty's Customs and Excise, King's Beam House, Mark Lane, London EC3R 7HE (01–626–1515)
Her Majesty's Customs and Excise Betting Duty Control Collections,
—— 21 India St, Glasgow G2 4PZ (041–221–3828)
—— Trafford Road, Salford M5 2RD (061–872–4282)

Her Majesty's Customs and Excise Chief Registrar of British Ships, Custom House, Lower Thames St, London EC3 R6EE (01–283–8633)
Her Majesty's Customs and Excise Collectors – look under Customs and Excise Collectors' Offices in local telephone directory
Her Majesty's Customs and Excise GCC4, Kent House, Upper Ground, London SE1 9PS
Her Majesty's Customs and Excise local offices – look under Customs and Excise in your local telephone directory
Her Majesty's Customs and Excise Statistics, Statistical Office, Portcullis House, 27 Victoria Ave, Southend-on-Sea SS2 6AL (0702–49421)
Her Majesty's Land Registry, Lincoln's Inn Fields, London WC2A 3PH (01–405–3488)
Her Majesty's Land Registry District Land Registries
—— Birmingham and West Midlands, Bruton Way, Gloucester GL1 1DQ (0452–28666)
—— Greater London (East) and East Anglia, Brickdale House, Danestrete, Stevenage, Herts SG1 1XG (0438–4488)
—— Greater London (North), Lyon House, Lyon Rd, Harrow, Middlesex HA1 2EU (01–427–8811)
—— Greater London (South), Sunley House, Bedford Park, Croydon CR9 3LE
—— Greater Manchester and the North West, Lytham St Annes, Lancs FY8 5AB (0253–736999)
—— North East, Aykley Heads, Durham DH1 5TR (0385–61361)
—— South East, Tunbridge Wells, Kent TN2 5AQ (0892–26141)
—— Wales and adjoining English counties, 37 The Kingsway, Swansea SA1 5LF (0792–50971)
—— West and South Yorkshire and East Midlands, Chalfont Drive, Nottingham NG8 3RN (0602–291111)
—— West Country, Railway Offices, North Rd, Plymouth PL4 6AD (0752–69381)
Her Majesty's Land Registry Land Charges Department, Burrington Way, Plymouth PL5 3LP (0752–779831)
Her Majesty's Stationery Office, Headquarters, Atlantic House, Holborn Viaduct, London EC1P 1BN (01–583–9876)
Her Majesty's Stationery Office, government bookshops
—— 80 Chichester St, Belfast BT1 4JY
—— 258 Broad St, Birmingham B1 2HE
—— Southery House, Wine St, Bristol BS1 2BQ
—— 41 The Hayes, Cardiff CF1 1JW
—— 13a Castle St, Edinburgh EH2 3AR
—— PO Box 569, London SE1 9NH (01–928–1321)
—— 49 High Holborn, London WC1V 6HB
—— Brazenose St, Manchester M60 8AS
Her Majesty's Treasury, Parliament St, London SW1P 3AG (01–233–3000)
Her Majesty's Treasury, Dividends Section, Parliament St, London SW1P 3AG (01–233–8752/7984/5900)
Herring Industry Board, Sea Fisheries House, 10 Young St, Edinburgh EH2 4JQ (031–225–2515)
High Court, The Strand, London WC1 (01–405–7641)
Highway Authority – for address contact your local authority
Hillcroft College, Southbank, Surbiton (01–399–2688)
Historic Buildings Councils
—— Historic Buildings Council for England, 25 Saville Row, London W1X 2BT (01–734–6010)
—— Historic Buildings Council for Wales, Welsh Office, Summit House, Windsor Place, Cardiff
—— Historic Buildings Council for Scotland, Argyle House, Edinburgh 3
Historic Monuments Centre, 36 Parliament St, Whitehall (01–839–7596)
HM Customs and Excise Collections – see Her Majesty's Customs and Excise Collectors
Hockey Association, 70 Brompton Rd, London SW3 1HB (01–584–2584)
Holiday Fellowship, Fellowship House, 142 Great North Way, London NW4 1EG (01–203–3381)
Home Grown Cereals Authority, Hamlyn House, Highgate Hill, London N19 5PR (01–263–3391)
Home Office, 50 Queen Anne's Gate, London SW1H 9AT (01–213–3000)
Home Office Broadcasting Department, 50 Queen Anne's Gate, London SW1H 9AT (01–213–3000)
Home Office Immigration and Nationality Department, Lunar House, Wellesley Rd, Croydon (01–686–0688)
Home Office Probation and After Care Department, 50 Queen Anne's Gate, London SW1H 9AT (01–213–3000)

Home Office Radio Regulatory Department, Waterloo Bridge House, Waterloo Rd, London SE1 8UA
Home Office Statistics, Tolworth Tower, Surbiton, Surrey KT6 7DS (01–399–5191 ex 298)
Home Secretary, Home Office, Whitehall, London SW1A 2AP (01–213–3000)
Honduras, Embassy of, 48 George St, London W1H 5RF (01–486–3380)
Hong Kong Government Office, 6 Grafton St, London W1X 3LB (01–499–9821)
Honorable Society of Cymmrodorion, 118 Newgate St, London EC1 (01–606–0840)
Hops Marketing Board, 61 Maidstone Rd, Paddock Wood, Tonbridge, Kent (089–283–3415)
Horserace Betting Levy Board, 17–23 Southampton Row, London WC2 (01–405–5346)
Horserace Totalisator Board, Tote House, New Bridge St, London EC4 (01–353–1066)
House of Commons, London SW1A 0AA (01–219–3000)
House of Lords, London SW1A 0PW (01–219–3000); Black Rod's Office (01–219–3100); Information Office (01–219–3107); Record Office (01–219–3074)
Houses of Parliament, Westminster, London SW1 (01–219–3000)
Housewife's Trust, 3 Sloane Terrace Mansions, London SW1X 9DG (01–730–2055)
Housing Corporation, 159 Tottenham Court Rd, London W1 (01–386–9466)
Hungarian Embassy, 35 Eaton Place, London SW1X 8BY (01–235 7191, 4048)
Hungarian Tourist Office 'Ibusz', 46 Eaton Place, London SW1 (01–235–8767)

I

Icelandic Embassy, 1 Eaton Terrace, London SW1W 8EY (01–730–5131)
Icelandic Tourist Information Bureau, 73 Grosvenor St, London W1 (01–499–9971)
Incorporated Association of Architects and Surveyors, 29 Belgrave Sq, London SW1 (01–235–3755)
Incorporated Association of Preparatory Schools, 138 Kensington High St, London W8 4BN (01–727–2316)
Incorporated Law Society of Northern Ireland, Royal Courts of Justice (Ulster), Chichester St, Belfast BT1 3JZ (0232–31614)
Incorporated Society of Valuers and Auctioneers, 3 Cadogan Gate, London SW1X 0AS (01–235–2282)
Independent Broadcasting Authority, 70 Brompton Rd, London SW3 1EY (01–584–7011)
Independent Broadcasting Authority Complaints Review Board, 70 Brompton Rd, London SW3 1EY (01–584–7011)
Independent Local Radio Programme Companies
—— Beacon Radio, PO Box 303, Wolverhampton WV6 0DQ (0902–757211)
—— BRMB Radio (Birmingham Broadcasting), Radio House, PO Box 555, Birmingham B6 4BX (021–359–4481)
—— Capital Radio, Euston Tower, London NW1 3DR (01–388–1288)
—— Downtown Radio, PO Box 293, Newtownards, Co. Down, Northern Ireland (0247–815555)
—— London Broadcasting Company, Communications House, Gough Sq, London EC4P 4LP (01–353–1010)
—— Metro Radio, Newcastle-upon-Tyne NE99 1BB (0632 884121)
—— Pennine Radio, PO Box 235, Pennine House, Forster Sq, Bradford BD1 5NP (0274–31521)
—— Piccadilly Radio, 127–131 The Piazza, Piccadilly Plaza, Manchester M1 4AW (061–236–9913)
—— Plymouth Sound, Earl's Acre, Alma Road, Plymouth PL3 4HX (0752–27272)
—— Radio City (Sound of Merseyside) Ltd, PO Box 194, 8–10 Stanley Street, Liverpool L69 1LD (051–227–5100)
—— Radio Clyde, Ranken House, Blythswood Court, Anderston Cross Centre, Glasgow G2 7LB (041–204–2555)
—— Radio Forth, Forth House, Forth Street, Edinburgh EH1 3LF (031–556–9255)
—— Radio Hallam, PO Box 194, Hartshead, Sheffield S1 1GP (0742–71188)
—— Radio Orwell, Electric House, Lloyds Avenue, Ipswich IP1 3HU (0473–216971)
—— Radio Tees, 74 Dovecot Street, Stockton-on-Tees (0642–615111)
—— Radio Trent, 29–31 Castle Gate, Nottingham NG1 7AP (0602–581731)
—— Radio Victory, PO Box 257, Portsmouth PO1 5RT (0705–27799)
—— Swansea Sound, Victoria Rd, Gowerton, Swansea SA4 3AB (0792–893751)

Independent Local Radio Programme Companies—cont.
—— Thames Valley Broadcasting, PO Box 210, Reading RG3 5RZ (0734–413131)
Independent Schools Information Service, 47 Victoria St, London SW1H 0EQ (01–222–7274)
Independent Television Companies Association, 52 Mortimer St, London W1N 8AN (01–636–6866)
Independent Television News Ltd (ITN), ITN House, 48 Wells St, London W1P 4DE (01–637–2424)
Independent Television Programme Companies
—— Anglia Television Ltd, Anglia House, Norwich NR1 3JG (0603–28366)
—— Associated Television Network Ltd, ATV Centre, Birmingham B1 2JP (021–643–9898)
—— Border Television Ltd, The Television Centre, Carlisle CA1 3NT (0228–25101)
—— Channel Television, The Television Centre, Rouge Bouillon, St Helier, Jersey, CI (0534–23451)
—— Grampian Television Ltd, Queen's Cross, Aberdeen AB9 2XJ (0224–53553)
—— Granada Television Ltd, Granada Television Centre, Manchester M60 9EA (061–832–7211)
—— Harlech Television Ltd, The Television Centre, Cardiff CF1 9XL (0222–21021)
—— London Weekend Television Ltd, South Bank Television Centre, Kent House, Upper Ground, London SE1 9LT (01–261–3434)
—— Scottish Television Ltd, Cowcaddens, Glasgow G2 3PB (041–332–9999)
—— Southern Television Ltd, Southern Television Centre, Northam, Southampton SO9 4YQ (0703–28582)
—— Thames Television Ltd, Thames Television House, 306–316 Euston Road, London NW1 3BB (01–387–9494)
—— Tyne Tees Television Ltd, The Television Centre, City Road, Newcastle-upon-Tyne NE1 2AL (0632–610181)
—— Ulster Television Ltd, Havelock House, Ormeau Road, Belfast BT7 1EB (0232 28122)
—— Westward Television Ltd, Derry's Cross, Plymouth, Devon PL1 2SP (0752–69311)
—— Yorkshire Television Ltd, The Television Centre, Leeds LS3 1JS (0532–38283)
India Office Library and Records, Orbit House, Blackfriars Rd, London SE1 (01–928–9531)
Indian Agricultural Research Institute, New Delhi 12, India
Indian High Commission, India House, Aldwych, London WC2 4NA (01–836–8484)
Indian Assistant High Commissioner's Offices
—— 86 New St, Birmingham 2 (021–643–0366)
—— Jaegar House (6th Floor), 62 Buchanan St, Glasgow G1 3JE (041–221–2801)
—— 4 Rodney St, Liverpool 1 (051–709–6630)
Indonesian Embassy, 38 Grosvenor Sq, London W1X 9AD (01–499–7661)
Industrial Commercial Finance Corporation, 91 Waterloo Rd, London SE1 8XP (01–928–7822)
Industrial Property and Copyright Department, 25 Southampton Buildings, Chancery Lane, London WC2A 1AY
Industrial Training Boards
—— Agricultural, Bourne House, 34 Beckenham House, Beckenham, Kent BR3 4PB (01–650–4890)
—— Air Transport and Travel, Staines House, 158 High St, Staines, Middx TW18 4AS (81–57171)
—— British Gas Corporation, Education and Training, 5 Grosvenor Crescent, London SW1 7EE (01–245–9651)
—— Carpet, Evelyn House, 32 Alderley Rd, Wilmslow, Cheshire SK9 1NX (099–64–27118)
—— Ceramics, Glass and Mineral Products, Bovis House, Northolt Rd, Harrow, Middx HA2 0EF (01–422–7101)
—— Chemical and Allied Products, Staines House, 158 High St, Middx TW18 4AT (81–51366)
—— Clothing and Allied Products, Tower House, Merrion Way, Leeds LS2 8NY (0532–41331)
—— Construction, Radnor House, London Rd, Norbury, London SW16 4EL (01–764–5060)
—— Cotton and Allied Textiles, 10th Floor, Sunlight House, Quay St, Manchester M3 3LH (061–832–9656)
—— Distributive, MacLaren House, Talbot Rd, Stretford, Manchester M32 0FP (061–872–2494)
—— Electricity Supply Industry Training Committee, 30 Millbank, London SW1P 4RD (01–834–2333)
—— Engineering, St Martin's House, 140 Tottenham Court Rd, London W1P 9LN (01–387–0501)
—— Food, Drink and Tobacco, Barton House, Barton St, Gloucester GL1 1QQ (0452–28621)
—— Footwear, Leather and Fur Skin, Maney Building, 29 Birmingham Rd, Sutton Coldfield, Warwick B72 1QE (021–355–3511)
—— Foundry Industry Training Committee, 50 Charlotte St, London W1P 2EL (01–580–0341)

Industrial Training Boards—*cont.*
—— Furniture and Timber, 31 Octagon Parade, High Wycombe, Bucks HP11 2JA (0494–32751)
—— Hotel and Catering, Ramsey House, Central Sq, Wembley, Middx HA9 7AP (01–902–8865)
—— Iron and Steel, 4 Little Essex St, London WC2R 3LR (01–240–2044)
—— Knitting, Lace and Net, 4 Hamilton Rd, Nottingham NG5 1AU (0602–61075)
—— Local Government, 8 The Arndale Centre, Luton, Beds LU1 2TS (0582–211111)
—— Man-made Fibres Producing, 3 Pond Place, London SW3 6QR (01–589–9008)
—— Merchant Navy, 146 Minories, London EC3N 1ND (01–481–8131)
—— National Water Council Training, Tadley Court, Tadley Common Rd, Tadley, Nr Basingstoke, Hants RG26 6TB (07356–3011)
—— Paper and Paper Products, Star House, Potters Bar, Herts EN6 2PG (77–50211)
—— Petroleum, York House, Empire Way, Wembley, Middx HA9 0PT (01–903–4161)
—— Printing and Publishing, Merit House, Edgware Rd, London NW9 5AG (01–205–0162)
—— Road Transport, Capital House, Empire Way, Wembley, Middx HA9 0NG (01–902–8880)
—— Rubber and Plastics Processing, Brent House, 950 Great West Rd, Brentford, Middx TW8 9ES (01–568–0731)
—— Shipbuilding, Raebarn House, Northolt Rd, South Harrow, Middx HA2 0DR (01–422–9581)
—— Wool, Jute and Flax, Butterfield House, Otley Rd, Baildon, Shipley, West Yorks ED17 7HE (0274–595511)
Industrial Tribunals' Central Offices
—— England and Wales, 93 Ebury Bridge Rd, London SW1 (01–730–9161)
—— Northern Ireland, 1 Shaftesbury Sq, Belfast BT2 7DD
—— Scotland, Saint Andrew House, 141 West Nile St, Glasgow G1 2RU (041–331–1601)
Industrial Tribunals' Regional Offices
—— Ashford, Tufton House, Tufton Street, Ashford, Kent TN23 1RJ (0233–21346)
—— Birmingham, Phoenix House, 1–3 Newhall St, Birmingham B3 3NH (021–236–6051)
—— Bristol, Prince House, 43–51 Prince St, Bristol BS1 4PE
—— Bury St Edmunds, 118 Northgate St, Bury St Edmunds, Suffolk IP33 1HQ
—— Cardiff, Caradog House, 1–6 St Andrews Place, Cardiff CF1 3BE (0222–372693)
—— Edinburgh, 11 Melville Crescent, Edinburgh 3 (031–226–5584)
—— Exeter, 10th Floor, Renslade House, Bonhay Rd, Exeter EX4 3BX (0392–79665)
—— Leeds, Minerva House, East Parade, Leeds LS1 5JZ (0532–459741)
—— Liverpool, No. 1 Union Court, Cook St, Liverpool L2 4UJ (051–236–9397)
—— London North, 19–29 Woburn Place, London WC1H 0LU (01–632–4921)
—— London South, 93 Ebury Bridge Rd, London SW1W 8RE (01–730–9161)
—— Manchester, Alexandra House, 14–22 The Parsonage, Manchester M3 2JA (061–833–0581)
—— Newcastle-upon-Tyne, Watson House (3rd Floor), Pilgrim St, Newcastle-upon-Tyne NE1 6RE (0632–28865)
—— Nottingham, 7th Floor, Birkbeck House, Trinity Sq, Nottingham (0602–45701)
—— Sheffield, Fargate Court (1st Floor), Fargate, Sheffield S1 2HD (0742–70348)
—— Southampton, 149A High St, Southampton (0703–31236)
Inland Revenue Headquarters, Somerset House, Strand, London WC2 (01–438–6622)
Inland Revenue Capital Taxes Offices
—— Law Court Buildings, Chichester St, Belfast BT1 3NU (0232–3511)
—— 47 Robbs Lane, Edinburgh EH14 1TX (031–443–8861)
—— Minford House, Rockley Rd, London W14 0DF (01–603–4622)
—— Lynwood Road, Thames Ditton, Surrey KT7 0EB (01–398–4242)
Inland Revenue Development Land Tax Office, Corporation House, 73–5 Albert Rd, Middlesbrough, Cleveland TS1 2RY (0642–241144)
Inland Revenue HM Collector of Taxes – for local office look under Inland Revenue, Taxes, Collectors of, in local telephone directory
Inland Revenue HM Inspector of Taxes – for local office look under Inland Revenue, Taxes, HM Inspector of, in local telephone directory
Inland Revenue PAYE Enquiry Offices – look in telephone directory under Inland Revenue, HM Inspector of Taxes
Inland Revenue Stamp Offices
—— Head Office, The Controller of Stamps, Bush House, South West Wing, Strand, London WC2B 4QN (01–438–6622)

Inland Revenue Stamp Offices—*cont.*
—— Adjudication Section, Controller of Stamps (D), West Block, Barrington Road, Worthing, West Sussex BN12 4SF (0903–502525)
—— Direct Post Section, Controller of Stamps (D), West Block, Barrington Road, Worthing, West Sussex BN12 4SF (0903–502525)
—— Branch Offices
    London (City Office), 61 Moorgate, London EC2R 6BH (01–438–6658)
    London (Stock Exchange), 26 Austin Friars, London EC2N 2EH (01–438–6906, 6907)
    Law Courts Buildings, Chichester St, Belfast BT1 3JH (0232–35111)
    First Floor, Edmund House, 12–22 Newhall St, Birmingham B3 3DU (021–643–4411)
    First Floor, The Pithay, All Saints St, Bristol BS1 2NY (0272–291071)
    Companies House, Crown Way, Cardiff CF4 3UR (0222–388588)
    Controller of Stamps (Scotland), Lauriston House, 80 Lauriston Place, Edinburgh EH3 9SL (031–229–9344)
    Distributor of Stamps, Montrose House, 187 George St, Glasgow, G1 1YU (041–552–4455)
    Stamp Office, 42 Eastgate, Leeds LS2 7LD (0532–448211)
    Tower Building, Water Street, Liverpool L3 1AE (051–236–4313)
    Albert Bridge House, 1 Bridge Street, Manchester M60 9BT (061–832–8311)
    Room 222, Aidan House, All Saints Office Centre, Newcastle-upon-Tyne NE1 2BG (0632–611991)
    Lower Ground Floor, Lambert House, Talbot St, Nottingham NG1 5NN (0602–40111)
    Stamp Office, Revenue Buildings, 123 West Street, Sheffield S1 3SP (0742–26431)
Inland Revenue Valuation Offices – for local offices look under Inland Revenue, Valuation Offices, in local telephone directory
Inn of Court of Northern Ireland, Royal Courts of Justice, Belfast BT1 3JF (0232–35111)
Insolvency Service, Thomas More Buildings, Royal Courts of Justice, Strand, London WC2A 2JY (01–405–7641)
Inspector of Ancient Monuments
—— Government Buildings, St Agnes Road, Gabalfa, Cardiff CF4 4YF
—— Argyle House, 3 Lady Lawson St, Edinburgh EH3 9SD
—— 23 Saville Row, London W1X 2AA
Inspector of Taxes – see Inland Revenue, HM Inspector of Taxes
Institut fur Ziorflanzonbau der TU, 3 Hannover-Herrenhauson, Herrenhauser Strasse 2, West Germany
Institute of Actuaries, Staple Inn Hall, High Holborn, London WC1V 7QJ (01–242–0106)
Institute of Chartered Accountants in England and Wales, PO Box 433, Chartered Accountant's Hall, Moorgate Place, London EC2P 2BJ (01–628–7060)
Institute of Chartered Accountants in Ireland, 7 Fitzwilliam Place, Dublin 2, Ireland (0001–760401)
Institute of Chartered Accountants of Scotland, 27 Queen St, Edinburgh EH2 1LA (031–225–3687)
Institute of Chartered Shipbrokers, 23 Bury St, London EC3 (01–283–1361)
Institute of Continuing Education of the New University of Ulster, Magee University College, Londonderry, Northern Ireland (Londonderry 65621)
Institute of Cost and Management Accountants, 63 Portland Place, London W1N 4AB (01–637–2311)
Institute of Freight Forwarders, Suffield House, 9 Paradise Rd, Richmond, Surrey (01–948–3141)
Institute of Fuel, 18 Devonshire St, Portland Place, London W1N 2AU (01–580–7124)
Institute of Marine Engineers, 76 Mark Lane, London EC3R 7JN (01–481–8493)
Institute of Medical Laboratory Sciences, 12 Queen Anne St, London W1 (01–636–8192)
Institute of Practitioners in Advertising, 44 Belgrave Sq, London SW1X 8QS (01–235–7020)
Institute of Professional Legal Studies, Queen's University, Belfast BT7 1NN (0232–45133)
Institute of Psycho-Analysis, 63 New Cavendish St, London W1N 7RD (01–580–4952)
Institute of Registered Architects – amalgamated with Secretariat of Architects and Surveyors, 15 St Mary St, Chippenham, Wilts (0249–5539)
Institute of Trade Mark Agents, 69 Cannon St, London EC4N 5AB (01–248–4444)
Institute of Trichologists (Incorporated), 228 Stockwell Rd, Brixton, London SW9 9SU (01–733–2056)
Institution of Chemical Engineers, 165–71 Railway Terrace, Rugby CV21 3HQ (0788–78214)
Institution of Civil Engineers, Great George St, London SW1P 3AA (01–839–3611)
Institution of Electrical Engineers, Savoy Place, London WC2R 0BL (01–240–1871)

Institution of Electronic and Radio Engineers, 8–9 Bedford Sq, London WC1B 3RG (01–637–2771)
Institution of Engineering Designers Ltd, Courtleigh, Westbury Leigh, Westbury, Wiltshire (0373–822801)
Institution of Gas Engineers, 17 Grosvenor Crescent, London SW1X 7ES (01–245–9811)
Institution of Mechanical Engineers, 1 Birdcage Walk, London SW1H 9JJ (01–839–1211)
Institution of Mining Engineers, Hobart House, Grosvenor Place, London SW1X 7AE (01–235–3691)
Institution of Mining and Metallurgy, 44 Portland Place, London W1N 4BR (01–580–3802)
Institution of Municipal Engineers, 25 Eccleston Sq, London SW1V 1NX (01–834–5083)
Institution of Production Engineers, Rochester House, 66 Little Ealing Lane, London W5 4XX (01–579–9411)
Institution of Structural Engineers, 11 Upper Belgrave St, London SW1X 8BH (01–235–4537)
International Agents Association, 18 Charing Cross Rd, London WC2 (01–240–1724)
International Air Transport Association
—— 41 Dover St, London W1 (01–493–6502)
—— PO Box 550, Montreal, Quebec, Canada H3A 2R4 (514–844–6311)
—— 26 Chemin de Joinville, PO Box 160, 1216 Cointrin, Geneva, Switzerland
International Amateur Athletic Federation, 162 Upper Richmond Rd, London SW15 (01–789–3853)
International Astronomical Union, Observatoire de Geneve, CH 1290 Sauverny, Switzerland
International Camellia Society, Oldfield, Moorlands Rd, Verwood, Dorset
International Catholic Girls Society, 39 Victoria St, London SW1 (01–799–4588)
International Commission of Jurists, 109 Route de Chene, 1224 Chene-Bougeries, Geneva, Switzerland (Geneva 35–19–73)
International Commodities Clearing House, Roman Wall House, 1/2 Crutched Friars, London EC3N 1AN (01–488–3200)
International Cricket Conference, Lord's Cricket Ground, London NW8 8QN (01–289–1611)
International Defence and Aid Fund for Southern Africa, 104–5 Newgate St, London EC1A 7AP (01–606–6123)
International Poplar Commission, Via della Terme de Carcalla, 00100 Rome, Italy
International Professional Skating Association, 61 Godalming Ave, Wallington, Surrey SM6 8NP
International Social Service of Great Britain, 39 Brixton Rd, London SW9 (01–582–9802)
International Society for Horticultural Science, Ministry of Agriculture and Fisheries, Bezuidenhoutseweg 73, The Hague, Netherlands
International Squash Players, 21 Hillside Rd, Heswall, Merseyside (051–342–2654)
International Tanker Owners (Pollution) Federation Ltd, Plantation House, 31–5 Fenchurch St, London EC3 (01–623–9487)
International Voluntary Service, 91 High St, London NW10 (01–965–1446)
International Women's Cricket Council, 95 St George's Drive, Ickenham, Uxbridge, Middlesex (71–32361)
Inter-University Council for Higher Education Overseas, 90–1 Tottenham Court Rd, London W1P 0DT (01–580–6572)
Intervention Board for Agricultural Produce Head Offices
—— Steel House, Tothill St, London SW1 (01–273–4378)
—— Fountain House, 2 West Mall, Reading, Berkshire RG1 7QW (0734–583626)
Intervention Board for Agricultural Produce Branch Offices
—— Annexe B, Dundonald House, Upper Newtownards Rd, Belfast BT4 3TS (023–121–4577)
—— Room 03, Block 2, Government Buildings, St Agnes Rd, Gabalfa, Cardiff CF4 4YN (0222–62131)
—— Chesser House, 500 Gorgie Rd, Edinburgh EH11 3AW (031–443–4020)
Intourist, 292 Regent St, London W1 (01–580–4974)
Iranian Missions to UK
—— Imperial Iranian Embassy, 16 Prince's Gate, London SW7 1PX (01–937–5225)
—— Iranian Consulate-General, 7 Booth St, Manchester M2 4AB (061–832–8529)
Iraq, Embassy of the Republic of, 21–2 Queen's Gate, London SW7 5JG (01–584–7141)
Irish Amateur Boxing Association (Ulster Council), 85 Elmfield Rd, Glengormley, Newtownabbey (023–13–5521)
Irish Amateur Rowing Union
—— Headquarters, 20 Burdett Ave, Sandycove, Co Dublin (0001–802003)
—— Ulster Branch, 16 Ulsterville Ave, Belfast BT9 4AQ (0232–660929)

Irish Amateur Swimming Association
—— Headquarters, 6 Maywood Crescent, Dublin 5
—— Ulster Branch, 13 Knockbrida Park, Belfast BT6 0HB (0232–642312)
Irish Bowling Association, 131 Haypark Avenue, Belfast BT7 3FG (Belfast 643–644)
Irish Cricket Union (Ulster Branch), Northern Ireland Cricket Association, c/o Sports Council for Northern Ireland, 39 Malone Rd, Belfast 9 (0232–663154)
Irish Embassy, 17 Grosvenor Place, London SW1X 7HR (01–235–2171)
Irish Football Association Ltd, 20 Windsor Ave, Belfast (0232–669458)
Irish Hockey Union, 21 Chestnut Grove, Ballinteer, Dublin 14 (Dublin 687211)
Irish Ladies' Golf Union, Northern Executive, 97 Ballybarnes Rd, Newtownards, Co Down (0247–2096)
Irish Ladies' Hockey Union,
—— Headquarters, 53 Dargle Rd, Blackrock, Co Dublin
—— Ulster Branch, 141 Stockman's Lane, Belfast 9 (0232–668637)
Irish Lawn Tennis Association, Ulster Branch, 20 Beechdere Gardens, Lisburn, Co Antrim (084–62–78574)
Irish Olympic Handball Association, c/o McAuley, Physical Education Centre, Queens University, Botanic Park, Belfast 9 (0232–661111)
Irish Rugby Football Union
—— Headquarters, 62 Lansdowne Rd, Dublin 4 (0001 684601)
—— Ulster Branch, Ravenhill Park, Belfast BT6 0D6 (0232–649141)
Irish Squash Rackets Association, Ulster Branch, 69 Greystone Ave, Belfast BT9 6UH (0232–624114)
Irish Table Tennis Association, 4 Fairhill Gardens, Donegall Park Ave, Belfast BT15 4FZ (0648–2385)
Irish Tourist Office, Ireland House, 150 New Bond St, London W1 (01–493–3201)
Irish Women's Bowling Association, Ulster Branch, 27 Ulsterdale St, Belfast (0232–654812)
Irish Women's Indoor Bowling Association, 89 Hamilton Rd, Bangor, Co Down
Irish Women's Squash Rackets Association, Ulster Branch, 5 Moira Road, Hillsborough, Co Down (0846–682436)
Isle of Man Snooker Association, Ballaquiggin, Santon, Isle of Man
Israel Government Tourist Office, 69 St James's St, London SW1 (01–493–2431)
Israeli Embassy, 2 Palace Green, Kensington, London W8 4QB (01–937–8050)
Italian Consular Agent, 15 West Bute St, Cardiff CF1 6EP (0222–29887/8)
Italian Consulate, 79 Oxford St, Manchester (061–236–9024)
Italian Consulate-General, 6 Melville Crescent, Edinburgh EH3 7AJ (031–226–3631)
Italian Embassy, 14 Three King's Yard, Davies St, London W1Y 2EH (01–629–8200)
Italian State Tourist Department, (ENIT) 201 Regent St, London W1 (01–734–4631)
Italian Vice-Consulates
—— 23 Allhallows, Bedford (0234–56647/8)
—— 22 Park Circus, Glasgow G3 6BE (041–332–3563)
Ivory Coast, Embassy of the, 2 Upper Belgrave St, London SW1X 8BJ (01–235–6991)

J

Jamaican Consulates
—— Scala House, Holloway Circus, Birmingham 1 (021–643–1691)
—— Faulkner House, Faulkner St, Manchester 1 (061–236–5264)
Jamaican High Commission, 48 Grosvenor St, London W1X 0BJ (01–499–8600)
Japanese Embassy, 43–6 Grosvenor St, London W1X 0BA (01–493–6030)
Jersey Zoological Park, Les Augres Manor, Trinity, Jersey
Job Centres – look in local telephone directory under Employment Service Agency Jobcentres
Jockey Club, 42 Portman Sq, London W1H 0EN (01–486–4921)
Joint Matriculation Board, Manchester M15 6EU (061–273–2565)
Jordanian Embassy, Embassy of the Hashemite Kingdom of Jordan, 6 Upper Phillimore Gardens, London W8 7HE (01–937–3685)

Joseph Rowntree Memorial Trust, The Family Fund, Beverley House, Shipton Rd, York YO3 6RB (0904–29241)
Judge Advocate General of the Forces, 6 Spring Gdns, London SW1A 2BQ (01–218–5134)
Judicial Committee of the Privy Council, Downing St, London SW1 (01–233–3000)

K

Karolinska Institute, Faculty of Medicine, Fack, S–10401 Stockholm 60, Sweden
Keep Fit Association, 70 Brompton Rd, London SW3 1HE (01–584–3271)
Keep Fit Association of Northern Ireland, 17 Fairview Park, Dunmurry, Belfast (0232–610933)
Keep Fit Association of Wales, Wenallt, Woodville Place, Rhondda Road, Ferndale, Rhondda, Mid Glamorgan
Keith Prowse Ltd, 24 Store St, London WC1 (01–637–3131)
Kennel Club, 1 Clarges St, London W1Y 8AB (01–493–6651)
Kensington Palace, London W8 (01–930–3141 – Princess Margaret; 01–937–6374 – Princess Alice Duchess of Gloucester and the Duke and Duchess of Gloucester; 01–937–5514 – Prince Michael; 01–937–5868 – Princess Alice Countess of Athlone)
Kenyan High Commission, 45 Portland Place, London W1N 4AS (01–636–2371)
Korean Embassy, 5 Palace Gate, London W8 5NF (01–581–0247)
Kuwait, Embassy of the State of, 40 Devonshire St, London W1N 2AX (01–580–8471)

L

Laboratory of the Government Chemist, Cornwall House, Stamford St, London SE1 9NQ (01–928–7900)
Labour Party Headquarters, Transport House, Smith Sq, London SW1P 3JA (01–834–9434)
Lake District Special Planning Board, County Hall, Kendal, Cumbria (0539–24555)
Lambeth Palace Library, Lambeth Palace, Lambeth Palace Rd, London SE1 (01–928–6222)
Land Authority for Wales, Brunel House, Cardiff
Land Settlement Association Ltd, 43 Cromwell Rd, London SW7 2EE (01–589–9066)
Lands Tribunal, 5 Chancery Lane, London WC2 (01–831–6611)
Landscape Institute incorporating the Institute of Landscape Architects, 12 Carlton House Terrace, London SW1Y 5AH (01–839–4044)
Laotian Embassy, Embassy of the People's Democratic Republic of Laos, 5 Palace Green, Kensington, London W8 4QA (01–937–9519)
Law Centres – look in telephone directory either under Law Centre or under the name of your local authority
Law Commission, Conquest House, 37–8 John St, Theobalds Rd, London WC1N 2BQ (01–242–0861)
Law Officers, Law Officers Department, Royal Courts of Justice, London WC2A 2LL (01–405–7641)
Law Society, 113 Chancery Lane, London WC2A 1PL (01–242–1222)
Law Society of Scotland, Law Society's Hall, 26 Drumsheugh Gardens, Edinburgh EH3 7YR (031–226–7411)
Lawn Tennis Association, Barons Court, West Kensington, London W14 9EG (01–385–2366)
Lawn Tennis Umpires' Association of Great Britain, 82 Tattenham Way, Burgh Heath, Tadworth, Surrey KT20 5NQ (25–50904)
Lebanese Embassy, 21 Kensington Palace Gardens, London W8 4QM (01–229–7265)
Lesotho, High Commission for the Kingdom of, 16A St James's St (1st Floor), London SW1A 1EU (01–839–1154)
Levy Exemption Referees, 162–8 Regent St, London W1R 6DE (01–214–6000)
Liberal Party Organisation, 1 Whitehall Place, London SW1A 2HE (01–839–4092)
Liberian Embassy, 21 Prince's Gate, London SW7 1QB (01–589–9405)

Library Association, 7 Ridgmount St, London WC1E 7AE (01–636–7543)
Libyan Embassy, 58 Prince's Gate, London SW7 2BW (01–589–5235)
Life Offices' Association, Aldermary House, Queen St, London EC4 (01–248–4477)
Liverpool Cotton Association Ltd, 620 Cotton Exchange Buildings, Edmund St, Liverpool L3 9LH (051–236–6041)
Lloyds Bank Ltd, Head Office, 71 Lombard St, London EC3 (01–626–1500)
Lloyd's Insurance Brokers' Association, 3–4 Lime St, London EC3M 7DQ (01–623–4555)
Lloyd's of London, Lime Street, London EC3M 7HA (01–623–7100)
Lloyd's of London Press Ltd, Sheepen Rd, Colchester, Essex (0206–69222)
Lloyd's Publications and Shipping Intelligence, Lime Street, London EC3M 7HA (01–623–7100)
Lloyd's Register of Shipping, 71 Fenchurch St, London EC3M 4BS (01–709–9166)
Local authorities – Address in local telephone directory under authority's name or from public libraries or Citizens' Advice Bureaux; see also text item Local authorities
Local Authority Education Welfare Officer – contact local education authorities
Local Education Authorities
—— Avon, PO Box 57, Avon House North, St James Barton, Bristol BS99 7EB (0272–290777)
—— Bedfordshire, County Hall, Bedford MK42 9AP (0234–63222)
—— Berkshire, Kennet House, 80–2 Kings Rd, Reading RG1 3BL (0734–55981)
—— Buckinghamshire, County Hall, Aylesbury HP20 1UZ (0296–5000)
—— Cambridgeshire, Shire Hall, Castle Hill, Cambridge CB3 0AP (0223–58811)
—— Cheshire, County Hall, Chester CH1 1SQ (0244–602424)
—— Cleveland, Woodlands Rd, Middlesbrough, Cleveland TS1 3BN (0642–248155)
—— Clwyd, Education Department, Shire Hall, Mold CH7 6ND (0352–2121)
—— Cornwall, Education Department, County Hall, Truro TR1 3BA (0872–4282)
—— Cumbria, 5 Portland Sq, Carlisle CA1 1PU (0228–32161)
—— Derbyshire, County Offices, Matlock DE4 3AG (0629–3411)
—— Devon, County Hall, Exeter EX2 4QG (0392–77977)
—— Dorset, County Hall, Dorchester DT1 1XJ (0305–3131)
—— Durham, County Hall, Durham DH1 5UJ (0385–64411)
—— Dyfed, County Hall, Carmarthen SA31 1JP (0267–4251)
—— Essex, PO Box 47, Threadneedle House, Market Rd, Chelmsford CM1 1LD (0245–67222)
—— Glamorgan, Mid, County Hall, Cathays Park, Cardiff CF1 3NF (0222–28033)
—— Glamorgan, South, Kingsway, Cardiff CF1 4JG (0222–31033)
—— Glamorgan, West, Princess House, Princess Way, Swansea SA1 4PD (0792–42024)
—— Gloucestershire, Shire Hall, Gloucester GL1 2TP (0452–21444)
—— Guernsey, PO Box 32, La Couperderie, St Peter Port (0481–23535)
—— Gwent, County Hall, Cwmbran NP4 2XG (06333–67711)
—— Gwynedd, Castle St, Caernarvon LL55 1SD (0286–4121)
—— Hampshire, The Castle, Winchester SO23 8UG (0962–4411)
—— Hereford and Worcester, Castle St, Worcester WR1 3AG (0905–27131)
—— Hertfordshire, County Hall, Hertford SG13 8DF (32–54242)
—— Humberside, County Hall, Beverley HU17 9BA (Beverley 887131)
—— Isle of Man, Government Buildings, Bucks Rd, Douglas (0624–26262)
—— Isle of Wight, County Hall, Newport PO30 1UD (098–381–4031)
—— Isles of Scilly, Town Hall, St Mary's TR21 0LW (072–04–537)
—— Jersey, PO Box 142, Highlands, St Saviour (0534–71065)
—— Kent, Springfield, Maidstone ME14 2LJ (0622–54371)
—— Lancashire, PO Box 61, County Hall, Preston PR1 8RJ (0772–54868)
—— Leicestershire, County Hall, Glenfield, Leicester LE3 8RF (0533–871313)
—— Lincolnshire, County Offices, Lincoln LN1 1YQ (0522–29931)
—— London
    Barking, Town Hall, Barking, Essex IG11 7LU (01–594–3880)
    Barnet, Town Hall, Friern Barnet, London N11 3DL (01–368–1255)
    Bexley, Town Hall, Crayford, Kent DA1 4EN (Crayford 526290)
    Brent, PO Box 1, Chesterfield House, 9 Park Lane, Wembley, Middlesex NA9 7RW (01–903–1400)
    Bromley, Sunnymead, Bromley Lane, Chislehurst BR7 6LH (01–467–5561)
    Croydon, Taverner House, Park Lane, Croydon CR9 1TP (01–686–4433)
    Ealing, Hadley House, 79–81 Uxbridge Rd, London W5 5SU (01–579–2424)

Local Education Authorities—London—*cont.*
    Enfield, PO Box 56, Civic Centre, Enfield EN1 3XQ (01–366–6565)
    Haringey, Somerset Rd, Tottenham, London N17 9EH (01–808–4500)
    Harrow, Civic Centre, Harrow, Middlesex HA1 2UW (01–863–5611)
    Havering, Mercury House, Mercury Gdns, Romford RM1 3DR (Romford 66999)
    Hillingdon, Civic Centre, Uxbridge, Middlesex UB8 1UW (Uxbridge 50111)
    Hounslow, Civic Centre, Lampton Rd, Hounslow, Middlesex TW3 4DN (01–570–7728)
    Inner London, County Hall, London SE1 7PB (01–633–5000)
    Kingston-upon-Thames, Tolworth Tower, Surbiton, Surrey KT6 7EE (01–399–5111)
    Merton, Station House, London Rd, Morden, Surrey SM4 5DR (01–542–8101)
    Newham, Broadway, Stratford, London E15 4BH (01–534–4545)
    Redbridge, Lynton House, 255–259 High Rd, Ilford, Essex IG1 1NN (01–478–3020)
    Richmond-upon-Thames, Regal House, London Rd, Twickenham, Middlesex TW1 3QB (01–892–4466)
    Sutton, The Grove, Carshalton, Surrey SM5 3AL (01–669–4499)
    Waltham Forest, Municipal Offices, Leyton High Rd, Leyton, London E1 5QJ (01–539–3650)
—— Manchester
    Bolton, PO Box 53, Paderborn House, Civic Centre, Bolton BL1 1JW (0204–22311)
    Bury, Athenaeum House, Market St, Bury BL9 0BN (061–761–5121)
    Manchester, Crown Square, Manchester M60 3BB (061–228–2191)
    Oldham, Old Town Hall, Middleton Rd, Chadderton, Oldham, Lancashire CL9 1PP (061–633–2181)
    Rochdale, Municipal Offices, Manchester Old Rd, Middleton, Manchester M24 4EA (061–643–5541)
    Salford, Chapel St, Salford M3 5LT (061–832–9751/8)
    Stockport, Stopford House, Stockport SK1 3XE (061–480–4949)
    Tameside, Town Hall, Dukinfield, Cheshire SK16 4LA (061–330–8300)
    Trafford, Town Hall, Sale, Cheshire M33 1ZF (061–973–2253)
    Wigan, Civic Centre, Millgate, Wigan WN1 1YD (0942–44991)
—— Merseyside
    Knowsley, Huyton Hay Rd, Huyton, Merseyside L36 5IH (051–480–5111)
    Liverpool, 14 St Thomas St, Liverpool L1 6BJ (051–236–5480)
    St Helens, Century House, Hardshaw St, St Helens WA10 1RN (0744–24061)
    Sefton, Burlington House, Crosby Rd North, Waterloo, Liverpool L22 OL6 (051–928–6677)
    Wirral, Municipal Offices, Cleveland St, Birkenhead L41 6NH (051–647–7020)
—— Midlands, West
    Birmingham, Council House, Margaret St, Birmingham B3 3BU (021–235–9944)
    Coventry, New Council Offices, Earl St, Coventry CV1 5RS (0203–25555)
    Dudley, 2 St James's Rd, Dudley DY1 3JQ (0384–214311)
    Sandwell, Highfields, High St, West Bromwich B70 8RG (021–553–6541)
    Solihull, PO Box 20, Council House, Solihull B91 3QU (021–705–6789)
    Walsall, Civic Centre, Darwell St, Walsall WS1 1DQ (0922–21244)
    Wolverhampton, St John's Sq, Wolverhampton WV2 4DB (0902–27811)
—— Norfolk, County Hall, Norwich NR1 2DL (0603–611122)
—— Northamptonshire, Northampton House, Northampton NN1 2HX (0604–34833)
—— Northumberland, Eldon House, Regent Centre, Gosforth, Newcastle-upon-Tyne NE3 3HZ (0632–850181)
—— Nottinghamshire, County Hall, West Bridgford, Nottingham NG2 7QP (0602–863366)
—— Oxfordshire, Macclesfield House, New Rd, Oxford OX1 1NA (0865–722422)
—— Powys, County Hall, Llandrindod Wells LD1 5LE (0597–3711)
—— Salop, Shirehall, Abbey Foregate, Shrewsbury SY2 6ND (0743–222100)
—— Somerset, County Hall, Taunton TA1 4DY (0823–3451)
—— Staffordshire, Tipping St, Stafford ST16 2LB (0785–3121)
—— Suffolk, Grimwade St, Ipswich IP4 2JS (0473–55801)
—— Surrey, County Hall, Kingston-upon-Thames KT1 2DJ (01–546–1050)
—— Sussex, East, PO Box 4, County Hall, Lewes BN7 1SG (07916–5400)
—— Sussex, West, County Hall, West St, Chichester PO19 1RF (0243–85100)
—— Tyne and Wear
    Gateshead, Prince Consort Rd South, Gateshead NE8 4LP (0632–783031)

Local Education Authorities—Tyne and Wear—*cont.*
  Newcastle-upon-Tyne, Civic Centre, Barras Bridge, Newcastle-upon-Tyne NE1 8PU (0632–28520)
  North Tyneside, The Chase, North Shields, NE29 0HW (08945–76621)
  South Tyneside, Town Hall, Jarrow, NE32 3LE (0632–898271)
  Sunderland, Town Hall and Civic Centre, Sunderland SR2 7DN (0783–76161)
—— Warwickshire, 22 Northgate St, Warwick CV34 4SR (0926–43431)
—— Wiltshire, County Hall, Trowbridge BA14 8JB (022–14–3641)
—— Yorkshire, North, County Hall, Northallerton DL7 8AE (0609–3123)
—— Yorkshire, South
  Barnsley, 50 Huddersfield Rd, Barnsley S75 1DP (0226–87621)
  Doncaster, Education Dept, Princegate, Doncaster DN1 3EP (0302–4041)
  Rotherham, Municipal Offices, Howard St, Rotherham S60 1QR (0709–2121)
  Sheffield, PO Box 67, Leopold St, Sheffield S1 1RJ (0742–26341)
—— Yorkshire, West
  Bradford, Provincial House, Tyrrel St, Bradford BD1 1NP (0274–29477)
  Calderdale, Alexandra Buildings, King Edward St, Halifax HX1 1EB (0422–57133)
  Kirklees, Oldgate House, Oldgate, Huddersfield HD1 6QW (0484–37399)
  Leeds, Great George St, Leeds LS1 3AE (0532–35361)
  Wakefield, 8 Bond St, Wakefield WF1 2QL (0924–70211)
Local Enterprise Development Unit
—— Headquarters, Lamont House, Purdy's Lane, Belfast BT8 4TB (0232–691031)
—— Eastern, 21 Linenall St, Belfast BT2 8BS (0232–47241)
—— Northern, 17 The Diamond, Londonderry BT48 6HW (0504–67257)
—— Southern, 5 Downshire Place, Newry (0693–2955)
—— Western, 14E Mountjoy Rd, Omagh (0662–45763)
Local (Gaming) Licensing Authority – contact local authority
Local Government Boundary Commission for England, 20 Albert Embankment, London SE1 7TJ (01–211–3000)
Local Government Boundary Commission for Scotland, 26–7 Royal Terrace, Edinburgh EH7 5AH (031–557–1900)
Local Government Boundary Commission for Wales, Queen's Court, Plymouth St, Cardiff CF1 4DA (0222–395031)
Location of Offices Bureau, 27 Chancery Lane, London WC2A 1NS (01–405–2921)
London borough councils – look in London telephone directory under name of borough
London Broadcasting Company, Communications House, Gough Sq, London EC4P 4LP (01–353–1010)
London Chamber of Commerce and Industry, 69 Cannon St, London EC4N 5AB (01–248–4444)
London Cocoa Terminal Market Association, Cereal House, 58 Mark Lane, London EC3R 7NE (01–488–3736)
London College of Osteopathy, 24–5 Dorset Sq, London NW1 (01–262–5250)
London Commodity Exchange, Cereal House, 58 Mark Lane, London EC3R 7NE (01–488–3736)
London Court of Arbitration of the London Chamber of Commerce and the City Corporation, 69 Cannon St, London EC4N 5AB (01–248–4444)
London Grain Futures Market and Clearing House, Baltic Exchange, 24/28 St Mary Axe, London EC3A 8EP (01–283–5146)
London Jute Association, 69 Cannon Street, London EC4N 5AB (01–248–4444)
London Maritime Arbitrators' Association, The Baltic Exchange, 14–20 St Mary Axe, London EC3A 8BU
London Metal Exchange, 1 Metal Exchange Buildings, Whittington Ave, London EC3 (01–626–1011)
London Rubber Terminal Market Association, Cereal House, 58 Mark Lane, London EC3R 7NE (01–488–3736)
London Tourist Board, 26 Grosvenor Gardens, London SW1 (01–730–3450)
London Transport Executive, 55 Broadway, London SW1H 0BD (01–222–5600)
London Transport Lost Property Office, 200 Baker St, London NW1 5RT
London Transport Passengers' Committee, 26 Old Queen St, London SW1 (01–930–8019)
London University Examination Board, 66–72 Gower St, London WC1E 6EE (01–636–8000)

London Vegetable Oil Terminal Market Association, Cereal House, 58 Mark Lane, London EC3R 7NE (01–488–3736)
London Weekend Television Ltd, South Bank Television Centre, Kent House, Upper Ground, London SE1 9LT (01–261–3434)
London Wool Terminal Market Association, Roman Wall House, 1 Crutched Friars, London EC3N 1AN (01–488–3200)
Long Distance Walkers Association, 11 Thorn Bank, Onslow Village, Guildford, Surrey
Lord Advocate's Department, Crown Office, 9 Parliament Sq, Edinburgh EH1 1RH (031–226–6831)
Lord Chamberlain, St James's Palace, London SW1 (01–930–9882)
Lord Chancellor's Office
—— 67 Tufton St, London SW1P 3RG (01–212–7676)
—— House of Lords, London SW1A 0PW (01–219–3232)
Los Angeles State and County Arboretum, 301 North Baldwin Ave, Arcadia, Cal. 91008, USA
Luxembourg, Embassy of, 27 Wilton Crescent, London SW1X 8SD (01–235–6963)
Luxembourg National Tourist Office, 66 Haymarket, London W1 (01–930–3361)

M

Madagascar, Embassy of, 1 Boulevard Suchet, Paris 16, France
Magistrates' Court – look in local telephone directory under Courts
Malawi, High Commission for the Republic of, 47 Great Cumberland Place, London W1H 8DB (01–723–6021)
Malaysian High Commission, 45 Belgrave Sq, London SW1X 8QT (01–245–9221)
Mali, Embassy of the Republic of, Rue C Lemmonier 112, B – 1060 Brussels, Belgium (45–75–89)
Malta Government Office, Malta House, Haymarket, London SW1 (01–930–9851)
Maltese High Commission, 24 Haymarket, London SW1Y 4DJ (01–930–9851)
Manchester Chamber of Commerce and Industry, PO Box 559, Ship Canal House, King St, Manchester M60 2HB (061–832–5574)
Manpower Services Commission, Selkirk House, 166 High Holborn, London WC1V 6PF (01–240–1706)
Marine Pollution Compensation Services Ltd, 15f Berkeley House, 15 Hay Hill, London W1X 7LH (01–493–4771)
Martial Arts Commission, 4–16 Deptford Bridge, London SE8 4SJ (01–691–3433)
Marwell Zoological Park, Colden Common, Winchester, Hants SO21 1JH
Marylebone Cricket Club, Lord's Cricket Ground, London NW8 8QN (01–289–1611)
Masters of Deerhounds Association, Honeymead, Simonsbath, Minehead, Somerset (0865–348)
Masters of Foxhounds Association, Parsloes Cottage, Bagendon, Cirencester, Gloucestershire (028–583–470)
Masters of Otterhounds Association, Upper House Farm, Hascombe, Godalming, Surrey (048–632–225)
Mauritanian diplomatic mission for UK, Embassy of the Islamic Republic of Mauritania, 5 Rue de Montevideo, Paris 16, France (504–88–54)
Mauritius High Commission, 32–3 Elvaston Place, London SW7 5NW (01–581–0294)
Meat and Livestock Commission Head Offices
—— PO Box 44, Queensway House, Bletchley, Milton Keynes, Bucks MK2 2EF (0908–74941)
—— Scotland, Craigie House, Craigie Knowes Rd, Perth PH2 0DQ (0738–27401)
Medical Council on Alcoholism, 8 Bourdon St, London W1X 9HY
Medical Defence Union, 3 Devonshire Place, London W1 (01–486–6181)
Medical Research Council, 20 Park Crescent, London W1N 4AL (01–636–5422)
Medicines Commission, Finsbury Square House, 33–37a Finsbury Sq, London EC2A 1PP (01–638–6020)
Mental Health Review Tribunals
—— Tyrone House, Ormeau Ave, Belfast BT2 8HH
—— Pearl Assurance House, Greyfriars Rd, Cardiff CF1 3RT (0222–44151)
—— Linacre House, Stanley Precinct, Bootle, Liverpool (051–933–9101)
—— 16–19 Gresse St, 2nd Floor, London W1P 1PS (01–637–9053)

Mental Health Review Tribunals—*cont.*
—— Spur A Block 5, Government Buildings, Chalfont Dr, Western Boulevard, Nottingham NG8 3RZ (0602–294222)
Meteorological Office, Bracknell, Berkshire RG12 2SZ (0344–20242)
Metrication Board, 22 Kingsway, London WC2B 6LE (01–242–6828)
Metro Radio, Newcastle-upon-Tyne NE99 1BB (0632–884121)
Metropolitan Police Force Headquarters, New Scotland Yard, Broadway, London SW1H 0BG (01–230–1212)
Metropolitan Police Lost Property Office, 15 Penton St, London N1 9PO
Metropolitan Regional Examinations Board, Lyon House, 104 Wandsworth High St, London SW18 4LF (01–870–2144)
Mexican Embassy, 8 Halkin St, London SW1X 7DW (01–235–6393)
Middlesex Regional Examining Board, 53–63 Wembley Hill Rd, Wembley, Middx HA9 8BH (01–903–3961)
Midland Bank Ltd, Head Office, Poultry Lane, London EC2 (01–606–9911)
Milk Marketing Board
—— England and Wales, Thames Ditton, Surrey KT7 0EL
—— Northern Ireland, 454–6 Antrim Rd, Belfast BT15 5GD (0232–779211)
—— Scotland, Underwood Rd, Paisley, Renfrewshire PA3 1TJ (041–887–1234)
—— Aberdeen and District, Twin Spires, Bucksburn, Aberdeen AB2 9NR (0224–43371)
—— North of Scotland, Claymore House, 29 Ardconnel Terrace, Inverness IV2 3AF
MIND, 22 Harley St, London W1N 2ED (01–637–0741)
Minister of Agriculture, Fisheries and Food, Whitehall Place West, London SW1A 2HH (01–839–7711)
Ministry of Agriculture, Fisheries and Food, Headquarters
—— Main Headquarters, Whitehall Place West, London SW1A 2HH (01–839–7711)
—— Headquarters (2), Great Westminster House, Horseferry Rd, London SW1 2AE (01–216–6311)
—— Welsh Department, Plas Crug, Aberystwyth, Dyfed SY23 1NG (0970–3162)
Ministry of Agriculture, Fisheries and Food, Agricultural Development: and Advisory Service Centres
—— Trawsgoed, Aberystwyth, Dyfed SY23 4HT (09743–255)
—— Block 3, Government Buildings, Burghill Rd, Westbury-on-Trym, Bristol PS10 6NJ (0272–500000)
—— Block C, Government Buildings, Brooklands Avenue, Cambridge CB2 2DR (0223–5891)
—— Shardlow Hall, Derby DE7 2GN (0332–792315)
—— Block 2, Government Buildings, Lawnswood, Leeds LS16 5PY (0532–67–4411)
—— Government Buildings, Kenton Bar, Newcastle-upon-Tyne NE1 2YA (0632–889811)
—— Block A, Government Offices, Coley Park, Reading RG1 6DT (0734–581222)
—— Woodthorne, Wolverhampton WV6 8TQ (0902–754190)
Ministry of Agriculture, Fisheries and Food, Animal Health Divisions
—— Division I, Division ID and Division II, Hook Rise South, Surbiton, Surrey KT6 7NF (01–337–6611)
—— Division IIIB and Division IIIC, Government Buildings, Garrison Lane, Chessington, Surrey KT9 2LW
—— Division IVB, Tolworth Tower, Surbiton, Surrey (01–339–5191)
Ministry of Agriculture, Fisheries and Food Divisional Offices
—— Lion House, Willowburn Trading Estate, Anwick (0665–2881)
—— St Mary's Manor, Beverley, HU17 8DN (0482–887201)
—— Southgate St, Bury St Edmunds IP33 2BD (0284–3271)
—— Government Buildings, St Agnes Rd, Gabalfa, Cardiff CF4 4YH (0222–62131)
—— Eden Bridge House, Lowther St, Carlisle CA3 8DX (0228–23400)
—— Government Buildings, Picton Terrace, Carmarthen, Dyfed SA31 3BT (0267–4545)
—— Beeches Rd, Chelmsford CM1 2RU (0245–53201)
—— Station Rd, Ruthin, Clwyd LL15 1BP (082–422611)
—— Berkeley Towers, Nantwich Rd, Crewe, Cheshire CW2 6PT (0270–69211)
—— Elvet House, Hallgarth St, Durham DH1 3LD (0385–64433)
—— Government Buildings, Alphington Rd, Alphington, Exeter EX2 8NQ (0392–77951)
—— Elmbridge Court, Cheltenham Rd, Gloucester GL3 1AG (0452–21421)

Ministry of Agriculture, Fisheries and Food Divisional Offices—*cont.*
—— Government Buildings, Epsom Rd, Guildford GU1 2LD (0483–62881)
—— Government Buildings, Penralt, Caernarfon, Gwynedd LL55 1EP (0286–4144)
—— Block 7, Government Buildings, St George's Rd, Harrogate HG2 9EG (0423–67351)
—— Government Offices, Chequers Court, Huntingdon PE18 6LT (0480–52161)
—— Ceres House, No 2 Searby Rd, Lincoln LN2 4DW (0522–29951)
—— Crown House, Sittingbourne Rd, Maidstone ME14 5EY (0622–54300)
—— Government Buildings, Crosby Rd, Northallerton DL6 1AD (0609–3751)
—— 122A Thrope Rd, Norwich NR1 1RN (0603–29881)
—— Government Buildings, Gladstone Rd, Northampton NN5 7QG (0604–52388)
—— Government Buildings, Marston Rd, New Marston, Oxford OX3 0TP (0865–44891)
—— The Lindens, Spa Rd, Llandrindod Wells, Powys LD1 5HA (0597–2771)
—— Government Buildings, Cop Lane, Penwortham, Preston PR1 0SP (0772–44123)
—— Whitehall, Monkmoor Road, Shrewsbury SY2 5AJ (0743–53961)
—— Quantock House, Paul St, Taunton TA1 3NX (0823–87922)
—— Agar Rd, Truro TR1 1JX (0872–3191)
—— Government Buildings, Christchurch Rd, Winchester SO23 9SZ (0962–63500)
—— Block C, Government Buildings, Whittington Rd, Worcester WR5 2LQ (0905–355355)
Ministry of Agriculture, Fisheries and Food, Publications Branch, Government Buildings, Tolcarne Dr, Pinner, Middx HA5 2DT (01–868–7161)
Ministry of Agriculture, Fisheries and Food, Regional Offices
—— Block 3, Government Buildings, Burghill Rd, Westbury-on-Trym, Bristol BS10 6NJ (0272–500000)
—— Block C, Government Buildings, Brooklands Ave, Cambridge CB2 2DR (0223–58911)
—— Block 2, Government Buildings, Lawnswood, Leeds LS16 5PY (0532–67–4411)
—— Government Buildings, Kenton Bar, Newcastle-upon-Tyne NE1 2YA (0632–869811)
—— Block 2, Government Buildings, Chalfont Dr, Nottingham NG8 3RH (0602–292251)
—— Block A, Government Offices, Coley Park, Reading RG1 6DT (0734–581222)
—— Woodthorne, Wolverhampton WV6 8TQ (0902–754190)
Ministry of Agriculture, Fisheries and Food Seeds Branch, White House Lane, Huntingdon Rd, Cambridge CB3 0LF (0223–77151)
Ministry of Agriculture, Fisheries and Food Statistics, Whitehall Place, London SW1A 2HH (01–839–7711/7000/7024)
Ministry of Agriculture, Fisheries and Food, Torry Research Station, 135 Abbey Rd, Aberdeen AB9 8DG (0224–877071)
Ministry of Defence
—— Headquarters, Main Building, Whitehall, London SW1A 2HB
—— S4 (Air), Main Building, Whitehall, London SW1A 2HB
—— Claims Commission, 41 Tothill St, London SW1
—— Dept PS12, Army Casualties, Room 304A, Lansdowne House, Berkeley Sq, London W1X 6AA
—— Hydrographic Department (Sales Branch), Taunton, Somerset TA1 2DN
—— Director of Marketing, Stuart House, 23–5 Soho Sq, London W1V 5FJ
—— Naval Law Division, Archway Block South, Old Admiralty Building, Spring Gardens, London SW1A 2BE
—— Navy, Old Admiralty Building, Whitehall, London SW1A 2BE
—— Procurement Executive, ER (Central), 1a, Main Building, London SW1A 2HB
—— Procurement Executive
    Director General of Defence Contracts, CB Admin 3, St George's Court, 14 New Oxford St, London WC1A 1EJ
    Sales Supply, St Christopher House, Southwark St, London SE1
—— Provost and Security Services UK, Government Building, Bromyard Ave, Acton, London W3
—— (RAF), AR9, Adastral House, Theobalds Rd, London WC1X 8RU
Ministry of Overseas Development
—— Head Office, Eland House, Stag Place, London SW1E 5DH (01–834–2377)
—— Appointments Officer, Room E301, Eland House, Stag Place, London SW1E 5DH (01–834–2377)
—— International Recruitment Unit, Eland House, Stag Place, London SW1E 5DH (01–834–2377)
—— Statistics, Eland House, Stag Place, London SW1E 5DH (01–834–7477)
Ministry of Transport, 2 Marsham St, London SW1P 3EB (01–212–3434)

Minor Counties Cricket Association, 4 Kingsland Ave, Oakhill, Stoke-on-Trent, Staffs ST4 5LA (0782–412733)
Modern Pentathlon Association of Great Britain, 1a Godstone Rd, Burley, Surrey CR2 2DH
Monaco Consulate-General, 4 Audley Sq, London W1Y 5DR (01–629–0734)
Monaco Information Centre, 34 Sackville St, London W1X 1DB (01–437–3660)
Mongolian Embassy, 7 Kensington Court, London W8 5DL (01–937–0150)
Monopolies and Mergers Commission, New Court, 48 Carey St, London WC2A 2JT (01–831–6111)
Moroccan Bank for Foreign Trade, 241 Boulevard Mohammed V, Casablanca, Morocco
Moroccan Embassy, 49 Queen's Gate Gardens, London SW7 5NE (01–584–8827)
Moroccan National Tourist Office, 20 Pall Mall, London SW1 (01–839–6235)
Motor Agents Association, 201 Great Portland St, London W1N 6AB (01–580–9122)
Motor Caravanners' Club Ltd, 29 Wimbledon Park Rd, London SW18 5SJ (01–874–1929)
Motorcycle Union of Ireland, 8 Martinville Park, Saintfield Rd, Belfast 8 (0232–646886)
Mount Everest Foundation, Middle Place, Heathwaite Manor, Windermre, Cumbria LA23 2NG (096–62–4019)
Mountaineering Council of Scotland, 11 Kirklee Quadrant, Glasgow G12 0TS
Music Week, 40 Longacre, Covent Garden, London WC2 (01–836–1522)
Musicians' Union, 29 Catherine Place, London SW1 (01–834–1348)
Muzzle Loaders Association of Great Britain, 12 Frances Rd, Bagginton, Coventry, Warwickshire (0203–301895)

N

National Air Rifle and Pistol Association, 20 Pytchley Way, New Duston, Northampton NN5 6RN (0604–712426)
National Air Traffic Services, Space House 43–59 Kingsway, London WC2B 6TE (01–379–7331)
National Anglers' Council, 5 Cowgate, Peterborough PE1 1LR (0733–54084)
National Army Museum, Royal Hospital Rd, London SW3 (01–730–0717)
National Association for the Care and Resettlement of Offenders, 125 Kennington Park Rd, London SE11 (01–582–7172)
National Association of Citizens Advice Bureaux, 26 Bedford Sq, London WC1B 3HU (01–636–4066)
National Association of Launderette Industry, 77 New Bond St, London W1Y 9DB (01–493–3321)
National Association of Pension Funds, Prudential House, Weelesley Rd, Croydon CR0 2AD (01–687–2017)
National Association of Prison Visitors, 47 Hartington St, Bedford
National Association of Retail Furnishers, 3 Berners St, London W1P 4JP (01–636–1778)
National Association of Shoe Repair Factories, Leather Trade House, 82 Borough High St, London SE1 1LL (01–407–1522)
National Blood Transfusion Service – look in telephone directory under Blood
National Bus Company, 25 New Street Sq, London EC4 (01–583–9177)
National Caravan Council, 40 Piccadilly, London W1V 0ND (01–734–3681)
National Caving Association, c/o Dept of Geography, The University, Box 363, Birmingham 15
National Chrysanthemum Society, 62 St Margaret's Ave, Whetstone, London N20
National Coal Board, Hobart House, Grosvenor Pl, London SW1 (01–235–2020)
National Coal Board local offices – look under National Coal Board in local telephone directory
National Consumer Council, 18 Queen Anne's Gate, London SW1 (01–930–5752)
National Consumer Protection Council, Hendon, London NW4 4NY (01–202–5787)
National Council for Civil Liberties, 186 Kings Cross Rd, London WC1X 9DE (01–278–4575)
National Council for Social Service, 26 Bedford Sq, London WC1 (01–636–4066)
National Council on Alcoholism, 45 Great Peter St, London SW1P 3LT
National Coursing Club, 32 Brixton Rd, London SW9 8BU (01–735–8541)
National Cricket Association, Lord's Cricket Ground, London NW8 8QN (01–289–1611)
National Enterprise Board, 12–18 Grosvenor Gardens, London SW1W 0DW
National Examinations Board of Embalmers, 181 High St, Erdington, Birmingham B23 6SY (021–373–0011)

National Farmers Union, Agriculture House, Knightsbridge, London SW1 (01–235–5077)
National Federation of Anglers, Haig House, 87 Green Lane, Derby (0332–362000)
National Federation of Consumer Groups, 61 Valentine Rd, Birmingham B14 7AJ (021–444–6010)
National Federation of Housing Associations, 86 The Strand, London WC2 (01–836–2741)
National Federation of Music Societies, 1 Montague St, London WC1B 5BF (01–530–4855)
National Federation of Sea Anglers, 26 Downview Crescent, Uckfield, Sussex (0825–3589)
National Film Finance Corporation, 27 Soho Sq, London W1 (01–437–4884)
National Front, 91 Connaught Rd, Teddington, Middlesex (01–977–2452)
National Fruit Trials, Brogdale Farm, Faversham, Kent
National Giro Centre, Bridle Rd, Bootle, Merseyside GIR 0AA (051–966–2146)
National Greyhound Racing Club Ltd, St Martin's House, 140 Tottenham Court Rd, London W1P 0AS (01–387–0705)
National Health Service – see Department of Health and Social Security
National Health Service Drug Dependence Centres
—— Ross Clinic, Royal Cornhill Hospital, Cornhill Rd, Aberdeen (0224–52411)
—— Park Prewett Hospital, Basingstoke (0256–3202)
—— St Catherine's Hospital, Church Rd, Birkenhead (051–652–2281)
—— All Saints' Hospital, Winson Green, Birmingham 18 (021–523–5151)
—— St Lawrence's Hospital, Bodmin (0208–3281)
—— St Ann's Hospital, Haven Rd, Canford Cliffs, Bournemouth (0202–708881)
—— Lynfield Mount Hospital, Heights Lane, Bradford (0274–48121)
—— Warley Hospital, Brentwood (0277–21–3241)
—— Herbert Hone Clinic, Upper Gloucester Rd, Brighton (0273–23395)
—— Glenside Hospital, Stapleton, Bristol (0272–65–3285)
—— Addenbrooke's Hospital, 2 Benet Place, Lensfield Rd, Cambridge (0223–55671)
—— St Augustine's Hospital, Chartham Down, Nr Canterbury (022–773–382)
—— Adfer Unit, Whitchurch Hospital, Cardiff (0222–62191)
—— Moston Hospital, Liverpool Rd, Chester CH2 4AA (0244–25202)
—— Royal Infirmary, Chester (0244–28261)
—— Graylingwell Hospital, Chichester (0243–85171)
—— Crawley Hospital, West Green Drive, Crawley (0293–27866)
—— Roundway Hospital, Devizes (0380–3592)
—— Herrison Hospital, Herrison, Dorchester (0305–3661)
—— Andrew Duncan Clinic, Royal Edinburgh Hospital, Morningside Terrace, Edinburgh (031–447–2011)
—— Spelthorne St Mary Hospital, Thorpe, Egham (655–3112)
—— Exe Vale Hospital, Digby Section, Woodwater Lane, Exeter (0392–74057)
—— Wonford Section, Dryden Rd, Exeter (0392–77358)
—— Knowle Hospital, Fareham (0329–32271)
—— Southern General Hospital, Glasgow (041–445–2466)
—— Eastern District Hospital, Glasgow (041–554–6267/8/9)
—— St Francis Hospital, Haywards Heath (0444–51881)
—— St Christopher's Day Hospital, Horsham (0403–4367)
—— Lady Chichester Hospital, Aldrington House, New Church Rd, Hove 3 (0273–778383)
—— Craig Dunain Hospital, Inverness (0463–34101)
—— Moorhaven Hospital, Ivybridge (0755–42411)
—— St John's Hospital, London Rd, Lincoln (0522–27401)
—— Day Hospital, 10 Croxteth Rd, Liverpool 8
—— Liverpool Psychiatric Day Hospital, 10 Croxteth Road, Liverpool L8 3SG
—— Sefton General Hospital, Smithdown Rd, Liverpool 15 (051–733–4020)
—— Walton Hospital, 107 Rice Lane, Liverpool 9 (051–525–3611)
—— London
    Banstead Hospital, Sutton, Surrey (01–642–6611)
    Bethlem Royal, Monks Orchard Rd, Eden Park, Beckenham, Kent (01–777–6611)
    Bexley Hospital, Dartford Heath, Bexley, Kent (29–26282)
    Bowden House Clinic, London Rd, Harrow-on-the-Hill, Middlesex (01–864–0221)
    Charing Cross Drug Dependency Unit, 57 Aspenlea Rd, W6 (01–385–8834)
    Hackney Drug Dependency Unit, Homerton High St, London E9 (01–986–6816)
    Lambeth Hospital, Brook Drive, London SE11 (01–735–8141)

National Health Service Drug Dependence Centres—London—*cont.*
    Maudsley Hospital, Denmark Hill, London SE5 (01–703–6333)
    Norwood and District Hospital, Hermitage Rd, London SE19 (01–820–2101)
    Paddington Clinic and Day Hospital, 217 Harrow Rd, London W12 (01–286–4800)
    Queen Mary's Hospital, Roehampton Lane, London SW15 (01–789–6611)
    St Bernard's Hospital, Southall, Middlesex (01–574–8141)
    St Clement's Hospital, Bow Rd, London E3 (01–980–4899)
    St George's Hospital, Blackshaw Rd, London SW17 (01–672–1255)
    St Luke's (Woodside) Hospital, Simmons House, Woodside Ave, London N10 (01–883–8498)
    St Mary's Drug Dependency Centre, Woodfield Rd, London W9 (01–286–7371/2)
    Tooting Bec Hospital, Tooting Bec Rd, London SW17 (01–672–3350)
    University College Hospital (National Temperance Hospital), 122 Hampstead Rd, London NW1 LT2 (01–387–9300)
    West Middlesex Hospital, Twickenham Rd, Isleworth, Middlesex (01–560–2121)
    Westminster Hospital, 52/53 Vincent Sq, London SW1 (01–828–9811)
    St Giles' Hospital, St Giles' Rd, Camberwell, London SE5 (01–703–0898)
    Guy's Hospital, St Thomas St, London SE1 (01–407–7600)
—— Prestwich Hospital, Prestwich, Manchester (061–773–2236)
—— Kingseat Hospital, Newmachar (065–17–253)
—— Newcastle General Hospital, Westgate Rd, Newcastle-upon-Tyne 4 (0632–38811)
—— Parkwood House, St Nicholas Hospital, Gosforth, Newcastle-upon-Tyne (0632–858181)
—— Belmont Day Centre, St Cadoc's Hospital, Caerleon, Newport (0633–421121)
—— St Andrew's Hospital, Thorpe, Norwich (0603–35151)
—— Ormskirk and District Hospital, Wigan Rd, Ormskirk (0695–75471)
—— Ley Clinic, Littlemore Hospital, Littlemore, Nr Oxford (0865–77891)
—— St James Hospital, Locksway Rd, Portsmouth (0705–35211)
—— Rochford General Hospital, Dalys Rd, Rochford (0702–544471)
—— Hill End Hospital, Hill End, St Albans (56–55555)
—— Southend General Hospital, Prittlewell Chase, Southend-on-Sea (0702–48911)
—— Drug Dependency Clinic, Mental Health Centre, Southampton (0703–27658)
—— Lister Hospital, Stevenage (0438–4333)
—— Ashfield Clinic, Kings Mill Hospital, Mansfield Rd, Sutton-in-Ashfield (0623–22515)
—— Seymour Clinic, Gorse Hill, Swindon (0793–5193)
—— Tone Vale Hospital, Morton Fitzwarren, Taunton (082–343–375)
—— Stanley Royd Hospital, Aberford Rd, Wakefield (0924–75217)
—— Queen Elizabeth II Hospital, Howlands, Welwyn Garden City (96–28111)
—— Brookwood Hospital, Knaphill, Woking (0486–74545)
—— Yeovil General Hospital, Higher Kingston, Yeovil (0935–5122)
—— Clifton Hospital, York (0904–24677)
National House Building Council, 58 Portland Pl, London W1N 4BU (01–387–7201)
National Indoor Bowls Council, 76 Argyle Rd, Saltcoats, Ayrshire
National Inspection Council for Electrical Installation Contracting, Alembic House, 93 Albert Embankment, London SE1 7TB (01–582–7746)
National Institute for Biological Standards and Control, Holly Hill, London NW3 (01–435–2232)
National Institute of Adult Education, 35 Queen Anne St, London W1 (01–637–4241)
National Institute of Agricultural Botany, Huntingdon Rd, Cambridge CB3 0LE (0223–76381)
National Insurance Commissioners – contact Local Department of Health and Social Security offices
National Joint Council of Approved Driving Instructor Organisations, 19 Shales Rd, Bitterne, Southampton
National Library for the Blind
—— 35 Great Smith St, London SW1 (01–222–2725)
—— 5 St John St, Manchester (061–834–0432, 061–834–0254)
National Library of Scotland, George IV Bridge, Edinburgh EH1 1EW (031–226–4531)
National Library of Wales, Aberwystwyth, Dyfed SY23 3BU (0970–3816)
National Park Information Centres
—— The Wharf, Aberdyfi (065–472–321)
—— Lower Mond St, Abergavenny (0873–3524)
—— Old Court House, Church St, Ambleside (096–63–3084)

National Park Information Centres—*cont.*
—— Car Park, Ambleside, Waterhead
—— Leyburn, Aysgarth Falls, Yorkshire Dales (096–93–424)
—— Market Hall, Bridge St, Bakewell, Peak District (062–981–3227)
—— The Old British School, High St, Bala (067–82–367)
—— Caerblaidd Office, Queen's Bridge, Blaenau Ffestiniog (076–681–360)
—— Bowness Bay, Glebe Rd, Bowness (096–62–2895)
—— 6 Glamorgan St, Brecon (0874–2763)
—— Pembrokeshire Countryside Unit, Car Park, Broad Haven (043–783–412)
—— St Ann's Well, The Crescent, Buxton, Peak District (0298–5106)
—— 9 Otterbarn Green, Byrness (0830–622)
—— Castle St, Castleton, Peak District (0433–20679)
—— Reading Room, Clapham (via Lancaster) (046–85–419)
—— Old Gas Showrooms, Conway (049–263–2248)
—— Danby Lodge National Park Centre, Nr Whitby, Danby (028–76–645)
—— Information Centre, Two Bridges, Dartmoor (082–289–253)
—— Bridge End, Dollgellau (0341–422888)
—— Beach Car Park, Combe Martin, Exmoor (027–188–3319)
—— Exmoor House, Dulverton, Exmoor (0398–665)
—— Parish Hall, Lynmouth, Exmoor
—— Town Hall, Fishguard (0348–3484)
—— Gwyddfor House, High St, Harlech (076–673–658)
—— County Museum, Haverfordwest Castle, Haverfordwest (0437–3708)
—— Station Yard, Hawes, Yorkshire Dales
—— Car Park, Hawkshead
—— Military Rd, Hexham (049–984–396)
—— Old School House, Ingram, Northumberland (066–578–248)
—— Moot Hall, Keswick
—— Kingsmoor Common, Kilgetty (0834–813672)
—— Mountain Centre, Libanus (0874–3366)
—— Community Centre, Llanberis (028–682–765)
—— Glan-y-Borth, Llanrwst (0492–640604)
—— 8 Broad St, Llandovery (0550–20693)
—— Town Hall, Milford Haven (064–62–4567)
—— Market House, The Parade, Minehead (0643–2984)
—— Drill Hall, Main St, Pembroke (064–63–2143)
—— National Park Residential Study Centre, Maentwrog, Plas Tanybwlch (076–685–324)
—— Church House, Church St, Rothby, Northumberland
—— City Hall, St Davids (043–788–392)
—— top of Sutton Bank by the A170, Sutton Bank
—— The Norton, Tenby (0834–3510)
—— Bank House, High St, Windermere (096–62–2498)
—— National Park Centre, Windermere Brockhole (096–62–2231)
—— Town Hall, Yorkshire Dales (3617)
National Ports Council, Commonwealth House, 1–19 New Oxford St, London WC1A 1DZ
National Register of Archives, Quality House, Quality Court, London WC2 (01–242–1198)
National Register of Archives (Scotland), HM General Register House, Edinburgh EH1 3YY (031–556–6585)
National Research Development Corporation, PO Box 236, Kingsgate House, 66–74 Victoria St, London SW13 6SL (01–828–3400)
National Rifle Association, Bisley Camp, Brookwood, Woking, Surrey GU24 0PB (04867–2213)
National Roller Hockey Association, c/o Newbury, 12 Oaklands Rise, Welwyn, Herts
National Savings Bank, Boydstone Rd, Cowglen, Glasgow G58 1SB (041–649–4555)
National Savings Stock Register, Bonds and Stock Office, Lytham St Annes, Lancs FY0 1YN (0253–721212)
National Schizophrenia Fellowship, 29 Victoria Rd, Surbiton, Surrey KT6 4JT
National Skating Association of Great Britain, Charterhouse, Charterhouse Sq, London EC1M 6AT (01–253–3824)
National Ski Federation of Great Britain, 118 Eaton Sq, London SW1 (01–235–8227)

National Small Bore Rifle Association, Codrington House, 113 Southwark St, London SE1 0JW (01-928-3262)
National Society for the Prevention of Cruelty to Children, National Headquarters, 1 Riding House St, London W1 (01-580-8812)
National Television Licence Records Office, Barbon House, Bond St, Bristol BS1 3NJ
National Tourist Offices – see text entry for each country
National Travel Association of Denmark, 169-73 Sceptre House, Regent St, London W1 (01-734-2637)
National Trust, Head Office, 42 Queen Annes's Gate, London SW1H 9AS (01-980-0211)
National Trust for Scotland, 5 Charlotte Sq, Edinburgh EH2 4DU (031-226-5922)
National Union of Conservative and Unionist Associations, 32 Smith Sq, London SW1 (01-222-9000)
National Water Council, 1 Queen Anne's Gate, London SW1 9BT (01-930-3100)
National Westminster Bank Ltd, Head Office, 41 Lothbury, London EC2 (01-606-6060)
National Zoological Association of Great Britain, Stowlangtoft, Bury St Edmunds IP31 3JW (0359-30623)
Natural Environment Research Council, Alhambra House, 27-33 Charing Cross Rd, London WC2H 0AX (01-930-9232)
Nature Conservancy Council
—— Great Britain Headquarters, 19-20 Belgrave Sq, London SW1X 8PY (01-235-3241)
—— Headquarters for England, Calthorpe House, Calthorpe St, Banbury, Oxon OX16 8EX (0295-57601)
—— Headquarters for Scotland, 12 Hope Terrace, Edinburgh EH9 2AS (031-447-4784)
—— Headquarters for Wales, Bangor Research Station, Ffordd Penrhos, Bangor, Gwynedd LL57 2LQ (0248-4001)
—— Grants Officer, Attingham Park, Shrewsbury, Salop SY4 4TW
Naval Liaison Officers
—— First Floor, 5 Bute Crescent, Cardiff CF1 6AN
—— Royal Liver Buildings, Liverpool 3
—— London Dock House, 1 Thomas More St, London E1 9AZ
—— No. 50 Berth, Eastern Docks, Southampton SO9 2TJ
Nepalese Embassy, 12A Kensington Palace Gardens, London W8 4QU (01-229-1594)
Netherlands Embassy, 38 Hyde Park Gate, London SW7 5DP (01-584-5040)
Netherlands National Touring Office, 143 New Bond St, London W1Y 5DR (01-499-9367)
New Town Development Corporations
—— Cuerdon Pavilion, Bamber Bridge, Preston PR5 6AZ
—— Gifford House, Basildon, Essex SS13 2EX
—— Farley Hall, Binfield, Bracknell, Berks RG12 5EU
—— Chisholm House, 9 Queen's Sq, Corby, Northants NN17 1PA
—— Cumbernauld House, Cumbernauld G67 3JH
—— Gwent House, Town Centre, Cwmbran, Gwent NP4 3XJ
—— Atholl House, East Kilbride, Lanarkshire G74 1LU
—— New Glenrothes House, Glenrothes, Fife KY7 5PR
—— Gate House, The High, Harlow, Essex CM20 1LJ
—— Perceton House, Irvine KA11 2AL
—— Livingston, West Lothian EH54 7AD
—— Wavendon Tower, Wavendon, Milton Keynes, Bucks MK17 8LX
—— Churchill House, Newton Aycliffe, Co Durham DL5 4LE
—— Ladywell House, Newtown, Powys SY16 1JB
—— Cliftonville House, Bedford Rd, Northampton NN4 0AY
—— PO Box 3, Touthill Close, City Rd, Peterborough PE1 1UJ
—— Lee House, Yoden Way, Peterlee SR8 1BB
—— 'Holmwood', Plymouth Rd, Redditch, Worcs B97 4PD
—— Chapel St, Runcorn, Cheshire WA7 5AR
—— Pennylands, Skelmersdale, Lancs WN8 8AR
—— Swingate House, Danestrete, Stevenage, Herts SG1 1XE
—— Priorslee Hall, Telford, Salop TF2 9NT
—— New Town House, Buttermarket St, PO Box No. 49, Warrington, Cheshire WA1 2LF
—— Usworth Hall, Stephenson, District 12, Washington, Tyne and Wear NE37 3HS

New Zealand High Commission, New Zealand House, Haymarket, London SW1Y 4TQ (01-930-8422)
Newbattle Abbey College, Dalkeith, Scotland (031-663-1921)
Newspaper Publishers Association Ltd, 6 Bouverie St, London EC4 (01-583-0132)
Newspaper Society, 6 Carmelite St, London EC4 (01-353-4722)
Nicaragua, Embassy of, 8 Gloucester Rd, London SW7 4RB (01-584-3231)
Niger diplomatic mission to UK, Embassy of the Republic of Niger, 154 Rue de Longchamps, Paris 16, France (504-8060)
Nigerian High Commission, Nigeria House, 9 Northumberland Ave, London WC2 5BX (01-839-1244)
Nobel Committee of the Norwegian Storting (Parliament), Drammensveien 19, Oslo 2, Norway
Nobel Foundation, Nobelhuset, Sturegatan 14, S-11436 Stockholm, Sweden
North American Gladiolus Society, 11345 Moreno Ave, Lakeside, Calif 92040, USA
North of England Zoological Society, Zoological Gardens, Chester
North of Scotland College of Agriculture, School of Agriculture, 581 King St, Aberdeen AB9 1UD (0224-40291)
North of Scotland Hydro Electric Board, 16 Rothesay Terrace, Edinburgh 3
North Regional Examinations Board, Wheatfield Rd, Westerhope, Newcastle-upon-Tyne NE5 5JZ (0632-862711)
North West Regional Examinations Board, Orbit House, Albert St, Eccles, Manchester M3 0WL (061-788-9521)
Northern Bank Ltd, 16 Victoria St, Belfast BT1 3GQ (0232-22271)
Northern Ice Hockey Association, Whitley Bay Ice Rink, Hillheads Rd, Whitley Bay, Tyne and Wear
Northern Ireland Agricultural Wages Board, Magnet House, 81-93 York St, Belfast BT15 1AD (0232-24681)
Northern Ireland Amateur Athletic Association, 20 Kernan Park, Portadown, County Armagh (0762-34652)
Northern Ireland Billiard and Snooker Control Council, 12 Ravernet Walk, Old Warren Estate, Lisburn, Co Antrim
Northern Ireland Commission for Administration, River House, 48 High St, Belfast BT1 2JT (0232-33821)
Northern Ireland Commissioner for Complaints, 48 High St, Belfast BT1 2JT (0232-33821)
Northern Ireland Consumer Council, 176 Newtownbreda Rd, Belfast BT8 4QS (0232-647151)
Northern Ireland Council for Nurses and Midwives, 216 Belmont Rd, Belfast BT4 2AT (0232-652713)
Northern Ireland Council of Physical Recreation, 49 Malone Rd, Belfast BT9 6RZ (0232-663154)
Northern Ireland Cycling Federation, 20 Thornleigh Gardens, Bangor, Co Down
Northern Ireland Department of Agriculture, Dundonald House, Upper Newtownards Rd, Belfast BT4 3SB (0232-650111)
Northern Ireland Department of Commerce, Chichester House, 64 Chichester St, Belfast BT1 4JX (0232-34488)
Northern Ireland Department of Health and Social Services, Dundonald House, Upper Newtownards Rd, Belfast BT4 35F (0232-650111)
Northern Ireland Electricity Consumer's Council, 120 Malone Rd, Belfast BT9 5HT (0232-66110)
Northern Ireland Electricity Service, 120 Malone Rd, Belfast BT9 5HT (0232-66110)
Northern Ireland Federation of Sub-Aqua Clubs, 59 Malone Ave, Belfast 9 (0232-666180)
Northern Ireland Fencing Union, 33 Ravenhill Park, Belfast BT6 0DG (0232-647830)
Northern Ireland Finance Corporation, 55 Royal Ave, Belfast 1 (0232-47125)
Northern Ireland Judo Federation, 39 Malone Rd, Belfast 9 (0232-668312)
Northern Ireland Labour Party, 1-5 Cheviot Ave, Belfast BT4 3AG (0232-650365)
Northern Ireland Mountain Centre, Tollymore, Byersford, Newcastle, Co Down (Newcastle 2623)
Northern Ireland Netball Association, 7 Hillcrest Ave, Newtownlands (4497)
Northern Ireland Office
—— Stormont Castle, Belfast BT4 3ST (0232-63011)
—— Great George St, London SW1P 3AJ (01-233-3000)
Northern Ireland Office, Personal Injuries Board, Windsor House, 9-13 Bedford St, Belfast BT2 7LT (0232-44821)
Northern Ireland Office Statistics, Stormont, Belfast BT4 3SW (0232-63210)
Northern Ireland Orienteering Association, 23 Ferndale Crescent, Newtonabbey BT36 8AN

Northern Ireland Paraplegic Association, 105 Irish Quarter South, Carrick Fergus (0231–63370)
Northern Ireland Parliamentary Commissioner for Administration, River House, 48 High St, Belfast BT1 2JT (0232–33821)
Northern Ireland Railways Co. Ltd, Central Station, Belfast
Northern Ireland Schools Examinations Council, Benhill House, 42 Benhill Road, Belfast BT8 4RS (0232–647261)
Northern Ireland Tourist Board, River House, High St, Belfast 1 (0232–31221)
Northern Ireland Trampolining Association, 8 Drumavoley Park, Ballycastle (026–57–62359)
Northern Ireland Tug-of-War Association, 44 Creevy Ave, Cilnahirk, Belfast BP5 7PN (0232–57771)
Northern Ireland Volleyball Association, Sports Council, 39 Malone Rd, Belfast BT9 6RZ (0232–663154)
Northern Ireland Women's Amateur Athletic Association, 22 Grange Ave, Ballymena, Co Antrim
Northern Ireland Women's Football Association, 14 Woodview Park (0762–36326 (B))
Norwegian Embassy, 25 Belgrave Sq, London SW1X 8QD (01–235–7151)
Norwegian National Tourist Office, 20 Pall Mall, London SW1Y 5NE (01–839–6235)
Nyndee Nomenclature Committee, Torokina Ave, St Ives, NSW, Australia

O

Occupational Pensions Board, Apex Tower, High St, New Malden, Surrey KT3 4DN
Office of Fair Trading
——— Northern Ireland Department of Commerce, 176 Newtownbreda Rd, Belfast BT1 4JX
——— 9 Hope St, Edinburgh EH2 4ET (031–225–3185)
——— Field House, Bream's Buildings, London EC4 1PR (01–242–2858)
Office of Law Reform, Parliament Buildings, Stormont, Belfast 4 (0232–63210)
Office of Manpower Economics, 22 Kingsway, London WC2B 6JY (01–405–5944)
Office of Population Censuses and Surveys, 10 Kingsway, London WC2B 6JP (01–242–0262)
Office of Population Censuses and Surveys, Statistics, St Catherine's House, Kingsway, London WC2B 6JP (01–242–0262 ex 2183)
Official Board of Ballroom Dancing, 87 Parkhurst Rd, London N7 0LP (01–609–1386)
Official Custodian for Charities, Charity Commission, St Alban's House, 57–60 Haymarket, London SW1Y 4QX (01–214–6000)
Official Seed Testing Station
——— 50 Houston Road, Crossnacreevey, Catlereagh, Belfast BT6 9SH (023–123–229, 434)
——— Huntingdon Road, Cambridge CB3 0LE
——— Agricultural Scientific Services, East Craigs, Corstorphine, Edinburgh EH12 8NJ (031–334–0355)
Official Solicitor, Official Solicitor's Department, 48–9 Chancery Lane, London WC2A 13R (01–405–7641)
Offshore Pollution Liability Ltd, Britannia House, Moor Lane, London EC2Y 9BR
Oman, Embassy of the Sultanate of, 64 Ennismore Gardens, London SW7 1NH (01–584–6782)
Open University, Walton Hall, Milton Keynes MK7 6AA (0908–74066)
Ordnance Survey, Romsey Rd, Maybush, Southampton SO9 4DH (0703–775555)
Ordnance Survey Copyright Branch, Romsey Rd, Maybush, Southampton SO9 4DH (0703–775555)
Ordnance Survey, Northern Ireland, Ministry of Finance, Laydas Drive, Belfast BT9 6FJ (06683–58225)
Oxford and Cambridge Schools Examination Board, Brook House, 10 Trumpington St, Cambridge CB2 1CB (0223–54421)
Oxford Delegacy of Local Examinations, Ewert Place, Summertown, Oxford (0865–54291)
Oxford Regional Health Authority, 2 Foredown Drive, Portslade, Brighton, Sussex BN4 2BB

P

Pakistani Consulate, Fraternal House, 45 Cheapside, Bradford (0274–21972, 21921)
Pakistani Embassy, 35 Lowndes Sq, London SW1X 9JN (01–235–2044)
Pakistani Vice-Consulates
—— 39 Corporation St, Birmingham 2 (021–643–5391)
—— 134 St Vincent St, Glasgow G2 (041–221–4785)
—— 86 Princess St, Manchester 1
Panamanian Embassy, c/o 39 Montpelier Sq, London SW7 (01–589–8751)
Panel on Take-overs and Mergers, PO Box No. 226, The Stock Exchange Building, London EC2P 2TX
Papua–New Guinea High Commission, 22 Garrick St, London WC2 (01–836–9460, 01–240–1780)
Paraguay, Embassy of, Braemar Lodge, Cornwall Gardens, London SW7 4AQ (01–937–1253)
Parliamentary Commissioner for Administration, Church House, Great Smith St, London SW1P 3BW (01–212–6271)
Parole Board for England and Wales, Queen Anne's Gate, London SW1H 9AT (01–213–3181)
Parole Board for Scotland, Broomhouse Drive, Edinburgh E11 3UY (031–443–4040)
Passenger Transport Executives
—— Glasgow, 14 St Vincent St, Glasgow G2 5TR (041–248–5971)
—— London, 55 Broadway, London SW1M 0BD (01–222–5600)
—— Manchester, Manchester M1 5AY (061–228–6511)
—— Merseyside, 24 Helton Gdn, Liverpool L3 2AN (051–236–7411)
—— Midland West, 16 Summer Lane, Birmingham B19 3SD (021–622–5151)
—— Tyne and Wear, Cuthbert House, All Saints, Newcastle-upon-Tyne (NE1 2DA (0632–610431)
—— Yorkshire South, Exchange St, Sheffield S2 5SZ (0742–78688)
—— Yorkshire West, Metro House, West Parade, Wakefield WF1 1NS (0924–78234)
Passport Agency, Marlborough House, 30 Victoria St, Belfast BT1 3LW (0232–32371)
Passport Offices
—— 1st Floor, Empire House, 131 West Nile Street, Glasgow G1 2RY (041–332–0271)
—— 5th Floor, India Buildings, Water Street, Liverpool L2 0Q2 (051–227–3461)
—— Clive House, 70 Petty France, London SW1H 9HD (01–222–8010)
—— Olympia House, Upper Dock St, Newport, Gwent NPT 1XA (Newport 52431)
—— 55 Westfield Rd, Peterborough PE3 6TG (Peterborough 263636)
Patent Office, 25 Southampton Buildings, London WC2 1AY (01–405–8721)
Peak Park Joint Planning Board, Aldern House, Bayslow Rd, Bakewell, Derbyshire DE4 1AE (Bakewell 062–981–2881)
Pennine Radio, PO Box 235, Pennine House, Forster Sq, Bradford BD1 5NP (0274–31521)
Performing Right Society Ltd, 29 Berners St, London W1 (01–580–5544)
Performing Right Tribunal, 25 Southampton Buildings, Chancery Lane, London WC2A 1AY (01–405–8721)
Periodical Publishers Association, Imperial House, Kingsway, London WC2 (01–836–7111)
Peruvian Embassy, 52 Sloane St, London SW1X 9SP (01–235 1917, 2545)
Pharmaceutical Society of Great Britain, Lambeth High St, London SE1 7JN (01–735–9141)
Philatelic Bureau, Lothian House, 124 Lothian Rd, Edinburgh EH3 9BB (031–556–8661)
Philippines Consulate, Cardiff – enquire at Philippines Embassy
Philippines Consulate-General, 26–7 Buckingham Terrace, Glasgow G12 8EE (041–334–4264)
Philippines, Embassy of the, 9A Palace Green, London W8 4QE (01–937 3646, 9158)
Piccadilly Radio, 127–31 The Piazza, Piccadilly Plaza, Manchester M1 4AW (061–236–9913)
Pigs and Poultry Division, Ministry of Agriculture, Fisheries and Food, Whitehall Place, London SW1A (01–839–7711)
Plaid Cymru Headquarters, 8 Heol y Frenhines, Cardiff (Cardiff 31944)
Plant Variety Rights Office, White House Lane, Huntingdon Rd, Cambridge CB3 0LF (0223–77151)
Plater College, Pullens Lane, Headington, Oxon (0865–67626)
Plymouth Sound, Earl's Acre, Alma Road, Plymouth PL3 4HX (0752–27272)

Police – in emergency dial 999 and ask for police; otherwise look for local police station under Police in telephone directory or contact your police force headquarters

Police Force Headquarters
—— Avon and Somerset Constabulary, PO Box No 188, Bristol BS99 7BH (0272–290721)
—— Bedfordshire Police, 55 Goldington Rd, Bedford MK40 3LS (Bedford 61301)
—— Cambridgeshire Constabulary, Hinchinbrooke Park, Huntingdon PE18 8NP (0480–56111)
—— Cheshire Constabulary, Castle Esplanade, Chester CH1 2PP (0244–315432)
—— Cleveland Constabulary, PO Box 670, Dunning Rd, Middlesbrough, Cleveland TS1 2AR (0642–248184)
—— Cumbria Constabulary, Carleton Hall, Penrith, Cumbria CA10 2AU (Penrith 4411)
—— Derbyshire Constabulary, Butterley Hall, Ripley, Derby DE5 3RS (0773–3551)
—— Devon and Cornwall Constabulary, Middlemoor, Exeter EX2 7HQ (Exeter 52101)
—— Dorset Police, Dorchester, Dorset (Dorchester 3011–7)
—— Durham Constabulary, Aykley Heads, Durham DH1 5TT (0385–64929)
—— Dyfed-Powys Police, Friar's Park, Carmarthen (Carmarthen 6444–7)
—— Essex Police, PO Box No 2, Springfield, Chelmsford, Essex CM2 2DA (Chelmsford 67267)
—— Gloucestershire Constabulary, Holland House, Lansdown Rd, Cheltenham, Glos. (Cheltenham 21321)
—— Greater Manchester Police, PO Box 51, Southmill St, Manchester M60 2NH (061–228–1212)
—— Guernsey, Channel Islands Police, The Grange, St Peter Port, Guernsey, CI (0481–25111)
—— Gwent Constabulary, Croesyceiliog, Cwmbran, Gwent NP4 2XJ (Cwmbran 2011)
—— Hampshire Constabulary, West Hill, Winchester, Hants (0962–68133)
—— Hertfordshire Constabulary, Stanborough Rd, Welwyn Garden City, Herts AL8 6XF (Welwyn Garden 31177)
—— Humberside Police, Queen's Gardens, Kingston-upon-Hull, Humberside HU1 3DJ (0482–26111)
—— Isle of Man Police, Douglas, Isle of Man (Douglas 4616)
—— Jersey, Channel Islands Police, Rouge Bouillon, St Helier, Jersey, CI (0534–25071)
—— Kent Constabulary, Sutton Road, Maidstone, Kent ME15 9BZ (Maidstone 65432)
—— Lancashire Constabulary, Hutton, Nr Preston PR4 5SB, Lancs. (0772–614444)
—— Leicestershire Constabulary, 'Ashleigh', 420 London Rd, Leicester LE2 2PT (Leicester 700911)
—— Lincolnshire Police, Church Lane, Lincoln (0522–29911)
—— London
    Metropolitan Police, New Scotland Yard, Broadway, London SW1H 0BG (01–230–1212)
    City of London, 26 Old Jewry, London, EC2R 8DJ (01–606–8866)
    Port of London Authority, Gallions Entrance, Royal Albert Dock Basin, London E16 2QD (01–476–6900)
—— Merseyside Police Force, PO Box 59, L69 1JD (051–709–6010)
—— Norfolk Constabulary, Martineau Lane, Norwich NR1 2DJ (Norwich 21234/7)
—— Northamptonshire Police, Wootton Hall, Northampton NN4 0JQ (Northampton 62111)
—— Northern Ireland, Royal Ulster Constabulary, 'Brooklyn', Knock Rd, Belfast BT5 6LE (0232–650222)
—— Northumbria Police, Ashington, Northumberland (Ashington 814511)
—— North Wales Police, Colwyn Bay (Colwyn Bay 57171)
—— North Yorkshire Police, Northallerton, Yorkshire DL7 8RB (Northallerton 3131)
—— Nottinghamshire Constabulary, Sherwood Lodge, Arnold, Nottingham NG5 8PP (0602–269700)
—— Scotland
    Central Scotland Police, Police Headquarters, Randolphfield, Stirling FK8 2HD (0786–3161)
    Dumfries and Galloway Constabulary, Loreburn St, Dumfries DG1 1HP (0387–2112–5)
    Fife Constabulary, Wemyss Rd, Dysart, Kirkcaldy, Fife (Kirkcaldy 52611–6)
    Grampian Police, Queen Street, Aberdeen AB9 1BA (0224–29933)
    Lothian and Borders Police, Fettes Ave, Edinburgh EH4 1RB (031–311–3131)
    Northern Constabulary, Perth Road, Inverness IV2 3SY (0463–39191)
    Strathclyde Police, Police Headquarters, 173 Pitt Street, Glasgow G2 4JS (041–204–2626)
    Tayside Police, PO Box 59, West Bell Street, Dundee, DD1 9JU (0382–23200)
—— South Wales Constabulary, Bridgend CF31 3SR (0656–55555)
—— South Yorkshire Police, PO Box 14, Sheffield S3 8LY (0742–78522)
—— Staffordshire Police, Cannock Rd, Stafford ST17 0QG (Stafford 57717)

Police Force Headquarters—*cont.*
—— Suffolk Constabulary, Martlesham Heath, Ipswich IP5 7QS (047–3624848)
—— Surrey Constabulary, Mount Browne, Sandy Lane, Guildford, Surrey (Guildford 71212)
—— Sussex Police, Malling House, Lewes, Sussex BN7 2DZ (Lewes 5432)
—— Thames Valley Police, Kidlington, Oxford OX5 2NX (08675–4343)
—— Warwickshire Constabulary, PO Box 14, Leek Wootton, Warwick CV35 7QB (Warwick 45431)
—— West Mersey Constabulary, Hindlip Hall, Hindley, Worcester WR3 8SP (Worcester 27188)
—— West Midlands Police, PO Box 52, Lloyd House, Colmore Circus, Queensway, Birmingham B4 6NQ (021–236–5000)
—— West Yorkshire Metropolitan Police, PO Box 9, Wakefield, Yorkshire (Wakefield 75222)
—— Wiltshire Constabulary, London Rd, Devizes, Wiltshire (0380–2341)
Polish Embassy, 47 Portland Pl, London W1N 3AG (01–580–4324)
Polish Travel Office 'Orbis', 313 Regent St, London W1 (01–580–8028)
Polytechnic of Central London, 309 Regent St, London W1 (01–580–2020)
Pony Club, National Equestrian Centre, Stoneleigh, Kenilworth, Warwickshire (0203–27192)
Portsmouth Royal Naval Museum, HM Dockyard, Portsmouth, Hants
Portuguese Consulate, 178 Cathedral Rd, Cardiff (0222–26991)
Portuguese Embassy, 11 Belgrave Sq, London SW1X 8PP (01–235–5331)
Portuguese State Information and Tourist Office, 20 Lower Regent St, London SW1Y 4PH (01–930–2455)
Post offices – for local offices look under Post Office Services (Principal Post Offices and District Post Offices) in local telephone directory
Post Office, Central Headquarters, 23 Howland St, London W1P 6HQ (01–631–2345)
Post Office Advisory Committee – address from the Post Office Users' Council or National Council, or in local telephone directory
Post Office District Postmaster – look in local telephone directory under Post Office Services, District Post Offices
Post Office External Telecommunications Executive, 2–12 Gresham St, London EC2 (01–432–1234)
Post Office Head Postmaster – look in local telephone directory under Post Office Services, Principal Post Offices
Post Office International and Maritime Telecommunications Region, Wireless Telegraph Section, Mercantile Marine Office, Union House, St Martins Le Grand, London EC1N 1AR
Post Office Telecommunications Headquarters, 2–12 Gresham St, London EC2V 7AG (01–357–3000)
Post Office Users' Council for Northern Ireland, Chamber of Commerce, 22 Gt Victoria St, Belfast BT2 7PU (Belfast 44113)
Post Office Users' Council for Scotland, Alhambra House, 45 Waterloo St, Glasgow G2 6AT (041–248–2855)
Post Office Users' Council for Wales, 142–3 St Helen's Rd, Swansea SA1 4DE (0792–54795)
Post Office Users' National Council for England, Waterloo Bridge House, Waterloo Bridge Rd, London SE1 8UA (01–928–9458)
Potato Marketing Board
—— 50 Hans Crescent, Knightsbridge, London SW1X 0NB (01–589–4874)
—— Scottish Division, 8 Manor Place, Edinburgh EH3 7DF (031–225–1466)
Pregnancy Advisory Service, 40 Margaret St, London W1 (01–409–2081)
Pre-School Playgroups Association, Alford House, Aveline St, London SE11 5DH (01–582–8871)
Pre-School Playgroups Association Regional Offices
—— East Midlands, Willson House, 25/29 Derby Rd, Nottingham NG1 5AW (0602–45906)
—— Eastern, 4th Floor, Sidney House, Sussex St, Cambridge CB1 1PF (0223–311908)
—— Greater London, 314/316 Vauxhall Bridge Rd, London SW1V 1AA (01–828–2417)
—— Inner London, 314/316 Vauxhall Bridge Rd, London SW1V 1AA (01–828–1401)
—— North West, Hotspur House, Gloucester St, Manchester M1 5QB (061–236–7847)
—— Northern, St Andrew's Kirk, 13 Grantham Rd, Newcastle-upon Tyne NE2 1QX (0632–20361)
—— Northern Ireland, 84 Donegall Pass, Belfast BT7 1BX, N. Ireland (0232–33385)
—— Scottish, Playgroup House, 7 Royal Terrace, Glasgow G3 7NT (041–331–1340)
—— South East, Neale House, Moat Rd, East Grinstead, W. Sussex (0342–312553)
—— South West, Room 15, Pearl Assurance House, 236 High St, Exeter, Devon EX4 3NN (0392–58623)

Pre-School Playgroups Association Regional Offices—*cont.*
—— Southern, St Mary's Centre, Chain St, Reading RG1 2HX (0734–594064)
—— Wales, Cartrefle College, Cefn Rd, Wrexham, Clwyd LL13 9NL (0978 58195)
—— West Midlands, 6 Prince's Chambers, 6 Corporation St, Birmingham B24 4RN (021–643–0063)
—— Yorkshire and North Humberside, Charlton House, Hunslet Rd, Leeds LS10 1EU (0532–452514)
Press Council, 1 Salisbury Sq, London EC4Y 8AE (01–353–1248)
Price Commission, Headquarters, Neville House, Page St, London SW1P 4LS (01–828–7070)
Price Commission Offices
—— 3rd Floor, Midland Hotel, Whitla St, Belfast BT15 1JU (0232–740493/4)
—— Bayliss House, Hurst St, Birmingham B5 4BS (021–622 3541/4)
—— 11 Park Place, Clifton, Bristol BS8 1LS (0272–299727)
—— Three Crowns House, 72–80 Hills Rd, Cambridge CB2 1LA (0223–59171/4)
—— 4th Floor, Westminster House, 95–7 St Mary St, Cardiff CF1 1DX (0222–41652/4)
—— Sussex House, High St, Crawley, Sussex RH10 1YR (0293–37352/4)
—— Trafalgar House, 75 Hope St, Glasgow G2 6NG (041–204–0577/9, 0570)
—— 3rd Floor, Royal Exchange House, Boar Lane, Leeds LS1 5NS (0532–38133)
—— Corn Exchange Building, Fenwick St, Liverpool L2 7QH (051–227–3607)
—— 2nd Floor, Wingate House, Shaftesbury Ave, London W1B 7AE (01–439–4401)
—— 5 Trinity St, London SE1 1DH (01–403–0565)
—— Warwickgate House, 7 Warwick Rd, Old Trafford, Manchester M16 0HP (061–872–6911/4)
—— Gunner House, Neville St, Newcastle-upon-Tyne NE1 5DN (0632–611331)
—— Spur E, Block 6, Government Buildings, Chalfont Dr, Nottingham NG8 3RP (0602–291111)
—— 10 Portman Rd, Battle Farm Trading Estate, Reading RG3 1JN (0734–598022/5)
Prime Minister's Office, 10 Downing St, London SW1 (01–233–3000)
Principal Registry of the Family Division, Somerset House, Strand, London WC2 (01–405–7641)
Privy Council Office, 68 Whitehall, London SW1A 2AT (01–233–3000)
Probate Registry, Principal Office, Somerset House, London WC2R 1LP (01–405–7641)
Probate Registry Regional Offices
—— South West Wing, Bush House, London WC2B 4QN (01–836–7366)
—— Garth Rd, Bangor LL57 1EA (0248–2410)
—— Royal Courts of Justice (Belfast), Chichester St, Belfast BT1 3JF (0232–35111)
—— Cavendish House, Waterloo St, Birmingham B2 5PS (021–236–6263)
—— Market St, Bodmin PL31 2JW (0208–2279)
—— 28 Richmond Place, Brighton BN2 2NA (0273–684071)
—— 4th Floor, 37–41 Prince St, Bristol BS1 4PX (0272–23915)
—— 49 Cardiff Rd, Llandaff, Cardiff CF5 2YW (0222–562422)
—— 2 Victoria Place, Carlisle CA1 1ER (0228–21751)
—— 14 King St, Carmarthen SA31 1BL (0267–6238)
—— 17 Cuppin St, Chester CH1 2DA (0244–20997)
—— 94 Fore St, Exeter EX4 3HZ (0392–74515)
—— 3 Pitt St, Gloucester GL1 2BJ (0452–22585)
—— 4th Floor, Commerce House, Paragon St, Hull HU1 3PW (0482–28807)
—— 15 Museum St, Ipswich IP1 1HG (0473–53724)
—— Mitre House, Church St, Lancaster LA1 1HE (0524–2791)
—— Devereux House, East Parade, Leeds LS1 2BA (0532–31505)
—— Government Buildings, Newark St, Leicester LE1 5SE (0533–546117)
—— Mill House, Brayford Side North, Lincoln LN1 1YW (0522–23648)
—— 3rd Floor, India Buildings, Water St, Liverpool L2 0QR (051–236–8264)
—— 3rd Floor, 5–11 London Rd, Maidstone ME16 8HP (0622–51737)
—— 9th Floor, Astley House, 23 Quay St, Manchester M3 4AT (061–834–4319)
—— 12–16 Woodlands Rd, Middlesbrough TS1 3BE (0642–44770)
—— 2nd Floor, Plummer House, Croft St, Newcastle-upon-Tyne NE1 6NP (0632–28543)
—— 65 Cathedral Close, Norwich NR1 4DN (0603–26648)
—— Castle Gate House, Castle Gate, Nottingham NG1 7BU (0602–51337)
—— 10A New Rd, Oxford OX1 1LY (0865–41163)
—— Clifton House, Broadway, Peterborough PE1 1SL (0733–62802)
—— 4th Floor, Belgrave House, Bank St, Sheffield S1 1QN (0742–29920)

Probate Registry Regional Offices—*cont.*
—— 2nd Floor, Norwich Union House, Trinity St, Hanley, Stoke-on-Trent ST1 5PZ (0682–23736)
—— 4–5 St Peter St, Winchester SO23 8BL (0962–3046)
—— Duncombe Place, York YO1 2EA (0904–24210)
Professional Footballers' Association, 12 Corn Exchange Buildings, Ranging Ditch, Manchester M4 3BN (061–834–7554)
Professional Golfers' Association, Kennington Oval, London SE11 (01–735–8803)
Professional Tennis Coaches' Association, 21 Glencairn Court, Landsown Road, Cheltenham, Glos (0242–27401)
Public Carriage Office, Penton St, London N1 (01–278–1744)
Public Libraries – listed under the name of your local authority in the telephone directory
Public Record Offices
—— Chancery Lane, London WC2A 1LR (01–405–0741)
—— Ruskin Ave, Kew, Surrey TW9 4DU (01–876–3444)
Public Record Office for Northern Ireland, 66 Balmoral Ave, Belfast BT9 6NY (0232–661621)
Public Trustee Office, 24 Kingsway, London WC2B 6JX (01–405–4300)

Q

Qatar, Embassy of the State of, 10 Reeves Mews, Grosvenor Sq, London W1Y 3PB (01–499–8831)
Queen's Awards Office, William National House, 11–13 Holborn Viaduct, London EC1A 1EL

R

Racecourse Association, 42 Portman Sq, London W1 (01–486–3082)
Racing Industry Liaison Committee, 42 Portman Sq, London W1 (01–486–4921)
Racing Information Bureau, 42 Portman Sq, London W1 (01–486–4571)
Radio and Television Retailers' Association, 100 St Martin's Lane, London WC2N 4BD (01–836–1463)
Radio City (Sound of Merseyside) Ltd, PO Box 194, 8–10 Stanley St, Liverpool L69 1LD (051–227–5100)
Radio Clyde, Ranken House, Blythswood Court, Anderston Cross Centre, Glasgow G2 7LB (041–204–2555)
Radio Forth, Forth House, Forth St, Edinburgh EH1 3LF (031–556–9255)
Radio Hallam, PO Box 194, Hartshead, Sheffield S1 1GP (0742–71188)
Radio Orwell, Electric House, Lloyds Ave, Ipswich IP1 3HU (0473–216971)
Radio Tees, 74 Dovecot St, Stockton-on-Tees (0642–615111)
Radio Trent, 29–31 Castle Gate, Nottingham NG1 7AP (0602–581731)
Radio Victory, PO Box 257, Portsmouth PO1 5RT (0705–27799)
RAF – see Royal Air Force
Ramblers' Association, 1–4 Crawford Mews, London W1H 1PT (01–262–1477)
Records and Recording, PO Box 294, 2–4 Old Pye St, London SW1 PLR (01–222–4112)
Red Deer Commission, Knowsley, 82 Fairfield Rd, Inverness IV3 5LH (0463–31751)
Regional Arts Associations
—— Eastern, 30 Station Rd, Cambridge CB1 2JH (0223–67707).
—— East Midlands, 1 Frederick St, Loughborough, Leicestershire LE11 3BH (0509–67136)
—— Greater London, 25–31 Tavistock Place, London WC1H 9SF (01–387–9541)

Regional Arts Associations—*cont.*
—— Lincolnshire and Humberside, Beaumont Lodge, Beaumont Fee, Lincoln LN1 1UN (0522–33555)
—— Merseyside, Bluecoat Chambers, School Lane, Liverpool L1 3BX (051–709–0671)
—— Northern, 31 New Bridge St, Newcastle-upon-Tyne NE1 8JY (0632–610446)
—— North West, 52 King St, Manchester M2 4LY (061–833–9471)
—— Southern, 19 Southgate St, Winchester, Hampshire SO23 7EB (0962–69422)
—— South East, 58 London Road, Southborough, Tunbridge Wells, Kent TN4 0PR (0892–38743)
—— South West, 23 Southernhay East, Exeter, Devon EX1 1QL (0392–70338)
—— West Midlands, Lloyds Bank Chambers, Market St, Stafford ST16 2AP (0785–2788)
—— Yorkshire, Glyde House, Glydegate, Bradford, Yorkshire BD5 0BQ (0274–23051)
—— North Wales, 10 Wellfield House, Bangor, Gwynedd LL57 1ER (0248–53248)
—— South East Wales, Victoria Street, Cwmbran, Gwent NP4 3JP (06333–67530)
—— West Wales, Dark Gate, Red St, Carmarthen, Dyfed (0267–4248)

Regional Economic Planning Boards
—— Eastern, Charles House, 375 Kensington High St, London W14 8QH (01–603–3444)
—— East Midlands, Cranbrook House, Cranbrook St, Nottingham NG1 1FB (0602–46121)
—— Northern, Gallowgate, Newcastle NE1 4TD (0632–27575)
—— North West, Sunley Buildings, 17th Floor, Piccadilly Plaza, Manchester M1 4BE (061–832–9111)
—— Scottish, St Andrew's House, Edinburgh EH1 3DD (031–556–8501)
—— South East, Charles House, 375 Kensington High St, London W14 8QH (01–603–3444)
—— South West, Froomsgate House, Rupert St, Bristol BS1 2QN (0272–297201)
—— Welsh, Cathays Park, Cardiff CF1 3NQ (0222–28066)
—— West Midlands, Five Ways House, Islington Row Middle Way, Birmingham B15 1SR (021–643–8191)
—— Yorkshire and Humberside, City House, Leeds LS1 4PS (0532–38232)

Regional Gas Consumers' Council – address from local gas showroom (look under gas in local telephone directory) or British Gas Corporation Region head office

Regional Health Authority, Alcoholism Treatment Units
—— East Anglia, Fulbourn Hospital, Cambridge
—— London
    Bethlem/Maudsley B6, Maudsley, Denmark Hill
    Elm Dean, Bexley Hospital
    West Park, Epsom
    Graylingham
    St Bernards, Southall
    Worlingham Park, Surrey
—— Mersey, Moston Hospital, Chester
—— North Western
    Lancaster Moor, Lancaster
    Springfield, Manchester
    Withington, Manchester
    Prestwich Hospital, Prestwich
—— Northern, St Nicholas, Gosforth
—— Oxford, Ley Clinic, Littlemore
—— South Western, Deepway House, Exminster Hospital, Exminster
—— Trent, Mapperley, Nottingham
—— Wales, Whitchurch Hospital, Cardiff
—— Wessex
    Park Prewitt, Basingstoke
    Saint James, Portsmouth
    Herbert Day Hospital, Westbourne
—— West Midlands
    All Saints, Birmingham
    Central Hospital, Hatton
    St George's, Stafford
—— Yorkshire
    Broadgate Hospital, Beverley
    Scalebor Park Hospital, Ilkley

Register of Companies – see Registrar of Companies
Registrar General of England and Wales, General Register Office, St Catherine's House, 10 Kingsway, London WC2B 6JP (01–242–0262)
Registrar General for Northern Ireland, General Register Office, Oxford House, 49–55 Chichester St, Belfast BT1 4HL
Registrar General for Scotland, General Register Office, New Register House, Edinburgh EH1 3YT (031–556–3952)
Registrar-General of Shipping and Seamen, Llantrisant Rd, Cardiff CF5 27S (0222–561–221)
Registrar of Births, Deaths and Marriages – look in telephone directory either under the name of your local authority or under 'Registration of Births, Deaths and Marriages' (district offices in Scotland and N. Ireland; sub-district offices in England and Wales)
Registrar of British Ships, Custom House, Lower Thames St, London EC3 6EE (01–283–8633)
Registrar of Business Names
—— England and Wales, Pembroke House, 40–56 City Rd, London EC1Y 2DN (01–253–9393)
—— Scotland, Exchequer Chambers, 102 George St, Edinburgh EH2 3DJ
Registrar of Companies
—— England and Wales, Crown Way, Maindy, Cardiff CF4 3UZ (0222–388588)
—— London Search Room, Companies House, 55–71 City Rd, London EC1Y 1BB (01–253–9393)
—— Northern Ireland, Department of Commerce, 43–7 Chichester St, Belfast BT1 4RJ (0232–34121/4)
—— Scotland, Exchequer Chambers, 102 George St, Edinburgh EH2 3DJ
Registrar of Titles, Land Registry, River House, 48 High St, Belfast BT1 4GA
Rent Assessment Committee – for address contact your local authority, or ask at a Citizens' Advice Bureau
Rent Officer – for address contact your local authority or ask at a Citizens' Advice Bureau
Rent Registration Office – see Scottish Rent Registration Offices
Rent Tribunals – for address contact your local authority or Citizens' Advice Bureau
Restrictive Practices Court, Royal Courts of Justice, Strand, London WC2A 2LL
Road Haulage Association, 22 Upper Woburn Place, London WC1 (01–387–9711)
Road Time Trials Council, 'Dallacre', Mill Rd, Yarwell, Peterborough PE8 6PS (0780–782464)
Road Transport Industry Training Board, Capitol House, Empire Way, Wembley HA9 0NG
Romanian Embassy, 4 Palace Green, London W8 4QD (01–937–9666)
Romanian Information Office, 98 Jermyn St, London SW1 (01–930–8812)
Rothschilds and Sons Ltd, Head Office, New Court, St Swithin's Lane, London EC4 (01–626–4356)
Royal Academy of Arts, Piccadilly, London W1V 0DS (01–734–9052)
Royal Aero Club, Kimberley House, Vaughan Way, Leicester (0533–51051)
Royal Aeronautical Society, 4 Hamilton Place, London W1V 0BQ (01–499–3515)
Royal Air Force, Inspectorate of Recruiting, Government Buildings, London Rd, Stanmore, Middlesex HA7 4PZ
Royal Air Force Participation Committee, MOD (S4d(Air)), Room 0/7 Metropole Building, Northumberland Ave, London WC2N 5BL
Royal Air Force Personnel Management Centre, Ministry of Defence, RAF Innsworth, Gloucester GL3 1E2
Royal Air Force Museum, Hendon Aerodrome, London NW9 (01–205–2266)
Royal and Ancient Golf Club of St Andrews, Fife KY16 9JD (033–481–2112)
Royal Archives, Windsor Castle, Berkshire
Royal Armoured Tank Museum, Royal Armoured Corps Centre, Bovington Camp, Nr Wareham, Dorset
Royal Association for Disability and Rehabilitation (RADAR), 34 Ecceston Sq, London SW1V 1PE
Royal Astronomical Society, Burlington House, Piccadilly, London W1V 0NL (01–734–4582)
Royal Automobile Club
—— Headquarters, PO Box 100, RAC House, Lansdowne Road, Croydon (01–686–2314)
—— 85 Pall Mall, London SW1Y 5HW
—— Motor Sports Division, 31 Belgrave Sq, London SW1X 8QH (01–235–8601)
—— Touring Services, PO Box 92, Lansdowne Rd, Croydon, Surrey (01–686–2525)
Royal Auxiliary Air Force, No. 1 Maritime Headquarters Unit, Valency House, Sandy Lane, Northwood, Middx (0293–26161 ex 647)
Royal Bank of Scotland Ltd, Head Office, PO Box 31, 42 St Andrews Sq, Edinburgh EH2 2YE (031–556–9151)

Royal Botanic Gardens, Kew, Surrey (01-940-1171)
Royal Botanical Gardens, Box 399, Hamilton, Canada L8N 3H8
Royal Caledonian Curling Club, 2 Coates Crescent, Edinburgh EH3 7AL (031-225-7083)
Royal College of Pathologists, 2 Carlton Terrace, London SW1 5AF
Royal College of Veterinary Surgeons, 32 Belgrave Sq, London SW1X 8PQ (01-235-4971)
Royal Commission on Historical Manuscripts, Quality House, Quality Court, London WC8 (01-242-1198)
Royal Commonwealth Society, 18 Northumberland Ave, London WC2N 5BJ (01-930-6733)
Royal Courts of Justice, Chichester St, Belfast BT1 3JF (Belfast 35111)
Royal Danish Embassy, 29 Pont St, London SW1X 0BA (01-584-0102)
Royal Fine Art Commission, 2 Carlton Gardens, London SW1Y 5AA (01-930-3935)
Royal Fine Art Commission for Scotland, 22 Melville St, Edinburgh EH3 7NS (031-225-5434)
Royal General Bulbgrowers' Society, Parklaan, Hillegom, The Netherlands
Royal Greenwich Observatory, Herstmonceux Castle, Hailsham, East Sussex BN27 1RP (032-181-3171)
Royal Horticultural Society, PO Box 313, Vincent Square, London SW1P 2PE (01-834-4333)
Royal Horticultural Society's Garden, Wisley, Woking, Surrey GU23 6QB
Royal Hospital, Chelsea, London SW3 4SL (01-730-0161)
Royal Incorporation of Architects in Scotland, 15 Rutland Square, Edinburgh (031-229-7205)
Royal Institute of British Architects, 66 Portland Place, London W1 (01-580-5533)
Royal Institution of Chartered Surveyors, 12 Great George St, Parliament Sq, London SW1P 3AD (01-839-5600)
Royal Institute of Chemistry, 30 Russell Sq, London WC1B 5DT (01-580-3482)
Royal Institution of Naval Architects, 10 Upper Belgrave St, London SW1X 8BQ (01-235-4622)
Royal Marines, Drafting and Records Office, HMS *Centurion*, Grange Rd, Gosport, Hants PO13 9XA
Royal Marines Museum, Eastney Barracks, Southsea, Hants
Royal Marines Reserve
—— City of London, 2 Old Jamaica Rd, Bermondsey, London SE16 4AN (01-237-4331)
—— Bristol, Dorset House, Litfield Place, Bristol BZ8 3NA (0272-33523)
—— Merseyside, Morpeth Dock, Birkenhead, Merseyside L41 1EQ (051-647-7815)
—— Tyne, Wingrove House, Westgate Rd, Newcastle-upon-Tyne NE4 9PQ (06327-31225)
—— Scotland, 1 Maxwell Rd, Eglington Toll, Glasgow G41 1PQ (041-423-5451)
Royal Mint
—— Headquarters, Tower Hill, London EC3N 4DR (01-488-3424)
—— Marketing Manager, Llantrisant, Pontyclun, Mid Glamorgan CF7 8YT (0443-222111)
—— Numismatic Bureau, PO Box 6, Pontyclun, Mid Glamorgan CF7 8YT (0443-223880)
Royal National Eisteddfod, Parks Department, Cardiff City Corporation, Heath Park, Cardiff (0222-750984)
Royal National Institute for the Blind, 224 Great Portland St, London W1
Royal National Lifeboat Institution, 21 Ebury St, London SW1 (01-730-0031)
Royal Naval Reserve Communications Training Centres
—— 275 Broad St, Birmingham B1 2DU
—— 75 Smith St, Coventry CV6 5EH
—— 158 Sidwell St, Exeter EX4 6RN
—— Harrogate Rd, Yeadon, Leeds S19 7XS
—— Townbury House, Blackfriars St, Manchester M3 5AJ
—— 46 Carrington St, Nottingham NG1 7GB
—— Drill Hall, 116 Hartington Rd, Preston PR1 8PQ
—— Cavendish Buildings, 218 West St, Sheffield S1 4EU
—— York Bank Chambers, Finkle St, Stockton TS18 1AR
—— Kings Dock, Swansea SA1 8QU
—— 524 London Rd, Westcliff-on-Sea SS0 9HS
Royal Naval Reserve Sea Training Centres
—— HMS *Caroline*, Milewater Basin, Belfast BT3 9AD
—— HMS *Flying Fox*, Winterstoke Rd, Bristol BS8 3NS
—— HMS *Cambria*, 245 East Dock (West Side), Cardiff CF1 5TS
—— HMS *Camperdown*, Marine Parade, Dundee DD1 3JB
—— HMS *Claverhouse*, Granton Sq, Edinburgh EH5 1HB

Royal Naval Reserve Sea Training Centres—*cont.*
—— HMS *Calliope*, South Shore Rd, Gateshead NE8 2BE
—— HMS *Graham*, 130 Whitefield Rd, Govan, Glasgow G51 2SA
—— HMS *Sussex*, Maxwell's Wharf, Wharf Rd, Hove, Sussex BN4 1WR
—— HMS *Eaglet*, Salthouse Dock, Liverpool L3 0AA
—— HMS *President*, King's Reach, London EC4Y 0HJ
—— HMS *Wessex*, No. 50 Berth, Eastern Docks, Southampton SO9 2TJ
Royal Naval Reserve Shore Headquarters Units
—— HMS *Southwick*, Fort Southwick, Fareham, Hants
—— HMS *Wildfire*, Medway Rd, Gillingham, Kent
—— HMS *Dalriada*, Navy Buildings, Eldon St, Greenock
—— HMS *Northwood*, Northwood, Middlesex HA6 3HT
—— HMS *Vivid*, Maritime Headquarters, Mount Wise, Plymouth, Devon PL1 4JH
—— HMS *Scotia*, Maritime Headquarters, Rosyth, Fife
Royal Navy, Director General of Defence Accounts, PP1 B11, HMS *Centurion*, Grange Road, Gosport, Hants PO13 9XA
Royal Navy, Director of Recruiting, Ministry of Defence, Old Admiralty Building, Spring Gardens, London SW1A 2BE
Royal Nepalese Embassy, 12A Kensington Palace Gdns, London W8 4QU (01–229–1594)
Royal New Zealand Institute of Horticulture Inc, Nomenclature Committee, PO Box 450, Wellington, New Zealand
Royal Observer Corps Headquarters, Bentley Priory, Stanmore, Middlesex
Royal Ocean Racing Club, 20 St James's Place, London SW1 (01–493–5252)
Royal Scottish Automobile Club, 11 Blythswood Sq, Glasgow G2 (041–221–3850)
Royal Scottish Country Dance Society, 12 Coates Crescent, Edinburgh EH3 7AF (031–225–3854)
Royal Society for the Prevention of Cruelty to Animals, National Headquarters, Manor House, The Causeway, Horsham, Sussex (0403–64181)
Royal Society of Arts, 8 John Adam St, London WC2 (01–839–2366)
Royal Society of London, 6 Carlton House Terrace, London SW1Y 5AG (01–839–5561)
Royal Swedish Embassy, 23 North Row, London W1R 2DN (01–499–9500)
Royal Yachting Association
—— 8 Frederick St, Edinburgh EH2 2HB (031–225–7320)
—— 24 Nant Bychan, Moelfre, Gwynedd
—— Craigaveagh, Skitrick Island, Killinchy, Co Down (0238–541579)
—— Victoria Way, Woking, Surrey (048–62–5022)
Royal Zoological Society of Scotland, Murrayfield, Edinburgh EH1 26TS
Rubber Trade Association of London, Cereal House, 58 Mark Lane, EC3R 7NE (01–480–5388)
Rugby Football League, 180 Chapeltown Rd, Leeds 7 (0532–634637)
Rugby Football Union, Twickenham, Middx (01–892–8161)
Ruskin College, Walton St, Oxford (0865–54331)
Rwanda Diplomatic Mission to the UK, Embassy of the Rwanda Republic, 101 Boulevard St Michel, Brussels 4, Belgium (02/34–17–63)

S

St Crispin's Boot Trades Association, St Crispin's House, Desborough, Nr Kettering, Northants (0536–760374)
St Dunstans, PO Box 58, 191 Old Marylebone Rd, London MS1 8QU (01–723–5021)
St James's Palace, York House, London SW1 (01–930–4872 – Duke and Duchess of Kent)
Salmon and Trout Association, Fishmongers' Hall, London EC4R (01–626–3531)
Salvation Army, Head Office, 101 Queen Victoria St, London EC4 (01–236–5222)
Samaritans
—— Headquarters, 39 Wallbrook, London EC4 (01–626–2277)
—— local branches – look in your local telephone directory under Samaritans
Saudi Arabian Embassy, 30 Belgrave Sq, London SW1X 8QB (01–235–0831)
School for Dental Auxiliaries, New Cross Hospital, Avonley Rd, London SE14 5ER (01–639–7761)

Schools Council, 160 Great Portland St, London W1N 6LL (01–580–0352)
Science Research Council, State House, High Holborn, London WC1R 4TA (01–242–1262)
Scientific Authority for Animals, c/o Countryside and Recreation Division 4, Department of the Environment, 17–19 Rochester Row, London SW1P 1LN (01–212–0417)
Scottish Agricultural Wages Board, Chester House, 500 Gorgie Rd, Edinburgh EH11 3AW (031–443–4020)
Scottish Amateur Athletic Association, 25 Bearsdon Rd, Glasgow G13 1YL
Scottish Amateur Ballroom Dancers Association, 23 Falloch Rd, Bearsden, Glasgow G61 1LH
Scottish Amateur Boxing Association, Heatherlea, West Bay, Dunoon, Argyll (0369–2887)
Scottish Amateur Fencing Union, 39 Ashton Lane, Glasgow G12 8SJ
Scottish Amateur Rowing Association, 139 Old Dalkeith Rd, Little France, Edinburgh EH16 4SZ (031–644–1070)
Scottish Amateur Swimming Association, Pathfoot Building, University of Stirling FK9 4LA (0786–70544)
Scottish Amateur Wrestling Association, 13 Kay Park Terrace, Kilmarnock
Scottish Archery Association, 6 Strand Head, Stewarton, Kilmarnock (Stewarton 2760)
Scottish Arts Council, 19 Charlotte Sq, Edinburgh EH2 4DF (031–226–6051)
Scottish Association of Opticians, 116 Blythswood St, Glasgow G2 4JQ (041–221–3492)
Scottish Association of Sand and Land Yacht Clubs, 11 Mavisbank Place, Polton, Lasswade CH13 1DQ
Scottish Auto-Cycle Union, Kippilaw, Longridge Rd, Whitburn, West Lothian (0501–42663)
Scottish Badminton Union, 8 Frederick St, Edinburgh EH2 2HB (031–226–5050)
Scottish Billiards Association and Control Council, Rubismore House, 2 Cambridge St, Edinburgh EH1 2DY (031–229–0444)
Scottish Bowling Association, 50 Wellington St, Glasgow G2 6EF (041–221–8999)
Scottish Braille Press, Craigmiller Park, Edinburgh (031–667–6230)
Scottish Bus Group Ltd, 6 New St, Edinburgh 8 (031–556–2515)
Scottish Canoe Association, 8 Frederick St, Edinburgh EH2 2HB (031–225–3993)
Scottish Clay Pigeon Association, 42 Hill St, Tillicoultry, Clackmannanshire
Scottish Conservative and Unionist Association, 11 Atholl Crescent, Edinburgh EH3 8HG (031–229–1342)
Scottish Conservative Party Headquarters, 11 Atholl Crescent, Edinburgh EH3 8HG (031–229–1342)
Scottish Consumer Council, 4 Somerset Place, Glasgow G3 (041–332–3377)
Scottish Council for Civil Liberties, 146 Holland St, Glasgow G2 (041–945–1380 evenings only)
Scottish Council on Disability, 18–19 Claremont Crescent, Edinburgh EH7 4QD
Scottish Courts Administration, PO Box 37, 28 North Bridge, Edinburgh EH1 1RA (031–226–5911)
Scottish Cricket Union, 8 Frederick St, Edinburgh EH2 2HB (031–225–3993)
Scottish Croquet Association, 17 Greygoran, New Sauchie, Alloa, Clackmannanshire (0259–213515)
Scottish Cyclists' Union, 293 Rosemount Place, Aberdeen
Scottish Daily Newspaper Society, 90 Mitchell St, Glasgow G1 (041–221–9741)
Scottish Design Centre, 72 St Vincent St, Glasgow G2 5TN (041–221–6121)
Scottish Development Agency, 120 Bothwell St, Glasgow G2 (041–248–2700)
Scottish Development Agency, Small Business Division, 102 Telford Rd, Edinburgh EH4 29P (031–343–1411)
Scottish Development Department, New St Andrews House, St James Centre, Edinburgh EH1 3SZ (031–556–8400)
Scottish Economic Planning Department
—— Head Office, New St Andrews House, Edinburgh (031–556 8400)
—— Industrial Development, Alhambra House, 45 Waterloo St, Glasgow G2 6AT (041–248–2855)
Scottish Education Department, New St Andrew's House, St James Centre, Edinburgh EH1 3SY (031–556–8400)
Scottish Federation of Coarse Angling, 11 Tarbert Ave, Priory Bridge, Blantyre G72 9PB
Scottish Federation of Housing Associations, 56 Hanover St, Edinburgh
Scottish Federation of Sea Anglers, 8 Frederick St, Edinburgh EH2 2HB (031–225–7611)
Scottish Field Archery Association, 10 Glenavon Drive, Cairneyhill, Dunfermline
Scottish Film Council, 16 Woodside Terrace, Glasgow C3 (041–332–5413)
Scottish Football Association Ltd, 6 Park Gardens, Glasgow G3 7YF (041–332–6372)
Scottish Football League, 188 West Regent St, Glasgow G2 4RY (041–248–3844)

Scottish Golf Union, c/o Bank of Scotland Building, 54 Shandwick Place, Edinburgh EH2 4RT (031–226–6711)
Scottish Handball Association, 311 Househillwood Rd, Craigbank, Glasgow G53 6SR
Scottish Health Education Unit, 21 Lansdowne Cresent, Edinburgh 12 (031–337–3251)
Scottish Highlands and Islands Development Board, Bridge House, 27 Bank St, Inverness IV1 1QR (0463–34171)
Scottish Hockey Association, 15 Cadogan Rd, Edinburgh EH16 6LY (031–225–6448)
Scottish Home and Health Department, New St Andrew's House, St James' Centre, Edinburgh EH1 3TF
Scottish Indoor Bowling Association, 3 Rowallan Crescent, Prestwick KA9 2HE
Scottish Information Office, Room 2/89, New St Andrew's House, Edinburgh EH1 3TD
Scottish Joint Committee for Anglers, 10 Corrennie Drive, Edinburgh EH10 6EQ
Scottish Judo Federation, 8 Frederick St, Edinburgh EH2 2HB (031–226–3566)
Scottish Labour Party, Room 267, 12 Waterloo St, Glasgow
Scottish Ladies Golfing Association, Heemsted, Gosford Road, Longuiddry, East Lothian
Scottish Ladies Lacrosse Association, 106 Beecha Ave, Newton Mearns, Glasgow G77 5BL (041–639–2970)
Scottish Law Commission, 140 Causewayside, Edinburgh EH9 1PR (031–668–2131)
Scottish Lawn Tennis Association, 1 Royal Terrace, Edinburgh EH7 5AD (031–556–6237)
Scottish Liberal Party Regional Offices
—— 68 Channel St, Galashiels (0896–2583)
—— 5 Wells St, Inverness (0463–32360)
Scottish Liberal Party Headquarters, 2 Atholl Place, Edinburgh EH3 8HP (031–229–7484)
Scottish Motor Trade Association, 3 Palmerston Place, Edinburgh EH12 5AQ (031–225–3643)
Scottish National Party Headquarters, 6 North Charlotte St, Edinburgh EH2 4JH (031–226–3661)
Scottish National Rifle Association, 119 Woodfield Ave, Colinton, Edinburgh, EH13 0QR
Scottish National Ski Council, The Barn, Balmore, Torrance, By Glasgow (03602–496)
Scottish Netball Association, 927 Aikenhead Rd, Glasgow 644 4QE
Scottish Newspaper Proprietors' Association, 10 York Place, Edinburgh (031–556–6787)
Scottish Office
—— New St Andrew's House, St James Centre, Edinburgh EH1 3SX (031–556–8400)
—— Dover House, Whitehall, London SW1A 2AU (01–930–6151)
—— Statistics, New St Andrew's House, Edinburgh (031–556–8400)
Scottish Official Board of Highland Dancing, PO Box 501, Falcon Road West, Edinburgh EH10 4EH
Scottish Orienteering Association, Gartincaber Lodge, Doune, Perthshire (Doune 712)
Scottish Photography Group, 58 High St, Edinburgh (031–557–1140)
Scottish Pistol Association, Gowan Brae, Blairgowrie, Perthshire
Scottish Records Advisory Council, HM General Register House, Edinburgh EH1 3YY (031–556–6585)
Scottish Record Office, HM General Register House, Edinburgh EH1 3YY (031–556–6585)
Scottish Rent Registration Offices
—— 47 Holburn St, Aberdeen AB1 6BR (0224–25288)
—— 26 East Dock St, Dundee DD1 3EY (0382–24082)
—— 6/7 Coates Place, Edinburgh EH3 7AA (031–225–1200)
—— St Andrew House, 141 West Nile St, Glasgow G1 2RN (041–332–6981)
—— 43 Civic Sq, Windmill Hill St, Motherwell, Lanarkshire (0698–65599)
Scottish Rights of Way Society, 6 Abercrombie Place, Edinburgh (031–556–3942)
Scottish Rugby Union, Murrayfield, Edinburgh EH12 5PJ (031–337–2346)
Scottish Sailing Association, 105 Clermiston Rd, Edinburgh EH12 6UR
Scottish Smallbore Rifle Association, 88 Southbrae Drive, Glasgow G13 1TZ
Scottish Sport Parachute Association, 99 West Torbain, Kirkcaldy, Fife (0592–200042)
Scottish Sports Association for the Disabled, Fife Institute of Physical and Recreational Education, Viewfield Rd, Glenrothes, Fife KY6 2RA
Scottish Sports Council, 1 St Colme St, Edinburgh EH3 6AA (031–225–8411)
Scottish Sports Council Sports Centres
—— Glenmore Lodge National Outdoor Training Centre, Aviemore, Inverness-shire PH22 1QU (Cairngorm 256)
—— Inverclyde National Sports Training Centre, Largs, Ayrshire KA30 8RW (047–567–2468)
—— Cumbrae National Water Sports Training Centre, Gt Cumbrae, Ayrshire (047–557–3757)

Scottish Squash Rackets Association, 8 Frederick St, Edinburgh EH2 2HB (031-225-3993)
Scottish Standing Conference on Sport, 1 St Colme St, Edinburgh EG3 6AA (031-225-8411)
Scottish Sub-Aqua Club, 16 Royal Crescent, Glasgow G3 7SL (041-332-9291)
Scottish Surfing Federation, 21 Fairway, Haddington, East Lothian EH41 4EW
Scottish Table Tennis Association, 151 Vancouver Dr, East Kilbride (041-339-8888)
Scottish Television Ltd, Cowcaddens, Glasgow G2 3PR (041-332-9999)
Scottish Tourist Board, 23 Ravelston Terrace, Edinburgh EH4 3EU (031-332-2433)
Scottish Trades Union Congress, 12 Woodlands Terrace, Glasgow 3 (041-332-4946)
Scottish Trampoline Association, 8 Frederick St, Edinburgh EH2 2HB (031-225-3993)
Scottish Volleyball Association, 8 Frederick St, Edinburgh EH2 2HB (031-225-7311)
Scottish Waterski Association, 9 Park Crescent, West Quarter, Falkirk, Stirlingshire
Scottish Women's Amateur Athletic Association, 8 Frederick St, Edinburgh EH2 2HB (031-225-7643)
Scottish Women's Bowling Association, 15 Cardonald Gardens, Glasgow G52 3PQ
Scottish Women's Football Association, 120 Cedar Rd, Abronhill, Cumbernauld, Glasgow G67 (023-67-27758)
Scottish Women's Hockey Association, 31 Dollar Ave, Falkirk, Stirlingshire FK2 7LF
Scottish Women's Indoor Bowling Association, 76 Chalmers Rd, Ayr
Scottish Women's Keep Fit Association, 18B Forrester Park Ave, Edinburgh EH12 9AN
Scottish Youth Hostels Association, 7 Glebe Crescent, Stirling FK8 2JA (0786-2821)
Secretary of State for Defence, Main Building, Whitehall, London SW1A 2HB (01-218-9000)
Secretary of State for Education and Science, Elizabeth House, York Rd, London SE1 7PH (01-928-9222)
Secretary of State for Employment, 8 St James Sq., London SW17 4JB (01-214-6000)
Secretary of State for Energy, Department of Energy, Thames House South, Millbank, London SW1P 4QJ (01-211-3000)
Secretary of State for the Environment, 2 Marsham St, London SW1P 3EB (01-212-3434)
Secretary of State for Foreign and Commonwealth Affairs, Downing St, London SW1A 2AL (01-233-3000)
Secretary of State for Health and Social Security, Alexander Fleming House, Elephant and Castle, London SE1 6BY (01-407-5522)
Secretary of State for Northern Ireland, Gt George St, London SW1P 3AJ (01-233-3000)
Secretary of State for Prices and Consumer Protection, 1 Victoria St, London, SW1H 0ET (01-215-7877)
Secretary of State for Scotland, Dover House, Whitehall, London SW1A 2AU (01-930-6151)
Secretary of State for Social Services, Alexander Fleming House, Elephant and Castle, London SE1 6BY (01-407-5522)
Secretary of State for Trade, Department of Trade, 1 Victoria St, London SW1H 0ET (01-215-7877)
Secretary of State for Transport, Department of Transport, 2 Marsham St, London SW1P 3EB (01-212-3434)
Secretary of State for Wales
—— Welsh Office, Gwydyr House, Whitehall, London SW1A 2ER (01-233-3000)
—— Welsh Office, Cathays Park, Cardiff (0222-28066)
Seed Potato Marketing Board for Northern Ireland, Pearl Assurance House, 2 Donegall Sq East, Belfast BT1 5GF (0232-33336)
Senate of the Inns of Court and the Bar, 11 South Sq, Gray's Inn, London WC1 (01-242-0082)
Senegal, Embassy of the Republic of, 11 Phillimore Gardens, London W8 7QG (01-937-0925)
Seychelles High Commission, 2 Mill St, London W1 (01-499-9951)
SHAC, 189a Old Brompton Rd, London SW5 0AR (01-373-7276)
Shelter National Campaign for the Homeless Ltd, 86 Strand, London WC2R 0EQ (01-836-2051)
Sheriffs' Court – in Scotland look in telephone directory under Courts
Sierra Leone High Commission, 33 Portland Pl, London W1N 3AG (01-636-6483)
Simplification of International Trade Procedures Board, 11-12 Waterloo Place, London SW1Y 4AU (01-839-3393)
Singapore, High Commission for the Republic of, 2 Wilton Crescent, London SW1X 8RW (01-235-8315)
Sinn Fein, the Workers' Party, 30 Gardiner Place, Dublin 1 (Dublin 741045)
Skateboarding Association, c/o Sports Council, 70 Brompton Rd, London SW3 1EX (01-589-3411)
Ski Club of Great Britain, 118 Eaton Sq, London SW1W 9AF (01-235-4711)

Ski Council of Wales, Castell Howell, Llandyssul, Dyfed (054–555–209)
Small Industries Council for Rural Areas of Scotland, 27 Walker St, Edinburgh EH3 7HZ (031–225–2846)
Social Democratic and Labour Party Headquarters, 38 University St, Belfast BT7 1FZ (0232–23428)
Social Science Research Council, 1 Temple Ave, London EC4Y 0BD (01–353–5252)
Socialist Party Head Office, 52 Clapham High St, London SW4 (01–622–3811)
Socialist Workers' Party, 6 Cottons Gardens, London E2 (01–739–1878)
Society for Education in Film and Television, 29 Old Compton St, London W1V 6AA (01–734–5455)
Society of Chiropodists, 8 Wimple St, London W1M 8BX (01–580–3228)
Society of Industrial Artists and Designers, Nash House, 12 Carlton House Terrace, London SW1Y 5AH (01–930–1911)
Society of Motor Manufacturers and Traders, Forbes House, Halkin St, London SW1 (01–235–7000)
Society of Radiographers, 14 Upper Wimpole St, London W1M 8BN (01–935–5726)
Society of Remedial Gymnasts, Physical Medicine Department, General Hospital, Cheyne Walk, Northampton NN1 5BD (0604–34700)
Solicitor General, Law Officers' Department, Royal Courts of Justice, London WC2A 2L (01–405–7641)
Somali Democratic Republic, Embassy of, 60 Portland Place, London W1N 3DG (01–580–7148)
South Africa Aloe Breeders Association, PO Box 16393, Pretoria North 0116, South Africa
South African Consulate-General, Stock Exchange House, 69 George's Place, Glasgow G2 1BX (041–221–3114)
South African Embassy, South Africa House, Trafalgar Sq, London WC2N 5DP (01–930–4488)
South-East Regional Examinations Board, Beloe House, 2–4 Mount Ephraim Rd, Tunbridge Wells, Kent TN1 1EU (0892–35311)
South Western Examinations Board, 23–9 Marsh St, Bristol BS1 4BP (0272–23434)
Southern Ice Hockey Association, 191 Pitshanger Lane, London W5
Southern Regional Examinations Board, 53 London Rd, Southampton SO9 4YL (0703–32312)
Southern Television Ltd, Southern Television Centre, Northam, Southampton SO9 4YQ (0703–28582)
Southern Universities Joint Board, Cotham Rd, Bristol BS6 6DD (0272–36042)
Soviet Union Embassy, 13 Kensington Palace Gardens, London W8 4QX (01–229–3628, 2666 and 6142)
Spanish Consulate-Generals
—— 21 Rodney St, Liverpool L1 9EF
—— Richmond House (1st Floor), Terminus Terrace, College St, Southampton
Spanish Embassy, 24 Belgrave Sq, London SW1X 8QA (01–235–5555)
Spanish Tourist Office (SSTD), Jermyn St, London SW1 (01–930–8578)
Speedway Control Board, 31 Belgrave Sq, London SW1X 8QJ (01–235–8601)
Sports Council
—— Headquarters, 70 Brompton Rd, London SW3 1EX (01–589–3411)
—— National Documentation Centre for Sport, Physical Education and Recreation, University of Birmingham, PO Box 363, Birmingham B15 2TT (021–472–7410)
Sports Centres
—— Bisham Abbey, National Sports Centre, Marlow, Bucks (662–84–2818)
—— Crystal Palace, National Sports Centre, Norwood, London SE19 (01–778–0131)
—— Holme Pierrepoint National Water Sports Centre, Adbolton Lane, Nottingham NG12 2LU (0602–866301)
—— Lilleshall Hall National Sports Centre, Nr Newport, Shropshire (0952–844253)
—— Cowes National Sailing Centre, Cowes, Isle of Wight (0983–82–2069)
—— Plas y Brenin National Mountaineering Centre, Capel Curig, North Wales (Capel Curig 214)
Sports Council for Northern Ireland, 49 Malone Rd, Belfast BT9 6RZ (0232–663154)
Sports Council for Wales
—— Headquarters, Sophia Gardens, Cardiff CF1 9SW (0222–397571)
—— Sports Centre for Wales, Sophia Gardens, Cardiff CF1 9SW (0222–397571)
Squash Rackets Association, 70 Brompton Rd, London SW1 1DX (01–584–2506/0094)
Squash Rackets Professionals' Association, 127 Old Bath Rd, Cheltenham, Gloucestershire GL53 7DH (0242–22898)
Sri Lanka, High Commission for the Republic of, 13 Hyde Park Gardens, London W2 2LX (01–262–1841)

Standing Conference on Drug Abuse (SCODA), Kingsbury House, 3 Blackburn Rd, London NW6 1XA
Statistics and Market Intelligence Library, Export House, Ludgate Hill, London EC4M 7HU (01-248-5757)
Stock Exchange, the, Old Broad St, London EC2N 1HP (01-588-2355)
Stock Exchange trading floors
—— Northern Bank House, 10 High St, Belfast BT1 2BP (0232-21094)
—— Margaret St, Birmingham B3 3JL (021-236-9181)
—— 12 Dublin St, Edinburgh EH1 3PP (031-556-9671)
—— Stock Exchange House, PO Box 141, 69 St George's Place, Glasgow G2 1BU (041-221-7060)
—— Silkhouse Court, Tithebarn St, Liverpool L2 2LT (051-236-0869)
—— Old Broad St, London EC2N 1HP (01-588-2355)
—— 4 Norfolk St, Manchester M2 1DS (061-833-0931)
—— Melrose House, 3 St Sampson's Sq, York YO1 2RL (0904-54982)
Submarine Museum, HMS *Dolphin*, Gosport, Hants (Portsmouth 22351)
Sudanese Embassy, 3 Cleveland Row, St James's, London SW1A 1DD (01-839-8080)
Sugar Association of London, Refined Sugar Association, Plantation House, Mincing Lane, London EC3M 3HT (01-626-1745)
Sunday Times, Thomson House, Gray's Inn Rd, London WCL (01-837-1234)
Superintendant Registrar of Births, Deaths and Marriages – look in telephone directory either under the name of your local authority or under Registration of Births, Deaths and Marriages (district offices)
Supplementary Benefits Commission, Headquarters, Division SB4B, New Court, Carey St, London WC2A 2LS
Supreme Court of Judicature, Central Office, Royal Courts of Justice, Strand, London WC2 (01-405-7641)
Surinam Embassy, The Hague, Netherlands
Swansea Sound, Victoria Rd, Gowerton, Swansea SA4 3AB (0792-893751)
Swaziland High Commission, 58 Pont St, London SW1X 0AE (01-589-5447)
Swedish Academy, källargränd 4, Börschuset, S–11129 Stockholm
Swiss Bank Corporation, 99 Gresham St, London EC2P 2BR (01-606-4000)
Swiss Embassy, 16–18 Montagu Place, London W1H 2BQ (01-723-0701)
Swiss National Tourist Office, New Coventry St, London W1 (01-734-1921)
Syrian Embassy, 5 Eaton Terrace, London SW1W 8EX (01-730-0384)

T

Table Tennis Association of Wales, 198 Cyncoed Rd, Cardiff CF2 6BQ (0222-757241)
Tanzanian High Commission, 43 Hertford St, London W1Y 8DB (01-499-8951)
Tattersalls Committee, PO Box 13, 7/9 Hatherley Rd, Reading, Berks (0734-65402)
Tea Centre, Sir John Lyon House, 5 High Timber St, Upper Thames St, London EC4V 3LR (01-236-3369)
Tea Trade Committee, Tamesis House, 9 Wapping Lane, London E1 9DA (01-481-3681)
Technical Education and Training Organisation for Overseas Countries, Grosvenor Gardens House, 35–7 Grosvenor Gardens, London SW1 0BS (01-834-3665)
Technician Education Council, 76 Portland Place, London W1N 4AA (01-580-3050)
Telephone Area Office – listed in your local telephone directory under Post Office Services
Telephone for the Blind Fund, Mynthust, Leigh, Nr Reigate, Surrey
Test and County Cricket Board, Lord's Cricket Ground, London NW8 8QN (01-289-1611)
Thai Embassy, 29–30 Queen's Gate, London SW7 5JB (01-589-0173)
Thames Television Ltd, Thames Television House, 306–16 Euston Rd, London NW1 3BB (01-387-9494)
Thames Valley Broadcasting, PO Box 210, Reading RG3 5RZ (0734-413131)
Thomas Nelson and Sons Ltd, 18 Dalkeith Rd, Edinburgh EH16 5BS (031-667-8818)
Timber Trade Federation, Clareville House, Whitcomb St, London WC2 (01-839-1891)

Togo diplomatic mission to UK, Embassy of the Republic of Togo, Ave de Tervueren, 264, 1150 Brussels, Belgium (770–53–63, 770–17–91)
Togo Hon. Consulate, 10 New Bond St, London W1Y 9PF (01–493–6970/9076)
Tonga High Commission, 17th Floor, New Zealand House, Haymarket, London SW1Y 4TE (01–839–3287)
Tour Operators' Study Group Trust Fund Ltd, 52 Lincoln's Inn Fields, London WC2A 3LZ (01–831–7611)
Tourist Boards
—— English, 4 Grosvenor Gdns, London SW1 (01–730–3400)
—— Scottish, 22 Ravelston Terrace, Edinburgh (031–332–2433)
—— Welsh, Welcome House, Llandaff, Cardiff (0222–27281)
—— Northern Ireland, River House, 48 High St, Belfast (0232–31221)
—— Cumbrian, Ellerthwaite, Windermere (096–62–4444)
—— East Anglian, 14 Museum St, Ipswich (0473–21421)
—— East Midlands, Bailgate, Lincoln (0522–31521)
—— Heart of England, The Old Bank House, 65 High St, Worcester (0905–29511)
—— Northumbrian, Prudential Building, 140–150 Pilgrim St, Newcastle-upon-Tyne (0632–28795)
—— North West, Lastrop Village, Bromley Cross, Bolton, Lancs (0204–591511)
—— South East, Cheviot House, 4–6 Monson Rd, Tunbridge Wells, Kent (0892–33066)
—— Southern, Old Town Hall, Leigh Rd, Eastleigh, Hampshire (0703–6027)
—— Thames and Chilterns, 8 The Market Place, Abingdon, Oxfordshire (0235–22711)
—— West Country, Trinity St, Southern Hay East, Exeter (0392–76357)
—— Yorkshire and Humberside, 312 Tadcaster Rd, York (0904–707961)
Trade Mark Patent and Design Federation, 21 Tothill St, London SW1M 9LP (01–222–0841)
Trades Union Congress, Congress House, Great Russell St, London WC1B 3LS (01–636–4030)
Trade Unions, Headquarters
—— Actors Equity Association, British, 8 Harley St, London W1N 2AB (01–636–6367)
—— Agricultural and Allied Workers, National Union of, 'Headland House,' 308 Gray's Inn Rd, London WC1X 8DS (01–278–7801)
—— Asphalt Workers, The Amalgamated Union of, Jenkin House, 173A Queens Rd, London SE15 2NF (01–639–1669)
—— Bakers' Food and Allied Workers' Union, Stanborough House, Gt North Rd, Stanborough, Welwyn Garden City, Herts AL8 7TA (30–60150)
—— Bakers and Allied Workers, Scottish Union of, 'Baxterlee,' 127 Fergus Drive, Glasgow G20 6AU (041–946–4213)
—— Bank Employees, The National Union of, Sheffield House, Portsmouth Rd, Esher, Surrey KT10 9BH (78–66624)
—— Beamers, Twisters and Drawers (Hand and Machine), Amalgamated Association of, 27 Every St, Nelson, Lancs. BB9 7NE (0282–64181)
—— Blastfurnacemen, Ore Miners, Coke Workers and Kindred Trades, The National Union of, 93 Borough Rd West, Middlesbrough, Cleveland TS1 3AJ (0642–242961)
—— Blind and Disabled, The National League of the, Tottenham Trades Hall, 7 Bruce Grove, London N17 6RA (01–808–6030)
—— Boilermakers, Shipwrights, Blacksmiths and Structural Workers, Amalgamated Society of, Lifton House, Eslington Rd, Newcastle-upon-Tyne NE2 4SB (0632–81–3205/6)
—— Boot, Shoe and Slipper Operatives, Rossendale Union of, 7 Tenterfield St, Waterfoot, Rossendale, Lancs. (07062–5657)
—— British Air Line Pilots' Association, 81 New Rd, Harlington, Middlesex UB3 5BG (01–759–9331)
—— Broadcasting Staff, Association of, Kings Court, 2 Goodge St, London, W1P 2AE (01–637–1261)
—— Brushmakers and General Workers, National Society of, 20 The Parade, Watford WD1 2AA (92–21950)
—— Building Technicians, Association of, Ucatt House, 177 Abbeville Rd, Clapham, London SW4 9RL (01–622–2442)
—— Card Setting Machine Tenters' Society, 36 Greenton Ave, Scholes, Cleckheaton, West Yorks. BD19 6DT (0277–670022)
—— Carpet Trade Union, Northern, 22 Clare Rd, Halifax HX1 2HX (0422–60492)

Trade Unions, Headquarters—*cont.*

—— Ceramic and Allied Trades Union, 5 Hillcrest St, Hanley, Stoke-on-Trent, ST1 2AB (0782–24201–3)

—— Cinematograph, Television and Allied Technicians, The Association of, 2 Soho Sq, London W1V 6DD (01–437–8506)

—— Civil and Public Services Association, 215 Balham High Rd, London SW17 7BQ (01–672–1299)

—— Civil and Public Servants, Society of, 124–126 Southwark St, London SE1 0TU (01–928–9671)

—— Civil Service Union, 17–21 Hatton Wall, London EC1N 8JP (01–242–2991)

—— Cloth Pressers' Society, 34 Southgate, Honley, nr Huddersfield HD7 2NT (0484–61175)

—— Colliery Overmen, Deputies and Shotfirers, National Association of, Argyle House, 29–31 Euston Rd, London NW1 2SP (01–837–0908)

—— Construction, Allied Trades and Technicians, Union of, 'Fairfields,' Roe Green, Kingsbury NW9 0PT (01–204–0273)

—— Co-operative Officials, National Association of, Saxone House, 56 Market St, Manchester M1 1PW (061–834–6029)

—— Coopers' Federation of Great Britain, 13 Gayfield Sq, Edinburgh (031–556–2109)

—— Domestic Appliance and General Metal Workers, National Union of, Imperial Building, High St, Rotherham S60 1PB (0709–2820)

—— Dyers, Bleachers and Textile Workers, National Union of, National House, Sunbridge Rd, Bradford BD1 2QB (0274–25642)

—— Electrical Electronic Telecommunication and Plumbing Union, Hayes Court, West Common Rd, Hayes, Bromley, Kent BR2 7AU (01–462–7755)

—— Electrical Power Engineers' Association, Station House, Fox Lane North, Chertsey, Surrey (093–28–64131)

—— Engineering Workers, Amalgamated Union of
  Construction Section, 190 Cedars Rd, Clapham, London SW4 0PP (01–622–4451)
  Engineering Section, 110 Peckham Rd, London SE15 5EL (01–703–4231)
  Foundry Section, 164 Chorlton Rd, Brook's Bar, Manchester M16 7NU (061–226–1151)
  Technical, Administrative and Supervisory Section, Onslow Hall, Little Green, Richmond, Surrey TW9 1QN (01–948–2271)

—— Felt Hatters and Allied Workers, Amalgamated Society of Journeymen, 14 Walker St, Denton, nr Manchester (061–336–2450)

—— Felt Hat Trimmers and Wool Formers, Amalgamated Association, 14 Walker St, Denton, nr Manchester (061–336–2450)

—— Film Artistes' Association, 61 Marloes Rd, London W8 6LF (01–937–4567/8)

—— Fire Brigades' Union, The, 59 Fulham High St, London SW6 3JN (01–736–2157)

—— Footwear, Leather and Allied Trades, National Union of the, The Grange, Earls Barton, Northampton NN6 0JH (0604–810326)

—— Funeral Service Operatives, National Union of, 16 Woolwich New Rd, London SE18 6HD (01–854–5870)

—— Furniture, Timber and Allied Trades Union, 'Fairfields,' Roe Green, Kingsbury NW9 0PT (01–204–0273)

—— General and Municipal Workers, National Union of, Thorne House, Ruxley Ridge, Claygate, Esher, Surrey KT10 0TL (78–62081–5)

—— Gold, Silver and Allied Trades, National Union of, Kean Chambers, 11 Mappin St, Sheffield S1 4DT (0742–21668)

—— Government Supervisors and Radio Officers, Association of, 90 Borough High St, London SE1 1LL (407–4866–7)

—— Graphical and Allied Trades, Society of, 274–283 London Road, Hadleigh, Benfleet, Essex (0702–553131)

—— Graphical Association, National, Graphic House, 63–67 Bromham Rd, Bedford MK10 2AG (0234–51521)

—— Greater London Council Staff Association, 164/168 Westminster Bridge Rd, London SE1 7RW (01–633–5927)

—— Healders' and Twisters' Trade and Friendly Society, Huddersfield, 20 Uppergate, Hepworth, Huddersfield HD7 1TG (048–489–4509)

Trade Unions, Headquarters—*cont.*
—— Health Service Employees, Confederation of, Glen House, High St, Banstead, Surrey SM7 2LH (25–53322)
—— Health Visitors' Association, 36 Eccleston Square, London SW1V 1PF (01–834–9523)
—— Hosiery and Knitwear Workers, National Union of, 55 New Walk, Leicester LE1 7EB (0533–56791)
—— Inland Revenue Staff Federation, General Secretary, 7–9 St George's Sq, London SW1V 2HY (01–834–8254)
—— Insurance Workers, National Union, 185 Woodhouse Rd, London N12 9BA (01–368–1098)
—— Iron and Steel Trades Confederation, Swinton House, 324 Gray's Inn Rd, London WC1X 8DD (01–837–6691)
—— Journalists, National Union of, Acorn House, 314–320 Gray's Inn Rd, London WC1X 8DP (01–278–7916)
—— Jute, Flax and Kindred Textile Operatives, Union of, 93 Nethergate, Dundee DD1 4DH (0382–22273)
—— Laminated and Coil Spring Workers' Union, 120 Burngreave Rd, Sheffield S3 9DE (0742 345787)
—— Licensed House Managers, National Association of, 9 Coombe Lane, London SW20 8NE (01–947–3080)
—— Lithographic Artists, Designers, Engravers and Process Workers, Society of, 55 Clapham Common, South Side, London SW4 9DF (01–720–7551)
—— Lock and Metal Workers, National Union of, Bellamy House, Wilkes St, Willenhall, Staffs. WV13 2BS (0902–66651/2)
—— Locomotive Engineers and Firemen, Associated Society of, 9 Arkwright Rd, Hampstead, London NW3 6AB (01–435–2160/6300)
—— Loom Overlookers, The General Union of Associations of, 6 St Mary's Place, Bury BL9 0DZ (061–764–4244)
—— Managers and Overlookers' Society, Textile Hall, Westgate, Bradford BD1 2RG (0274–27967)
—— Merchant Navy and Air Line Officers' Association, 'Oceanair House,' 750–760 High Rd, London E11 3BB (01–989–6677)
—— Metal Mechanics, National Society of, 70 Lionel St, Birmingham B3 1JG (01–236–0726)
—— Metalworkers' Union Associated, 92 Deansgate, Manchester M3 2QG (061–834–6891)
—— Military and Orchestral Musical Instrument Makers' Trade Society, 56 Avondale Crescent, Enfield, Middx.
—— Mineworkers, National Union of, 222 Euston Rd, London NW1 2BX (01–387–7631)
—— Musicians' Union, 29 Catherine Place, Buckingham Gate, London SW1 (01–834–1348)
—— National and Local Government Officers' Association, 1 Mabledon Place, London WC1H 9AJ (01–388–2366)
—— Pattern Weavers' Society, 21 Kaye Lane, Almondbury, Huddersfield HD5 8XP (0484–25657)
—— Patternmakers and Allied Craftsmen, Association of, 15 Cleve Rd, West Hampstead, London NW6 1YA (01–624–7085)
—— Post Office Engineering Union, Greystoke House, Hanger Lane, Ealing, London W5 1ER (01–998–6521)
—— Post Office Executives, Society of, 116 Richmond Rd, Kingston-on-Thames KT2 5HL (01–549–3323)
—— Post Office Management Staffs Association, L. F. Pratt, 52 Broadway, Bracknell, Berks. RG12 1AJ (0344 24061)
—— Post Office Workers, Union of, U.P.W. House, Crescent Lane, Clapham Common, London SW4 9RN (01–622–9977)
—— Power Loom Carpet Weavers' and Textile Workers' Association, Carpet Weavers Hall, Callows Lane, Kidderminster (0562 3192)
—— Power Loom Overlookers, Scottish Union of, 1 Osnaburgh St, Forfar, Angus DD8 2AA (0307–5709)
—— Power Loom Overlookers, Yorkshire Association of, Textile Hall, Westgate, Bradford BD1 2RG (0274–27966)
—— Printers, Graphical and Media Personnel, National Society of Operative, Caxton House, 13–16 Borough Rd, St George's Circus, London SE1 0AL (01–928–1481)
—— Prison Officers' Association, Cronin House, 245 Church St, London N9 9HW (01–807–3383/3101)

Trade Unions, Headquarters—*cont.*

—— Professional Civil Servants, Institution of, 3/7 Northumberland St, London WC2N 5BS (01–930–9755)
—— Professional, Executive, Clerical and Computer Staff, Association of, 22 Worple Rd, London SW19 4DF (01–947–3131/6)
—— Public Employees, National Union of, Civic House, 8 Aberdeen Terrace, Blackheath, London SE3 0QY (01–852–2842)
—— Radio and Electronic Officers' Union, 4–6 Branfil Rd, Upminster, Essex RM14 2XX (86–22321–2)
—— Railwaymen, National Union of, Unity House, Euston Rd, London NW1 2BL (01–387–4771)
—— Roll Turners' Trade Society, British, 44 Collingwood Ave, Corby, Northants (05366–2617)
—— Sawmakers' Protection Society, Sheffield, 27 Main Ave, Totley, Sheffield (0742–361044)
—— Scalemakers, National Union of, 195 Walworth Rd, London SE17 1RP (01–703–8008)
—— Schoolmasters and Union of Women Teachers, National Association of, Swan Court, Waterhouse St, Hemel Hempstead, Herts. HP1 1DT (0442–2971–4)
—— Scientific, Technical and Managerial Staffs, Association of, and Medical Practitioners' Section, 10–26A Jamestown Rd, London NW1 7DT (01–267–4422)
—— Screw, Nut, Bolt and Rivet Trade Union, 368 Dudley Rd, Birmingham B18 4HH (021–558–2001)
—— Seamen, National Union of, Maritime House, Old Town, Clapham, London SW4 0JP (01–622–5581)
—— Sheet Metal Workers, Coppersmiths, Heating and Domestic Engineers, National Union of, 75–77 West Heath Rd, London NW3 7TL (01–455–0053/5)
—— Shop, Distributive and Allied Workers, Union of, 'Oakley,' 188 Wilmslow Rd, Fallowfield, Manchester M14 6LJ (061–224–2804)
—— Shuttlemakers, Society of, 21 Buchan Towers, Manchester Rd, Bradford
—— Spring Trapmakers' Society, Bellamy House, Wilkes St, Willenhall, Staffs WV13 2BS (0902–66651)
—— Tailors and Garment Workers, National Union of, Radlett House, West Hill, Aspley Guise, Milton Keynes MK17 8DT (0908–583099)
—— Teachers in Further and Higher Education, National Association of, Hamilton House, Mabledon Place, London WC1H 9BH (01–387–6806)
—— Teachers, National Union of, Hamilton House, Mabledon Place, London WC1H 9BD (01–387–2442)
—— Textile Workers and Kindred Trades, Amalgamated Society, 'Foxlowe,' Market Place, Leek, Staffs. ST13 6AD (0538–382068)
—— Textile Workers' Union, Amalgamated, Textile Union Centre, 5 Caton St, Rochdale OL16 1QJ (07–06–59551 and 58367)
—— Theatrical, Television and Kine Employees, The National Association of, 155 Kennington Park Rd, London SE11 4JU (01–735–9068)
—— Tobacco Mechanics Association, 9 Wootton Crescent, St Anne's Park, Bristol BS4 4AN (0272–773848)
—— Tobacco Workers' Union, The, 9 Station Parade, High St, London E11 1QF (01–989–1107)
—— Transport and General Workers' Union, Transport House, Smith Sq, London SW1P 3JB (01–838–7788)
—— Transport Salaried Staffs' Association, Walkden House, 10 Melton St, London NW1 2EJ (01–387–2101)
—— Transport Union, The United Road, 76 High Lane, Chorlton-cum-Hardy, Manchester M21 1FD (061–881–6245)
—— University Teachers, Association of, United House, 1 Pembridge Rd, London W11 3HJ (01–221–4370)
—— Wallcoverings, Decorative and Allied Trades, National Union of, 223 Bury New Rd, Whitefield, nr Manchester M25 6GW (061–766–3645/6)
—— Wire Drawers and Kindred Workers, The Amalgamated Society of, Prospect House, Alma St, Sheffield S3 8SA (0742–21674)
—— Wool, Shear Workers' Trade Union, Sheffield, 19 Rivelin Park Drive, Malin Bridge, Sheffield 6
—— Wool Sorters' Society, National, 40 Little Horton Lane, Bradford BD5 0AL (0274–20392)
—— Writers' Guild of Great Britain, 430 Edgware Rd, London W2 1EH (01–723–8074/5/6)

Traffic Commissioners
—— Greyfriars House, Gallowgate, Aberdeen AB9 2ZS (0224–23411)
—— Cumberland House, 200 Broad St, Birmingham B15 1T9 (021–643–5011)
—— The Gaunts House, Denmark St, Bristol BS1 5DR (0272–297221)
—— Terrington House, 13–15 Hills Rd, Cambridge CB2 1NP (0223–58922)
—— Caradog House, 1–5 St Andrew's Place, Cardiff CF1 3PW (0222–24801/8)
—— Ivy House, 3 Ivy Terrace, Eastbourne, East Sussex BN4 QP (0323–21471)
—— 24 Torphichen St, Edinburgh EH5 8HD (031–229–9166)
—— Hillcrest House, 386 Harehills Lane, Leeds LS9 6NF (0532–38144)
—— Government Buildings, Bromyard Ave, Acton, London W3 7AY
—— Arkwright House, Parsonage Gardens, Deansgate, Manchester M60 9AN (061–832–8644)
—— Low Friar House, 36–42 Low Friar St, Newcastle-upon-Tyne NE1 5XR (0632–610031)
—— Birkbeck House, 14–16 Trinity Sq, Nottingham NG1 4BA (0602–45511)
Training Services Agency
—— Ebury Bridge House, Ebury Bridge Rd, London SW1W 8PY (01–730–9661)
—— 162–8 Regent St, London W1R 6DE (01–214–6000)
—— 95 Wigmore St, London W1H 9AA (01–486–6688)
Transport Tribunal, Watergate House, 15 York Buildings, London WC2 (01–839–7194)
Transport Users Committee, Belfast, Royal Exchange, Cross St, Belfast (061–834–5245)
Transport Users' Consultative Committee – address from notices at railway stations, or in telephone directory
Tree Council, 17–19 Rochester Row, London SW1P 1LN (01–212–0984)
Trinidad and Tobago High Commission, 42 Belgrave Sq, London SW1X 8NT (01–245–9351)
Trinity College, College Green, Dublin 2 (0001–772941)
Trinity House Pilotage Service, Trinity House, Tower Hill, London EC3N 4DH (01–480–6601)
Trustee Savings Bank, Head Office, 49–53 Surrey Row, London SE1 0BY (01–633–9344)
Trustee Savings Banks – find them in the local telephone directory under Trustee Savings Banks; booklet of branches from Trustee Savings Bank, Head Office
Trustee Savings Bank Association Ltd, 3 Gracechurch St, London EC3 (01–283–8533)
Tug of War Association, Calf House, Manor Rd, Stourpaine, Blandford, Dorset (025–82–2566)
Tunisian Embassy, 29 Prince's Gate, London SW7 1QG (01–584–8117)
Tunisian Tourist Centre, Stafford St, London SW1 (01–493–2952)
Turkish Embassy, 43 Belgrave Sq, London SW1X 8PA (01–235–5252)
Turkish Tourism Information Office, Conduit St, London W1 (01–734–8681)
Twycross Zoo Park Ltd, Norton-juxta-Twycross, Nr Atherstone, Warwicks
Tyne Tees Television Ltd, The Television Centre, City Rd, Newcastle-upon-Tyne NE1 2AL (0632–610181)

U

UK Assay Offices
—— New Hall St, Birmingham B3 1SB
—— Goldsmiths Hall, 15 Queen St, Edinburgh EH2 1JE
—— Goldsmiths Hall, Gutter Lane, London EC2V 8AQ
—— 137 Portobello St, Sheffield S1 4DR
UK Atomic Energy Authority, 11 Charles II St, London W1 (01–930–6262)
UK Immigrants Advisory Service, Brettenham House, 14 Lancaster Place, London WC2 (01–240–5176)
Ulster Angling Federation Ltd, 27 Sandyknowes Park, Glengormley, Newtownabbey, Co Antrim (023–13–5252)
Ulster Archery Association, 17 Dellmount Ave, Bangor, Co Down (0247–67315)
Ulster Automobile Club, 3 Botanic Ave, Belfast BT7 1JG (0232–21607)
Ulster Bank Ltd, 35–9 Waring St, Belfast BT1 2ER (0232–35232)
Ulster Clay Pigeon Shooting Association, 6 Springhill Ave, Bangor, Co. Down (Bangor 63153)
Ulster Counties Small Bore Shooting Association, 64 Glencregagh Park, Belfast 6 (0232–643796)
Ulster Defence Regiment Headquarters, Magheralave Rd, Lisburn, Northern Ireland

Ulster Hang Gliding Club, 32 Jericho Rd, Artigan, Killyleagh, Co Down (039–682245)
Ulster Liberal Party, 5 Windsor Ave, Belfast BT9 6EE (0232–669395)
Ulster Province Irish Federation of Sea Anglers, 274 Bangor Rd, Whitespots, Newtownards
Ulster Rifle Association, 271 Holywood Rd, Belfast BT4 2EW (Belfast 650408)
Ulster Savings Branch, Crown Buildings, Artillery Rd, Coleraine, Co Londonderry
Ulster Ski Federation, 9 Norfolk Drive, Belfast 11 (0232–614356)
Ulster Society for the Prevention of Cruelty to Animals, Knockeen, 11 Drumview Rd, Lisburn, Co Antrim BT2 76YF (Carryduff 813126)
Ulster Society of Amateur Dancers, 82 Owenvanagh Park, Belfast 11 (0232–616942)
Ulster Television Ltd, Havelock House, Ormeau Rd, Belfast BT7 1EB (0232–28122)
Ulster Unionist Headquarters, 41–3 Waring St, Belfast BT1 2EY (0232–24601)
Union Bank of Switzerland, 117 Old Broad St, London EC2N 1AJ (01–588–3861)
Union Movement, 76A Rochester Row, London SW1 (01–834–2500)
United Arab Emirates, Embassy of the, 30 Prince's Gate, London SW7 1PT (01–581–1281)
United Nations Association International Service, 23 New Quebec St, London W1 (01–402–9029)
United States Consulate-Generals
—— Queen's House, 14 Queen St, Belfast BT1 6EQ (0232–28239)
—— 3 Regent Terrace, Edinburgh EH7 5BW (031–556–8315)
United States Embassy, Grosvenor Sq, London W1A 1AE (01–499–9000)
United States National Arboretum, Washington DC 20002, USA
United Terminal Sugar Market Association, Cereal House, 58 Mark Lane, London EC3R 7NE (01–488–3736)
Universities Central Council on Admissions, PO Box 28, Cheltenham, Gloucestershire GL50 1HY (0242–59041)
University College at Buckingham, Buckingham MK18 1EG (02802–4161)
University Entrance and Schools Examinations Council, University of London, 66–72 Gower St, London WC1E 6EE (01–636–8000)
University Grants Committee, 14 Park Crescent, London W1N 4DH (01–636–7799)
University Library, 9 West Rd, Cambridge CB3 9DR (0223–61441)
University of London, 66–72 Gower St, London WC1E 6EE (01–636–8000)
Upper Volta Hon Consulate, 104 Park St, London W1Y 3RJ (01–491–7351)
Uruguayan Consulate, Liver Buildings, Liverpool
Uruguayan Embassy, 48 Lennox Gardens, London SW1X 0DL (01–589–8835)

V

VAT Tribunals Headquarters, 17 North Audley St, London W16 2PX (01–629–5542)
Venezuelan Consulate-General, 1 Faulkner Sq, Liverpool L8 7NU (051–708–0376)
Venezuelan Embassy, Flat 6, 3 Hans Crescent, London SW1X 0LX (01–584–4206)
Vietnamese Embassy, 12–14 Victoria Rd, London W8 (01–937–1912)
Vintners Company, Black Swan House, Kennet Wharf Lane, London EC4 (01–236–1863)
Voluntary Service Overseas, 14 Bishops Bridge Rd, London W2 (01–262–2611)

W

Wales Council for the Disabled, Crescent Rd, Caerphilly, Mid Glamorgan (0222–869224)
Wales Tourist Board, Welcome House, High St, Llandaff, Cardiff CF5 2YZ (0222–567701)
Water Authorities
—— Anglian, Diploma House, Grammar School Walk, Huntingdon PE18 6NZ (0480–56181)
—— North West, Dawson House, Great Sankey, Warrington, Cheshire WA5 3LW (092–572–4321)
—— Northumbrian, Northumbria House, Regent Centre, Gosforth, Newcastle-upon-Tyne NE3 3PX (0632–843151)

Water Authorities—*cont.*
—— Severn Trent, Abelson House, 2297 Coventry Rd, Sheldon, Birmingham B26 3PS (021–743–4222)
—— South West, 3–5 Barnfield Rd, Exeter EX1 1RE (0392–50861)
—— Southern, Guildbourne House, Worthing, Sussex BN11 1LD (0903–205252)
—— Thames, New River Head, Rosebery Ave, London EC1R 4TP (01–837–3300)
—— Welsh National Water Development Authority, Cambrian Way, Brecon, Powys LD3 7HP (0874–3181)
—— Wessex, Techno House, Redcliffe Way, Bristol BS1 6NY (0272–25491)
—— Yorkshire, West Riding House, 67 Albion St, Leeds LS1 5AA (0532–448201)
Water Companies Association, 14 Great College St, London SW1P 3RX (01–222–0644)
Water Companies
—— Bournemouth and District, Alderney Waterworks, Francis Ave, Bournemouth BH11 8NB (020–16–2261)
—— Bristol, PO Box No. 218, Bridgwater Rd, Bristol BS99 7AU (0272–665881)
—— Cambridge, Rustat Rd, Cambridge CB1 3QS (0223–47351)
—— Cheadle, 43 Chapel St, Cheadle, Staffordshire (05384–2388)
—— Chester, Aqua House, 45 Boughton, Chester CH3 5AU
—— Cholderton and District, Estate Office, Cholderton, Salisbury, Wilts (098–064–203)
—— Colne Valley, Blackwell House, Aldenham Rd, Watford, Herts WD2 2EY (92–23333)
—— Corby (Northants) and District, Stamion Lane, Corby, Northants NN18 8ES (053–66–2121)
—— East Anglian, 163 High St, Lowestoft (0502–2406)
—— East Worcestershire, 46 New Rd, Bromsgrove, Worcs B60 2JT (0527–75151)
—— East Surrey, London Road, Redhill RH1 1LJ (91–66333)
—— Eastbourne, 14 Upperton Rd, Eastbourne, Sussex BN21 1EP (0323–21371)
—— Essex, 324 South St, Romford, Essex RM1 1AL (70–46076)
—— Folkestone and District, The Cherry Garden, Cherry Garden Lane, Folkstone, Kent CT19 4QB (0303–76951)
—— Hartlepool, 3 Lancaster Rd, Hartlepool TS24 8LW (0429–4405/6)
—— Jersey, PO Box 22, 2 Mulcaster St, St Helier, Jersey (Jersey Central 32501)
—— Lee Valley, PO Box 48, Bishops Rise, Hatfield, Herts AL10 (30–64311)
—— Mid Kent, PO Box 45, High St, Snodland, Kent ME6 5AH (0634–240313)
—— Mid Southern, Frimley Green, Camberley, Surrey GU16 6HZ (025–16–5031)
—— Mid-Sussex, PO Box 129, 1 Church Rd, Haywards Heath, Sussex RH16 3DX (0444–57111)
—— Newcastle and Gateshead, PO Box 10, Allendale Rd, Newcastle-upon-Tyne NE6 2SW (0632–654144)
—— North Surrey, The Causeway, Staines, Middlesex TW18 3BX (81–55464)
—— Portsmouth, PO Box 8, West St, Havant, Hants PO9 1LG (070–12–6333)
—— Rickmansworth and Uxbridge Valley, Rickmansworth, Herts WD3 1LB
—— South Staffordshire, 50 Sheepcote St, Birmingham B16 8AR (021–643–8131)
—— Sunderland and South Shields, 29 St John St, Sunderland SR1 1JT (0783–57123)
—— Sutton District, 59 Gander Green Lane, Cheam, Surrey SM1 2EP (01–643–8050)
—— Tendring Hundred Waterworks Company, Manningtree, Essex CO11 2AZ (020–639–2155)
—— Weld Estate, Lulworth Castle, Wareham, Dorset (092–941–352)
—— West Hampshire, Knapp Mill Road, Christchurch, Dorset BH23 2LU (020–15–3361)
—— West Kent, Cramptons Rd, Sevenoaks, Kent TN14 5DG (0732–52307)
—— Wrexham and East Denbighshire, 21 Egerton St, Wrexham LL11 1ND (09878–2259)
—— Yorks, Lendal Tower, York YO1 2DL (0904–22171)
Weatherbys, 42 Portman Sq, London W1 (01–486–4921)
Welsh Academy, Museum Place, Cardiff CF1 3NX (0222–394711)
Welsh Amateur Athletic Association, Winterbourne, Greenway Close, Penarth, South Glamorgan
Welsh Amateur Basketball Association, 28 Brundall Crescent, Cardiff (0222–593518)
Welsh Amateur Boxing Association, Erw Wen, Rhiwhina, Cardiff (0222–63566)
Welsh Amateur Fencing Union, 62 Melbourne Way, Newport, Gwent NPT 3RG
Welsh Amateur Swimming Association, 21 Old Vicarage Close, Llanishen, Cardiff (0222–753448)
Welsh Anglers' Council, 16 Cambria Rd, Old Colwyn, Clwyd LL29 9AG (Colwyn Bay 55666)
Welsh Archery Federation, Brook Cottage, Lisvaney Rd, Llanishen, Cardiff (0222–752488)
Welsh Association of Sub-Aqua Clubs, 5 Tynmawr Close, Rumney, Cardiff CF3 8BU (0222–77507)
Welsh Badminton Union, 7 Romsey Court, St Dials, Cwmbran

Welsh Baseball Union, 39 Pentyrch St, Cathays, Cardiff
Welsh Billiards and Snooker Association and Control Council, 80 Shirley Dr, Heolgerrig, Merthyr Tydfil, Mid Glamorgan
Welsh Books Scheme, University of Wales Press Board, Cathays Park, Cardiff (0222–28066)
Welsh Bowling Association, Holford, Courtland Terrace, Merthyl Tydfil, Mid-Glamorgan (0685–2062)
Welsh Canoeing Association, Nant BH Outdoor Centre, Nant BH, Llanrwst, Gwynedd (0492–640735)
Welsh Clay Pigeon Shooting Association, Ivy Cottage, Ogmore-by-Sea, Bridgend, Mid Glamorgan (0656–4440)
Welsh Consumer Council, 8 St Andrew's Place, Cardiff (0222–25416)
Welsh Council for the Disabled, Llys Ifor, Crescent Rd, Caerphilly, Mid Glamorgan
Welsh Cricket Association, 19 Gower St, Briton Ferry, Neath, West Glamorgan
Welsh Cross-Country Association, Harriers Haunt, 40 Twyni Teg, Killay, Swansea, West Glamorgan
Welsh Curling Association, 16 Gele Ave, Gwersyllt, Wrexham, Clwyd
Welsh Cycling Union, Mount Pleasant Stores, Alltwen, Pontardawe, Swansea (0792–862220)
Welsh Development Agency, Treforest Industrial Estate, Pontypridd, Mid Glamorgan CF37 5UT (044–385–2666)
Welsh Education Department
—— Elizabeth House, York Rd, London SE1 7PH (01–928–9222)
—— 31 Cathedral Rd, Cardiff CF1 9UJ (0222–42661)
Welsh Federation of Coarse Anglers, 16 White Rock Close, Graigwen, Pontypridd, Mid Glamorgan CF37 2EN
Welsh Federation of Sea Anglers, 2 Coed Bach, Highlight Park, Barry, South Glamorgan (0446–736892)
Welsh Fly Fishing Association, Gwyn Teifi, Pontrhydfendigaid, Ystrad Meurig, Dyfed
Welsh Folk Dance Society, 369 Gower Rd, Killay, Swansea, West Glamorgan SA2 7AH (0792–23338)
Welsh Golfing Union, 2 Isfryn, Burry Port, Dyfed SA16 0BY (055–46–2595)
Welsh Handball Association, c/o Knight, Bridgend Sports Centre, Bridgend, Glamorgan
Welsh Hang Gliding Club, 35 Worcester Close, Llanyrafon, Cwmbran, Gwent
Welsh Hockey Association, Bank House, Llanidloes, Powys SY18 6BW (055–12–2567)
Welsh Indoor Bowling Association, 24 Coryton Rise, Whitchurch, Cardiff (0222–41441)
Welsh Joint Education Committee, 245 Western Ave, Cardiff CF5 2YX (0222–561231)
Welsh Judo Association, 39 Beachley Drive, Fairwater, Cardiff
Welsh Ladies' Golf Union, Ysgoldy Gynt, Llanhennock, Newport, Gwent NP6 1LT (0633–420642)
Welsh Ladies Indoor Bowling Association, 43 Court Rd, Caerphilly, Mid Glamorgan
Welsh Lawn Tennis Association, The Chimes, Heol-y-Bryn, The Knap, Barry, South Glamorgan (0446–2074)
Welsh League of Youth, Plas Glanleyn, Llanuwchllyn (067–84–607)
Welsh Liberal Party Headquarters, Dumfries Chambers 15–17, 91 St Mary's St, Cardiff (0222–22210)
Welsh Liberal Party Regional Offices
—— Aberystwyth, Dyfed (0907–7686)
—— Newtown, Powys (0686–25527)
Welsh National Party, Plaid Cymru Headquarters, 8 Heol y Frenhines, Cardiff (0222–31944)
Welsh National Water Development Authority, Cambrian Way, Brecon, Powys LD3 7HP (0874–3181)
Welsh Netball Association, 64 Awel Mor, Llanedeyrn, Cardiff (0222–750722)
Welsh Office
—— London Head Office, Gwydyr House, Whitehall, London SW1A 2ER (01–233–3000)
—— Cardiff Head Office, Cathays Park, Cardiff CF1 3NQ (0222–28066)
—— Conservation and Land Division, 22nd Floor, Pearl House, Greyfriars Road, Cardiff
—— Health and Social Security Work Department, Government Buildings, Gabalfa, Cardiff CF4 4YL (0222–62131)
—— Industry Department, Government Buildings, Gabalfa, Cardiff CF4 4YL (0222–62131)
—— Statistics, Cathays Park, Cardiff CF1 3NQ (0222–28066)
—— Translation Unit, Oxford House, Cardiff (0222–44171)

Welsh Orienteering Association, Psychology Department, North Arts Building, University College of Swansea, Singleton Park, Swansea SA2 8PP
Welsh Rifle Association, 63 Lewis Rd, Neath, West Glamorgan (0639–3109)
Welsh Rugby Union, Royal London House, 28–31 St Mary St, Cardiff (0222–32015)
Welsh Smallbore Shooting Union, 52 Parc-y-Felin, Creigian, Cardiff CF4 8PA
Welsh Sports and Games Association, National Sports Centre for Wales, Sophia Gardens, Cardiff CF1 9SW (0222–397571)
Welsh Sports Association for the Disabled, Council for Social Services, The Crescent, Caerphilly, Mid Glamorgan
Welsh Squash Rackets Association, 19 Berkley Drive, Penarth (0222–703496)
Welsh Surfing Federation, The Marloes, 35 Sker Walk, Rest Bay, Porthcawl, Mid Glamorgan
Welsh Tourist Board, Welcome House, High St, Llandaff, Cardiff CF5 2YZ (0222–567701)
Welsh Trampolining Association (British Trampoline Federation, Wales Division), 17 Silver St, Roath, Cardiff (0222–499–811)
Welsh Tug-of-War Association, 8 Bryn Illtyd, Llanmaes Rd, Llantwit Major, South Glamorgan CF6 9XD (044–65–2923)
Welsh Volleyball Association, Nantyglo Leisure Centre, Pond Road, Nantyglo, Gwent (0495–310785)
Welsh Water Ski Committee, 17 Hadfield Close, Deeside, Clywd (0244–814355)
Welsh Women's Amateur Athletic Association, 19 Coed Bach, Highlight Park, Barry (0446–743126)
Welsh Women's Amateur Athletic Association, 11 Cedar Rd, St Athan, Nr Barry, South Glamorgan
Welsh Women's Bowling Association, Monnington, Park Crescent, Abergavenny, Gwent (0873–3607)
Welsh Women's Hockey Association, 7 Pleasant View, Llahilleth, Abertillery, Gwent (049–532–292)
West Midlands Examinations Board, Norfolk House, Smallbrook Queensway, Birmingham B54N (021–643–2081)
West of England Amateur Rowing Association, Long Reach, Tor Hill, Marldon, Paignton, Devon
West of Scotland Agricultural College, Auchincruive, Ayr KA6 5HW (029–252–331)
West Yorkshire and Lindsey Regional Examining Board, Scarsdale House, 136 Derbyshire Lane, Sheffield S8 8SE (0742–57436)
Westward Television Ltd, Derry's Cross, Plymouth, Devon PL1 2SP (0752–69311)
White Fish Authority, Sea Fisheries House, 10 Young St, Edinburgh EH2 4JQ (031–225–2515)
Wildfowlers' Association of Great Britain and Ireland, Marford Hill, Rossett, Clwyd LL12 0HL (0244–570881)
Wildfowl Trust Headquarters, Slimbridge, Gloucester GL2 7BT
William and Glyn's Bank Ltd, Head Office, 20 Birchin Lane, London EC3 (01–623–4356)
Wine Standards Board of the Vintners' Company, 68 Upper Thames St, London EC4V 3BJ (01–236–9512)
Women's Amateur Athletic Association, 70 Brompton Rd, London SW3 1EE (01–584–6876)
Women's Cricket Association, 70 Brompton Rd, London SW3 1HA (01–584–7213)
Women's Football Association, 7 Mayfield Rd, London N8 9LL (01–340–6641)
Women's Hockey Board of Great Britain and Ireland, c/o Mrs Crisp, Cumbergate, Peterborough (0733–68532)
Women's National Commission, Queen Anne's Chambers, 41 Tothill St, London SW1H 9JX (01–273–4601)
Women's Squash Rackets Association, 345 Upper Richmond Rd West, Sheen, London SW14 8QN (01–876–6219)
Workers' Educational Association, 9 Upper Berkeley St, London W1 (01–402–5608)
World Health Organisation
—— Ave Appia, Geneva 27, Switzerland
—— Registered Office (Europe), 8 Scherfigsvej, Copenhagen, Denmark
Worshipful Company of Spectacle Makers, Apothecaries' Hall, Blackfriars Lane, London EC4V 6EL (01–236–2932)

Y

Yellow Fever Vaccination Centres
—— Aberdeen: Beach Boulevard Clinic, Beach Boulevard, Aberdeen (0224–29427)
—— Ballymena: Northern Health and Social Services Board, Yellow Fever Vaccination Centre, 51 Castle St, Ballymena (0266–6324, 2108)
—— Barnsley: Medical Services Clinic, New St, Barnsley, South Yorkshire (0226–3525)
—— Belfast: Eastern Health and Social Services Board, Yellow Fever Vaccination Centre, Lincoln Avenue Clinic, Antrim Rd, Belfast BT14 6AZ (0232–41771)
—— Birmingham: Immunisation Section, Congreve Passage, Birmingham B3 3DH (021–235–3428)
—— Blackburn: Lancashire Area Health Authority, Blackburn District, Larkhill Health Centre, Mount Pleasant, Blackburn BB1 5BJ (0254–63611)
—— Bournemouth: Avebury Child Health Clinic, Maderia Rd, Bournemouth. (Wednesday from 2 pm – appointment only.) (0202–76161)
—— Bradford: Edmund Street Clinic, 26 Edmund St, Bradford, West Yorkshire BD5 0BJ (0274–28421)
—— Brighton: Royal York Buildings, Old Steine, Brighton BN1 1NP (0273–23344)
—— Bristol: Central Health Clinic, Tower Hill, Bristol BS99 7BQ (0272–291010)
—— Cambridge: Medical Examination and Yellow Fever Clinic, Old Addenbrooke's Hospital, Trumpington St, Cambridge (Cambridge 45151)
—— Cardiff: Riverside Health Centre, Wellington Street, Canton, Cardiff (0222–31033)
—— Carlisle: Central Clinic, Victoria Place, Carlisle CA3 8QG (0228–23411)
—— Chelmsford: Medical Centre, Ground Floor, Block A, County Hall, Chelmsford CM1 1LX (0245–67222)
—— Coventry: Room 4, Out-Patients Department, Coventry and Warwickshire Hospital, Stoney Stanton Rd, Coventry CV1 4FN (0203–25555)
—— Derby: Derbyshire County Council Clinic, Cathedral Rd, Derby DE1 3PE (0332–45934)
—— Doncaster: Health Clinic, Chequer Rd, Doncaster DN1 2AD (0302–67051)
—— Dundee: King's Cross Hospital, Clepington Rd, Dundee (0382–85241)
—— Edinburgh: Central Vaccination Clinic, 9 Johnston Terrace, Edinburgh EH1 2PP (031–225–8474)
—— Exeter: School Health Service, 1A Southernhay West, Exeter EX1 1JN (0392–77888)
—— Glasgow: Vaccination Clinic, 20 Cochrane St, Glasgow G1 1JA (041–221–9600)
—— Gloucester: Gloucestershire Royal Hospital, Great Western Rd, Gloucester GL1 3NN (0452–23584)
—— Grimsby: The Clinic, 34 Dudley St, Grimsby, South Humberside (0472–3070) (mornings only)
—— Haverfordwest: Preseli – South Pembrokeshire, District Health Office, Merlins Hill, Haverfordwest, Dyfed SA61 1PG (0437–3345)
—— Kingston upon Hull: Central Clinic, 74 Beverley Rd, Kingston upon Hull HU3 1YD (0482–223191)
—— Lancaster: Ashton Road Clinic, Lancaster (0524–2558)
—— Leeds: 8 Park Square East, Leeds LS1 2LH (0532–30661)
—— Leicester: Princess House, 20 Princess Rd, Leicester LE1 6TP (0533–51281)
—— Lincoln: Community Health Services, St Mark's House, St Mark's Station Yard, Lincoln (0522–27196)
—— Liverpool:
   Vaccination Centre, Health Department, Hatton Garden, Liverpool L3 2AW (051–227–3911)
   School of Tropical Medicine, Pembroke Place, Liverpool L3 5QA (051–709–2298)
—— London:
   Yellow Fever Vaccination Service, Hospital for Tropical Diseases, 4 St Pancras Way, London NW1 0PE (01–387–4411)
   Health Centre, 3 The Manor Drive, Worcester Park, Surrey (01–337–0246)

Yellow Fever Vaccination Centres—London—*cont.*
    Yellow Fever Vaccination Service, Medical Department, Unilever House, Blackfriars, London EC4P 4BQ (01-353-7474)
    Yellow Fever Vaccination Service, 53 Great Cumberland Place, London W1H 7LH (01-262-6456)
    Vaccination Centre, St George's Hospital Medical School, Hyde Park Corner, London SW1X 7EZ (01-235-4343)
—— Maidstone: Area Health Authority, Springfield, Sandling Rd, Maidstone (0622-54371)
—— Manchester: Health Department, 3rd Floor, Town Hall Extension, Manchester M60 2JS (061-236-3377)
—— Middlesbrough: The Clinic, Carlow St, Middlesbrough (0642-49141)
—— Newcastle-upon-Tyne: Shieldfield Health and Social Services Centre, 4 Clarence Walk (off Stoddart Street), Newcastle-upon-Tyne NE2 1AL (0632-38811)
—— Newport: Gwent Area Health Authority, 1st Floor, Sovereign House, Kingsway Centre, Newport, Gwent (0633-63313)
—— Northampton: Northampton Yellow Fever Centre, 67 Giles St, Northampton (0604-34833)
—— Norwich: West Pottergate Health Centre, West Pottergate, Norwich NR2 4BX (0603-611911)
—— Nottingham: Radford Welfare Centre, Grant St, Nottingham NG7 3GS (0602-50551)
—— Omagh: Western Health and Social Services Board, Yellow Fever Vaccination Centre, The Health Centre, Mountjoy Rd, Omagh (0662-3521)
—— Oxford: Health Department, 103 Banbury Rd, Oxford OX2 6JZ (0865-511451)
—— Penzance: Health Clinic Bellair, Alverton, Penzance (0736-2321)
—— Plymouth: Environmental Health Department, Civic Centre, Plymouth (0752-68000)
—— Sheffield: Central Health Clinic, Mulberry St, Sheffield S1 2PJ (0742-731661)
—— Shrewsbury: County Health Department, 2nd Floor, North Block, Shirehall, Abbey Foregate, Shrewsbury (0743-52211)
—— Southampton: Central Health Clinic, East Park Terrace, Southampton (0703-34321)
—— Southend-on-Sea: Warrior Square Clinic, Warrior Square, Southend-on-Sea (0702-49451)
—— Swansea: Public Health Department, 21 Orchard Street, Swansea SA1 5AQ (0792-51501)
—— Taunton: Health Centre, Tower Lane, Taunton (0823-82251)
—— Truro: Health Area Office, The Leats, Truro (0872-2202)
—— York: Health Service Centre, 33 Monkgate, York (0904-59881)
Yemen Arab Republic, Embassy of the, 40 South St, London W1Y 5PD (01-629-2085)
Yemen People's Democratic Republic, Consulate of the, 60 Wordsworth Rd, Smallheath, Birmingham B10 (021-772-0957)
Yemen People's Democratic Republic, Embassy of the, 57 Cromwell Rd, London SW7 2ED (01-584-6607)
Yorkshire Bank Ltd, Head Office, Infirmary St, Leeds LS1 1QT (0542-450-841)
Yorkshire Regional Examinations Board, 31-3 Springfield Ave, Harrogate HG1 2HW (0423-66991)
Yorkshire Television Ltd, The Television Centre, Leeds LS3 1JS (0532-38283)
Young Womens Christian Association of Great Britain, 2 Weymouth St, London W1 (01-636-9722)
Youth Hostels Association (England & Wales), Trevelyan House, St Stephen's Hill, St Albans, Herts AL1 2DY (56-55215)
Yugoslav Embassy, 5 Lexham Gardens, London W8 5JJ (01-370-6105-9, 6100)
Yugoslav National Tourist Office, Regent St, London W1 (01-580-4974)

Z

Zaire, Embassy of the Republic of, 26 Chesham Pl, London SW1X 8HH (01-235-6137)
Zambia, High Commission for the Republic of, 7-11 Cavendish Place, London W1M 0HB (01-580-0691)
Zirnostenska Bank, 104-6 Leadenhall St, London EC3
Zoological Society of London, Regent's Park, London NW1 4RY (01-722-3333)

INDEX

Abandoned children, 141
Abattoirs, 1
Abortion, 1
Abortion Act (1967), 1
Abroad, Animals, 13; Artists, 17; Death, 87–8;
  Detention, 172; Education, 110;
  Employment, 117–18; Exporting, 124–7;
  Gifts, 147; Hospitals, 159; Illness, 169;
  Imprisonment, 172; Motoring, 227; Payment,
  256; Property, compensation, 273; Property,
  exchange control, 273
Abstraction, water, 352
Access, to countryside, rambling, 281; to
  debates, Parliament, 251–2
Accident Book, 174
Accidents, Aircraft, 9–10; Industrial, 174;
  Road, 291–2; Shipping, 308
Accommodation, temporary, 69
Accounts, annual company's, 63–4; Bank, 22;
  Overseas, 22–3
Accountants, 1–2
Acetylene cylinders, approval of, 124
Acquisition, Firearms, 133
Action Areas, housing, 160–1
Activities, Trade Union, 336
Actors, secondment, 333
Acts of Parliament, 2, 79, 91, 109, 194, 203, 233;
  see also individual Acts
Actuaries, 2
Acupuncture, 2
Addiction, narcotic, 107
Additives, food, 136
Addresses, accommodation, 1
Administration of Justice Act (1970), 55
Admiralty Court, 55
Admission, schools, 300–1
Adoption, 3–4
Adult education, 4; Publications, 4
Adultery, 103
Advertising, Controls, 4–5, 74; Practitioners, 5;
  Sandwich boards, 5; Sex discrimination, 306
Advice, 5; Housing, 164; Legal aid, 197
Advocacy services, 24–5
Aerodrome, firearms, 134
Aeronautical radios, 280
Aeroplanes, 136
Aesthetics, 14
Afghanistan, 5
African horse sickness, 13
After-care, prison, 272
Agencies, Employment, 119; Theatrical, 334
Agents, Election, 113; Estate, 122; Overseas,
  247; Parliamentary, 252; Patent, 256
Agriculture, 5–9; Food, EEC intervention,
  136–7; Research, 288; Overseas, 303
Aid, Centres, housing, 165; Disablement, 96;
  Government, 349; Hearing, 74, 154; Legal,
  196
Aided schools, 302
Aikido, 215
Air, Fares, 8–9; Navigators, 8–9; Pilots, 8–9;
  Pollution, 9; Rescue, 287–8; Traffic control,
  9; Travel, 9; Weapons, 34
Aircraft, Accidents, 9–10; Charter, 10; Firearms
  on, 134; Noise, 237; Private, light, 136;
  Purchase, 10; Registration, 10; Sale, 10
Airfreight containers, 10
Airports and aerodromes, 10; VIP lounges,
  10–11
Albania, 11
Alcohol, 11; Ethyl, 122
Alcoholism, 11, 154
Aldermen, Court of, 53
Alderney Islet, 44
'A' levels, 146
Algeria, 11
Aliens Employment Act (1955), 58
Alliance Party of Northern Ireland, 11
Allocation of housing, 162
Allotments, 11–12

Allowances, Armed forces, 15; Duty-free, 108; Exchange, 110; Hill livestock, 155–6; Maternity, 215; Rent, 287
Ambulances, 42, 159
Amateur, Films, 131; Radio, 285
American roulette, 144
Ammunition, 134
Amortisation finance, industry, 177
Amnesty International, Human rights, 165
Amphetamine, 106
Analysis, Chemical, 45; Public, 274
Ancient Monuments, 12
Andorra, 12
Anglican Churches, marriages, 212
Angling, 12
Angola, 12–13
Animals, Abroad, 13; Birds, 13–14; Cruelty to, 82; Dangerous, 14; Diseases, 13; Experiments, 13; Exporting, 124; Health Offices, 100; Performing, 257; Pets, 13–14; Products, exporting, 127; Slaughter of, 1; Stray, 323; Welfare, 13; Wild, 354
Anthrax, 13
Antiques, Exporting, 125; Firearms, 134; Importation, 14
Appeal, Court of, 55, 78–9
Appeals, 2–3, to Privy Council, 178
Apple production, 14
Appliances, Gas, 146; Prescription charges, 218
Appointments, Crown, 51; Judicial, 186; Ministers, 149
Apprenticeship, 177; Training, 155
Approval, shipping, 308
Approved place, detention in, 94
Arbitration, 175; Maritime, 211
Archaeology, 166; Finds, 14
Archbishops, of Canterbury and York, 159; Special licence, 212
Archery, 14
Architects, 14; Landscape, 192; Naval, 234
Architects (Registration) Acts (1931 to 1969), 14
Architecture, 166; Aesthetics, 14–15
Archives, Film, 131; Royal, 295
Argentine Republic, 15
Armed Forces, Allowances, 15; Criminal justice, 79–80; Discipline, 79–80; Display teams, 15; Medals 216; Museums, 228; Pay, 15; Recruitment, 15
Armorial Bearings, 15–16
Arms, Purchase, 16; Royal, 295; Sale, 16
Army, Careers Information Office, 289; Volunteer Reserve, 289
Arrangements, Au Pair, 20; Electoral, local government, 206; Manufacture under licence abroad, 126
Arrest, of Suspects, 16; Unlawful, 55
Art, 166
Arthritis, 95

Articles of Association, Companies, 64
Artificial insemination, Cattle, 16; Human, 16–17; Pigs, 16
Artificial limbs, 96
Artists, Abroad, 17; Industrial, 174
Arts, Administration training, 17; Centres, 17; Community, 62; Martial, 215; Royal Academy of, 17; Support, 17–18; Tours overseas, 17
Ascot, Royal, 17
Assisted areas, 17–18
Associations, Housing, 161
Astronauts, 18
Asylum, political, 263
Athletics, 18
Attachments, telephone, 330
Attack on the UK, 19
Attendance, Centres, 19; School, 299–300
Auctioneers, 122
Auctions, military surplus, 223
Auditions, 20
Automobile Association, 227
Au Pair arrangements, 19
Australia, 20
Austria, 20
Authorities, Education, 110; Health, 153; Local, 203–6
Autobiography, publishers of, 202
Auxiliaries, dental, 91
Auxiliary Forces, 289–90
Avant-garde films, 131
Awards, Design, 93; Gallantry, 143; Queen's, 278

Baccarat, 144
Badgers, 21
Badges, car, for disabled persons, 96
Badminton, 21
Bagatelle Boards, 26–7
Bags, Post Office, 266–7
Bahamas, 21
Bahrain, 21
Bailiff's Warrant, 163
Balance of payments, 171
Ballooning, 21–2
Ballroom dancing, 87
Baltic Exchange, 22
Bananas, 171
Bangladesh, 22
Banks, 24; Accounts, 22; Authorised, 123; of England, 95; Holidays, 23; Loans, 23; Notes, 23; Overseas, 22–3; Rate, 23; Swiss, 327–8
Bankruptcy, 23–4
Banns, publication of, 212
Barbados, 24
Bar Council, 25
Barley, 43–4
Barristers, 24–5

Baseball, 25
Basketball, 25
Bearer, gun, 134
Bed of the sea, ownership, 140
Beef, 42–3; Certificates of Entitlement, 137
Beekeeping, 25
Beer, 123
Benefits, Maternity, 215; Sickness, 310; Social Security, 313–14; Supplementary, 325–6; Unemployment, 343; Widows, 354
Benin, 26
Bequests under Wills, 148
Bermuda, 26
Bestsellers, books, 30–1
Betting, Businesses, 26; Duty, 26; Racecourse, 279
Betting, Gaming and Lotteries Act (1963), 279
Betting Levy Boards Act (1972), 279
Big six, 144
Billiards, 27; Tables, 26
Bills, Electricity, 116; Gas, 116
Bingo, 27; Clubs, 143–4
Biography, publishers of, 202
Birds, Importation, 13–14; Pests, 257; Wild, 354–7
Birth, 27; Certificates, 27; Records, 283; Registration, 27–8, 285; Sterilisation, 321
Bishops of London, Durham and Winchester, 159
Blackcurrant bushes, 158
Black jack, 144
Blindness, 28–9, 95; Aids, 29; Books, 29; Children, 98; Eye donation, 128; Postal services, 29
Blood Donors, 29
Bloodstock, breeding of, 158
Blown glass, 76
Blue Ensign, 135
Boarding houses, 133
Boats, 29, 40
Boating, 29
Bobsleigh, 29–30
Bodies, dead, 89
Bolivia, 30
Bombs, 30
Bonded warehouses, 30
Bonds, premium, 148, 268
Bookbinding, 76
Bookmakers, 158; Levy, 30; Licences, 30
Books, Art, 16; Bestsellers, 30–1; Rent, 163
Boroughs, 31
Borrowing, foreign, 138
Borstal training, 31
Botanical characteristics, 136
Botswana, 31
Boule, 144
Boundaries, 31; Local government, 206
Bowls, 31–2

Boxes, Post Office, 266–7
Boxing, 32
Braille, 29; Writing machines, 97
Brazil, 32–3
Breath tests, 33
Brecon Beacons, 232
Breeding, Dogs, 105; Greyhounds, 149; Hens, 112; Plants, 261
Breeding of Dogs Act (1973), 105
Brewers, 33
Bridleways, 138
British Broadcasting Corporation, 331–2
British Code of Advertising Practice, 4
British Collective Passports, 256
British Council, 111
British Library, 17; Medical information service, 216; Translating service, 338; Reading room, 33
British Museum, 232
British Nationality Act (1948), 52, 255
British Protected Persons, 33
British Savings Bonds, 33
British Standard Passports, 254–5
British Standards, 33–4, 115
British Summertime, 34
British Visitors Passports, 255–6
British Waterways Board, 12, 161
Broadcast Charity Appeals, 34
Broadcasting contracts, radio and television, 331
Broadcast Relay Systems licences, 34
Broadcasts, Party political, 254
Broadleaved trees, 140
Brokers, Bullion, 148; Insurance, 181; Securities, 304–5
Brucellosis, 42
Brunei, 34–5
Buckingham Palace, 35
Builders, house, VAT, 161
Building, 35, 74
Buildings, Architectural interest, 35–6; Buying, 191; Historic, 12; Selling, 191
Building Societies, 225
Bulgaria, 36
Bullion, 148
Bursaries, state, 4
Burial, 36; Abroad, 88; at Sea, 37
Burma, 37
Burning grass and heather, 149
Burundi, 37
Bus Conductors, 37; Services, 37–8; Subsidies, 37–8
Buses, London, 207–8
Business, Names, 38; Registration, VAT, 38; Security, keys, 38; Small, 38; Small in Wales, 311
Butter, Certificates of entitlement, 137
Buying Land, Houses and other buildings, 91
Byelaws, 38

Cadet Corps, 134
Calf subsidies, 42–3
Calibration, 39
Calligraphy, 76
Cameroon, 39
Camping, 39–40
Canada, 40
Canals, 40, 161
Canal boat children, 299–300
Candidates, 113; Local government, 206–7; Parliamentary, 253
Canine societies, 105
Cannabis, 106
Canoeing, 40–1
Canterbury, 109
Capital Gains Tax, 41
Caravanning, 40
Caravans, 74
Car badges for disabled persons, 96
Carcasses, badger, 20
Carcinogens, 335
Cardiff festivals, 130
Cards, Cheque, 45; Credit, 76
Care, Child, 45–6; Order, 50
Cargo at sea, 42
Cargo gear, survey, 1
Carnations, 158
Carnets, International Camping, 39
Carpets, 74
Car, Drivers, 74; Motor, 106; Sales, 41–2
Cartography, 211
Carving, wood, 76
Car wash plant, 42
Cassettes, loans, 283
Cattle, 42–3, 155–6; Plague, 13
Caving, 43
Cellar flaps, 43
Censorship, film, 131
Censuses, 43
Central African Empire, 43
Centres, Attendance, 19–20; Day, 87; Film, 131; Law, 193
Cereals, 43–4
Certificates, Birth, 27; City and Guilds, 53; Death, 88; Education, General, 146; Fair rents, 163; Film, censorship, 131–2; Firearms, 134; Origin, 44, 125; Machinery, 210; Secondary Education, 44
Certification, documents and records, 283
Cesspits, 306
Chad, 44
Chancery division of High Court, 54
Channel Islands, 44, 52
Charges, Dental, 91–2; Rent, 287; Unregistered land, 190–1
Charity, 45; Appeals, broadcast, 134; Entertainments, 132; Football pools, 138
Charter, Aircraft, 10; Royal, 295; Ships, 307

Chelsea, Flower show, 45; Pensioners, 45
Chemical analysis, 45
Chemin de fer, 144
Cheques, 45
Chewing tobacco, 334
Children, 45–50; Books, 202; Criminal justice, 80–1; Cruelty to, 82; Deafness, 87; Entertainment, 132; Family fund for the disabled, 97; Fostering, 140–1; Handicapped, 97–8; Mental disability, 219; School attendance, 299–300; School crossings, 300; Still born, 321–2
Chile, 50
China, 51
Chiltern Hundreds, 50–1
Chiropodists, 51
Chiropracters, 2
Choreographers, 228
Christmas mail, 51
Chronically Sick and Disabled Persons Act (1970), 95
Chuck-a-luck, 144
Church of England, 51, 109, 159
Church of Ireland, 213–14
Cider, 51, 123
Cigarettes, 334; Lighters, 201
Cigars, 334
Cinemas, 51; Public, 131
Cinematograph Act (1909), 51
Circuit Judge, 54
Circuses, 14
Cities, 52
Citizenship, dual, 107
Citizenship of the UK and colonies, 52–3
City and Guilds Certificates, 53
City of London, 53
Civil court proceedings, 197
Civil defence, 53–4
Civil gallantry awards, 143
Civil honours, 157
Civil law disputes, 54–8
Civil Liberties, National Council for, 166
Civil servants, 58, 118
Claims against foreign governments, 58; against UK government by foreigners, 58
Claims, conflicting, Peerage, 256
Claims, Ministry of Defence, 90–1
Claims, small, 311–12
Classics, 166
Clean Air Acts (1956 and 1968), 312
Cleanliness at work, 167
Cleaning, 74
Clinics, Child health, 49; Drug addiction, 107; Family planning, 74
Closed shop, 58–9
Clothing, School, 129, 302; Work, 59
Clubs, Film, 132; Flying, 136; Gambling, 143–4; Liquor licensing, 59
Coal and Steel Community, European, 111

Coal mining, 59; Subsidence, 224
Coarse fishing, 12
Coastguard, 287–8
Cocaine, 106–7
Cocoa, exporting, 126
Code, firework, 134
Coins, 59; Transactions, 148
Cold stores, 59
Coldwater fish, 134
Collection, Street, 323; Tax, 172; Waste food, 352
Collections, Permanent, 132
College of Arms, 155
Colleges of Art, 142
Colleges of Education, 110
Colleges of Technology, 142
Columbia, 59
Colonies, citizenship, 52–3
Colorado beetle, 261
Colour television sets, 171
Commerce, 177
Commercial, Disputes, Exporting, 124; Divers, 103; Law, 127; List, 55
Committees, Parliamentary, 252–3
Commodity markets, 59–60
Common Council, Court of, 53
Common Entrance Examinations, 60
Common Hall, Court of, 53
Common land, 61
Common Market, 111
Commonwealth, countries, 52–3, 61–2; Navy, 135; see also individual countries
Commonwealth Development Corporation, 94
Communist Party, 62
Community, Arts, 62; Centres, 62; Homes, children, 47, 50; Land Scheme, 62; Service Orders, 63; Transit, EEC, 111; Village halls, 62
Companies, 63–8; Dance, 228; Dividends, 103; Music, 228; Opera, 228; Overseas, 248; Theatre, 333–4
Companies Acts (1948 to 1976), 1, 64, 66, 68
Companies (Accounts) Regulations (1971), 65
Compensation, Criminal injuries, 79; Compulsory purchase, 69; From criminals, 68; Property abroad, 273
Competition and events, flying, 136
Composers, 228
Computers, privacy, 70
Concert agencies, 70
Concessions, travel, 338
Conciliation, 175
Conditions and terms, employment, 120
Conductors, bus, 37
Confravision, 330
Congenital deformity, 95
Congo, 70
Conflicting claims, Peerage, 256

Conscience, prisoners of, 165
Conservation, Beauty spots, 70; Coasts, 70; Countryside, 75–6; Energy, 121; Supplies, exporting, 126; Wildlife, 120
Conservation of Wild Creatures and Wild Plants Act (1975), 354, 356
Conservative Party, 70–1; Scottish, 303
Constituency boundaries, European assembly, 71
Construction, Safety, 72; Sites, 237–8; Works in tidal waters, 72
Consular invoices and fees, exporting, 127
Consulate, British, 52
Consuls, 72
Consultant, 159
Consumer, Credit, 72–3; Products, design, 93
Consumer Credit Act, 73
Consumer Protection Act (1961), 299, 274
Consumer Protection Act Northern Ireland (1965), 299
Contacts abroad, exporting, 125
Contractors, Building, 161; Electrical, 115
Contracts, Public preference, 274–5; Radio, 331; Television, 331; Tenancy, 163
Contraception, 74
Contributions, National Insurance, 231
Controlled tenancy, 163
Control of Pollution Act (1974), 264, 274
Control order, houses, 161
Controls, Aircraft, 84; ATA carnets, 83; Cargo, 83–4; Customs, 83; Dividend, 103; Drugs, 106; Explosives, 124; Pests, 257; Shipping 84; Smoke, 312; Travellers, 84
Convention, European, human rights, 165
Conversion grants, 160–1
Converting properties into flats, 160
Convictions, criminal, 286
Co-operative Party, 74
Co-operatives, housing, 161
Co-ownership schemes, housing, 161–2
Copyright, 75; Crown, 82
Copyright Act (1911), 199; (1956), 75, 82, 275
Coroners, 89–90
Corporation, City, 53; Tax, 75
Corps museums, 228
Correspondence colleges, 75
Corridor area, 276
Corrosive materials, 335
Costa Rica, 75
Costs, court, 56
Council, Design, 174; Europe, 166; Ministers, 111
Councillors, 205–6
Councils, Local, 204–6; Queen's, 278
Country Code, 75
County, Councils, 204–6; Courts, 54; Planning, 335
Countryside Act (1968), 61

Coursing, 76
Court, Civil, 54; Contempt of, 56; Criminal, 78–9; European, 122; Legal Aid, 197; Martial, 80
Coypus, 224
Crafts, 76
Craps, 144
Creative artists, 228
Credit, Cards, 76; Foreign Currency, 138–9; Reference agencies, 76–7; Sex discrimination, 307
Cremation, 36; Abroad, 88
Cricket, 77
Crime prevention, 77
Criminal court proceedings, 77; Legal aid, 197
Criminal Injuries Compensation Board, 56, 79
Criminal, injustice, 178
Criminal Law Act (1977), 132, 319
Criminals, compensation from, 68–9
Crofting, 8
Crops, horticultural, 158
Croquet, 82
Crossings, school, 300
Crown Agents, 94, 247
Crown and Anchor, 144
Crown, Appointments, Church of England, 51; Copyright, 82; Court, 78; Estates, 82
Crude gold, 148
Cruelty to animals, 82
Crufts, 105
Cruising, 29
Crutches, 96
Cuba, 82
Cup Final, 82; Scottish, 303
Curling, 82
Currency, foreign, Credit, 138–9; Decorations, 139; Exchange market, 139–40; Investment, 182; Medals, 139; Securities, 139
Curricula, schools, 301
Customs, 83–5; Exporting, 124; Post, 266–7
Cuts in films, 132
Cutting trees down, 339–40
Cycling, 85; Motor, 227
Cyprus, 85–6
Czechoslovakia, 86

Dancing premises, 228
Dangerous, Drugs, control, 106; Substances, transport, 338
Dangerous Wild Animals Act (1976), 14, 363
Dartmoor, 232
Data Projection Authority, 70
Day care, Centres, 49; Child, 48
Day centres, 86
Day nurseries, 87
Day-patients, 159
Dead, war, 351
Deafness, 87, 95, 98, 201; Benefit, 176

Dealers, Firearms, 134; Gold, 148; Spirits, 316
Death, 87–90; Post mortem, 266; Records, 283; Registration, 285; Wills, 357
Debts owing to employees, 117
Declarations, 101–2
Decorating, 74
Decorations, foreign, 139
Deed of Covenant, 76
Deer, red, 284
Defamation, 55
Defence, Civil, 53–4; Ministry, 90–1; Research facilities, 91
Degree equivalents, 91
Degrees, 91
Delivery, oil, 244
Demonstrations, 91
Denmark, 91
Dental, Auxiliaries, 91; Charges, 91–2; Hygienists, 91; Services, 48; Treatment, 92, 129
Dentures, 129
Department of Energy and Trade, 103
Deportation from the UK, 93
Depositaries, authorised, 126
Deposits, returnable, 163
Design Advisory Service, 174
Design, Awards, 93; Construction of high dams, 121; Consumer products, 93; Industrial, 174
Design Council, 73
Designers, 333; Lyric theatre, 228
Despair, 325
Detention, Abroad, 172; Approved place, 94; Centres, 93–4
Developers, 122
Developing countries, Employment abroad, 118; Fish, 135; Training, agricultural, 94
Development, Aid, Certificates, Industrial, 174; Commonwealth Development Corporation, 94; Crown agents, 94; Industrial, 176; Invention, 182; Permits, 242
Development and Road Improvement Funds Acts (1909 and 1910), 297
Development Land Tax, 94
Devolution, Scottish, 302
Diagnosis, 159
Diamonds, exporting, 126
Dies, 216
Dietitians, 94
Dinghies, inflatable, 40
Diplomatic Privileges Act (1964), 94–5
Diplomatic Immunity, 94–5
Direct investment, exchange control, 95
Direct taxes, 181
Directories, telephone, 330–1
Directors, companies, 64; Stage, 333
Disablement, 95–9; Benefit, 175–6; Mental, 219–21
Disabled, sport for the, 318

Disasters, Military assistance, 223; Overseas, 99
Discharge, prison, 270–1
Discipline, Employment, 119; Schools, 301
Disclaimants to House of Lords, 159–60
Disconnections, telephone, 331
Discrimination, Racial, 279–80; Sexual, 306–7
Disease, Animal, 13; Fish, 134–5; Industrial, 89, 175–6; Plants, 261
Disinfectants, 99–100
Dismissal, 100–2
Dispersants, oil, 244
Display teams, armed forces, 15
Disputes, Civil law, 54; Dockwork, 103; Exporting, 124; Industrial, 175; Public authorities, 100–3
District Councils, 204–6; Royal Charter, 31
Districts, polling, 264
Distillers licences, spirits, 316
Dividend control, 103
Diving, 103
Divorce, 55, 103
Divorced women, 49
D notices, 235
Docks, Safety, 307–8; Survey, 103
Docks and Harbours Act (1966), 103
Doctors, National Health Service, 103–5, 158–9
Documents, 283–4
Documentary, Films, 131; Material, 126
Documentation procedures, exporting, 125
Dogs, 105; Guard, 150
Dominican Republic, 105
Donors, Blood, 29; Eye, 128; Kidney, 188
Doping, prevention of, 158
Dourine, 13
Down's syndrome, 219
Drainage, land, 35
Drawback, 123
Drinking water at work, 107
Drivers and cars, 74
Driving, Heavy Goods Vehicle, 154; Instructors, 105; Licences, 105–6; Permits, international, 5, 106; Tests, 106
Drought, 106
Drugs, 262; Control, 106; Dependence, 106–7; Exporting, 127
Dual Citizenship, 107; Nationality, 107
Duke of Edinburgh's Award Scheme for Young People, 107–8
Dumbness, 95, 98
Dumping at Sea Act (1974), 72, 108
Dust, health hazards, 108
Duty, Betting, 26; Customs, 84–5; Death, 88; Excise, 123; -free allowances, 108; -free stores, yachts, 360; Remission of, ethanol, 122; Stamp, 319

Earnings Related Supplement, 109

Ecclesiastical Law, 109
Economic and Social Council of the United Nations, 166
Economic regulator, 123
Ecuador, 109–10
Edinburgh Gazette, 295
Edinburgh International Festival, 130
Education, Abroad, 110; Adult, 4; Authorities, 110; Entertainments, 132; General Certificate, 146; Film, 132; Handicapped children, 97–8; Nursery, 239; Sex discrimination, 306; Technology, 111; *see also* school attendance
Eggs, 112; Fish, 134–5; Wild birds, 354–5
Egypt, 113
Eire (Irish Republic), 113
Eisteddfod, Llangollen International Musical, 130
Elderly people, day centres, 87
Elections, 113–15; Local government, 206–7; Parliamentary, 253
Electoral Law Act (Northern Ireland) (1962), 207
Electoral Registration Officer, 99
Electricity, 115–16; Bills, 116; Contractors, 115; Disconnections, 145; Goods, 74; Lines, 115
Electronic calculators, 171
El Salvador, 113
Embalmers, 117
Emblems, royal, 295
Embroidery, 76
Emergencies overseas, 99
Emergency legislation, 166
Emigration, 117
Employers' Grants, 117; Insolvency, 117; Work permits, 358
Employment, 117–20, 129, 185; Immigration, 170; Medical advisory service, 358; Merchant Navy, 221–2; of the disabled, 97; Sex discrimination, 306–7; Transfer scheme, 286
Employment Agencies Act (1973), 70, 334
Employment Protection Act (1975), 119, 336–7
Endangered species, 120
Energy, Conservation, 120; Department of, 116
Engineering Projects, Industrial, 175
Engineers, 121; Flight, 136
England, Church of, 51
English, 166; Language teaching, 121–2; Law, 194
Engraved glass, 76
Ensign, blue, 135
Entertaining, Parliamentary, 253; Rural areas, 132
Entry, Certificates, 349; Points, Customs, 85
Environment, Department of, 116; Maps, 211; Photographs, 211
Epileptic children, 98
Episcopalian church, 213

Epizootic lymphangitis, 13
Equal Pay Act (1970), 307, 350
Equal pay, wages, 350
Equine encephalomyelitis, 13
Equine infectious anaemia, 13
Equipment, Aid for the disabled, 96; Electrical, approvable marks, 115
Estate, Agents, 122; Crown, 82; Duty, 88
Ethanol, remission of duty, 122
Ethiopia, 122
Ethyl alcohol, control of sale, 122
Eurodollars, 139
European, Assembly, 71; Atomic Energy Community (Euratom), 111; Economic Community, 111–12; Company law, 68; Convention, human rights, 165; Court, 122; Finance, industry, 177; Intervention, food, 136–7; Law, 193–4; Space programme, 18; *see also* individual countries
European Communities Act (1972), 193; (1976), 68
Euthanasia, 122
Evening institutions, 142
Evidence, fresh, criminal injustice, 78
Ewes, 156
Examination, Certificate of Secondary Education, 42; Common entrance, 60
Exchange control, 122–3; Direct investment, 95; Employment abroad, 118; Emigration, 117; Exporting, 125; Investment, 182; Immigration, 170; Property abroad, 273; Imports, 171–2; Sterling securities, 321; Travel, 338
Exchange Control Act (1947), 148
Exchange market, foreign, 139–40
Exchanges, student, 324; Youth, 324
Excise, Duty, 123; Licence, 11; Motor vehicle, 226
Exclusion, schools, 300–1
Ex-directory telephone numbers, 331
Exhibitions, Film, 131; Fine Art, 32–3; Import duty, 123
Exhumation, 123
Exmoor, 232
Expansion, industrial, advice, 175
Expenses, Election, 113; Removal, 286–7
Experiments upon animals, 13
Exploration, Gas, 243; Mineral, 223; Oil, 243
Explosives, 124
Explosives (Age of Purchase) Act (1976), 134
Exporting, 124–7; Food, 137; Training courses, 124; Livestock, 202; Queen's awards, 278
Expulsion, schools, 300–1
Extradition from the UK, 127–8
Eye, Donations, 128; Treatment, 128

Fabric, Printing, 76; Supports, 96

Facilities, recreational, 284
Factories, 129; Explosives, 124; Fire safety, 133
Fair Employment Act (Northern Ireland) 279
Fairs, Children, 299–300; Pleasure, 142
Fair rents, 163
Fair Trading Act (1973), 224
Fair Wages Resolution, 350
False imprisonment, 55
Family, Division of the High Court, 54; Fund, Children's, 97; Income supplement, 129–30; Planning clinics, 74; Practitioner committees, 179
Farcy, 13
Fares, air, 8–9
Farm, Capital grant schemes, 140; Feed stuffs, sale, 130; Fertilisers, sale, 130; Livestock, welfare, 202–3
Farmers, 155–6
Faro and farobank, 144
Father of illegitimate children, 168–9
Fat sheep guarantee scheme, 307
Feeding livestock, 202–3
Feed stuffs, sale, 130
Fees, school, 173
Fellowship Party, 130
Fencing, 130
Fertilisers, sale, 130
Festivals, financial support, 130; Film, 132
Fiction, publishers of, 202
Field sports, 130
Fiji, 130
Film, 130–2, 200
Finance Act (1975), 88
Finance, EEC for industry, 177; Exporting, 124–6; Gas fields, 243; Oil fields, 243
Fine Arts, financial support, 132–3
Fingerprints, 133
Finland, 133
Firearms Act (1968), 133–4
Fire at work, 133
Fire blight disease, 261
Fireworks, 134
Fish, 134–5; White, 353–4
Fishguard festival, 130
Fishing, 12
Fittings, costs, 164
Five hundred tree scheme, 140
Fixtures, costs, 164
Flags, 135
Flammable substances, 133
Flapping racecourses, 149
Flaps, cellar, 43
Flats, leased, 162
Fleece, 357–8
Flight crew licences, 136
Flooding, 135
Flower, Show, Chelsea, 45; Trials, 135–6
Fluoridation of water, 352

Flying, 136
Food, 136–7; Additives, 136; and Agricultural Organisation, 118; Waste, 352
Food and Drug Acts (1955), 136, 274, 299
Food and Drugs Act, Northern Ireland (1956), 298
Foodstuffs, regulations, exporting, 127
Football, 137–8; Poll betting, 265; Rugby, 296
Foot and mouth disease, 13
Footpaths, 138
Foreign, Banks, 24; Borrowing, 138; Controlled companies, 95; Credit, 138–9; Currency, 138–9; Currency resources, 123; Currency securities, 139; Governments, claim against, 58
Foreigners, education in UK, 342
Foreshore, ownership, 140
Forestry planting grants, 140
Formation of companies, 66
Fortification of wine, 357
Foster(ing), Local authorities, 140–1; Parents, 50; Private, 141
Foundlings, 141
Fowl pest, 13
Fowl plague, 13
France, 141
Franking machines, 141
Fraud, 55
Freehold, housing, 162
Free, Milk, 223; Parking, 96; Tickets to BBC shows, 331–2
Freight, rail, 281
French roulette, 144
Freshwater fish, 134–5
Fruit trees, 158
Fuel, 142
Fugitive offenders, extradition, 127–8
Fundamental freedoms, 165
Fund, Commonwealth, technical co-operation, 61; Redundancy, 284
Funeral directors, 117
Funerals, 89
Funfares, 142
Furniture, 74; Making, 76
Further education, 142; Disablement, 97

Gabon, 143
Gallantry awards, 143
Galleries, National, 232; Press, Parliament, 251–2
Gambia, The, 143
Gambling clubs, 143–4
Game, Fishing, 12; Licences, 144
Gamekeeper licences, 144
Games, Commonwealth, 62; Olympic, 244–5
Gaming Act (1968), 143–5
Garden, Parties, Royal, 295; Plants, 145; Sprinklers, 158

Gas, Bills, 116; Cylinders, 338; Disconnections, 145; Leaks, 145–6; Natural, 243–4; Oil, 142; Offshore, 1; Regulations, 146; see also electricity bills
General Certificate of Education, 146; Examination, 60–1
Generating stations, 115
George Cross, 143
George Medal, 142
German Democratic Republic, 146
German Federal Republic, 147
General improvement areas, 160–1
Ghana, 147
Gibraltar, 147
Gifts abroad, 147–8
Giro, national, 230
Glanders, 13
Glass, crafts, 76
Glasses, 129, 316; see also Spectacles
Gliding, 148; Hang, 153
Gold, 148, 152; Resources, 123
Golf, 148
Goods, Containerised, 85; Sex discrimination, 307; Unsolicited, 148–9; Vehicles, 85, 106
Goods Vehicle (Operators' Licences) Regulations (1969), 154
Government, Aid, voluntary services, 349; Foreign, claims against, 58; Injustice, 178–9; Ministers, appointment, 149; News media, 235; Services, exporting, 124; Stock, purchase, 149; Stock, sale, 149
Government of Ireland Act (1920), 194
Grants, Agricultural, 5–6; Arts, 17; Crafts, 76; Death, 88–9; Forestry planting, 140; House renovation, 160; Maternity, 215; Recreation, 75–6; Regional developments, 18, 285; Research, 288–9; Rural development, 297; Students, 4, 324–5; Training, 337–8; Tree planting, 340
Grapes, growers of, 357
Grass, Burning, 149; Skiing, 311
Greater horseshoe bat, 354
Greece, 149
Green cards for motor insurance, see specific country
Green pound, 137
Grenada, 149
Greyhound racing, 149, 265
Grey squirrels, 224
Grievances, 150
Grounds, sports, 318
Guard Dogs Act (1975), 150
Guardianship, 150
Guarding of machinery, 210
Guatemala, 150
Guernsey, 44
Guides, London, 150; Post Office, 267
Guilds, City and, certificates, 53

Guinea, 150
Guinea-Bissau, 150
Guyana, 150
Gymnastics, 150
Gypsy children, 299–300
Gyroplane, 136

Haiti, 152
Hallmarking Act (1973), 152
Handball, 152
Handicapped, Children, 97; People, day centres, 87; Post office aids, 331
Handmade paper, 76
Hang gliding, 153
Harbours Act (1964), 266
Harbours, fishing, 135
Hazard, 144
Hazardous substances, Branch A, 124, 338; Branch B, 133, 237; Branch C, 335; Branch D, 167; Division, 358
Haulage, road, international permits, 292
Hayward Gallery, 132
Health, 153–4; at work, 358; Authorities, 153; Hazards, dust, 108; Injustice, 179–80; National, 230; Protection, travel, 339; Regulations for livestock, 127; Services, child, 48–9
Health and Safety at Work Act (1974), 119, 133, 307, 358
Health and Safety (Agriculture) Poisonous Substances Regulations (1975), 257
Hearing aids, 154
Heather burning, 149
Heavy Goods Vehicle, Drivers' licence, 154; Operators', licence, 154–5
Heavy Goods Vehicles (Plating and Testing) Regulations (1971), 227
Heavy oil, 142
Helicopters, 136
Help, Home, 156; with installation of telephone, television, radio, 129
Henley Royal Regatta, 155
Herm islet, 44
Heralds, 155
Herbal, Cigarettes, 334; Medicines, 217
Hereditary, Peerages, 159–60; Titles, 155
Heritage coasts scheme, 70
Herring, 135, 155
Heroin, 107
High Court, 54, 78–9; of Chivalry, 155
Higher National Certificates, 245
Highlands, Scottish, 303
Highway Acts, 293
Hill livestock, 155–6
Historical records, 283
Historic buildings, 12, 17, 35–6
History, 166; Local, 207
Her Majesty's Forces, 118
Hockey, 156; Ice, 168

Holidays, Bank, 23; Centres, fire safety, 133; for the severely handicapped, 99
Home Help, 156; for the handicapped, 99
Homelessness, 156
Home Secretary, 53
Home tuition for handicapped children, 98
Homosexuals, rights of, 166
Honduras, 157
Honours, 157; Royal, 295
Hop plants, 157–8
Horserace Betting Levy Board, 158
Horseracing, 158, 265
Horses, 158, 203
Horticultural, Crops, 158; Development scheme, 5; Society, Royal, 295
Hosepipes, 158
Hospitals, Abroad, 159; Death in, 89; Emergencies, 217; Patients, 219; Treatment under NHS, 158–9
Hotels, fire safety, 133
Hounds' licences, 159
Houseboats, 40, 161
Housebuilders, VAT, 161
House of Commons, 160
House of Lords, 56, 78, 159–60
Houses, 156–7, 161–5; Advisory service, 225; Buying, 191; for the disabled, 98; Lodging, 207; Renovation grants, 160–1; Sex discrimination, 307; Sharing, 161
House-to-house Collections Act (1939), 208
House-to-house Regulation (1947), 208
Housing Act (1974), 161
Housing Rents and Subsidies Act (1975), 161
Hovercraft, 165
Humanities, 166
Human rights, 165–6
Hungary, 167
Hunting, 167
Hydrocarbon oils, 123, 142
Hygiene at work, 167
Hygienists, dental, 91
Hypnosis, 167
Hypnotism Act (1952), 167
Hypnotherapists, 167

Iceland, 168
Ice Hockey, 168; Skating, 311
Illegitimate children, 168–9
Illness, Abroad, 169; Mental, 219–21
Immigration, 169–70; Rules for control of entry, 358
Immigration Act (1971), 169–70, 358
Immunisation, 49
Immunity, diplomatic, 94–5
Imperial War Museum, 232
Import, 171–2; Duty, 123, 127; Fish, 134–5; Food, 137; Licences, 171; Livestock, 203; Postal customs clearance, 267; Training courses, 124

Imprisonment abroad, 172
Improvement grant, 160–1
Income, family, supplement, 129–30
Income tax, 172–3; Relief, mortgages, 225–6
Incorporation, 64
Independent, Schools, 173; Trade Unions, 337; Wheelchair housing, 98
Index, design, 93
Indexed-linked National Savings, 173
India, 173–4
Indirect, Discrimination, 279–80; Taxes, 181
Indonesia, 174
Indoor chair, 96
Industry, 174–81; Disease, 89; Invention, 182; Nationalised, 74; Noise, 237; Permits, 242; Tourist, 334–5; Therapy organisation, 219; Tribunal, 100, 119
Information, Disclosure of, trade unions, 336–7; Survey, 326
Injunctions, 101
Injury, Benefit, 175; Compensation, criminal, 79; Industrial, 175–6
Injustice, 178–81
Inland Revenue, 181; Stamps, 319
Inns of Court, 25
Insolvency, Employers', 117; Stamps, 319
Installation, Industrial, 176; of television, telephone and radio, help with, 129
Instructors, Driving, 105; Flying, 136
Insulation against noise, compensation, 69
Insurance, Brokers, 181; Companies, 181; Exporting, 124–6; Investment, abroad, 182; Stamps, National, 232
Insurance Companies Act (1972), 181
International, Atomic Energy Agency, 118; Camping carnets, 40; Commission of Jurists, 165–6; Cricket Conference, 77; Defence and Aid Fund for Southern Africa, 116; Development Association, 118; Driving permits, 106, 227; Finance Corporation, 118; Labour Office, 110; Labour organisations' Special List of Non-governmental Organisations, 166; Monetary fund, 118; Olympic committee, 244–5; Organisations, employment abroad, 118; Publications, 181; Safeguards, employment rights, 120; System of limits, 222
Interpol, 181
Interpreters for deaf students, 97
Introductions to contacts abroad, 125
Invalid, Care allowance, 99; Carriages, 106; Pension, 181; Vehicle, 96
Invasion of privacy, 332
Inventions, development, 182
Investigation of companies, 66
Investment, 182–3; Direct, exchange control, 95
Iran, 183
Iraq, 183

Irish Republic, Citizen of, 53; Eire, 113; Traditional arts, 183
Ironstone land, 183
Isle of Man, 52, 183–4
Israel, 184
Italy, 184
Ivory Coast, 184

Jamaica, 185
Japan, 185
Jersey, 44
Jethou islet, 44
Jewish marriages, 213
Job centres, 119
Jobs, 185
Jockey Club, 158
Jockeys, 158
Jordan, 185–6
Judges, High Court, 55
Judicial, Appointments, 186; Committee, 178; Procedure, 55–6; Separation, 103
Judo, 186
Ju jitsu, 215
Jurists, International Commission of, 165–6
Jury service, 186–7
Justice, criminal, 79–82
Juvenile courts, 80–1

Kampuchea, 188
Karate, 215
Keep fit, 189
Kendo, 215
'Kennel Gazette', 105
Kenya, 188
Key money, 164
Kidney donations, 188
Kiosks, telephone, 330
Knackers' yards, 1
Knitting, 76
Korean, Republic, 188; Martial Arts, 215
Kung fu, 215
Kuwait, 188–9

Labelling requirements, exporting, 127
Labour Office, International, 120
Labour Party, 190, 312; Northern Ireland, 239; Scottish, 303–4
Lack of capability, 100
Lacrosse, 190
Lake District, 232
Land, 191–2; Drainage, 135; Ironstone, 183; Registry stamps, 319; Rescue, 287–8; Scheme, community, 62–3; Use, planning, 260; Yachting, 299
Land Compensation Act (1961), 273
Landlords, 162–4
Landscape architects, 192
Language, of instruction, schools, 301; Schools 192; Teaching, English, 121–2

Large blue butterfly, 354
Late Night Refreshment Houses Act (1969), 236
Lauderettes, 192–3
Laundry, 74; Service for disabled people, 98
Law, 166, 193–6; Centres, 193; Civil disputes, 54; Company and EEC, 68; Ecclesiastical, 109; Rule of, 165–6
Lawn tennis, 332–3, 357
Leader of the Opposition, 196
Leaks, gas, 145–6
Leasehold, housing, 162
Leave, maternity, 215
Lebanon, 196
Legacy duty, 88; Exemption from, 196
Legal aid, 196–7; Sex discrimination, 307
Legal problems overseas, 197
Legislation, 197–8; Process, EEC, 11–12
Legitimacy, 198
Lesotho, 198
Lettering, 76
Letters of consent for entry, 349
Letters patent, 52
Letting, 162–4
Levy, Bookmakers, 30; Film, 132; Herrings, 155
Liabilities of public authorities, 101
Liberal party, 198–9
Liberia, 199
Librarianship, 199
Libraries, 199–200
Libya, 200
Licences, Bookmaking, 30; Dogs, 105; Driving, 105–6, 154; Export, 125–6; Flying, 136; Gaming machines, 144–5; Grass and heather burning, 149; HGV, 154; Hosepipes and garden sprinklers, 158; Hounds, 159; Liquor, 201–2; Radio, 280; Ships, 308–9; Shoe black, 309; Television, 332
Licensing hours, 200
Liechtenstein, 200–1
Life assurance companies, 225
Life Peerages Act (1958), 159
Life peerages, 159–60, 201
Life sentences, parole, 254
Lifting gear, 201
Lifts, 201
Lighters, Cigarette, 201; Mechanical, 123
Lighting at work, 167
Lines, electric, 115
Linguistics, 166
Lip reading, 201
Liquidation, 23–4
Liquor, 11; Clubs, 59; Licences, 201–2; Wine, 357
List, Doctor's, 159; Honours, 157; Lloyd's, 203; Navy, 135
List, 99, 330
Listing, stock exchange, 322
Literature, Financial support, 202

Live animals, Exporting, 126; Health regulations for, 127
Live shows, television and radio, 331
Livery stables, 291
Livestock, 202–3; Allowances, 155–6
Llandaff festival, 130
Llangollen International Musical Eisteddfod, 130
Lloyd's of London, 203; Register of shipping, 308
Loans, Abroad, 147; Bank, 23
Laos, 192
Lobbies, 91
Lobbying Parliament, 203
Local Authority, 203–6; Housing, 162; Mortgages, 225
Local, conditions, advice about, 124–5; Government, 206–7; History, 207; Injustice, 180–1; Officials, introductions to, 124–5; Radio, tickets, 332
Local Education Authorities, 4, 119, 300–1; Courses, 142
Local Government Act (1933), 206; (1972), 38, 206
Local Government Miscellaneous Provisions Act (1976), 329
Location, office, 242
Lockouts, 100
Lodging houses, 207
London Cab Order (1934 amended in 1955), 329
London, Buses, 207–8; City, 53; Guides, 150; Foreign exchange market, 139; Gazette, 69, 201, 295
Long lease, 162
Lord Chancellor, 160
Lord Lyon King at Arms, 155
Lord Mayor of London, 53
Lords, House of, 159–60
Lords of Appeal in Ordinary, 159
Lost property, 208
Lotteries, 208–9
Lotteries and Amusements Act (1976), 144
Loudspeakers, noise, 238
Low incomes, families on, 129–30
Luxembourg, 209
Lyric theatre designers, 228

Machines, 210
Madagascar, 210
Magazines, explosive, 124
Magistrates' courts, 54, 78–9
Mail, Christmas, 51; Order, 74
Mains, electricity, 115–16
Maintenance, prices, 270
Maisonettes, leased, 162
Maladjusted children, 98
Malawi, 210
Malaysia, 210–11

Mali, 211
Malta, 211
Management, Export of, Advice, 124; Mines and quarries, 121; Schools, 301–2
Mange, parasitic, 13
Manpower Services Commission, 96
Manual workers, wages, 350–1
Maps, environmental, 211; Ordnance survey, 246
Marathon races, 211
Marches, public, 91
Maritime, Arbitration, 211; Radios, 280
Markets, Commodity, 59; Exporting, 124; Foreign exchange, 139–40; Milk, 223
Marking requirements, exporting, 127
Marks, on precious metal, 152
Marriage, 211–15; Records, 283; Register of, 285
Marriage (Scotland) Act (1977), 214
Martial arts, 215
Mass protests, 91
Matches, 123, 215
Maternity, 215–16; Allowance, 109
Mature students, 325
Maundy, Royal, 295
Mauritius, 216
Mauritania, 216
Meals, on wheels, 216; School, 302
Meat, exporting, 127
Mechanical lighters, 122
Medals, 216; Foreign, 139
Media and government, news, 235
Mediation, 175
Medical, Card, National Health Service, 230; Information service, British Library, 216; Register, 105; Research, 288; Sciences postgraduate awards, 288; Specialist overseas, 216; Suspension, 119; Treatment, emergency, 216–17
Medicines, 217–18
Medicines Act (1968), 217, 348
Members of Parliament, 218–19
Membership, Trade Union, 336
Memorandum of Association, Companies, 66
Mental disability, 219–21
Mental Health Act (1959), 220
Mentally disordered persons, 95–6
Mercantile exchange, 22
Merchant banks, 24
Merchant Navy, 221–2; Ships, 135
Merchant Shipping Act (1894), 308, 360
Merchant Shipping Notices, 42
Mergers, 224, 329
Messages, SOS, 315
Messengers, street, 323
Metal dealers, Scrap, 304
Metal detectors, 280
Metalwork, 76

Meters, Electricity, 116; Gas, 146
Methylated spirits, 222
Metrication, 222
Metropolitan counties, 204
Metropolitan Police Act (1839), 43
Metropolitan Public Carriage Act (1869), 329
Mexico, 222
Mice, control, 257
Midwives, 222–3
Military assistance, 223; Gallantry awards, 143; Honours, 157; Surplus, 223
Milk, 223; Free, 129; Schools, 302
Minders, Child 49
Mines, 223–4
Mineral exploration, 223
Mineral Exploration and Investment Grants Act (1972), 223
Mining, Coal, 59; Gold, 148
Minimum wage, 350
Ministerial appointments, 149, 224
Ministry of Defence, claims, 90–1
Mink, 224
Misconduct, 100; Doctors, 104
Missing persons, 224
Misuse of Drugs Act (1971), 105
Mixing oil, 244
M notices, 308
Mobility allowance, 99; Housing, 98
Modern languages, 166
Moles, 244
Monaco, 244
Monetary compensatory amounts, 137
Moneylenders, 224
Mongolia, 224
Monopolies, 224–5
Monuments, ancient, 12, 17
Moon, books in, 29
Mooring, canals and rivers, 40
Mopeds, 106
Morocco, 225
Morphine, 106
Mortgages, 225–6; Industry, 177
Most Distinguished Order of St Michael and St George, 157
Mother, illegitimate children, 168
Motor cars, 106; Racing, 226; Rallying, 226
Motor cycles, 42, 106; Speedway racing, 227
Motor horns, illegal use of, 238
Motoring abroad, 227
Motor vehicle, 226–7
Motor Vehicles (Tests) Regulation (1976), 226
MOT licences, 226
Mozambique, 228
Mountaineering, 227–8
Mouse-eared bat, 354
Multiple occupation, 161
Museums, National, 232; Armed Forces, 228

Music, 166; Premises, 228; Financial support, 228
Musical scores, commissioning, 228
Musicians, street, 323
Musk-rats, 224
Mutilated banknotes, 22

Names, 229; Business, 38
Narcotic addiction, 107
National Council for Civil Liberties, 166
National Film Archive, 131
National Front, 229–30
National Gallery, 232
National Giro, 230
National Health Service, 230
National Health Service Act (1946), 48
National Insurance, 231–2; Stamps, 319
Nationality, 53; Dual, 107
Nationalised industry, 74, 176–7
National Maritime Museum, 232
National parks, 232
National Portrait Gallery, 232
National Savings Bank Accounts, 232–3
National Savings certificates, 233
National Savings, index-linked, 173
National security, 233
National Stud, 158
National Trust, 233
Natterjack toad, 354
Natural environment research, grants, 228
Natural History Museum, 232
Naturalisation, 233
Natural Science postgraduates, grants, 288
Nature, Conservation, 233–4; Reserves, 234
Naturopath, 2
Naval architects, 234
Navigators, Air, 8–9; Flight, 136
Navy, Royal, 135
Nepal, 234
Nests, wild birds, 354–5
Netball, 234
Netherlands, 234–5
Network television, independent, tickets to, 331–2
Newcastle disease, 13
News media and government, 235–6
Newsreels, 131
New Towns, 235
New varieties of garden plants, 145
New Zealand, 235
Nicaragua, 236
Niger, 236
Nigeria, 236
Night Refreshment Houses, 236
Nobel Prizes, 236–7
Noise, 237–8; Insulation, compensation, 71
Nomadic children, 299–300
Non-custodial sentences, criminal, 81–2

Non-indigenous rabbits, 224
Non-patrials, Immigration, 170–1
Non-trading companies, 68
Northern Ireland, Agriculture, 8; Alliance Party of, 11; Law, 194–5; Labour Party, 239; Marriage, 212–13
Northumberland, 232
North Wales festivals, 130
North York moors, 232
Norway, 239
Notices, shipping, 308
Notification of livestock diseases, 13; Fish diseases, 135
Nuclear, Attack, warning, 19; Installations, 239
Nuclear Installations Act, 239
Number plates, 239
Nurseries and Childminders Regulation Act (1948), 48
Nurseries, day, 87
Nursery education, 239
Nurses, 2, 239
Nursing, at home, 239–40; Care, 159
Nuisance, noise, 238

Oaths, 241
Obedience classes, dogs, 105
Obscene Publications Act (1959, 1964), 132, 241
Obscenity, 240
Occupational, Activities, 96; Guidance, 241; Pension schemes, 240–1; Therapists, 242
Offenders, young adult, 361
Office Development Permits, 242
Offices, Fire safety, 133; Location, 242
Official, Publications, 242; Secrecy, 166; Solicitor, 242–3
Official Secrets Act (1920), 1
Offshore operations, oil and gas, 243–4
Oil, Crude, 243–4; Heavy, 142; Off-shore, 1
Oil Pollution Act (1971), 264
Old people, 244
'O' levels, 146
Olympic Games, 244–5
Oman, 245
Ombudsman, 180
Opening hours, shops, 309–10
Open spaces, 61
Operation and maintenance of ships and aircraft, 121
Operators' licences, Heavy Goods Vehicles, 154–5
Opium, 106
Opposition, leader, 196
Ophthalmic medical practitioners, 128
Opticians, 128, 245
Option mortgages, 225–6
Orchestras, professional, 228
Order, drought, 106

Order of the British Empire, 157
Order of the Companions of Honour, 157
Order of the Garter, 155, 157, 295
Order of Merit, 157, 295
Order of the Bath, 157
Order of the Thistle, 295
Orders for arrest, 16
Orders, Prohibition, 272
Ordinary National Certificates and Diplomas, 245
Ordnance Survey Maps and Services, 246
Organisation for Economic Co-operation and Development, 118
Orienteering, 246
Origin, Certificates of, 44, 125
Orphans, 246–7
Osteopaths, 2, 247
Orthoptists, 247
Out-patients, 159
Overcrowding, 162
Overhead electrical supplies, 116
Overseas, Academic exchange, 248; Agents, 247; Agriculture, 303; Agricultural training, 94; Arts tours, 18; Awards to British students, 247–8; British equivalents, 248; Charities, 45; Companies, 248; Disasters, 99; Emergencies, 99; Estate administration, 248; Exporting, 124–7; Food aid, 248; Legal problems, 197; Libraries, 199–200; Marriage, 214; Motoring, 227; Professional visits, 248; Qualifications, 248; Registration of births and deaths, 285–6; Science, 303; Sterling area, 249; Students in UK, 249; Teaching, 330; Technology, 303; Visitors, medical treatment, 217; Workers, employed in UK, 358
Ownership, Greyhounds, 149; Land, registered title, 191–2; Securities, 304

Painted glass, 76
Pakistan, 250
Panama, 250
Paper, handmade, 76
Papua, New Guinea, 250
Parachuting, 250
Paraguay, 250–1
Parasitic mange, 13
Pardons, 251
Parents, Foster, 140–1; Rights, schools, 302–3
Parish council, 52
Paris Treaty (1951), 111
Parking, Concessions for disabled persons, 96; Restrictions, 251
Parks, Country, 75; National, 232
Parliament, 251–3; Lobbying, 203; Members of, 218–19; Petitions to, 258
Parliamentary Agents, 252; Elections, 114
Parliamentary Commissioner Act, 179
Parole, 253–4

Partial sight, 98
Partially deaf children, 98
Partnerships, 254
Passenger ships, 254
Passports, 254–6
Patent agents, 256
Patrials, immigration, 171
Patronage, Royal, 296
Party political broadcasts, 254
Pawnbrokers, 224
Pay, 350–1; Armed forces, 15; Dentists, 104; Doctors, 104; Maternity, 215–16
Pay As You Earn, 172
Payments, Abroad, 256; for imports, 171–2
Peak district, 232
Pear production, 14
Pedigrees, 256
Peerage Act (1963), 159
Peerage, Claims, 256; Life, 201
Peeresses, 159–60
Peers, 159–60
Pembrokeshire coast, 232
Pennine Way, 138
Pensions, 242; Invalidity, 181; Retirement, 290–2
Pentathlon, 256–7
Performances, public, 275
Performing Animals Regulation Act (1925), 257
Perfumes, Excise duty, 123; Manufacture of, 122
Permission, Planning, 261
Permits, International, road haulage, 292; Pool betting, 265; Work, 358
Perry, 51, 123
Personal problems, 257
Peru, 257
Pest, Control, 257–8; Plants, 261
Petitions to Parliament, 258
Petroleum spirit tank wagons, 338
Petrol, Concessions, motoring abroad, 227; Storage, 258
Pets, Importation, 13–14; Shops, 258
Pharmaceuticals, exporting, 127
Pharmacists, 258
Philippines, 258–9
Philosophy, 166
Phone calls, obscene, 241
Phosphate fertilisers, 171
Photographic material, 126
Photography, Environment, 211; Financial support, 259
Physically handicapped children, 98
Physiotherapists, 2, 259
Pig Health Scheme, 259
Pilotage, 259
Pilots, Air, 8–9; Gliding, 148; Licences, 136; Trinity House, 341
Pipelines, 259–60
Pipes, gas, 146

Piprado, 106
Pistols, 134
Plaid Cymru, 260
Planning, and noise, 237; Country, 335; Industrial, 176; Land use, 260–1; Permission, 175; Roads, 292–4; Town, 335
Planting, Forests, grants, 140; Maintenance of woodlands scheme, 140; Trees, grants, 340
Plants, Breeding, 261; Diseases, 261; Exporting, 127; Garden, 145; Wild, 356–7
Platinum, 152
Play groups, 262
Plays, 333
Pleasure fairs, 144
Pleuro-pneumonia, 13
Plumbing, water, 352
Plum Pox (Sharka disease), 261
Plutonium, 280
Poetry, publishers of, 202
Poisons, 262
Poisoning, industrial, 89
Poker dice, 144
Poland, 262
Poles, telegraph, 330
Police, 262–3; Photographs, 133
Police Acts (1964), 274
Policy, employment, 119
Political, Asylum, 263; Broadcasts, party, 255; Levies, 263–4
Polling stations, 264
Pollution, 264–5
Polytechnics, 265
Pontoon, 144
Pool Competitions Act (1971), 138
Pool Competitions (Continuance) Order (1977), 138
Pools, football, Betting, 279; Charity, 138; Duty, 265
Pools, swimming, 327
Population statistics, 265–6
Ports, 266
Portugal, 266
Possession of firearms, 133
Post mortems, 90, 266
Post Office, 51, 266–7; Aids for the handicapped, 331; Ballot papers, 114; Telecommunications, 330; Telephones, 280; Stamps, 319
Potatoes, 171, 267–8
Pottery, 76
Poultry, 13–14, 26
Powerboat racing, 268
Power stations, 175
Precious metals, 153
Preference, public contracts, 275
Pregnancy, 268
Premium Bonds, 145, 268
Pre-release Employment Scheme, prison, 271

Prerogative order, 101
Presbyterian Church, 213–14
Prescriptions, Charge refunds, 268; For glasses, 129
Preservation Orders, trees, 340
Presses, private, 76
Press, Galleries, Parliament, 251–2; Malpractice, 268–9
Pressure boiler plants, 321
Prevention of Fraud (Investments) Act (1958), 322, 344
Prevention of Oil Pollution Act (1971), 264
Price Act (1974), 298
Price Commission Act (1977), 298
Price, Controls, 269–70; Maintenance, 270; Securities, 304–5
Principal Registry of the Family Division, 103
Prison, 270–2
Prisoners, of conscience, 165; Rights of, 166
Privacy, Computers, 70; Individual, 166; Invasion, 332
Private, Dancing schools, 228; Fostering, 141; Light aircraft, 136; Mobile radio systems, 280; Presses, 76; Railways, 281; Rented tenancies, 163; Stables, 291
Privy Council, appeal to, injustice, 178
Prize medals, 216
Probate, 272; Duty, 88
Probation, 272
Problems, personal, 257
Procedures, exporting, 127
Processors of waste food, 352
Product, consumer, 73
Production, loans, Film, 131; Gas, 243; Milk, 223; Oil, 243; Wine, 357
Professional, Artists, 133; Qualification, EEC, 112
Professions supplementary to medicine, 272–3; grants, 325
Professors, Regius, 286
Profit controls, 269–70
Programmes, television and radio, 332
Progressive wilt disease of hops, 261
Prohibited weapons, 133
Prohibition, 101
Proofing of firearms, 133
Property, 273–4; Lost and found, 208
Property abroad, compensation, 273
Prosecutions, 273–4
Protected persons, British, 33
Protected state, British, 52
Protection, consumer, 73–4
Protection of Animals Act (1911), 82
Protection of Birds Act (1954, 1967), 355
Protection of Human Rights and Fundamental Freedoms, 165
Protective clothing, 59
Protectorate, British, 52

Protests, mass, 91
Proxy votes, 114
Psychoanalysis, 274
Psychotherapists, 274
Public Analysts, 274
Public Appointments Unit, 224
Public Authorities, disputes with, 100–3
Publications, Adult, 4; International, 181; Obscene, 241; Official, 242; Parliament, 252
Public, Contracts, 274–5; Health, danger to, 162; Health legislation, 101; Marches, 91; Performances, 275; Radio, 332; Records, 283–4; Rights of way, 138, 275; Servants, top salaries, 275; Schools, 173; Service TV, 332; Service vehicle driving licences, 275; Trustee, 276
Public Health Act (1936), 265
Publicity, overseas, exporting, 127
Punto banco, 144
Puppet theatres, 333–4
Purchase, Aircraft, 10; Arms, 16; Government stock, 149; Securities, 305; Ships, 309

Qualifications, Doctors', 104–5; Professional, EEC, 112
Quarries, 223–4
Quatar, 278
Queen, 61; Awards, 278; Bench Division of the High Court, 54–6; Commendation for Brave Conduct, 143; Council, 278; Gallantry medal, 143; University of Belfast Festival, 130
Questioning of suspects, 16
Quick Advice Service, Energy, 121
Quotas, exporting, 127

Rabbits, non-indigenous, 224
Rabies, 13, 339
Racecourses, 158; Betting, 279; Greyhound, 149
Race discrimination, 166, 279–80
Race Relations Act (1976), 279
Race Relations Board, 54
Racing, Greyhound, 149; Horse, 158; Motor car, 226; Powerboat, 268; Yachts, 360
Radio, 74, 331–2; Help with installation of, 129; Licences, 280
Radio-active materials, 280–1
Radioactive Substances Act (1960), 108
Radiographers, 281
Rail, 281; Fire safety, 133; Private, 281
Rallying, motor car, 226
Rambling, 281
Rare plants, 356–7
Raspberry canes, 158
Rateable value, 162
Rates, 282–3; Bank, 23; Rebate, 281–2; Support grant, 282
Ratings, flying, 136
Rats, control, 257
Readers for blind students, 97

Rebates, Rate, 281–2; Rent, 287
Recognition, Trade Union, 336
Records, 283–4; Parliament, 252
Recreational facilities, 284
Recreation grants, countryside conservation, 75–6
Recruitment, Armed Forces, 15; EEC, 112; Police, 263
Red core diseases of strawberries, 261
Red Deer, 284
Reduction, 102
Redundancy, 100; Fund, 117, 284
Reference agencies, credit, 76–7
Refineries, oil, 244
Reform, law, 195
Refreshment houses, night, 236
Refugees, 284–5
Refunds, prescription charge, 268
Regatta, Henley Royal, 155; Royal, 294
Regimental museums, 228
Regional Development grants, 285
Registrar of County Court, 54
Registration, Aircraft, 10; Adopted children, 3–4; Birth, 27–8, 285; Charities, 45; Citizenship, 52–3; Companies, 66; Changes, 66–7; Death, 89–90, 285; Dogs, 105; Electoral, 114; for customs, 127; Fishing vessels, 135; Marriages, 285; Motor vehicle, 226; National insurance, 232; Shipping, 308; Title, land ownership, 191–2; with the police, 170; Yachts, 360
Regius Professors, 286
Regulated tenancy, 163
Regulations, Exporting, 127; Gas, 146; Livestock, health, 127; VAT, 347
Rehabilitation, Medical, 96; Offenders, 286
Rehabilitation of Offenders Act (1974), 100, 286
Relations, industrial, 176
Religious instruction, 301
Remedial gymnasts, 159, 286
Remedies in disputes with public authorities, 101–2
Remission of Duty, Ethanol, 122
Removal expenses, 286–7
Renovation, house, grants, 160–1
Rents, 162–3, 287; Factories, 129
Rented accommodation, tied to employment, 164
Rent Act, 54
Rent (Agriculture) Act (1976), 164
Re-organisation of secondary school system, 303
Repairs, Essential house, 160–1; Shoes, 74
Repatriation, from the UK, 287; of remains, 88; to the UK, 287
Reports, prices, 270
Repossession, housing, 163
Representation of the People Act (1949), 206

Requirements, technical and legal export, 124
Resale Prices Act (1976), 270
Rescue, Air, land and sea, 287–8
Research, Defence, 91; Employment, 119–20; Energy, 121; Fish, 135; Grants, 288; Industrial, 176
Reserve forces, 289–90
Reserves, nature, 234
Residence, EEC, 112; Permit, 170
Residential accommodation for disabled people, 98–9
Restrictions, parking, 251
Restrictive covenants on land, 290
Results, election, 113–14
Retirement pension, 290–2
Returns, annual, companies, 63–4
Revenue list, 54
Revolvers, 134
Rheumatism, disabled by, 95
Rhodesia, 291; Exporting, 126
Rifles, 134
Rights, Employment, International safeguards, 120; Export of advice about, 124; Human 165–6; of way, 138; Parents', schools, 302–3; Public, 275
Rivers, 40; Houseboats, 161; Work, 352
Road, Accidents, 291–2; Haulage, International permits, 292; Land acquisition, 294; Planning, 292–4; Safety, 294
Road Traffic Act (1972), 222, 226, 274
Roller skating, 311
Roman Catholic Church, 213–14
Romania, 294
Rome Treaty (1957), 111
Rowing, 294
Royal, 294; Academy of Arts, 17, 294; Archives, 295; Arms and Emblems, 295; Ascot, 17; Automobile Association, 227; Auxiliary Air Force, 289; Charter, 91, 295; Courts of Justice, 55; Garden parties, 295; Honours, 295; Horticultural Society, 295; Marines, reserve, 290; Maundy, 295; National Eisteddfod of Wales, 130; Navy, 3, 135, 290, 296; Observer Corps, 289–90; Patronage, 296; Victorian Chain, 295; Victorian Order, 157, 295; Visits, 296; Warrants of Appointment, 296
Royalty supplements for new initiatives in creative writing, 333
Rugby football, 296
Rural development aid, 296–7
Rwanda, 296

Safari parks, 363–4
Safety, at work, 358; Construction, 72; Docks, 307–8; Electrical, 115; Explosives, 124; Fire, 133; Gas, 146, 244; General division, 358; International employment rights, 120; Machine, 210; Oil, 244; Pleasure fairs, 142; Road, 249; Shipbuilding, 307
Salaries, public servants, 275
Sale, Aircraft, 10; Arms, 16; Goods, 298; Government stock, 149; Record, 283; Securities, 305; Ships, 309
Sale of Goods Act (1893), 298
Salmon, 134–5
Samaritans, 299
Samples, import, 127
Sand lizard, 354
Sandwich boards, 5
Sand yachting, 299
Sanitary conveniences, work, 167
San Marino, 299
Sark islet, 44
Saudi Arabia, 299
Saving Loan Scheme, energy, 121
Savings bank accounts, National, 232–3
Savings bonds, British, 33
Savings, Certificates, 148; National, 233
Scholarship plan, Commonwealth, 62
Schools, 299–300; Flying, 136; Health service, 49; Independent, 173; Language, 192; Private dancing, 228
Sciences, 166; Overseas, 303; Reports, 303; Research grants, 388–9; Sites of special interest, 234
Scores, musical, 228
Scotland, 303–4; Agriculture, 8; Assembly, 71; Law, 195–6; Marriage, 214–15
Scrap metal dealers, 304
Screening of young children, 219
Scrub Clearance Scheme, 140
Sea, Death at, 88; Fishing, 12; Flooding from, 135; Pollution, 264; Rescue, 287–8
Seabed, ownership, 140
Seafish, 135
Seals, 216
Seaworthiness, 308; Offshore operations, 243
Secondary school system, reorganisation of, 303
Secretaries of companies, 64
Securities, 304–5; Foreign currency, 139; Sterling, exchange control, 321
Security, Export, 126; Racing, 158; National, 233
Seed potatoes, 158
Seeds, 305; Exporting, 127
Segregation, 279–80
Self-employment, 231–2
Selling land, houses and other buildings, 191
Senegal, 305
Sentences, Criminal, 81–2; Prison, 271
Separation, judicial, 103
Serpentine Gallery, 132
Servants, civil, 58
Services, Employment, 119; Jury, 186–7; Mental disability, 319; Orders, community,

Services, Employment—*cont.*
63; Ordnance survey, 246; Sex discrimination, 307; Training, 337–8; Unsolicited, 149; Water, 352
Sewerage, 305–6; Disposal, 352
Seychelles, 307
Sex discrimination, 166, 306–7
Sex Discrimination Act (1975), 306–7, 222
Sex Discrimination (Northern Ireland) Order (1976), 307
Sexually-transmitted diseases, 154
Shares, companies, 322
Sharing, house, 161
Sheep, 156, 307; Scab, 13; Pox, 13; Wool, 357–8
Sheltered houses, 98
Sheriff Court (Scotland) Act, 58
Shipping exchange, 22
Ships, 308–9; Brokers, 307; Building, safety, 307–8; Charter, 307; Firearms on, 134; Passenger, 254; -worthy goods, 309
Shoeblack, licence, 309
Shoes, 74
Shooting, 309
Shop, Closed, 58–9; Fire safety, 133; Opening hours, 309–10; Pet, 258; Stewards, 310
Shops Act (1950), 309
Short Stay Crisis Centre, 107
Shot guns, 134
Shows, dog, 105
Sickness benefit, 310
Sight testing, 128
Silver, 152; Mining, 148
Sierra Leone, 310
Singapore, 310
Sinn Fein, The Worker's Party, 310–11
Sites, Camping, 39; Caravanning, 40, 74; of special scientific interest, 234
Skateboarding, 311
Skating, 311
Skiing, 311; Water, 352
Skill centres, 97, 119
Skips for waste removal, 311
Slaughterers, 1, 13
Slaughter houses, 1
Sleigh, bob, 29
Small, Businesses in Wales, 311; Claims, 311–12; Holdings, 312; Vehicles, 106; Woods Scheme, 140
Smoke control, 312
Smoking, 154
Smooth snake, 354
Snooker, *see* Billiards
Snowdonia, 232
Snuff, 334
Social Demoeratic and Labour Party, 312
Social, Inquiry reports, 81; Science research grants, 289; Security benefits, 99, 313–14; Workers, 159, 314

Social Security Act (1975), 323
Social Security Pensions Act (1975), 120
Socialist Party of Great Britain, 314
Socialist Workers Party, 314
Socialist International, 239
Societies, Film, 132; Housing, 161
Solicitors, 24–5, 55, 74, 314
Somali Democratic Republic, 315
SOS messages, 315
South Africa, 315; International Defence and Aid Fund, 166
Soviet Union, 315
Spain, 315–16
Speaker of the House, 160
Special, Agreement, schools, 302; Allowance, child, 49–50; Betting days, 149; Clinic, 348; Constables, police recruitment, 263; Licence, 212
Specialists, overseas, medical, 216
Species, endangered, 120
Spectacles, 128, 316
Speech, Defects, children suffering from, 98; Therapists, 316
Speedway racing, motorcycle, 227
Spirits, Dealers' and distillers' licences, 316; Methylated, 222
Spiritual, Lords, 159
Sponsored visits to UK, 317
Sport, 317–18; Aerobatics, 150–1; Field, 130
Sports Ground Act (1975), 318
Sprinklers, garden, 158
Squash, 318–19
Squatting, 319
Squirrels, grey, 224
Sri Lanka, 319
Stable staff, 158
Stallions, 158
Stamps, 319; National insurance, 232
Standards, British, 33–4
State Certified Midwife, 222
Stationary, companies, 67–8
Stations, Generators, 115; Polling, 264
Statistics, 319–21
Statutory tenant, 163
Strawberry plants, 158
Steam boiler, plants, 321
Sterilisation, 321
Sterling securities, exchange control, 321
Still-births, 321–2
Stock, 322–3
Storage, oil, 244
Stranded people, 323
Strangers Gallery, 251
Stray animals, 323
Street, Filming, 132; Collections, 322; Messengers, 323; Musicians, 323; Trading, 323
Strikes, 100, 323–4

Students, 324–5; British, overseas awards to, 247–8; Tenancies, 163
Subjects, British, 34
Sub-postmasters, 267
Subsidence, mining, 224
Subsidies, calves, 42–3
Succession duty, 88
Suicide, 325
Sudan, 325
Suez Canal Certificate, 325
Sugar Beet, 325
Suggestions, Post Office, 267; Rail travel, 281
Summer exhibition, Royal Academy, 284
Summer time, British, 34
Supplement, earnings related, 108; Family income, 129–30
Supplementary Benefits Act (1976), 156
Suppliers, trees, 340
Supply, Electricity, 116; Gas, 146; Royal Navy, 296; Water, 352
Support, for cattle and beef, 42; Grant, rate, 282
Supreme Court, Solicitors, 314
Surfing, 326
Surinam, 326
Surplus, military, 223
Survey information, 326
Surveyors, 122, 326
Surveys, Yacht, 360
Suspects, arrest and questioning, 16
Suspended prison sentences, 271
Swans, 327
Swansea festival, 130
Swaziland, 327
Sweden, 327
Swimming, 327
Swine fever, 13
Swine vesicular disease, 13
Switzerland, 328
Syria, 328

Table tennis, 328
Take-overs, 329
Talking Book service, 199
Tankers, oil, 264
Tanzania, 329
Tapping, telephone, 331
Target practice, 134
Tariffs, exporting, 127
Tate Gallery, 232
Tax, Capital gains, 41; Capital transfer, 41; Car, 41–2; Covenants, 76; Corporation, 75; Exemption from road excise, 96; Free allowances, 108; Income, 44, 172–3; Land development, 94; Rates, 282–3; Stamp duty, 319
Taxi-cabs, 329
Teachers, 329–30
Teaching, English language, 121–2

Technology, Advice, export of, 124; Colleges, 142; Education, 111; Overseas, 303; Queen's awards, 127–8
Telecommunications, 330
Telegraph poles and system, 330
Telephones, 330–1; Calls, obscene, 241; Disabled persons, 96; Help with installation, 129; Radio, 280
Television, 74, 331–2; Help with installation, 129; Licence stamps, 319
Temporary, Accommodation compensation, 9; Employment subsidy, 117; Resident, 230; Work, 185
Ten pin bowling, 333
Tenant, Controlled, 163; Letting, 164–5; of residential accommodation, compensation, 69–70; Statutory, 163
Tennis, 332–3
Terms and conditions, employment, 120
Territorial Volunteer Reserve, 289
Teschen disease of pigs, 13
Test certificates, motor vehicle, 226
Tests, Breath, 33; Driving, 106; Textiles, 171
Thailand, 333
Theatres, 333–4; Children, 300
Theatres Act (1968), 333
Theatrical agencies, 334
Theology, 166
Therapists, speech, 316
Therapy, industrial organisation, 219
Thermal environment, at work, 167
Tidal waters, construction works, 72
Tied rented accommodation, 164
Time, British Summer, 34; Trials, 85
Titles, Hereditary, 155; Registered and unregistered, 191–2
Tobacco manufacturers, 334
Togo, 334
Toilet preparations, manufacture of, 122
Tonga, 334
Top salaries, public servants, 275
Totalisators, 149, 158, 279
Tote board, see totalisators
Tourist, Information for disabled people, 99; Industry, 334–5; Parliament, 252
Tours, Artistic, 228; Overseas, 18
Town and Country Planning Acts, 59; (1971), 242
Town planning, 335
Town Police Clauses Act (1847), 329
Town twinning, 335
Towpaths, canal, 40
Toxic materials, 335
Toys, 74
Track betting licences, 149
Trade Descriptions Act (1968), 274, 299
Trade restrictions, exporting, 127
Trade Unions, 176, 336–7

Trade Union and Labour Relations Act (1974), 58–9, 100
Trading, Companies, 68; Street, 323
Trading Standards Officers, 73
Traditional arts, Irish, 183
Trainers, greyhound, 149; Race horses, 158; Services and grants, 337–8
Training, boards, industrial, 176–7; Borstal, 31; of the disabled, 97; Racehorse, 158
Trampolining, 338
Tramp ships, 307
Transit, community, EEC, 111
Translation service, British Library, 338
Transmission facilities, 331
Transplants, kidney, 188
Transport, Dangerous substances, 338; Schools, 302
Transportable pressure vessels, 338
Travel, 74, 338–9; Expenses to hospital, 159; Rail, 281
Treasure trove, 339
Treaties, exporting, 127
Treatment, Dental, 92, 129; Eye, 128; Medical, 58–9
Trees, 339–40
Trente et quarante, 144
Trials, flower and vegetable, 135–6
Tribunals, Administrative, 2; Industrial, 100, 119, 177; Land, 290
Tribunals and Inquiries Act (1971), 2
Trichologists, 340
Tricycles, non-powered, 96
Trinidad and Tobago, 340
Trinity House Pilots, 340–1
Tropical fish, 134
Trustee, public, 276–7
Truck Acts, 350
Trust, National, 233; Territory, British, 52
Trusts, unit, 344
Tuberculosis, bovine, 13, 21, 42
Tug of war, 341
Tunisia, 341
Turkey, 341
Twin towns, 335

Uganda, 342
United Kingdom, Citizenship, 52–3; Documents abroad, verification, 342; Education, foreigners, 342; Parliament, constituency boundaries, 71–2; Warning and monitoring organisations, 19
Ulster, Defence Regiment, 289; Liberal Party, 342; Unionist Party, 342–3
Underground, London, 207–8
Underwater swimming, 343
Unemployment, 185, 343–4; Benefit, 119
UNESCO, 118, 166
Unidentified flying objects, 344

Uniform, schools, 301
Union Movement, 344
Unit Trusts, 344
United Arab Emirates, 344
United Nations, 118
United States, 344
Universal Declaration of Human Rights, 166
Universities, 344–5; Humanities, 166
Unlawful arrest, 55
Unregistered land, land charges on, 190–2
Unsolicited Goods and Services Act (1971), 148–9
Upper Volta, 345
Uranium, 280
Uruguay, 345
Use of firearms, 133

Vacancies, 346
Vaccinations, 48, 346; *see also* individual countries
Vagrancy Act (1824) (Northern Ireland), 333
Vagrant children, 299–300
Vale of Glamorgan festival, 130
Valuations, property, 273–4
Valuation list, 282
Value-added tax, 41, 346–7
Valuers, 122
Vampire bats, 13
Vegetables, Fresh, 171; Trials, 135
Vehicles, Abandoned, 1; Commercial, 42; Excise licence, 266; Gas, 347–8; Noise, 238–9; Parking, loading and unloading, 251; Public service, 276; Testing stations, 226–7, 347
Venereal disease, 348
Venezuela, 348
Ventilation at work, 167
Verification, UK documents abroad, 342
Vessels, Accommodation, 1; Fishing, 135
Veterinarians, 149, 348–9
Veterinary, Medicinal products, 348; Research, 288; Surgeons, 149, 348–9
Victorian Chain, Royal, 295
Victorian Order, Royal, 295
Video projects, independent, 131
VIP lounges at airports, 10–11
Vienna Convention on Diplomatic Relations, 94
Vietnam, Socialist Republic of, 349
Village halls, 62
Vingt-et-un, 144
Visas, 349
Visitors, Health, 154; Prison, 271–2
Visits, Royal, 296; Stock exchange, 322; to UK, sponsored, 317
Vitamins, 349; Free, 129
Vocational training of disabled, 97
Volley ball, 349

Voluntary, Organisations, 45; Service, employment abroad, 118; Services, government aid, 349
Voting, 114; Disabled people, 99

Wages, 350–1
Wales, Companies registered in, 66; Party of, 260; Small businesses in, 311
Walking, Frames, 96; Sticks, 96
Walks, 351
Wallace Collection, 232
War, Dead, 351; Disablement, 351; Widows, 351
Wards of Court, 351–2
Warehouses, bonded, 30
Warrants, for arrest, 16; of Appointment, Royal, 296; Ministry of Defence, 135
Wart disease of potatoes, 261
Washing facilities at work, 167
Waste, Food, 352; Removal, skips for, 311
Water, skiing, 352; Pollution, 265
Weapons, prohibited, 133
Weather services, 352–3
Weaving, 76
Weight lifting, 353
Weights and Measures Act (1963), 298
Weights and Measures Regulations, 222
Welfare, Animal, 13; Child, 45–50; on farms, livestock, 203
Welsh, Assembly, Constituency boundaries, 71; Language, 353; Law, 194; Liberal Party, 353
West Highlands Way, 138
Westminster Hall, 252
Wheat, 43–4
Wheelchairs, 96, 98
Wheel of Fortune, 144
White fish, 135, 353–4
'Who's Who', 354
Widowers, 354
Widow's, Allowance, 109; Benefit, 354
Wild, Animals, 354; Birds, 354–7; Plants, 356–7
Wildlife park, 363–4

Wills, 148, 357
Wimbledon, 357
Wine, 123, 357
Wireless Telegraphy Act (1949), 280
Wisley, 136
Women, Divorced, 49; and government, 357
Woodland, 140
Woodturning, 76
Wool marketing, 357–8
Work, Clothing, 59; Fire at, 133; Health, 358; Hygiene at, 167; Machines, 210; Noise at, 237; Permit, 117–18, 170, 358; Residence, EEC, 112; Safety, 358
Workers, social, 314
Working dog trials, 105
Workshops, film, 131
Work to rule, 324
World Bank, 118
Wrecks, 358–9
Wrestling, 359; Premises, 32
Writers for the theatre, 333

Yachting, 360; Land and sand, 299
Yachts, 135, 308
Yemen Arab Republic, 360
Yemen, Peoples' Democratic Republic, 361
York, 109
Yorkshire Dales, 232
Young, Adult offenders, 361; Communist League, 62; Conservative Association, 71; Peoples' Orders, 50; People, unemployment, 343–4
Youth, Employment subsidy, 117; Exchanges, 324
Yugoslavia, 361–2

Zaire, 363
Zambia, 363
Zero-rating for VAT, 347
Zip fasteners, 171
Zoos, 14, 363

MIX
Papier aus verantwortungsvollen Quellen
Paper from responsible sources
FSC® C105338

If you have any concerns about our products,
you can contact us on
ProductSafety@springernature.com

In case Publisher is established outside the EU,
the EU authorized representative is:
**Springer Nature Customer Service Center GmbH
Europaplatz 3, 69115 Heidelberg, Germany**

Printed by Libri Plureos GmbH
in Hamburg, Germany